LEARNING TO PROGRAM IN C++

D1164168

ISBN 0-13-032410-8

9 780130 324108

LEARNING TO PROGRAM IN C++

Steve Heller

Prentice Hall PTR

PRENTICE HALL PTR
UPPER SADDLE RIVER, NJ 07458
WWW.PHPTR.COM

Library of Congress Cataloging-in-Publication Data

CIP Data Available

Editorial/production supervision: *Mary Sudul*
Cover design: *Anthony Gemmellarõ*
Cover design director: *Jerry Votta*
Manufacturing manager: *Alexis R. Heydt*
Marketing manager: *Bryan Gambrel*
Acquisitions editor: *Paul Petralia*
Editorial Assistant: *Justin Somma*

 © 2001 Prentice Hall PTR
Prentice-Hall, Inc.
Upper Saddle River, NJ 07458

The publisher offers discounts on this book when ordered in bulk quantities.
For more information, contact
Corporate Sales Department,
Prentice Hall PTR
One Lake Street
Upper Saddle River, NJ 07458
Phone: 800-382-3419; FAX: 201-236-714
E-mail (Internet): corpsales@prenhall.com

Printed in the United States of America

10 9 8 7 6 5 4 3 2 1

ISBN 0-13-032410-8

Prentice-Hall International (UK) Limited, *London*
Prentice-Hall of Australia Pty. Limited, *Sydney*
Prentice-Hall Canada Inc., *Toronto*
Prentice-Hall Hispanoamericana, S.A., *Mexico*
Prentice-Hall of India Private Limited, *New Delhi*
Prentice-Hall of Japan, Inc., *Tokyo*
Simon & Schuster Asia Pte. Ltd., *Singapore*
Editora Prentice-Hall do Brasil, Ltda., *Rio de Janeiro*

Dedication

This book is dedicated to Susan Patricia Caffee Heller, the light of my life. Without her, this book would not be what it is; even more important, I would not be what I am: a happy man.

Contents

CHAPTER 5   *Functional Literacy*   *215*

CHAPTER 6

Taking Inventory *303*

CHAPTER 7

Stringing Along   *409*

CHAPTER 8

Down the Garden Path   **479**

CHAPTER 9

Stocking Up **565**

CHAPTER 10 *Pretty Poly* *657*

CHAPTER 12   *Homeward Bound   859*

CHAPTER 13

Stealing Home   *913*

Foreword

The fundamental problem with most technical books is that the authors are just too smart for their readers' good. By the time one becomes an expert at a highly technical field, such as C++ programming, one has usually lost the knack of identifying with the poor struggling newbie. Also—it has to be said—most techies are not very good writers.

Fortunately, the most able 10% of programmers also tend to be rather good writers—and my old friend Steve Heller is well up in both categories. He's also clever enough to know that he's not really very good at thinking like a programming newbie, and to go find help from people who are.

But the book you're holding in your hands isn't just clever; it has a special, serendipitous magic that makes it one of the most remarkable technical books I've ever seen. Because Steve found a writing partner whose intelligence matched his own, and whose eager, questioning ignorance was the perfect complement of his seasoned expertise.

This book, besides being an omnibus of the books Steve and Susan have written together, is also the story of the meeting of two very remarkable minds. Their continuing dialogue gives it a human texture that is sadly absent from most technical tutorials. They bring out the best in each other; Steve continually challenges Susan to think and learn and grow, and Susan draws Steve out of the high fastnesses of abstraction into generating examples and analogies that are grounded in everyday experience.

The result is a lovely fugue in two voices that weaves together many themes. Steve's unfolding of the mysteries of C++ intertwines with Susan's developing understanding of the language. Their growing affection and respect for each other complements the tale of bytes and silicon as they explore the inner world of the computer together. Susan discovers what she did not know, and Steve re-discovers what he does. Both processes are a pleasure to behold.

How many introductions to programming are there that are also love stories? This may well be the only one. I won't spoil the ending for you -- but I will say that if nothing else, Steve and Susan's relationship has produced work that is not merely top-caliber technical instruction but arguably art of a high and subtle order.

It is an honor to know these two human beings, and a privilege to introduce their book. I hope you find that their journey of discovery guides you on one of your own.

Eric S. Raymond
August, 2000

Preface

Is this book for you? If you're a programmer in a language other than C++ and you want to upgrade your skills, then you shouldn't have much difficulty figuring that out for yourself by reading a few pages. But what if you have no previous programming experience? In that case, here's a little quiz that may help you decide:

1. Do you want to know how the programs in your computer work inside and how to write some of your own?

2. Are you willing to exert yourself mentally to learn a complex technical subject?

3. Do you have a sense of humor?

If you've answered yes to these questions and follow through with the effort required, then you will get a lot out of this book.

The common wisdom states that programming is a difficult subject that should be reserved for a small number of specialists. One of the main reasons that I have written this book is that I believe this attitude is wrong; it is possible, and even desirable, for you to learn how programs work and how to write them. Those who don't understand how computers perform their seemingly magical feats are at an increasing disadvantage in a society ever more dependent on these extraordinary machines.

Regardless of the topic, I can see no valid reason for a book to be stuffy and dry, and I've done everything possible to make this one approachable. However, don't let the casual tone fool you into thinking that the subject is easy; there is no royal road to programming, any more than there is to geometry. Especially if you have no prior experience in programming, C++ will stretch your mind more than virtually any other area of study.

But why should you read *this* book rather than any of dozens of other introductory C++ books? The ingredient that makes this book unique is the participation of a real, live person who didn't already know the material before reading it: Susan Heller, my wife. Her main contribution has been to read every line of the first draft of the book and to ask questions via e-mail about anything she didn't understand. I answered her questions, also by e-mail, until both of us were satisfied that she understood the material in question and that the text was clear. After the text was otherwise complete, I extracted appropriate parts of the e-mail exchanges, edited them for spelling, punctuation, and so forth, and included them in the text where they will be most useful to the reader.

Of course, these exchanges do take up room in the book that might otherwise be filled with more information about C++ and programming. Therefore, if you want to get the absolute maximum of new information per page, you might want to select another book such as Bjarne Stroustrup's excellent book, *The C++ Programming Language*, 3rd Edition (ISBN 0-201-88954-4). However, the vast majority of messages I've received from readers of my other books for beginners have indicated that they found my approach very helpful, and I suspect that most readers of this book will feel the same.

Susan has written an account of her involvement in this project, which immediately follows this Preface. I recommend that you read that account before continuing with the technical material following it, as it explains how and why she contributed to making your task easier and more enjoyable.

Speaking of Susan, here is a bit of correspondence between us on the topic of how one should read this book, which occurred after her first reading of what is now Chapter 2, "Hardware Fundamentals", and Chapter 3, "Basics of Programming".

Susan: Let me say this: to feel like I would truly understand it, I would really need to *study* this about two more times. Now, I could do this, but I am not sure you would want me to do so. I think reading a chapter once is enough for most people.

Steve: As a matter of fact, I would expect the reader of my book to read and study this chapter several times if necessary; for someone completely new to programming, I imagine that it *would* be necessary. Programming is one of the most complex human disciplines, although it doesn't take the mathematical skills of a subject such as nuclear physics, for example. I've tried to make my explanations as simple as possible, but there's no way to learn programming (or any other complex subject) without investing a significant amount of work and thought.

After she had gone through the text a number of times and had learned a lot from the process, we continued this discussion as follows:

Susan: Well then, maybe this should be pointed out in a Preface or something. Of course, it would eventually be obvious to the reader as it was to me, but it took me a while to come to that conclusion. The advantage of knowing this in advance is that maybe I would not be so discouraged that I was not brilliant after one read of a chapter.

Steve: I will indeed mention in the preface that the reader shouldn't be fooled by the casual tone into thinking that this is going to be a walk in the park. In any event, please don't be discouraged. It seems to me that you have absorbed a fair amount of very technical material with no previous background; that's something to be proud of!

We'll be hearing from Susan many more times in the course of the book. She will be checking in frequently in the form of extracts from the e-mail discussion we engaged in during the testing and revising process. I hope you will find her comments and my replies add a personal touch to your study of this technical material.

While we're on the topic of your studying, this would be a good time to tell you how to get updates and help with any errors you might find in the book or with any other questions you might have. The best way is to visit my WWW site, *http://www.steveheller.com.* My email address is *steve@steveheller.com.*

In the event that you enjoy this book and would like to tell others about it, you might want to write an online review on *Amazon.com*, which you can do by visiting my home page and following the links to the "customer reviews" on Amazon.

I should also tell you how the various typefaces are used in the book. Helvetica is used for program listings, for terms used in programs, and for words defined by the C++ language. *Italics* are used primarily for technical terms that are found in the glossary, although they are also used for emphasis in some places. The first time that a particular technical term is used, it is in **bold** face; if it is a term defined in the C++ language, it will be in **bold Helvetica**.

Now that those preliminaries are out of the way, let's proceed. The next voice you will hear is that of Susan, my test reader. I hope you get as much out of her participation in this book as I have.

Acknowledgments

I'd like to thank all the fine people who work at Associated Solutions, Inc., especially Dennis Harvey, Chief Technology Officer, for letting me apply my knowledge of C++ to help make our forms processing products among the best in the world.

I'd also like to thank all the readers of my previous books who have written to me with praise and sometimes with corrections. Of course, I appreciate the former very much, but I appreciate the latter as well; every correction a reader sends me makes the next version of the book that much better.

Finally, I'd like to thank my mother, Sali Neff, and father, the late Leonard Heller. They had that rare but invaluable characteristic among parents: the courage and patience to let me do it my way.

Letter from a Novice

One day in March, 1995, I found myself reading this little message on my computer monitor:

```
[#: 288196 S10/Have You Heard?]
[25-Mar-95 20:34:55]
[Sb: Readers for my new book]
[Fm: Steve Heller 71101,1702]
[To: all]

Hi!
I'm looking for some readers for a book I'm working on,
which teaches people how to program, using C++ as the
language. The ideal candidate is someone who wants to
learn how to program, but has little or no knowledge or
experience in programming. I can't pay anything, but
participants will learn how to program, and will be
acknowledged in the book, as well as getting an
autographed copy. If you're interested, please reply by
e-mail.

Steve
```

As I considered my response to this message I felt a little trepidation for what was to come. I have known only one profession: nursing. I had owned and used a computer for only a little over two years at the time and thought DOS was too difficult to understand. Not only had I no prior knowledge of programming, I had very little knowledge of computers in general. Yet, what knowledge I did have of the computer fed my curiosity for more, and as my love of the computer grew, it soon was apparent I had no choice. I replied by e-mail, waited impatiently for several days, and then...

I jumped to the sound of an ominous knock at my front door. A sense of foreboding heightened with every step I made toward the sound. Cracking it open, I saw dark bluish-grey clouds hanging low overhead, threatening to unleash their contents at any moment. The tenseness of the postal worker's expression changed suddenly to an implacable smile as he quickly slipped a large envelope into my unsuspecting hands. Almost as soon as I realized I held the envelope, I looked up again to find the postman gone. The sky began to swirl, though there was only a hint of a breeze on my face. A slow shudder engulfed me as I quickly locked the door.

Half dazed, I was left standing at my doorway, staring at my name on the envelope, written in a handwriting nearly identical to my own. Confused, but with a penetrating sense of courage, I tore open the mysterious yellow mailer. It in turn seemed to be the catalyst for the rupturing of the sky, and my roof and heart pounded in unison. As the contents of the envelope spilled out on my lap, I caught a glimpse of the words "Who's Afraid of C++?" on the looseleaf manuscript. I was briefly frozen by a paralyzing shiver that gripped my body, as I began to wonder what would become of me. What did this mean? What was C++ and why should I be afraid of it? What was I getting myself into?

And one more question, most mysterious of all: *Who is Steve Heller?*

Never in my wildest dreams would I have ever expected that I would end up reading every page of this book with utmost attention to detail, leaving no word unturned, no concept overlooked, no hair on my head left unpulled for the next nine months of my life. But, if we were going to make this book as clear as possible for anyone who wanted to read it, there was no other way.

The process of writing this book was an enormous effort on both our parts. Neither Steve nor I could have ever imagined the type of dialogue that would ensue. It just happened; as I asked the questions, he answered the questions and I asked again. The exchange would continue until we were both satisfied that I "had it". When that happened, Steve knew the right wording for the book, and I could move on to the next concept. It was an experience like no other in my life. It was a time filled with confusion, frustration, anger, acceptance, understanding, and joy. The process often gave cause for others to question my motivation for doing it. Admittedly, at times my frustration was such that I wanted to give up. But it became my mountain, and I had to climb it. I would not accept defeat.

The material was not the only source of my frustration. There was the inherent difficulty that Steve and I had in keeping communication flowing and speaking the same language. We found we had very different writing styles, which added another obstacle to our undertaking. He, the ultimate professional, and I, the incorrigible misfit, finally managed a happy medium. We corresponded on a daily basis, almost exclusively by e-mail. Through that medium it was our challenge to get into each other's minds. He had to learn how I thought and I had to learn how he thought — not an easy task for an expert and a novice who were total strangers.

What you are about to read is the refinement of the writings of the mind of a genius filtered through the mind of a novice. Ideally, the result of this combination has produced the best possible information, written in the most understandable form. The book as you see it is considerably different from the original version, as a result of this filtering process. For that same reason, it is also different from any other book of its kind. To our knowledge, this is the first time that someone with no previous background in programming has been enlisted in the creation of such a book. Of course, it took tutoring, but that tutoring is what led to the simplification of the text so that future novices could enjoy a relatively pain-free reading experience.

During the first few months of this process, I had to take it on faith that somehow all of this material would eventually make sense. But late one quiet night while first reading about object-oriented programming, (the creation of "classes") I was abruptly shaken by the most incredible feeling. I was held spellbound for a few moments, I gasped and was gripped with the sudden realization and awe of the profound beauty of the code. I had finally caught a glimpse of what programming was *really* all about. This experience later led me to write the following in a letter to my sister:

> Programming is SOOOO gorgeous. So fine, so delicate. It is so beautifully spun with silk threads, tiny and intricate. Yet like silk it can be strong and powerful, it all depends on how you use it.

At last, I had "gotten it". Within these pages the beauty lies dormant, waiting to be viewed only when the work has been done and the mountain scaled by those who embark on the task of learning. It is an exquisite panorama and a most worthy journey.

2000: A Space Odyssey

That was in 1995. As I write this in April 2000, I have gained further insight into the art of programming. When Steve Heller asked me to help with the writing of the second part of this book, originally published as *Who's Afraid of More C++?*, I felt that shiver down my back again. I groaned, knowing full well this time what I was getting myself into and wondering if I had the stamina to do it again.

Well, I did and we had another book. I also have the answers to the questions that I asked myself five years ago.

I have learned what C++ is. It is a computer programming language. It is an immense language, it is a complicated language, and it is a very powerful language. I learned through the writing of this book that C++ can be molded and shaped to do just about anything you want it to do. It convolutes, twists and turns corners. You can play hide and seek with it. Yet, in the hands of an expert, it is amazing to see it come to life.

As Steve and I wrote this book, I became more than a test reader, I also became a usability tester. Through this role I saw just how complicated writing a program is. I had already seen all the source code for the home inventory program that Steve wrote for this book, and was amazed to see just this one little screen of words to show for all our efforts. I knew what was underneath that screen. I knew all the hours, the false starts, the redos, the polishing that it took to get to where we were in the program, and I could not believe that so little showed for our efforts.

Just when Steve thought he was done with it, I was quick to inform him that indeed he was not. It didn't take me long to "break" the program, causing more redos. Then there were things I wanted in the program to make it just a little easier, or a just little prettier. Back Steve went to the compiler. Actually, I think this was as much of a lesson on software design as it was on "more C++". There is so much to think about when writing a program; you have to program not only what you want it to do, but also what you don't want it to do.

I can't say that there is no reason to fear C++. It is a difficult thing to learn, but no more so than any other language, including human spoken ones. It takes interest, work, and practice. But I think that as with any difficult subject, it can be mastered with the right learning tools and a competent teacher. I believe Steve to be a natural teacher and in this book, he has created an excellent learning tool.

As for the other question, *Who is Steve Heller?*: he is now my husband. Even after all the trouble he caused me with C++, I figured anyone who has the same handwriting as I do must be my soulmate.

Susan Patricia Caffee Heller
Sulphur Springs, Texas
April, 2000

CHAPTER 1

Introduction to Programming

"Begin at the beginning, and go on till you come to the end: then stop." This method of telling a story is as good today as it was when the King of Hearts prescribed it to the White Rabbit. In this book, we must begin with you, the reader, since my job is to explain a technical subject to you. It might appear that I'm at a severe disadvantage; after all, I've never met you.

Nevertheless, I can make some pretty good guesses about you. You almost certainly own a computer and know how to use its most common application, word processing. If you use the computer in business, you probably also have an acquaintance with spreadsheets and perhaps some database experience as well. Now you have decided to learn how to program the computer yourself rather than relying completely on programs written by others. On the other hand, you might be a student using this book as a text in an introductory course on programming. In that case, you'll be happy to know that this book isn't written in the dry, overly academic style employed by many textbook writers. I hope that you will enjoy reading it, as my previous readers have.

Whether you are using this book on your own or in school, there are many good reasons to learn how to program. You may have a problem that hasn't been solved by commercial software; you may want a better understanding of how commercial programs function so you can figure out how to get around their shortcomings and peculiarities; or perhaps you're just curious about how computers perform their seemingly magical feats. Whatever the initial reason, I hope you come to appreciate the great creative possibilities opened up by this most ubiquitous of modern inventions.[1]

Before we begin, however, we should agree on definitions for some fundamental words in the computing field. Susan had some incisive observations about the power of words. Here is our exchange on that issue:

> **Susan:** I will read something usually at face value, but often there is much more to it; that is why I don't get it. Then, when I go back and really think about what those words mean, it will make more sense. This book almost needs to be written in ALL CAPS to get the novice to pay closer attention to each and every word.

> **Steve:** IMAGINE WRITING A BOOK IN ALL CAPS! THAT WOULD BE VERY DIFFICULT TO READ, DON'T YOU THINK?

Many of the technical words used in this book are in the glossary at the end of the book; it is also very helpful to have a good technical dictionary of computer terms, as well as a good English dictionary.

Of course, you may not be able to remember all of these technical definitions the first time through. If you can't recall the exact meaning of one of these terms, just look up the word or phrase in the index, and it will direct you to the page where the definition is stated.

---

1.   Of course, it's also possible that you already know how to program in another language and are using this book to learn how to do so in C++. If so, you'll have a head start; I hope that you'll learn enough to repay the effort of wading through some material you already know.

Before we continue, let's check in again with Susan. The following is from her first letter to me about the contents of this book:

Susan: I like the one-on-one feel of your text, like you are talking just to me. Now, you did make a few references to how simple some things were which I didn't catch on to, so it kinda made me feel I was not too bright for not seeing how apparently simple those things were...

I think maybe it would have been helpful if you could have stated from the onset of this book just what direction you were taking, at least chapter by chapter. I would have liked to have seen a goal stated or a least a summary of objectives from the beginning. I often would have the feeling I was just suddenly thrown into something as I was reading along. Also (maybe you should call this C++ *for Dummies*, or is that taken already?)[2], you might even *define* what programming is! What a concept! Because it did occur to me that since I have never seen it done, I really don't know what programming *is*! I just know it's something that nerds do.

Susan's wish is my command, so I have provided a list of objectives at the beginning of each chapter after this one. I've also fulfilled her request for a definition of some programming terms.

Definitions

An **algorithm** is a set of precisely defined steps to calculate an answer to a problem or set of problems, and which is guaranteed to arrive at such an answer eventually. As this implies, a set of steps that might never end is *not* an algorithm.

---

2. As it happens, that title is indeed taken. However, I'm not sure it's been applied appropriately, since the book with that title assumes previous knowledge of C! What that says about C programmers is better left to the imagination.

Programming is the art and science of solving problems by the following procedure:[3]

1. Find or invent a general solution to a class of problems.

2. Express this solution as an algorithm or set of algorithms.

3. Translate the algorithm(s) into terms so simple that a stupid machine like a computer can follow them to calculate the specific answer for any specific problem in the class.

At this point, let's see what Susan had to say about the above definition and my response.

> **Susan:** Very descriptive. How about this definition: Programming is the process of being creative using the tools of science such as incremental problem solving to make a stupid computer do what you want it to. That I understand!
>
> Your definition is just fine. A definition has to be concise and descriptive, and that you have done — and covered all the bases. But you know what is lacking? An example of what it looks like. Maybe just a little statement that really looks bizarre to me, and then say that by the end of the chapter you, the reader, will actually know what this stuff really means! Sort of like a coming attraction type of thing.
>
> **Steve:** I understand the idea of trying to draw the reader into the "game". However, I think that presenting a bunch of apparent gibberish with no warning could frighten readers as easily as it

---

3. This definition is possibly somewhat misleading since it implies that the development of a program is straightforward and linear, with no revisions required. This is known as the "waterfall model" of programming, since water going over a waterfall follows a preordained course in one direction. However, real-life programming doesn't usually work this way; rather, most programs are written in an incremental process as assumptions are changed and errors are found and corrected.

might intrigue them. I think it's better to delay showing examples until they have some background.

Now let's return to our list of definitions:

Hardware refers to the physical components of a computer, the ones you can touch. Examples include the keyboard, the monitor, the printer.

Software refers to the nonphysical components of a computer, the ones you cannot touch. If you can install it on your hard disk, it's software. Examples include a spreadsheet, a word processor, a database program.

Source code is a program in a form suitable for reading and writing by a human being.

An **executable program** (or an *executable*, for short) is a program in a form suitable for running on a computer.

Object code is a portion of a program in a form suitable for incorporation into an executable program.

Compilation is the process of translating source code into object code. Almost all of the software on your computer was created by this process.

A **compiler** is a program that performs compilation as defined above.

How to Write a Program

Now you have a definition of programming. Unfortunately, however, this doesn't tell you how to write a program. The process of solving a problem by programming in C++ follows these steps:

1. Problem: After discussions between the user and the programmer, the programmer defines the problem precisely.

2. Algorithms: The programmer finds or creates algorithms that will solve the problem.

3. C++: The programmer implements these algorithms as source code in C++.

4. Executable: The programmer runs the C++ compiler, which must already be present on the programmer's machine, to translate the source code into an executable program.

5. Hardware: The user runs the resulting executable program on a computer.

These steps advance from the most abstract to the most concrete, which is perfectly appropriate for an experienced C++ programmer. However, if you're using this book to learn how to program in C++, obviously you're not an experienced C++ programmer, so before you can follow this path to solving a problem you're going to need a fairly thorough grounding in all of these steps.

This description is actually a bit oversimplified, as we'll see in the discussion of *linking* in Chapter 5, "Functional Literacy". For now, let's see what Susan thinks about this issue.

> **Susan:** With all the new concepts and all the new language and terms, it is so hard to know what one thing has to do with the other and where things are supposed to fit into the big picture. Anyway, you have to understand; for someone like me, this is an enormous amount of new material to be introduced to all at once. When you are bombarded with so many new terms and so many abstract concepts, it is a little hard to sort out what is what. Will you have guidelines for each of the steps? Since I know a little about this already, the more I look at the steps, I just know that what is coming is going to be a big deal. For example, take step 1; you have to give the ingredients for properly defining a problem. If something is left out, then everything that follows won't work.

Steve: I hope you won't find it that frustrating, because I explain all of the steps carefully as I do them. Of course, it's possible that I haven't been careful enough, but in that case you can let me know and I'll explain it further.

Unfortunately, it's not possible for me to provide a thorough guide to all of those steps, as that would be a series of books in itself. However, there's a wonderful small book called *How to Solve It* by G. Polya, that you should be able to get at your local library. It was written to help students solve geometry problems, but the techniques are applicable in areas other than geometry. I'm going to recommend that readers of my book read it if they have any trouble with general problem solving.

The steps for solving a problem via programming might sound reasonable in the abstract, but that doesn't mean that you can follow them easily without practice. Assuming that you already have a pretty good idea of what the problem is that you're trying to solve, the algorithms step is likely to be the biggest stumbling block. Therefore, it might be very helpful to go into that step in a bit more detail.

Baby Steps

If we already understand the problem we're going to solve, the next step is to figure out a plan of attack, which we will then break down into small enough steps to be expressed in C++. This is called **stepwise refinement**, since we start out with a "coarse" solution and refine it until the steps are within the capability of the C++ language. For a complex problem, this may take several intermediate steps, but let's start out with a simple example. Say that we want to know how much older one person is than another. We might start with the following general outline:

1. Get two ages from user.

2. Calculate difference of ages.

3. Print the result.

This in turn can be broken down further, as follows:

1. Get two ages from user.

   a. Ask user for first age.

   b. Ask user for second age.

2. Subtract second age from first age.

3. Print result.

This looks okay, except that if the first person is younger than the second one, then the result will be negative. That may be acceptable. If so, we're just about done, since these steps are simple enough for us to translate them into C++ fairly directly. Otherwise, we'll have to modify our program to do something different, depending on which age is higher. For example,

1. Get two ages from user.

   a. Ask user for first age.

   b. Ask user for second age.

2. Compute difference of ages.

   a. If first age is greater than second, subtract second age from first age.

   b. Otherwise, subtract first age from second age.

3. Print result.

You've probably noticed that this is a much more detailed description than would be needed to tell a human being what you want to do. That's because the computer is extremely stupid and literal: it does only what you tell it to do, not what you meant to tell it to do.

Unfortunately, it's very easy to get one of the steps wrong, especially in a complex program. In that case, the computer will do something ridiculous, and you'll have to figure out what you did wrong. This debugging, as it's called, is one of the hardest parts of programming. Actually, it shouldn't be too difficult to understand why that is the case. After all, you're looking for a mistake you've made yourself. If you knew exactly what you were doing, you wouldn't have made the mistake in the first place.

I hope that this brief discussion has made the process of programming a little less mysterious. In the final analysis, it's basically just logical thinking.[4]

On with the Show

Now that you have some idea how programming works, it's time to see exactly how the computer actually performs the steps in a program, which is the topic of Chapter 2, "Hardware Fundamentals".

---

4. Of course, the word *just* in this sentence is a bit misleading; taking logical thinking for granted is a sure recipe for trouble.

CHAPTER 2   *Hardware Fundamentals*

Like any complex tool, the computer can be understood on several levels. For example, it's entirely possible to learn to drive an automobile without having the slightest idea how it works. The analogy with computers is that it's relatively easy to learn how to use a word processor without having any notion of how such programs work. On the other hand, programming is much more closely analogous to designing an automobile than it is to driving one; therefore, we're going to have to go into some detail about the internal workings of a computer, not at the level of electronic components, but at the lowest level accessible to a programmer.

This is a book on learning to program in C++, not on how a computer works.[1] Therefore, it might seem better to start there and eliminate this detour, and indeed many (perhaps most) books on C++ do exactly that. However, in working out in detail how I'm going to

---

1. Some people believe that you should learn C before you learn C++. Obviously, I'm not one of those people; for that matter, neither is the inventor of C++, Bjarne Stroustrup. On page 169 of his book, *The Design and Evolution of C++*, he says "Learn C++ first. The C subset is easier to learn for C/C++ novices and easier to use than C itself".

explain C++ to you, I've come to the conclusion that it would be virtually impossible to explain *why* certain features of the language exist and how they actually work, without your understanding *how* they relate to the underlying computer hardware.

I haven't come to this position by pure logical deduction, either. In fact, I've worked backward from the concepts that you will need to know to program in C++ to the specific underlying information that you will have to understand first. I'm thinking in particular of one specific concept, the *pointer*, that is supposed to be extremely difficult for a beginning programmer in C++ to grasp. With the approach we're taking, you shouldn't have much trouble understanding this concept by the time you get to it in Chapter 7, "Stringing Along". It's noted as such in the discussion there. I'd be interested to know how you find my explanation there, given the background that you'll have by that point; don't hesitate to e-mail me about this topic (or any other, for that matter).

On the other hand, if you're an experienced programmer, a lot of this will be just review for you. Nonetheless, it can't hurt to go over the basics one more time before diving into the ideas and techniques that make C++ different from other languages.

Now let's begin with some definitions and objectives for this chapter.

Definitions

A **digit** is one of the characters used in any positional numbering system to represent all numbers starting at 0 and ending at one less than the base of the numbering system. In the decimal system, there are ten digits, 0–9, and in the hexadecimal system there are sixteen digits, 0–9 and a–f.

A **binary** number system is one that uses only two digits, 0 and 1.

A **hexadecimal** number system is one that uses sixteen digits, 0–9 and a–f.

CPU is an abbreviation for central processing unit. This is the "active" part of your computer, which executes all the *machine instructions* that make the computer do useful work.

A **machine instruction** is one of the fundamental operations that a *CPU* can perform. Some examples of these operations are addition, subtraction, or other arithmetic operations; other possibilities include operations that control what instruction will be executed next. All C++ programs must be converted into machine instructions by a *compiler* before they can be executed by the *CPU*.

An **assembly language** program is the human-readable representation of a set of *machine instruction*s; each assembly language statement corresponds to one machine instruction. By contrast, a C++ program consists of much higher-level operations which cannot be directly translated one-for-one into machine instructions.

Objectives of This Chapter

By the end of this chapter, you should

- Understand the programmer's view of the most important pieces of software in your computer.

- Understand the programmer's view of the most important pieces of hardware in your computer.

- Be able to solve simple problems using both the binary and hexadecimal number systems.

- Understand how whole numbers are stored in the computer.

Behind the Curtain

First we'll need to expand on the definition of *hardware*. As noted earlier, *hardware* means the physical components of a computer, the ones you can touch.[2] Examples are the monitor, which displays your document while you're working on it, the keyboard, the printer, and all of the interesting electronic and electromechanical components inside the case of your computer.[3] Right now, we're concerned with the programmer's view of the hardware. The hardware components of a computer with which you'll be primarily concerned are the disk, RAM (Random Access Memory), and last but certainly not least, the CPU.[4] We'll take up each of these topics in turn.

Disk

When you sit down at your computer in the morning, before you turn it on, where are the programs you're going to run? To make this more specific, suppose you're going to use a word processor to revise a letter you wrote yesterday before you turned the computer off. Where is the letter, and where is the word processing program?

You probably know the answer to this question; they are stored on a *disk* inside the case of your computer. Technically, this is a *hard*

---

2. Whenever I refer to a *computer*, I mean a modern microcomputer capable of running MS-DOS or some version of Windows; these are commonly referred to as *PCs*. Most of the fundamental concepts are the same in other kinds of computers, but the details differ.

3. Although it's entirely possible to program without ever seeing the inside of a computer, you might want to look in there anyway, just to see what the CPU, RAM chips, disk drives, and other components, look like. Some familiarization with the components will give you a head start if you ever want to expand the capacity of your machine.

4. Other hardware components can be important to programmers of specialized applications; for example, game programmers need extremely fine control of how information is displayed on the monitor. However, we have enough to keep us busy learning how to write general data-handling programs. You can always learn how to write games later, if you're interested in doing so.

disk, to differentiate it from a *floppy disk*, the removable storage medium often used to distribute software or transfer files from one computer to another.[5] Disks use magnetic recording media, much like the material used to record speech and music on cassette tapes, to store information in a way that will not be lost when power is turned off. How exactly is this information (which may be either executable programs or data such as word processing documents) stored?

We don't have to go into excruciating detail on the storage mechanism, but it is important to understand some of its characteristics. A disk consists of one or more circular *platters*, which are extremely flat and smooth pieces of metal or glass covered with a material that can be very rapidly and accurately magnetized in either of two directions, "north" and "south". To store large amounts of data, each platter is divided into many millions of small regions, each of which can be magnetized in either direction, independent of the other regions. The magnetization is detected and modified by *recording heads*, similar in principle to those used in tape cassette decks. However, in contrast to the cassette heads, which make contact with the tape while they are recording or playing back music or speech, the disk heads "fly" a few millionths of an inch away from the platters, which rotate at very high velocity.[6]

The separately magnetizable regions used to store information are arranged in groups called *sectors*, which are in turn arranged in

---

5.   Although at one time, many small computers used floppy disks for their main storage, the tremendous decrease in hard disk prices means that today even the most inexpensive computer stores programs and data on a hard disk.

6.   The heads have to be as close as possible to the platters because the influence of a magnet (called the *magnetic field*) drops off very rapidly with distance. Thus, the closer the heads are, the more powerful the magnetic field is and the smaller the region that can be used to store data so that it can be retrieved reliably, and therefore the more data that can be stored in the same physical space. Of course, this leaves open the question of why the heads aren't in contact with the surface; that would certainly solve the problem of being too far away. Unfortunately, this seemingly simple solution would not work at all. There is a name for the contact of heads and disk surface while the disk is spinning, *head crash*. The friction caused by such an event destroys both the heads and disk surface almost instantly.

concentric circles called *tracks*. All tracks on one side of a given platter (a *recording surface*) can be accessed by a recording head dedicated to that recording surface; each sector is used to store some number of *bytes* of the data, generally a few hundred to a few thousand. *Byte* is a coined word meaning a group of 8 *bi*nary digi*ts*, or *bits* for short.[7] You may wonder why the data aren't stored in the more familiar decimal system, which of course uses the digits from 0–9. This is not an arbitrary decision; on the contrary, there are a couple of very good reasons that data on a disk are stored using the binary system, in which each digit has only two possible states, 0 and 1. One of these reasons is that it's a lot easier to determine reliably whether a particular area on a disk is magnetized "north" or "south" than it is to determine 1 of 10 possible levels of magnetization. Another reason is that the binary system is also the natural system for data storage using electronic circuitry, which is used to store data in the rest of the computer.

While magnetic storage devices have been around in one form or another since the very early days of computing, the advances in technology just in the last 15 years have been staggering. To comprehend just how large these advances have been, we need to define the term used to describe storage capacities: the megabyte. The standard engineering meaning of *mega* is "multiply by 1 million", which would make a megabyte equal to 1 million (1,000,000) bytes. As we have just seen, however, the natural number system in the computer field is binary. Therefore, *one megabyte* is often used instead to specify the nearest round number in the binary system, which is 2^{20} (2 to the power of 20), or 1,048,576 bytes. This wasn't obvious to Susan, so I explained it some more:

> **Susan:** Just how important is it to really understand that the megabyte is 2^{20} (1,048,576) bytes? I know that a meg is not really a meg; that is, it's more than a million. But I don't understand 2^{20}, so

---

7. In some old machines, bytes sometimes contained more or less than 8 bits, but the 8-bit byte is virtually universal today.

is it enough to just take your word on this and not get bogged down as to why I didn't go any further than plane geometry in high school? You see, it makes me worry and upsets me that I don't understand how you "round" a binary number.

Steve: 2^{20} would be 2 to the power of 20; that is, 20 twos multiplied together. This is a "round" number in binary, just as 10 * 10 * 10 (1000) is a "round" number in decimal.

1985: A Space Odyssey

With that detail out of the way, we can see just how far we've come in a relatively short time. In 1985, I purchased a 20 megabyte disk for $900 ($45 per megabyte); its **access time**, which measures how long it takes to retrieve data, was approximately 100 milliseconds (milli = 1/1000, so a millisecond is 1/1000 of a second). In April 2000, a 17000 megabyte disk cost as little as $154, or approximately 1 *cent* per megabyte; in addition to delivering 4500 times as much storage per dollar, this disk had an access time of 9 milliseconds, which is approximately 11 times as fast as the old disk. Of course, this significantly understates the amount of progress in technology in both economic and technical terms. For one thing, a 2000 dollar is worth considerably less than a 1985 dollar. In addition, the new drive is superior in every other measure as well. It is much smaller than the old one, consumes much less power, and has many times the projected reliability of the old drive.

This tremendous increase in performance and decrease in price has prevented the long-predicted demise of disk drives in favor of new technology. However, the inherent speed limitations of disks still require us to restrict their role to the storage and retrieval of data for which we can afford to wait a relatively long time.

You see, while 9 milliseconds isn't very long by human standards, it is a long time indeed to a modern computer. This will become more evident as we examine the next essential component of the computer, the *RAM*.

RAM

The working storage of the computer, where data and programs are stored while we're using them is called **RAM**, which is an acronym for random access memory. For example, your word processor is stored in RAM while you're using it. The document you're working on is likely to be there as well unless it's too large to fit all at once, in which case parts of it will be retrieved from the disk as needed. Since we have already seen that both the word processor and the document are stored on the disk in the first place, why not leave them there and use them in place, rather than copying them into RAM?

The answer, in a word, is *speed*. RAM, which is sometimes called "internal storage", as opposed to "external storage" (the disk), is physically composed of millions of microscopic switches on a small piece of silicon known as a *chip*: a 4-megabit RAM chip has approximately 4 million of them.[8] Each of these switches can be either on or off; we consider a switch that is on to be storing a 1, and a switch that is off to be storing a 0. Just as in storing information on a disk, where it is easier to magnetize a region in either of two directions, it's a lot easier to make a switch that can be turned on or off reliably and quickly than one that can be set to any value from 0–9 reliably and quickly. This is particularly important when you're manufacturing millions of them on a silicon chip the size of your fingernail.

A main difference between disk and RAM is what steps are needed to access different areas of storage. In the case of the disk, the head has to be moved to the right track (an operation known as a *seek*), and then we have to wait for the platter to spin so that the region we want to access is under the head (called *rotational delay*). On the other hand, with RAM, the entire process is electronic; we can read or write any byte immediately as long as we know which byte

---

8. Each switch is made of several transistors. Unfortunately, an explanation of how a transistor works would take us too far afield. Consult any good encyclopedia, such as the *Encyclopedia Britannica*, for this explanation.

we want. To specify a given byte, we have to supply a unique number, called its **memory address,** or just **address** for short.

Return to Sender, Address Unknown

What is an address good for? Let's see how my discussion with Susan on this topic started.

> **Susan:** About memory addresses, are you saying that each little itty bitty tiny byte of RAM is a separate address? Well, this is a little hard to imagine.

> **Steve:** Actually, each byte of RAM *has* a separate address, which doesn't change, and a value, which does.

In case the notion of an address of a byte of memory on a piece of silicon is too abstract, it might help to think of an address as a set of directions to find the byte being addressed, much like directions to someone's house. For example, "Go three streets down, then turn left. It's the second house on the right". With such directions, the house number wouldn't need to be written on the house. Similarly, the memory storage areas in RAM are addressed by position; you can think of the address as telling the hardware which street and house you want, by giving directions similar in concept to the preceding example. Therefore, it's not necessary to encode the addresses into the RAM explicitly.

Susan wanted a better picture of this somewhat abstract idea:

> **Susan:** Where are the bytes on the RAM, and what do they look like?

> **Steve:** Each byte corresponds to a microscopic region of the RAM chip. As to what they look like, have you ever seen a printed circuit board such as the ones inside your computer? Imagine the lines on that circuit board reduced thousands of times in size to microscopic

dimensions, and you'll have an idea of what a RAM chip looks like inside.

Since it has no moving parts, storing and retrieving data in RAM is much faster than waiting for the mechanical motion of a disk platter turning.[9] As we've just seen, disk access times are measured in milliseconds, or thousandths of a second. However, RAM access times are measured in *nanoseconds* (*ns*); *nano* means one-billionth. In early 2000, a typical speed for RAM was 10 ns, which means that it is possible to read a given data item from RAM about 1,000,000 times as quickly as from a disk. In that case, why not use disks only for permanent storage, and read everything into RAM in the morning when we turn on the machine?

The reason is cost. In early 2000, the cost of 128 megabytes of RAM was approximately $150. For that same amount of money, you could have bought over 16000 megabytes of disk space! Therefore, we must reserve RAM for tasks where speed is all-important, such as running your word processing program and holding a letter while you're working on it. Also, since RAM is an electronic storage medium (rather than a magnetic one), it does not maintain its contents when the power is turned off. This means that if you had a power failure while working with data only in RAM, you would lose everything you had been doing.[10] This is not merely a theoretical

---

9. There's also another kind of electronic storage, called **ROM**, for read-only memory; as its name indicates, you can read from it, but you can't write to it. This is used for storing permanent information, such as the program that allows your computer to read a small program from your *boot disk*; that program, in turn, reads in the rest of the data and programs needed to start up the computer. This process, as you probably know, is called *booting* the computer. In case you're wondering where that term came from, it's an abbreviation for *bootstrapping*, which is intended to suggest the fanciful notion of pulling yourself up by your bootstraps. Also, you may have noticed that the terms RAM and ROM aren't symmetrical; why isn't RAM called RWM, read-write memory? Probably because it's too hard to pronounce.

10. The same disaster would happen if your system were to crash, which is not that unlikely if you're using certain popular PC graphically oriented operating environments whose names start with "W".

problem, by the way; if you don't remember to save what you're doing in your word processor once in a while, you might lose a whole day's work from a power outage of a few seconds.[11]

Before we get to how a program actually works, we need to develop a better picture of how RAM is used. As I've mentioned before, you can think of RAM as consisting of a large number of bytes, each of which has a unique identifier called an *address*. This address can be used to specify which byte we mean, so the program might specify that it wants to read the value in byte 148257, or change the value in byte 66666. Susan wanted to make sure she had the correct understanding of this topic:

> **Susan:** Are the values changed in RAM depending on what program is loaded in it?

> **Steve:** Yes, and they also change while the program is executing. RAM is used to store both the program itself and the values it manipulates.

This is all very well, but it doesn't answer the question of how the program actually uses or changes values in RAM, or performs arithmetic and other operations; that's the job of the CPU, which we will take up next.

The CPU

The **CPU** (central processing unit) is the "active" component in the computer. Like RAM, it is physically composed of millions of microscopic transistors on a chip; however, the organization of these transistors in a CPU is much more complex than on a RAM chip, as the latter's functions are limited to the storage and retrieval of data.

---

11. Most modern word processors can automatically save your work once in a while, for this very reason. I heartily recommend using this facility; it's saved my bacon more than once.

The CPU, on the other hand, is capable of performing dozens or hundreds of different fundamental operations called *machine instructions*, or *instructions* for short. While each instruction performs a very simple function, the tremendous power of the computer lies in the fact that the CPU can perform (or *execute*) tens or hundreds of millions of these instructions per second.

These instructions fall into a number of categories: instructions that perform arithmetic operations such as adding, subtracting, multiplying, and dividing; instructions that move information from one place to another in RAM; instructions that compare two quantities to help make a determination as to which instructions need to be executed next and instructions that implement that decision; and other, more specialized types of instructions.[12]

Of course, adding two numbers together, for example, requires that the numbers be available for use. Possibly the most straightforward way of making them available is to store them in and retrieve them from RAM whenever they are needed, and indeed this is done sometimes. However, as fast as RAM is compared to disk drives (not to mention human beings), it's still pretty slow compared to modern CPUs. For example, the computer I'm using right now has a 500 megahertz (MHz)[13] Pentium III CPU, which can execute an instruction in 2 ns.

To see why RAM is a bottleneck, let's calculate how long it would take to execute an instruction if all the data had to come from and go back to RAM. A typical instruction would have to read some

---

12. Each type of CPU has a different set of instructions, so programs compiled for one CPU cannot in general be run on a different CPU. Some CPUs, such as the very popular Pentium series from Intel, fall into a "family" of CPUs in which each new CPU can execute all of the instructions of the previous family members. This allows upgrading to a new CPU without having to throw out all of your old programs, but limits the ways in which the new CPU can be improved without affecting this "family compatibility".

13. Since frequency is measured in decimal units rather than in binary units, the *mega* in megahertz means one million (10^6), not 1,048,576 (2^{20}) as it does when referring to memory and disk capacity. I'm sorry if this is confusing, but it can't be helped.

data from RAM, and write its result back there; first, though, the instruction itself has to be loaded (or *fetched*) into the CPU before it can be executed. Let's suppose we have an instruction in RAM, reading and writing data also in RAM. Then the minimum timing to do such an instruction could be calculated as in Figure 2.1.

To compute the effective speed of a CPU, we divide 1 second by the time it takes to execute one instruction.[14] Given the assumptions in this example, the CPU could execute only about 31 MIPS (million instructions per second), which is a far cry from the 500 MIPS or more that we might expect.[15] This seems very wasteful; is there a way to get more speed?

FIGURE 2.1. **RAM vs. CPU speeds.**

Time	Function
10 ns	Read instruction from RAM
10 ns	Read data from RAM
2 ns	Execute instruction
10 ns	Write result back to RAM
32 ns	Total instruction execution time

In fact, there is. As a result of a lot of research and development, both in academia and in the semiconductor industry, it is possible to approach the rated performance of fast CPUs, as will be illustrated in Figure 2.12. Some of these techniques have been around for as long as we've had computers; others have fairly recently trickled down from supercomputers to microcomputer CPUs. One of the most important of these techniques is the use of a number of different kinds

---

14. In fact, the Pentium III can actually execute more than one instruction at a time if conditions are right. I'll ignore this detail in my analysis, but if I considered it, the discrepancy between memory speeds and CPU speeds would be even greater.

15. 1 second/32 ns per instruction = 31,250,000 instructions per second.

of storage devices having different performance characteristics; the arrangement of these devices is called the **memory hierarchy**. Figure 2.2 illustrates the memory hierarchy of my home machine. Susan and I had a short discussion about the layout of this figure.

> **Susan:** OK, just one question on Figure 2.2. If you are going to include the disk in this hierarchy, I don't know why you have placed it over to the side of RAM and not above it, since it is slower and you appear to be presenting this figure in ascending order of speed from the top of the figure downward. Did you do this because it is external rather than internal memory and it doesn't "deserve" to be in the same lineage as the others?

> **Steve:** Yes; it's not the same as "real" memory, so I wanted to distinguish it.

Before we get to the diagram, I should explain that a **cache** is a small amount of fast memory where frequently used data are stored temporarily. According to this definition, RAM functions more or less as a cache for the disk; after all, we have to copy data from a slow disk into fast RAM before we can use it for anything. However, while this is a valid analogy, I should point out that the situations aren't quite parallel. Our programs usually read data from disk into RAM explicitly; that is, we're aware of whether it's on the disk or in RAM, and we have to issue commands to transfer it from one place to the other. On the other hand, caches are "automatic" in their functioning. We don't have to worry about them, and our programs work in exactly the same way with them as without them, except faster. In any event, the basic idea is the same: to use a faster type of memory to speed up repetitive access to data usually stored on a slower storage device.

We've already seen that the disk is necessary to store data and programs when the machine is turned off, while RAM is needed for its higher speed in accessing data and programs we're currently using.[16] But why do we need the *external cache*?

Actually, we've been around this track before when we questioned why everything isn't loaded into RAM rather than read from the disk as needed; we're trading speed for cost. To have a cost-effective computer with good performance requires the designer to choose the correct amount of each storage medium.

So just as with the disk vs. RAM trade-off, the reason that we use the external cache is to improve performance. While RAM can be accessed about 100 million times per second, the external cache is made from a faster type of memory chip, which can be accessed about 250 million times per second. While not as extreme as the speed differential between disk and RAM, it is still significant.

However, we can't afford to use external cache exclusively instead of RAM because there isn't enough of it. Therefore, we must reserve external cache for tasks where speed is all-important, such as supplying frequently used data or programs to the CPU.

The same analysis applies to the trade-off between the external cache and the *internal cache*. The internal cache's characteristics are similar to those of the external cache, but to a greater degree; it's even smaller and faster, allowing access at the rated speed of the CPU. Both characteristics have to do with its privileged position on the same chip as the CPU; this reduces the delays in communication between the internal cache and the CPU, but means that chip area devoted to the cache has to compete with area for the CPU, as long as the total chip size is held constant.

Unfortunately, we can't just increase the size of the chip to accommodate more internal cache because of the expense of doing so. Larger chips are more difficult to make, which reduces their *yield*, or the percentage of good chips. In addition, fewer of them fit on one *wafer*, which is the unit of manufacturing. Both of these attributes make larger chips more expensive to make.

---

16. These complementary roles played by RAM and the disk explain why the speed of the disk is also illustrated in the memory hierarchy.

FIGURE 2.2. A memory hierarchy.

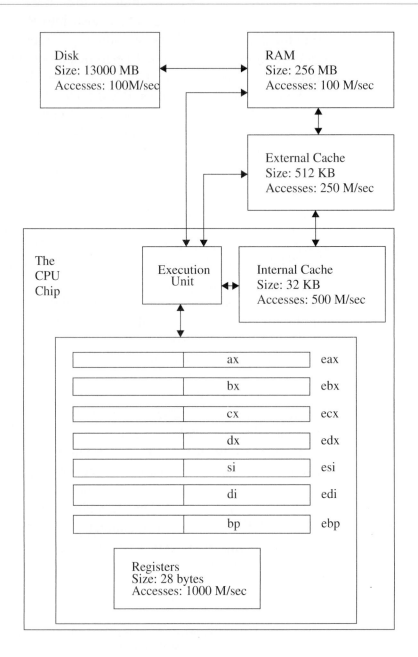

Caching In

To oversimplify a bit, here's how caching reduces the effects of slow RAM. Whenever a data item is requested by the CPU, there are three possibilities.

1. It is already in the internal cache. In this case, the value is sent to the CPU without referring to RAM at all.

2. It is in the external cache. In this case, it will be "promoted" to the internal cache and sent to the CPU at the same time.

3. It is not in either the internal or external cache. In this case, it has to be entered into a location in the internal cache. If there is nothing already stored in that cache location, the new item is simply added to the cache. However, if there is a data item already in that cache location, then the old item is displaced to the external cache, and the new item is written in its place.[17] If the external cache location is empty, that ends the activity; if it is not empty, then the item previously in that location is written out to RAM and its slot is used for the one displaced from the internal cache.[18]

Please Register Here

Another way to improve performance that has been employed for many years is to create a small number of private storage areas, called **registers**, that are on the same chip as the CPU itself.[19] Programs use

---

17. It's also possible to have a cache that stores more than one item in a location, in which case one of the other items already there will be displaced to make room for the new one. The one selected is usually the one that hasn't been accessed for the longest time, on the theory that it's probably not going to be accessed again soon; this is called the *least recently used* (abbreviated LRU) replacement algorithm.

18. This is fairly close to the actual way caches are used to reduce the time it takes to get frequently used data from RAM (known as *caching reads*); reducing the time needed to write changed values back to RAM (*caching writes*) is more complicated.

these registers to hold data items that are actively in use; data in registers can be accessed within the time allocated to instruction execution (2 ns in our example), rather than in the much longer time needed to access data in RAM. This means that the time needed to access data in registers is predictable, unlike data that may have been displaced from the internal cache by more recent arrivals and thus must be reloaded from the external cache or even from RAM. Most CPUs have some **dedicated registers**, which aren't available to application programmers (that's us), but are reserved for the operating system (e.g., DOS, UNIX, OS/2) or have special functions dictated by the hardware design; however, we will be concerned primarily with the **general registers** intended for our use.[20] These are used to hold working copies of data items called **variables**, which otherwise reside in RAM during the execution of the program. These variables represent specific items of data, that we wish to keep track of in our programs.

The notion of using registers to hold temporary copies of variables wasn't crystal clear to Susan. Here's our discussion:

> **Susan:** Here we go, getting lost. When you say, "The general registers are used to hold working copies of data items called variables, which reside in RAM", are you saying RAM stores info when not in use?

---

19. In case you're wondering how a small number of registers can help the speed of a large program, I should point out that no matter how large a program is, the vast majority of instructions and data items in the program are inactive at any given moment. In fact, perhaps only a dozen instructions are in various stages of execution at any given time even in the most advanced microprocessor CPU available in 2000. The computer's apparent ability to run several distinct programs simultaneously is an illusion produced by the extremely high rate of execution of instructions.

20. All of the registers are physically similar, being just a collection of circuits in the CPU used to hold a value. As indicated here, some registers are dedicated to certain uses by the design of the CPU, whereas others are generally usable. In the case of the general registers, which are all functionally similar or identical, a compiler often uses them in a conventional way; this stylized usage simplifies the compiler writer's job.

Steve: During execution of a program, when data aren't in the general registers, they are generally stored in RAM.

Susan: I didn't think RAM stores anything when turned off.

Steve: You're correct; RAM doesn't retain information when the machine is turned off. However, it is used to keep the "real" copies of data that we want to process but won't fit in the registers.[21]

You can put something in a variable, and it will stay there until you store something else there; you can also look at it to find out what's in it. As you might expect, several types of variables are used to hold different kinds of data; the first ones we will look at are variables representing whole numbers (the so-called **integer variables**), which are a subset of the category called **numeric variables**. As this suggests, other variable types can represent numbers with fractional parts. We'll use these so-called *floating-point* variables later.

Different types of variables require different amounts of RAM to store them, depending on the amount of data they contain; a very common type of numeric variable, known as a **short**, requires 16 bits (that is, 2 bytes) of RAM to hold any of 65536 different values, from −32768 to 32767, including 0. As we will see shortly, these odd-looking numbers are the result of using the binary system. By no coincidence at all, the early Intel CPUs such as the 8086 had general registers that contained 16 bits each; these registers were named ax, bx, cx, dx, si, di, and bp. Why does it matter how many bits each register holds? Because the number (and size) of instructions it takes to process a variable is much less if the variable fits in a register; therefore, most programming languages, C++ included, relate the size of a variable to the size of the registers available to hold it. A short is exactly the right size to fit into a 16-bit register and therefore

---

21. Since RAM doesn't maintain its contents when power is turned off, anything that a program needs to keep around for a long time, such as inventory data to be used later, should be saved on the disk. We'll see how that is accomplished in a future chapter.

can be processed efficiently by the early Intel machines, whereas longer variables had to be handled in pieces, causing a great decline in efficiency of the program.

Progress marches on; More recent Intel CPUs, starting with the 80386, have 32-bit general registers; these registers are called eax, ebx, ecx, edx, esi, edi, and ebp. You may have noticed that these names are simply the names of the old 16-bit registers with an e tacked onto the front. The reason for the name change is that when Intel increased the size of the registers to 32 bits with the advent of the 80386, it didn't want to change the behavior of previously existing programs that (of course) used the old names for the 16-bit registers. So the old names, as illustrated in Figure 2.2, now refer to the bottom halves of the "real" (that is, 32-bit) registers; instructions using these old names behave exactly as though they were accessing the 16-bit registers on earlier machines. To refer to the 32-bit registers, you use the new names eax, ebx, and so on, for *extended* ax, *extended* bx, and so forth.

What does it mean to say that instructions using the 16-bit register names behave exactly as though they were accessing the 16-bit registers on earlier machines? Before I can explain this, you'll have to understand the binary number system on which all modern computers are based. To make this number system more intelligible, I have written the following little fable.

Odometer Trouble

Once upon a time, the Acme company had a factory that made golf carts. One day, Bob, the president of Acme, decided to add an odometer to the carts so that the purchaser of the cart could estimate when to recharge the battery. To save money, Bob decided to buy the little numbered wheels for the odometers and have his employees put the odometers together. The minimum order was for a thousand odometer wheels, which was more than he needed for his initial run of 50 odometers. When he got the wheels, however, he noticed that they were defective. Instead of the numbers 0–9, each wheel had only two numbers, 0 and 1. Of course, he was quite irritated by this error and attempted to contact the company from which he had purchased the wheels, but it had closed down for a month for summer vacation. What was he to do until it reopened?

While he was fretting about this problem, the employee who had been assigned the task of putting the odometers together from the wheels came up with a possible solution. This employee, Jim, came into Bob's office and said, "Bob, I have an idea. Since we have lots of orders for these odometer-equipped carts, maybe we can make an odometer with these funny wheels and tell the customers how to read the numbers on the odometer".

Bob was taken aback by this idea. "What do you mean, Jim? How can anyone read those screwy odometers"?

Jim had given this some thought. "Let's take a look at what one of these odometers, say with five wheels, can display. Obviously, it would start out reading 00000, just like a normal odometer. Then when one mile has elapsed, the rightmost wheel turns to 1, so the whole display is 00001; again, this is just like a normal odometer".

"Now we come to the tricky part. The rightmost wheel goes back to 0, not having any more numbers to display, and pushes the 'tens' wheel to 1; the whole number now reads 00010. Obviously, one more mile makes it 00011, which gives the situation shown in Figure 2.3."

FIGURE 2.3. The first few numbers.

Normal odometer	Funny odometer
00000	00000
00001	00001
00002	00010
00003	00011

Jim continued, "What's next"? This time, the rightmost wheel turns over again to 0, triggering the second wheel to its next position. However, this time, the second wheel is already at its highest value, 1; therefore, it also turns over to 0 and increments the third wheel. It's not hard to follow this for a few more miles, as shown in Figure 2.4."

Bob said, "I get it. It's almost as though we were counting normally, except that you skip all the numbers that have anything but 0s or 1s in them".

FIGURE 2.4. **The next few numbers.**

Normal odometer	Funny odometer
00004	00100
00005	00101
00006	00110
00007	00111

"That's right, Bob. So I suppose we could make up a list of the 'real' numbers and give it to the customers to use until we can replace these odometers with normal ones. Perhaps they'll be willing to work with us on this problem".

"Okay, Jim, if you think they'll buy it. Let's get a few of the customers we know best and ask them if they'll try it; we won't charge them for the odometers until we have the real ones, but maybe they'll stick with us until then. Perhaps any odometer would be better than no odometer at all".

Jim went to work, making some odometers out of the defective wheels; however, he soon figured out that he had to use more than five wheels because that allowed only numbers from 0 to 31. How did he know this?

Each wheel has two numbers, 0 and 1. So with one wheel, we have a total of two combinations. Two wheels can have either a 0 or a 1 for the first number, and for each position of the first wheel there are two possibilities for the second; $2*2 = 4$, so there are a total of four combinations for two wheels. With three wheels, the same analysis holds: two numbers for the first wheel * two for the second wheel * two for the third wheel, or eight possibilities in all; actually, they are the same eight possibilities we saw in Figures 2.3 and 2.4.

A pattern is beginning to develop. For each added wheel, we get twice as many possible combinations. To see how this continues, take a look at Figure 2.5[22], which shows the count of combinations vs. the number of wheels for all wheel counts up to 16 (i.e., quantities that can be expressed by 16-bit numbers).

Jim decided that 14 wheels would do the job, since the lifespan of the golf cart probably wouldn't exceed 16383 miles, and so he made up the odometers. The selected customers turned out to be agreeable and soon found that having even a weird odometer was better than none, especially since they didn't have to pay for it. However, one customer did have a complaint. The numbers on the wheels didn't seem to make sense when translated with the chart supplied by Acme.

The customer estimated that he had driven the cart about 9 miles, but the odometer displayed

11111111110111

which, according to his translation chart, was 16375 miles. What could have gone wrong?

Jim decided to have the cart brought in for a checkup, and what he discovered was that the odometer cable had been hooked up backwards. That is, instead of turning the wheels forward, they were going backwards. That was part of the solution, but why was the value 16375? Just like a car odometer, in which 99999 (or 999999, if you have a six-wheel odometer) is followed by 0, going backwards from 0 reverses that progression. Similarly, the number

---

22. If you think that last number in Figure 2.5 looks familiar, you're right. It's the number of different values that I said could be stored in a type of numeric variable called a short. This is no coincidence; read on for the detailed explanation.

11111111111111 on the funny odometers would be followed by 00000000000000, since the "carry" off to the leftmost digit is lost.

FIGURE 2.5. How many combinations?

Number of wheels	Number of combinations
1	2
2	4
3	8
4	16
5	32
6	64
7	128
8	256
9	512
10	1024
11	2048
12	4096
13	8192
14	16384
15	32768
16	65536

Therefore, if you start out at 0 and go backward 1 mile, you'll get

11111111111111

The next mile will turn the last digit back to 0, producing

11111111111110

What happens next? The last wheel turns back to 1 and triggers the second wheel to switch as well, with the result

111111111101

The next few "backward" numbers look like this:

111111111100
111111111011
111111111010
111111111001
111111111000
111111110111

and so on. If you look at the right-hand end of these numbers, you'll see that the progression is just the opposite of the "forward" numbers.

As for the customer's actual mileage, the last one of these is the number the customer saw on his backward odometer. Apparently, he was right about the distance driven, since this is the ninth "backward" number. So Jim fixed the backward odometer cable and reset the value to the correct number, 00000000001001, or 9 miles.

Eventually, Acme got the right odometer wheels with 0–9 on them, replaced the peculiar ones, and everyone lived happily ever after.

THE END

Back to the Future

Since the wheels that made up the funny odometers contain only two digits, 0 and 1, the odometers use the binary system for counting. Now it should be obvious why we will see numbers like 65536 and 32768 in our discussions of the number of possible different values that a variable can hold; variables are stored in RAM as collections of bytes, each of which contains 8 bits. As the list of combinations indicates, 8 bits (1 byte) provide 256 different combinations, while 16 bits (2 bytes) can represent 65536 different possible values.

But what about the "backward" numbers with a lot of 1s on the left? As the fable suggests, they correspond to negative numbers. That is, if moving 2 miles forward from 0 registers as 00000000000010, and moving 2 miles backward from 0 registers as 11111111111110, then the latter number is in some sense equivalent to –2 miles. This in fact is the way that negative integers are stored in the computer; integer variables that can store either positive or negative values are called *signed variables*. If we don't specify whether we want to be able to store either positive or negative values in a given variable, the C++ language assumes that we want that ability, and provides it for us by default.

However, adding the ability to represent negative numbers has a drawback: you can't represent as many positive numbers. This should be fairly obvious, since if we interpret some of the possible patterns as negative, they can't also be used for positive values. Of course, we don't have to worry about negative numbers when counting, for example, how many employees our company has; in such cases, we can specify that we want to use *unsigned variables*, which will always be interpreted as positive (or 0) values. An example is an unsigned short variable, which uses 16 bits (that is, 2 bytes) to hold any number from 0 to 65535, which totals 65536 different values. This capacity can be calculated as follows: since each byte is 8 bits, 2 bytes contain a total of 16 bits, and 2^{16} is 65536.

It's important to understand that the difference between a short (that is, a signed short) and an unsigned short is exactly which 65536 values each can hold. An unsigned short can hold any whole number from 0 to 65535, whereas a short can hold any value from –32768 to +32767.

I hope this is clear to you, but in case it isn't, let's see how Susan and I worked over this point.

Susan: I really don't think I understand what a short is besides being 2 bytes of RAM, and I don't really know what signed and unsigned mean.

Steve: A short is indeed 2 bytes (that is, 16 bits) of RAM. This means that it can hold any of 2^{16} (65536) different values. This is a very nice range of values for holding the number of pounds that a pumpkin weighs (for example). You'll see some more uses for this type of variable later.

The difference between a (signed) short and an unsigned short is exactly which 65536 values each can hold. An unsigned short can hold any whole number from 0 to 65535, whereas a (signed) short can hold any value from -32768 to $+32767$. The difference between these is *solely* in the interpretation that we (and the compiler) give to the values. In other words, it's not possible to tell whether a given 2 bytes of RAM represent a short or an unsigned short by looking at the contents of those bytes; you have to know how the variable was defined in the program.

Susan: OK, let's start over. A short is 2 bytes of RAM. A short is a variable. A short is a numeric variable. It can be signed (why is that a default?), meaning its value can be -32768 to $+32767$, or unsigned, meaning its value can be 0–65535. How's that?

Steve: That's fine. Since you've asked, the reason signed is the default is because that's the way it was in C, and changing it in C++ would "break" C programs that depend on this default. Bjarne Stroustrup, the inventor of C++, has a rule that C++ must be as close to C as possible but no closer. In this case, there's no real reason to change the default, so it wasn't changed.

Susan: Oh, why is it that every time you say something is fairly obvious, my mind just shuts down? When you say "if we interpret some of the possible patterns as negative, they can't also be used for positive values." Huh? Then if that is the case, would not the reverse also be true? I can see how this explains the values of the signed and unsigned short, but really, I don't think I have grasped this concept.

Steve: What I was trying to explain is that you have to choose one of the following two possibilities:[23]

1. (signed) short range: -32768 to $+32767$

2. unsigned short range: 0 to 65535

In other words, you have to decide whether you want a given variable to represent

1. Any of 65536 values from -32768 to $+32767$, including 0.

2. Any of 65536 values numbers from 0 to 65535.

If you want a variable with a range like that in selection 1, use a (signed) short; if you prefer the range in selection 2, use an unsigned short. For example, for the number of lines in a text file, you could use an unsigned short, since the maximum number of lines could be limited to less than 65000 lines and couldn't ever be negative. On the other hand, to represent the number of copies of a book that have been sold in the last month, including the possibility of returns exceeding sales, a signed short would be better, since the value could be either positive or negative.

Susan: In other words, if you are going to be using variables that might have a negative value, then use a signed short, and if you want strictly positive numbers, including 0 as "positive", then use an unsigned short. Right?

Steve: Exactly!

---

23. If neither of these does what you want, don't despair. Other types of numeric variables have different ranges, as we'll see starting in Chapter 9.

Susan: Well, then, how do you write a short to indicate that it is signed or unsigned?

Steve: When you define it, you have to specify that it is unsigned if you want it to be unsigned; the default is signed. In other words, if we define a variable x as short x;, it will be signed, whereas if we want a variable called x that is an unsigned short, we have to say unsigned short x;.

Susan: So does it make any difference if your variable is going to overlap the signed and unsigned short ranges? For example, if you are using numbers from 10000 to 30000, would it matter which short you used? It falls under the definition of both.

Steve: You can use whichever you wish in that case.

Over-Hexed

You may have noticed that it's tedious and error prone to represent numbers in binary; a long string of 0s and 1s is hard to remember or to copy. For this reason, the pure binary system is hardly ever used to specify numbers in computing. However, we have already seen that binary is much more "natural" for computers than the more familiar decimal system. Is there a number system that we humans can use a little more easily than binary, while retaining the advantages of binary for describing internal events in the computer?

As it happens, there is. It's called **hexadecimal**, which means "base 16". As a rule, the term *hexadecimal* is abbreviated to *hex*. Since there are 16 possible combinations of 4 bits (2*2*2*2), hexadecimal notation allows 4 bits of a binary number to be represented by one hex digit. Unfortunately, however, there are only 10 "normal" digits, 0–9.[24] To represent a number in any base, you need as many different digit values as the base, so that any number

---

24. Paging Dr. Seuss...

less than the base can be represented by one digit. For example, in base 2, you need only two digits, 0 and 1. In base 8 (*octal*), you need eight digits, 0–7.[25] So far, so good. But what about base 16? To use this base, we need 16 digits. Since only 10 numeric digits are available, hex notation needs a source for the other six digits. Because letters of the alphabet are available and familiar, the first six letters, a–f, were adopted for this service.[26]

Although the notion of a base-16 numbering system doesn't seem strange to people who are familiar with it, it can really throw someone who learned normal decimal arithmetic solely by rote, without understanding the concepts on which it is based. This topic of hexadecimal notation occupied Susan and me for quite awhile; here's some of the discussion we had about it:

> **Susan:** I don't get this at all! What is the deal with the letters in the hex system? I guess it would be okay if 16 wasn't represented by 10!

> **Steve:** Well, there are only 10 "normal" digits, 0–9. To represent a number in any base, you need as many "digits" as the base, so that any number less than the base can be represented by one "digit". This is no problem with a base less than ten, such as octal, but what about base 16? To use this base we need 16 digits, 0–9 and a–f. One way to remember this is to imagine that the "hex" in "hexadecimal" stands for the six letters a–f and the "decimal" stands for the 10 digits 0–9.

> **Susan:** OK, so a hex digit represents 16 bits? So then is hex equal to 2 bytes? According to the preceding a hex digit is 4 bits.

---

25. In the early days of computing, base 8 was sometimes used instead of base 16, especially on machines that used 12-bit and 36-bit registers; however, it has fallen into disuse because almost all modern machines have 32-bit registers.

26. Either upper- or lowercase letters are acceptable to most programs (and programmers). I'll use lower case because such letters are easier to distinguish than upper case ones; besides, I find them less irritating to look at.

Steve: Yes, a hex digit represents 4 bits. Let's try a new approach. First, let me define a new term, a *hexit*. That's short for "hex digit", just like "bit" is short for "binary digit".

1. How many one-digit decimal numbers exist?

2. How many two-digit decimal numbers exist?

3. How many three-digit decimal numbers exist?

4. How many four-digit decimal numbers exist?

5. How many one-bit binary numbers exist?

6. How many two-bit binary numbers exist?

7. How many three-bit binary numbers exist?

8. How many four-bit binary numbers exist?

9. How many one-hexit hexadecimal numbers exist?

10. How many two-hexit hexadecimal numbers exist?

11. How many three-hexit hexadecimal numbers exist?

12. How many four-hexit hexadecimal numbers exist?

The answers are:

1. 10

2. 100

3. 1000

4. 10000

5. 2

6. 4

7. 8

8. 16

9. 16

10. 256

11. 4096

12. 65536

What do all these answers have in common? Let's look at the answers a little differently, in powers of 10, 2, and 16, respectively:

1. $10 = 10\text{\textasciicircum}1$

2. $100 = 10\text{\textasciicircum}2$

3. $1000 = 10\text{\textasciicircum}3$

4. $10000 = 10\text{\textasciicircum}4$

5. $2 = 2\text{\textasciicircum}1$

6. $4 = 2\text{\textasciicircum}2$

7. $8 = 2\text{\textasciicircum}3$

8. $16 = 2\text{\textasciicircum}4$

9. $16 = 16\text{\textasciicircum}1$

10. $256 = 16\text{\textasciicircum}2$

11. $4096 = 16\text{\textasciicircum}3$

12. $65536 = 16\text{\textasciicircum}4$

That is, a number that has one digit can represent "base" different values, where "base" is 2, 10, or 16 (in our examples). Every time we increase the size of the number by one more digit, we can represent "base" times as many possible different values, or in other words, we multiply the range of values that the number can represent by the base. Thus, a two-digit number can represent any of "base*base" values, a three-digit number can represent any of "base*base*base" values, and so on. That's the way positional number systems such as decimal, binary, and hex work. If you need a bigger number, you just add more digits.

Okay, so what does this have to do with hex? If you look at the above table, you'll see that 2^4 (16) is equal to 16^1. That means that 4 bits are exactly equivalent to one hexit in their ability to represent different numbers: exactly 16 possible numbers can be represented by four bits, and exactly 16 possible numbers can be represented by one hexit.

This means that you can write one hexit wherever you would otherwise have to use four bits, as illustrated in Figure 2.6.

So an 8-bit number, such as:
0101 1011
can be translated directly into a hex value, like this:
5   b

For this reason, binary is almost never used. Instead, we use hex as a shortcut to eliminate the necessity of reading, writing, and remembering long strings of bits.

Susan: A hex digit or hexit is like a four-wheel odometer in binary. Since each wheel is capable of only one of two values, being either (1) or (0), then the total number of possible values is 16. Thus your 2*2*2*2 = 16. I think I've got this down.

Steve: You certainly do!

Susan: If it has 4 bits and you have 2 of them then won't there be eight "wheels" and so forth? So 2 hex would hold XXXXXXXX places and 3 hex would hold XXXXXXXXXXXX places.

Steve: Correct. A one-hexit number is analogous to a one-digit decimal number. A one-hexit number contains 4 bits and therefore can represent any of 16 values. A two-hexit number contains 8 bits and therefore can represent any of 256 values.

Now that we've seen how each hex digit corresponds exactly to a group of four binary digits, here's an exercise you can use to improve your understanding of this topic: Invent a random string of four binary digits and see where it is in Figure 2.6. I guarantee it'll be there somewhere! Then look at the "hex" column and see what "digit" it corresponds to. There's nothing really mysterious about hex; since we have run out of digits after 9, we have to use letters to represent the numbers 'ten', 'eleven', 'twelve', 'thirteen', 'fourteen', and 'fifteen'.

FIGURE 2.6. **Binary to hex conversion table**

4-bit value	1-hexit value
0000	0
0001	1
0010	2
0011	3
0100	4
0101	5
0110	6
0111	7
1000	8
1001	9
1010	a
1011	b
1100	c
1101	d
1110	e
1111	f

Another reason to use hex rather than decimal is that byte values expressed as hex digits can be combined directly to produce larger values, which is not true with decimal digits. In case this isn't obvious, let's go over it in more detail. Since each hex digit (0–f) represents exactly 4 bits, two of them (00–ff) represent 8 bits, or one byte. Similarly, 4 hex digits (0000–ffff) represent 16 bits, or a short value; the first two digits represent the first byte of the 2-byte value, and the last two digits, the second byte. This can be extended to any number of bytes. On the other hand, representing 4 bits requires two decimal digits, as the values range from 00–15, whereas it takes three digits (000–255) to represent one byte. A 2-byte value requires five decimal digits, since the value can be from 00000 to 65535. As you can see, there's no simple relationship between the decimal digits representing each byte and the decimal representation of a 2-byte value.

Figure 2.7 is a table showing the correspondence between some decimal, hex, and binary numbers, with the values of each digit position in each number base indicated, and the calculation of the total of all of the bit values in the binary representation.

FIGURE 2.7. Different representations of the same numbers

Decimal Place Values 10 1	Hexadecimal Place Values 16 1	Binary Place Values 16 8 4 2 1		Sum of binary digit values
0	0 0	0 0 0 0 0	=	0 + 0 + 0 + 0 + 0
1	0 1	0 0 0 0 1	=	0 + 0 + 0 + 0 + 1
2	0 2	0 0 0 1 0	=	0 + 0 + 0 + 2 + 0
3	0 3	0 0 0 1 1	=	0 + 0 + 0 + 2 + 1
4	0 4	0 0 1 0 0	=	0 + 0 + 4 + 0 + 0
5	0 5	0 0 1 0 1	=	0 + 0 + 4 + 0 + 1
6	0 6	0 0 1 1 0	=	0 + 0 + 4 + 2 + 0
7	0 7	0 0 1 1 1	=	0 + 0 + 4 + 2 + 1
8	0 8	0 1 0 0 0	=	0 + 8 + 0 + 0 + 0
9	0 9	0 1 0 0 1	=	0 + 8 + 0 + 0 + 1
1 0	0 a	0 1 0 1 0	=	0 + 8 + 0 + 2 + 0
1 1	0 b	0 1 0 1 1	=	0 + 8 + 0 + 2 + 1
1 2	0 c	0 1 1 0 0	=	0 + 8 + 4 + 0 + 0
1 3	0 d	0 1 1 0 1	=	0 + 8 + 4 + 0 + 1
1 4	0 e	0 1 1 1 0	=	0 + 8 + 4 + 2 + 0
1 5	0 f	0 1 1 1 1	=	0 + 8 + 4 + 2 + 1
1 6	1 0	1 0 0 0 0	=	16 + 0 + 0 + 0 + 0
1 7	1 1	1 0 0 0 1	=	16 + 0 + 0 + 0 + 1
1 8	1 2	1 0 0 1 0	=	16 + 0 + 0 + 2 + 0
1 9	1 3	1 0 0 1 1	=	16 + 0 + 0 + 2 + 1

Susan had some more thoughts on the hexadecimal number system. Let's listen in:

Susan: I think you need to spend a little more time reviewing the hex system, like an entire chapter. Well, I am getting the impression that we are going to be working with hex, so I am trying to concentrate my understanding on that instead of binary. I think this all moves a little too fast for me. I don't know what your other reviewers are saying but I just feel like I get a definition of a abstract concept, and the next thing I know I am supposed to be doing something with it, like make it work. Ha! I personally need to digest new concepts, I really need to think them over a bit, to take them in and absorb them. I just can't start working with it right away.

As usual, I've complied with her request; the results are immediately ahead.

Exercises

Here are some exercises that you can use to check your understanding of the binary and hexadecimal number systems.[27] I've limited the examples to addition and subtraction, as that is all that you're ever likely to have to do in these number systems. These operations are exactly like their equivalents in the decimal system, except that as we have already seen, the hexadecimal system has six extra digits after 9: a, b, c, d, e, and f. We have to take these into account in our calculations: for example, adding 9 and 5, rather than producing 14, produces e.

---

27. Please note that the ability to do binary or hexadecimal arithmetic is *not* essential to further reading in this book.

1. Using the hexadecimal system, answer these problems:

   a. $1a + 2e = ?$

   b. $12 + 18 = ?$

   c. $50 - 12 = ?$

2. In the binary system, answer these problems:

   a. $101 + 110 = ?$

   b. $111 + 1001 = ?$

   c. $1010 - 11 = ?$

Consider the two types of numeric variables we've encountered so far, short and unsigned short. Let's suppose that x is a short, and y is an unsigned short, both of them currently holding the value 32767, or 7fff in hex.

3. What is the result of adding 1 to y, in both decimal and hex?

4. What is the result of adding 1 to x, in both decimal and hex?

Answers to exercises can be found at the end of the chapter.

Registering Relief

Before we took this detour into the binary and hexadecimal number systems, I promised to explain what it means to say that the instructions using the 16-bit register names "behave exactly as though they were accessing the 16-bit registers on earlier machines". After a bit more preparation, we'll be ready for that explanation.

First, let's take a look at some characteristics of the human-readable version of machine instructions: assembly language instructions. The **assembly language** instructions we will look at have a fairly simple format.[28] The name of the operation is given first, followed by one or more spaces. The next element is the "destination", which is the register or RAM location that will be affected by the instruction's execution. The last element in an instruction is the "source", which represents another register, a RAM location, or a constant value to be used in the calculation. The source and destination are separated by a comma.[29] Here's an example of a simple assembly language instruction:

```
add    ax,1
```

In this instruction, add is the operation, ax is the destination, and the constant value 1 is the source. Thus, add ax,1 means to add 1 to the contents of ax, replacing the old contents of ax with the result.

Let's see what Susan has to say about the makeup of an assembly language instruction:

Susan: So the destination can be a register, cache, or RAM?

Steve: Yes, that's right. However, the cache is transparent to the programmer. That is, you don't say "write to the cache" or "read from the cache"; you just use RAM addresses and the hardware uses the cache as appropriate to speed up access to frequently used locations. On the other hand, you do have to address registers explicitly when writing an assembly language program.

---

28. I'm simplifying here. There are instructions that follow other formats, but we'll stick with the simple ones for the time being.

29. Of course, the actual machine instructions being executed in the CPU don't have commas, register names, or any other human-readable form; they consist of fixed-format sequences of bits stored in RAM. The CPU actually executes machine language instructions rather than assembly language ones; a program called an *assembler* takes care of translating the assembly language instructions into machine instructions. However, we can usually ignore this step, because each assembly language instruction corresponds to one machine instruction. This correspondence is quite unlike the relationship between C++ statements and machine instructions, which is far more complex.

Now we're finally ready to see what the statement about using the 16-bit register names on a 32-bit machine means. Suppose we have the register contents shown in Figure 2.8 (indicated in hexadecimal). If we were to add 1 to register ax, by executing the instruction add ax,1, the result would be as shown in Figure 2.9.

FIGURE 2.8. 32 and 16 bit registers, before add ax,1

32-bit register	32-bit contents	16-bit register	16-bit contents
eax	1235ffff	ax	ffff

FIGURE 2.9. 32 and 16 bit registers, after add ax,1

32-bit register	32-bit contents	16-bit register	16-bit contents
eax	12350000	ax	0000

In case this makes no sense, consider what happens when you add 1 to 9999 on a four digit counter such as an odometer. It "turns over" to 0000, doesn't it? The same applies here: ffff is the largest number that can be represented as four hex digits, so if you add 1 to a register that has only four (hex) digits of storage available, the result is 0000.

As you might imagine, Susan was quite intrigued with the above detail; here is her reaction.

> **Susan:** I have a understanding retention half-life of about 30 nanoseconds, but while I was reading this I was understanding it except I am boggled as to how adding 1 to ffff makes 0000, see, I am still not clear on Hex. Question: When you show the contents of a 32-bit register as being 12350000, then is the 1235 the upper half and the 0000 the lower half? Is that what you are saying?

> **Steve:** That's right!

As this illustrates, instructions that refer to ax have no effect whatever on the upper part of eax; they behave exactly as though the upper part of eax did not exist. However, if we were to execute the instruction add eax,1 instead of add ax,1, the result would look like Figure 2.10.

FIGURE 2.10. **32 and 16 bit registers, after** add eax,1

32-bit register	32-bit contents	16-bit register	16-bit contents
eax	12360000	ax	0000

In this case, eax is treated as a whole. Similar results apply to the other 32-bit registers and their 16-bit counterparts.

On a RAMpage

Unfortunately, it isn't possible to use only registers and avoid references to RAM entirely, if only because we'll run out of registers sooner or later. This is a good time to look back at the diagram of the "memory hierarchy" (Figure 2.2) and examine the relative speed and size of each different kind of memory.

The "size" attribute of the disk and RAM are specified in megabytes, whereas the size of an external cache is generally in the range from 64 kilobytes to 1 megabyte. As I mentioned before, the internal cache is considerably smaller, usually in the 8 to 16 kilobyte range. The registers, however, provide a total of 28 *bytes* of storage; this should make clear that they are the scarcest memory resource. To try to clarify why the registers are so important to the performance of programs, I've listed the "speed" attribute in number of accesses per second, rather than in milliseconds, nanoseconds, and so forth. In the case of the disk, this is about 100 accesses per second. Normal RAM can be accessed about 100 million times per second, while the external cache allows about 250 million accesses per second. The clear winners, though, are the internal cache and the registers, which can be accessed 500 million times per second and 1 billion times per second, respectively.

Registering Bewilderment

In a way, the latter figure (1 billion accesses per second for registers) overstates the advantages of registers relative to the cache. You see, any given register can be accessed only 500 million times per second[30]; however, many instructions refer to two registers and still execute in one CPU cycle. Therefore, the maximum number of references per second is more than the number of instructions per second.

However, this leads to another question: Why not use instructions that can refer to more than one memory address (known as *memory-to-memory* instructions) and still execute in one CPU cycle? In that case, we wouldn't have to worry about registers; since there's (relatively) a lot of cache and very few registers, it would seem to make more sense to eliminate the middleman and simply refer to data in the cache.[31] Of course, there is a good reason for the provision of both registers and cache. The main drawback of registers is that there are so few of them; on the other hand, one of their main advantages is also that there are so few of them. Why is this?

The main reason to use registers is that they make instructions shorter: since there are only a few registers, we don't have to use up a lot of bits specifying which register(s) to use. That is, with eight registers, we only need 3 bits to specify which register we need. In fact, there are standardized 3-bit codes that might be thought of as "register addresses", which are used to specify each register when it

---

30. As before, we are ignoring the ability of the CPU to execute more than one instruction simultaneously.

31. Perhaps I should remind you that the programmer doesn't explicitly refer to the cache; you can just use normal RAM addresses and let the hardware take care of making sure that the most frequently referenced data ends up in the cache.

---

is used to hold a variable. Figure 2.11 is the table of these register codes.[32]

FIGURE 2.11. 32- and 16-bit register codes

Register address	16-bit register	32-bit register
000	ax	eax
001	cx	ecx
010	dx	edx
011	bx	ebx
100	sp	esp
101	bp	ebp
110	si	esi
111	di	edi

By contrast, with a "memory-to-memory" architecture, each instruction would need at least 2 bytes for the source address, and 2 bytes for the destination address.[33] Adding 1 byte to specify what the instruction is going to do, this would make the minimum instruction size 5 bytes, whereas some instructions that use only registers can be as short as 1 byte. This makes a big difference in performance because the caches are quite limited in size; big programs don't fit in the caches, and therefore require a large number of RAM accesses. As a result, they execute much more slowly than small programs.

---

32. Don't blame me for the seemingly scrambled order of the codes; that's the way Intel's CPU architects assigned them to registers when they designed the 8086 and it's much too late to change them now. Luckily, we almost never have to worry about their values, because the assembler takes care of the translation of register names to register addresses.

33. If we want to be able to access more than 64 kilobytes worth of data, which is necessary in most modern programs, we'll need even more room to store addresses.

Slimming the Program

This explains why we want our programs to be smaller. However, it may not be obvious why using registers reduces the size of instructions, so here's an explanation.

Most of the data in use by a program are stored in RAM. When using a 32-bit CPU, it is theoretically possible to have over 4 billion bytes of memory (2^{32} is the exact number). Therefore, that many distinct addresses for a given byte of data are possible; to specify any of these requires 32 bits. Since there are only a few registers, specifying which one you want to use takes only a few bits; therefore, programs use register addresses instead of memory addresses wherever possible, to reduce the number of bits in each instruction required to specify addresses.

I hope this is clear, but it might not be. It certainly wasn't to Susan. Here's the conversation we had on this topic:

> **Susan:** I see that you are trying to make a point about why registers are more efficient in terms of making instructions shorter, but I just am not picturing exactly how they do this. How do you go from "make the instructions much shorter" to "we don't have to use up a lot of bits specifying which registers to use"?

> **Steve:** Let's suppose that we want to move data from one place to another in memory. In that case, we'll have to specify two addresses: the "from" address and the "to" address. One way to do this is to store the addresses in the machine language instruction. Since each address is at least 16 bits, an instruction that contains two addresses needs to occupy at least 32 bits just for the addresses, as well as some more bits to specify exactly what instruction we want to perform. Of course, if we're using 32-bit addresses, then a "two-address" instruction would require 64 bits just for the two addresses, in addition to whatever bits were needed to specify the type of instruction.

> **Susan:** OK. . . think I got this. . .

Steve: On the other hand, if we use registers to hold the addresses of the data, we need only enough bits to specify each of two registers. Since there aren't that many registers, we don't need as many bits to specify which ones we're referring to. Even on a machine that has 32 general registers, we'd need only 10 bits to specify two registers; on the Intel machines, with their shortage of registers, even fewer bits are needed to specify which register we're referring to.

Susan: Are you talking about the bits that are needed to define the instruction?

Steve: Yes.

Susan: How would you know how many bits are needed to specify the two registers?

Steve: If you have 32 different possibilities to select from, you need 5 bits to specify one of them, because 32 is 2 to the fifth power. If we have 32 registers, and any of them can be selected, that takes 5 bits to select any one of them. If we have to select two registers on a CPU with 32 registers, we need 10 bits to specify both registers.

Susan: So what does that have to do with it? All we are talking about is the instruction that indicates "select register" right? So that instruction should be the same and contain the same number of bits whether you have 1 or 32 registers.

Steve: There is no "select register" instruction. Every instruction has to specify whatever register or registers it uses. It takes 5 bits to select 1 of 32 items and only 3 bits to select 1 of 8 items; therefore, a CPU design that has 32 registers needs longer instructions than one that has only 8 registers.

Susan: I don't see why the number of registers should have an effect on the number of bits one instruction should have.

Steve: If you have two possibilities, how many bits does it take to select one of them? 1 bit. If you have four possibilities, how many bits does it take to select one of them? 2 bits. Eight possibilities require 3 bits; 16 possibilities require 4 bits; and finally 32 possibilities require 5 bits.

Susan: Some machines have 32 registers?

Steve: Yes. The PowerPC, for example. Some machines have even more registers than that.

Susan: If the instructions to specify a register are the same, then why would they differ just because one machine has more registers than another?

Steve: They aren't the same from one machine to another. Although every CPU that I'm familiar with has registers, each type of machine has its own way of executing instructions, including how you specify the registers.

Susan: OK, and in doing so it is selecting a register, right? An instruction should contain the same number of bits no matter how many registers it has to call on.

Steve: Let's take the example of an **add** instruction, which as its name implies, adds two numbers. The name of the instruction is the same length, no matter how many registers there are; that's true. However, the actual representation of the instruction in machine language has to have room for enough bits to specify which register(s) are being used in the instruction.

Susan: They are statements right? So why should they be bigger or smaller if there are more or fewer registers?

Steve: They are actually machine instructions, not C++ statements. The computer doesn't know how to execute C++ statements, so the C++ compiler is needed to convert C++ statements into machine instructions. Machine instructions need bits to specify which register(s) they are using; so, with more registers available, more bits in the instructions have to be used to specify the register(s) that the instructions are using.

Susan: Do all the statements change the values of bits they contain depending on the number of registers that are on the CPU?

Steve: Yes, they certainly do. To be more precise, the machine language instructions that execute a statement are larger or smaller depending on the number of registers in the machine, because they need more bits to specify one of a larger number of registers.

Susan: "It takes five bits to select one of 32 items..."

"...and only three bits to select one of eight items". Why?

Steve: What is a bit? It is the amount of information needed to select one of two alternatives. For example, suppose you have to say whether a light is on or off. How many possibilities exist? Two. Since a single bit has two possible states, 0 or 1, we can represent "on" by 1 and "off" by 0 and thus represent the possible states of the light by one bit.

Now suppose that we have a fan that has four settings: low, medium, high, and off. Is one bit enough to specify the current setting of the fan? No, because one bit has only two possible states, while the fan has four. However, if we use two bits, then it will work. We can represent the states by bits as follows:

```
bits  state
----  -----
00    off
01    low
10    medium
11    high
```

Note that this is an arbitrary mapping; there's no reason that it couldn't be like this instead:

```
bits   state
----   -----
00     medium
01     high
10     off
11     low
```

However, having the lowest "speed" (that is, off) represented by the lowest binary value (00) and the increasing speeds corresponding to increasing binary values makes more sense and therefore is easier to remember.

This same process can be extended to represent any number of possibilities. If we have eight registers, for example, we can represent each one by 3 bits, as noted previously in Figure 2.11 on page 52. That is the actual representation in the Intel architecture; however, whatever representation might have been used, it would require 3 bits to select among eight possibilities. The same is true for a machine that has 32 registers, except that you need 5 bits instead of 3.

Susan: Okay, so then does that mean that more than one register can be in use at a time? Wait, where is the room that you are talking about?

Steve: Some instructions specify only one register (a "one-register" instruction), while others specify two (a "two-register" instruction); some don't specify any registers. For example, most "branch" instructions are in the last category; they specify which address to continue execution from. These are used to implement if statements, for loops, and other flow control statements.

Susan: So, when you create an instruction you have to open up enough "room" to talk to all the registers at once?

Steve: No, you have to have enough room to specify any one register, for a one-register instruction, or any two registers for a two-register instruction.

Susan: Well, this still has me confused. If you need to specify only one register at any given time, then why do you always need to have all the room available? Anyway, where is this room? Is it in RAM or is it in the registers themselves? Let's say you are going to specify an instruction that uses only 1 of 32 registers. Are you saying that even though you are going to use just one register you have to make room for all 32?

Steve: The "room" that I'm referring to is the bits in the instruction that specify which register the instruction is using. That is, if there are eight registers and you want to use one of them in an instruction, 3 bits need to be set aside in the instruction to indicate which register you're referring to.

Susan: So you need the bits to represent the address of a register?

Steve: Right. However, don't confuse the "address of a register" with a memory address. They have nothing to do with one another, except that they both specify one of a number of possible places to store information. That is, register `ax` doesn't correspond to memory address 0, and so on.

Susan: Yes, I understand the bit numbers in relation to the number of registers.

Steve: That's good.

Susan: So the "address of a register" is just where the CPU can locate the register in the CPU, not an address in RAM. Is that right?

Steve: Right. The address of a register merely specifies which of the registers you're referring to; all of them are in the CPU.

After that comedy routine, let's go back to Susan's reaction to something I said earlier about registers and variables:

> **Susan:** The registers hold only variables... Okay, I know what is bothering me! What else is there besides variables? Besides nonvariables, please don't tell me that. (Actually that would be good, now that I think of it.) But this is where I am having problems. You are talking about data, and a variable is a type of data. I need to know what else is out there so I have something else to compare it with. When you say a register can hold a variable, that is meaningless to me, unless I know what the alternatives are and where they are held.

> **Steve:** What else is there besides variables? Well, there are constants, like the number 5 in the statement x = 5;. Constants can also be stored in registers. For example, let's suppose that the variable x, which is a short, is stored in location 1237. In that case, the statement x = 5; might generate an instruction sequence that looks like this:

```
mov ax,5
mov [1237],ax
```

> where the number in the [] is the address of the variable x. The first of these instructions loads 5 into register ax, and the second one stores the contents of ax (5, in this case) into the memory location 1237.

> Sometimes, however, constants aren't loaded into registers as in this case but are stored in the instructions that use them. This is the case in the following instruction:

```
add ax,3
```

> This means to add 3 to whatever was formerly in register ax. The 3 never gets into a register but is stored as part of the instruction.[34]

A Fetching Tale

Another way of reducing overhead is to read instructions from RAM in chunks, rather than one at a time, and feed them into the CPU as it needs them; this is called *prefetching*. This mechanism operates in parallel with instruction execution, loading instructions from RAM into special dedicated registers in the CPU before they're actually needed; these registers are known collectively as the *prefetch queue*. Since the prefetching is done by a separate unit in the CPU, the time to do the prefetching doesn't increase the time needed for instruction execution. When the CPU is ready to execute another instruction, it can get it from the prefetch queue almost instantly, rather than having to wait for the slow RAM to provide each instruction. Of course, it does take a small amount of time to retrieve the next instruction from the prefetch queue, but that amount of time is included in the normal instruction execution time.

> **Susan:** I don't understand prefetching. What are "chunks"? I mean I understand what you have written, but I can't visualize this. So, there is just no time used to read an instruction when something is prefetched?

> **Steve:** A separate piece of the CPU does the prefetching at the same time as instructions are being executed, so instructions that have already been fetched are available without delay when the execution unit is ready to "do" them.

The effect of combining the use of registers and prefetching the instructions can be very significant. In our example, if we use an instruction that has already been loaded, which reads data from and writes data only to registers, the timing reduces to that shown in Figure 2.12.

---

34. We'll go into this whole notion of using registers to represent and manipulate variables in grotesque detail in Chapter 3.

FIGURE 2.12. **Instruction execution time, using registers and prefetching**

Time	Function
0 ns	Read instruction from RAM
0 ns	Read data from RAM
2 ns	Execute instruction
0 ns	Write result back to RAM
2 ns	Total instruction execution time

As I indicated near the beginning of this chapter, the manufacturers aren't lying to us; if we design our programs to take advantage of these (and other similar) efficiency measures taken by the manufacturer, we can often approach the maximum theoretical performance figures. You've just been subjected to a barrage of information on how a computer works. Let's go over it again before continuing.

Review

The main components of the computer of most significance to programmers are disk, RAM, and the CPU; the first two of these store programs and data that are used by the CPU.

Computers represent pieces of information (or data) as binary digits, universally referred to as *bits*. Each bit can have the value 0 or 1. The binary system is used instead of the more familiar decimal system because it is much easier to make devices that can store and retrieve 1 of 2 values than 1 of 10. Bits are grouped into sets of eight, called *bytes*.

The disk uses magnetic recording heads to store and retrieve groups of a few hundred bytes on rapidly spinning platters in a few milliseconds. The contents of the disk are not lost when the power is turned off, so it is suitable for more or less permanent storage of programs and data.

RAM, which is an acronym for Random Access Memory, is used to hold programs and data while they're in use. It is made of millions of microscopic transistors on a piece of silicon called a *chip*. Each bit is stored using a few of these transistors. RAM does not retain its contents when power is removed, so it is not good for permanent storage. However, any byte in a RAM chip can be accessed in about 10 nanoseconds (billionths of a second), which is about one million times as fast as accessing a disk. Each byte in a RAM chip can be independently stored and retrieved without affecting other bytes, by providing the unique memory address belonging to the byte you want to access.

The CPU (also called the *processor*) is the active component in the computer. It is also made of millions of microscopic transistors on a chip. The CPU executes programs consisting of instructions stored in RAM, using data also stored in RAM. However, the CPU is so fast that even the typical RAM access time of 10 nanoseconds is a bottleneck; therefore, computer manufacturers have added both *external cache* and *internal cache*, which are faster types of memory used to reduce the amount of time that the CPU has to wait. The internal cache resides on the same chip as the CPU and can be accessed without delay. The external cache sits between the CPU and the regular RAM; it's faster than the latter, but not as fast as the internal cache. Finally, a very small part of the on-chip memory is organized as *registers*, which can be accessed within the normal cycle time of the CPU, thus allowing the fastest possible processing.

Conclusion

In this chapter, we've covered a lot of material on how a computer actually works. As you'll see, this background is essential if you're going to understand what really happens inside a program. In the next chapter, we'll get to the "real thing": how to write a program to make all this hardware do something useful.

Answers to Exercises

1. Hexadecimal arithmetic

   a. 48

   You probably won't be surprised to hear that Susan didn't care much for this answer originally. Here's the discussion on that topic:

   Susan: Problem 1a. My answer is 38. Why? My own personal way of thinking: If a = 10 right? and if e = 14 and if 1 * 10= 10 and if 2 * 14 = 28 then if you add 10 + 28 you get 38. So please inform me how you arrived at 48? I didn't bother with the rest of the problems. If I couldn't get the first one right, then what was the point?

   Steve: Here's how you do this problem:

   ```
   1(1 * 16) + a(10 * 1)
   2(2 * 16) + e(14 * 1)
   ------------------
   3(3 * 16) + 18(24 * 1 = 1 * 16 + 8 * 1)
   ```

   Carry the 1 from the low digit to the high digit of the answer, to produce:

   4(4 * 16) + 8(8 * 1), or 48 hex, which is the answer.

     b. 2a

     c. 3e

2. Binary arithmetic

     a. 1011

     b. 10000

     c. 111

3. 32768 decimal, or 8000 in hex

4. –32768, or 8000 in hex

Why is the same hex value rendered here as –32768, while it was 32768 in question 3? The only difference between short and unsigned short variables is how their values are interpreted. In particular, short variables having hexadecimal values from 8000 to ffff are considered negative, while unsigned short values in that range are positive. That's why the range of short values is –32768 to +32767, whereas unsigned short variables can range from 0 to 65535.

By the way, whenever the number system being used isn't obvious, the convention is to add the letter h to the end of hexadecimal numbers. Thus, if it wasn't obvious that the number "8000" we were referring in the previous paragraph was hexadecimal, we could write it as 8000h to make it perfectly clear.

CHAPTER 3 — *Basics of Programming*

After that necessary detour into the workings of the hardware, we can now resume our regularly scheduled explanation of the creative possibilities of computers. It may sound odd to describe computers as providing grand scope for creative activities: Aren't they monotonous, dull, unintelligent, and extremely limited? Yes, they are. However, they have two redeeming virtues that make them ideal as the canvas of invention: They are extraordinarily fast and spectacularly reliable. These characteristics allow the creator of a program to weave intricate chains of thought and have a fantastic number of steps carried out without fail. We'll begin to explore how this is possible after we go over some definitions and objectives for this chapter.

Definitions

An **identifier** is a user defined name; variable names are identifiers. Identifiers must not be spelled the same as keywords such as if and while; for example, you cannot create a variable with the name while.

A **keyword** is a word defined in the C++ language, such as if and while. It is illegal to define an identifier such as a variable name that is spelled the same as a keyword.

Objectives of This Chapter

By the end of this chapter, you should

1. Understand what a program is and have some idea how one works.

2. Understand how to get information into and out of a program.

3. Understand how to use if and while to control the execution of a program.[1]

4. Understand how a portion of a program can be marked off so that it will be treated as one unit.

5. Be able to read and understand a simple program I've written in C++.

---

1. Please note that capitalization counts in C++, so IF and WHILE are not the same as if and while. You have to use the latter versions.

Speed Demon

The most impressive attribute of modern computers, of course, is their speed; as we have already seen, this is measured in MIPS (millions of instructions per second).

Of course, raw speed is not very valuable if we can't rely on the results we get. ENIAC, one of the first electronic computers, had a failure every few hours, on the average; since the problems it was solving took about that long to run, the likelihood that the results were correct wasn't very high. Particularly critical calculations were often run several times, and if the users got the same answer twice, they figured it was probably correct. By contrast, modern computers are almost incomprehensibly reliable. With almost any other machine, a failure rate of one in every million operations would be considered phenomenally low, but a computer with such a failure rate would make hundreds of errors per second.[2]

Blaming It on the Computer

On the other hand, if computers are so reliable, why are they blamed for so much that goes wrong with modern life? Who among us has not been the victim of an erroneous credit report, or a bill sent to the wrong address, or been put on hold for a long time because "the computer is down"? The answer is fairly simple: It's almost certainly not the computer. More precisely, it's very unlikely that the CPU was at fault; it may be the software, other equipment such as telephone lines, tape or disk drives, or any of the myriad "peripheral devices" that the computer uses to store and retrieve information and interact with the outside world. Usually, it's the software; when customer

---

2. However, we haven't yet completely eliminated the possibility of hardware errors, as the floating-point flaw in early versions of the Pentium™ processor illustrates. In rare cases, the result of the divide instruction in those processors was accurate to only about 5 decimal places rather than the normal 16 to 17 decimal places.

service representatives tell you that they can't do something obviously reasonable, you can count on its being the software. For example, I once belonged to a 401K plan whose administrators provided statements only every three months, about three months after the end of the quarter; in other words, in July I found out how much my account had been worth at the end of March. The only way to estimate how much I had in the meantime was to look up the share values in the newspaper and multiply by the number of shares. Of course, the mutual fund that issued the shares could tell its shareholders their account balances at any time of the day or night; however, the company that administered the 401K plan didn't bother to provide such a service, as it would have required doing some work.[3] Needless to say, whenever I hear that "the computer can't do that" as an excuse for such poor service, I reply "Then you need some different programmers".

That Does Not Compute

All of this emphasis on computation, however, should not blind us to the fact that computers are not solely arithmetic engines. The most common application for which PCs are used is word processing, hardly a hotbed of arithmetical calculation. While we have so far considered only numeric data, this is a good illustration of the fact that computers also deal with another kind of information, which is commonly referred to by the imaginative term **nonnumeric variables**. Numeric variables are those suited for use in calculations, such as in totalling a set of weights. On the other hand, nonnumeric data are items that are not used in calculations like adding, multiplying, or subtracting: Examples are names, addresses, telephone numbers, Social Security numbers, bank account numbers, or driver's license numbers. Note that just because something is called a *number*, or even is composed entirely of the digits 0–9, does

---

3.   This was apparently against the plan administrator's principles.

not make it numeric data by our standards; the question is how the item is used. No one adds, multiplies, or subtracts driver's license numbers, for example; they serve solely as identifiers and could just as easily have letters in them, as indeed some do.

For the present, though, let's stick with numeric variables. Now that we have defined a couple of types of these variables, short and unsigned short, what can we do with them? To do anything with them, we have to write a C++ program, which consists primarily of a list of operations to be performed by the computer, along with directions that influence how these operations are to be translated into machine instructions.

This raises an interesting point: Why does our C++ program have to be translated into machine instructions? Isn't the computer's job to execute (or *run*) our program?

Lost in Translation

Yes, but it can't run a C++ program. The only kind of program any computer can run is one made of machine instructions; this is called a *machine language* program, for obvious reasons. Therefore, to get our C++ program to run, we have to translate it into a machine language program. Don't worry, you won't have to do it yourself; that's why we have a program called a *compiler.*[4] The most basic tasks that the compiler performs are the following:

----

4. How is the compiler itself translated into machine language so it can be executed? The most common method is to write the compiler in the same language it compiles and use the previous version of the compiler to compile the newest version! Of course, this looks like an infinite regress; how did the first compiler get compiled? By manual translation into *assembly language*, which was then translated by an *assembler* into machine language. To answer the obvious question, at some point an assembler was coded directly in machine language.

1. Assigning memory addresses to variables. This allows us to use names for variables, rather than having to keep track of the address of each variable ourselves.

2. Translating arithmetic and other operations (such as +, –, etc.) into the equivalent machine instructions, including the addresses of variables assigned in the previous step.[5]

This is probably a bit too abstract to be easily grasped, so let's look at an example as soon as we have defined some terms. Each complete operation understood by the compiler is called a *statement*, and ends with a semicolon (;).[6] Figure 3.1 shows some sample statements that do arithmetic calculations.[7]

FIGURE 3.1. A little numeric calculation

```
short i;
short j;
short k;
short m;

i = 5;
j = i * 3;          // j is now 15
k = j - i;          // k is now 10
```

---

5. The compiler also does a lot of other work for us, which we'll get into later.

6. By the way, blank lines are ignored by the compiler; in fact, because of the trailing semicolon on each statement, you can even run all the statements together on one line if you want to, without confusing the compiler. However, that will make it much harder for someone reading your code later to understand what you're trying to do. Programs aren't written just for the compiler's benefit but to be read by other people; therefore, it is important to write them so that they can be understood by those other people. One very good reason for this is that more often than you might think, those "other people" turn out to be *you*, six months later.

7. The // marks the beginning of a *comment*, which is a note to you or another programmer; it is ignored by the compiler. For those of you with BASIC experience, this is just like REM (the "remark" keyword in that language); anything after it on a line is ignored.

```
m = (k + j) / 5;        // m is now 5
i = i + 1;              // i is now 6
```

To enter such statements in the first place, you can use any text editor that generates "plain" text files, such as the EDIT program that comes with DOS or Windows' Notepad. Whichever text editor you use, make sure that it produces files that contain only what you type; stay away from programs like Windows Write™ or Word for Windows™, as they add some of their own information to indicate fonts, type sizes, and the like to your file, which will foul up the compiler.

Once we have entered the statements for our program, we use the compiler to translate the programs we write into a form that the computer can perform; as defined in Chapter 1, the form we create is called *source code*, since it is the source of the program logic, while the form of our program that the computer can execute is called an *executable program*, or just an *executable* for short.

As I've mentioned before, there are several types of variables, the short being only one of these types. Therefore, the compiler needs some explanatory material so that it can tell what types of variables you're using; that's what the first four lines of our little sample program fragment are for. Each line tells the compiler that the type of the variable i, j, k, or m is short; that is, it can contain values from -32768 to $+32767$.[8]

After this introductory material, we move into the list of operations to be performed. This is called the *executable* portion of the program, as it actually causes the computer to do something when the program is executed; the operations to be performed, as mentioned above, are called **statements**. The first one, i = 5;, sets the variable i to the value 5. A value such as 5, which doesn't have a name, but represents itself in a literal manner, is called (appropriately enough) a **literal** value.

---

8. Other kinds of variables can hold larger (and smaller) values; we'll go over them in some detail in future chapters.

This is as good a time as any for me to mention something that experienced C programmers take for granted but has a tendency to confuse novices. This is the choice of the = sign to indicate the operation of setting a variable to a value, which is known technically as **assignment**. As far as I'm concerned, an assignment operation would be more properly indicated by some symbol suggesting movement of data, such as 5 => i;, meaning "store the value 5 into variable i". Unfortunately, it's too late to change the notation for the **assignment statement**, as such a statement is called, so you'll just have to get used to it. The = means "set the variable on the left to the value on the right".[9]

Now that I've warned you about that possible confusion, let's continue looking at the operations in the program. The next one, j = i * 3;, specifies that the variable j is to be set to the result of multiplying the current value of i by the literal value 3. The one after that, k = j − i;, tells the computer to set k to the amount by which j is greater than i; that is, j − i. The most complicated line in our little program fragment, m = (k + j) / 5;, calculates m as the sum of adding k and j and dividing the result by the literal value 5. Finally, the line i = i + 1; sets i to the value of i plus the literal value 1.

This last may be somewhat puzzling; how can i be equal to i + 1? The answer is that an assignment statement is *not* an algebraic equality, no matter how much it may resemble one. It is a command telling the computer to assign a value to a variable. Therefore, what i = i + 1; actually means is "Take the current value of i, add 1 to it, and store the result back into i." In other words, a C++ variable is a place to store a value; the variable i can take on any number of values, but

---

9. At the risk of boring experienced C programmers, let me reiterate that = *does not mean* "is equal to"; it means "set the variable to the left of the = to the value of the expression to the right of the =. In fact, there is *no* equivalent in C++ to the mathematical notion of equality. We have only the assignment operator = and the comparison operator ==, which we will encounter in the next chapter. The latter is used in if statements to determine whether two expressions have the same value. All of the valid comparison operators are listed in Figure 4.5.

only one at a time; any former value is lost when a new one is assigned.

This notion of assignment was the topic of quite a few messages with Susan. Let's go to the first round:

Susan: I am confused with the statement i = i + 1; when you have stated previously that i = 5;. So, which one is it? How can there be two values for i?

Steve: There can't; that is, not at one time. However, i, like any other variable, can take on any number of values, one after another. First, we set it to 5; then we set it to 1 more than it was before (i + 1), so it ends up as 6.

Susan: Well, the example made it look as if the two values of i were available to be used by the computer at the same time. They were both lumped together as executable material.

Steve: After the statement i = 5;, and before the statement i = i + 1;, the value of i is 5. After the statement i = i + 1;, the value of i is 6. The key here is that a variable such as i is just our name for some area of memory that can hold only one value at one time. Does that clear it up?

Susan: So, it is not like algebra? Then i is equal to an address of memory and does not really equate with a numerical value? Well, I guess it does when you assign a numerical value to it. Is that it?

Steve: Very close. A variable in C++ isn't really like an algebraic variable, which has a value that has to be figured out and doesn't change in a given problem. A programming language variable is just a name for a storage location that can contain a value.

With any luck, that point has been pounded into the ground, so you won't have the same trouble that Susan did. Now let's look at exactly what an assignment statement does. If the value of i before the statement i = i + 1; is 5 (for example), then that statement will cause the CPU to perform the following steps:[10]

1. Take the current value of i (5).

2. Add one to that value (6).

3. Store the result back into i.

After the execution of this statement, i will have the value 6.

What's Going on Underneath?

In a moment we're going to dive a little deeper into how the CPU accomplishes its task of manipulating data, such as we are doing here with our arithmetic program. First, though, it's time for a little pep talk for those of you who might be wondering exactly why this apparent digression is necessary. It's because if you don't understand what is going on under the surface, you won't be able to get past the "Sunday driver" stage of programming in C++. In some languages it's neither necessary or perhaps even possible to find out what the computer actually does to execute your program, but C++ isn't one of them. A good C++ programmer needs an intimate acquaintance with the internal workings of the language, for reasons which will become very apparent when we get to Chapter 6. For the moment, you'll just

---

10. If you have any programming experience whatever, you may think that I'm spending too much effort on this very simple point. I can report from personal experience that it's not necessarily easy for a complete novice to grasp. Furthermore, without a solid understanding of the difference between an algebraic equality and an assignment statement, that novice will be unable to understand how to write a program.

have to take my word that working through these intricacies is essential; the payoff for a thorough grounding in these fundamental concepts of computing will be worth the struggle.

Now let's get to the task of exploring how the CPU actually stores and manipulates data in memory. As we saw previously, each memory location in RAM has a unique *memory address*; *machine instructions* that refer to RAM use this address to specify which *byte* or bytes of memory they wish to retrieve or modify. This is fairly straightforward in the case of a 1-byte variable, where the instruction merely specifies the byte that corresponds to the variable. On the other hand, the situation isn't quite as simple in the case of a variable that occupies more than 1 byte. Of course, no law of nature says that an instruction couldn't contain a number of addresses, one for each byte of the variable. However, this solution is never adopted in practice, as it would make instructions much longer than they need to be. Instead, the address in such an instruction specifies the first byte of RAM occupied by the variable, and the other bytes are assumed to follow immediately after the first one. For example, in the case of a short variable, which as we have seen occupies 2 bytes of RAM, the instruction would specify the address of the first byte of the area of RAM in which the variable is stored. However, there's one point that I haven't brought up yet: how the data for a given variable are actually arranged in memory. For example, suppose that the contents of a small section of RAM (specified as two hex digits per byte) look like Figure 3.2.

FIGURE 3.2. A small section of RAM

Address	Hex byte value
1000	41
1001	42
1002	43
1003	44
1004	00

Also suppose that a short variable i is stored starting at address 1000. To do much with a variableup a, we're going to have to load it into a *general register*, one of the small number of named data storage locations in the CPU intended for general use by the programmer; this proximity allows the CPU to operate on data in the registers at maximum speed. You may recall that there are seven general registers in the 386 CPU (and its successors); they're named eax, ebx, ecx, edx, esi, edi, and ebp.[11] Unfortunately, there's another complication here; these registers are designed to operate on 4-byte quantities, while our variable i, being of type short, is only two bytes long. Are we out of luck? No, but we do have to specify how long the variable is that we want to load. This problem is not unique to Intel CPUs, since any CPU has to have the ability to load different-sized variables into registers. Different CPUs use different methods of specifying this important piece of information; in the Intel CPUs, one way to do this is to alter the register name.[12] As we saw in the discussion of the development of Intel machines, we can remove the leading e from the register name to specify that we're dealing with 2-byte values; the resulting name refers to the lower two bytes of the 4-byte register. Therefore, if we wanted to load the value of i into register ax (that is, the lower half of register eax), the instruction could be written as follows:[13]

mov ax,[1000][14]

---

11. Besides these general registers, a dedicated register called esp plays an important role in the execution of real programs. We'll see how it does this in Chapter 5.

12. This is not the only possible solution to this problem nor necessarily the best one; for example, in many Motorola CPUs, you specify the length of the variable directly in the instruction, so loading a *word* (i.e., 2-byte) variable might be specified by the instruction move.w, where the .w means "word". Similarly, a *longword* (i.e., 4-byte) load might be specified as move.l, where the .l means "long word".

13. It's also possible to load a 2-byte value into a 32-bit (i.e., 4-byte) register such as eax and have the high part of that register set to 0 in one instruction, by using an instruction designed specifically for that purpose. This approach has the advantage that further processing can be done with the 32-bit registers.

As usual, our resident novice Susan had some questions on this topic. Here is our conversation:

Susan: If you put something into 1000 that is "too big" for it, then it spills over to the next address?

Steve: Sort of. When you "put something into 1000", you have to specify exactly what it is you're "putting in". That is, it must be either a short, a char, or some other type of variable that has a defined size.

Susan: Is that how it works? Why then is it not necessary to specify that it is going to have to go into 1000 and 1001? So what you put in is not really in 1000 anymore, it is in 1000 *and* 1001? How do you refer to its REAL address? What if there is no room in 1001? Would it go to 2003 if that is the next available space?

Steve: Because the rule is that you always specify the starting address of any item (variable or constant) that is too big to fit in 1 byte. The other bytes of the item are always stored immediately following the address you specify. No bytes will be skipped when storing (or loading) one item; if the item needs 4 bytes and is to be stored starting at 1000, it will be stored in 1000–1003.

Susan: I see. In other words, the compiler will always use the next bytes of RAM, however many need to be used to store the item?

Steve: Right.

---

14. The number inside the brackets [ ] represents a memory address.

Who's on First?

Now I have a question for you. After we execute the assembly language statement mov ax,[1000] to load the value of i into ax, what's in register ax? That may seem like a silly question; the answer is obviously the value of i. Yes, but what is that value exactly? The first byte of i, at location 1000, has the value 41 hexadecimal (abbreviated 41h), and the second byte, at location 1001, has the value 42h. But the value of i is 2 bytes long; is it 4142h or 4241h? These are clearly not the same!

That was a trick question; there's no way for you to deduce the answer with only the information I've given you so far. The answer happens to be 4241h, because that's the way Intel decided to do it; that is, the low part of the value is stored in the byte of RAM where the variable starts. Some other CPUs, e.g., Motorola's 680x0 series, do it the opposite way, where the high part of the value is stored in the byte of RAM where the variable starts; this is called *big-endian*, since the big end of the value is first, while the Intel way is correspondingly called *little-endian*. And some machines, such as the Power PC, can use either of these methods according to how they are started up. This makes it easier for them to run software written for either memory orientation.

As you might have surmised, the same system applies to 4-byte values; therefore, if we wrote the instruction mov eax,[1000], since we're on a little-endian machine, it would load the eax register with the value 44434241h; that is, the four bytes 41, 42, 43, and 44 (hex) would be loaded into the eax register, with the byte having the lowest address loaded into the low end of the register.

Here's another example. A little-endian system would represent the number 1234 (hex) stored at address 5000 as in Figure 3.3,whereas a big-endian system would represent the same value 1234 (hex) as illustrated in Figure 3.4.

FIGURE 3.3. **One little endian**

Address   Value

5000   34
5001   12

FIGURE 3.4. **A big endian example**

Address   Value

5000   12
5001   34

This really isn't much of a problem as long as we don't try to move data from one type of machine to another; however, when such data transportation is necessary, dealing with mixed endianness can be a real nuisance.[15] Before going on, let's practice a bit with this notion of how data are stored in memory.

Exercises, First Set

1. Assume that a short variable named z starts at location 1001 in a little-endian machine. Using Figure 3.5 for the contents of memory, what is the value of z, in hex?

---

15. Luckily, we won't run into this problem in this book. However, it is very common in dealing with networks of computers, and there are industry standards set up to allow diverse types of computers to coexist in a network.

FIGURE 3.5. Exercise 1

Address	Hex byte value
1000	3a
1001	43
1002	3c
1003	99
1004	00

Underware?

I can almost hear the wailing and tooth gnashing out there. Do I expect you to deal with these instructions and addresses by yourself? You'll undoubtedly be happy to know that this isn't necessary, as the compiler takes care of these details. However, if you don't have some idea of how a compiler works, you'll be at a disadvantage when you're trying to figure out how to make it do what you want. Therefore, we're going to spend the next few pages "playing compiler"; that is, I'll examine each statement and indicate what action the compiler might take as a result. I'll simplify the statements a bit to make the explanation simpler; you should still get the idea. Figure 3.6 illustrates the set of statements that I'll compile:[16]

FIGURE 3.6. A really little numeric calculation

```
short i;
short j;

i = 5;
j = i + 3;
```

---

16. As I've mentioned previously, blank lines are ignored by the compiler; you can put them in freely to improve readability.

Here are the rules of this game:

1. All numbers in the C++ program are decimal; all addresses and numbers in the machine instructions are hexadecimal.[17]

2. All addresses are 2 bytes long.[18]

3. Variables are stored at addresses starting at 1000.

4. Machine instructions are stored at addresses starting at 2000.[19]

5. A number *not* enclosed in [] is a literal value, which represents itself. For example, the instruction mov ax,1000 means to move the value 1000 into the ax register.

6. A number enclosed in [] is an address, which specifies where data are to be stored or retrieved. For example, the instruction mov ax,[1000] means to move 2 bytes of data starting at location 1000, *not* the value 1000 itself, into the ax register.

Now let's start compiling. The first statement, short i; says to allocate storage for a 2-byte variable called i that will be treated as signed (because that's the default). Since no value has been assigned to this variable yet, the resulting "memory map" looks like Figure 3.7.

FIGURE 3.7. Compiling, part 1

Address	Variable Name
1000	i

---

17. However, I've cheated here by using small enough numbers in the C++ program that they are the same in hex as in decimal.

18. The real compiler on the CD-ROM actually uses 4-byte addresses, but this doesn't change any of the concepts involved.

19. These addresses are arbitrary; a real compiler will assign addresses to variables and machine instructions by its own rules.

As you might have guessed, this exercise was the topic of a considerable amount of discussion with Susan. Here's how it started:

Susan: So the first thing we do with a variable is to tell the address that its name is i, but no one is home, right? It has to get ready to accept a value. Could you put a value in it without naming it, just saying address 1000 has a value of 5? Why does it have to be called i first?

Steve: The reason that we use names instead of addresses is because it's much easier for people to keep track of names than it is to keep track of addresses. Thus, one of the main functions of a compiler is to allow us to use names that are translated into addresses for the computer's use.

The second statement, short j; tells me to allocate storage for a 2-byte variable called j that will be treated as signed (because that's the default). Since no value has been assigned to this variable yet, the resulting "memory map" looks like Figure 3.8.

FIGURE 3.8. **Compiling, part 2**

Address	Variable Name
1000	i
1002	j

Here's the exchange about this step:

Susan: Why isn't the address for j 1001?

Steve: Because a short is 2 bytes, not 1. Therefore, if i is at address 1000, j can't start before 1002; otherwise, the second byte of i would have the same address as the first byte of j, which would cause chaos in the program. Imagine changing i and having j change by itself!

Susan: Okay. I just thought that each address represented 2 bytes for some reason. Then in reality each address always has just 1 byte?

Steve: Every byte of RAM has a distinct address, and there is one address for each byte of RAM. However, it is often necessary to read or write more than one byte at a time, as in the case of a short, which is 2 bytes in length. The machine instructions that read or write more than 1 byte specify only the address of the first byte of the item to be read or written; the other byte or bytes of that item follow the first byte immediately in memory.

Susan: Okay, this is why I was confused. I thought when you specified that the RAM address 1000 was a short (2 bytes), it just made room for 2 bytes. So when you specify address 1000 as a short, you know that 1001 will also be occupied with what you put in 1000.

Steve: Or to be more precise, location 1001 will contain the second byte of the short value that starts in byte 1000.

The next line is blank, so we skip it. This brings us to the statement i = 5; which is an executable statement, so we need to generate one or more machine instructions to execute it. We have already assigned address 1000 to i, so we have to generate instructions that will set the 2 bytes at address 1000 to the value that represents 5. One way to do this is to start by setting ax to 5, by the instruction mov ax,5, then storing the contents of ax (5, of course) into the location where the value of i is kept, namely 1000, via the instruction mov [1000],ax.

Figure 3.9 shows what our "memory map" looks like so far.

FIGURE 3.9. Compiling, part 3

Address	Variable Name	
1000	i	
1002	j	

Address	Machine Instruction	Assembly Language Equivalent
2000	b8 05 00	mov ax, 5
2003	a9 00 10	mov [1000],ax

Here's the next installment of my discussion with Susan on this topic:

Susan: When you use ax in an instruction, that is a register, not RAM?

Steve: Yes.

Susan: How do you know you want that register and not another one? What are the differences in the registers? Is ax the first register that data will go into?

Steve: For our current purposes, all of the 16-bit general registers (ax, bx, cx, dx, si, di, bp) are the same. Some of them have other uses, but all of them can be used for simple arithmetic such as we're doing here.

Susan: How do you know that you are not overwriting something more important than what you are presently writing?

Steve: In assembly language, the programmer has to keep track of that; in the case of a compiled language, the compiler takes care of register allocation for you, which is another reason to use a compiler rather than writing assembly language programs yourself.

Susan: If it overwrites, you said important data will go somewhere else. How will you know where it went? How does it know whether what is being overwritten is important? Wait. If something is overwritten, it isn't gone, is it? It is just moved, right?

Steve: The automatic movement of data that you're referring to applies only to cached data being transferred to RAM. That is, if a slot in the cache is needed, the data that it previously held is written out to RAM without the programmer's intervention. However, the content of registers is explicitly controlled by the programmer (or the compiler, in the case of a compiled language). If you write something into a register, whatever was there before is gone. So don't do that if you need the previous contents!

Susan: How do you know that 5 will require 2 bytes?

Steve: In C++, because it's a short. In assembly language, because I'm loading it into ax, which is a 2-byte register.

Susan: Why do the variable addresses start at 1000 and the machine addresses start at 2000?

Steve: It's arbitrary; I picked those numbers out of the air. In a real program, the compiler decides where to put things.

Susan: What do you mean by machine address? What is the machine? Where are the machine addresses?

Steve: A machine address is a RAM address. The machine is the CPU. Machine addresses are stored in the instructions so the CPU knows which RAM location we're referring to.

Susan: We talked about storing instructions before; is this what we are doing here? Are those instructions the "machine instructions"?

Steve: Yes.

Susan: Now, this may sound like a very dumb question, but please tell me where 5 comes from? I mean if you are going to move the value of 5 into the register ax, where is 5 hiding to take it from and to put it in ax? Is it stored somewhere in memory that has to be moved, or is it simply a function of the user just typing in that value?

Steve: It is stored in the instruction as a literal value. If you look at the assembly language illustration on page 84, you will see that the mov ax,5 instruction translates into the three bytes b8 05 00; the 05 00 is the 5 in "little-endian" notation.

Susan: Now, what is so magical about ax (or any register for that matter) that will transform the address 1000 to hold the value of 5?

Steve: The register doesn't do it; the execution of the instruction mov [1000],ax is what sets the memory starting at address 1000 to the value 5.

Susan: What are those numbers supposed to be in the machine instruction box? Those are bytes? Bytes of what? Why are they there? What do they do?

Steve: They represent the actual machine language program as it is executed by the CPU. This is where "the rubber meets the road". All of our C++ or even assembly language programs have to be translated into machine language before they can be executed by the CPU.

Susan: So this is where 5 comes from? I can't believe that there seems to be more code. What is b8 supposed to be? Is it some other type of machine language?

Steve: Machine language is exactly what it is. The first byte of each instruction is the "operation code", or "op code" for short. That tells the CPU what kind of instruction to execute; in this case, b8 specifies a "load register ax with a literal value" instruction. The literal value is the next 2 bytes, which represent the value 5 in "little-endian" notation; therefore, the full translation of the instruction is "load ax with the literal value 5".

Susan: So that is the "op code"? Okay, this makes sense. I don't like it, but it makes sense. Will the machine instructions always start with an op code?

Steve: Yes, there's always an op code first; that's what tells the CPU what the rest of the bytes in the instruction mean.

Susan: Then I noticed that the remaining bytes seem to hold either a literal value or a variable address. Are those the only possibilities?

Steve: Those are the ones that we will need to concern ourselves with.

Susan: I don't understand why machine addresses aren't in 2-byte increments like variable addresses.

Steve: Variable addresses aren't always in 2-byte increments either; it just happens that short variables take up 2 bytes. Other kinds of variables can and often do have other lengths.

Susan: So even though variable addresses are the same as instruction addresses they really aren't because they can't share the same actual address. That is why you distinguish the two by starting the instruction addresses at 2000 in the example and variable addresses at 1000, right?

Steve: Right. A particular memory location can hold only one data item at a time. As far as RAM is concerned, machine instructions are just another kind of data. Therefore, if a particular location is used to store one data item, you can't store anything else there at the same time, whether it's instructions or data.

The last statement, j = i + 3; is the most complicated statement in our program, and it's not that complicated. As with the previous statement, it's executable, which means we need to generate machine instructions to execute it. Because we haven't changed ax since we used it to initialize the variable i with the value 5, it still has that value. Therefore, to calculate the value of j, we can just add 3 to the value in ax by executing the instruction add ax,3. After the execution of this instruction, ax will contain i + 3. Now all we have to do is to store that value in j. As indicated in the translation of the statement short j; the address used to hold the value of j is 1002. Therefore, we can set j to the value in ax by executing the instruction mov [1002],ax.

Figure 3.10 shows what the "memory map" looks like now.

FIGURE 3.10. **Compiling, part 4**

Address	Variable Name	
1000	i	
1002	j	

Address	Machine Instruction	Assembly Language Equivalent
2000	b8 05 00	mov ax, 5
2003	a9 00 10	mov [1000],ax
2006	05 03 00	add ax,3
2009	a9 02 10	mov [1002],ax

By the way, don't be misled by this example into thinking that all machine language instructions are 3 bytes in length. It's just a coincidence that all of the ones I've used here are of that length. The actual size of an instruction on the Intel CPUs can vary considerably, from 1 byte to a theoretical maximum of 12 bytes. Most instructions in common use, however, range from 1 to 5 bytes.

Here's the rest of the discussion that we had about this little exercise:

Susan: In this case mov means add, right?

Steve: No, mov means "move" and add means "add". When we write mov ax,5, it means "move the value 5 into the ax register". The instruction add ax,3 means "add 3 to the current contents of ax, replacing the old contents with this new value".

Susan: So you're moving 5 but adding 3? How do you know when to use mov and when to use add if they both kind of mean the same thing?

Steve: It depends on whether you want to replace the contents of a register without reference to whatever the contents were before (mov) or add something to the contents of the register (add).

Susan: Okay, here is what gets me: how do you get from address 1000 and i=5 to ax? No, that's not it; I want you to tell me what is the relationship between ax and address 1000. I see ax as a register and that should contain the addresses, but here you are adding ax to the address. This doesn't make sense to me. Where are these places? Is address 1000 in RAM?

Steve: The ax register doesn't contain an address. It contains data. After the instruction mov ax,5, ax contains the number 5. After the instruction mov [1000],ax, memory location 1000 contains a copy of the 2-byte value in register ax; in this case, that is the value of the short variable i.

Susan: So do the machine addresses represent actual bytes?

Steve: The machine addresses specify the RAM locations where data (and programs) are stored.

Execution Is Everything

Having examined what the compiler does at *compile time* with the preceding little program fragment, let's see what happens when the compiled program is executed at *run time*. When we start out, the sections of RAM we're concerned with will look like Figure 3.11.

First, a couple of rules for this part of the "game":

1. The *italic* text indicates the next instruction to be executed.

2. We put ?? in the variable and register contents to start out with, to indicate that we haven't stored anything in them yet, and so we don't know what they contain.

FIGURE 3.11. Before execution

Address	Variable Name	Contents
1000	i	?? ??
1002	j	?? ??
--	ax	?? ??

Address	Machine Instruction	Assembly Language Equivalent
2000	*b8 05 00*	*mov ax, 5*
2003	a9 00 10	mov [1000],ax
2006	05 03 00	add ax,3
2009	a9 02 10	mov [1002],ax

Now let's start executing the program. The first instruction, mov ax,5, as we saw earlier, means "set the contents of ax to the value 5".

Figure 3.12 shows the situation after mov ax,5 is executed.

FIGURE 3.12. After the first instruction is executed

Address	Variable Name	Contents
1000	i	?? ??
1002	j	?? ??
--	ax	5

Address	Machine Instruction	Assembly Language Equivalent
2000	b8 05 00	mov ax, 5
2003	*a9 00 10*	*mov [1000],ax*
2006	05 03 00	add ax,3
2009	a9 02 10	mov [1002],ax

As you can see, executing mov ax,5 has updated the contents of ax, and we've advanced to the next instruction, mov [1000],ax. When we have executed that instruction, the situation looks like Figure 3.13, with the variable i set to 5. Figure 3.14 shows the result after the following instruction, add ax,3, is executed.

FIGURE 3.13. After execution of second instruction

Address	Variable Name	Contents
1000	i	5
1002	j	?? ??
--	ax	5

Address	Machine Instruction	Assembly Language Equivalent
2000	b8 05 00	mov ax, 5
2003	a9 00 10	mov [1000],ax
2006	*05 03 00*	*add ax,3*
2009	a9 02 10	mov [1002],ax

Learning to Program in C++   **91**

FIGURE 3.14. **After execution of third instruction**

Address	Variable Name	Contents
1000	i	5
1002	j	?? ??
--	ax	8

Address	Machine Instruction	Assembly Language Equivalent
2000	b8 05 00	mov ax, 5
2003	a9 00 10	mov [1000],ax
2006	05 03 00	add ax,3
2009	a9 02 10	mov [1002],ax

As expected, add ax,3 has increased the contents of ax by the value 3, producing 8. Now we're ready for the final instruction.

FIGURE 3.15. **After execution of final instruction**

Address	Variable Name	Contents
1000	i	5
1002	j	8
--	ax	8

Address	Machine Instruction	Assembly Language Equivalent
2000	b8 05 00	mov ax, 5
2003	a9 00 10	mov [1000],ax
2006	05 03 00	add ax,3
2009	a9 02 10	mov [1002],ax

Figure 3.15 shows the situation after the final instruction, mov [1002],ax, has been executed.

After executing the final instruction, mov [1002],ax, the variable i has the value 5 and the variable j has the value 8.

A Cast of Characters

This should give you some idea of how numeric variables and values work. But what about nonnumeric ones?

This brings us to the subject of two new variable types and the values they can contain. These are the char (short for "character") and its relative, the string. What are these good for, and how do they work?[20]

A variable of type char corresponds to 1 byte of storage. Since a byte has 8 bits, it can hold any of 256 (2^8) values; the exact values depend on whether it is signed or unsigned, as with the short variables we have seen before. Going strictly according to this description, you might get the idea that a char is just a "really short" numeric variable. A char indeed can be used for this purpose in cases where no more than 256 different numeric values are to be represented. In fact, this explains why you might want a signed char. Such a variable can be used to hold numbers from –128 to +127; an unsigned char, on the other hand, has a range from 0 to 255. This facility isn't used very much any more, but in the early days of C, memory was very expensive and scarce, so it was sometimes worth the effort to use 1-byte variables to hold small values.

However, the main purpose of a char is to represent an individual letter, digit, punctuation mark, "special character" (e.g., $, @, #, %, and so on) or one of the other "printable" and displayable units from which words, sentences, and other textual data such as this paragraph are composed.[21]

---

20. In case you were wondering, the most common pronunciation of char has an *a* like the a in "married", while the *ch* sounds like "k".

These 256 different possibilities are plenty to represent any character in English, as well as a number of other European languages, but the written forms of "ideographic" languages such as Chinese consist of far more than 256 characters, so 1 byte isn't big enough to hold a character in these languages. While they have been supported to some extent by schemes that switch among a number of sets of 256 characters each, such clumsy approaches to the problem made programs much more complicated and error prone. As the international market for software is increasing rapidly, it has become more important to have a convenient method of handling large *character sets*; as a result, a standard method of representing the characters of such languages by using 2 bytes per character has been developed. It's called the "Unicode standard". There's even a proposed solution that uses 32 bits per character, for the day when Unicode doesn't have sufficient capacity.[22]

Since one char isn't good for much by itself, we often use groups of them, called strings, to make them easier to handle. Just as with numeric values, these variables can be set to literal values, which represent themselves. Figure 3.16 is an example of how to specify and use each of these types we've just encountered. This is the first complete program we've seen, so there are a couple of new constructs that I'll have to explain to you.

By the way, in case the program in Figure 3.16 doesn't seem very useful, that's because it isn't; it's just an example of the syntax of defining and using variables and literal values. However, we'll use these constructs to do useful work later, so going over them now isn't a waste of time.

---

21. As we will see shortly, not all characters have visible representations; some of these "nonprintable" characters are useful in controlling how our printed or displayed information looks.

22. That should take care of any languages that aliens civilizations might introduce to our planet.

FIGURE 3.16. Some real characters and strings (code\basic00.cc)

```
#include "string6.h"

int main()
{
    char c1;
    char c2;
    string s1;
    string s2;

    c1 = 'A';
    c2 = c1;

    s1 = "This is a test ";
    s2 = "and so is this.";

    return 0;
}
```

Why do we need the line #include "string6.h"? Because we have to tell the compiler how to manipulate strings. They aren't built in to its knowledge base. For the moment, it's enough to know that the contents of the file string6.h are needed to tell the compiler how to use strings; we'll get into the details of this mechanism later, starting in Chapter 7.

However, since we're already on the subject of files, this would be a good time to point out that the two main types of files in C++ are implementation files (also known as source files), which in our case have the extension .cc, and header files, which by convention have the extension .h.[23] Implementation files contain statements that result in executable code, while each header file contains information that allows us to access a set of language features.

---

23. Other compilers sometimes use other extensions for implementation files, such as .cpp, and for header files, such as .hpp.

The next construct we have to examine is the line int main(), which has two new components. The first is the "return type", which specifies the type of value that will be returned from the program when it ends. In this case, that type is int, which is an integral type exactly like short, except that its size depends on the compiler that you're using. With a 32-bit compiler like the one on the CD-ROM in this book, an int is 32 bits, or twice the size of a short. With a 16-bit compiler such as Borland C++ version 3.1, an int is the same size as a short. I don't like to use ints, because I want my code to work in the same way on both 16- and 32-bit compilers. However, we don't have much choice here, because the C++ language specifies that main has to have the return type int.

This brings us to the meaning of main(). This tells the compiler where to start executing the code: C++ has a rule that execution always starts at the place called main.

We'll get into this in more detail in Chapter 5. For now, you'll just have to take my word that this is necessary; I promise I'll explain what it really means when you have enough background to understand the explanation.

You may also be puzzled by the function of the other statements in this program. If so, you're not alone. Let's see the discussion that Susan and I had about that topic.

> **Susan:** Okay, in the example *why* did you have to write c2 = c1;? Why not B? Why make one thing the same thing as the other? Make it different. Why would you even want c2=c1; and not just say c1 twice, if that is what you want?

> **Steve:** It's very hard to think up examples that are both simple enough to explain and realistic enough to make sense. You're right that this example doesn't do anything useful; I'm just trying to introduce what both the char type and the string type look like.

> **Susan:** Come to think of it, what does c1='A'; have to do with the statement s1= "This is a test ";? I don't see any relationship between one thing and the other.

Steve: This is the same problem as the last one. They have nothing to do with one another; I'm using an admittedly contrived example to show how these variables are used.

Susan: I am glad now that your example of chars and strings (put together) didn't make sense to me. That is progress; it wasn't supposed to.

What does this useless but hopefully instructive program do? As is always the case, we have to tell the compiler what the types of our variables are before we can use them. In this case, c1 and c2 are of type char, whereas s1 and s2 are strings. After taking care of these formalities, we can start to use the variables. In the first executable statement, c1 = 'A'; we set the char variable c1 to a literal value, in this case a capital *A*; we need to surround this with single quotation marks (') to tell the compiler that we mean the letter *A* rather than a variable named A. In the next line, c2 = c1; we set c2 to the same value as c1 holds, which of course is 'A' in this case. The next executable statement s1 = "This is a test "; as you might expect, sets the string variable s1 to the value "This is a test ",[24] which is a literal of a type called a **C string**. Don't confuse a C string literal with a string. A C string literal is a type of literal that we use to assign values to variables of type string. In the statement s1 = "This is a test "; we use a quotation mark, in this case the double quote ("), to tell the compiler where the literal value starts and ends.

You may be wondering why we need two different kinds of quotes in these two cases. The reason is that there are actually two types of nonnumeric data, *fixed-length data* and *variable-length data*. Fixed-length data are relatively easy to handle in a program, as the compiler can set aside the correct amount of space in advance. Variables of type char are 1 byte long and can thus contain exactly one character; as a result, when we set a char to a literal value, as we

---

24. Please note that there is a *space* (blank) character at the end of that C string literal, after the word "test". That space is part of the literal value.

do in the line c1 = 'A'; the code that executes that statement has the simple task of copying exactly 1 byte representing the literal 'A' to the address reserved for variable c1.[25]

However, C string literals such as "This is a test " are variable-length data, and dealing with such data isn't so easy. Since there could be any number of characters in a C string, the code that does the assignment of a literal value like "This is a test " to a string variable has to have some way to tell where the literal value ends. One possible way to provide this needed information would be for the compiler to store the length of the C string literal in the memory location immediately before the first character in the literal. I would prefer this method; unfortunately, it is not the method used in the C language (and its descendant, the C++ language). To be fair, the inventors of C didn't make an arbitrary choice; they had reasons for their decision on how to indicate the length of a string. You see, if we were to reserve only 1 byte to store the actual length in bytes of the character data in the string, then the maximum length of a string would be limited to 255 bytes. This is because the maximum value that could be stored in the length byte, as in any other byte, is 255. Thus, if we had a string longer than 255 bytes, we would not be able to store the length of the string in the 1 byte reserved for that purpose. On the other hand, if we were to reserve 2 bytes for the length of each string, then programs that contain many strings would take more memory than they otherwise would.

---

25. Warning: Every character inside the quotes has an effect on the value of the literal, whether the quotes are single or double; even "invisible" characters such as the *space* (' ') will change the literal's value. In other words, the line c1 = 'A'; is *not* the same as the line c1 = 'A '; . The latter statement may or may not be legal, depending on the compiler you're using, but it is virtually certain not to give you what you want, which is to set the variable c1 to the value equivalent to the character 'A'. Instead, c1 will have some weird value resulting from combining the 'A' and the space character. In the case of a string value contained in double quotes, multiple characters are allowed, so "A B" and "AB" both make sense, but the space still makes a difference; namely, it keeps the 'A' and 'B' from being next to one another.

While the extra memory consumption that would be caused by using a 2-byte length code may not seem significant today, the situation was considerably different when C was invented. At that time, conserving memory was very important; the inventors of C therefore chose to mark the end of a C string by a byte containing the value 0, which is called a **null byte**.[26] This solution has the advantage that only one extra byte is needed to indicate the end of a C string of any length. However, it also has some serious drawbacks. First, this solution makes it impossible to have a byte containing the value 0 in the middle of a C string, as all of the C string manipulation routines would treat that null byte as being the end of the C string. Second, it is a nontrivial operation to determine the length of a C string; the only way to do it is to scan through the C string until you find a null byte. As you can probably tell, I'm not particularly impressed with this mechanism; nevertheless, as it has been adopted into C++ for compatibility with C, we're stuck with it for literal strings in our programs.[27] Therefore, the literal string "ABCD" would occupy 5 bytes, 1 for each character, and 1 for the null byte that the compiler adds automatically at the end of the literal. But we've skipped one step: How do we represent characters in memory? There's no intuitively obvious way to convert the character 'A' into a value that can be stored in 1 byte of memory.

The answer, at least for our purposes in English, is called the **ASCII code** standard. This stands for American Standard Code for Information Interchange, which as the name suggests was invented to allow the interchange of data between different programs and makes of computers. Before the invention of ASCII, such interchange was difficult or impossible, since every manufacturer made up its own

---

26. I don't want to mislead you about this notion of a byte having the value 0; it is *not* the same as the representation of the decimal digit "0". As we'll see, each displayable character (and a number of invisible ones) is assigned a value to represent it when it's part of a string or literal value (i.e., a C string literal or char literal). The 0 byte I'm referring to is a byte with the binary value 0.

27. Happily, we can improve on it in most other circumstances, as you'll see later.

code or codes. Here are the specific character codes that we have to be concerned with for the purposes of this book:

1. The codes for the capital letters start with hex 41 for 'A', and run consecutively to hex 5a for 'Z'.

2. The codes for the lower case letters start with hex 61 for 'a', and run consecutively to hex 7a for 'z'.[28]

3. The codes for the numeric digits start with hex 30 for '0', and run consecutively to hex 39 for '9'.

Given these rules, the memory representation of the string "ABCD" might look something like Figure 3.17.

FIGURE 3.17. Yet another small section of RAM

Address	Hex byte value
1000	41
1001	42
1002	43
1003	44
1004	00 (null byte; that is, end of C string)

Now that we see how strings are represented in memory, I can explain why we need two kinds of quotes. The double quotes tell the compiler to add the null byte at the end of the string literal, so that when the assignment statement s1 = "This is a test "; is executed, the program knows when to stop copying the value to the string variable.

---

28. You may wonder why I have to specify that the codes for each case of letters run consecutively. Believe it or not, there are a number of slightly differing codes collectively called EBCDIC (Extended Binary Coded Decimal Interchange Code), in which this is not true! Eric Raymond's amusing and interesting book, *The New Hacker's Dictionary*, has details on this and many other historical facts.

A Byte by Any Other Name...

Have you noticed that I've played a little trick here? The illustration of the string "ABCD" should look a bit familiar; its memory contents are exactly the same as in Figure 3.2, where we were discussing numeric variables. I did this to illustrate an important point: the contents of memory actually consists of uninterpreted bytes, which have meaning only when used in a particular way by a program. That is, the same bytes can represent numeric data or characters, depending on how they are referred to.

This is one of the main reasons why we need to tell the C++ compiler what types our variables have. Some languages allow variables to be used in different ways at different times, but in C++ any given variable always has the same type; for example, a char variable can't change into a short. At first glance, it seems that it would be much easier for programmers to be able to use variables any way they like; why is C++ so restrictive?

The C++ **type system**, as this feature of a language is called, is specifically designed to minimize the risk of misinterpreting or otherwise misusing a variable. It's entirely too easy in some languages to change the type of a variable without meaning to; the resulting bugs can be very difficult to find, especially in a large program. In C++, the usage of a variable can be checked by the compiler. Such **static type checking** allows the compiler to tell you about many errors that otherwise would not be detected until the program is running (**dynamic type checking**). This is particularly important in systems that need to run continuously for long periods of time. While you can reboot your machine if your word processor crashes due to a run-time error, this is not acceptable as a solution for errors in the telephone network, for example.

Of course, you probably won't be writing programs demanding that degree of reliability any time soon, but strict static type checking is still worthwhile in helping eliminate errors at the earliest possible stage in the development of our programs.

Some Strings Attached

After that infomercial for the advantages of static type checking, we can resume our examination of strings. You may have noticed that there's a **space** character at the end of the string "This is a test ". That's another reason why we have to use a special character like " (the double quote) to mark the beginning and end of a string; how else would the compiler know whether that space is supposed to be part of the string or not? The space character is one of the **nonprinting character**s (or **nondisplay character**s) that controls the format of our displayed or printed information; imagine how hard it would be to read this book without space characters! While we're on the subject, I should also tell you about some other characters that have special meaning to the compiler. They are listed in Figure 3.18.

I'll be more specific about the uses of parentheses later, when we have seen some examples. As for the backslash, if you wanted to (for example) insert a " in a string, you would have to use \", because just a plain " would indicate the end of the string. That is, if you wanted to display This is a "string"., you would have to write the value of the string as "This is a \"string\"."

I compiled Figure 3.18 at the instigation of guess who:

Susan: How about you line up all your cute little " ' \ ; things and just list their meanings? I forget what they are by the time I get to the next one. Your explanations of them are fine, but they are scattered all over the place; I just want one place that has all the explanations.

Steve: That's a good idea. As usual, you're doing a good job representing the novices; keep up the good work!

Our next task, after a little bit of practice with the memory representation of a C string, will be to see how we get the values of our strings to show up on the screen.

FIGURE 3.18. Special characters for program text

Name	Graphic	Purpose
Single quote	'	surrounds a single character value
Double quote	"	surrounds a multi-character value
Semicolon	;	ends a statement
Curly braces	{ }	groups statements together
Parentheses	( )	surrounds part of a statement
Backslash	\	Tells the compiler that the next character should be treated differently from the way that it would normally be treated.

Exercises, Second Set

2. Assume that a C string literal starts at memory location 1001. If the contents of memory are as illustrated in Figure 3.19, what is the value of the C string?

FIGURE 3.19. A small section of RAM

Address	Hex byte value
1000	44
1001	48
1002	45
1003	4c
1004	4c
1005	4f
1006	00

In and Out

Most programs need to interact with their users, both to ask them what they want and to present the results when they are available. The computer term for this topic is **I/O** (short for "input/output"). We'll start by getting information from the keyboard and displaying it on the screen; later, we'll go over the more complex I/O functions that allow us to read and write data on the disk.

The program in Figure 3.20 displays the text "This is a test and so is this.". The meaning of << is suggested by its arrowlike shape: The information on its right is sent to the "output target" on its left. In this case, we're sending the information to one of the predefined destinations, cout, which stands for "character output".[29] Characters sent to cout are displayed on the screen.

FIGURE 3.20. **Some simple output (code\basic01.cc)**

```
#include <iostream.h>
#include "string6.h"

int main()
{
    string s1;
    string s2;

    s1 = "This is a test ";
    s2 = "and so is this.";

    cout << s1;
    cout << s2;

    return 0;
}
```

29. The line #include <iostream.h> is necessary here to tell the compiler about cout and how it works. We'll get into this in a bit more detail shortly.

This program will send the following output to the screen:

This is a test and so is this.

So much for simple output. Input from the keyboard can be just as simple. Modifying our little sample to use it results in Figure 3.21.

FIGURE 3.21. **Some simple input and output (code\basic02.cc)**

```cpp
#include <iostream.h>
#include "string6.h"

int main()
{
    string s1;
    string s2;

    cin >> s1;
    cin >> s2;

    cout << s1;
    cout << " ";
    cout << s2;

    return 0;
}
```

As you might have guessed, cin (shorthand for "character input") is the counterpart to cout as >> is the counterpart to <<; cin supplies characters from the keyboard to the program via the >> operator.[30] This program will wait for you to type in the first string, ended by hitting the ENTER key, then do the same for the second string. When you hit ENTER the second time, the program will display the first string, then a blank, and then the second string.

---

30. In case you were wondering, cout is pronounced "see out", while cin is pronounced "see in".

Susan had some questions about these little programs, beginning with the question of case sensitivity:

Susan: Are the words such as cout and cin case sensitive? I had capitalized a few of them just out of habit because they begin the sentence and I am not sure if that was the reason the compiler gave me so many error messages. I think after I changed them I reduced a few messages.

Steve: *Everything* in C++ is case sensitive. That includes keywords like if, for, do, and so on, as well as your own variables. That is, if you have a variable called Name and another one called name, those are completely different and unrelated to one another. You have to write cin and cout just as they appear here, or the compiler won't understand you.

If Only You Knew

In our examples so far, the program always executes the same statements in the same order. However, any real program is going to need to alter its behavior according to the data it is processing. For example, in a banking application, it might be necessary to send out a notice to a depositor whenever the balance in a particular account drops below a certain level; or perhaps the depositor would just be charged some exorbitant fee in that case. Either way, the program has to do something different depending on the balance. In particular, let's suppose that the "First Absconders and Defaulters National Bank" has a minimum balance of $10,000. Furthermore, let's assume that if you have less than that amount on deposit, you are charged a $20 "service charge". However, if you are foolish enough to leave that ridiculous amount of money on deposit, then they will graciously allow you to get away with not paying them while they're using your money (without paying you interest, of course). To determine whether or not you should be charged for your checking account, the bank can use an if statement, as shown in Figure 3.22.

FIGURE 3.22. **Using an if statement (code\basic03.cc)**

```
#include <iostream.h>

int main()
{
    short balance;

    cout << "Please enter your bank balance: ";
    cin >> balance;

    if (balance < 10000)
        cout << "Please remit $20 service charge." << endl;
    else
        cout << "Have a nice day!" << endl;

    return 0;
}
```

This program starts by displaying the line

Please enter your bank balance:

on the screen. Then it waits for you to type in your balance, followed by the ENTER key (so it knows when you're done). The conditional statement checks whether you're a "good customer". If your balance is less than $10,000, the next statement is executed, which displays the line

Please remit $20 service charge.[31]

The phrase << endl is new here. It means "we're done with this line of output; send it out to the screen". You could also use the special character '\n', which means much the same thing; its official name is "newline".

Now let's get back to our regularly scheduled program. If the condition is false (that is, you have at least $10,000 in the bank), the computer skips the statement that asks you to remit $20; instead, it executes the one after the else, which tells you to have a nice day. That's what else is for; it specifies what to do if the condition specified in the if statement is false (that is, not true). If you typed in a number 10,000 or higher, the program would display the line

Have a nice day!

You don't have to specify an else if you don't want to. In that case, if the if condition isn't true, the program just goes to the next statement as though the if had never been executed.

While We're on the Subject

The while statement is another way of affecting the order of program execution. This conditional statement executes the statement under its control as long as a certain condition is true. Such potentially repeated execution is called a **loop**; a loop controlled by a while statement is called, logically enough, a while loop. Figure 3.23 is a program that uses a while loop to challenge the user to guess a secret number from 0–9, and keeps asking for guesses until the correct answer is entered.

---

31. This explanation assumes that the "10,000" is the balance in dollars. Of course, this doesn't account for the possibility of balances that aren't a whole number of dollars, and there's also the problem of balances greater than $32767, which wouldn't fit into a short. As we'll see in Chapter 9, both of these problems can be solved by using a different data type called double.

FIGURE 3.23. Using a while statement (code\basic04.cc)

```cpp
#include <iostream.h>

int main()
{
    short Secret;
    short Guess;

    Secret = 3;

    cout << "Try and guess my number. Hint: It's from 0 to 9" << endl;
    cin >> Guess;

    while (Guess != Secret)
        {
        cout << "Sorry, that's not correct." << endl;
        cin >> Guess;
        }

    cout << "You guessed right!" << endl;

    return 0;
}
```

There are a few wrinkles here that we haven't seen before. Although the while statement itself is fairly straightforward, the meaning of its condition, !=, isn't intuitively obvious. However, if you consider the problem we're trying to solve, you'll probably come to the (correct) conclusion that != means "not equal", since we want to keep asking for more guesses while the Guess is not equal to our Secret number.[32] Since there is a comparison operator that tests for "not equal", you

---

32. Why do we need parentheses around the expression Guess != Secret? The conditional expression has to be in parentheses so that the compiler can tell where it ends and the statement to be controlled by the while begins.

might wonder how to test for "equal" as well; as is explained in some detail in the next chapter, in C++ we have to use == rather than = to compare whether two values are equal.

You might also be wondering whether an if statement with an else clause would serve as well as the while; after all, if is used to select one of two alternatives, and the else could select the other one. The answer is that this would allow the user to take only one guess before the program ends; the while loop lets the user try again as many times as needed to get the right answer.

Now you should have enough information to be able to write a simple program of your own. Susan asked for an assignment to do just that:

> **Susan:** Based on what you have presented in the book so far, send me a setup, an exercise for me to try to figure out how to program, and I will give it a try. I guess that is the only way to do it. I can't even figure out a programmable situation on my own. So if you do that, I will do my best with it, and that will help teach me to think. (Can that be?) Now, if you do this, make it simple, and no tricks.

Of course, I did give her the exercise she asked for (exercise 3), but also of course, that didn't end the matter. She decided to add her own flourish, which resulted in exercise 4. These exercises follow below, right after some instructions on the mechanics of creating a program. The instructions assume that you've installed the software from the CD-ROM in the back of this book. Otherwise, follow the instructions in the back of the book to install the software, and then come back to these instructions.

1. Change to the "\shcppg\code" directory on the drive where you installed the compiler.

2. Type RHIDE to start the compiler's integrated development environment (IDE). Use RHIDE's editor to create a source code file containing the source code for your program. To do this, select the File menu and click New. Then type in the code for your program, which we'll assume will be called "myprog".

3. When you get done writing the source code for your program, you will have to save it. To do this, select the File menu and click on Save. This will bring up a dialog box into which you will type the name of your file, which we'll assume is "myprog.cc" (without the quotes), and hit ENTER.

4. Once you have written the source code for your program, you will need to create a "project" to keep track of the various parts of the program. To do this, select the "Project" menu, click on "Open project", and then type in the name of the project that you want to create. If you want to call your project "myprog", you'll type "myprog" (without the quotes) and hit ENTER.

5. Now you will need to add the source file you just created to the project list so that it will be compiled. To do this, select the Project menu, then click on "Add item". Type in the name of your file, which is "myprog.cc", and hit ENTER.

6. The next step is to tell RHIDE to include the files that define how strings and vectors[33] work. You can skip this step if you aren't using any strings or vectors, but most programs will eventually need to use one or more of these data types even if they don't need them at the start, so you might as well include these files. To do this, select the Project menu, then click on "Add item". Type in "string7.cc" and hit ENTER, then type in "wassert.cc" and hit ENTER.

7. When you have finished adding files to the project, click on the CANCEL button to close the "Add item" dialog box.

---

33. The vector is a data type we'll start using in Chapter 4.

8. To compile your program, select the "Compile" menu and click "Make". This will compile any source files that haven't been compiled since they were written or last changed.

9. To run your program normally from a DOS prompt, make sure you are in the "\shcppg\code" directory, and then type the name of the program, without the extension. In this case, you would just type "myprog".

10. To run your program under the debugger, make sure you are in the "\shcppg\code" directory, and then type RHIDE myprog (substituting the name of your program for "myprog"). Again, do *not* add the ".cc" to the end of the file name. Once RHIDE has started up, you can step through the program by hitting F8, which will treat any function call as one statement, or by hitting F7, which will step into any function call. Any time you want to see the display that the user would see when running the program normally, hit ALT-F5, then ENTER to get back to the debugger. The debugger also has a lot of other features, including displaying the values of variables during program execution, which I encourage you to explore.

Now here are the programs Susan came up with, along with some others that fall in the same category.

Exercises, Third Set

3. Write a program that asks the user to type in the number of people that are expected for dinner, not counting the user. Assuming that the number typed in is n, display a message that says "A table for (n+1) is ready.". For example, if the user types 3, display "A table for 4 is ready.".

4. Modify the program from exercise 3 to display an error message if the number of guests is more than 20.

5. Write a program that asks the user to type in his or her name and age. If the age is less than 47, then indicate that the user is a youngster; otherwise, that he or she is getting on in years.

6. Write a program that asks the user whether Susan is the world's most tenacious novice. If the answer is "true", then acknowledge the user's correct answer; if the answer is "false", then indicate that the answer is erroneous. If neither "true" nor "false" is typed in, chastise the user for not following directions.

7. Write a program that calculates how much allowance a teenager can earn by doing extra chores. Her allowance is calculated as $10 if she does no extra chores; she gets $1 additional for each extra chore she does.

Just up the Block

Our most recent programming example has contributed another item to our arsenal of programming weapons: namely, the ability to group several statements into one logical section of a program. That's the function of the **curly braces**, { and }. The first one of these starts such a section, called a **block**, and the second one ends the block. Because the two statements after the while are part of the same block, they are treated as a unit; both are executed if the condition in the while is true, and neither is executed if it is false. A block can be used anywhere that a statement can be used, and is treated in exactly the same way as if it were one statement.[34]

---

34. If you look at someone else's C++ program, you're likely to see a different style for lining up the {} to indicate where a block begins and ends. As you'll notice, my style puts the { and } on separate lines rather than running them together with the code they enclose, to make them stand out, and indents them further than the conditional statement. I find this the clearest, but this is a matter where there is no consensus. The compiler doesn't care how you indent your code or whether you do so at all; it's a stylistic issue.

At the Fair

Now we're ready to write a program that vaguely resembles a solution to a real problem. We'll start with a simple, rural type of programming problem.

Imagine that you are at a county fair. The contest for the heaviest pumpkin is about to get underway, and the judges have asked for your help in operating the "pumpkin scoreboard". This device has a slot for the current pumpkin weight (the CurrentWeight slot), and another slot for the highest weight so far (the HighestWeight slot); each slot can hold three digits from 0–9 and therefore can indicate any weight from 0–999. The judges want you to maintain an up-to-date display of the current weight and of the highest weight seen so far. The weights are expressed to the nearest pound. How would you go about this task?

Probably the best way to start is by setting the number in both slots to the weight of the first pumpkin called out. Then, as each new weight is called out, you change the number in the CurrentWeight slot to match the current weight; if it's higher than the number in the HighestWeight slot, you change that one to match as well. Of course, you don't have to do anything to the HighestWeight slot when a weight less than the previous maximum weight is called out, because a pumpkin with a lesser weight can't be the winner. How do we know when we are done? Since a pumpkin entered in this contest has to have a weight of at least 1 pound, the weigher calls out 0 as the weight when the weighing is finished. At that point, the number in the HighestWeight slot is the weight of the winner.

The procedure you have just imagined performing can be expressed a bit more precisely by the following algorithm:

1. Ask for the first weight.

2. Set the number in the CurrentWeight slot to this value.

3. Copy the number in the CurrentWeight slot to the HighestWeight slot.

4. Display both the current weight and the highest weight so far (which are the same, at this point).

5. While the CurrentWeight value is greater than 0 (that is, there are more pumpkins to be weighed), do steps a to d:

   a. Ask for the next weight.

   b. Set the number in the CurrentWeight slot to this weight.

   c. If the number in the CurrentWeight slot is greater than the number in the HighestWeight slot, copy the number in the CurrentWeight slot to the HighestWeight slot.

   d. Display the current weight and the highest weight so far.

6. Stop. The number in the HighestWeight slot is the weight of the winner.

Figure 3.24 is the translation of our little problem into C++. You've already seen most of the constructs that this program contains, but let's examine the role of the *preprocessor directive* #include <iostream.h>. This tells the compiler that we want to use the standard C++ I/O library. The term *preprocessor directive* is a holdover from the days when a separate program called the *preprocessor* handled functions such as #include before handing the program over to the compiler; these days, these facilities are provided by the compiler, but the name has stuck.

The #include command has the same effect as copying all of the code from a file called iostream.h into our file; iostream.h defines the I/O functions and variables cout, cin, <<, and >>, along with others that we haven't used yet. If we left this line out, none of our I/O statements would work.

FIGURE 3.24. A C++ Program (code\pump1.cc)

English	C++
First, we have to tell the compiler what we're up to in this program	
Define the standard input and output functionality	#include <iostream.h>
This is the main part of the program	int main()
Start of program	{
Define variables	short CurrentWeight; short HighestWeight;
Here's the start of the "working" code	
Ask for the first weight	cout << "Please enter the first weight: ";
Set the number in the CurrentWeight slot to the value entered by the user	cin >> CurrentWeight;
Copy the number in the CurrentWeight slot to the HighestWeight slot	HighestWeight = CurrentWeight;
Display the current and highest weights	cout << "Current weight " << CurrentWeight << endl; cout << "Highest weight " << HighestWeight << endl;
While the number in the CurrentWeight slot is greater than 0 (i.e., there are more pumpkins to be weighed)	while (CurrentWeight > 0)
Start repeated steps	{
Ask for the next weight	cout << "Please enter the next weight: ";
Set the number in the CurrentWeight slot to this value	cin >> CurrentWeight;

English	C++
If the number in the CurrentWeight slot is more than the number in the HighestWeight slot,	if (CurrentWeight > HighestWeight)
then copy the number in the CurrentWeight slot to the Highest-Weight slot	HighestWeight = CurrentWeight;
Display the current and highest weights	cout << "Current weight " << CurrentWeight << endl; cout << "Highest weight " << HighestWeight << endl;
End repeated steps in while loop	}
We've finished the job; now to clean up	
Tell the rest of the system we're okay	return 0;
End of program	}

Susan had some questions about variable names.

Susan: Tell me again what the different shorts mean in this figure. I am confused, I just thought a short held a variable like i. What is going on when you declare HighestWeight a short? So do the "words" HighestWeight work in the same way as i?

Steve: A short is a variable. The name of a short, like the name of any other variable, is made up of one or more characters; the first character must be a letter or an underscore (_), while any character after the first must be either a letter, an underscore, or a digit from 0–9. To define a short, you write a line that gives the name of the short. This is an example:

short HighestWeight;

Susan: Okay, but then how does i take 2 bytes of memory and how does HighestWeight take up 2 bytes of memory? They look so different, how do you know that HighestWeight will fit into a short?

Steve: The length of the names that you give variables has nothing to do with the amount of storage that the variables take up. After the compiler gets through with your program, there aren't any variable names; each variable that you define in your source program is represented by the address of some area of storage. If the variable is a short, that area of storage is 2 bytes long; if it's a char, the area of storage is 1 byte long.

Susan: Then where do the names go? They don't go "into" the short?

Steve: A variable name doesn't "go" anywhere; it tells the compiler to set aside an area of memory of a particular length that you will refer to by a given name. If you write short xyz; you're telling the compiler that you are going to use a short (that is, 2 bytes of memory) called xyz.

Susan: If that is the case, then why bother defining the short at all?

Steve: So that you (the programmer) can use a name that makes sense to you. Without this mechanism, you'd have to specify everything as an address. Isn't it easier to say

```
HighestWeight = CurrentWeight;
```

rather than

```
mov ax,[1000]
mov [1002],ax
```

or something similar?

Susan also had a question about the formatting of the output statement cout << "Highest weight " << HighestWeight << endl;.

> **Susan:** Why do we need both "Highest weight" and HighestWeight in this line?

> **Steve:** Because "Highest weight" is displayed on the screen to tell the user that the following number is supposed to represent the highest weight seen so far. On the other hand, HighestWeight is the name of the variable that holds that information, so including HighestWeight in the output statement will result in displaying the highest weight we've seen so far on the screen. Of course, the same analysis applies to the next line, which displays the label "Current weight" and the value of the variable CurrentWeight.

The topic of #include statements was the cause of some discussion with Susan. Here's the play by play:

> **Susan:** Is the include command the only time you will use the # symbol?

> **Steve:** There are other uses for #, but you won't see any of them for a long time.[35]

> **Susan:** So #include is a command.

> **Steve:** Right; it's a command to the compiler.

> **Susan:** Then what are the words we have been using for the most part called? Are those just called *code* or just *statements*? Can you make a list of commands to review?

---

35. Not until "Definitions" on page 860 in Chapter 12, to be exact.

Steve: The words that are defined in the language, such as if, while, for, and the like are called *keywords*. User defined names such as function and variable names are called *identifiers*.

Susan: So iostream.h is a header file telling the compiler that it is using info from the iostreams library?

Steve: Essentially correct; to be more precise, when we include iostream.h, we're telling the compiler to look into iostream.h for definitions that we're going to use.

Susan: Then the header file contains the secondary code of machine language to transform cin and cout into something workable?

Steve: Close, but not quite right. The machine code that makes cin and cout do their thing is in the iostreams library; the header file gives the compiler the information it needs to compile your references to cout, cin, <<, and >> into references to the machine code in the library.

Susan: So the header file directs the compiler to that section in the library where that machine code is stored? In other words, it is like telling the compiler to look in section XXX to find the machine code?

Steve: The header file tells the compiler what a particular part of the library does, while the library contains the machine code that actually does it.

If you have previous experience as a programmer (other than in C), you may wonder why we have to tell the compiler that we want to use the standard I/O library. Why doesn't the compiler know to use that library automatically? This seeming oversight is actually the result of a decision made very early in the evolution of C: to keep the language itself (and therefore the compiler) as simple as possible, adding functionality with the aid of standard libraries. Since a large part of the libraries can be written in C (or C++), this decision reduces the amount of work needed to "port" the C (or C++) language from one machine architecture or operating system to another. Once the compiler has been ported, it's not too difficult to get the libraries to work on the new machine. In fact, even the C (or C++) compiler can be written in C (or C++), which makes the whole language quite portable. This may seem impossible. How do you get started? In fact, the process is called *bootstrapping*, from the impossible task of trying to lift yourself by your own bootstraps.[36] The secret is to have one compiler that's already running; then you use that compiler to compile the compiler for the new machine. Once you have the new compiler running, it is common to use it to compile itself, so that you know it's working. After all, a compiler is a fairly complex program, so getting it to compile and execute properly is a pretty good indication that it's producing the right code when it compiles itself.

Most of the rest of the program should be fairly easy to understand, except for the two lines int main() and return 0;, which have related functions. Let's start with the line int main(). As we've already seen, the purpose of the main() part of this line is to tell the compiler where to start execution; the C++ language definition specifies that execution always starts at a block called main. This may seem redundant, as you might expect the compiler to assume that we want to start execution at the beginning of the program. However, C++ is intended to be useful in the writing of very large programs; such programs can and usually do consist of several implementation files, each of which contains some of the functionality of the program. Without such a rule, the compiler wouldn't know which module should be executed first.

The int part of this same line specifies the type of the *exit code* that will be returned from the program by a return statement when the program is finished executing; in this case, that type is int. The exit

---

36. If this term sounds familiar, we've already seen it in the context of how we start up a computer when it's turned on, starting from a small *boot program* in the *ROM*, or Read-Only Memory.

code can be used by a *batch file* to determine whether our program finished executing correctly; an exit code of 0, by convention, means that it did.[37] The final statement in the program is return 0;. This is the return statement just mentioned, whose purpose is to return an exit code of 0 when our program stops running. The value that is returned, 0, is an acceptable value of the type we declared in the line int main(), namely, int; if it didn't match, the compiler would tell us we had made an error.

Finally, the closing curly brace, }, tells the compiler that it can stop compiling the current block, which in this case is the one called main. Without this marker, the compiler would tell us that we have a missing }, which of course would be true.

Novice Alert

Susan decided a little later in our collaboration that she wanted to try to reproduce this program just by considering the English description, without looking at my solution. She didn't quite make it without peeking, but the results are illuminating nevertheless.

> **Susan:** What I did was to cover your code with a sheet of paper and just tried to get the next line without looking, and then if I was totally stumped then I would look. Anyway, when I saw that if statement then I knew what the next statement would be but I am still having problems with writing backwards. For example
>
> ```
> if (CurrentWeight > HighestWeight)
>   HighestWeight = CurrentWeight;
> ```
>
> That is just so confusing because we just want to say that if the current weight is higher than the highest weight, then the current weight will be the new highest weight, so I want to write

---

37. A *batch file* is a text file that directs the execution of a number of programs, one after the other, without manual intervention. A similar facility is available in most operating systems.

CurrentWeight = HighestWeight. Anyway, when I really think about it I know it makes sense to do it the right way; I'm just having a hard time thinking like that. Any suggestions on how to think backward?

Steve: What that statement means is "*set* HighestWeight *to the current value of* CurrentWeight." The point here is that = does *not* mean "is equal to"; it means "set the variable to the left of the = to the value of the expression to the right of the =". It may not be a very clear way of saying that, but that's what it means.

Susan: With all the { and } all over the place, I was not sure where and when the return 0; came in. So is it always right before the last }? OK, now that I think about it, I guess it always would be.

Steve: You have to put the return statement at a place where the program is finished whatever it was doing. That's because whenever that statement is executed, the program is going to stop running. Usually, as in this case, you want to do that at the physical end of main.

Susan: Anyway, then maybe I am doing something wrong, and I am tired, but after I compiled the program and ran it, I saw that the HighestWeight label was run in together with the highest number and the next sentence, which said "Please enter the next weight". All those things were on the same line and I thought that looked weird; I tried to fix it but the best I had the stamina for at the moment was to put a space between the " and the P, to at least make a separation.

Steve: It sounds as though you need some endls in there to separate the lines.

Take It for a Spin

Assuming that you've installed the software from the CD-ROM in the back of this book, you can try out this program by following these steps:

1. Change to the "code" subdirectory of the directory where you copied the example programs. If you've been following the directions as written, this will be "c:\shcppg\code".

2. Start the Integrated Development Environment (IDE) for the compiler by typing its name, RHIDE, followed by the name of the program to be compiled. For example, to compile "pump1", type

    RHIDE pump1

3. Then select "Make" from the "Compile" menu. The compiled version will be placed in the "\shcppg\code" directory.

4. Once you are done compiling, you can exit to DOS by selecting the File menu and clicking on Exit. Then you can execute the program by typing the name of the program you want to run at the DOS prompt, first making sure that you are in the directory where you copied the example programs. For example, to run "pump1", exit to DOS, make sure you are in "\shcppg\code" and type:

    pump1

5. To run your program under the debugger, make sure you are in the "\shcppg\code" directory, and then type RHIDE pump1. Again, do *not* add the ".cc" to the end of the file name. Once RHIDE has started up, you can step through the program by hitting F8, which will treat any function call as one statement, or by hitting F7, which will step into any function call. Any time you want to see the display that the user would see when running the program normally, hit ALT-F5, then ENTER to get back to the debugger. The

debugger also has a lot of other features, including displaying the values of variables during program execution, which I encourage you to explore.

By the way, if you're confused about the seemingly meaningless values that the debugger shows for variables before the first statement that sets each one to a value, let me assure you that they are indeed meaningless. I'll explain why that is in the next chapter.

We're almost done with this chapter, but first let's practice a little more with chars and strings.

Exercises, Fourth Set

8. Here are four possible versions of an output statement. Assuming that the value of the string variable called name is "Joe Smith", what does each one of them do?

```
cout << "That is very old, " << name << ". " << endl;

cout << "That is very old, " << name << '. ' << endl;

cout << "That is very old, " << name << "." << endl;

cout << "That is very old, " << name << '.' << endl;
```

Now it's time for some review on what we've covered in this chapter.

Review

We started out by discussing the tremendous reliability of computers; whenever you hear "it's the computer's fault", the overwhelming likelihood is that the software is to blame rather than the hardware. Then we took a look at the fact that, although computers are calculating engines, many of the functions for which we use them don't have much to do with numeric calculations; for example, the most common use of computers is probably word processing. Nevertheless, we started out our investigation of programming with *numeric variables*, which are easier to understand than non-numeric ones. To use variables, we need to write a *C++ program*, which consists primarily of a list of operations to be performed by the computer, along with directions that influence how these operations are to be translated into machine instructions.

That led us into a discussion of why and how our C++ program is translated into machine instructions by a *compiler*. We examined an example program that contained simple *source code statements*, including some that define variables and others that use those variables and constants to calculate results. We covered the symbols that are used to represent the operations of addition, subtraction, multiplication, division, and *assignment*, which are +, −, *, /, and = respectively. While the first four of these should be familiar to you, the last one is a programming notion rather than a mathematical one. This may be confusing because the operation of assignment is expressed by the = sign, but is *not* the same as mathematical equality. For example, the statement x = 3; does *not* mean "*x* is equal to 3", but rather "set the variable x to the value 3". After this discussion of the structure of statements in C++, we started an exploration of how the CPU actually stores and manipulates data in memory. The topics covered in this section included the order in which multibyte data items are stored in memory and the use of *general registers* to manipulate data efficiently.

Then we spent some time pretending to be a compiler, to see how a simple C++ program looks from that point of view, in order to improve our understanding of what the compiler does with our programs. This exercise involved keeping track of the addresses of variables and instructions and watching the effect of the instructions on the general registers and memory locations. During this exploration of the machine, we got acquainted with the *machine language* representation of instructions, which is the actual form that our executable programs take in memory. After a thorough examination of what the compiler does with our source code at *compile time*, we followed what would happen to the registers and memory locations at *run time* (that is, if the sample program were actually executed).

Then we began to look at two data types that can hold nonnumeric data, namely the char and the string. The char corresponds to 1 byte of storage, and therefore can hold one character of data. Examples of appropriate values for a char variable include letters (a–z, A–Z), digits (0–9), and special characters (e.g., , . ! @ # $ %). A char can also represent a number of other "nonprintable" characters such as the "space", which causes the output position on the screen to move to the next character. Actually, a char can also be used as a "really short" numeric variable, but that's mostly a holdover from the days when memory was a lot more expensive, and every byte counted.

One char isn't much information, so we often want to deal with groups of them as a single unit; an example would be a person's name. This is the province of the string variable type: Variables of this type can handle an indefinitely long group of chars.

At the beginning of our sample program for strings and chars, we encountered a new construct, the #include *statement*. This tells the compiler where to find instructions on how to handle data types such as strings, about which it doesn't have any built-in knowledge. Then we came across the line int main(), which indicates where we want to start executing our program. A C++ program always starts execution at the place indicated by such a line. We also investigated the meaning of int, which is the *return type* of main. The return type tells the compiler what sort of data this program returns to the operating system when it finishes executing; the return value can be used to determine what action a *batch file* should take next.

As we continued looking at the sample program for strings and chars, we saw how to assign literal values to both of these types, and noted that two different types of quotes are used to mark off the literal values: the single quote ('), which is used in pairs to surround a literal char value consisting of exactly one char, such as 'a'; and the double quote ("), which is used in pairs to surround a literal string value of the *C string* type, such as "This is a test". We also investigated the reason for these two different types of literal values, which involves the notion of a *null byte* (a byte with the value 0); this null byte is used to mark the end of a C string in memory.

This led us to the discussion of the *ASCII code*, which is used to represent characters by binary values. We also looked at the fact that the same bytes can represent either a numeric value or a C string, depending on how we use those bytes in our program. That's why it's so important to tell the compiler which of these possibilities we have in mind when we write our programs. The way in which the compiler regulates our access to variables by their type, which is defined at compile time, is called the *type system*; the fact that C++ uses this *static type checking* is one of the reasons that C++ programs can be made more robust than programs written in languages that use *dynamic type checking*, where these errors are not detected until run time.

After a short discussion of some of the special characters that have a predefined meaning to the compiler, we took an initial glance at the mechanisms that allow us to get information into and out of the computer, known as *I/O*. We looked at the << function, which provides display on the screen when coupled with the built-in destination called cout. Immediately afterwards, we encountered the corresponding input function >> and its partner cin, which team up to give us input from the keyboard.

Next, we went over some program organization concepts, including the if statement, which allows a program to choose between two alternatives; the while statement, which causes another statement to be executed while some condition is true; and the *block*, which allows several statements to be grouped together into one logical statement. Blocks are commonly used to enable several statements to be controlled by an if or while statement.

At last we were ready to write a simple program that does something resembling useful work, and we did just that. The starting point for this program, as with all programs, was to define exactly what the program should do; in this case, the task was to keep track of the pumpkin with the highest weight at a county fair. The next step was to define a solution to this problem in precise terms. Next, we broke the solution down into steps small enough to be translated directly into C++. Of course, the next step after that was to do that translation. Finally, we went over the C++ code, line by line, to see what each line of the program did.

Now that the review is out of the way, we're about ready to continue with some more C++. First, though, let's step back a bit and see where we are right now.

Conclusion

We've come a long way from the beginning of this chapter. Starting from basic information on how the hardware works, we've made it through our first actual, runnable program. By now, you should have a much better idea whether you're going to enjoy programming (and this book). Assuming you aren't discouraged on either of these points, let's proceed to gather some more tools, so we can undertake a bigger project.

Answers to Exercises

1. 3c43. In case you got a different result, here's a little help:

    a. If you got the result 433a, you started at the wrong address.

    b. If you got the result 433c, you had the bytes reversed.

    c. Finally, if you got 3a43, you made both of these mistakes.

If you made one or more of these mistakes, don't feel too bad; even experienced programmers have trouble with hexadecimal values once in awhile. That's one reason we use compilers and assemblers rather than writing everything in hex!

2. "HELLO". If you couldn't figure out what the "D" at the beginning was for, you started at the wrong place.

3. Figure 3.25 is Susan's answer to this problem.

FIGURE 3.25. First dinner party program (code\basic05.cc)

```
#include <iostream.h>

int main()
{
    short n;

    cout << "Please type in the number of guests ";
    cout << "of your dinner party. ";
    cin >> n;

    cout << "A table for " << n+1 << "is ready. ";

    return 0;
}
```

By the way, the reason that this program uses two lines to produce the sentence "Please type in the number of guests of your dinner party." is so that the program listing will fit on the page properly. If you prefer, you can combine those into one line that says:

```
cout << "Please type in the number of guests of your dinner party. ";.
```

Of course, this also applies to the next exercise. Here's the discussion that Susan and I had about this exercise:

Susan: I would have sent it sooner had I not had the last cout arrows going like this >> (details).<G> Also, it just didn't like the use of endl; at the end of the last cout statement. It just kept saying "parse error".

Steve: If you wrote something like

```
cout  <<  "A table for "  << n+1 <<  "is ready. " << "endl;"
```

then it wouldn't work for two reasons. First, "endl;" is just a character string, not anything recognized by <<. Second, you're missing a closing ;, because characters inside quotes are treated as just plain characters by the compiler, not as having any effect on program structure.

The correct way to use endl in your second output statement is as follows:

```
cout << "A table for " << n+1 << "is ready. " << endl;
```

By the way, you might want to add a " " in front of the is in is ready, so that the number doesn't run up against the is. That would make the line look like this:

```
cout << "A table for " << n+1 << " is ready. " << "endl;"
```

Susan: Okay.

4. Figure 3.26 is Susan's answer to this problem, followed by our discussion.

FIGURE 3.26. Second dinner party program (code\basic06.cc)

```
#include <iostream.h>

int main()
{
    short n;
```

```
cout << "Excluding yourself, please type the ";
cout << "number of guests in your dinner party.\n";

cin >> n;

if (n>20)
    cout << "Sorry, your party is too large. ";
else
    cout << "A table for " << n+1 << " is ready. ";

return 0;
}
```

Steve: Congratulations on getting your program to work!

Susan: Now, let me ask you this: can you ever modify else? That is, could I have written else (n>20), or does else always stand alone?

Steve: You can say something like Figure 3.27.

FIGURE 3.27. else if **example**

```
if (x < y)
  {
  cout << "x is less than y" << endl;
  }
else
    {
    if (x > y)
      cout << "x is greater than y" << endl;
    else
      cout << "x must be equal to y!" << endl;
    }
```

In other words, the controlled block of an if statement or an else statement can have another if or else inside it. In fact, you can have as many "nested" if or else statements as you wish; however, it's best to avoid very deep nesting because it tends to confuse the next programmer who has to read the program.

5. The answer to this problem should look like Figure 3.28.

FIGURE 3.28. Name and age program (code\basic07.cc)

```
#include <iostream.h>
#include "string6.h"

int main()
{
    string name;
    short age;

    cout << "What is your name? ";
    cin >> name;

    cout << "Thank you, " << name << endl;

    cout << "What is your age? ";
    cin >> age;

    if (age < 47)
        cout << "My, what a youngster!" << endl;
    else
        cout << "Hi, Granny!" << endl;

    return 0;
}
```

One point that might be a bit puzzling in this program is why it's not necessary to add an << endl to the end of the lines that send data to cout before we ask the user for input. For example, in the sequence:

```
cout << "What is your name? ";
cin >> name;
```

how do we know that the C string "What is your name? " has been displayed on the terminal before the user has to type in the answer? Obviously, it would be hard for the user to answer our request for information without a clue as to what we're asking for.

As it happens, this is a common enough situation that the designers of the iostreams library have anticipated it and solved it for us. When we use that library to do output to the screen and input from the keyboard, we can be sure that any screen output we have already requested will be displayed before any input is requested from the user via the keyboard.

6. Figure 3.29 shows Susan's program, which is followed by our discussion.

FIGURE 3.29. Novice program (code\basic08.cc)

```
#include <iostream.h>
#include "string6.h"

int main()
{
    string answer;

    cout << "Please respond to the following statement ";
    cout << "with either true or false\n";

    cout << "Susan is the world's most tenacious novice.\n";
    cin >> answer;

    if (answer != "true")
        if (answer != "false")
            cout << "Please answer with either true or false.";

    if (answer == "true")
        cout << "Your answer is correct\n";

    if (answer == "false")
```

```
        cout << "Your answer is erroneous\n";

    return 0;
}
```

Susan: Steve, look at this. It even runs!

Also, I wanted to ask you one more question about this program. I wanted to put double quotes around the words true and false in the 3rd output statement because I wanted to emphasize those words, but I didn't know if the compiler could deal with that so I left it out. Would that have worked if I had?

Steve: Not if you just added quotes, because " is a special character that means "beginning or end of C string". Here's what you would have to do to make it work:

```
cout << "Please answer with either \"true\" or \"false\".";
```

The \ is a way of telling the compiler to treat the next character differently from its normal usage. In this case, we are telling the compiler to treat the special character " as "not special"; that is, \" means "just the character double quote, please, and no nonsense". This is called an *escape*, because it allows you to get out of the trap of having a " mean something special. We also use the \ to tell the compiler to treat a "nonspecial" character as "special"; for example, we use it to make up special characters that don't have any visual representation. You've already seen '\n', the "newline" character, which means "start a new line on the screen".

Susan: So if we want to write some character that means something "special", then we have to use a \ in front of it to tell the compiler to treat it like a "regular" character?

Steve: Right.

Susan: And if we want to write some character that is "regular" and make it do something "special", then we have to use a \ in front of it to tell the compiler that it means something "special"? That's weird.

Steve: It may be weird, but that's the way it works.

Susan: I now just got it. I was going to say, why would you put the first quotation mark before the slash, but now I see. Since you are doing a endline character, you have to have quotes on both sides to surround it which you don't usually have to do because the first quotes are usually started at the beginning of the sentence, and in this case the quote was already ended. Ok, thanks for clearing that up.

Steve: You've got it.

Susan: Another thing I forgot is how you refer to the statements in () next to the "if" keywords; what do you call the info that is in there?

Steve: The condition.

7. Figure 3.30 is Susan's version of this program. Actually, it was her idea in the first place.

FIGURE 3.30. **Allowance program (code\basic09.cc)**

```cpp
#include <iostream.h>
#include "string6.h"

int main()
{
    short x;

    cout << "Elena can increase her $10 allowance each week ";
    cout << "by adding new chores." << endl;

    cout << "For every extra chore Elena does, she gets ";
```

```
cout << "another dollar." << endl;

cout << "How many extra chores were done? " << endl;
cin >> x;

if (x==0)
   {
   cout << "There is no extra allowance for Elena ";
   cout << "this week. " << endl;
   }
else
   {
   cout << "Elena will now earn " << 10 + x;
   cout << " dollars this week." << endl;
   }

return 0;
}
```

8. You'll be happy (or at least unsurprised) to hear that Susan and I had quite a discussion about this problem.

> **Susan:** Remember on my "test" program how I finally got that period in there? Then I got to thinking that maybe it should have been surrounded by single quotes ' instead of double quotes. It worked with a double quote but since it was only one character it should have been a single quote, so I went back and changed it to a single quote and the compiler *didn't like that at all*. So I put it back to the double. So what is the deal?

> **Steve:** You should be able to use 'x' or "x" more or less interchangeably with <<, because it can handle both of those data types (char and C string, respectively). However, they are indeed different types. The first one specifies a literal char value, whereas the second specifies a literal C string value. A char value can only contain one character, but a C string can be as long as you want, from none to hundreds or thousands of characters.

Susan: Here's the line that gave me the trouble:

```
cout << "That is very old, " << name << ". " << endl;
```

Remember I wanted to put that period in at the end in that last line? It runs like this but not with the single quotes around it. That I don't understand. This should have been an error. But I did something right by mistake. Anyway, is there something special about the way a period is handled?

Steve: I understand your problem now. No, it's not the period; it's the space after the period. Here are four possible versions of that line:

```
1. cout << "That is very old, " << name << ". " << endl;
2. cout << "That is very old, " << name << '. ' << endl;
3. cout << "That is very old, " << name << "." << endl;
4. cout << "That is very old, " << name << '.' << endl;
```

None of these is exactly the same as any of the others. However, 1, 3, and 4 will do what you expect, whereas 2 will produce weird looking output, with some bizarre number where the "." should be. Why is this? It's not because "." is handled specially, but because the space (" "), when inside quotes, either single or double, is a character like any other character. Thus, the expression '. ' in line 2 is a "multicharacter constant", which has a value dependent on the compiler; in this case, you'll get a short value equal to (256 * the ASCII value of the period) + the ASCII value of the space. This comes out to 11808, as I calculate it. So the line you see on the screen may look like this:

```
That is very old, Joe Smith11808
```

Now why do all of the other lines work? Well, 1 works because a C string can have any number of characters and be sent to cout correctly; 3 works for the same reason; and 4 works because '.' is a valid one-character constant, which is another type that << can handle.

I realize it's hard to think of the space as a character, when it doesn't look like anything; in addition, you can add spaces freely between variables, expressions, and so forth, in the program text. However, once you're dealing with C strings and literal character values, the space is just like any other character.

Susan: So it is okay to use single characters in double quotes? If so, why bother with single quotes?

Steve: Single quotes surround a literal of type char. This is a 1-byte value that can be thought of (and even used) as a very short number. Double quotes surround a literal of type "C string". This is a multibyte value terminated by a 0 byte, which cannot be used or treated as a number.

Susan: I am not too clear on what exactly the difference is between the char and "C string". I thought a char was like a alpha letter, and a string was just a bunch of letters.

Steve: Right. The difference is that a C string is variable length, and a char isn't; this makes a lot of difference in how they can be manipulated.

Susan: Am I right in thinking that a char could also be a small number that is not being used for calculations?

Steve: Or that is used for (very small) calculations; for instance, if you add 1 to the value 'A', you get the value for 'B'. At least that's logical.

Susan: What do you mean by "terminated by a 0 byte"? That sounds familiar; was that something from an earlier chapter which is now ancient history?

Steve: Yes, we covered that some time ago. The way the program can tell that it's at the end of a C string (which is of variable length, remember) is that it gets to a byte with the value 0. This wouldn't be my preferred way to specify the size of a variable-length string, in my opinion, but it's too late to do anything about it; it's built into the compiler.

Susan: When you say a C string, do you mean the C programming language in contrast to other languages?

Steve: Yes.

Susan: All right, then the 0 byte used to terminate a C string is the same thing as a null byte?

Steve: Yes.

Susan: Then you mean that each C string must end in a 0 so that the compiler will know when to stop processing the data for the string?

Steve: Yes.

Susan: Could you also just put 0? Hey, it doesn't hurt to ask. I don't see the problem with the word *hello*; it ends with an o and not a 0. But what if you do need to end the sentence with a 0?

Steve: It's not the digit '0', which has the ASCII code 30h, but a byte with a 0 value. You can't type in a null byte directly, although you can create one with a special character sequence if you want to. However, there's no point in doing that usually, because all literal C strings such as "hello" always have an invisible 0 byte added automatically by the compiler. If for some reason you need to explicitly create a null byte, you can write it as '\0', as in

```
char x = '\0';
```

which emphasizes that you really mean a null byte and not just a plain old 0 like this:

```
char x = 0;
```

The difference between these two is solely for the benefit of the next programmer to look at your code; they're exactly the same to the compiler.

CHAPTER 4

More Basics

Now that we have seen how to write a simple program in C++, it's time to acquire some more tools. We'll extend our example program from Chapter 3 for finding the heaviest pumpkin. Eventually, we want to provide the weights of the three heaviest pumpkins, so that first, second, and third prizes can be awarded. It might seem that this would require just a minor modification of the previous program, in which we would keep track of the heaviest so far, second heaviest so far, and third heaviest so far, rather than merely the heaviest so far. However, this modification turns out to be a bit more complicated than it seems. Since this book is intended to teach you how to program using C++, rather than just how to use the C++ language, it's worth investigating why this is so. First, though, here are the objectives for this chapter.

Objectives of This Chapter

By the end of this chapter, you should

1. Understand the likelihood of error in even a small change to a program.

2. Be aware that even seemingly small changes in a problem can result in large changes in the program that solves the problem.

3. Have some understanding of the type of thinking needed to solve problems with programming.

4. Understand the selection sorting algorithm for arranging values in order.

5. Understand how to use a vector to maintain a number of values under one name.

6. Be able to use the for statement to execute program statements a (possibly varying) number of times.

7. Be familiar with the arithmetic operators ++ and +=, which are used to modify the value of variables.

Algorithmic Thinking

Let's take our program modification one step at a time, starting with just the top two weights. Figure 4.1 is one possible way to handle this version of the problem.

FIGURE 4.1. Finding the top two weights, first try (code\pump1a.cc)

```
int main()
{
  short CurrentWeight;
  short HighestWeight;
  short SecondHighestWeight;

  cout << "Please enter the first weight: ";
  cin >> CurrentWeight;
  HighestWeight = CurrentWeight;
```

Learning to Program in C++

```
SecondHighestWeight = 0;
cout << "Current weight " << CurrentWeight << endl;
cout << "Highest weight " << HighestWeight << endl;

while (CurrentWeight > 0)
  {
  cout << "Please enter the next weight: ";
  cin >> CurrentWeight;
  if (CurrentWeight > HighestWeight)
    {
    SecondHighestWeight = HighestWeight;
    HighestWeight = CurrentWeight;
    }
  cout << "Current weight " << CurrentWeight << endl;
  cout << "Highest weight " << HighestWeight << endl;
  cout << "Second highest weight " << SecondHighestWeight << endl;
  }

return 0;
}
```

The reasons behind some of the new code, shown in **bold**, should be fairly obvious, but we'll go over them anyway. First, of course, we need a new variable, SecondHighestWeight, to hold the current value of the second highest weight we've seen so far. Then, when the first weight is entered, the statement SecondHighestWeight = 0; sets the SecondHighestWeight to 0. After all, there isn't any second-highest weight when we've only seen one weight. The first nonobvious change is the addition of the statement SecondHighestWeight = HighestWeight;, which copies the old HighestWeight to SecondHighestWeight, whenever there's a new highest weight. On reflection, however, this should make sense; when a new high is detected, the old high must be the second highest value (so far). Also, we have to copy the old HighestWeight to SecondHighestWeight before we change HighestWeight. After we have set HighestWeight to a new value, it's too late to copy its old value into SecondHighestWeight.

First, let's see how Susan viewed this solution:

Susan: I noticed that you separate out the main program {} from the other {} by indenting. Is that how the compiler knows which set of {} goes to which statements and doesn't confuse them with the main ones that are the body of the program?

Steve: The compiler doesn't care about indentation at all; that's just for the people reading the program. All the compiler cares about is the number of { it has seen so far without matching }. There aren't any hard rules about this; it's a "religious" issue in C++, where different programmers can't agree on the best way.

Susan: Now on this thing with setting SecondHighestWeight to 0. Is that initializing it? See, I know what you are doing, and yet I can't see the purpose of doing this clearly, unless it is initializing, and then it makes sense.

Steve: That's correct.

Susan: How do you know how to order your statements? For example, why did you put the "SecondHighestWeight = HighestWeight;" above the other statement? What would happen if you reversed that order?

Steve: Think about it. Let's suppose that:

CurrentWeight is 40
HighestWeight is 30
SecondHighestWeight is 15

and the statements were executed in the following order:

1. HighestWeight = CurrentWeight

2. SecondHighestWeight = HighestWeight

What would happen to the values? Well, statement 1 would set HighestWeight to CurrentWeight, so the values would be like this:

CurrentWeight is 40
HighestWeight is 40
SecondHighestWeight is 15

Then statement 2 would set SecondHighestWeight to HighestWeight, leaving the situation as follows:

CurrentWeight is 40
HighestWeight is 40
SecondHighestWeight is 40

This is clearly wrong. The problem is that we need the value of HighestWeight *before* it is set to the value of CurrentWeight, not afterward. After that occurs, the previous value is lost.

Susan: Yes, that is apparent; I was just wondering if the computer had to read it in the order that you wrote it, being that it was grouped together in the {}. For example, you said that the compiler doesn't read the {} as we write them, so I was wondering if it read those statements as we write them. Obviously it has to. So then everything descends in a progression downward and outward, as you get more detailed in the instructions.

Assuming that you've installed the software from the CD-ROM in the back of this book, you can try out this program. First, you have to compile it by changing to the code subdirectory under the main directory where you installed the software, and typing RHIDE pump1a, then using the "Make" command from the "Compile" menu. Then exit back to DOS and type pump1a to run the program. It will ask you for weights and keep track of the highest weight and second-highest weight that you've entered. Type 0 and hit ENTER to end the program.

To run it under the debugger, make sure you are in the code subdirectory, and then type RHIDE pump1a. Again, do *not* add the ".cc" to the end of the file name. Once RHIDE has started up, you can step through the program by hitting F8, which will treat any function

call as one statement, or by hitting F7, which will step into any function call. Any time you want to see the display that the user would see when running the program normally, hit ALT-F5, then ENTER to get back to the debugger.

A Prize Catch

This program may seem to keep track of the highest and second highest weights correctly, but in fact there's a hole in the logic. To be exact, it doesn't work correctly when the user enters a new value that's less than the previous high value but more than the previous second-high value. In that case, the new value should be the second-high value, even though there's no new high value. For example, suppose that you enter the following weights: 5 2 11 3 7. If we were to update SecondHighestWeight only when we see a new high, our program would indicate that 11 was the high, and 5 the second highest; since neither 3 nor 7 is a new high, SecondHighestWeight would remain as it was when the 11 was entered.

Here's what ensued when Susan tried out the program and discovered this problem:

> **Susan:** Steve, the program! I have been playing with it. Hey this is fun, but look, it took me awhile. I had to go over it and over it, and then I was having trouble getting it to put current weights that were higher than second weights into the second weight slot. For example, if I had a highest weight of 40 and the second highest weight of 30 and then selected 35 for a current weight, it wouldn't accept 35 as the second-highest weight. It increased the highest weights just fine and it didn't change anything if I selected a lower number of the two for a current weight. Or did you mean to do that to make a point? I am supposed to find the problem? I bet that is what you are doing.

> **Steve:** Yep, and I'm not sorry, either.\<G\>

Susan: You just had to do this to me, didn't you? OK, what you need to do is to put in a statement that says if the current weight is greater than the second-highest weight, then set the second-highest weight to the current weight (as illustrated in Figure 4.2).

FIGURE 4.2. Susan's solution to the bug in the first attempt

```
else
  {
  if (CurrentWeight > Second HighestWeight)
    Second HighestWeight = CurrentWeight;
  }
```

I hope you are satisfied.

Steve: Satisfied? Well, no, I wouldn't use that word. How about ecstatic? You have just figured out a bug in a program, and determined what the solution is. Don't tell me you don't understand how a program works.

Now I have to point out something about your code. I understood what you wrote perfectly. Unfortunately, compilers aren't very smart, and therefore have to be extremely picky. So you have to make sure to spell the variable names correctly, that is, with no spaces between the words that make up a variable name. This would make your answer like the if clause shown in Figure 4.3.

Congratulations again.

As Susan figured out, we have to add an else clause to our if statement, so that the corrected version of the statement looks like Figure 4.3.

FIGURE 4.3. Using an if statement with an else clause

```
if (CurrentWeight > HighestWeight)
  {
```

```
        SecondHighestWeight = HighestWeight;
        HighestWeight = CurrentWeight;
        }
      else
        {
        if (CurrentWeight > SecondHighestWeight)
          SecondHighestWeight = CurrentWeight;
        }
```

In this case, the condition in the first if is checking whether CurrentWeight is greater than the previous HighestWeight; when this is true, we have a new HighestWeight and we can update both HighestWeight and SecondHighestWeight. However, if CurrentWeight is not greater than HighestWeight, the else clause is executed. It contains another if; this one checks whether CurrentWeight is greater than the old SecondHighestWeight. If so, SecondHighestWeight is set to the value of CurrentWeight.

What happens if two (or more) pumpkins are tied for the highest weight? In that case, the first one of them to be encountered is going to set HighestWeight, as it will be the highest yet encountered. When the second pumpkin of the same weight is seen, it won't trigger a change to HighestWeight, since it's not higher than the current occupant of that variable. It will pass the test in the else clause, if (CurrentWeight > SecondHighestWeight), however, which will cause SecondHighestWeight to be set to the same value as HighestWeight. This is reasonable behavior, unlikely to startle the (hypothetical) user of the program, and therefore is good enough for our purposes. In a real application program, we'd have to try to determine what the user of this program would want us to do.

Figure 4.4 shows the corrected program.

FIGURE 4.4. Finding the top two weights (code\pump2.cc)

```
#include <iostream.h>

int main()
{
```

```
        short CurrentWeight;
        short HighestWeight;
        short SecondHighestWeight;

        cout << "Please enter the first weight: ";
        cin >> CurrentWeight;
        HighestWeight = CurrentWeight;
        SecondHighestWeight = 0;
        cout << "Current weight " << CurrentWeight << endl;
        cout << "Highest weight " << HighestWeight << endl;

        while (CurrentWeight > 0)
           {
           cout << "Please enter the next weight: ";
           cin >> CurrentWeight;
           if (CurrentWeight > HighestWeight)
              {
              SecondHighestWeight = HighestWeight;
              HighestWeight = CurrentWeight;
              }
           else
              {
              if (CurrentWeight > SecondHighestWeight)
                  SecondHighestWeight = CurrentWeight;
              }
           cout << "Current weight " << CurrentWeight << endl;
           cout << "Highest weight " << HighestWeight << endl;
           cout << "Second highest weight " << SecondHighestWeight << endl;
           }

        return 0;
     }
```

Assuming that you've installed the software from the CD-ROM in the back of this book, you can try out this program. First, compile it by changing to the code subdirectory under the main directory where you installed the software, and typing RHIDE pump1a, then using the "Make" command from the "Compile" menu. Then exit back to DOS and type pump1a to run the program. It will ask you for weights and keep track of the highest weight and second-highest weight that you've entered. Type 0 and hit ENTER to end the program.

To run it under the debugger, make sure you are in the code subdirectory, and then type RHIDE pump1a. Again, do *not* add the ".cc" to the end of the file name. Once RHIDE has started up, you can step through the program by hitting F8, which will treat any function call as one statement, or by hitting F7, which will step into any function call. Any time you want to see the display that the user would see when running the program normally, hit ALT-F5, then ENTER to get back to the debugger.

When you are asked for a weight, type one in and hit ENTER just as when executing normally. When you enter a 0 weight, the program will stop looping and execution will take the path to the end }.

By the way, since we've just been using the if statement pretty heavily, this would be a good time to list all of the conditions that it can test. We've already seen some of them, but it can't hurt to have them all in one place. Figure 4.5 lists these conditions, with translations.

FIGURE 4.5. What if?

Symbol	Controlled block will be executed if:
>	First item is larger than second item
<	First item is smaller than second item
>=	First item is larger than or equal to second item
<=	First item is smaller than or equal to second item
!=	First item differs from second item
==	First item has the same value as the second item

You may wonder why we have to use == to test for equality rather than just =. That's because = means "assign right hand value to variable on left", rather than "compare two items for equality". This is a "feature" of C++ (and C) that allows us to accidentally write if (a = b) when we mean if (a == b). What does if (a = b) mean? It means the following:

1. Assign the value of b to a.

2. If that value is 0, then the result of the expression in parentheses is false, so the controlled block of the if is not executed.

3. Otherwise, the result of the expression in parentheses is true, so the controlled block of the if is executed.

Some people find this useful; I don't. Therefore, whenever possible I enable the compiler warning that tells you when you use a = inside an if statement in a way that looks like you meant to test for equality.

What a Tangled Web We Weave...

I hope this excursion has given you some appreciation of the subtleties that await in even the simplest change to a working program; many experienced programmers still underestimate such difficulties and the amount of time that may be needed to ensure that the changes are correct. I don't think it's necessary to continue along the same path with a program that can award three prizes. The principle is the same, although the complexity of the code grows with the number of special cases we have to handle. Obviously, a solution that could handle any number of prizes without special cases would be a big improvement, but it will require some major changes in the organization of the program. That's what we'll take up next.

You May Already Have Won

One of the primary advantages of the method we've used so far to find the heaviest pumpkin(s) is that we didn't have to save the weights of all the pumpkins as we went along. If we don't mind saving all the weights, then we can solve the "three prize" problem in a different way. Let's assume for the purpose of simplicity that there are only five weights to be saved, in which case the solution looks like this:

1. Read in all of the weights.

2. Make a list consisting of the three highest weights in descending order.

3. Award the first, second, and third prizes, in that order, to the three entries in the list of highest weights.

Now let's break those down into substeps which can be more easily translated into C++:

1. Read in all of the weights.

    a. Read first number

    b. Read next number

    c. If we haven't read five weights yet, go back to 1b

2. Make a list consisting of the three highest weights in descending order.

    a. Find the largest number in the original list of weights

    b. Copy it to the sorted list

    c. If we haven't found the three highest numbers, go back to 2a

Oops. That's not going to work, since we'll get the same number each time.[1] To prevent that from happening, we have to mark off each number as we select it. Here's the revised version of step 2:

2. Make a list consisting of the three highest weights in descending order.

   a. Find the largest number in the original list of weights

   b. Copy it to the sorted list

   c. Mark it off in the original list of weights, so we don't select it again

   d. If we haven't found the three highest numbers, go back to 2a

3. Award the first, second, and third prizes, in that order, to the three entries in the list of highest weights.

   a. Display first number in the list

   b. Display next number in list

   c. If we haven't displayed them all, go back to 3b

Unlike our previous approach, this obviously can be generalized to handle any number of prizes. However, we have to address two problems before we can use this approach: First, how do we keep track of the weights? And, second, how do we select out the highest three weights? Both of these problems are much easier to solve if we don't have a separate variable for each weight.

---

1. I realize I'm breaking a cardinal rule of textbooks: Never admit that the solution to a problem is anything but obvious, so the student feels like an idiot if it in fact isn't obvious. In reality, even a simple program is difficult to get right, and indicating the sort of thought processes that go into analyzing a programming problem might help demystify this difficult task.

Variables, by the Numbers

The answer to our first question is that we can use a **vector**.[2] This is a variable containing a number of "sub-variables" that can be addressed by position in the vector; each of these sub-variables is called an *element*. A vector has a name, just like a regular variable, but the elements do not. Instead, each element has a number, corresponding to its position in the vector. For example, we might want to create a vector of short values called Weight, with five elements. To do this, we would write this line: vector<short> Weight(5);.[3]

We haven't heard from Susan for awhile, but the following exchange should make up for that.

Susan: Okay, why do we need another header (#include "vector.h")?[4]

Steve: Each header contains definitions for a specific purpose. For example, iostream.h contains definitions that allow us to get information in (I) and out (O) of the computer. On the other hand, vector.h contains definitions that allow us to use vectors.

Susan: So then using a vector is just another way of writing this same program, only making it a little more efficient?

2. In order to use vectors, we have to #include the header file vector.h; otherwise, the compiler won't understand that type of variable.

3. A vector actually contains some additional information beyond the elements themselves. Unfortunately, how a vector actually works is too complicated to go into in this book.

4. Note that the #include statement for vector.h in Figure 4.6 uses "" rather than <> around the file name. The use of "" tells the compiler to search for vector.h in the current directory first, and then the "normal" places that header files supplied with the compiler are located. This is necessary because vector.h in fact is in the current directory. If we had written #include <vector.h>, the compiler would look only in the "normal" places, and therefore would not find vector.h.

Steve: In this case, the new program can do more than the old program could: The new program can easily be changed to handle virtually any number of prizes, whereas the old program couldn't.

Susan: So there is more than one way to write a program that does basically the same thing?

Steve: As many ways as there are to write a book about the same topic.

Susan: I find this to be very odd. I mean, on one hand the code seems to be so unrelentingly exact; on the other, it can be done in as many ways as there are artists to paint the same flower. That must be where the creativity comes in. Then I would expect that the programs should behave in different manners, yet accomplish the same goal.

Steve: It's possible for two programs to produce similar (or even exactly the same) results from the user's perspective and yet work very differently internally. For example, the "vectorized" version of the weighing program, if we had it display only the top two weights, would produce exactly the same final results as the final "non-vectorized" version, even though the method of finding the top two weights was quite different.

Now we can refer to the individual elements of the vector called Weight by using their numbers, enclosed in **square brackets** ([ ]); the number in the brackets is called the **index**.[5] Here are some examples:

```
Weight[1] = 123;
Weight[2] = 456;
Weight[3] = Weight[1] + Weight[2];
Weight[i+1] = Weight[i] + 5;
```

5. By the way, if you're wondering how to pronounce Weight[i], it's "weight sub i". "Sub" is short for **subscript**, which is an old term for "index".

As these examples indicate, an element of a vector can be used anywhere a "regular" variable can be used.[6] But an element of a vector has an attribute that makes it much more valuable than a "regular" variable for our purposes here: We can vary which element we are referring to in a given statement, by varying its index. Take a look at the last sample line, in which two elements of the vector Weight are used; the first one is element i+1 and the other is element i. As this indicates, we don't have to use a constant value for the element number but can calculate it while the program is executing; in this case, if i is 0, the two elements referred to are element 1 and element 0, while if i is 5, the two elements are elements 6 and 5, respectively.

The ability to refer to an element of a vector by number rather than by name allows us to write statements that can refer to any element in a vector, depending on the value of the index variable in the statements. To see how this works in practice, let's look at Figure 4.6, which solves our three-prize problem.

FIGURE 4.6. Using a vector (code\vect1.cc)

```
#include <iostream.h>
#include "vector.h"

int main()
{
    vector<short> Weight(5);
    vector<short> SortedWeight(3);
    short HighestWeight;
    short HighestIndex;
    short i;
    short k;

    cout << "I'm going to ask you to type in five weights, in pounds." << endl;
```

---

6. What I'm calling a "regular" variable here is technically known as a *scalar variable*; that is, one with only one value at any given time.

```
for (i = 0; i < 5; i ++)
  {
  cout << "Please type in weight #" << i+1 << ": ";
  cin >> Weight[i];
  }

for (i = 0; i < 3; i ++)
    {
    HighestWeight = 0;
    for (k = 0; k < 5; k ++)
      {
      if (Weight[k] > HighestWeight)
        {
        HighestWeight = Weight[k];
        HighestIndex = k;
        }
      }
    SortedWeight[i] = HighestWeight;
    Weight[HighestIndex] = 0;
    }

cout << "The highest weight was: " << SortedWeight[0] << endl;
cout << "The second highest weight was: " << SortedWeight[1] << endl;
cout << "The third highest weight was: " << SortedWeight[2] << endl;

return 0;
}
```

Assuming that you've installed the software from the CD-ROM in the back of this book, you can try out this program. First, you have to compile it by changing to the code subdirectory under the main directory where you installed the software, and typing RHIDE vect1, then using the "Make" command from the "Compile" menu. Then exit back to DOS and type vect1 to run the program. It will ask you for five weights. After you've entered five weights, the program will sort them and display the top three.

To run it under the debugger, make sure you are in the code subdirectory, and then type RHIDE vect1. Again, do *not* add the ".cc" to the end of the file name. Once RHIDE has started up, you can step through the program by hitting F8, which will treat any function

call as one statement, or by hitting F7, which will step into any function call. Any time you want to see the display that the user would see when running the program normally, hit ALT-F5, then ENTER to get back to the debugger.

When you are asked for a weight, type one in and hit ENTER just as when executing normally. After you've entered 5 weights, the program will start the sorting process. When the sorted results have been displayed (or when you're tired of tracing the program), type q (for *quit*) and hit ENTER to exit from the debugger.

This program uses several new features of C++ which need some explanation. First, of course, there is the line that defines the vector Weight:

```
vector<short> Weight(5);
```

As you might have guessed, this means that we want a vector of five elements, each of which is a short. As we have already seen, this means that there are five distinct index values each of which refers to one element. However, what isn't so obvious is what those five distinct index values actually are. You might expect them to be 1, 2, 3, 4 and 5; actually, they are 0, 1, 2, 3, and 4.

This method of referring to elements in a vector is called **zero-based indexing**. Although it might seem arbitrary to start counting at 0 rather than at 1, assembly language programmers find it perfectly natural, because the calculation of the address of an element is simpler with such indexing; the formula is "(address of first element) + (element number) * (size of element)".

This bit of history is relevant because C, the predecessor of C++, was originally intended to replace assembly language so that programs could be moved from one machine architecture to another with as little difficulty as possible. One reason for some of the eccentricities of C++ is that it has to be able to replace C as a "portable assembly language" that doesn't depend on any specific machine architecture. This explains, for example, the great concern of the inventor of C++ for *run-time efficiency*, as he wished to allow programmers to avoid the use of C or assembly language for efficiency.[7] Since C++ was intended to replace C completely, it has to be as efficient as possible; otherwise, programmers might switch back from C++ to C whenever they were concerned about the speed and size of their programs.

Zero Isn't Nothing

While we're on the topic of zero-based indexing, I'd like to mention a case where the inventors of a commonly used facility should have used zero-based indexing, but didn't. We're still suffering from the annoyances of this one.

Long ago, there was no standard calendar, with year numbers progressing from one to the next, when January 1st came around. Instead, years were numbered relative to the reign of the current monarch; for example, the Bible might refer to "the third year of Herod's reign". This was fine in antiquity, when most people really didn't care what year it was. There weren't very many retirement plans or 50th wedding anniversaries to celebrate anyway. However, eventually historians realized that it was a major nuisance to try to calculate the age of someone who was born in the fourth year of someone's reign and died in the tenth year of someone else's. According to Grolier's Multimedia Encyclopedia:

> 'About AD 525, a monk named Dionysius Exiguus suggested that years be counted from the birth of Christ, which was designated AD (anno Domini, "the year of the Lord") 1. This proposal came to be adopted throughout Christendom during the next 500 years. The year before AD 1 is designated 1 BC (before Christ).'

---

7. *Run-time efficiency* means the amount of time a program takes to run, as well as how much memory it uses. These issues are very significant when writing a program to be sold to or used by others, as an inefficient program may be unacceptable to the users.

The encyclopedia doesn't state when the use of the term BC started, but the fact that its translation is English is a suspicious sign indicating that this development was considerably later. In any event, this numbering system made matters considerably easier. Now, you could tell that someone who was born in AD 600 and died in AD 650 was approximately 50 years old at death.

Unfortunately, however, there was still a small problem. Zero hadn't yet made it to Europe from Asia when the new plan was adopted, so the new calendar numbered the years starting with 1, rather than 0; that is, the year after 1 BC was 1 AD. While this may seem reasonable, it accounts for a number of oddities of our current calendar:

1. Date ranges spanning AD and BC are hard to calculate, since you can't just treat BC as negative. For example, if someone were born in 1 BC and died in 1 AD, how old was that person? You might think that this could be calculated as 1 − (-1), or 2; however, the last day of 1 BC immediately preceded the first day of 1 AD, so the person might have been only a few days old.

2. The 20th century consists of the years 1901 to 2000; the year numbers of all but the last year of that century actually start with the digits *19* rather than *20*.

3. Similarly, the third millennium starts on January 1, 2001, not 2000.

The reason for the second and third of these oddities is that since the first century started in 1 AD, the second century had to start in 101 AD; if it started in 100 AD, the first century would have consisted of only 99 years (1–99), rather than 100.

If only they had known about the zero! Then the zeroth century would have started at the beginning of 0 AD and ended on the last day of 99 AD. The first century would have started at 100 AD, and so on; coming up to current time, we would be living through the last years of the 19th century, which would be defined as all of those years whose year numbers started with *19*. The second millennium would start on January 1, 2000, as everyone would expect.

Index Variables

There's not much we can do about that now, so let's get back to our discussion of the revised pumpkin-weighing program. The last two lines in the variable definition phase define two variables, called i and k, which have been traditional names for **index variable**s (i.e., variables used to hold indexes) since at least the invention of FORTRAN in the 1950s. The inventors of FORTRAN used a fairly simple method of determining the type of a variable: if it began with one of the letters I–N, it was an integer. Otherwise, it was a **floating-point variable** (i.e., one that can hold values that contain a fractional part, such as 3.876). This rule was later changed so that the user could specify the type of the variable regardless of its name, as in C++, but the default rules were the same as in the earlier versions of FORTRAN, to allow programs using the old rules to continue to compile and run correctly.

Needless to say, Susan had some questions about the names of index variables:

Susan: So whenever you see i or k you know you are dealing with a vector?

Steve: Not necessarily. Variables named i and k are commonly used as indexes, but they are also used for other purposes sometimes.

Susan: Anyway, if i and k are sometimes used for other purposes, then the compiler doesn't care what you use as indexes? Again, no rules, just customs?

Steve: Right. It's just for the benefit of other programmers, who will see i and say "oh, this is probably an index variable".

I suspect one reason for the durability of these short names is that they're easy to type, and many programmers aren't very good typists.[8] In C++, the letters i, j, k, m and n are commonly used as indexes; however, l (the letter "ell") generally isn't, because it looks too much like a 1 (the numeral one). The compiler doesn't get confused by this resemblance, but programmers very well might.

After the variable definitions are out of the way, we can proceed to the executable portion of our program. First, we type out a note to the user, stating what to expect. Then we get to the code in Figure 4.7.

FIGURE 4.7. Using a for statement (from code\vect1.cc)

```
for (i = 0; i < 5; i ++)
    {
cout << "Please type in weight #" << i+1 << ": ";
cin >> Weight[i];
    }
```

---

8. I strongly recommend learning how to type (i.e., touch type). I was a professional programmer without typing skills for over 10 years before agreeing to type (someone else's) book manuscript. At that point, I decided to teach myself to touch-type, so I wrote a *Dvorak keyboard* driver for my Radio Shack Model III computer and started typing. In about a month I could type faster than with my previous two finger method and eventually got up to 80+ words per minute on English text. If you've never heard of the Dvorak keyboard, it's the one that has the letters laid out in an efficient manner; the "home row" keys are AOEUIDHTNS rather than the absurd set ASDFGHJKL;. This "new" (1930s) keyboard layout reduces effort and increases speed and accuracy compared to the old QWERTY keyboard, which was invented in the 1880s to prevent people from typing two keys in rapid succession and jamming the typebars together. This problem has been nonexistent since the invention of the IBM® Selectric typewriter (which uses a ball rather than typebars) in 1960, but inertia keeps the old layout in use even though it is very inefficient. In any event, since I learned to type, writing documentation has required much less effort. This applies especially to writing articles or books, which would be a painful process otherwise.

The first line here is called a *for statement*, which is used to control a *for loop*; this is a loop control facility similar to the *while loop* we encountered in Chapter 3. The difference between these two statements is that a for loop allows us to specify more than just the condition under which the **controlled block** will be repetitively executed.[9] A for statement specifies three expressions (separated by ";") that control the execution of the for loop: a *starting expression*, a *continuation expression*, and a *modification expression*. In our case, these are i = 0, i < 5, and i ++, respectively. Let's look at the function and meaning of each of these components.

First, the **starting expression**, in this case i = 0. The starting expression is executed once before the block controlled by the for statement is executed. In this case, we use it to set our index variable, i, to 0, which will refer to the first element of our Weight vector.

Next, the **continuation expression**, in this case i < 5. As long as this expression is true, the controlled block of the for will be executed; in this case, we will continue executing the controlled blocked as long as the value of i is less than 5. Note: The continuation expression is actually executed *before* every execution of the controlled block; thus, if the continuation expression is false when the loop is entered for the first time, the controlled block will not be executed at all.

The notion of the continuation expression is apparently confusing to some novices. Susan fell into that group.

Susan: In your definition of for, how come there is no ending expression? Why is it only a modification expression? Is there never a case for a conclusion?

Steve: The "continuation expression" tells the compiler when you want to continue the loop; if the continuation expression comes out

---

9. You may sometimes see the term *controlled statement* used in place of *controlled block*; since, as we have already seen, a block can be used anywhere that a single statement can be used, *controlled statement* and *controlled block* are actually just two ways of saying the same thing.

false, then the loop terminates. That serves the same purpose as an "ending expression" might, but in reverse.

Finally, let's consider the **modification expression**, i ++.[10] This is exactly equivalent to i = i + 1, which means "set i to one more than its current value", an operation technically referred to as **incrementing a variable**. You may wonder why we need two ways to say the same thing; actually, there are a few reasons. One is that ++ requires less typing, which as I've already mentioned isn't a strong point of many programmers; also, the ++ (pronounced "plus plus") operator doesn't allow the possibility of mistyping the statement as, for example, i = j + 1; when you really meant to increment i. Another reason why this feature was added to the C language is that, in the early days of C, compiler technology wasn't very advanced, and the ++ operator allowed the production of more efficient programs. You see, many machines can add one to a memory location by a single machine language instruction, usually called something like inc, shorthand for *increment memory*. Even a simple compiler can generate an "increment memory" instruction as a translation of i ++, while it takes a bit more sophistication for the compiler to recognize i = i + 1 as an increment operation. Since incrementing a variable is a very common operation in C++, this was worth handling specially.[11]

Here's an English translation of our sample for statement:

1. Set the index variable i to 0.

2. If the value of i is less than 5, execute the following block (in this case, the block with the cout and cin statements). Otherwise, skip to the next statement after the end of the controlled block; that is, the one following the closing }.

---

10. You don't need a space between the variable name and the **++** operator; however, I think it's easier to read this way.

11. By the way, the name C++ is sort of a pun using this notation; it's supposed to mean "the language following C". In case you're not doubled over with laughter, you're not alone. I guess you had to be there.

3. Add one to the value of i and go back to step 2.

Susan didn't think these steps were very clear. Let's listen in on the conversation that ensued:

> **Susan:** Where in the for statement does it say to skip to the next statement after the end of the controlled block when i is 5 or more?

> **Steve:** It doesn't have to. Remember, the point of {} is to make a group of statements act like one. A for statement always controls exactly one "statement", which can be a block contained in {}. Therefore, when the continuation expression is no longer true, the next "statement" to be executed is whatever follows the } at the end of the block.

> **Susan:** Okay, now I get it. The {} curly brackets work together with the < 5 to determine that the program should go on to the next statement.

> **Steve:** Right.

> **Susan:** Now, on the "controlled block" — so other statements can be considered controlled blocks too? I mean is a controlled block basically just the same thing as a block? I reviewed your definition of *block*, and it seems to me that they are. I guess it is just a statement that in this case is being controlled by for.

> **Steve:** Correct. It's called a *controlled block* because it's under the control of another statement.

> **Susan:** So if we used while before the { } then that would be a while controlled block?

> **Steve:** Right.

> **Susan:** Then where in step 3 or in i++ does it say to go back to step 2?

Steve: Again, the for statement executes one block (the *controlled block*) repeatedly until the continuation expression is false. Since a block is equivalent to one statement, the controlled block can also be referred to as the *controlled statement*. In the current example, the block that is controlled by the for loop consists of the four lines starting with the opening { on the next line after the for statement itself and ending with the closing } after the line that says cin >> Weight[i];.

Susan: Okay. But now I am a little confused about something else here. I thought that cout statements were just things that you would type in to be seen on the screen.

Steve: That's correct, except that cout is a variable used for I/O, not a statement.

Susan: So then why is << i+1 << put in at this point? I understand what it does now but I don't understand why it is where it is.

Steve: Because we want to produce an output line that varies depending on the value of i. The first time, it should say

Please enter weight #1:

The second time, it should say

Please enter weight #2:

and so on. The number of the weight we're asking for is one more than i; therefore we insert the expression << i + 1 << in the output statement so that it will stick the correct number into the output line at that point.

Susan: How does << i+1 << end up as #1 ?

Steve: The first time, i is 0; therefore, i + 1 is 1. The # comes from the end of the preceding part of the output statement.

Now let's continue with the next step in the description of our for loop, the modification expression i ++. In our example, this will be executed five times. The first time, i will be 0, then 1, 2, 3, and finally 4. When the loop is executed for the fifth time, i will be incremented to 5; therefore, step 2 will end the loop by skipping to the next statement after the controlled block.[12] A bit of terminology is useful here: Each time through the loop is called an *iteration*.

Let's hear Susan's thoughts on this matter.

> **Susan:** When you say that "step 2 will end the loop by skipping to the next statement after the controlled block", does that mean it is now going on to the next for statement? So when i is no longer less than 5, the completion of the loop signals the next controlled block?

> **Steve:** In general, after all the iterations in a loop have been performed, execution proceeds to whatever statement follows the controlled block. In this case, the next statement is indeed a for statement, so that's the next statement that is performed after the end of the current loop.

The discussion of the for statement led to some more questions about loop control facilities and the use of parentheses:

> **Susan:** How do you know when to use () ? Is it only with if and for and while and else and stuff like that, whatever these statements are called? I mean they appear to be modifiers of some sort; is there a special name for them?

> **Steve:** The term **loop control** applies to statements that control loops that can execute controlled blocks a (possibly varying)

---

12. Why is the value of i at the end of this loop 5 rather than 4? Because at the end of each pass through the loop, the modification expression (i ++) is executed before the continuation expression that determines whether the next execution will take place (i < 5). Thus, at the end of the fifth pass through the loop, i is incremented to 5 and then tested to see if it is still less than 5. Since it isn't, the loop terminates at that point.

---

number of times; these include for and while. The if and else statements are somewhat different, since their controlled blocks are executed either once or not at all. The () are needed in those cases to indicate where the controlling expression(s) end and the controlled block begins. You can also use () to control the order of evaluation of an arithmetic expression: The part of the expression inside parentheses is executed first, regardless of normal ordering rules. For example, 2*5+3 is 13, while 2*(5+3) is 16.

Susan: So then if you just wrote while CurrentWeight > 0 with no () then the compiler couldn't read it?

Steve: Correct.

Susan: Actually it is beginning to look to me as I scan over a few figures that almost everything has a caption of some sort surrounding it. Everything either has a " " or () or {} or [] or <> around it. Is that how it is going to be? I am still not clear on the different uses of () and {}; does it depend on the control loop?

Steve: The {} are used to mark the controlled block, while the () are used to mark the conditional expression(s) for the if, while, for, and the like. Unfortunately, () also have other meanings in C++, which we'll get to eventually. The inventor of the language considers them to have been overused for too many different meanings, and I agree.

Susan: Okay, I think I have it: {} define blocks and () define expressions. How am I to know when a new block starts? I mean if I were doing the writing, it would be like a new paragraph in English, right? So are there any rules for knowing when to stop one block and start another?

Steve: It depends entirely on what you're trying to accomplish. The main purpose of a block is to make a group of statements act like one statement; therefore, for example, when you want to control a group of statements by one if or for, you group those statements into a block.

Now that we've examined the for statement in excruciating detail, what about the block it controls? The first statement in the block:

```
cout << "Please type in weight #" << i+1 << ": ";
```

doesn't contain anything much we haven't seen before; it just displays a request to enter a weight. The only difference from previous uses we've made of the cout facility is that we're inserting a numeric expression containing a variable, i+1, into the output. This causes the expression to be translated into a human-readable form consisting of digits. All of the expressions being sent to cout in one statement are strung together to make one line of output, if we don't specify otherwise. Therefore, when this statement is executed during the first iteration of the loop, the user of this program will see:

```
Please type in weight #1:
```

Then the user will type in the first weight. The same request, with a different value for the weight number, will show up each time the user hits ENTER, until five values have been accepted.

The second statement in the controlled block,

```
cin >> Weight[i];
```

is a little different. Here, we're reading the number the user has typed in at the keyboard and storing it in a variable. But the variable we're using is different each time through the loop: it's the "ith" element of the Weight vector. So, on the first iteration, the value the user types in will go into Weight[0]; the value accepted on the second iteration will go into Weight[1]; and so on, until on the fifth and last iteration, the typed-in value will be stored in Weight[4].

Here's Susan's take on this.

Susan: What do you mean by the ith element? So does Weight[i] mean you are directing the number that the user types in to a certain location in memory?

Steve: Yes, to the element whose number is the current value of i.

Susan: When you say cin >> Weight[i] does that mean you are telling the computer to place that variable in the index? So this serves two functions, displaying the weight the user types in and associating it to the index?

Steve: No, that statement has the sole function of telling the computer to place the value read in from the keyboard into element i of vector Weight.

Susan: What I am confusing is what is being seen on the screen at the time that the user types in the input. So, the user sees the number on the screen but then it isn't displayed anywhere after that number is entered? Then, the statement cin >> weight [i] directs it to a location somewhere in memory with a group of other numbers that the user types in?

Steve: Correct. This will be illustrated under the contents of Weight heading in Figures 4.10–4.13.

Now that we have stored all of the weights, we want to find the three highest of the weights. We'll use a sorting algorithm called a **selection sort**, which can be expressed in English as follows:

1. Repeat the following steps three times, once through for each weight that we want to select.

2. Search through the list (i.e., the Weight vector), keeping track of the highest weight seen so far in the list and the index of that highest weight.

3. When we get to the end of the list, store the highest weight we've found in another list (the "output list", which in this case is the vector SortedWeight).

4. Finally, set the highest weight we've found in the original list to 0, so we won't select it as the highest value again on the next pass through the list.

Let's take a look at the portion of our C++ program that implements this sort, in Figure 4.8.

FIGURE 4.8. Sorting the weights (from code\vect1.cc)

```
for (i = 0; i < 3; i ++)
  {
  HighestWeight = 0;
  for (k = 0; k < 5; k ++)
    {
    if (Weight[k] > HighestWeight)
      {
      HighestWeight = Weight[k];
      HighestIndex = k;
      }
    }
  SortedWeight[i] = HighestWeight;
  Weight[HighestIndex] = 0;
  }
```

Susan had some interesting comments and questions on this algorithm. Let's take a look at our discussion of the use of the variable i:

Susan: Now I understand why you used the example of $i = i + 1$; in Chapter 3; before, it didn't make sense why you would do that silly thing. Anyway, now let me get this straight. To say that, in the context of this exercise, means you can keep adding 1 to the value of i? I am finding it hard to see where this works for the number 7, say, or anything above 5 for that matter. So, it just means you can have 4 +1 or + another 1, and so on? See where I am having trouble?

Steve: Remember, a short variable such as i is just a name for a 2-byte area of RAM, which can hold any value between −32768 and +32767. Therefore, the statement i ++; means that we want to recalculate the contents of that area of RAM by adding 1 to its former contents.

Susan: No, that is not the answer to my question. Yes, I know all that. What I am saying is this: I assume that i ++; is the expression that handles any value over 4, right? Then let's say that you have pumpkins that weigh 1, 2, 3, 4, and 5 pounds consecutively. No problem, but what if the next pumpkin was not 6 but say 7 pounds? If at that point, the highest value for i was only 5 and you could only add 1 to it, how does that work? It just doesn't yet have the base of 6 to add 1 to. Now do you understand what I am saying?

Steve: I think I see the problem you're having now. We're using the variable i to indicate which weight we're talking about, not the weight itself. In other words, the first weight is Weight[0], the second is Weight[1], the third is Weight[2], the fourth is Weight[3], and the fifth is Weight[4]. The actual values of the weights are whatever the user of the program types in. For example, if the user types in 3 for the first weight, 9 for the second one, 6 for the third, 12 for the fourth, and 1 for the fifth, then the vector will look like Figure 4.9.

The value of i has to increase by only one each time because it indicates which element of the vector Weight is to store the current value being typed in by the user. Does this clear up your confusion?

Susan: I think so. Then it can have any whole number value 0 or higher (well, up to 32767); adding the 1 means you are permitting the addition of at least 1 to any existing value, thereby allowing it to increase. Is that it?

FIGURE 4.9. Elements vs. values

Element	Value
Weight[0]	3
Weight[1]	9
Weight[2]	6
Weight[3]	12
Weight[4]	1

Steve: No, I'm not permitting an addition; I'm performing it. Let's suppose i is 0. In that case, Weight[i] means Weight[0], or the first element of the Weight vector. When I add 1 to i, i becomes 1. Therefore, Weight[i] now means Weight[1]. The next execution of i ++; sets i to 2; therefore, Weight[i] now means Weight[2]. Any time an i is used in an expression, for example, Weight[i], i + j, or i + 1 you can replace the i by whatever the current value of i is. The only place where you can't replace a variable such as i by its current value is when it is being modified, as in i ++ or the i in i = j + 1. In those cases, i means the address where the value of the variable i is stored.

Susan: Okay, then i is not the number of the value typed in by the user; it is the location of an element in the Weight vector, and that is why it can increase by 1, because of the i ++?

Steve: Correct, except that I would say "that is why it *does* increase by 1". This may just be terminology.

Susan: But in this case it can increase no more than 4 because of the i < 5 thing?

Steve: Correct.

Susan: But it has to start with a 0 because of the i = 0 thing?

Steve: Correct.

Susan: So then cin >> Weight [i] means that the number the user is typing has to go into one of those locations but the only word that says what that location could be is Weight; it puts no limitations on the location in that Weight vector other than when you defined the index variable as short i;. This means the index cannot be more than 32767.

Steve: Correct. The current value of i is what determines which element of Weight the user's input goes into.

Susan: I think I was not understanding this because I kept thinking that i was what the user typed in and we were defining its limitations. Instead we are telling it where to go.

Steve: Correct.

Having beaten that topic into the ground, let's look at the correspondence between the English description of the algorithm and the code:

1. Repeat the following steps once through for each prize:

   for (i = 0; i < 3; i ++)

   During this process the variable i is the index into the SortedWeight vector where we're going to store the weight for the current prize we're working on. While we're looking for the highest weight, i is 0; for the second-highest weight, i is 1; finally, when we're getting ready to award a third prize, i will be 2.

2. Initialize the variable that we will use to keep track of the highest weight for this pass through the data:

   HighestWeight = 0;

3. Step through the input list:

   for (k = 0; k < 5; k ++)

4. For each element of the list Weight, we check whether that element (Weight[k]) is greater than the highest weight seen so far in the list (HighestWeight). If that is the case, then we reset HighestWeight to the value of the current element (Weight[k]) and the index of the highest weight so far (HighestIndex) to the index of the current element (k):

```
if (Weight[k] > HighestWeight)
    {
    HighestWeight = Weight[k];
    HighestIndex = k;
    }
```

5. When we get to the end of the input list, HighestWeight is the highest weight in the list, and HighestIndex is the index of that element of the list that had the highest weight. Therefore, we can copy the highest weight to the current element of another list (the "output list"). As mentioned earlier, i is the index of the current element in the output list. Its value is the number of times we have been through the outer loop before; that is, the highest weight, which we will identify first, goes in position 0 of the output list, the next highest in position 1, and so on:

```
SortedWeight[i] = HighestWeight;
```

6. Finally, set the highest weight in the input list to 0, so we won't select it as the highest value again on the next pass through the list.

```
Weight[HighestIndex] = 0;
```

This statement is the reason that we have to keep track of the "highest index"; that is, the index of the highest weight. Otherwise, we wouldn't know which element of the original Weight vector we've used and therefore wouldn't be able to set it to 0 to prevent its being used again.

Here's Susan's rendition of this algorithm:

Susan: Okay, let me repeat this back to you in English. The result of this program is that after scanning the list of user input weights the weights are put in another list, which is an ordering list, named k. The program starts by finding the highest weight in the input list. It then takes it out, puts it in k, and replaces that value it took out with a 0, so it won't be picked up again. Then it comes back to find the next highest weight and does the same thing all over again until nothing is left to order. Actually this is more than that one statement. But is this what you mean? That one statement is responsible for finding the highest weight in the user input list and placing it in k. Is this right?

Steve: It's almost exactly right. The only error is that the list that the weights are moved to is the SortedWeight vector, rather than k. The variable k is used to keep track of which is the next entry to be put into the SortedWeight vector.

Susan: Okay. There was also something else I didn't understand when tracing through the program. I did see at one point during the execution of the tracing version of this program that i=5. Well, first I didn't know how that could be because i is supposed to be < 5, but then I remembered that i ++ expression in the for loop, so I wondered if that is how this happened. I forgot where I was at that point, but I think it was after I had just completed entering 5 values and i was incrementing with each value. But see, it really should not have been more than 4 because if you start at 0 then that is where it should have ended up.

Steve: The reason that i gets to be 5 after the end of the loop is that at the end of each pass through the loop, the modification expression (i ++) is executed before the continuation expression (i < 5). So, at the end of the fifth pass through the loop, i is incremented to 5 and then tested to see if it is still less than 5. Since it isn't, the loop terminates at that point.

Susan: I get that. But I still have a question about the statement if Weight[k] > highest weight. Well, the first time through, this will definitely be true because we've initialized HighestWeight to 0, since any weight would be greater than 0. Is that right?

Steve: Yes. Every time through the outer (i) loop, as we get to the top of the inner loop, the 0 that we've just put in HighestWeight should be replaced by the first element of Weight; that is, Weight[0], except of course if we've already replaced Weight[0] by 0 during a previous pass. It would also be possible to initialize HighestWeight to Weight[0] and then start the loop by setting k to 1 rather than 0. That would cause the inner (k) loop to be executed only four times per outer loop execution, rather than five, and therefore would be more efficient.

Susan: Then HighestIndex=k; is the statement that sets the placement of the highest number to its rank?

Steve: Right.

Susan: Then I thought about this. It seems that the highest weight is set first, then the sorting takes place so it makes four passes (actually five) to stop the loop.

Steve: The sorting is the whole process. Each pass through the outer loop locates one more element to be put into the SortedWeight vector.

Susan: Then the statement Weight[HighestIndex] = 0; comes into play, replacing the highest number selected on that pass to 0.

Steve: Correct.

Susan: Oh, when k is going through the sorting process why does i increment though each pass? It seems that k should be incrementing.

Steve: Actually, k increments on each pass through the inner loop, or 15 times in all. It's reset to 0 on each pass through the outer loop, so that we look at all of the elements again when we're trying to find the highest remaining weight. On the other hand, i is incremented on each pass through the outer loop or three times in all, once for each "highest" weight that gets put into the SortedWeight vector.

Susan: Okay, I get the idea with i, but what is the deal with k? I mean I see it was defined as a short, but what is it supposed to represent, and how did you know in advance that you were going to need it?

Steve: It represents the position in the original list, as indicated in the description of the algorithm.

Susan: I still don't understand where k fits into this picture. What does it do?

Steve: It's the index in the "inner loop", which steps through the elements looking for the highest one that's still there. We get one "highest" value every time through the "outer loop", so we have to execute that outer loop three times. Each time through the outer loop, we execute the inner loop five times, once for each entry in the input list.

Susan: Too many terms again. Which is the "outer loop" and which was the "inner loop"?

Steve: The outer loop executes once for each "highest" weight we're locating. Each time we find one, we set it to 0 (at the end of the loop) so that it won't be found again the next time through.

Susan: Okay, but now I am confused with the statement: if (Weight[k] > HighestWeight). This is what gets me: If I understand this right (and obviously I don't) how could Weight[k] ever be greater than HighestWeight, since every possible value of k represents one of the elements in the Weight vector, and HighestWeight is the highest weight in that vector? For this reason

I am having a hard time understanding the code for step 2, but not the concept.

Steve: The value of HighestWeight at any time is equal to the highest weight that has been seen *so far*. At the beginning of each execution of the outer loop, HighestWeight is set to 0. Then, every time that the current weight (Weight[k]) is higher than the current value of HighestWeight, we reset HighestWeight to the value of the current weight.

Susan: I still don't understand this statement. Help.

Steve: Remember that HighestWeight is reset to 0 on each pass through the outer loop. Thus, this if statement checks whether the kth element of the Weight vector exceeds the highest weight we've seen before in this pass. If that is true, obviously our "highest" weight isn't really the highest, so we have to reset the highest weight to the value of the kth element; if the kth element isn't the true highest weight, at least it's higher than what we had before. Since we replace the "highest" weight value with the kth value any time that the kth value is higher than the current "highest" weight, at the end of the inner loop, the number remaining in HighestWeight will be the true highest weight left in Weight. This is essentially the same algorithm as we used to find the highest weight in the original version of this program, but now we apply it several times to find successively lower "highest" weights.

Susan: Okay, I understand now, i increments to show how many times it has looped through to find the highest number. You are doing a loop within a loop, really, it is not side by side is it?

Steve: Correct.

Susan: So, when you first enter your numbers they are placed in an index called i, then they are going to be cycled through again, placing them in a corresponding index named k, looking for the top three numbers. To start out tharough each pass, you first set the highest weight to the first weight since you have preset the highest weight to 0. But, to find the top three numbers you have to look at each place or element in the index. At the end of each loop you sort out the highest number and then set that removed element to 0 so it won't be selected again. You do this whole thing three times.

Steve: That's right, except for some terminology: where you say "an index called i", you should say "a vector called Weight", and where you say "an index called k", you should say "a vector called SortedWeight". The variables i and k are used to step through the vectors, but they are not the vectors themselves.

Susan: Okay, then the index variables just are the working representation of what is going on in those vectors. But are not the numbers "assigned" an index? Let's see; if you lined up your five numbers you could refer to each number as to its placement in a vector. Could you then have the column of weights in the middle of the two indexes of i and k to each side?

Steve: If I understand your suggestion, it wouldn't work, because k and i vary at different speeds. During the first pass of the outer loop, i is 0, while k varies from 0 to 5; on the second pass of the outer loop, i is 1, while k varies from 0 to 5 again, and the same for the third pass of the outer loop. The value of i is used to refer to an individual element of the SortedWeight vector, the one that will receive the next "highest" weight we locate. The value of k is used to refer to an individual element of the Weight vector, the one we're examining to see if it's higher than the current HighestWeight.

Susan: This is what gets me, how do you know in advance that you are going to have to set HighestIndex to k? I see it in the program as it happens and I understand it then, but how would you know that the program wouldn't run without doing that? Trial and error? Experience? Rule books?

Steve: Logic. Let's look at the problem again. The sorting algorithm that we're using here is called *selection sort*, because each time through the outer loop it selects one element out of the input vector and moves it to the output vector. To prevent our selecting the same weight (i.e., the highest one in the original input) every time through the outer loop, we have to clear each weight to 0 as we select it. But, to do that, we have to keep track of which one we selected; that's why we need to save HighestIndex.

Being a glutton for punishment, Susan brought up the general problem of how to create an algorithm in the first place.

Susan: Do they make instruction sheets with directions of paths to follow? How do you identify problems? I mean, don't you encounter pretty much the same types of problems frequently in programming and can they not be identified some way so that if you knew a certain problem could be categorized as a Type C problem, let's say, you would approach it with a Type C methodology to the solution? Does that make sense? Probably not.

Steve: It does make sense, but for some reason such "handbooks" are rare. Actually, another book of mine, *Optimizing C++*, is designed to provide something like you're suggesting, with solutions to common problems at the algorithmic level. There's also a book called *Design Patterns* that tries to provide tested solutions to common design problems, at a much higher level.

Details, Details

Let's go back and look at the steps of the algorithm more closely (they start on page 176). Steps 1 through 3 should be fairly self-explanatory, once you're familiar with the syntax of the for statement; they start the outer loop, initialize the highest weight value for the current loop, and start the inner loop.

Step 4 is quite similar to the process we went through to find the highest weight in our previous two programs; however, the reason for the HighestIndex variable may not be obvious. We need to keep track of which element of the original vector (i.e., Weight) we have decided is the highest so far, so that this element won't be selected as the highest weight on *every* pass through the Weight vector. To prevent this error, step 4 sets each "highest" weight to a value that won't be selected on a succeeding pass. Since we know there should be no 0 weights in the Weight vector, we can set each selected element to 0 after it has been selected, to prevent its reselection. Figure 4.10 shows a picture of the situation before the first pass through the data, with ??? in SortedWeight to indicate that those locations contain unknown data, as they haven't been initialized yet.

FIGURE 4.10. Initial situation

Index	Contents of Weight	Contents of SortedWeight
0	5	???
1	2	???
2	11	???
3	3	
4	7	

In Figure 4.10, the highest value is 11 in Weight[2]. After we've located it and copied its value to SortedWeight[0], we set Weight[2] to 0, yielding the situation in Figure 4.11.

FIGURE 4.11. After the first pass

Index	Contents of Weight	Contents of SortedWeight
0	5	11
1	2	???
2	0	???
3	3	
4	7	

Now we're ready for the second pass. This time, the highest value is the 7 in Weight[4]. After we copy the 7 to SortedWeight[1], we set Weight[4] to 0, leaving the situation in Figure 4.12.

FIGURE 4.12. After the second pass

Index	Contents of Weight	Contents of SortedWeight
0	5	11
1	2	7
2	0	???
3	3	
4	0	

On the third and final pass, we locate the 5 in Weight[0], copy it to SortedWeight[2], and set Weight[0] to 0. As you can see in Figure 4.13, SortedWeight now has the results we were looking for: the top three weights, in descending order.

FIGURE 4.13. Final situation

Index	Contents of Weight	Contents of SortedWeight
0	0	11
1	2	7
2	0	5
3	3	
4	0	

To Err Is Human...

That accounts for all of the steps in the sorting algorithm. However, our implementation of the algorithm has a weak spot that we should fix. If you want to try to find it yourself, look at the code and explanation again before going on. Ready?

The key word in the explanation is "should" in the following sentence: "Since we know there *should* be no 0 weights in the Weight vector, we can set each selected element to 0 after it has been selected, to prevent its reselection". How do we *know* that there are no 0 weights? We don't, unless we screen for them when we accept input. In the first pumpkin-weighing program, we stopped the input when we got a 0, but in the programs in this chapter we ask for a set number of weights. If one of them is 0, the program will continue along happily.[13] Before we change the program, though, let's try to figure out what would happen if the user types in a 0 for every weight.

You can try this scenario out yourself. First, you have to compile the program by changing to the code subdirectory under the main directory where you installed the software, and typing RHIDE vect1, then using the "Make" command from the "Compile" menu. Then exit back to DOS and type vect1 to run the program. When it asks for weights, enter a 0 for each of the five weights.

To run it under the debugger, make sure you are in the code subdirectory, and then type RHIDE vect1. Again, do *not* add the ".cc" to the end of the file name. Once RHIDE has started up, you can step through the program by hitting F8, which will treat any function call as one statement, or by hitting F7, which will step into any function call. Any time you want to see the display that the user would see when running the program normally, hit ALT-F5, then ENTER to get back to the debugger. After you've entered a 0 for each of the five weights, the program will start the sorting process.

In case you're reading this away from your computer, Figure 4.14 shows what might happen (although the element number in the message may not be the same)[14].

---

13. For that matter, what if someone types in a negative weight, such as −5? Of course, this doesn't make any sense, but it's a good idea to try to prevent errors, rather than assuming that users of a program will always act sensibly.

14. It's even possible that you won't get an error message at all, and the program will run correctly. However, if this happens, it just means that you're lucky. As you'll see later, you shouldn't count on that sort of luck.

FIGURE 4.14. A possible error message

You have tried to use element 51082 of a vector which has only 5 elements.

Why doesn't the program work in this case? Because we have an **uninitialized variable**; that is, one that has never been set to a valid value. In this case, it's HighestIndex. Let's look at the sorting code one more time, in Figure 4.15.[15]

FIGURE 4.15. Sorting the weights, again (from code\vect1.cc)

```
for (i = 0; i < 3; i ++)
  {
  HighestWeight = 0;
  for (k = 0; k < 5; k ++)
    {
    if (Weight[k] > HighestWeight)
      {
      HighestWeight = Weight[k];
      HighestIndex = k;
      }
    }
  SortedWeight[i] = HighestWeight;
  Weight[HighestIndex] = 0;
  }
```

---

15. You may have noticed a slight oddity in this code. The block controlled by the for statement consists of exactly one statement; namely, the if that checks for a new HighestWeight value. According to the rules I've provided, that means we don't have to put curly braces ({}) around it to make it a block. While this is true, long experience has indicated that it's a very good idea to make it a block anyway, as a preventive measure. It's very common to revisit old code to fix bugs or add new functions, and in so doing we might add another statement after the if statement at a later time, intending it to be controlled by the for. The results wouldn't be correct, since the added statement would be executed exactly one time after the loop was finished, rather than once each time through the loop. Such errors are very difficult to find, because the code looks all right when inspected casually; therefore, a little extra caution when writing the program in the first place often pays off handsomely.

It's clear that HighestWeight is **initialized** (i.e., given a valid value) before it is ever used; the statement HighestWeight = 0; is the first statement in the block controlled by the outer for loop. However, the same is not true of HighestIndex. Whenever the condition in the if statement is true, both HighestWeight and HighestIndex will indeed be set to legitimate values: HighestWeight will be the highest weight seen so far on this pass, and HighestIndex will be the index of that weight in the Weight vector. However, what happens if the condition in the if statement never becomes true? In that case, HighestIndex will have whatever random value it started out with at the beginning of the program; it's very unlikely that such a value will be correct or even refer to an actual element in the Weight vector.

Here's the discussion that Susan and I had on this topic:

Susan: You say that HighestIndex isn't initialized properly. But what about when you set k equal to 0 and then HighestIndex is set equal to k? Is that not initialized?

Steve: The problem is that the statement HighestIndex = k; is executed only when Weight[k] is greater than HighestWeight. If that never occurs, then HighestIndex is left in some random state.

Susan: Okay, then why didn't you say so in the first place? I understand that. However, I still don't understand why the program would fail if all the weights the user typed in were 0. To me it would just have a very boring outcome.

Steve: That's the case in which HighestIndex would never be initialized; therefore, it would contain random garbage and would cause the program to try to display an element at some random index value.

Susan: I traced through the program again briefly tonight and that reminds me to ask you why you put the highest weight value to 1596 and the second-highest weight value to 1614?

Steve: I didn't. Those just happened to be the values that those memory locations had in them before they were initialized.

Susan: I was totally confused right from the beginning when I saw that. But did you do that to show that those were just the first two weights, and that they have not been, how would you say this, "ordered" yet? I don't know the language for this in computerese, but I am sure you know what I am saying.

Steve: Not exactly; they haven't been initialized at that point, so whatever values they might contain would be garbage.

Susan: So at that point they were just the first and second weights, or did you just arbitrarily put those weights in there to get it started? Anyway, that was baffling when I saw that.

Steve: Before you set a variable to a particular value, it will have some kind of random junk in it. That's what you're seeing at the beginning of the program, before the variables have been initialized.

Susan: Okay, I am glad this happened, I can see this better, but whose computer did that? Was it yours or mine? I mean did you run it first and your computer did it, or was it my computer that came up with those values?

Steve: It's your computer. The program starts out with "undefined" values for all of the uninitialized variables. What this means in practice is that their values are whatever happened to be left around in memory at those addresses. This is quite likely to be different on your machine from what it is on mine or even on yours at a different time.

Susan: So something has to be there; and if you don't tell it what it is, the old contents of memory just comes up?

Steve: Right.

Susan: If it had worked out that the higher number had been in first place, then I would have just assumed that you put that there as a starting point. I am really glad that this happened but I was not too happy about it when I was trying to figure it out.

Steve: See, it's all for your own good.

Susan: If that were the case, I would think it nearly impossible that we have the same values at any given address. How could they ever be remotely the same?

Steve: It's very unlikely that they would, unless the address were one that was used by very basic software such as DOS or Windows, which might be the same on our computers.

Susan: Anyway, then you must have known I was going to get "garbage" in those two variables, didn't you? Why didn't you advise me at least about that? Do you know how confusing it was to see that first thing?

Steve: Yes, but it's better for you to figure it out yourself. Now you really know it, whereas if I had told you about it in advance, you would have relied on my knowledge rather than developing your own.

I hope that has cleared up the confusion about the effect of an uninitialized variable in this example. But, why do we have to initialize variables ourselves? Surely they must have some value at any given time. Let's listen in on the conversation that Susan and I had about this point:

Susan: So, each bit in RAM is capable of being turned on or off by a 1 or a 0? Which one is on and which one is off? Or does that matter? How does this work electronically? I mean how does the presence of a 0 or a 1 throw the RAM into a different electronic state?

Steve: To be more exact, each "switch" is capable of existing in either the "on" or "off" state. The assignment of states to 1s and 0s is our notion, which doesn't affect the fact that there are exactly two distinct states the switch can assume, just like a light switch (without a dimmer). We say that if the switch is off, it's storing a 0, and if it's on, it's storing a 1.

Susan: What is the "normal state" of RAM: on or off?

Steve: It's indeterminate. That's one reason why we need to explicitly set our variables to a known state before we use them.

Susan: That didn't make sense to me originally, but I woke up this morning and the first thing that came to my mind was the light switch analogy. I think I know what you meant by *indeterminate*.

If we consider the light switch as imposed with our parental and financial values, it is tempting to view the "normal state" of a light switch as off. Hey, does the light switch really care? It could sit there for 100 years in the on position as easily as in the off position. Who is to say what is normal? The only consequence is that the light bulb will have been long burned out. So it doesn't matter, it really doesn't have a normal state, unless people decide that there is one.

Steve: What you've said is correct. The switch doesn't care whether it's on or off. In that sense, the "normal" position doesn't really have a definition other than one we give it.

However, what I meant by *indeterminate* is slightly different: When power is applied to the RAM, each bit (or to be more precise, a switch that represents that bit) could just as easily start out on as off. It's actually either one or the other, but which one is pretty much random, so we have to set it to something before we know its value.

Susan: Oh, you broke my heart, when I thought I had it all figured out! Well, I guess it was okay, at least as far as the light switch was concerned, but then RAM and a light switch are not created equal. So RAM is pretty easy to please, I guess...

After that bit of comic relief, let's get back to the analysis of this program. It should be fairly obvious that if the user types in even one weight greater than 0, the if statement will be true when that weight is encountered, so the program will work. However, if the user typed in all 0 weights, the program would fail, as we saw before, because the condition in the if statement would never become true. To prevent this from causing program failure, all we have to do is to add one more line, the one in **bold** in Figure 4.16.

FIGURE 4.16. Sorting the weights, with correct initialization (from code\vect2.cc)

```
for (i = 0; i < 3; i ++)
  {
  HighestWeight = 0;
  HighestIndex = 0;
  for (k = 0; k < 5; k ++)
    {
    if (Weight[k] > HighestWeight)
      {
      HighestWeight = Weight[k];
      HighestIndex = k;
      }
    }
  SortedWeight[i] = HighestWeight;
  Weight[HighestIndex] = 0;
  }
```

Now we can be sure that HighestIndex always has a value that corresponds to some element of the Weight vector, so we won't see the program fail as the previous one would.

Assuming that you've installed the software from the CD-ROM in the back of this book, you can run the corrected program to test that it works as advertised. First, you have to compile it by changing to the code subdirectory under the main directory where you installed the software, and typing RHIDE vect2, then using the "Make" command from the "Compile" menu. Then exit back to DOS and type vect2 to run the program. After you've entered 5 weights, the program will start the sorting process.

To run it under the debugger, make sure you are in the code subdirectory, and then type RHIDE vect2. Again, do *not* add the ".cc" to the end of the file name. Once RHIDE has started up, you can step through the program by hitting F8, which will treat any function call as one statement, or by hitting F7, which will step into any function call. Any time you want to see the display that the user would see when running the program normally, hit ALT-F5, then ENTER to get back to the debugger.

After you've entered 5 weights, the program will start the sorting process. This time, entering five 0 weights will produce the expected result: The top three weights will all be 0.

By the way, it's also possible to initialize a variable at the same time as you define it. For example, the statement short i = 12; defines a short variable called i and sets it to the value 12 at the same time. This is generally a good practice to follow when possible; if you initialize the variable when you define it, you don't have to remember to write a separate statement to do the initialization.

To Really Foul Things Up Requires a Computer

We should pay some more attention to the notion of program failure, as it's very important. The first question, of course, is what it means to say that a program "fails". The best answer is that it doesn't work correctly, but that isn't very specific.

As you can imagine, this notion was the topic of some discussion with Susan:

> **Susan:** What do you mean by a program failing? I know it means it won't work, but what happens? Do you just get error messages, and it won't do anything? Or is it like the message that you have on page 187?

> **Steve:** In general, a program "failing" means that it does something unexpected and erroneous. Because I have put some safety features into the implementation of vector, you'll get an error message if you misuse a vector by referring to a nonexistent element.

In general, a program failure may or may not produce an error message. In the specific case that we've just seen, we'll probably get an error message while trying to access a nonexistent element of the Weight vector. However, it's entirely possible for a program to just "hang" (run endlessly), "crash" your system, produce an obviously ridiculous answer, or worst of all, provide a seemingly correct but actually erroneous result.

The causes of program failures are legion. A few of the possibilities are these:

1. Problems isolated to our code.

   a. The original problem could have been stated incorrectly.

   b. The algorithm(s) we're using could have been inappropriate for the problem.

   c. The algorithm(s) might have been implemented incorrectly.

   d. An input value might be outside the expected range.

   And so on...

2. Problems interacting with other programs.

a. We might be misusing a function supplied by the system, like the << operator.

b. The documentation for a system function might be incorrect or incomplete. This is especially common in "guru"-oriented operating systems, where the users are supposed to know everything.

c. A system function might be unreliable. This is more common than it should be.

d. The compiler might be generating the wrong instructions. I've seen this on a few rare occasions.

e. Another program in the system might be interfering with our program. This is quite common in some popular operating environments that allow several programs to be executing concurrently.[16]

And so on...

With a simple program such as the ones we're writing here, errors such as the ones listed under problems with our code are more likely, as we have relatively little interaction with the rest of the system. As we start to use more sophisticated mechanisms in C++, we're more likely to run into instances of interaction problems.

What, Me Worry?

After that excursion into the sources of program failure, let's get back to our question about initializing variables. Why do we have to worry about this at all? It would seem perfectly reasonable for the compiler to make sure that our variables were always initialized to some

---

16. Especially those whose names begin with "W".

reasonable value; in the case of numeric variables such as a short, 0 would be a good choice. Surely Bjarne Stroustrup, the designer of C++, didn't overlook this.

No, he didn't; he made a conscious decision not to provide this facility. It's not due to cruelty or unconcern with the needs of programmers. On the contrary, he stated in the Preface to the First Edition of *The C++ Programming Language* that "C++ is a general-purpose programming language designed to make programming more enjoyable for the serious programmer".[17] To allow C++ to replace C completely, he could not add features that would penalize efficiency for programs that do not use these features. Adding initialization as a built-in function of the language would make programs larger and slower if the programmer had already initialized all variables as needed. This may not be obvious, but we'll see in a later section why it is so.

Here's Susan's reaction to these points about C++:

Susan: What is run-time efficiency?

Steve: How long it takes to run the program and how much memory it uses.

Susan: So are you saying that C++ is totally different from C? That one is not based on the other?

Steve: No, C++ is a descendant of C. However, C++ provides much more flexibility to programmers than C.

Susan: Now, about what Bjarne said back in 1986: Who enjoys this, and if C++ is intended for a serious programmer, why am I reading this book? What is a serious programmer? Would you not think a serious programmer should have at least taken Computer Programming 101?

---

17. *The C++ Programming Language, 2nd Edition.* v.

Steve: This book should be a pretty good substitute for Computer Programming 101. You probably know considerably more than the usual graduate of such a course, although the e-mail tutoring has been a major contributor to your understanding. Anyway, if you want to learn how to program, you have to start somewhere, and it might as well be with the intention of being a serious programmer.

Garbage in, Garbage Out

In the meantime, there's something else we should do if we want the program to work as it should. As the old saying "Garbage in, garbage out" suggests, by far the best solution to handling spurious input values is to prevent them from being entered in the first place. What we want to do is to check each input value and warn the user if it's invalid. Figure 4.17 illustrates a new input routine that looks like it should do the trick.

FIGURE 4.17. **Garbage prevention, first attempt (from code\vect2a.cc)**

```
for (i = 0; i < 5; i ++)
  {
  cout << "Please type in weight #" << i+1 << ": ";
  cin >> Weight[i];
  if (Weight[i] <= 0)
    {
    cout << "I'm sorry, " << Weight[i] << " is not a valid weight.";
    cout << endl;
    }
  }
```

Assuming that you've installed the software from the CD-ROM in the back of this book, you can try out this program. First, you have to compile it by changing to the code subdirectory under the main directory where you installed the software, and typing RHIDE vect2a, then using the "Make" command from the "Compile" menu. Then exit back to DOS and type vect2a to run the program. It will ask you for five weights and sort them after you have entered them.

To run it under the debugger, make sure you are in the code subdirectory, and then type RHIDE vect2a. Again, do *not* add the ".cc" to the end of the file name. Once RHIDE has started up, you can step through the program by hitting F8, which will treat any function call as one statement, or by hitting F7, which will step into any function call. Any time you want to see the display that the user would see when running the program normally, hit ALT-F5, then ENTER to get back to the debugger.

When you are asked for a weight, type one in and hit ENTER just as when executing normally. After you've entered 5 weights, the program will start the sorting process. When finished, it will display the top three weights of the five that were entered.

Most of this should be familiar; the only line that has a new construct in it is the if statement. The condition <= means "less than or equal to", which is reasonably intuitive.

Unfortunately, this program won't really solve the problem of bad input. The problem is what happens after the error message is displayed; namely, the loop continues at the top with the next weight, and we never correct the erroneous input. Susan didn't have much trouble figuring out exactly what that last statement meant:

> **Susan:** When you say that "we never correct the erroneous input", does that mean that it is added to the list and not ignored?

> **Steve:** Right.

To fix this problem completely, we need to use an approach similar to the one shown in the final version of this program (Figure 4.18). Assuming that you've installed the software from the CD-ROM in the back of this book, you can try out this program. First, you have to compile it by changing to the code subdirectory under the main directory where you installed the software, and typing RHIDE vect3, then using the "Make" command from the "Compile" menu. Then exit back to DOS and type vect3 to run the program. It will ask you for five weights and sort them after you have entered them.

To run it under the debugger, make sure you are in the code subdirectory, and then type RHIDE vect3. Again, do *not* add the ".cc" to the end of the file name. Once RHIDE has started up, you can step through the program by hitting F8, which will treat any function call as one statement, or by hitting F7, which will step into any function call. Any time you want to see the display that the user would see when running the program normally, hit ALT-F5, then ENTER to get back to the debugger.

When you are asked for a weight, type one in and hit ENTER just as when executing normally. After you've entered five weights, the program will start the sorting process, and will display the results when finished.

FIGURE 4.18. Finding the top three weights using vectors **(code\vect3.cc)**

```cpp
#include <iostream.h>
#include "vector.h"

int main()
{
    vector<short> Weight(5);
    vector<short> SortedWeight(3);
    short HighestWeight;
    short HighestIndex;
    short i;
    short k;

    cout << "I'm going to ask you to type in five weights, in pounds." << endl;

    for (i = 0; i < 5; )
     {
     cout << "Please type in weight #" << i+1 << ": ";
     cin >> Weight[i];
     if (Weight[i] <= 0)
       {
       cout << "I'm sorry, " << Weight[i] << " is not a valid weight.";
       cout << endl;
```

```
        }
      else
       i ++;
      }

   for (i = 0; i < 3; i ++)
      {
      HighestIndex = 0;
      HighestWeight = 0;
      for (k = 0; k < 5; k ++)
         {
         if (Weight[k] > HighestWeight)
            {
            HighestWeight = Weight[k];
            HighestIndex = k;
            }
         }
      SortedWeight[i] = HighestWeight;
      Weight[HighestIndex] = 0;
      }

   cout << "The highest weight was: " << SortedWeight[0] << endl;
   cout << "The second highest weight was: " << SortedWeight[1] << endl;
   cout << "The third highest weight was: " << SortedWeight[2] << endl;

   return 0;
   }
```

Now let's look at the changes that we've made to the program from the last revision. The first change is that the for loop where the input is accepted from the user has only two sections rather than three in its control definition (inside the ()). As you may recall, the first section specifies the initial condition of the index variable; in this case, we're starting i out at 0, as is usual in C and C++. The second section indicates when we should continue executing the loop; here, it's as long as i is less than 5. But the third section, which usually indicates what to do to the index variable, is missing. The reason for this is that we're going to adjust the index variable manually in the loop, depending on what the user enters.

In this case, if the user enters an invalid value (i.e., less than or equal to 0), we display an error message and leave i as it was, so that the next time through the loop, the value will go into the same element in the Weight vector. When the user enters a valid value, the else clause increments i so that the next value will go into the next element in the vector. This fixes the error in our previous version that left incorrect entries in the vector. Now that we have beaten the pumpkin weighing example to a pulp[18], let's review the mass of information to which I've subjected you so far in this chapter.

Review

We started out by extending our pumpkin weighing program to tell us the highest two weights rather than just the highest one. During this exercise, we learned the use of the else clause of an if statement. We also saw that making even an apparently simple change to a working program can introduce an error; in this case we were copying the highest weight to the next highest weight only when a new high weight was detected. This would produce an incorrect result if a value higher than the previous second highest but lower than the current highest weight were entered.

Next we extended the program again, this time to handle any number of prizes to be given to the highest weight, second-highest weight, third-highest weights, and so on. This inspired a complete reorganization of the program; the new version used the *selection sort* algorithm to produce a list of as many of the highest weights as we need, in descending order. To do this, we had to use a vector, or set of values with a common name, to store all of the weights as they were read in. When they had all been entered, we searched through them three times, once to find each of the top three elements. A vector, just like a regular variable, has a name. However, unlike a regular variable, a vector does not have a single value, but rather consists of a number of *elements*, each of which has a separate value. An element

---

18. Pumpkin pie, anyone?

is referred to by a number, called an *index*, rather than by a unique name; each element has a different index. The lowest index is 0, and the highest index is 1 less than the number of elements in the vector; for example, with a 10 element vector, the legal indexes are 0 through 9. The ability to refer to an element by its index allows us to vary the element we are referring to in a statement by varying the index; we put this facility to good use in our implementation of the selection sort, which we'll review shortly.

We then added the for statement to our repertoire of loop control facilities. This statement provides more precise control than the while statement. Using for, we can specify a *starting expression*, a *continuation expression*, and a *modification expression*. The starting expression sets up the initial conditions for the loop. Before each possible execution of the controlled block, the continuation expression is checked, and if it is true, the controlled block will be executed; otherwise, the for loop will terminate. Finally, the modification expression is executed after each execution of the controlled block. Most commonly, the starting expression sets the initial value of a variable, the continuation expression tests whether that variable is still in the range we are interested in, and the modification expression changes the value of the variable. For example, in the for statement

```
for (i = 0; i < 5; i ++)
```

the starting expression is i = 0, the continuation expression is i < 5, and the modification expression is i ++. Therefore, the block controlled by the for statement will be executed first with the variable i set to 0; at the end of the block, the variable i will be incremented by 1, and the loop will continue if i is still less than 5.

Then we used the for statement and a couple of vectors to implement a *selection sort*. This algorithm goes through an "input list" of n elements once for each desired "result element". In our case, we want the top three elements of the sorted list, so the input list has to be scanned three times. On each time through, the algorithm picks the highest value remaining in the list and adds that to the end of a new "output list". Then it removes the found value from the input list. At the end of this process, the output list has all of the desired values from the input list, in descending order of size. When going over the program, we found a weak spot in the first version: If all the weights the user typed were less than or equal to 0, the program would fail because one of the variables in the program would never be *initialized*; that is, set to a known value.

This led to a discussion of why variable initialization isn't done automatically in C++. Adding this feature to programs would make them slower and larger than C programs doing the same task, and C++ was intended to replace C completely. If C++ programs were significantly less efficient than equivalent C programs, this would not be possible, so Bjarne Stroustrup omitted this feature.

While it's important to insure that our programs work correctly even when given unreasonable input, it's even better to prevent this situation from occurring in the first place. So the next improvement we made to our pumpkin weighing program was to tell the user when an invalid value had been entered and ask for a valid value in its place. This involved a for loop without a modification expression, since we wanted to increment the index variable i to point to the next element of the vector only when the user typed in a valid entry; if an illegal value was typed in, we requested a legal value for the same element of the vector.

Exercises

So that you can test your understanding of this material, here are some exercises.

1. If the program in Figure 4.19 is run, what will be displayed?

FIGURE 4.19. Exercise 1 (code\morbas00.cc)

```cpp
#include <iostream.h>
#include "vector.h"

int main()
{
   vector<short> x(5);
   short Result;
   short i;

   for (i = 0; i < 5; i ++)
      {
      x[i] = 2 * i;
      }

   for (i = 0; i < 5; i ++)
      {
      Result = Result + x[i];
      }

   cout << Result << endl;

   return 0;
}
```

2. If the program in Figure 4.20 is run, what will be displayed?

FIGURE 4.20. Exercise 2 (code\morbas01.cc)

```cpp
#include <iostream.h>
#include "vector.h"

int main()
{
   vector<short> x(4);
   short Result;
   short i;
```

```
x[0] = 3;
for (i = 1; i < 4; i ++)
    x[i] = x[i-1] * 2;

Result = 0;
for (i = 0; i < 4; i ++)
    Result = Result + x[i];

cout << Result << endl;

return 0;
}
```

3. Write a program that asks the user to type in a weight, and display the weight on the screen.

4. Modify the program from exercise 3 to ask the user to type as many weights as desired, stopping as soon as a 0 is entered. Add up all of the weights entered and display the total on the screen at the end of the program.

Answers to exercises can be found at the end of the chapter.

Conclusion

We've covered a lot of material in this chapter in our quest for better pumpkin weighing, ranging from sorting data into order based on numeric value through the anatomy of vectors. Next, we'll take up some more of the language features you will need to write any significant C++ programs.

Answers to Exercises

1. The correct answer is: "Who knows?" If you said "30", you forgot that the loop variable values are from 0 through 4, rather than from 1 through 5. On the other hand, if you said "20", you had the right total of the numbers 0, 2, 4, 6, and 8, but didn't notice that the variable Result was never initialized. Of course, adding anything to an unknown value makes the final value unpredictable. Most current compilers, including the one on the CD-ROM in the back of this book, are capable of warning you about such problems; if you compiled the program with this warning turned on, you'd see a message something like this:

morbas00.cc:7: warning: 'short result' may be used uninitialized in this function.

This is the easiest way to find such errors, especially in a large program. Unfortunately, the compiler may produce such warnings even when they are not valid, so the final decision is still up to you.

Assuming that you've installed the software from the CD-ROM in the back of this book, you can try this program out. First, you have to compile it by changing to the code subdirectory under the main directory where you installed the software, and typing RHIDE morbas00, then using the "Make" command from the "Compile" menu. Then exit back to DOS and type morbas00 to run the program.

Running this program normally isn't likely to give you much information. To run it under the debugger, make sure you are in the code subdirectory, and then type RHIDE morbas00. Again, do *not* add the ".cc" to the end of the file name. Once RHIDE has started up, you can step through the program by hitting F8, which will treat any function call as one statement, or by hitting F7, which will step into any function call. Any time you want to see the display that the user would see when running the program normally, hit ALT-F5, then ENTER to get back to the debugger.

2. The correct answer is 45. In case this isn't obvious, consider the following:

   a. The value of x[0] is set to 3.

   b. In the first for loop, the value of i starts out at 1.

   c. Therefore, the first execution of the assignment statement x[i] = x[i−1] * 2; is equivalent to x[1] = x[0] * 2;. This clearly sets x[1] to 6.

   d. The next time through the loop i is 2, so that same assignment statement x[i] = x[i−1] * 2; is equivalent to x[2] = x[1] * 2;. This sets x[2] to 12.

   e. Finally, on the last pass through the loop, the value of i is 3, so that assignment statement x[i] = x[i−1] * 2; is equivalent to x[3] = x[2] * 2; This sets x[3] to 24.

   f. The second for loop just adds up the values of all the entries in the x vector; this time, we remembered to initialize the total, Result, to 0, so the total is calculated and displayed correctly.

   Running this program normally isn't likely to give you much information, but you might want to run it under control of the debugger. You can do this in exactly the same way as you did the previous program, except athat you would type RHIDE morbas01 rather than RHIDE morbas00.

3. Let's start with Susan's proposed solution to this problem, in Figure 4.21, and the questions that came up during the process.

   FIGURE 4.21. Weight requesting program, first try (code\morbas02.cc)

```cpp
#include <iostream.h>

int main()
{
    short weight;
```

```
cout << "Please write your weight here. "\n;

cin >> weight

return 0;
}
```

Susan: Would this work? Right now by just doing this it brought up several things that I have not thought about before.

First, is the # standard for no matter what type of program you are doing?

Steve: The iostream.h header file is needed if you want to use <<, >>, cin and cout, which most programs do, but not all.

Susan: Okay, but I meant the actual pound sign (#), is that always a part of iostream.h?

Steve: It's not part of the filename, it's part of the #include command, which tells the compiler that you want it to pretend that you've just typed in the entire iostream.h file in your program at that point.

Susan: So then this header is declaring that all you are going to be doing is input and output?

Steve: Not exactly. It tells the compiler how to understand input and output via << and >>. Each header tells the compiler how to interpret some type of library functions; iostream.h is the one for input and output.

Susan: Where is the word iostream derived from? (Okay, io, but what about stream?)

Steve: A stream is C++ talk for "a place to get or put characters". A given stream is usually either an istream (input stream) or an ostream (output stream). As these names suggest, you can read from an istream or write to an ostream.

Susan: Second, is the \n really necessary here, or would the program work without it?

Steve: It's optional; however, if you want to use it, the \n should be inside the quotes, since it's used to control the appearance of the output. It can't do that if it's not sent to cout. Without the \n, the user would type the answer to the question on the same line as the question; with the \n, the answer would be typed on the next line, as the \n would cause the active screen position to move to the next line at the end of the question.

Susan: Okay, that is good, since I intended for the weight to be typed on a different line. Now I understand this much better. As far as why I didn't include the \n inside the quotes, I can't tell you other than the time of night I was writing or it was an oversight or a typo. I was following your examples and I am not a stickler for details type person.

Now that that's settled, I have another question: Is "return 0" the same thing as an ENTER on the keyboard with nothing left to process?

Steve: Sort of. It means that you're done with whatever processing you were doing and are returning control to the operating system (the C: prompt).

Susan: How does the program handle the ENTER? I don't see where it comes into the programs you have written. It just seems that at the end of any pause that an ENTER would be appropriate. So is the ENTER something that is part of the compiler that it just knows that by the way the code is written an ENTER will necessarily come next?

Steve: The istream input mechanism lets you type until you hit an ENTER, then takes the result up to that point.

One more point. We never tell the user that we have received the information. I've added that to your example.

Figure 4.22 illustrates the compiler's output for that erroneous program.

FIGURE 4.22. Error messages from the erroneous weight program (code\morbas02.cc)

```
morbas02.cc: In function 'int main()':
morbas02.cc:7: stray '\' in program
morbas02.cc:11: parse error before 'return'
```

And Figure 4.23 shows the corrected program.

FIGURE 4.23. The corrected weight program (code\morbas03.cc)

```cpp
#include  <iostream.h>

int main()
{
    short weight;

    cout << "Please write your weight here: ";

    cin >> weight;

    cout << "I wish I only weighed " << weight << " pounds.";

    return 0;
}
```

4. This was an offshoot of the previous question, which occurred when Susan wondered when the program in Figure 4.23 would terminate. Let's start from that point in the conversation:

Susan: Would this only run once? If so how would you get it to repeat?

Steve: We could use a while loop. Let's suppose that we wanted to add up all the weights that were entered. Then the program might look like Figure 4.24.

FIGURE 4.24. The weight totalling program (code\morbas04.cc)

```
#include <iostream.h>
int main()
{
    short weight;
    short total;

    cout << "Please type in your weight, typing 0 to end:";
    cin >> weight;

    total = weight;

    while (weight > 0)
        {
        cout << "Please type in your weight, typing 0 to end:";
        cin >> weight;
        total = total + weight;
        }

    cout << "The total is: " << total << endl;
    return 0;
}
```

In case you were wondering, the reason we have to duplicate the statements to read in the weight is that we need an initial value for the variable weight before we start the while loop so that the condition in the while will be calculated correctly.

By the way, there's another way to write the statement

```
total = total + weight;
```

that uses an operator analogous to ++, the increment operator: total += weight;. This new operator, += operator, means "add what's on the *right* to what's on the *left*". The motivation for this shortcut, as you might imagine, is the same as that for ++: It requires less typing, is more likely to be correct, and is easier to compile to efficient code. Just like the "increment memory" instruction, many machines have an "add (something) to memory" instruction, and it's easier to figure out that such an instruction should be used for an expression like x += y than in the case of the equivalent x = x + y. Let's see what Susan has to say about this notation:

Susan: Now I did find something that was very confusing. You say that += means to "add what's on the right to what's on the left" but your example shows that it is the other way around. Unless this is supposed to be mirror imaged or something, I don't get it.

Steve: No, the example is correct. total += weight; is the same as total = total + weight;, so we're adding the value on the right of the += (i.e., weight) to the variable on the left (i.e., total). Is that clearer now?

Susan: Okay, I think I got it now, I guess if it were more like an equation, you would have to subtract total from the other side when you moved it. Why is it that the math recollection that I have instead of helping me just confuses me?

Steve: Because, unfortunately, the = is the same symbol used to mean "is equal to" in mathematics. The = in C++ means something completely different: "set the thing on the left to the value on the right".

Running this program normally isn't likely to give you much information, so you might want to run it under control of the debugger. You can do this in exactly the same way as you did the previous two programs, except that you would type RHIDE morbas04 to start.

CHAPTER 5

Functional Literacy

C++ was intended to be useful in writing large programs. Such programs are usually composed of many *implementation files*, as I mentioned in Chapter 3.

In such a case, we must have some way of creating an executable program (sometimes abbreviated to just an *executable*) from a number of implementation files. We also need some way for code in one module to refer to code in another one. Similarly, we have to be able to specify where execution of our program should start; this is taken care of by the C++ rule that execution always starts at the block called main.

As we've already seen, the computer can't execute source code. Therefore, any implementation files we write have to be translated into *object code*; the result of such translation is an *object code module*. One other kind of module we're interested in is the *library module*, which contains the object code from several implementation files.

The idea of various types of modules led to the following discussion with Susan:

Susan: So an object file is like some kind of interface between your code and the binary numbers of the machine? I am confused.

Steve: Each implementation file is translated by the compiler into one object file. Then these object files will be combined along with some previously prepared library files, to make an executable program.

Susan: iostreams is a library? So are these already written programs that you can refer to like a real library?

Steve: Yes.

Susan: The libraries contain code segments that are generalized, and the other modules contain code segments that are program specific?

Steve: Right. One point that should be emphasized, though, is that a library contains object code, not source code.

Susan: Where is the library? I am serious.

Steve: You can have more than one library, including ones written for more specialized purposes by different companies. The main library for the djgpp compiler is in a file called libgpp.a, which is in the DJGPP/lib subdirectory. However, the name of the main library file is dependent on which compiler you're using; in some cases, the library code is broken down into more than one file.

Susan: So what is an "implementation file"? Is it a set of code written by the programmer?

Steve: It's a file containing part of a program, in source code. Most significant programs consist of a number of modules (files), rather than one big module (file), partly because it's easier to find and edit one logical segment of a program than a whole bunch of code all in one big file.

Susan: Okay then, so a module is just a big logical segment? How is it delineated from the rest of the program? Is it named? How do you find it? Can you just tell by looking where a module starts and ends?

Steve: A module, in C++ terminology, is a file. Therefore, an implementation module is an implementation file, which contains program statements. It has a name, which is the name of the file.

Susan: So an implementation file is like a library, only as we have discussed it is more specific than a library; it is for the program that you are working on?

Steve: Right.

Susan: Where are these modules and how do they get there?

Steve: Wherever you (or whoever wrote the code) put them. In the case of your "weight-writing" program, the code you wrote is in an implementation file. That module is compiled to make an object code module, which is then combined with other object code modules that I have written, and library module(s) that come with the compiler, to make an executable file that can be run.

Susan: So then the implementation file is a "miniprogram" within a program that holds the source code to be later compiled?

Steve: It contains part of the source code of a program, which needs to be compiled and combined with other previously compiled code before it can be used. I think that's the same as what you're saying.

Actually, I've misused C++ terminology a little here in the interests of comprehensibility. The term *block* isn't quite correct as applied to main(); the correct term is *function*. Let's take a look at the difference between these two concepts, some other related definitions, and the objectives for this chapter.

Definitions

An **implementation file** is a file that contains source code for a program. Almost every part of every program starts out as an implementation file.

Compilation of an implementation file produces a file called an **object code module** (or **object file**), which contains object (machine) code.

Several object code modules of a generally useful nature can be combined to make a file called a **library module**, usually abbreviated to **library**.

A **block** is a section of code that acts like one statement, as far as the language is concerned; that is, wherever a statement can occur, a block can be substituted, and it will be treated as one statement for the purposes of program organization.

A **function** is also a section of code, but its characteristics are different from those of a block. For one thing, you can't substitute a function for a statement; also, a function has a name, whereas blocks are anonymous. This name enables one function to start execution of another one.

A **function call** (or just "call" for short) causes execution to be transferred temporarily from the current function to the one named in the call.

A **called function** is a function that starts execution as a result of a function call.

A **calling function** is a function that suspends execution as a result of a function call.

A return statement is the mechanism used by a called function to return to the calling function, which picks up just where it left off.

Objectives of This Chapter

By the end of this chapter, you should

1. Understand how and when to use functions to reduce the amount of code you have to write.

2. Understand what software really is.

3. Understand how your source code is turned into an executable program.

4. Understand how storage is assigned to different types of variables.

5. Understand how functions can call one another.

Functioning Normally

Susan had a question about this new notion of a function, as related to modules:

> **Susan:** So a module has nothing to do with blocks and functions? If a function only "calls" another function, then how do you call a module?

> **Steve:** You can't call a module. In fact, although a few language features apply to modules rather than functions, modules don't really have much significance in C++ other than as places to store related functions.

When we call a function, we usually have to provide it with input (for example, some values to be averaged) and it usually produces output which we use in further processing (for example, the average of the input values). Some functions, though, have only one or the other. For example, some functions are organized in pairs consisting of one **storage function** and one **retrieval function**; the first stores data for the second to retrieve later. In that case, the storage function may not give us anything back when we call it, and the retrieving function may not need any input from us.

To see how and why we might use a function, let's take a look at a program having some duplicated code (Figure 5.1).

FIGURE 5.1. A sample program with duplicated code (code\nofunc.cc)

```cpp
#include <iostream.h>

int main()
{
    short FirstWeight;
    short SecondWeight;
    short FirstAge;
    short SecondAge;
    short AverageWeight;
    short AverageAge;

    cout << "Please type in the first weight: ";
    cin >> FirstWeight;

    cout << "Please type in the second weight: ";
    cin >> SecondWeight;

    AverageWeight = (FirstWeight + SecondWeight) / 2;

    cout << "Please type in the first age: ";
    cin >> FirstAge;

    cout << "Please type in the second age: ";
```

```
    cin >> SecondAge;

    AverageAge = (FirstAge + SecondAge) / 2;

    cout << "The average weight was: " << AverageWeight << endl;
    cout << "The average age was: " << AverageAge << endl;

    return 0;
}
```

I'd like you to look particularly at this line,

```
    AverageWeight = (FirstWeight + SecondWeight) / 2;
```

and this one,

```
    AverageAge = (FirstAge + SecondAge) / 2;
```

These two lines are awfully similar; the only difference between them is that one of them averages two weights and the other averages two ages. While this particular example doesn't take too much code to duplicate, it may not be too difficult for you to imagine the inefficiency and nuisance of having to copy and edit many lines of code every time we want to do exactly the same thing with different data. Instead of copying the code and editing it to change the name of the variables, we can write a function that averages whatever data we give it.

Figure 5.2 is a picture of a function call. The calling function (**1**) is main; the function call is at position (**2**). The called function is Average (**3**), and the return is at position (**4**); the returned value is stored in the variable AvgAge, as indicated by the assignment operator = in the statement

```
    AvgAge = Average(FirstAge,SecondAge);
```

and the calling function, main, resumes execution at line (**5**).

FIGURE 5.2. A function call

```
short Average(short First, short Second) //(3)
{
  short Result;
  Result = (First + Second)/2;
  return Result; //(4)
}


int main() //(1)
{
  short FirstAge;
  short SecondAge;
  short AvgAge;
  FirstAge = 5;
  SecondAge = 9;

  AvgAge = Average(FirstAge, SecondAge); //(2)
  cout << AvgAge << endl; //(5)
  return 0;
}
```

By the way, it's important to distinguish between returning a value from a function, which is optional, and returning control from a called function to the calling function, which always happens at the end of the called function (unless the program has terminated due to an error in the called function).[1]

While we're on the subject of the calling function, in case you're wondering why we started the example at the beginning of main, it's because every C++ program starts executing at that point. When the main function calls another function, such as Average, then main is suspended until Average is finished. When Average finishes, main resumes where it left off.

This isn't limited to one "level" of calls. The same thing can happen if Average (for example) calls another function, let's say Funcx; Average will wait until Funcx returns before continuing. Then when Average finishes, it will return to main, which will take up where it left off.

This idea of calling and returning from functions led to the following discussion with Susan:

> **Susan:** So if you wanted to be really mean you could get into someone's work in progress and stick a return somewhere in the middle of it and it would end the program right there? Now that I am thinking about it, I am sure you could do a whole lot worse than that. Of course, I would never do such a thing, but what I am saying is that whatever you are doing when the program gets to the return statement, then it is *the end*? Next stop, C:\?

> **Steve:** If you're in the main program, then a return statement means "back to the DOS prompt". If you're in a function other than main, it means "back to the function that called this function". In the case of a function that returns a value, the expression in the return statement tells the compiler what value to use in place of the function call. For example, the statement AvgAge = Average(i,j); sets AvgAge to the result in the return statement of the function Average. As you can see by looking at that function, the returned value is the average of the two input values, so that is the value that AvgAge is set to by this statement.

---

1. If you don't provide a return statement in a function that you're calling, then the called function will just return to the calling function when it gets to its closing }. However, this is not legal for a function that is defined to return a value. This of course leads to the question of why we'd call a function that doesn't return a value. One possibility is that the function exists only to produce output on the screen, rather than to return any results. The actions that a function performs other than returning a value are called ***side effects***.

Susan: Okay, but what about the return 0; at the end of the main program? Why should it be 0?

Steve: The return statement in the main program can return a different value if you wish. However, the custom is to return 0 from the main program to mean "everything went well" and some value greater than 0 to mean "there's a problem". This isn't entirely arbitrary, because a batch file can test that return value and use it to alter the flow of execution of commands in the batch file.

Susan: Okay, let's see if I have this right: The return statement has to match the main statement. This is so confusing. Look, when you say "The value that is returned, 0, is an acceptable value of the type we declared in the line int main ()" — since I see no 0 anywhere around int main () — you are referring to the int. An int can have a value of 0, right?

Steve: Right, the 0 has to match the int. That's because a function can have a return type, just like the type of a variable. In this case, int is the type of the main function, and the value is filled in by the return statement.

Susan: Okay, then all this is saying is that the value that is produced is the same type as that declared at the beginning of a program. Since we declared the type of main as an int, if the value produced were a letter or a picture of a cow, then you would get an error message?

Steve: Well, actually a letter (i.e., a char) would be acceptable as an int, due to rules left over from C. Otherwise, you're exactly correct.

Susan: Hey, where is the 0 coming from to be returned?

Steve: It's specified as a literal value in the return statement; you could put any legal int value in there instead, if you wanted to.

Susan: So the return value doesn't have to be a 0?

Steve: Right.

Susan: So 0 could be another int value, but it can't be a variable? Even I don't know what I am talking about now!

Steve: I think I've confused you unnecessarily. You can certainly return a value that is specified as a variable, such as return i;. What I meant was that the 0 we're returning in this case is a constant, not a variable.

Susan: The picture helps with the calling confusion. But I don't understand why int main is the calling function if the calling function suspends execution. How can you initiate a function if it starts out suspended? But I am serious.

Steve: The main function starts execution as the first function in your program. Therefore, it isn't suspended unless and until it calls another function.

Above Average

I think it's time for a more detailed example of how we would use a function. Suppose we want to average sets of two numbers and we don't want to write the averaging code more than once. The Average function just illustrated provides this service; its input is the two numbers we want to average, and its output is the average. Figure 5.3 shows the code for the function Average without all the lines and arrows:

FIGURE 5.3. A function to average two values

```
short Average(short First, short Second)
  {
  short Result;
```

```
Result = (First + Second) / 2;

return Result;
}
```

Assuming that you've installed the software from the CD-ROM in the back of this book, you can try out this function in a running program.[2] First, you have to compile it by changing to the code subdirectory under the main directory where you installed the software, and typing RHIDE func1, then using the "Make" command from the "Compile" menu. Then exit back to DOS and type func1 to run the program.

To run it under the debugger, make sure you are in the code subdirectory, and then type RHIDE func1. Again, do *not* add the ".cc" to the end of the file name. Once RHIDE has started up, you can step through the program by hitting F8, which will treat any function call as one statement, or by hitting F7, which will step into any function call. Any time you want to see the display that the user would see when running the program normally, hit ALT-F5, then ENTER to get back to the debugger.[3] As had become routine, I couldn't sneak this idea (of writing a function) past Susan without a discussion.

Susan: Where you say "and we don't want to write the averaging code more than once", are you just saying if you didn't do the

---

2. If you want to see the whole program that this function is used in, it's in Figure 5.5 on page 235.

3. Please don't be confused by the seemingly random values that all of the variables start out with when tracing the program. These are just the garbage values that happen to be lying around in memory where those variables reside; as we've already seen, variables that haven't yet been assigned a value are called *uninitialized variables*. The variables in this program are all initialized before they are used, but the tracing program starts to display them before the initializing statements have been executed; therefore, they appear uninitialized at the beginning of the trace. We'll see later in this chapter exactly why we have to initialize all of our variables before we use them.

Average function thing then you would have to write this program twice? I mean for example would you have to write a program separately for weights and then another one from the beginning for ages?

Steve: We wouldn't have to write an entirely separate program; however, we would have to write the averaging code twice. One of the main purposes for writing a function is so that we don't have to repeat code.

To analyze this piece of code, let's start at the beginning. Every function starts with a **function declaration**, which tells the compiler some vital statistics of the function. The function declaration consists of three parts:

1. A *return type*;

2. The function's name;

3. An *argument list*.

In the case of our Average function, the function declaration is short Average(short First, short Second). The return type is short, the name of the function is Average, and the argument list is (short First, short Second). Let's take these one at a time.

Return to Sender

The first part of the function declaration is the **return type**, in this case short. This indicates that the function Average will provide a value of type short to the calling function when the Average function returns. Looking at the end of the function, you will see a statement that says return Result;. Checking back to the variable definition part of the function, we see that Result is indeed a short, so the value we're returning is of the correct type. If that were not the case, the compiler would tell us that we had a discrepancy between the declared return type of our function and the type actually returned in the code. This is another example where the compiler helps us out with *static type checking*, as mentioned in Chapter 3; if we say we want to return a short and then return some other incompatible type such as a string, we've made a mistake.[4] It's much easier for the compiler to catch this and warn us than it is for us to locate the error ourselves when the program doesn't work correctly.

Susan wanted to know more about the return type. Here's the conversation that ensued:

> **Susan:** This return type thing — it will have to be the same type of value as the output is?

> **Steve:** For our purposes here, the answer is yes. As I've already mentioned, there are exceptions to this rule, but we won't need to worry about them.

> **Susan:** Do you always use the word return when you write a function?

> **Steve:** Yes, except that some functions have no return value. They don't have to have an explicit return statement, but can just "fall off the end" of the function, which acts like a return; statement. This is considered poor form, though; it's better to have a return statement.

The function name (in this case, Average) follows the same rules as a variable name. This is not a coincidence, because both function names and variable names are *identifiers*, which is a fancy word for "user defined names". The rules for constructing an identifier are pretty simple, as specified in the *C++ Draft Standard*: "An identifier

---

4. What do I mean by an *incompatible type*? C++ has rules that, for example, allow us to return a char variable where a short (or an int) is expected; the compiler will convert the char into either of those types for us automatically. This is convenient sometimes, but it reduces the chances of catching an error of this kind, and therefore is less safe than it could be. This practice is a legacy from C, which means that it can't be changed for practical reasons, even though it is less than desirable theoretically.

is an arbitrarily long sequence of letters and digits. The first character is a letter; the underscore _ counts as a letter. Upper- and lower-case letters are different. All characters are significant." In other words:

1. Your identifiers can be as long as you wish. The the compiler is required to distinguish between two identifiers, no matter how many identical characters they contain, as long as at least one character is different in the two names.[5]

2. They can be made of any combination of letters and digits, as long as the first character is a letter. For historical reasons, the underscore character _ counts as a letter.[6]

3. The upper and lower case versions of the same character aren't considered equal as far as names are concerned; that is, the variable xyz is a different variable from Xyz, while XYZ is yet another variable. Of course, *you* may get confused by having three variables with those names, but the compiler considers them all distinct.

By the way, the reason that the first character of an identifier can't be a digit is to make it easier for the compiler to figure out what's a number and what isn't. Another rule is that user defined names cannot conflict with names defined by the C++ language (*keywords*); some examples of keywords that we've already seen are if and short.

Finally, we have the **argument list**. In this case, it contains two *arguments*, a short called First, which holds the first number that our Average function uses to calculate its result; the second argument (also a short) is called Second, which of course is the other number needed to calculate the average. In other cases, there might be several

---

5. You don't have to worry about wasting space in your program by using long identifiers. They go away when your program is compiled and are replaced by addresses of the variables or functions to which they refer.

6. You should avoid starting your variable or function names with an underscore, as such names are "reserved" for use by compiler writers and other language implementers.

entries in the argument list, each of which provides some information to the called function. But what exactly *is* an argument?

For the Sake of Argument

The question of what is an argument is more subtle than it may appear. An argument is a value that is supplied by a function (the *calling function*) that wishes to use the services of another function (the *called function*). For example, the calling function might be our main function, and the called function might be our Average function, while the arguments are two short values to be averaged. Arguments like the ones here are actually copies of values from the calling function; that is, the compiler will initialize the variable named in the argument list of the called function to the value supplied by the calling function. This process of making a copy of the calling function's argument is referred to as *call by value*, and the resulting copy is called a **value argument**.[7] Figure 5.4 is an example of this argument passing mechanism at work with only one argument.

FIGURE 5.4. Argument passing with one argument (code\birthday.cc)

```
#include <iostream.h>

short Birthday(short age)
{
  age ++;
  return age;
}

int main()
{
```

---

7.   This discussion might make you wonder whether there's another type of argument besides a value argument. There is, and we'll find out about it in Chapter 6.

```
short x;
short y;

x = 46;
y = Birthday(x);

cout << "Your age was: " << x << endl;
cout << "Happy Birthday: your age is now " << y << endl;

return 0;
}
```

In this program, main sets x to 46 and then calls Birthday with x as the argument. When Birthday starts, a new variable called age is created, and set to 46, because that's the value of x, the argument with which main called Birthday. Birthday adds one to its variable age, and then returns the new value of that variable to main. What number will be printed for the variable age by the line cout << "Your age was: " << x << endl;? Answer: 46, because the variable age in Birthday was a *copy* of the argument from main, not the actual variable x named in the call to Birthday. On the other hand, the value of y in the main program will be 47, because that is the return value from Birthday.

As you might have guessed, the notion of copying the argument when a function is called occasioned an intense conversation with Susan.

> **Susan:** This is tough. I don't get it at all. Does this mean the value of the short named x will then be copied to another location in the function named Birthday?

> **Steve:** Yes, the value in the short named x will be copied to another short called age before the execution of the first line in the function Birthday. This means that the original value of x in main won't be affected by anything that Birthday does.

> **Susan:** Now for the really confusing part. I don't understand where you say "An argument like the one here (short age) is actually a

copy of a value in the calling function". Now, I have read this over and over and nothing helped. I thought I understood it for a second or two and then I would lose it; finally I have decided that there is very little in this section that I do understand. Help.

Steve: When you write a function, the normal behavior of the compiler is to insert code at the beginning of the function to make a copy of the data that the calling function supplies. This copy of the data is what the called function actually refers to, not the original. Therefore, if you change the value of an argument, it doesn't do anything to the original data in the calling function.

If you (the programmer of the function) actually want to refer to the data in the calling function and not a copy of it, you can specify this when you write the function. There are cases in which this makes sense, and we'll see some of them in Chapter 6.

Susan: I don't understand why it is a copy of the calling function and not the called function.

Steve: It's not a copy of the calling function; it's a copy of the value from the calling function, for the use of the called function. In the sample program, main sets x to 46 and then calls Birthday with x as the argument. When Birthday starts, a new variable called age is created, and set to 46, because that's the value of x, the argument with which main called Birthday. Birthday adds 1 to its variable age, and returns the new value of age to main. What will be printed by the line "cout << x << endl;"? Answer: 46, because the variable age in Birthday was a *copy* of the value of the argument from main, not the actual variable (x) specified in the call to Birthday. Does this explanation clarify this point?

Susan: I still don't understand the program. It doesn't make any sense. If x = 46, then it will always be 46 no matter what is going on in the called function. So why call a function? You know what, I think my biggest problem is that I don't understand the argument list. I think that is where I am hung up on this.

Steve: The arguments to the function call (x, in the case of the function call Birthday(x)) are transferred to the value of the argument in the function itself (the short variable age, in the case of the function Birthday(short age)).

Susan: In that case, why bother putting an x there, why just not put 46? Would it not do the same thing in the called function, since it is already set to 46?

Steve: Yes, but what if you wanted to call this function from another place where the value was 97 rather than 46? The reason that the argument is a variable is so you can use whatever value you want.

Susan: If we called Birthday with the value 46, then the 46 would be 46++, right?

Steve: 46++ is a syntax error, because you can't change the value of a literal constant. Only a variable can be modified.

Susan: So if you want to state a literal value, do you always have to declare a variable first and then set a variable to that literal value?

Steve: No, sometimes you can use a literal value directly without storing it in a variable. For example,

cout << 15;

or

cout << "Hello, my name is Steve Heller";

What I was trying to say is that you can't *change* a literal value. Thus, 15++; is not legal because a literal value such as 15 represents itself, that is, the value 15. If you could write 15++;, what should it do? Change all occurrences of 15 to 16 in the program?

Susan: I get that. Now, how does age get initialized to the value of x?

Steve: The compiler does that when it starts the function, because you have declared in the function declaration that the argument to the function is called age, and you have called the function with an argument called x. So the compiler copies the value from x into age right before it starts executing the function.

Susan: Oh, okay. That makes sense, because maybe later on you want to call the same function again and change only a little part of it, but you still need the original to be the same, so you can just change the copy instead of the original. Is that the purpose?

Steve: The reason that the called function gets a copy of data rather than the original is so that the person writing the calling function knows that the original variable hasn't been changed by calling a function. This makes it easier to create programs by combining your own functions with functions that have already been written (such as in the library). Is that what you meant?

Susan: So is everything copied? I am getting confused again, are you going to talk a little more about copying in the book? Have I just not gotten there? Anyway, if you haven't mentioned this more, I think you should, it explains hidden stuff.

Steve: Don't worry, we're going to go into *much* more detail about how this works. In fact, it's a major topic in the rest of the book.

General Delivery

The same analysis that we have just applied to the Birthday function applies also to the Average function that we started out with; the arguments First and Second are copies of the values specified in the call to Average.

Now that we have accounted for the Average function's input and output, we can examine how it does its work. First, we have a variable definition for Result, which will hold the value we will return to the calling function; namely, the average of the two input values.

Then we calculate that average, with the statement

Result = (First + Second) / 2;

Once the average has been calculated, we're ready to return it to the calling program, which is accomplished by the line return Result;. Finally, we reach the closing }, which tells the compiler that the function is done.

Using a Function

Now that we have seen how to write the Average function, let's see how to use it to solve our original problem. The program in Figure 5.5 uses our Average function twice, once to average two weights, and once to average two ages.

FIGURE 5.5. Using the Average function (code\func1.cc)

```cpp
#include <iostream.h>

short Average(short First, short Second)
{
    short Result;

    Result = (First + Second) / 2;

    return Result;
}

int main()
```

```
{
    short FirstWeight;
    short SecondWeight;
    short FirstAge;
    short SecondAge;
    short AverageWeight;
    short AverageAge;

    cout << "Please type in the first weight: ";
    cin >> FirstWeight;

    cout << "Please type in the second weight: ";
    cin >> SecondWeight;

    AverageWeight = Average(FirstWeight, SecondWeight);

    cout << "Please type in the first age: ";
    cin >> FirstAge;

    cout << "Please type in the second age: ";
    cin >> SecondAge;

    AverageAge = Average(FirstAge, SecondAge);

    cout << "The average weight was: " << AverageWeight << endl;
    cout << "The average age was: " << AverageAge << endl;

    return 0;
}
```

As always, calling a function requires specifying its name and its argument(s) and doing something with the return value, if any. In this case, we call Average with the arguments FirstWeight and SecondWeight, and store the result in AverageWeight. This is accomplished via the line AverageWeight = Average(FirstWeight,

SecondWeight);. Later, we call Average with the arguments FirstAge and SecondAge, and store the result in AverageAge. We do this via the line AverageAge = Average(FirstAge, SecondAge);.

The value of writing a function to average two numbers wasn't obvious to Susan at first. After some discussion, however, she agreed that it was valuable. Here's the conversation that convinced her:

> **Susan:** In general, I just don't understand why you even need to call the Average function in the first place; it looks like extra steps to me. It seems to me that all you need are your two input values, which end up just giving you the results right there for weight and age. I think that this is what bothers me the most. For example, when you get done with the set of weights, you should just have your results right then and there instead of calling the function of Average.

> **Steve:** But what is the result you want? You want the average of the weights. Where is that calculated?

> **Susan:** After you are done with that, then you already have written a set of ages so you can just use the result of that. It just seems like you are going in circles unnecessarily with this program. That is why I don't understand it.

> **Steve:** Again, just because you have a set of ages doesn't mean that you have the average age; some code somewhere has to calculate that average.

Susan still had a lot of trouble with visualizing the way this function worked. However, running it in "trace" mode got her moving again, resulting in the following discussion:

> **Susan:** Why does everything start out initialized to 0 except Result, which appears to hold an address in memory?

> **Steve:** The values of uninitialized variables are not reliable. In this case, I'm getting a similar value of Result to the one you're getting;

however, you cannot count on this. There's also no reason to think that the contents of Result are a memory address; they're just garbage until the variable is initialized.

Susan: Steve, I don't understand this; first you tell me that those numbers are garbage but represent addresses in memory and now you tell me that they are just garbage, but that they are not reliable. I don't understand, if they are uninitialized, how they ever *could* be reliable. This implies that at some time you could get an expected value even if they are uninitialized. They should always be garbage. So, when do those numbers represent memory addresses and when not?

Steve: Apparently I've confused you unnecessarily again. Here are the facts:

1. The contents of an uninitialized variable are garbage.

2. Since they are garbage, they represent nothing.

3. Since they are garbage, they can have any value, which may or may not appear to have meaning. Regardless of appearances, the value of an uninitialized variable is meaningless.

Then our discussion returned to the topic of how the main program works:

Susan: Oh, okay, so AverageWeight = Average(FirstWeight, SecondWeight); is the part that starts the Average function running?

Steve: Right.

Susan: Then after averaging the weights, why does Result go to 0? It looks to me that Result has no value at these points and I don't understand why.

Steve: Because you're looking at the next call to Average, where its variable Result is uninitialized again. By default, variables are uninitialized whenever they are created, which occurs each time the function where they "live" is entered. The "old" Result from the first call to Average "died" when the first call to Average was finished, and the new Result that is created on the second call is uninitialized until we set it to some known value.

The next topic we discussed was how to create a new program and get it to run.

Susan: Now when you start out a new program; are all the new implementation files named with a .cc extension?

Steve: Yes.

Susan: So this code in Average is where the real averaging takes place, right? Is this the "Average command"? I thought Average meant to average, so what is the deal?

Steve: The deal is that something has to do the averaging; rather than writing the same code every time we need to average another set of two numbers, we put that code in one place (the Average function) and call it whenever we need its assistance.

Susan: Okay, then this brings up another one of my questions. How come you write the Average function before the main function?

Steve: So that the main function knows how to call the Average function. There's another way to allow a function to call another one that doesn't come before it in the file, but I thought it was easier to show it this way at first.

Susan: If the main function is going to be executed first, then how come the Average function is written first? Does the compiler always look for main first?

Steve: Yes.

Susan: Yeah, but could the Average function then just be written after main instead of before it? Just to be there when it is needed, instead of before it is needed? Am I right that you still would not have to write it twice; it would still be there for the next time it is needed, right?

Steve: The Average function can be anywhere, even in a different module, but at the point that you try to use it, the compiler has to know about it; to be precise, you have to specify its name, return type, and what arguments it takes. Otherwise, the program won't compile. On the other hand, the compiled version of the Average function doesn't have to be available until the executable is created;[8] if it's not available at that point, you'll get an error saying that you have referenced an undefined function.

Susan: So does that mean you could put the Average function anywhere you want? Then could it or any "subfunction" be put anywhere you want because the main function would always be executed first? Or could you mess up the code if you put it in a really ridiculous place like inside an output or input statement. . . or could the compiler be able to ignore something like that and go about business as usual? I guess because of the brackets it should ignore such a thing but I am not sure. See, these are the things that we novices are obliged to ponder.

Steve: You can't start a function definition in the middle of another function. That's called a *nested function* and it's not allowed in C++. The rule can be stated approximately as "You can start a function definition anywhere except in the middle of another definition."

8.　This is done by the *linker*, which we'll get to later in this chapter.

Susan: So then the "cue" for the Average function to begin is the word Average (weight) or (age), when the compiler sees that word it just begins that separate function to start its little calculation.

Steve: That's right, except that it needs two arguments, not just one.

Susan: And that function since it was named Average causes the averaging function to work. Is that how it goes?

Steve: If I understand your question, it's not the name that makes the Average function do the averaging, it's the code that adds up the two values and divides by 2. We could replace all the references to Average with the word Glorp and the compiler wouldn't care; however, a future programmer trying to read the program probably wouldn't be amused by that name.

Susan: Oh, so there is nothing magical about the word Average, I thought it might trigger a function of averaging. Well, that sounds reasonable; it's more for us humans than the computer. And then that brings up another question, along the same line of thinking. After the Average function has done its thing, how does the program go from return Result; to the next output statement that asks for the ages? What triggers that change? I am not seeing this in the code.

Steve: The return keyword tells the compiler to hand back control to the function that called the one where the return is, as indicated in Figure 5.2.

This discussion didn't slake her thirst for knowledge about how to write a program. Here is how we continued:

Susan: Can I mix shorts with strings using the headers that are already stated in the test program?

Steve: Mixing shorts with strings is a dubious proposition, sort of like adding apples and oranges together; could you be more specific about what you're trying to do?

Susan: What if you wanted to add a numerical value to your program such as test: You have to put in a short, right? So if you added a short, what else would you have to do to make it work? Or would you have to start over with another main function after the first part and then declare new variables? I tried that too, and the compiler did not like that either. Very inflexible it is. I will tell you after one more try what I am doing. This will keep you in suspense.

Steve: It depends on what you're trying to do with the short. It's usually best to have a specific problem in mind that you're trying to solve by writing a program. Then you may see how to use these facilities (shorts, strings, vectors, etc.) to solve your problem; if not, you can ask me how they would fit into the solution.

As for your second suggestion, you're not allowed to have more than one main function in a program, because the compiler wouldn't know which one to use as the starting address for the program.

Susan: I am not really trying to solve anything, I just want to have the user type in more info and that info is a number — wait!! That is it, in that case it will be like an ASCII character and it doesn't need a short, right? That's right. I can still use a string. We are not crunching any numbers with this.

Steve: As long as you don't try to do any calculations, you can read the data into a string, even data that looks like a number; of course, that data entry method is pretty loose, since if the user types "abc" as an age, the program will accept it.

Susan: Can you define a string without a word but with just a wildcard type of variable like when we use i in shorts? In other words, does it matter what we call a variable?

Steve: A variable is always a "wildcard", whether it's a short or a string. For example, a **short** variable always has a name, such as i, or **index**, or whatever makes sense to you, and a value, which is a number such as 14 or 99. A **string** variable also has a name, such as **FirstName**, or **street**, or whatever makes sense to you, and a value, which consists of characters rather than a number, such as "Susan" or "Wesley".

A Convincing Argument

As you can see, using a function isn't very difficult. We have to provide it with the material to work on (its input arguments) and can store its return value in a variable for further processing (or use it directly, if we wish). But there's a little more here than meets the eye. How does the variable FirstWeight, for example, get transformed into the variable First that we used when writing the function?

This explanation requires us to to look at some more underlying software technology: To be precise, we're going to spend some time examining the infrastructure that makes computers usable for programmers. First, though, we have to consider a more general notion, that of a "virtual computer".

The Man behind the Curtain

Unlike many words in the vocabulary of computing, *virtual* has more or less retained its standard English definition: "That is so in essence or effect, although not formally or actually; admitting of being called by the name so far as the effect or result is concerned."[9] In other words, a virtual computer would be something that acts just like a computer, but really isn't one. Who would want such a thing?

---

9. *Oxford English Dictionary*, first current definition (4).

Apparently everyone, since *virtual computer* is just another name for what we have been calling *software*. This may seem a rash statement, but it really isn't. One of the most important mathematical discoveries (inventions?) of the twentieth century was Alan Turing's demonstration that it was possible to create a fairly simple computing device (called a *Turing machine* for some reason) that could imitate *any* other computing device. This machine works in the following way: You provide it with a description of the other computer you want it to imitate, and it follows those directions. Suppose we want a computer that calculates only trigonometric functions. Then we could theoretically write a set of instructions as to how such a computer would behave, feed it into a Turing machine, and have the Turing machine imitate the behavior of this theoretical "trigonometric computer".

This is undoubtedly interesting, but you may be wondering what it has to do with programming. Well, what do we do when we write a program? In the case of our pumpkin weighing program, we're describing the actions that would be taken by a hypothetical "pumpkin weighing computer". When we run the program, the real computer simulates these actions. In other words, we have created a virtual pumpkin weighing computer.

The same analysis applies to any program. A program can most fundamentally be defined as instructions to a "universal computer", telling it how to simulate the specialized computer you actually want to use. When the universal computer executes these instructions, it behaves exactly as the hypothetical specialized computer would.

Of course, real computers aren't really universal; they have limits in the amount of memory or disk space they contain and the speed of their execution. However, for problems that can be solved within those limits, they are truly universal computing devices that can be tailored to a particular problem by programming.

The Object of My Affections

Now let's take a look at one of these areas of software technology. We've already seen that the function of a compiler is to convert our human-readable C++ program into machine instructions that can be executed by the computer. However, the compiler doesn't actually produce an executable program that can stand by itself; instead, it translates each implementation file into a machine language file called an *object code module* (or *object file*). This file contains the instructions that correspond to the source code statements you've written, but not the "infrastructure" needed to allow them to be executed. We'll see what that infrastructure does for us shortly.

The creation of an object file rather than a complete executable program isn't a universal characteristic of compilers, dictated by nature. In fact, one of the most popular compilers in the early history of the PC, the Turbo Pascal™ compiler, did create an executable file directly from source code. This appears much simpler, so we have to ask why this approach has been abandoned with C++. As I've mentioned before, C++ was intended to be useful in writing large programs. Such programs can consist of hundreds or even thousands of modules (sections of source code) each containing hundreds or thousands of lines of code. Once all the modules are compiled, the object files resulting from the compilation are run through a program called the *linker*. The linker combines information from all of the object files, along with some previously prepared files called *library modules* (or *libraries*), to produce an executable program; this is called *linking* the program. One reason for this two-step approach is that we wouldn't want to have to recompile every module in a large program every time we made a change in one section; therefore, only those modules that have been affected are recompiled.[10] When all of

---

10. The alert reader may wonder why I referred to modules that have been "affected" rather than "changed". The reason is that even if we don't change a particular module, we must recompile it if a header file that it uses is changed. This is a serious maintenance problem in large systems but can be handled by special programming methods which are beyond the scope of this book.

the affected modules have been recompiled, the program is relinked to produce an updated executable.

To make such a system work, it's necessary to set up conventions as to which parts will be executed first, where data needed by more than one module will be stored, and so on. Also, a lot of operations aren't supplied as part of the language itself but are very handy in writing programs, such as the I/O functions that we've already seen. These make up the infrastructure needed to execute C++ programs.

Figure 5.6 is a picture of the process of turning source code into an executable file.

FIGURE 5.6. Making an executable

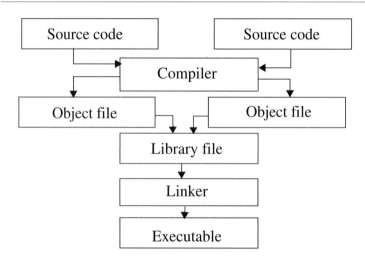

Susan found this explanation and diagram to be helpful.

Susan: This is beginning to come into focus. So you write your source code, it has a middle man called a object file and that just passes the buck over to a linker, which gathers info the program may need from the libraries, and then the program is ready to be read by the machine. Close?

Steve: Yes, very close indeed.

Operating Systematically

As is often the case in programming, this infrastructure is divided into several layers, the higher ones depending on the lower ones for more fundamental services. The lowest level of the infrastructure is supplied by the *operating system*, a program that deals with the actual hardware of your computer. By far the most common operating system for Intel CPUs, as this is written, is some variant of Microsoft Windows™, with Linux coming on strong. All of these provide some of the same facilities; for example, you are accustomed to dealing with files and directories when using application programs such as word processors and spreadsheets. However, the disk drive in your computer doesn't know anything about files or directories. As we have seen in Chapter 2, all it can do is to store and retrieve fixed-size pieces of data called *sectors*, given an absolute address on the disk described by a platter, track number, and sector number. Files are a creation of the operating system, which keeps track of which parts of which files are stored where on the disk.[11]

A modern operating system provides many more facilities than just keeping track of file storage. For example, it arranges for code and data to be stored in separate areas of RAM with different *access rights*, so that code can't be accidentally overwritten by a runaway program; that is, one that writes outside the memory areas it is supposed to use. This is a valuable service, as errors of this kind are quite difficult to find and can cause havoc when they occur.

That's the good news. The bad news is that MS-DOS, which is still the basis of all versions of Windows before Windows NT and Windows 2000, was created before the widespread availability of reasonably priced CPUs with memory protection facilities. For this

---

11. You might say that files are "virtual"; that is, they're a figment of the operating system's imagination. Nonetheless, they are quite useful. This reminds me of the story about the man who went to a doctor, complaining that his brother had thought he was a hen for many years. The doctor asked why the family hadn't tried to help the brother before, and the man replied, "We needed the eggs".

reason, when using those earlier operating systems, it's entirely possible for a runaway program to destroy anything else in memory. Theoretically, we should all be running "real" operating systems by the time you read this; so far, though, the rumors of the demise of MS-DOS have been greatly exaggerated.

This notion intrigued Susan. Here's how that conversation went:

Susan: What is a runaway program?

Steve: One that is writing in areas that it shouldn't, thus destroying data or programs outside its assigned memory areas.

Susan: How would an operating system actually separate code from data areas? Would it be a physical thing?

Steve: What makes this possible are certain hardware mechanisms built into all modern CPUs, so that certain areas of memory can be assigned to specific programs for use in predefined ways. When these mechanisms are used, a program can't write (or read, in some cases) outside its assigned area. This prevents one program from interfering with another.

Using Your Library Card

The next level of the infrastructure is supplied by the aforementioned *library modules*, which contain standardized segments of code that can perform I/O, mathematical functions, and other commonly used operations. So far, we have used the iostreams library, which provided the keyboard input and screen output in our example programs. We've also relied implicitly on the "startup" library, which sets up the conditions necessary for any C++ program to execute properly.[12]

Susan wasn't going to let me get away with this nonsense about the startup library without an explanation:

---

12. Two other libraries that we've used are the string and vector libraries.

Susan: I don't know what you are talking about when you say that we have also used a startup library. When did we do that? At startup? Well, is it something that you are actually using without knowing you are using it?

Steve: Yes. It initializes the I/O system, and generally makes the environment safe for C++ programs; they're more fragile than assembly language programs and have to have everything set up for them before they can venture out.

To understand the necessity for the startup library, we have to take a look at the way variables are assigned to memory locations. So far, we have just assumed that a particular variable had a certain address, but how is this address determined in the real world?

There are several possible ways for this to occur; the particular one employed for any given variable is determined by the variable's *storage class*. The simplest of these is the static storage class; variables of this class are assigned memory addresses in the executable program when the program is linked. The most common way to put a variable in the static storage class is to define it outside any function.[13] Such a variable will be initialized only once before main starts executing. We can specify the initial value if we wish; if we don't specify it, a default value (0 for numeric variables) will be assigned. An example of such a definition would be writing the line short x = 3; outside any function; this would cause x to be set to 3 before main starts executing. We can change the value of such a variable whenever we wish, just as with any other variable. The distinction I'm making here is that a static variable is always initialized before main begins executing. As you will see, this seemingly obvious characteristic of static variables is not shared with variables of other storage classes.

---

13. Another way to make a variable static is to state explicitly that the variable is static. However, this only works for variables defined inside functions. For the time being, we'll restrict the discussion to statically allocated variables defined outside any function.

This idea of assigning storage at link time led to the following discussion with Susan:

Susan: If you declare a variable with only one value then it isn't a variable anymore, is it?

Steve: A static variable can have its value changed, so it's a genuine variable. I was saying that it's possible to specify what its initial value should be before main starts executing.

Susan: Are you trying to say where in memory this variable is to be stored? Isn't the compiler supposed to worry about that?

Steve: I'm not specifying a location, but rather an attribute of the variable. A static variable behaves differently from the "normal" variables that we've seen up till now. One difference is that a static variable is always initialized to a known value before main starts executing.

Automatic Pilot

The notion of storage classes is essential to the solution of another mystery. You may recall that I mentioned some time ago that C++ doesn't provide automatic initialization of all variables because that facility would make a program bigger and slower. I'll admit that the truth of this isn't intuitively obvious to the casual observer; after all, a variable (or more exactly, the storage location it occupies) has to have *some* value, so why not something reasonable? As we have just seen, this *is* done for static variables. However, there is another storage class for which such a facility isn't quite as easy or inexpensive to implement;[14] that's the auto (short for "automatic") storage class,

---

14. "Inexpensive", in programming parlance, means "not using up much time and/or space".

which is the default class used for variables defined in functions. An auto variable is not initialized until the function in which it is defined starts execution and even then has no known value until we specifically assign a value to it.[15]

This notion led to a fair amount of discussion between Susan and me.

> **Susan:** Then so far I know about two types of variables, static and auto, is this correct?

> **Steve:** Right, those are the two "storage classes" that we've used so far.

> **Susan:** The auto variables are made up of garbage and the static variables are made up of something understandable, right?

> **Steve:** The auto variables are uninitialized by default, and the static variables are initialized to 0 (if they're numeric, at least).

> **Susan:** When you say that the auto class is used for functions by default does this mean you don't use static ones ever?

> **Steve:** *Default* means "what you get if you don't specify otherwise". For example, these days, if you buy almost any type of car and don't specify that you want a manual transmission, you will get an automatic.

> **Susan:** So, since we have used auto variables up to this point, then I am confused when we initialize them to a value. If we do, would that not make them static?

---

15. I'm oversimplifying a bit here. Variables can actually be declared inside any block, not just any function. An auto variable that is declared inside a block is born when the block is entered and lives until that block is finished executing. A static variable that is declared inside a block is initialized when that block is entered for the first time. It retains its value from that point on unless it is explicitly changed, as with any other statically allocated variable.

Steve: This is a difficult topic, so it's not surprising that you're having trouble. I didn't realize quite how difficult until I tried to answer your question and ended up with the essay found under the heading "Static Cling" on page 264.

Susan: How do you know what the address will be to assign to a variable? Okay, I mean this makes it sound like you, the programmer, know exactly which address in memory will be used for the variable and you assign it to that location.

Steve: You don't have to know the address; however, you do have to know that the address is fixed at link time. That's what makes it possible to initialize a static variable before main starts (if outside all functions) or just once when the function starts (if inside a function). On the other hand, auto variables can't be initialized until their functions start, because their addresses can change between executions of the function.

Susan: I am having a hard time trying to figure out what you mean by using static variables outside functions. If most of what we have been doing up to this point has been outside a function then why did you say that every variable we have used up to this point is auto? Or, I have meant to ask you this, is main really a function even if you don't have anything to call? For example, in the first pumpkin weighing program, we didn't have to call another function but I have been wondering if main is really a function that just has nothing to call? So in that case, the variables used in main would be auto?

Steve: You are correct that main is a function. To be precise, it's the first function executed in any C++ program. If it calls other functions, that's fine, but it doesn't have to. As with any other function, the variables used in main are auto by default; in the case of the pumpkin weighing program, since we didn't make any of them static, they're all auto in fact.

So far, all of our variables have been auto, and in most programs the vast majority of all variables are of this class.[16] Why should we use these variables when static ones have an initialization feature built in?

The first clue to this mystery is in the name auto. When we define a variable of the auto class, its address is assigned *auto*matically when its function is entered; the address is valid for the duration of that function.[17] Since the address of the variable isn't known until its function is entered, it can't be initialized until then, unlike the case with static variables. Therefore, if auto variables were automatically initialized, every function would have to start with some extra code to initialize every auto variable, which would make the program both slower and larger. Since Bjarne Stroustrup's design goals required that a C++ program should have the same run-time performance as a C program and as little space overhead as possible, such a feature was unacceptable. Luckily, forgetting to initialize an auto variable is something that can be detected at compile time, so it's possible for the compiler to warn us if we make this error. In general, it's a good idea to tell the compiler to warn you about dubious practices. Although not all of them may be real errors, some will be, and this is by far the fastest and best way to find them.[18]

Now we've seen why auto variables aren't initialized by default: Their addresses aren't known until entering the function in which they're defined. But that doesn't explain the advantage of assigning the addresses then. Wouldn't it be simpler (and faster) to assign them all during the linking process, as is done with static variables?

16. You may have noticed that we haven't defined any variables as auto. That's because, while auto and static are both storage classes and equivalent in that regard, there's almost never any reason to explicitly mark a variable as auto; instead, any variables defined within a function and not marked as static are set to the default class, auto.

17. This is why variables defined outside a function are static rather than auto; if they were auto, when would their addresses be assigned?

18. There are also commercial tools that help locate errors of this type, as well as other errors that can be found by analyzing the source code for inconsistencies.

Stacking the Deck

To understand why auto variables aren't assigned addresses during the linking process, we have to look at the way functions relate to one another. In particular, it is very common for a statement in one function to call another function; this is called *nesting* functions, and can continue to any number of levels.

Susan explained this in her inimitable way.

> **Susan:** Nesting of functions—does that mean a whole bunch of functions calling each other?

> **Steve:** Yes.

Although functions can call one another, it is very unlikely that every function in a large program will be in the midst of execution at any given time. This means that reserving space in the executable program for all of the variables in all of the functions will make that executable considerably larger than it otherwise would be.

If we had only static variables, this wasteful situation would indeed occur. The alternative, of course, is to use auto variables, which as we have just noted are assigned storage at run time. But where is that storage assigned, if not in the executable program?

While all static variables are assigned storage in the executable program when it is linked, auto variables are instead stored in a data structure called a **stack**; the name is intended to suggest the notion of stacking clean plates on a spring-loaded holder such as you might see in a cafeteria. The last plate deposited on the stack of plates will be the first one to be removed when a customer needs a fresh plate. Back in the world of programming, a stack with one entry might look something like Figure 5.7.

FIGURE 5.7. A stack with one entry

Name	Value
TOP	1234

If we add (or **push**) another value on to the stack, say 999, the result would look like Figure 5.8.

FIGURE 5.8. A stack with two entries

Name	Value
TOP	999
2nd	1234

If we were to push one more item, this time with the value 1666, the result would look like Figure 5.9. Now, if we retrieve (or **pop**) a value, we'll get the one on top; namely 1666. Then the stack will look like it did in Figure 5.8. The next value to be popped off the stack will be the 999, leaving us with the situation in Figure 5.7 again. If we continue for one more round, we'll get the value 1234, leaving us with an **empty stack**.

FIGURE 5.9. A stack with three entries

Name	Value
TOP	1666
2nd	999
3rd	1234

The reason that stacks are used to store auto variables is that the way items are pushed onto or popped off a stack exactly parallels what happens when one function calls another. Let's look at this stack idea again, but this time from the point of view of keeping track of where we are in one function when it calls another one, as well as allocating storage for auto variables.[19]

Don't Call Me, I'll Call You

In Figure 5.5, there are two calls to the function Average: The first one is used to average two weights and the other to average two ages. One point I didn't stress was exactly how the Average function "knew" which call was which; that is, how did Average return to the right place after each time it was called? In principle, the answer is fairly simple: The calling function somehow notifies the called function of the address of the next instruction that should be executed after the called function is finished (the **return address**). There are several possible ways to solve this problem. The simplest solution is to store the return address at some standardized position in the code of the called function; at the end of the called function, that address is used to get back to the caller. While this used to be standard practice, it has a number of drawbacks that have relegated it to the history books. A major problem with this approach is that it requires changing data that are stored with the code of the called routine; as we've already seen, when running a program on a modern CPU under a modern operating system, code and data areas of memory are treated differently, and changing the contents of code areas at run time is not allowed.

Luckily, there is another convenient place to store return addresses: on the stack. This is such an important mechanism that all modern CPUs have a dedicated register, usually called the **stack pointer**, to make it easy and efficient to store and retrieve return

---

19. The actual memory locations used to hold the items in the stack are just like any other locations in RAM; what makes them part of the stack is how they are used. Of course, as always, one memory location can hold only one item at a given time, so the locations used to hold entries on the stack cannot be simultaneously used for something else like machine instructions.

addresses and other data that are of interest only during the execution of a particular function. In the case of the Intel CPUs, the stack pointer's name is esp.[20] A machine instruction named call is designed to push the return address on the stack and jump to the beginning of the function being called.[21] The call instruction isn't very complex in its operation, but before going into that explanation, you'll need some background information about how the CPU executes instructions.

How does the CPU "know" what instruction is the next to be executed? By using another dedicated register that we haven't discussed before, the **program counter**, which holds the address of the next instruction to be executed. Normally, this is the instruction physically following the one currently being executed; however, when we want to change the sequence of execution, as in an if statement or a function call, the program counter is loaded with the address of the instruction that *logically* follows the present one. Whatever instruction is at the address specified in the program counter is by definition the next instruction that will be executed; therefore, changing the address in the program counter to the address of any instruction causes that instruction to be the next one to be executed.

Here are the actual steps that the call instruction performs:

1. It saves the contents of the program counter on the stack.

2. Then it loads the program counter with the address of the first instruction of the called function.

What does this sequence of events achieve? Well, since the program counter always points to the next instruction to be executed, the address stored on the stack by the first step is the address of the next

---

20. That's the 32-bit stack pointer; as in the case of the other registers, there's a 16-bit stack pointer called sp, which consists of the 16 lower bits of the "real" stack pointer esp.

21. That is, its name is call on Intel® machines and many others; all modern CPUs have an equivalent instruction, although it may have a different name.

instruction after the call. Therefore, the last instruction in the called function can resume execution of the calling function by loading the program counter with the stored value on the stack. This will restart execution of the calling function at the next instruction after the call, which is exactly what we want to achieve.

The effect of the second step is to continue execution of the program with the first instruction of the called function; that's because the program counter is the register that specifies the address of the next instruction to be executed.

How It All Stacks Up

As we'll see, the actual way that a stack is implemented is a bit different than is suggested by the "stack of plates" analogy, although the effect is exactly the same. Rather than keeping the top of the stack where it is and moving the data (a slow operation), the data are left where they are and the address stored in the stack pointer is changed, which is a much faster operation. In other words, whatever address the stack pointer is pointing to is by definition the "top of the stack".[22]

For example, suppose that we start with an empty stack, with the stack pointer at 20001ffe, and ???? to indicate that we don't know the contents of that memory location. Thus, the stack will look like Figure 5.10.

FIGURE 5.10. **An empty stack**

Address	Contents	Meaning
20001ffe	????	none

---

22. Please note that the address that the stack occupies in these diagrams is arbitrary. The actual address where the stack is located in your program is determined by the linker and the operating system.

Then, the user types in the two values "2" and "4" as the values of FirstWeight and SecondWeight, and the first call to Average occurs; let's suppose that call is at location 10001000.[23] The actual sequence of events is something like this:[24]

1. The address of the next instruction to be executed (say, 10001005) is pushed onto the stack, along with the values for the arguments First and Second, which are copies of the arguments FirstWeight and SecondWeight. In the process, the CPU will subtract eight (the size of one address added to the size of two shorts, in bytes) from the stack pointer (which is then 20001ff6) and store the return address at the address currently pointed to by the stack pointer. Thus, the stack looks like Figure 5.11.[25]

FIGURE 5.11. **The stack immediately after the call to** Average

Address	Contents	Meaning
20001ff2	????	none
20001ff4	????	none
20001ff6	10001005	return address in main
20001ffa	0004	Second
20001ffc	0002	First
20001ffe	????	none

23. As usual, all addresses are in hexadecimal.
24. The details will vary with the compiler, but the principles are as illustrated here.
25. The "Top of Stack" address, that is, the address where the stack pointer is pointing, will be **bold**. Also note that when we push items on the stack the stack pointer will move *upward* in the diagram. That's because lower addresses appear first in the diagram, and new items pushed onto the stack go at lower addresses. Anything in the diagram "above" the stack pointer (i.e., at a lower address than the stack pointer's current value) is not a meaningful value, as indicated in the "meaning" column.

2. Execution starts in the Average function. However, before the code we write can be executed, we have to reserve space on the stack for the auto variable(s) defined in Average (other than the arguments First and Second, which have already been allocated); in this case, there is only one, namely Result. Since this variable is a short, it takes 2 bytes, so the stack pointer has to be reduced by 2. After this operation is completed, the stack will look like Figure 5.12.

Wait a minute. What are those ???? doing at location 20001ff4? They represent an uninitialized memory location. We don't know what's in that location, because that depends on what it was used for previously, which could be almost anything. The C++ compiler uses stack-based addressing for auto variables, as well as copies of arguments passed in from the calling function; that is, the addresses of such variables are relative to the stack pointer, rather than being fixed addresses. In this case, the address of Result would be [esp], or the current value of the stack pointer; Second would be referred to in the object file as [esp+6] (i.e, 6 more than the current value of the stack pointer, to leave room for the return address and Result). Similarly, the address of First would be [esp+8], or 8 more than the current value of the stack pointer.[26] Since the actual addresses occupied by these variables aren't known until the setup code at the beginning of the function is actually executed, there's no way to clear the variables out before then. That's why auto variables aren't automatically initialized.

26. The actual mechanism used to refer to variables on the stack in a real compiler is likely to be different from this one, and indeed can vary among compilers. However, this implementation is similar in principle to the mechanisms using compilers.

FIGURE 5.12. The stack after auto variable allocation

Address	Contents	Meaning
20001ff2	????	none
20001ff4	????	Result
20001ff6	10001005	return address in main
20001ffa	0004	Second
20001ffc	0002	First
20001ffe	????	none

As you might have guessed, Susan and I went over this in gory detail. Here's the play by play.

Susan: Yes, I think this is what has confused me in the past about functions. I never fully understood how the mechanism worked as how one function calls another. I still don't. But I guess it is by the position of the next address in a stack?

Steve: The stack is used to pass arguments and get return values from functions, but its most important use is to keep track of the return address where the calling function is supposed to continue after the called function is done.

Susan: This is how I am visualizing the use of the stack pointer. In one of my other books it showed how the clock worked in the CPU and it seemed to cycle by pointing in different directions as to what was to happen next in a program. So it was sort of a pointer. Is this how this pointer works? So let me get this straight. All CPUs have some kind of stack pointer, but they are used only for calling functions? Exactly where is the instruction call? It sounds to me like it is in the hardware, and I am having a very difficult time understanding how a piece of hardware can have an instruction.

Steve: All of the instructions executed in a program are executed by the hardware. The call instruction, in particular, does two things:

1. It saves the address of the next instruction (the contents of the program counter) on the stack.

2. It changes the program counter to point to the first instruction of the called function.

The return instruction is used to return to the calling function. It does this by the following steps:

1. It retrieves the saved value of the program counter from the stack;[27]

2. It sets the program counter back to that value.

The result of this is that execution of the program continues with the next instruction in the calling function.

Susan: Are you saying that, rather than the pointer of a stack actually pointing to the top of the physical stack, wherever it points to by definition will be the top of the stack, even if it really doesn't look like it?

Steve: Exactly.

Susan: Now I see why we have to know what a short is. So then the pointer is pointing to 20001ff4 as the top of the stack even though it doesn't look like it?

Steve: Absolutely correct.

---

27. Note that the compiler may be required to adjust the stack pointer before retrieving the saved value of the program counter, to allow for the space used by local variables in the function. In our example we have to add 2 to the esp register to skip over the local variable storage and point to the return address saved on the stack.

Scoped Out

Now let's look at another distinct way to categorize variables: the **scope** of a variable is the part of the program in which it can be accessed. Here, we are concerned with *local scope* and *global scope*. Variables with **global scope** are called *global variables*. These variables are defined outside any function and therefore by default can be accessed from any function.[28] Global variables are always in the static storage class, as we have already seen. Variables with **local scope** are called *local variables*. These variables are defined in a function and are accessible only while that function is executing; they can be either static or auto and are auto by default.

Figure 5.13 shows the valid combinations of scope and storage class.

FIGURE 5.13. Scope vs. storage class

Scope	Storage class	
	static	auto
local	Y	Y
global	Y	N

Susan had some comments on this topic.

Susan: On this scope stuff; I think you are going to have to help me understand exactly what is inside a function and what is outside a function. I am not too sure I know what the difference is.

Steve: All code is inside a function. However, some variables (global variables) are outside all functions and therefore shareable by all functions. Variables that are defined inside functions are

---

28. Variables can be defined either inside a function (local variables) or outside a function (global variables); by contrast, code must always be inside a function.

called *local*, because they are available only to the code that's in that function.

Susan: I am validating this with you now. Please correct any misconceptions.

1. Only variables are declared outside functions.

2. No code is written outside functions.

3. Up to this point I am not to be aware of anything else going on outside a function.

Steve: Correct.

Before we get deeper into the notion of scope, I think we should revisit the question of variable initialization in the light of the notion of global and local variables. This is a difficult topic, so it wouldn't be surprising if you don't find it obvious; Susan didn't. I wrote the next section to explain this topic to her.

Static Cling

What makes a variable static or auto is when its storage is assigned, and therefore when its address is known. In the case of a static variable, this happens at link time. In the case of an auto variable it happens when the function where it is defined is entered.[29]

This distinction affects initialization because it's impossible to initialize something until you know where it is. Therefore, an auto variable cannot be initialized until the function where it is defined is entered. This also means that you cannot assume that an auto variable will retain its value from one execution of the function where it's

---

29. By the way, if you were worried about keeping track of the address of every variable, that's the compiler's problem, not yours. The important distinction between a static and an auto variable is *when* the address is assigned, not what the actual address is.

defined to the next execution of that function, because the variable might be at a different location the next time.

These restrictions do not apply to static variables, because their addresses are known at link time and don't change thereafter. A variable defined outside all functions (a *global* variable) is automatically in the static storage class, because otherwise its address would never be assigned.[30] Since its address is known at link time, the initialization of such a variable can be and is performed before the start of main.

A static variable that is defined inside a function is different from one defined globally, in that it is not initialized until the function where it is defined is entered for the first time. However, its value is retained from one execution of its function to another, because its address is fixed rather than possibly varying from one call of the function to the next as can occur with an auto variable. For this property to be of use, the initialization of a static variable in a function must be performed only once; if it were performed on each entry to the function, the value from the previous execution would be lost. Therefore, that initialization is done only once, when the function is first entered.

Susan wanted some more explanation of what happens at link time, and the related question of why we would want to use static variables.

Susan: Will you tell me again what happens at link time? Let's see, I think it goes like this: The source code is translated into an object file and then the object file is linked to the hardware to make executable code. Is that how it goes?

Steve: Not quite. The object file is linked with library files containing predefined functions in compiled form.

---

30. Since all global variables are already in the static storage class, you don't have to (and *shouldn't*) use the keyword static when declaring a global variable. In another confusing legacy from C, the word static has an entirely different and unrelated meaning when used for a global variable.

Susan: Now, tell me again why you would want a variable to be static? What is the advantage to that? Does it just take up less room and be more efficient?

Steve: The advantage is that a static variable keeps its value from one function call to the next. For example, suppose you wanted to count the number of times that a function was called. You could use a static variable in the function, initialize it to 0, and add 1 to it every time the function was called. When the program was done, the value of that variable would be the number of times the function was called. Obviously, we couldn't use an auto variable to do that, as it would have to be initialized every time the function started or we'd have an uninitialized variable.

Susan: I can see how using a static variable would work but I don't see why an auto variable couldn't do the same thing. Well, I guess it would change each time the function would be used. Are you saying in this case that the variable has to be global?

Steve: Not exactly. Although we could use a global variable, we could also use a static local variable. Figure 5.14 through 5.18 are some sample programs to illustrate the situation.

FIGURE 5.14. Using an auto variable and initializing it (code\count1.cc)

```
#include <iostream.h>

short counter()
{
    short count = 0;

    count ++;

    cout << count << " ";

    return 0;
}
```

```
int main()
{
   short i;

   for (i = 0; i < 10; i ++)
      counter();

   return 0;
}
```

FIGURE 5.15. Using an auto variable and not initializing it (code\count2.cc)

```
#include <iostream.h>

short counter()
{
   short count;

   count ++;

   cout << count << " ";

   return 0;
}
int main()
{
   short i;

   for (i = 0; i < 10; i ++)
      counter();

   return 0;
}
```

FIGURE 5.16. Using a local static variable and initializing it (code\count3.cc)

```cpp
#include <iostream.h>

short counter()
{
    static short count = 0;

    count ++;

    cout << count << " ";

    return 0;
}

int main()
{
    short i;

    for (i = 0; i < 10; i ++)
        counter();

    return 0;
}
```

FIGURE 5.17. Using a local static variable and not initializing it (code\count4.cc)

```cpp
#include <iostream.h>

short counter()
{
    static short count;

    count ++;

    cout << count << " ";
```

```
    return 0;
}

int main()
{
    short i;

    for (i = 0; i < 10; i ++)
        counter();

    return 0;
}
```

FIGURE 5.18. Using a global variable and not initializing it (code\count6.cc)

```
#include <iostream.h>

short count;

short counter()
{
    count ++;

    cout << count << " ";

    return 0;
}

int main()
{
    short i;

    for (i = 0; i < 10; i ++)
        counter();

    return 0;
}
```

What will each of these programs do when run?

> **Susan:** Now, let me think about this. Variables are: static or auto, global or local.
>
> Local is for use only within functions. These variables are mostly auto, and will be auto by default, but they can be static; in the latter case, they will be initialized to 0.
>
> **Steve:** Correct; a static numeric variable is initialized to 0 if no other provision is made by the programmer to initialize it. One fine point: a local variable can be used only within one function.
>
> **Susan:** Global variables are declared only outside functions. They are always allocated storage at link time, like static local variables.
>
> **Steve:** Correct.
>
> **Susan:** Variables with static allocation are fixed because they are initialized at link time and thus are done just once and never change. But they can be local or global.
>
> **Steve:** The address of a statically allocated variable is set once and never changes; its value can change just like an auto variable can.
>
> **Susan:** That's what I had mixed up. I was confusing addresses with values.
>
> **Steve:** Okay, as long as you're straightened out now.
>
> **Susan:** An auto variable is assigned an address when the function where it is defined is entered. All auto variables are local.
>
> **Steve:** Correct.

Susan: Now, here is where I am confused. What is the difference between *at link time* and *when the function where it is defined is entered*? Does *at link time* mean when you are done with your source code and you are making an executable?

Steve: Yes.

Susan: And does *when the function where it is defined is entered* mean when the program is already made into an executable and you are running the program?

Steve: Yes.

Susan: I am confused about what we mean by *initialization*. I am confusing declaring a value for a variable and the designation of an address for a variable. It almost seems as if we are using these two meanings for the same term. I always thought that *initializing a variable* meant just assigning a value to it.

Steve: Initializing a variable means assigning an initial value to it. In the case of an auto variable, this must be done every time the function where it is declared is entered, whereas with a static variable it is done once.

Susan: Okay, this is what I imagined this to mean<?>. Then how come, in your figure of a stack, you have values assigned to the places where the variables are?

Steve: Those values are present only *after* the variables to which they correspond have been initialized. In Figure 5.12, for example, the contents of the address corresponding to Result are shown as ???, rather than as a valid value, whereas the values of First and Second are shown as initialized, because they have already been set to values equal to the input arguments provided by the caller.

Susan: Remember when I started tracing the "sorting" program? It had random numbers in the places where numbers are supposed to go, and when I actually entered a value then those random numbers were replaced by that value. And is that why you put ??? there, because you know that something is there but you don't know exactly what? It is just whatever until you can put a real value into those slots.

Steve: Right.

Susan: So if you leave it alone by not initializing it, then it keeps the last value it had each time it goes through the loop and therefore the count goes up?

Steve: Yes, except that the initial value isn't reliable in that case. In the case of the example count programs, that value happened to be 0, but there's no reason to expect that in general.

Susan: I want you to know that it was not immediately apparent to me just what the code in the example programs was doing; it really does look kinda strange. Then I noticed that this code called a function named counter. Why? Couldn't this work without using a function call?

Steve: No, it wouldn't work without a function call, because the whole point is that when a function is called, the auto variables defined in that function have unknown values. How would I show that without a function call?

Susan: I see that. One more point, there was no 5, which I assumed you to mean to be a global initialized variable, so I made one myself by just copying 6 and assigning the value of 0 to count. So this is just about all this exercise did for me. . . . I still don't get it. Why? Because they all did the same thing except 1. The results for that were the following: 1 1 1 1 1 1 1 1 1 1. The results for the rest of the programs were all the same, being 1 2 3 4 5 6 7 8 9 10. So, if they all do the same thing, then what is the point? Now, what really makes me mad about this is why 1 has that result. This bothers me. Obviously it is not incrementing itself by 1 after the first increment, it is just staying at one. Oh, wait, okay, okay, maybe. . . how about this: If you initialize it to 0 then each time it comes up through the loop it is always 0 and then it will always add 1 to 0 and it has to do that 10 times.

Steve: Right. By the way, Figure 5.19 is the missing example.

FIGURE 5.19. Using a global variable and initializing it (code\count5.cc)

```cpp
#include <iostream.h>

short count = 0;

short counter()
{
   count ++;

   cout << count << " ";

   return 0;
}

int main()
{
   short i;

   for (i = 0; i < 10; i ++)
      counter();

   return 0;
}
```

Susan: Then on the initialized local static variable, why does it work? Because it is static, and because its address is one place and won't budge; that means its value can increment. Well, would that mean it isn't written over in its location every time the function is called so we can add a value to it each time through?

Steve: Right.

Susan: And then the uninitialized static one works for the same reason the auto uninitialized one works.

Steve: Not quite. A static local variable is *always* initialized to something, just like a global variable is. If you don't specify an initial value for a static local numeric variable, it will be initialized to 0 during the first execution of the function where it is defined.

Susan: Now as for global, this is hard. Let me guess. Do the global initialized and uninitialized work for the same reasons I said earlier?

Steve: The global variables are always initialized, whether you specify an initial value or not; if you don't specify one, it will be 0.

Susan: That's what you said about static numeric variables. Are they the same? Well, they have to be the same because only static variables can be global, right?

Steve: Correct. Global variables are always statically allocated.

Susan: So if you don't initialize a numeric variable then it can become any number unless it is a static numeric without explicit initialization and then it will be 0 by default?

Steve: Correct.

Susan: Okay, let me see if I have this. All static really means is that the variable is put in an address of memory that can't be overwritten by another variable but can be overwritten when we change the variable's value?

Steve: Right.

Susan: These are tricks, and you know I don't like tricks. If they are global numeric variables, whether explicitly initialized or not, they are static; therefore they will at least have a value of 0. In example 5 this is stated explicitly but not in example 6, so the variable also will take the value of 0 by default, therefore these two programs are effectively identical, just like 3 and 4. That is why examples 3, 4, 5, and 6 have the same results.

Steve: Well, obviously the trick didn't work; you crossed me up by getting the right answers anyway.

Let's pause here to look at a sample program that has examples of all the types of variables and initialization states we've just discussed. These are:[31]

1. global, not explicitly initialized

2. global, explicitly initialized

3. auto, uninitialized

4. auto, initialized

5. local static, not explicitly initialized

6. local static, explicitly initialized

Careful examination of the sample program shown in Figure 5.20 will help you to visualize how and where each of these variable types might be used.

FIGURE 5.20. Using variables of different scopes and storage classes (code\scopclas.cc)

```
#include <iostream.h>
```

---

31. Remember, there aren't any global auto variables, because they would never be initialized.

```
short count1; // A global variable, not explicitly initialized
short count2 = 5; // A global variable, explicitly initialized

short func1()
{
  short count3; // A local auto variable, not explicitly initialized
  short count4 = 22; // A local auto variable, explicitly initialized
static short count5; // A local static variable, not explicitly initialized
static short count6 = 9; // A local static variable, explicitly initialized

  count1 ++; // Incrementing the global variable count1.
  count2 ++; // Incrementing the global variable count2.
  count3 ++; // Incrementing the local uninitialized auto variable count3.
  count4 ++; // Incrementing the local auto variable count4.
  count5 ++; // Incrementing the local static variable count5.
  count6 ++; // Incrementing the local static variable count6.

  cout << "count1 = " << count1 << endl;
  cout << "count2 = " << count2 << endl;
  cout << "count3 = " << count3 << endl;
  cout << "count4 = " << count4 << endl;
  cout << "count5 = " << count5 << endl;
  cout << "count6 = " << count6 << endl;
  cout << endl;

  return 0;
}

int main()
{
  func1();
  func1();

  return 0;
}
```

Assuming that you've installed the software from the CD-ROM in the back of this book, you can try out this program. First, you have to compile it by changing to the code subdirectory under the main directory where you installed the software, and typing RHIDE scopclas, then using the "Make" command from the "Compile" menu. Then exit back to DOS and type scopclas to run the program.

To run it under the debugger, make sure you are in the code subdirectory, and then type RHIDE scopclas. Again, do *not* add the ".cc" to the end of the file name. Once RHIDE has started up, you can step through the program by hitting F8, which will treat any function call as one statement, or by hitting F7, which will step into any function call. Any time you want to see the display that the user would see when running the program normally, hit ALT-F5, then ENTER to get back to the debugger.

FIGURE 5.21. The results of using variables of different scopes and storage classes (code\scopclas.out)

```
count1 = 1
count2 = 6
count3 = -32768
count4 = 23
count5 = 1
count6 = 10

count1 = 2
count2 = 7
count3 = -32767
count4 = 23
count5 = 2
count6 = 11
```

The results shown should help to answer the question of when we would want to use a static variable rather than an auto variable: whenever we need a variable that keeps its value from one execution of a function to another. You may be wondering where that weird value for count3 came from. Since we never initialized it, we can't complain when its value is meaningless. Although the compiler can warn us about such problems in some cases, they are still a significant source of errors in C++ programs, so it's worthwhile doing some additional exercises to help drive the point home.

Exercises, First Set

1. What will each of the programs in Figure 5.22 through 5.27 do when run?

FIGURE 5.22. Exercise 1a (code\inita.cc)

```
//auto local variable, initialized

#include <iostream.h>

short mess()
{
  short xyz;

  xyz = 5;

  return 0;
}

short counter()
{
  short count = 0;

  count ++;

  cout << count << " ";

  return 0;
}

int main()
```

```
{
  short i;

  for (i = 0; i < 10; i ++)
    {
    mess();
    counter();
    }

  cout << endl;

  return 0;
}
```

FIGURE 5.23. Exercise 1b (code\initb.cc)

```
//auto local variable, uninitialized

#include <iostream.h>

short mess()
{
  short xyz;

  xyz = 5;

  return 0;
}

short counter()
{
  short count;

  count ++;

  cout << count << " ";
```

```
    return 0;
  }

  int main()
  {
    short i;

    for (i = 0; i < 10; i ++)
      {
      mess();
      counter();
      }

    cout << endl;

    return 0;
  }
```

FIGURE 5.24. Exercise 1c (code\initc.cc)

```
//static local variable, explicitly initialized

#include <iostream.h>

short mess()
{
  short xyz;

  xyz = 5;

  return 0;
}

short counter()
{
  static short count = 0;
```

```
   count ++;

  cout << count << " ";

  return 0;
}

int main()
{
  short i;

  for (i = 0; i < 10; i ++)
   {
    mess();
    counter();
   }

  cout << endl;

  return 0;
}
```

FIGURE 5.25. Exercise 1d (code\initd.cc)

```
//static local variable, not explicitly initialized

#include <iostream.h>

short mess()
{
  short xyz;

  xyz = 5;

  return 0;
}
```

```
short counter()
{
  static short count;

  count ++;

  cout << count << " ";

  return 0;
}

int main()
{
  short i;

  for (i = 0; i < 10; i ++)
    {
    mess();
    counter();
    }

  cout << endl;

  return 0;
}
```

FIGURE 5.26. Exercise 1e (code\inite.cc)

```
//global variable, explicitly initialized

short count = 0;

#include <iostream.h>

short mess()
{
  short xyz;
```

```
  xyz = 5;

  return 0;
}

short counter()
{
 count ++;

 cout << count << " ";

 return 0;
}

int main()
{
 short i;

 for (i = 0; i < 10; i ++)
   {
   mess();
   counter();
   }

 cout << endl;

 return 0;
}
```

FIGURE 5.27. Exercise 1f (code\initf.cc)

```
//global variable, not explicitly initialized

short count;

#include <iostream.h>
```

```
short mess()
{
  short xyz;

  xyz = 5;

  return 0;
}

short counter()
{
  count ++;

  cout << count << " ";

  return 0;
}

int main()
{
  short i;

  for (i = 0; i < 10; i ++)
    {
    mess();
    counter();
    }

  cout << endl;

  return 0;
}
```

Answers to exercises can be found at the end of the chapter.

Think Globally?

Now that, I hope, we've cleared up the question of when different types of variables are initialized, let's continue with the distinction between global and local variables. You may be surprised that a programmer would accept the limitation of allowing certain variables to be accessed only in certain functions. Surely it's more powerful to be able to access anything anywhere. Isn't it?

Let me tell you a little story about the "power' of global variables. Unlike the one about the funny odometers, this one is true.

A BASIC Difficulty

In the late 1970s, I worked for a (very) small software house where I developed a database program for the Radio Shack TRS-80 Model III computer. This computer was fairly powerful for the time; it had two 79K floppy disks and a maximum of 48K memory. The database program had to be able to find a subset of the few thousand records in the database in a minute or so. The speed of the floppy drive was the limiting factor. The only high-level language that was available was a BASIC interpreter clearly related by ancestry to QBASIC, the BASIC that comes with MS-DOS, but much more primitive; for example, variable names were limited to 2 characters.[32] There was also an assembler, but even at that time I wasn't thrilled with the idea of writing a significant application program in assembly language. So we were stuck with BASIC.

Actually, that wasn't so bad. Even then, BASIC then had pretty good string manipulation functions, much better than the ones that come with C, and the file access functions, although primitive, weren't too hard to work with for the application in question. You

---

32. That is, two significant characters; you could have names as long as you wanted, but any two variables that had the same first two characters were actually the same variable.

could read or write a fixed number of bytes anywhere in a disk file, and since all of the records in a given database were in fact the same length, that was good enough for our purposes. However, there were a couple of (related) glaring flaws in the language: there were no named subroutines (analogous to functions in C++), and all variables were global.

Instead of names, subroutines were addressed by line number. In TRS-80 BASIC, each line had a number, and you could call a subroutine that started at line 1000 by writing "GOSUB 1000". At the end of the subroutine, a "RETURN" statement would cause control to return to the next statement after the GOSUB.

While this was functional in a moronic way, it had some serious drawbacks. First, of course, a number isn't as mnemonic as a name. Remembering that line 1000 is the beginning of the invoice printing routine, for example, isn't as easy as remembering the name PrintInvoice. In addition, if you "renumbered" the program to make room for inserting new lines between previously existing lines, the line numbers would change. The second drawback was that, as the example suggests, there was no way to pass arguments to a subroutine when it was called. Therefore, the only way for a subroutine to get input or produce output was by using and changing global variables. Yet another problem with this line-numbered subroutine facility was that you could call any line as a subroutine; no block structure such as we have in C++ was available to impose some order on the flow of control.

With such an arrangement, it was almost impossible to make a change anywhere in even a moderately large program without breaking some subroutine. One reason for this fragility was that a variable could be used or changed anywhere in the program; another was that it was impossible to identify subroutines except by adding comments to the program, which could be out of date. For both these reasons, almost any change could have effects throughout the program.

I Say "Live It, or Live With It"

After some time struggling with this problem, I decided to end it, once and for all, by adding named subroutines with arguments and local variables to the language. This made it possible to maintain the program, and we ended up selling several hundred copies of it over the course of a couple of years. Besides, fixing the language was fun.[33]

The moral? There's almost always a way around a limitation of a computer language, although it may not be worth the effort to find it. Luckily, with C++, adding functionality is a bit easier than patching BASIC in assembly language.

Nesting Instinct

After that (theoretically) instructive anecdote, it's time to get back to our regularly scheduled text, where we were examining the function of the stack in storing information needed during execution of a function. The next statement in our example program (Figure 5.5 on page 235) is Result = (First + Second) / 2;. Since we've assumed that First is 2, and Second is 4, the value of Result will be (4+2)/2, or 3. After this statement is executed, the stack looks like Figure 5.28.

---

33. Unfortunately, the details of this adventure are both too technical and not very relevant to the task at hand. Also, I've forgotten exactly how I did it; after all, it was about 20 years ago.

FIGURE 5.28. **The stack after the initialization of** Result

Address	Contents	Meaning
20001ff2	????	none
20001ff4	0003	Result
20001ff6	10001005	return address in main
20001ffa	0004	Second
20001ffc	0002	First
20001ffe	????	none

Finally, at the end of the function, the stack pointer will be incremented to point to the stored return address. Then the return instruction will reload the program counter with the stored return address, which in this case is 10001005. Then the value of Result will be made available to the calling function and the stack pointer will be adjusted so the stack looks as it did before we called Average.

After the return, the stack will be empty, as we no longer need the arguments, the auto variable Result, or the return address from the Average function. Figure 5.29 shows what the stack looks like now.

FIGURE 5.29. **The stack after exiting from** Average

Address	Contents	Meaning
20001ff2	????	none
20001ff4	0003	none
20001ff6	10001005	none
20001ffa	0004	none
20001ffc	0002	none
20001ffe	????	none

Do not be fooled by the casual statement "the stack is empty". That means only that the stack pointer (esp) is pointing to the same place it was when we started our excursion into the Average function; namely,

20001ffe. The values that were stored in the memory locations used by Average for its auto variables haven't been erased by changing the stack pointer. This illustrates one very good reason why we can't rely on the values of auto variables until they've been initialized; we don't know how the memory locations they occupy might have been used previously.

The previous discussion of how arguments are copied into local variables when a function is called applies directly to our Average function; if we try to change the input arguments, we will change only the copies of those arguments on the stack, and the corresponding variables in the calling function won't be altered. That's perfectly acceptable here, since we don't want to change the values in the calling function; we just want to calculate their average and provide the result to the calling function. An argument that is handled this way is called a *value argument*, as its value is copied into a newly created variable in the called function, rather than allowing the called function access to the "real" argument in the calling function.[34]

One thing we haven't really discussed here is how the return value gets back to the caller. In the cases we've examined so far, using the compiler that accompanies this book, it's stored in a register (eax, to be precise), which is then available to the calling routine after we get back.[35] This is a very easy and fast way to pass a return value back to the caller. However, it has a drawback: a register can only hold one value of 32 bits. Sometimes this is not enough, in which case another mechanism will have to be used. However, the compiler takes care of these details for us, so we don't have to worry about them. In any event, it's time to go over the material we've covered in this chapter.

---

34. It's also possible to define a function that has access to an actual variable in the calling function; we'll see how and when to do that at the appropriate time.

35. In case you're wondering how I know which register is used to pass back the return value, it's simple. I cheated by examining the compiled code in the debugger. Different compilers do this differently, but they provide the same functionality to the C++ programmer.

Review

First, we added the fundamental programming concept of the *function*. A function is a piece of code that can "stand alone"; it can be compiled separately from other functions, and provides some service that we can use via a mechanism known as a *function call*. The function that makes the call is known as the *calling function*, and the one it calls is known as the *called function*. Before we can call a function, we need to know what input values it needs and what it returns. This information is provided by a *function declaration* at the beginning of each function. This includes an *argument list*, which specifies input values that the called function uses (if any), and a *return type*, which specifies the type of the value that it produces when it's finished (if any). When we call a function, it executes until it reaches the end of its code or reaches a return statement, whichever comes first. When either of these events happens, the program continues execution in the calling function immediately after the place where the function call occurs. Ordinarily, as in our example, an argument to a function is actually a copy of the variable in the calling program, so that the called function can't modify the "real" value in the caller. Such an argument is called a *value argument*.[36]

We also saw that function and variable names can be of any length, consisting of upper or lower case characters (or both), digits, and the special character underscore (_). To make it easier for the compiler to distinguish numbers from variable names, the first character can't be a digit. Also, a variable name can't be the same as a *keyword*, or name defined by the language; examples of keywords we've seen so far include if, for, and short.

After finishing the construction of our Average function, we saw how to use it by making a function call. Then we launched into an examination of the way that values in the calling function are

---

36. As this might suggest, there is another type of argument, which we'll get to in Chapter 6.

converted into arguments in the called function, which required a detour into the software infrastructure.

We started this excursion by looking at the *linker*, which is used to construct programs from a number of functions compiled into separate *object files*. Next, we explored the notion of *storage class*, which determines the working lifetime of a variable. The simplest storage class is static. Variables of this class, which includes all variables defined outside any function, have storage assigned to them by the linker and retain the same address during the lifetime of the program. On the other hand, auto (for "automatic") variables are always defined in a function and are assigned storage on the *stack* when that function starts execution. The stack is the data structure that stores function arguments and *return addresses* during the execution of a function; it's called that because it behaves like a spring-loaded stack of plates in a cafeteria, where the last one put on the top is the first one to be removed. Don't take this analogy too literally; most of the diagrams in this chapter show data being added and removed at the bottom rather than the top of the stack, but that doesn't affect its behavior.

Then we noted that each variable, in addition to a storage class, has a *scope*, which is the part of a program in which the variable can be accessed. At this point, the scopes that are important to us are *local scope* and *global scope*. As you might guess, a global variable can be referred to anywhere, while a local variable can be accessed only in the function where it is defined. Although it may seem limiting to use local variables rather than global ones, programs that rely on global variables are very difficult to maintain, as a change anywhere can affect the rest of the program. Programs that limit the scope of their variables, on the other hand, minimize the amount of code that can be affected by a change in one place. Because local variables are only usable while in the function where they are defined, they can be stored on the stack; therefore, they don't occupy memory during the entire lifetime of the program.

Of course, local variables take up room while they're being used, which means that the stack has to have enough storage to hold all of the local variables for the current function and all of the functions that haven't finished executing. That is, the stack has to have enough room for all of the variables in the current function, the function that called the current function, the one that called that one, and so on up to the main function. which is always the top-level function in a C++ program. Since the amount of memory that is allocated to the stack is not unlimited, it's possible to run out of space, in which case your program will stop working. This is called a *stack overflow*, by analogy with what happens if you put too many plates on the cafeteria plate stack: It falls over and makes a mess. When using the DJGPP compiler that comes with this book, it's unlikely that you'll ever run out of stack space unless you have a bug in your program. Some other compilers aren't as generous in their space allotments, so the likelihood of a stack overflow is less remote. The solution to this problem, should it arise, is to use another kind of storage allocation called *dynamic storage*; we'll see an example of this mechanism in Chapter 6.

Now that we've gone through that review, it's time to do another exercise to drive home some points about scope and storage classes.

Exercises, Second Set

2. If the program in Figure 5.30 is run, what will be displayed?

FIGURE 5.30. Exercise 2 (code\calc1.cc)

```
#include <iostream.h>

short i;

short Calc(short x, short y)
{
static short j = 0;
```

```
        cout << "The value of j in Calc is: " << j << endl;

        i ++;

        j = x + y + j;

        return j;
    }

int main()
{
    short j;

    for (i = 0; i < 5; i ++)
        {
        j = Calc(i + 5, i * 2) + 7;
        cout << "The value of j in main is: " << j << endl;
        }

    return 0;
}
```

Answers to exercises can be found at the end of the chapter.

Conclusion

We've covered a lot of material in this chapter, ranging from the anatomy of functions through a lot more information on what's going on "underneath the covers" of even a fairly simple C++ program. Next, we'll see how to write a realistic, although simplified, application program using some more advanced concepts in C++.

Answers to Exercises

1. Here are the answers for each of the programs in Figure 5.22 through 5.27:

   a. 1 1 1 1 1 1 1 1 1 1 1

   b. 6 6 6 6 6 6 6 6 6 6

   c. 1 2 3 4 5 6 7 8 9 10

   d. 1 2 3 4 5 6 7 8 9 10

   e. 1 2 3 4 5 6 7 8 9 10

   f. 1 2 3 4 5 6 7 8 9 10

   Why are these the way they are? Well, let's take them in order, except for b, which I'll take up last.

   The reason for the results from a should be fairly obvious; since we set the variable count to 0 every time we enter the counter function, incrementing it always gives the answer 1.

   As for c–f, they all produce the same answer; namely, the output value starts at 1 and increments by 1 each time. This is because the variable named count is statically allocated in each of these cases, which has two consequences: The initialization of the variable is done only once and it retains its value from one call of the counter function to the next. However, the reason for this behavior differs slightly in each of these cases, as follows:

   c. In initc.cc, count is a static variable defined in the counter function, which is explicitly initialized to 0.

   d. In initd.cc, count is a static variable defined in the counter function, which is not explicitly initialized. Statically allocated numeric variables are initialized to 0 if no other initial value is specified.[37]

   e. In inite.cc, count is a global variable explicitly initialized to 0.[38]

f. In initf.cc, count is a global variable not explicitly initialized. As in initd.cc, this will work because the default value of a statically allocated numeric variable is 0.

Now let's see why b is different.

b. In initb.cc, count is a local *uninitialized variable*. Here's where we see the reason for the mess function, which apparently does nothing useful; that function is there solely to supply a value that will use the same memory location as the counter function will use to store its count variable after the mess function returns to the main program. In other words, in the DJGPP compiler that comes with this book, the variable xyz in the mess function happens to land in the same memory location that the variable count occupies in the counter function. Therefore, whatever value happened to be in xyz at the end of the mess function will appear as if by magic in count when counter starts. If we were to initialize count before we used it in counter, we would never see this leftover value, but since we just use count without initializing it, we get whatever value that memory location had left in it from before.

In case this point isn't yet apparent to you, I've drawn a set of pictures that might help clear it up. At the point in main where mess is about to be called, let's suppose that the stack is empty, with the stack

---

37. You can count on this, because it's part of the language definition, although it's nicer for the next programmer if you specify what you mean explicitly.

38. Note that the keyword static is not used to specify that this variable is statically allocated; since globals are always statically allocated, the keyword static means something different when applied to a global variable or function. Even though we won't be using static for global variables or functions, it's possible that you will run into it in other programs, so it might be useful for you to have some idea of its meaning in those situations. An approximate translation of static for global functions or variables is that the function or variable is available for use only in the same file where it is defined, following the point of its definition.

pointer pointing to 20001ffe. The call instruction is at location 10001000, and is 5 bytes long, so the next instruction after the call starts at location 10001005. Before the call to mess occurs, the stack looks like Figure 5.31.[39]

FIGURE 5.31. The stack immediately before the call to mess

Address	Contents	Meaning
20001ff2	????	none
20001ff4	????	none
20001ff6	????	none
20001ff8	????	none
20001ffa	????	none
20001ffe	????	none

Then the call to mess occurs, which leaves the stack looking like Figure 5.32.

Next, mess declares a variable called xyz, which is an auto variable and therefore has to be stored on the stack. Since xyz is a short, it occupies 2 bytes on the stack, so the stack now looks like Figure 5.33.

---

39. As usual, the **bold** address indicates the current value of the stack pointer.

FIGURE 5.32. **Immediately before executing the first instruction in** mess

Address	Contents	Meaning
20001ff2	????	none
20001ff4	????	none
20001ff6	????	none
20001ff8	????	none
20001ffa	10001005	return address in main
20001ffe	????	none

FIGURE 5.33. **The stack after** mess **has declared the** auto **variable** xyz

Address	Contents	Meaning
20001ff2	????	none
20001ff4	????	none
20001ff6	????	none
20001ff8	????	xyz (uninitialized)
20001ffa	10001005	return address in main
20001ffe	????	none

So far, so good. Now xyz is assigned the value 5, which leaves the stack looking like Figure 5.34.

Then mess returns to main, so the stack is empty again. But here's the tricky part: to say "the stack is empty" merely means that the stack pointer has been reset back to 20001ffe. The data stored in locations 20001ff8-20001ffc have not been changed in any way.[40] So, before counter is called, the situation looks like Figure 5.35.

---

40. This statement is true when running the DJGPP compiler on an Intel machine; it may not be true on other systems. However, that possibility only reinforces the point that you should not rely on such behavior, as it is outside the definition of the C++ language.

Learning to Program in C++   **297**

FIGURE 5.34. **The stack after** xyz **has been initialized**

Address	Contents	Meaning
20001ff2	????	none
20001ff4	????	none
20001ff6	????	none
20001ff8	0005	xyz (uninitialized)
20001ffa	10001005	return address in main
20001ffe	????	none

FIGURE 5.35. **The stack before** counter **is called**

Address	Contents	Meaning
20001ff2	????	none
20001ff4	????	none
20001ff6	????	none
20001ff8	0005	none
20001ffa	10001005	none
20001ffe	????	none

When counter is called, let's assume the return address in main is now 10001013. After this is stored on the stack, we have the situation illustrated in Figure 5.36 upon entry to counter.

The first thing that counter does is to allocate storage for its one auto variable, count, by subtracting 2 from the stack pointer. After this is done, the situation is as illustrated in Figure 5.37.

That is, the variable count is assigned the storage location that previously held the value of xyz; this storage location (20001ff8) still has the value 5 left over from xyz. Of course, if we initialize count as we should, we'll never see that old value. However, this program doesn't initialize count; thus, count starts out with the leftover value 5 from xyz before counter increments count.

FIGURE 5.36. Immediately upon entry to counter

Address	Contents	Meaning
20001ff2	????	none
20001ff4	????	none
20001ff6	????	none
20001ff8	0005	none
20001ffa	10001013	return address in main
20001ffe	????	none

FIGURE 5.37. Before execution of the first instruction in counter

Address	Contents	Meaning
20001ff2	????	none
20001ff4	????	none
20001ff6	????	none
20001ff8	0005	count (uninitialized)
20001ffa	10001013	return address in main
20001ffe	????	none

The moral of the story is "always initialize your auto variables before use"; otherwise, you'll get whatever junk happens to be lying around in memory at the location where they are assigned when the function starts.

As you might guess, this set of problems led to a discussion with Susan.

Susan: Steve, what I don't get is what does the function called mess (aptly named) do? See, since I am still sketchy on function calls this really bothers me. Am I to assume that the mess function call comes first and then the counter function call comes second, and what does one have to do with the other?

Steve: As we've discussed before, all the lines in a given function (like main) are executed in sequential order from top to bottom, unless you use a flow control construct like if, while, or for, to change that order.

Susan: If it weren't for problem 1b, I would think that you were playing a trick on me and that this call was just a distraction and not utilized at all but I see it does do something, but what I am not sure.

Steve: You're correct that it does do something. One of the rules in figuring out a program is that everything does something; the question is often exactly what it is doing. Once you have that figured out, the rest is often pretty easy to determine.

2. If you got this one right, congratulations! It's just *filled* with tricks, but they're all things that you might run into in a real (poorly written) program. Here's the answer:

```
The value of j in Calc is: 0
The value of j in main is: 12
The value of j in Calc is: 5
The value of j in main is: 23
The value of j in Calc is: 16
The value of j in main is: 40
```

Let's see how this came about. The first question is why there are only three values displayed by each output statement. The for loop that calls the Calc routine and displays the results should execute 5 times, shouldn't it?

This is the first trick. Since i is a global variable, the statement i ++; in the Calc function affects its value. Therefore, i starts out at 0 in the main function, as usual, but when the Calc function is called, i is incremented to 1. So the next time the modification expression i ++ in the for statement is executed, i is already 1 and is changed to 2. Now the controlled block of the for statement is executed again, with i set to 2. Again, the call to Calc results in i being incremented an extra time, to 3, so the next execution of the for loop sets i to 4. The final call to Calc increments the value of i to 5, so the for loop terminates, having executed only three times rather than the five you would expect by looking at it. Now you can see why global variables are dangerous!

Now what about the values of j? Well, since the j in Calc is a static variable, it is initialized only once. Because it is a local static variable, that initialization is performed when Calc is called for the first time. So the first time Calc is called, j is set to 0. The arguments specified by main on the first call to Calc are 5 and 0; this means that, inside Calc, x and y have those values, respectively. Then the new value of j is calculated by the statement j = x + y + j;, or 5 in total. The return j; statement specifies this as the return value of Calc; this value is then added to 7 as specified by the assignment statement j = Calc(i + 5, i * 2) + 7; in main. That explains why the output statement in main displays the value of j as 12 the first time.

It's very important to note that the variable j in main is completely unrelated to the variable j in Calc. Since they are local variables, they have nothing in common but their names. There is no risk of confusion (at least on the compiler's part), since we can access a local variable only in the function in which it is defined. Therefore, when we refer to j in main, we mean the one defined there; and when we refer to j in Calc, we mean the one defined there.

Next, we call Calc again with the arguments 7 and 4. To compute these arguments from the expressions i + 5 and i * 2, you have to remember that i has been modified by Calc and is now 2, not 1 as we would expect normally. When we get to Calc, it displays the old value of j (5), left over from the previous execution of this function. This is because j is a local static variable; thus, the initialization statement static short j = 0; is executed only once, upon the first call to the function where it is defined. Once j has been set to a value in Calc, it will retain that value even in a subsequent call to Calc; this is quite unlike a normal auto variable, which has no known value at the beginning of execution of the function where it is defined. A new value of j is now calculated as 7 + 4 + 5, or 16, and returned to main.

On return from Calc, the value of j in main is 23, as set by the assignment statement j = Calc(i + 5, i * 2) + 7;. We also don't want to forget that i is now 3, having been changed in Calc.

Exactly the same steps occur for the last pass through the for loop: we call Calc with the new values of i + 5 and i * 2, which are 9 and 8, respectively, since i has been incremented to 4 by the for statement's modification expression i ++. Then Calc displays the old value of j, which is 16, and calculates the new value, which is 33. This is added to the literal value 7 and stored in j in main, resulting in the value 40, which is then displayed by the output statement.

Don't get discouraged if you didn't get this one, especially the effects caused by a global i. Even experienced programmers can be taken by surprise by programs that use global variables in such error-prone ways.

CHAPTER 6

Taking Inventory

Now we have enough of the fundamentals of programming under our belts to look at some of the more powerful features of C++. As I've mentioned before, C++ is the successor to C. What I haven't told you is *why* it was invented. One of the main reasons was to improve on C's support for user defined data types. What are these, and why are they so important?

As is the case with C++, the data types available in C are divided into two groups: **native** (i.e., defined in the language itself) and **user defined** (i.e., defined by the programmer). However, there is a major difference between C and C++ in the support provided to user defined types. In C, variables of the native types are fully supported by the language, while variables of user defined types are not; the native types that we've been using are char, short, and unsigned short (and int, but only for the return type of main), all of which have been inherited from C.[1]

By **fully supported**, I mean that native variables in both C and C++ can be defined, initialized, assigned values, passed as arguments and return values, and compared to other values of the same type. Such a variable can be assigned storage in either the static or auto storage classes: If a variable is auto, the storage is assigned at entry to the function where it is defined, and released automatically at exit from that function; if it is static, it is initialized to some reasonable value either at link time (for a *global* variable) or upon the first entry to the function where it is defined (for a *local* variable).[2] However, most of these facilities aren't available to user defined data types in C. For example, variables of such types can't be compared; this limitation results from the fact that the C compiler has no idea how to compare two variables of a type that you define. Similarly, what is a reasonable default value for a variable of a user defined type? Presumably, the user (i.e., the programmer) knows, but the C compiler doesn't.

In this chapter, we'll see how to give a C++ of compiler enough information to allow data types that we define to behave just like the native types. Let's start out with some definitions and objectives. Susan had a revealing question here:

> **Susan:** I think I need to find out something here. I am getting the impression that what is "native" is C and what is "user defined" is C++. Is that right? And if so, why?

> **Steve:** Pretty much so. As to why, the answer is pretty simple: the reason that C++ was invented in the first place was to add good support for user defined types to the efficiency of C.

---

1. There are actually several other native C++ types that we haven't used: long, float, double, and bool. The long type is useful for storing whole-number values that are larger than will fit into a short (hence the name), while float and double are able to store values that have fractional parts as well as integral values. These are useful in scientific and engineering calculations; we'll use all of them except for float later in the book. The bool type, a relatively recent addition to C++, is useful for keeping track of a true/false condition. We'll see how to use this variable type later in this chapter.

2. Please note that the terms class and *storage class* have nothing to do with one another. This is another case where C++ reuses the same word for different concepts, although at least "storage class" isn't a keyword. We should be grateful for such small favors.

Definitions

A **class** is a user defined type.

A **class interface** tells the compiler what facilities the class provides. This interface is usually found in a header file, which by convention has the extension .h.

A **class implementation** tells the compiler how to implement the facilities defined in the class interface. This is usually found in a source code file, which in the case of the compiler on the CD-ROM in the back of this book usually has the extension .cc.

An **object** is a variable of a class type. Its behavior is defined by the header file and implementation of the class.

A **member function** is a function that is part of the definition of a class.

A **member variable** is a variable that is part of the definition of a class.

Object-oriented programming is the organization of programs as collections of objects exhibiting user-defined behavior, rather than as collections of functions operating on variables of native data types.

Encapsulation is the concept of hiding the details of a class inside the implementation of that class rather than exposing them in the interface. This is one of the primary organizing principles that characterize object-oriented programming.

Internals, in the case of native data types, refers to details of the implementation of these types in the compiler. In the case of class types, *internals* means the details of implementation of the type rather than what it does for the user.

Objectives of This Chapter

By the end of this chapter, you should

1. Understand what a user defined type (a class) is, and how it is defined.

2. Understand how variables of some simple classes are created, destroyed, and copied.

3. Understand how and why access to the *internals* of a class is controlled.

Pay Some Attention to the Man Behind the Curtain

In C++, a user defined variable is called an *object*. Each object has a type, just like variables of native types (short, char, etc.). For example, if we define a class called StockItem (as we will do in this chapter), then an object can be of type StockItem, just as a native variable can be of type short. However, an additional step is required when we want to use user defined types. Since the compiler has no intrinsic knowledge of these types, we have to tell it exactly what they are and how they work. We do this by defining a class, which specifies both the data contained in the user defined variable and what operations can be performed on these data.

Here's how Susan reacted upon her first encounter with this idea.

> **Susan:** I can tell that there is only one thing that I think that I understand about this. That is, that C++ is not a language. You have to *make it up* as you go along. . . .

That may be overdoing it a bit, but there is a grain of truth in her observation: C++ is more of a "language kit" than it is a language. What do I mean by this?

I mean that to use C++ in the most effective way, rather than merely as a "better C", it is necessary to create data types and tell the compiler how to treat them as though they were native data types. So far in this book, we have been using data types that were previously defined, either by the compiler and language (native types, e.g., short, char) or by libraries (class types, e.g., string). Now we're going to actually make up our own types that will be usable just like native types; the difference between using variables and making up new variable types is analogous to the difference between using a program and writing a program, but carried to the next higher level.

In the event that you find this notion hard to understand, you're not alone; neither did Susan.

> **Susan:** This is an outrage! I didn't understand one other word as I was far beyond anything that could even be described as shock. I think I did faint. I may as well have been in a coma.

Interestingly enough, she did in fact understand this idea of making up our own data types, so perhaps she was overestimating the degree of her shock.

Before we get back to the technical explanation of how we create new data types, I'm sure one more question is burning in your mind: *Why* should we do this? What's wrong with the native types like char and short? The answer is simple: We make up types so that we can match the language to the needs of the problem we're trying to solve. For example, suppose we want to write a program to do inventory control for a small business like a grocery store. Such a program needs objects representing items in the store, which have prices, names, and so on. We need to define each of these types of objects so that it can display the behavior appropriate to the thing it represents. The availability of objects that have relevance to the problem being solved makes it much easier to write (and *read*) a program to handle inventory than if everything has to be made of shorts and chars.

I suspect that the advantages of making up one's own data types may still not be apparent to you, so let me make an analogy with natural languages. Making up new data types in C++ is in some ways quite similar to making up new words in English (for example). You might think that if everyone made up new words, the result would be chaos. Actually, this is correct, with the very important exception of technical jargon and other vocabularies that are shared by people who have more in common than simply being speakers of English. For example, physicians have their own "language" in the form of medical terminology. Of course, a cynical observer might conclude that the reason for such specialized vocabulary is to befuddle or impress the naive listener, and of course it can be used for that purpose. However, there is also a much more significant and valid reason: To make it possible for experts in a field to communicate with one another quickly and precisely. The same is true of creating our own data types; they enable us to write programs that are more understandable to those who are conversant with the problems being solved. It's much easier to talk to a store owner about inventory objects than about shorts and chars!

Here's the discussion that Susan and I had on this topic:

Susan: Why should we have user defined data types?

Steve: So that you can match the language to the needs of the problem you're trying to solve. For example, if you were writing a nurse's station program in C++, you would want to have objects that represented nurses, doctors, patients, various sorts of equipment, and so on. Each of these objects would display the behavior appropriate to the thing or person it was representing.

Susan: Why do you need that? What if each individual who spoke English made up a unique version of English (well, it is user defined, right?), how could we communicate? This is garbage.

Steve: We need user-defined types for the same reason that specialists need jargon in their technical fields. For example, why do you health-care professionals need words like *tachycardia*? Why don't you just say "a fast heartbeat" in simple English?

Hey, that's not a bad way to explain this: Adding classes is like adding specialized vocabulary to English. I don't remember ever seeing that explanation before; what do you think of it?

Susan: Huh? Then you are saying that, by defining a class of objects, they can take on more realistic qualities than just abstract notions? That is, if I wanted to define *nurse* in a program, then I would do it with a class named nurse and then I can define in that program the activities and functions that the nurse objects would be doing. Is this how you keep everything straight, and not mix them up with other objects?

Steve: Yes, that's one of the main benefits of object-oriented programming. You might be surprised how hard it is to teach an old-line C programmer the importance of this point.

Susan: So is this what object-oriented programming is? I have heard of it, but never knew what it meant. Could it also be described as user-defined programming? I guess there are advantages to teaching a novice; you don't have to undo old ideas to make way for newer ones. So, anything that is user defined is a class? That is, native variables are not classes?

Steve: Every user-defined type is a class; data items of a class type are called *objects*. Variables of native types are not objects in the object-oriented sense.

Susan: Okay, so if I want to make up something, then what I make up is called a class as opposed to the other type of stuff that isn't made up and is really C++; that is called *native*. That is intuitive, thank you. Then the class is made up of data items? And what about native variables; are they objects? I guess just the variables of the class are called *objects* because I just read your definition for *object*. So native variables are not objects, they are just variables. Am I am talking in circles again?

Steve: No, you're not; you're making perfect sense. The only point you have missed is that there are functions in the objects, as well as data items. We'll get into that shortly.

Susan: So Steve, tell me: What have I been doing up to this point? How does this new stuff compare to the old stuff and which one is it that the programmer really uses? (Let's see, do I want curtain 1 or 3; which one holds the prize?) I just want to get a little sense of direction here; I don't think that is a whole lot to ask, do you?

Steve: What you've been doing up to this point is *using* classes (string, vector) as well as native types like short and char. This new stuff shows how to *create* classes like string, rather than just using them.[3]

Assuming that I've sold you on the advantages of making up our own data types, let's see how we can actually do it. Each data type is represented by a class, whose full definition is composed of two parts: the **interface** definition (usually contained in a file with the extension .h), and the **implementation** definition (usually contained in a file with the extension .cc). The interface definition tells the compiler (and the class user) *what* the class does, while the implementation definition tells the compiler *how* the objects of that class actually perform the functions specified in the interface definition. Let's take a look at a step-by-step description of how to create and use a class.

1. Write the class interface definition, which will be stored in a file with the extension .h. In our example of a StockItem class, we'll use item1.h to hold our first version of this interface definition.

---

3. In case you were wondering, you can't create new native types.

This definition tells the compiler the names and types of the member functions and member variables that make up the objects of the class, which gives the compiler enough information to create objects of this class in a user's program.

2. Write the class implementation definition, which will be stored in a file with the extension .cc; in our example, the first one of these will be stored in the file item1.cc. This definition is the code that tells the compiler how to perform the operations that the interface definition refers to. The implementation definition file must #include the interface definition file (item1.h, in this case) so that the compiler has access to the interface that is being implemented.

3. Write the program that uses objects in the class to do some work; the first such program we'll write will be itemtst1.cc. This program also needs to #include the interface definition file, so that the compiler can tell how to create objects of this class.

4. Compile the class implementation definition to produce an object file (item1.o). This makes the class available to the user program.

5. Compile the user program to produce an object file (itemtst1.o).

6. Link the object file from the user program, the object file from the class implementation definition, and any necessary libraries together to form a finished executable; our first sample will be called itemtst1.exe.

A couple of items in this list need some more discussion. Let's see how Susan brought them to my attention.

> **Susan:** I have a problem here. First under item 2, you put "The class implementation definition file must #include"; excuse me, but that doesn't make sense. What do you mean by #include? How do you say that, "pound include"?

Steve: Yes, that's how it's pronounced. You could also leave off the "pound" and just say "include", and every C and C++ programmer would understand you.

Susan: Section 6 that stuff with the linking. . .isn't that done by the compiler; if not, how do you do it?

Steve: The linker does it, but the compiler is generally capable of calling the linker automatically for you; that's why we haven't needed to worry about this before.

Susan: Okay, where is the linker? Is it not part of the compiler software? If not, where does it come from?

Steve: Every compiler comes with one, but you can also buy one separately if you prefer.

Susan: Who puts it in your computer? Also, how do you "call" the linker if you have always had the compiler do it for you?

Steve: It is installed along with the compiler. You can tell the compiler not to call it automatically if you prefer to do it manually; there are reasons to do that sometimes. For example, when you're making a change that affects only one module in a large program, you recompile only that one module, then relink all the object files again to make the executable.

Susan: How do you do that?

Steve: It varies according to what compiler you're using. With the RHIDE GUI, you specify source files and object files in your project. The compiler will compile the source files and then link them with the object files.

Taking Stock

Now let's start on our first class definition, which is designed to help solve the problem of maintaining inventory in a small grocery store. We need to keep track of all the items that we carry, so we're going to define a class called StockItem. The StockItem class, like other classes, is composed of a number of functions and variables. As I suggested earlier, to make this more concrete, think of something like Lego™ blocks, which you can put together to make parts that can in turn be used to build bigger structures. The smallest Legos are the native types, and the bigger, composite ones are class types.

For the compiler to be able to define an object correctly, we'll have to tell it the names and types of the member variables that will be used to store the information about each StockItem; this enables the compiler to allocate memory for a StockItem.

So how do we identify these member variables? By considering what member variables each StockItem object will need to keep track of its corresponding item in the stock of the store. After some thought, I've come up with the following list of member variables:

1. The name of the item (m_Name),

2. The number in stock (m_InStock),

3. The distributor that we purchase it from (m_Distributor),

4. The price we charge (m_Price), and

5. The item number, or UPC (m_UPC).

What I mean by *an item* is actually something like "chunky chicken soup, 16 oz.", rather than a specific object like a particular can of soup. In other words, every can of soup with the same item number is considered equivalent to every other can of soup with the same item number, so all we have to keep track of for each item can be described by the above data. For the item number, we'll use the Universal

Product Code (UPC), which is printed as a bar code on almost every product other than fresh produce; it's a 10-digit number, which we'll represent as a string for convenience.

Susan took me to task about the notion of a StockItem object vs. a specific object like a particular can of soup. It didn't take too long to clear this one up:

> **Susan:** When you say "rather than a specific object", how much more specific can you get than "chunky chicken soup, 16 oz."?

> **Steve:** Each can of chunky chicken soup is at least slightly different from every other one; at least they are in different places.

Let's recap what we know about a StockItem so far. We need a member variable in the StockItem class definition for each value in the above description: the name of the item (m_Name), its price (m_Price), the number of items in stock (m_InStock), the name of the distributor (m_Distributor), and the UPC (m_UPC) of the item. Of course, merely storing these data isn't very useful unless we can do something with them. Therefore, objects of the StockItem class also need to be able to perform several operations on their data; we'll start by giving them the ability to display their contents. Figure 6.1 illustrates a very simple way that this class might be used.

FIGURE 6.1. The initial sample program for the StockItem class
(code\itemtst1.cc)

```cpp
#include <iostream.h>
#include "string6.h"
#include "item1.h"

int main()
{
    StockItem soup;

    soup = StockItem("Chunky Chicken",32,129,
```

```
        "Bob's Distribution","123456789");

        soup.Display();

        return 0;
    }
```

This program defines a StockItem named soup, assigns it some data, displays it on the screen via a function called Display, and finally terminates normally. By the time we're done with this chapter, you'll understand exactly how every operation in this program is performed by the StockItem class. Before we get too deeply into this particular class, however, we should look at the functions that almost all classes have in common. First, we'll need some more definitions to clarify the terms that we'll need for the discussion.

More Definitions

A **concrete data type** is a class whose objects behave like variables of native data types. That is, the class gives the compiler enough information that its objects can be created, copied, assigned, and automatically destroyed just as native variables are. The StockItem class that we will construct in this chapter is a concrete data type.

A **constructor** is a member function that creates new variables of the class to which it belongs. All constructors have the same name as the class for which they are constructors; therefore, the constructors for StockItem variables also have the name StockItem.

A **default constructor** is a constructor that is used when no initial value is specified for an object. Because it is a constructor, it has the same name as the class; since it is used when no initial value is specified, it has no arguments. Thus, StockItem() is the default constructor for the StockItem class.

A **copy constructor** is a constructor that makes a new object with the same contents as an existing object of the same type.

An **assignment operator** is a member function that sets a pre-existing object to the same value as another object of the same type.

A **destructor** is a member function that cleans up when an object expires; for a local object, this occurs at the end of the block where that object is defined.

. (period) is the **object member access** operator. It separates an object name, on its left, from the member variable or member function on its right.

:: is the class **membership operator**, which indicates the class a variable or function belongs to.

Common Behavior

While different classes vary considerably in the facilities that they provide, there are significant benefits to a class whose objects behave like those of native types. As I've just mentioned, such a class is called a *concrete data type*. To make a class a concrete data type, we must define certain member functions that allow creation, copying, and deletion to behave as with a native variable.

Susan wanted to see a chart illustrating the correspondence between what the compiler does for a native type and what we have to do to allow a new data type that we define to behave in the same way as a native data type; that is, to make our new type a concrete data type. Of course, I complied with her request: the result is Figure 6.2.

FIGURE 6.2. Comparison between native and user-defined types

The Native Problem	A Concrete Plan
Here are the essential facilities that the compiler provides for every native type:	To make a concrete data type, we have to provide each of these facilities for our new type. By no coincidence, there is a specific type of member function to provide each of them. Here are the official names and descriptions of each of these four functions:
1. The ability to create a variable with no specified initial value , e.g., short x;.	**1**. A *default constructor* that can create an object when there is no initial value specified for the object.
2. The ability to pass a variable as an argument to a function; in this case, the compiler has to make a copy of the variable so that the called function doesn't change the value of the variable in the calling function.	**2**. A *copy constructor* that can make a new object with the same contents as an existing object of the same type.
3. The ability to assign a value of an appropriate type to an existing variable such as x = 22; or x = z;.	**3**. An *assignment operator* that is used to set an existing object to the value of another object of the same type.
4. Reclaiming the storage assigned to a variable when it ceases to exist, so that those memory addresses can be reallocated to other uses. In the case of auto variables, this is at the end of the block where they were created; with static variables, it's at the end of execution of the program.	**4**. A *destructor* that cleans up when an object ceases to exist, including releasing the memory that the object has occupied; for an auto object, this occurs at the end of the block where the object was created; with static variables, it's at the end of execution of the program.

Because these member functions are so fundamental to the proper operation of a class, the compiler will generate a version of each of them for us if we don't write them ourselves, just as the corresponding behavior is automatically supplied for the native types. As we will see in Chapter 7, the compiler-generated functions are generally too simplistic to be used in a complex class. In such a case we need to create our own versions of these functions; I'll illustrate how to do that at the appropriate time. However, with a simple class such as the one we're creating here, the compiler-generated versions of the assignment operator, copy constructor, and destructor are perfectly adequate, so we won't be creating our own versions of these functions for StockItem.

Susan was a bit confused about the distinction between the compiler-generated versions of these essential functions and the compiler's built-in knowledge of the native types:

Susan: Aren't the compiler-generated versions the same thing as the native versions?

Steve: No, they're analogous but not the same. The compiler-generated functions are created only for objects, not for native types. The behavior of the native types is implemented directly in the compiler, not by means of functions.

Susan: I'm confused. Maybe it would help if you explained what you mean by "implemented directly in the compiler". Are you just saying that objects are implemented only by functions, whereas the native types are implemented by the built-in facilities of the compiler?

Steve: You're not confused, you're correct.

Susan: Okay, here we go again. About the assignment operator, what is this "version"? I thought you said earlier that if you don't write your own assignment operator it will use the native operator. So I don't get this.

Steve: There is no native assignment operator for any class type; instead, the compiler will generate an assignment operator for a class if we don't do it ourselves.

Susan: Then how can the compiler create an assignment operator if it doesn't know what it is doing?

Steve: All the compiler-generated assignment operator does is to copy all of the members of the right-hand variable to the left-hand variable. This is good enough with the StockItem class. We'll see in Chapter 7 why this isn't always acceptable.

Susan: Isn't a simple copy all that the native assignment operator does?

Steve: The only native assignment operators that exist are for native types. Once we define our own types, the compiler has to generate assignment operators for us if we don't do it ourselves; otherwise, it would be impossible to copy the value of one variable of a class type to another without writing an assignment operator explicitly.

Susan: Okay, this is what confused me, I just thought that the natives would be used as a default if we didn't define our own in the class type, even though they would not work well.

Steve: They will. That's what the compiler-generated assignment operator does. I think we have a semantic problem here, not a substantive one.

Susan: Why doesn't it default to the native assignment operator if it doesn't have any other information to direct it to make a class type operator? This is most distressing to me.

Steve: There isn't any native assignment operator for a StockItem. How could there be? The compiler has never heard of a StockItem until we define that class.

Susan: So it would be a third type of assignment operator. At this point, I am aware of the native type, the user defined type and a compiler-generated type.

Steve: Right. The native type is built into the compiler, the user defined type is defined by ... the user, and the compiler-generated type is created by the compiler for user defined types where the user didn't define his own.

Susan: Then the native and the compiler-generated assignment operator are the same? If so, why did you agree with me that there must be three different types of assignment operators? In that case there would really only be two.

Steve: No, there is a difference. Here is the rundown:

1. (Native assignment) The knowledge of how to assign values of every native type is built into the compiler; whenever such an assignment is needed, the compiler emits prewritten code that copies the value from the source variable to the destination variable.

2. (Compiler-generated assignment) The knowledge of how to create a defaults assignment operator for any class type is built into the compiler; if we don't define an assignment operator for a given class, the compiler generates code for an assignment operator that merely copies all of the members of the source variable to the destination variable. Note that this is slightly different from 1, where the compiler copies canned the instructions directly into the object file whenever the assignment is done; here, it generates an assignment operator for the specific class in question and then uses that operator whenever an assignment is done.

3. (User defined assignment) This does exactly what we define it to do.

Susan: Did you ever discuss the source variable and the destination variable? I don't recall that concept in past discussions. I like this. All I remember is when you said that = means to set the variable on the left to the value on the right. Does this mean that the variable on the left is the destination variable and the value on the right is the source variable?

Steve: Yes, if the value on the right is a variable; it could also be an expression such as "x + 2".

Susan: But how could it be a variable if it is a known value?

Steve: It's not its value that is known, but its name. Its value can vary at run time, depending on how the program has executed up till this point.

Susan: So the main difference is that in 1 the instructions are already there to be used. In 2 the instructions for the assignment operator have to be generated before they can be used.

Steve: That's a good explanation.

After my explanation of the advantages of a concrete data type, Susan became completely convinced, so much so that she wondered why we would ever want anything else.

Susan: On your definition for concrete data types. . . this is fine, but what I am thinking is that if something *wasn't* a concrete data type, then it wouldn't work, that is unless it was native. So what would a workable alternative to a concrete data type be?

Steve: Usually, we do want our objects to be concrete data types. However, there are times when, say, we don't want to copy a given object. For example, in the case of an object representing a window on the screen, copying such an object might cause another window to be displayed, which is probably not what we would want to happen.

Susan: Okay, so what would you call an object that isn't of a concrete data type?

Steve: There's no special name for an object that *isn't* of a concrete data type.

Susan: So things that are not of a concrete data type have no names?

Steve: No, they have names; I was just saying that there's no term like *non-concrete data type*, meaning one that doesn't act like a native variable. There is a term *abstract data type*, but that means something else.

Susan: See, this is where I am still not clear. Again, if something is *not* a concrete data type, then what is it?

Steve: There's no special term for a class that doesn't act like a native variable type. If something isn't a concrete data type, then you can't treat it like a native variable. Either you can't copy it, or you can't assign to it, or you can't construct it by default, or you can't destruct it automatically at the end of the function (or some combination of these). The lack of any of those features prevents a class from being a concrete data type.

Susan: Of what use would it be to have a class of a non-concrete data type? To me, it just sounds like an error.

Steve: Sometimes it does make sense. For example, you might want to create a class that has no default constructor; to create an element of such a class, you would have to supply one or more arguments. This is useful in preventing the use of an object that doesn't have any meaningful content; however, the lack of a default constructor does restrict the applicability of such a class, so it's best to provide such a constructor if possible.

Before we can implement the member functions for our StockItem class, we have to define what a StockItem is in more detail than my previous sketch.[4] Let's start with the initial version of the interface specification for that class in Figure 6.3, which includes the specification of the default constructor, the display function, and another constructor that is specific to the StockItem class.

I strongly recommend that you print out the files that contain this interface and its implementation, as well as the test program, for reference as you are going through this part of the chapter; those files are item1.h, item1.cc, and itemtst1.cc, respectively.

FIGURE 6.3. The initial interface of the StockItem class (**code\item1.h**)

```
class StockItem
{
public:
    StockItem();

    StockItem(string Name, short InStock, short Price,
    string Distributor, string UPC);

    void Display();

private:
    short m_InStock;
    short m_Price;
    string m_Name;
    string m_Distributor;
    string m_UPC;
};
```

Your first reaction is probably something like "What a bunch of malarkey!" Let's take it a little at a time, and you'll see that this seeming gibberish actually has a rhyme and reason to it. First we have the line class StockItem. This tells the compiler that what follows is

---

4. By the way, in using a functional class such as StockItem to illustrate these concepts, I'm violating a venerable tradition in C++ tutorials. Normally, example classes represent zoo animals, or shapes, or something equally useful in common programming situations.

the definition of a class interface, which as we have already seen is a description of the operations that can be performed on objects of a given user defined type; in this case, the type is StockItem. So that the compiler knows where this description begins and ends, it is enclosed in {}, just like any other block of information that is to be treated as one item.

After the opening {, the next line says public:. This is a new type of declaration called an **access specifier**, which tells the compiler the "security classification" of the item(s) following it, up to the next access specifier. This particular access specifier, public, means that any part of the program, whether it is defined in this class or not, can use the items starting immediately after the public declaration, and continuing until there is another access specifier. In the current case, all of the items following the public specifier are operations that we wish to perform on StockItem objects. Since they are public, we can use them anywhere in our programs. You may be wondering why everything isn't public; why should we prevent ourselves (or users of our classes) from using everything in the classes? It's not just hardheartedness; it's actually a way of improving the reliability and flexibility of our software, as I'll explain later.

As you might imagine, this notion of access specifiers didn't get past Susan without a battle. Here's the blow-by-blow account.

> **Susan:** So, is public a word that is used often or is it just something you made up for this example?

> **Steve:** It's a keyword of the C++ language, which has intrinsic meaning to the compiler. In this context, it means "any function, inside or outside this class, can access the following stuff, up to the next access specifier (if any)". Because it is a keyword, you can't have a variable named public, just as you can't have one named if.

> **Susan:** These access specifiers: What are they, anyway? Are they always used in classes?

> **Steve:** Yes.

Susan: Why aren't they needed for native variables?

Steve: Because you can't affect the implementation of native types; their internals are all predefined in the compiler.

Susan: What does *internals* mean? Do you mean stuff that is done by the compiler rather than stuff that can be done by the programmer?

Steve: Yes, in the case of native data types. In the case of class types, *internals* means the details of implementation of the type rather than what it does for the user.

Susan: You know, I understand what you are saying about *internals*; that is, I know what the words mean, but I just can't picture what you are doing when you say *implementation*. I don't see what is actually happening at this point.

Steve: The implementation of a class is the code that is responsible for actually doing the things that the interface says the objects of the class can do. All of the code in the item1.cc file is part of the implementation of StockItem. In addition, the private member variables in the header file are logically part of the implementation, since the user of the class can't access them directly.

Susan: Why is a class function called a *member function*? I like class function better; it is more intuitive.

Steve: Sorry, I didn't make up the terminology. However, I think *member function* is actually more descriptive, because these functions are members (parts) of the objects of the class.

Susan: So on these variables, that m_ stuff; do you just do that to differentiate them from a native variable? If so, why would there be a confusion, since you have already told the compiler you are defining a class? Therefore, all that is in that class should already be understood to be in the class rather than the native language. I don't like to look at that m_ stuff; it's too cryptic.

Steve: It's true that the compiler can tell whether a variable is a member variable or a global variable. However, it can still be useful to give a different name to a member variable so that the *programmer* can tell which is which. Remember, a member variable looks like a global variable in a class implementation, because you don't declare it as you would an argument or a local variable.

Now we're up to the line that says StockItem();. This is the declaration for a function called a *constructor*, which tells the compiler what to do when we define a variable of a user defined type. This particular constructor is the *default constructor* for the StockItem class. It's called the "default" constructor because it is used when no initial value is specified by the user; the empty parentheses after the name of the function indicate the lack of arguments to the function. The name of the function is the clue that it's a constructor; the name of a constructor is always the same as the name of the class for which it's a constructor, to make it easier for the compiler to identify constructors among all of the possible functions in a class.

This idea of having variables and functions "inside" objects wasn't intuitively obvious to Susan:

Susan: Now, where you talk about mixing a string and a short in the same function, can this not be done in the native language?

Steve: It's not in the same function but in the same variable. We are creating a user defined variable that can be used just like a native variable.

Susan: Okay, so you have a class StockItem. And it has a function called StockItem. But a StockItem is a variable, so in this respect a function can be inside a variable?

Steve: Correct. A StockItem is a variable that is composed of a number of functions and other variables.

Susan: Okay, I think I am seeing the big picture now. But you know that this seems like such a departure from what I thought was going on before, where we used native types in functions rather than the other way around. Like when I wrote my little program, it would have shorts in it but they would be in the function main. So this is a complete turnabout from the way I used to think about them; this is hard.

Steve: Yes, that is a difficult transition to make. Interestingly enough, experience isn't necessarily an advantage here; you haven't had as much trouble with it as some professional programmers who have a lot more experience in writing functions as "stand-alone" things with no intrinsic ties to data structures. However, it is one of the essentials in object-oriented programming; most functions live "inside" objects, and do the bidding of those objects, rather than being wild and free.

Why do we need to write our own default constructor? Well, although we have already specified the member variables used by the class, so that the compiler can assign storage as with any other static or auto variable, that isn't enough information for the compiler to know how to initialize the objects of the class correctly.[5] Unlike a native variable, the compiler can't set a newly created StockItem to a reasonable value, since it doesn't understand what the member variables of a StockItem are used for. That is, it can't do the

---

5.   In case it isn't obvious how the compiler can figure out the size of the object, consider that the class definition specifies all of the variables that are used to implement the objects of the class. When we define a new class, the types of all of the member variables of the class must already be defined. Therefore, the compiler can calculate the size of our class variables based on the sizes of those member variables. By the way, the size of our object isn't necessarily the sum of the sizes of its member variables; the compiler often has to add some other information to the objects. We'll see one of the reasons for this later in this book.

initialization without help from us. In the code for our default constructor, we will initialize the member variables to legitimate values, so that we don't have to worry about having an uninitialized StockItem lying around as we did with a short in a previous example. Figure 6.4 shows what the code to our first default constructor looks like.

FIGURE 6.4. The default constructor for the StockItem class **(from code\item1.cc)**

```
StockItem::StockItem()
: m_InStock(0), m_Price(0), m_Name(), m_Distributor(), m_UPC()
{
}
```

Let's use this example of a StockItem class to illuminate the distinction between interface and implementation. As I've already mentioned, the implementation of a claass is the code that is responsible for actually doing the things promised by the interface of that class. The interface was laid out in Figure 6.3. With the exception of the test program that illustrates the use of the StockItem class, all of the code that we will examine in this chapter is part of the implementation. This includes the constructors and the Display member function.

So you can keep track of where this fits into the "big picture", the code in Figure 6.4 is the implementation of the function StockItem::StockItem() (i.e., the default constructor for the class StockItem), whose interface was defined in Figure 6.3. Now, how does it work? Actually, this function isn't all that different from a "regular" function, but there are some important differences. First of all, the name looks sort of funny: Why is StockItem repeated?

The answer is that, unlike "regular" (technically, *global*) functions, a *member function* always belongs to a particular class. That is, such a function has special access to the data and other functions in the class. To mark its membership, its name consists of the name of the class (in this case, StockItem), followed by the class membership operator ::, followed by the name of the function (which in this case, is also StockItem); as we have already seen, the name of a constructor is always the same as the name of its class. Figure 6.5 shows how each component of the function declaration contributes to the whole.[6]

FIGURE 6.5. Declaring the default constructor for the StockItem class

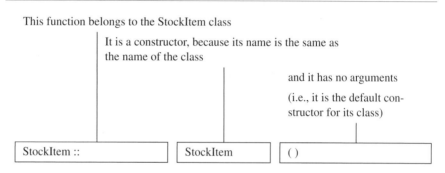

If you've really been paying attention, there's one thing that you may have noticed about this declaration as compared with the original declaration of this function in the class interface definition for StockItem (Figure 6.3). In that figure, we declared this same function as StockItem();, without the additional StockItem:: on the front. Why didn't we need to use the StockItem:: class membership notation in the class interface definition? Because inside the declaration of a class, we don't have to specify what class the member functions belong to; by definition, they belong to the class we're defining. Thus, StockItem() in the class interface declaration means "the member function StockItem, having no arguments"; i.e., the default constructor for the StockItem class.

Susan didn't have any trouble with this point, which was quite a relief to me, as I was dreading a big argument.

---

6.   By the way, spaces between components of the name aren't significant; that is, we can include them as in Figure 6.5, or leave them out as in Figure 6.4.

Susan: Oh, so you don't have to write StockItem::StockItem in the interface definition because it is implied by the class StockItem declaration?

Steve: Right.

Now let's look at the part of the constructor that initializes the member variables of the StockItem class, the *member initialization list*. The start of a member initialization list is signified by a : after the closing) of the constructor declaration, and the expressions in the list are separated by commas. A member initialization list can be used only with constructors, not any other type of functions.

The member initialization list of the default StockItem constructor is: : m_InStock(0), m_Price(0), m_Name(), m_Distributor(), m_UPC(). What does this mean exactly? Well, as its name indicates, it is a list of *member initialization expressions*, each of which initializes one member variable. In the case of a member variable of a native type such as short, a member initialization expression is equivalent to creating the variable with the initial value specified in the parentheses. In the case of a member variable of a class type, a member initialization expression is equivalent to creating the variable by calling the constructor that matches the type(s) of argument(s) specified in the parentheses, or the default constructor if there are no arguments specified. So the expression m_InStock(0) is equivalent to the creation and simultaneous initialization of a local variable by the statement short m_InStock = 0;. Similarly, the expression m_Name() is equivalent to the creation and simultaneous initialization of a local variable by the statement string m_Name;. Such a statement, of course, would initialize the string m_Name to the default value for a string, which happens to be the empty C string "".

Using a member initialization list is the best way to set up member variables in a constructor, for two reasons. First, it's more efficient than using assignment statements to set the values of member variables. For example, suppose that we were to write this constructor as shown in Figure 6.6.

FIGURE 6.6. **Another way to write the default** StockItem **constructor**

```
StockItem:: StockItem ()
{
  m_InStock = 0;
  m_Price = 0;
  m_Name = "";
  m_Distributor = "";
  m_UPC = "";
}
```

If we wrote the constructor that way, before we got to the opening {
of the constructor, all of the member variables that had constructors
(here, the strings) would be initialized to their default values. After
the {, they would be set to the values we specified in the code for the
constructor. It's true that we could solve this problem in this specific
example by simply not initializing the strings at all, as that would
mean that they would be initialized to their default values anyway, but
that solution wouldn't apply in other constructors such as the one in
Figure 6.7, where the member variables have specified values rather
than default ones.

The second reason that we should use a member initialization list
to initialize our member variables is that some member "variables"
aren't variables at all but constants. We'll see how to define consts, as
they are called in C++, in a later chapter. For now, it's enough to
know that you can't assign a value to a const, but you can (and indeed
have to) initialize it; therefore, when dealing with member consts, a
member initialization list isn't just a good idea, it's the law.

There is one fine point that isn't obvious from looking at the code
for this constructor: The expressions in a member initialization list
are executed in the order in which the member variables being
initialized are declared in the class definition, which is *not*
necessarily the order in which the expressions appear in the list. In
our example, since m_InStock appears before m_Name in the class
definition, the member initialization expression for m_InStock will be

executed before the expression initializing m_Name. This doesn't matter right now, but it will be important in Chapter 7, where we will be using initialization expressions whose order of execution is important.

You may have noticed that the executable part of the function shown in Figure 6.4 is empty, because all of the work has already been done by the member initialization list. This is fairly common, but not universal; as we'll see in Chapter 7, sometimes a constructor has to do something other than initialize member variables, in which case we need some code inside the {}.

Susan objected to my cavalier use of the empty C string "":

Susan: Excuse me, but what kind of value is " " ? Do you know how annoying it is to keep working with nothing?

Steve: It's not " ", but "". The former has a space between the quotes, and the latter does not; the former is a one-character C string consisting of one space, while the latter is a zero-character C string.

Susan: Okay, so "" is an empty C string, but could you please explain how this works?

Steve: The "" means that we have a C string with no data in it. The compiler generates a literal C string consisting of just the terminating null byte.

Susan: What good does that do? I don't get it.

Steve: Well, a string has to have some value for its char* to point to; if we don't have any real data, then using an empty C string for that purpose is analogous to setting a numeric value to 0.

Susan: Okay, so this is only setting the strings in the default constructor to a value that the compiler can understand so you don't get an error message, although there is no real data. We're trying to fool the compiler, right?

Steve: Close, but not quite. Basically, we want to make sure that we know the state of the strings in a default StockItem. We don't want to have trouble with uninitialized variables; remember how much trouble they can cause?

Susan: Yes, I remember. So this is just the way to initialize a string when you don't know what real value it will end up having?

Steve: Yes, that's how we're using it here.

Now let's get back to the member variables of StockItem. One important characteristic of any variable is its scope, so we should pay attention to the scope of these variables. In Chapter 5, we saw two scopes in which a variable could be defined: *local* (i.e., available only within the block where it was defined) and *global* (i.e., available anywhere in the program). Well, these variables aren't arguments (which have local scope) since they don't appear in the function's header, and they aren't defined in the function; therefore, they aren't local variables. Surely they can't be global variables, after I showed you how treacherous those can be.

Go to the Head of the class

I haven't misled you on that point; there is another scope called class scope, which applies to all member variables of a class. Variables with class scope occupy separate memory locations for each object of a given class; i.e., each object has its own separate set of member variables distinct from the member variables of any other objects of the same type.[7] In the case of StockItem, this set of member variables consists of m_InStock, m_Price, m_Name, m_Distributor, and m_UPC.

Member functions of a class can access member variables of objects of that class without defining them, as though they were global variables.

In addition to scope, each member variable has another attribute we have already encountered: an access specifier. The access of nonmember functions to any member variable or member function depends on the access specifier in effect when the member variable or function was declared. If you look back at Figure 6.3, you'll see that the line private: precedes the declaration of the member variables in the StockItem class. The keyword private is an access specifier, like public; however, where a public access specifier allows any function to access the items that follow it, a private access specifier allows only member functions to access items that follow it.

Susan had some more questions about access specifiers, including this new one, private:

Susan: It seems to me that the access specifiers act more like scope than anything. Are they about the same?

Steve: Yes, the difference between public and private is somewhat analogous to the difference between global and local variables, but the latter distinction affects where a variable is stored and when it is initialized, whereas an access specifier controls what functions can access the variable. However, because member variables are defined inside classes, they can't be global, nor can they be local in the sense that a "regular" (i.e., nonmember) variable can be; a member variable must always live inside a single occurrence of an object of its class.

But although scope rules and access specifiers are similar in some ways, in that they affect where a variable can be used, they aren't exactly the same. Scope defines where a variable is visible, whereas

---

7. Actually, I'm describing "normal" member variables here. There is another kind of member variable, called a *static member variable*, of which only one exists for a given class. We won't be using this type of member variable in this book.

access specifiers control where a variable (or function) is accessible. That is, if you write a program that tries to read or modify a private variable from outside the class implementation, the compiler knows what you're trying to do but won't let you do it. On the other hand, if you try to access a local variable from a function where it isn't defined, the compiler just tells you it never heard of that variable, which indeed it hasn't in that context. For example, let's suppose that the local variable x defined in function abc has no existence in any other function; in that case, if you try to access a variable named x in another function, say def, where it hasn't been defined, you'll get an error message from the compiler telling you that there is no variable x in function def. However, if there is a private member variable called x defined in class ghi, and you try to access that member variable from a nonmember function, the compiler will tell you that you're trying to do something illegal. It knows which x you mean, but it won't let you access it because you don't have permission.

Susan: Are they necessary for every class?

Steve: Pretty much. The default specifier for a class is private; that is, everything you declare in a class interface before the first explicit access specifier is private. Of course, this also means that if you don't ever provide an explicit access specifier in a given class, then everything declared in that class will be private. This isn't usually very useful, because without any public functions it's hard to use a class at all.

Susan: There is a default? Then why would the default be the least useful?

Steve: To make the programmer specify what should be publicly accessible rather than have it happen automatically. In general, it's best to keep as much as possible private, to reduce the dependency of external code on the internal implementation of the class. This makes it easier to change that implementation without causing trouble for the users of the class.

Susan: Okay, that makes sense now. Are there any other kinds of access specifiers or are these the only two?

Steve: Actually, there's one more called protected, that is sort of in between public and private; we'll start using it in Chapter 9.

Susan also wanted some more details about this new class scope.

Susan: How about explaining the difference between a class scope and a public access specifier?

Steve: Variables declared in a class, regardless of their access specifier, have class scope; that means that they live as long as the object that contains them. The access specifier determines who can access these variables, but does not affect their lifetime.

Of course, the constructor StockItem::StockItem(), by virtue of being a member function, has access to all member variables, so the private access specifier doesn't apply to it. We'll see later how that access specifier comes into play.

Now that we know what kind of variables the StockItem::StockItem() function deals with, its behavior isn't very mysterious: it simply initializes the member variables to 0 or the default string value (""), whichever is appropriate to their types. That's all very well, but it doesn't answer a very important question: What exactly do these member variables do? The answer is that they don't do anything by themselves; rather, they are the "raw material" the member functions use to implement the behavior that we want a StockItem to display. If you recall the discussion of interface vs. implementation, then you'll appreciate that the private member variables are also essentially part of the implementation and not part of the interface: Even though they are defined in the header file, the user of the class can't access them directly.

That's why we call variables that are declared inside the class definition *member variables*, and functions that are declared inside the class definition *member functions*; They "belong" to the class that we're defining. The member functions set, change, and use the values of the member variables in the course of implementing the behaviors that the StockItem class interface definition promises.[8]

Susan wasn't buying all this malarkey about member variables without a fight. Here's how it went.

> **Susan:** What do m_InStock and m_Price and the others actually do? It seems we are missing a verb here.

> **Steve:** They don't do anything by themselves. They are the member variables used to store the count and price of the goods described by a StockItem object, respectively. In the default constructor, they are both set to 0, indicating a StockItem with no content. This is the equivalent of the value 0 that is used to initialize statically allocated numeric variables and is used in the same way; that is, any StockItem that is created without a value is set to this empty state. Notice that this doesn't apply only to statically allocated StockItems, but to all StockItems; this is an example where a user defined type is superior to a native type. That is, we don't have to worry about having an uninitialized StockItem, because the default constructor ensures that every StockItem is set to a known value when it is created.

> **Susan:** Ugh. Don't remind me about uninitialized variables. Okay, that makes more sense now.

So much for the "high-altitude" description of what a class does. Now let's get back to the details that make it work, starting with a little puzzle: figuring out where the StockItem::StockItem() function is used in the test program in Figure 6.1. Believe it or not, this

---

8. The special status of member functions and variables as implementation aids explains why access specifiers such as public are applicable only to data or functions declared in a class, since the purpose of access specifiers is to control "outside" access to variables and functions used to implement a class. You can't apply access specifiers to native types, because the way they are implemented is not accessible to the programmer.

constructor is actually used in that program: To be exact, the line StockItem soup; calls it. Remember that the basic idea of constructing a class is to add data types to the language that aren't available "out of the box". One of the functions that we have to help the compiler with is initialization; a main purpose for the StockItem::StockItem() constructor is to initialize variables of the StockItem type that aren't explicitly initialized. That's why it's called a *default constructor*.

Susan didn't immediately cotton to the idea of calling a default constructor by simply defining a variable of that class.

> **Susan:** Sure, defining an object is simple if you don't lose your mind defining the classes first.

> **Steve:** It *is* simple for the application programmer (the user of the class). We're doing the hard part so he can just use the objects without having to worry about any of this stuff.

> **Susan:** Huh? Isn't the the "user of the class" always the same as the "writer of the class"?

> **Steve:** Not necessarily. You've been using strings (and vectors, for that matter) for some time now without having to be concerned about how they work. This is not unusual.

> **Susan:** Yeah, but if you are a programmer you will be a class writer, not just a user.

> **Steve:** Probably not with respect to all classes. You may very well write your own application-specific classes but use existing ones for all of the low-level stuff like vectors, strings, etc.

You should generally write a default constructor for every class you define, to guarantee the state of any "default constructed" variable. If you don't declare a default constructor, the compiler will supply one for you; however, since it doesn't know much about your class, it won't be able to guarantee very much about the initial state of one of your variables. The moral is that you should define your own default constructor. As you can see from our example, it's not much work.

So why did I say "generally", rather than "always"? Because there are some times when you don't want to allow an object to be created unless the "real" data for it are available. As with the copy constructor, the compiler will generate a default constructor for you automatically; to prevent this, you can declare a private default constructor that will cause a compiler error in any user code that tries to define an object of that class without specifying an initial value. You don't have to implement this constructor, because a program that tries to use it won't compile and thus will never be linked.

Susan thought that the idea of having to define a default constructor for each class was a bit off the wall.

> **Susan:** When you say that "you should define one of these (default constructors) for every class you define..." my question is how? What are you talking about? I thought a default meant just that, it was a default, you don't have to do anything with it, it is set to a preassigned value.

> **Steve:** It's true that the class user doesn't have to do anything with the default constructors. However, the class writer (that's us, in this case) has to define the default constructor so that when the class user defines an object without initializing it, the new object has a reasonable state for an "empty" object. This prevents problems like those caused by uninitialized variables of native types.

Shop till You Drop

Now let's continue with our analysis of the class interface (Figure 6.3 on page 323). Before we can do anything with an inventory record, we have to enter the inventory data. This means that we need another constructor that actually sets the values into the object. We also need some way to display the data for a StockItem on the screen, which means writing a Display function.

The next line of that figure is the declaration of the constructor that creates an object with actual data:

StockItem(string Name, short InStock, short Price, string Distributor, string UPC);

We can tell that this function is a constructor because its name, StockItem, is the same as the name of the class. If you're a C programmer, you may be surprised to see two functions that have the same name, differing only in the types of their arguments. This is not legal in C, but it is in C++; it's called **function overloading**, and as you'll see, it's a very handy facility that isn't limited to constructors. The combination of the function name and argument types is called the **signature** of a function; two functions that have the same name but differ in the type of at least one argument are distinct functions.[9] In the case of the default constructor, there are no arguments, so that constructor is used where no initial data are specified for the object. The statement StockItem soup; in the sample program (Figure 6.1) fits that description, so the default constructor is used. However, in the next statement of the sample program, we have the expression:

StockItem("Chunky Chicken", 32, 129, "Bob's Distribution", "123456789");

This is clearly a call to a constructor, because the name of the function is the name of a class, StockItem. Therefore, the compiler looks for a constructor that can handle the set of arguments in this call, and finds the following declaration:

---

9. Note that the names of the arguments are not part of the signature; in fact, you don't have to specify them in the function declaration. However, you should use meaningful argument names in the function declaration so the user of the function has some idea what the arguments to the function might represent. After all, the declaration StockItem(string, short, short, string, string); doesn't provide much information on what its arguments actually mean.

StockItem(string Name, short InStock, short Price, string Distributor, string UPC);

The first, fourth, and fifth arguments to the constructor are strings, while the second and third are shorts. Since these types all match those specified in the expression in the sample program, the compiler can translate that expression into a call to this constructor.

Figure 6.7 shows the code for that constructor.

FIGURE 6.7. Another constructor for the StockItem class **(from code\item1.cc)**

```
StockItem:: StockItem (string Name, short InStock,
short Price, string Distributor, string UPC)
: m_Name(Name), m_InStock(InStock), m_Price(Price),
m_Distributor(Distributor), m_UPC(UPC)
{
}
```

As you can see, nothing about this constructor is terribly complex; it merely uses the member initialization list to set the member variables of the object being constructed to the values of their corresponding arguments.

But why do we need more than one constructor? Susan had that same question, and I had some answers for her.

Susan: How many constructors do you need to say the same thing?

Steve: They don't say exactly the same thing. It's true that every constructor in the StockItem class makes a StockItem; however, each argument list varies. The default constructor makes an empty StockItem and therefore doesn't need any arguments, whereas the constructor StockItem::StockItem(string Name, short InStock, short Price, string Distributor, string UPC) makes a StockItem with the values specified by the Name, InStock, Price, Distributor, and UPC arguments in the constructor call.

Susan: Are you saying that in defining a class you can have two functions that have the same name, but they are different in only their arguments and that makes them unique?

Steve: Exactly. This is the language feature called *function overloading*.

Susan: So StockItem soup; is the default constructor in case you need something that can create uninitialized objects?

Steve: Not quite; the default constructor for the StockItem class is StockItem::StockItem(), which doesn't need any arguments, because it constructs an empty StockItem. The line StockItem soup; causes the default constructor to be called to create an empty StockItem.

Susan: And the line StockItem("Chunky Chicken",32,129,"Bob's Distribution","123456789"); is a constructor that finally gets around to telling us what we are trying to accomplish here?

Steve: No, that line causes a StockItem with the specified contents to be created, by calling the constructor StockItem::StockItem (string Name, short InStock, short Price, string Distributor, string UPC);.

Susan: So are you saying that for every new StockItem you have to have a new constructor for it?

Steve: No, there's one constructor for each way that we can construct a StockItem. One for situations where we don't have any initial data (the default constructor), one for those where we're copying one StockItem to another (the compiler-generated copy constructor), and one for those where we are supplying the data for a StockItem. There could be other ones too, but those are all we have right now.

Once that expression has been translated, the compiler has to figure out how to assign the result of the expression to the StockItem object called soup, as requested in the whole statement:

soup = StockItem("Chunky Chicken", 32, 129, "Bob's Distribution", "123456789");

Since the compiler has generated its own version of the assignment operator = for the StockItem class, it can translate that part of the statement as well, which results in the StockItem object named soup having the value produced by the constructor.

Finally, we have the line soup.Display(); which displays the value of soup on the screen. Figure 6.8 shows the code for that function.

FIGURE 6.8. Display **member function for the** StockItem class **(from code\item1.cc)**

```
void StockItem:: Display ()
{
  cout << "Name: ";
  cout << m_Name << endl;
  cout << "Number in stock: ";
  cout << m_InStock << endl;
  cout << "Price: ";
  cout << m_Price << endl;
  cout << "Distributor: ";
  cout << m_Distributor << endl;
  cout << "UPC: ";
  cout << m_UPC << endl;
}
```

This is also not very complicated; it just uses << to copy each of the parts of the StockItem object to cout, along with some identifying information that makes it easier to figure out what the values represent.

Susan wanted to know how we could use << without defining a special version for this class.

Susan: Hey, how come you don't have to define << as a class operator? Does the compiler just use the native <<? And that works okay?

Steve: We're using << only for types that already have it defined, which includes all of the native types, as well as the one I provided as part of the string class. If we wanted to apply << to a StockItem, we'd have to write our own version; you'll see how we do that when we go into the implementation of string.

Susan: Then please explain to me why << is being used in Figure 6.8, which is for the StockItem class.

Steve: It's being used for strings and shorts, not objects of the StockItem class. The fact that the strings and shorts are inside the StockItem class is irrelevant in this context; they're still strings and shorts, and therefore can be displayed by the << operators that handle strings and shorts.

Susan: So the stuff you get out of the standard library is only for the use of class types? Not native?

Steve: The iostreams library is designed to be able to handle both native types and class types; however, the latter use requires the class writer to do some extra work, as we'll see when we add these functions to the string class in Chapter 8.

Susan: So that means that the library is set up to understand things we make up for our class types?

Steve: Not exactly. However, if we follow the library's rules when creating our own versions of << and >>, then we'll be able to use those operators to read and write our data as though the ability to handle those types was built into the library.

That should clear up most of the potential problems with the meaning of this Display function. However, it does contain one construct that we haven't seen before: void. This is the return type of the Display function, as might be apparent from its position immediately before the class name StockItem. But what sort of return value is a void? In this context, it means simply that this function doesn't supply a return value at all.

You won't be surprised to learn that Susan had a few questions about this idea of functions that return no value.

Susan: How can a function not return a value? Then what is the point? Then would it "have no function"?

Steve: Now you're telling programming jokes? Seriously, though, the point of calling a function that returns no value is that it causes something to happen. The Display function is one example; it causes the value of a StockItem object to be displayed on the screen. Another example is a "storage function"; calling such a function can cause it to modify the value of some piece of data it is maintaining, so when you call the corresponding "retrieval function", you'll get back the value the "storage function" put away. Such lasting effects of a function call (other than returning a value) are called *side effects*.

Susan: But even a side effect is a change, so then it does do something after all, right?

Steve: Sure, it does something; every function should do something, or you wouldn't write (or call) it. However, some functions don't return any value to the calling program, in which case we specify their return type as void.

That takes care of the public part of the class definition. Now what about the private part? As I mentioned before in the discussion of how a class is defined, the access specifier private means that only member functions of the class can access the items after that specifier. It's almost always a good idea to mark all the member variables in a class as private, for two reasons.

1. If we know that only member functions of a class can change the values of member data, then we know where to look if the values of the data are incorrect. This can be extremely useful when debugging a program.

2. Marking member variables as private simplifies the task of changing or deleting those member variables should that become necessary. If the member variables are public, then we have no idea what functions are relying on their values. That means that changing or deleting these member variables can cause havoc anywhere in the system. Allowing access only by member functions means that we can make changes freely as long as all of the member functions are kept up to date.

Both of these advantages of keeping member variables private can be summed up in the term *of*, which means "hiding the details inside the class implementation rather than exposing them in the interface". This is one of the primary organizing principles that characterizes object-oriented programming.

Now that we've covered all of the member functions and variables of the StockItem class, Figure 6.9 shows the interface for the StockItem class again. As noted previously, the test program for this class, itemtst1.cc, is shown in Figure 6.1.

FIGURE 6.9. The initial interface of the StockItem class (code\item1.h)

```
class StockItem
{
public:
    StockItem();

    StockItem(string Name, short InStock, short Price,
        string Distributor, string UPC);
```

```
    void Display();

private:
    short m_InStock;
    short m_Price;
    string m_Name;
    string m_Distributor;
    string m_UPC;
};
```

There's only one more point about the member variables in the StockItem class that needs clarification; surely the price of an object in the store should be in dollars and cents, and yet we have only a short to represent it. As you know by now, a short can hold only a whole number, from –32768 to 32767. What's going on here?

Only that I've decided to store the price in cents rather than dollars and cents. That is, when someone types in a price, I'll assume that it's in cents, so "246" would mean 246 cents, or $2.46. This would of course not be acceptable in a real program, but for now it's okay.

This "trick" allows prices up to $327.67 (as well as negative numbers for things like coupons), which should be acceptable for our hypothetical grocery store. In Chapter 9, I'll give you some tips on using a different kind of numeric variable that can hold a greater variety of values. For now, though, let's stick with the short.

Figure 6.10 shows the implementation for the StockItem class.

FIGURE 6.10. The initial implementation of the StockItem class **(code\item1.cc)**

```
#include <iostream.h>
#include "string6.h"
#include "item1.h"

StockItem::StockItem()
: m_Name(), m_InStock(0), m_Price(0), m_Distributor(), m_UPC()
```

```
{
}

StockItem::StockItem(string Name, short InStock,
short Price, string Distributor, string UPC)
: m_Name(Name), m_InStock(InStock), m_Price(Price),
  m_Distributor(Distributor), m_UPC(UPC)
{
}

void StockItem::Display()
{
    cout << "Name: ";
    cout << m_Name << endl;
    cout << "Number in stock: ";
    cout << m_InStock << endl;
    cout << "Price: ";
    cout << m_Price << endl;
    cout << "Distributor: ";
    cout << m_Distributor << endl;
    cout << "UPC: ";
    cout << m_UPC << endl;
}
```

Susan had a few questions about the way that we specified the header files in this program:

Susan: Where did the #include "string6.h" come from?

Steve: I wrote it; it's the final version of the string header file as defined in Chapter 8.

Susan: So then it has not been covered up to this point? Then you might have to explain how it mysteriously appears in this code.

Steve: I'll tell the reader to expect a nauseatingly detailed description later on.

Susan: Oh, and how come this and the #include item1.h are in ""
instead of <>? I thought all header files are in <>?

Steve: Putting an include file name in "" tells the compiler to start
looking for the file in the current directory, and then search the
"standard places"; using the <> tells the compiler to skip the current
directory and start with the "standard places"; that is, where the
header files are that come with the compiler. What the "standard
places" are depends on the compiler.

Susan: I know I have not been the most focused test reader in the
last week, but did I miss something here? Did you explain way back
in an earlier chapter and I just forgot? I want to make sure that you
have explained this in the book, and even if you had earlier it would
not be a bad idea to remind the reader about this.

Steve: No, I believe it was my omission. Actually, you've been
quite focused, although not in quite the same area.

Assuming that you've installed the software from the CD-ROM in the
back of this book, you can try out this program. First, you have to
compile it by changing to the code subdirectory under the main
directory where you installed the software, and typing RHIDE
itemtst1, then using the "Make" command from the "Compile" menu.
Then exit back to DOS and type itemtst1 to run the program. You'll
see that it indeed prints out the information in the StockItem object.

To run it under the debugger, make sure you are in the code
subdirectory, and then type RHIDE itemtst1. Again, do *not* add the
".cc" to the end of the file name. Once RHIDE has started up, you can
step through the program by hitting F8, which will treat any function
call as one statement, or by hitting F7, which will step into any
function call. Any time you want to see the display that the user
would see when running the program normally, hit ALT-F5, then
ENTER to get back to the debugger.

That's good as far as it goes, but how do we use this class to keep track of all of the items in the store? Surely we aren't going to have a separately named StockItem variable for each one.

Vectoring In

This is another application for our old friend the vector; specifically, we need a vector of StockItems to store the data for all the StockItems in the store. In a real application we would need to be able to vary the number of elements in the vector, unlike our previous use of vectors. After all, the number of items in a store can vary from time to time.

As it happens, the vector data type that we are using can be resized after it is created. However, in our example program we'll ignore this complication and just use a vector that can hold 100 StockItems.[10] Even with this limitation, we will have to keep track of the number of items that are in use, so that we can store each new StockItem in its own vector element and keep track of how many items we may have to search through to find a particular StockItem. Finally, we need something to read the data for each StockItem from the inventory file where it's stored when we're not running the program.

Susan had some questions about these details of the test program:

Susan: In the paragraph when you are talking about the number of items, I am a little confused. That is, do you mean the number of different products that the store carries or the quantity of an individual item available in the store at any given time?

Steve: The number of different products, which is the same as the number of StockItems. Remember, each StockItem represents any number of objects of that exact description.

Susan: So what you're referring to is basically all the inventory in the store at any given period of time?

---

10. We'll see how to change the size of a vector in Chapter 11.

Steve: Exactly.

Susan: What do you mean by "need something to read the data" and "where it's stored when we're not running the program." I don't know what you are talking about, I don't know where that place would be.

Steve: Well, where are the data when we're not running the program? The disk. Therefore, we have to be able to read the information for the StockItems from the disk when we start the program.

Susan: Okay, that makes sense now.

Steve: I'm glad to hear it.

Figure 6.11 is a little program that shows the code necessary to read the data for the StockItem vector into memory when the program starts up.

FIGURE 6.11. Reading and displaying a vector of StockItems **(code\itemtst2.cc)**

```
#include <iostream.h>
#include <fstream.h>
#include "vector.h"
#include "string6.h"
#include "item2.h"

int main()
{
    ifstream ShopInfo("shop2.in");
    vector<StockItem> AllItems(100);
    short i;
    short InventoryCount;

    for (i = 0; i < 100; i ++)
```

```
    {
    AllItems[i].Read(ShopInfo);
    if (ShopInfo.fail() != 0)
        break;
    }

InventoryCount = i;

for (i = 0; i < InventoryCount; i ++)
    {
    AllItems[i].Display();
    }

return 0;
}
```

This program has a number of new features that need examination. First, we've had to add the "file stream" header file fstream.h to the list of include files, so that we will be able to read data in from a file. The way we do this is to create an ifstream object that is "attached" to a file when the object is constructed. In this case, the line ifstream ShopInfo("shop2.in"); creates an ifstream object called ShopInfo, and connects it to the file named shop2.in.

The next line is AllItems[i].Read(ShopInfo);, which calls the function Read for the ith StockItem in the AllItems vector, passing the ShopInfo ifstream object to a new StockItem member function called Read, which uses ShopInfo to get data from the file and store it into its StockItem (i.e., the ith element in the vector).

This whole process was anything but obvious to Susan.

Susan: How does just adding the header file fstream.h, enable you to read data in from a file?

Steve: The file fstream.h contains the declaration of the ifstream class.

Susan: Where did the ifstream class come from?

Steve: From the standard library that comes with the compiler.

Susan: Where did it come from and how did it get there? Who defined it and when was it written? Your only reference to this is just "The way we do this is to create an ifstream object that is `attached' to a file when the object is constructed". If this is just something that you wrote to aid this program that we don't have to worry about at this time, then please mention this.

Steve: I didn't write it, but we don't have to worry about it very much. I'll explain it to the minimum extent necessary.

After that bit of comic relief, let's get back to reality. Figure 6.12 is the implementation of the new Read function.

FIGURE 6.12. The Read **function for the** StockItem class **(from code\item2.cc)**

```
void StockItem:: Read (ifstream& s)
{
  s >> m_Name;
  s >> m_InStock;
  s >> m_Price;
  s >> m_Distributor;
  s >> m_UPC;
}
```

As you can see, the Read function is pretty simple; it just reads the data for one StockItem in from the file by way of the ifstream object s, using one >> expression to read each member variable's value. However, there's one construct here we haven't seen before: the & in ifstream&. As soon as we take a look at the new interface to the StockItem class (Figure 6.13), we'll see exactly what that means. I strongly recommend that you print out the files that contain this interface and its implementation, as well as the test program, for reference as you are going through this part of the chapter; those files are item2.h, item2.cc, and itemtst2.cc, respectively.

FIGURE 6.13. **The second version of the interface for the** StockItem class
(code\item2.h)

```
class StockItem
{
public:
    StockItem();

    StockItem(string Name, short InStock, short Price,
    string Distributor, string UPC);

    void Display();
    void Read(ifstream& s);

private:
    short m_InStock;
    short m_Price;
    string m_Name;
    string m_Distributor;
    string m_UPC;
};
```

The &, as used here in the context of declaring an argument to a
function, means that the argument to which it refers is a **reference
argument**, rather than a "normal" argument. It's important to
understand this concept thoroughly, so let's go into it in detail.

References Required

As you may recall from Chapter 5, when we call a function, the
arguments to that function are actually copies of the data passed in
from the calling function; that is, a new local variable is created and
initialized to the value of each expression from the calling function
and the called function works on that local variable. Such a local
variable is called a *value argument*, because it is a new variable with

the same value as the caller's original argument. There's nothing wrong with this in many cases; sometimes, though, as in the present case, we have to do it a bit differently. A reference argument, such as the ifstream& argument to Read, is *not* a copy of the caller's argument, but another name for the actual argument passed by the caller.

Reference arguments are often more efficient than value arguments, because the overhead of making a copy for the called function is avoided. Another difference between value arguments and reference arguments is that any changes made to a reference argument change the caller's argument as well, which in turn means that the caller's actual argument must be a variable, not an expression like x + 3; changing the value of such an expression wouldn't make much sense. This characteristic of reference arguments can confuse the readers of the calling function; there's no way to tell just by looking at the calling function that some of its variables can be changed by calling another function. This means that we should limit the use of reference arguments to those cases where they are necessary.

In this case, however, it *is* necessary to change the ifstream object that is the actual argument to the Read function, because that object contains the information about what data we've already read from the stream. If we passed the ifstream as a value argument, then the internal state of the "real" ifstream in the calling function wouldn't be altered to reflect the data we've read in our Read function, so every time we called Read, we would get the same input again. Therefore, we have to pass the ifstream as a reference argument.

The complete decoding of the function declaration void StockItem::Read(ifstream& s) is shown in Figure 6.14.

FIGURE 6.14. The declaration of StockItem::Read **in code\item2.h**

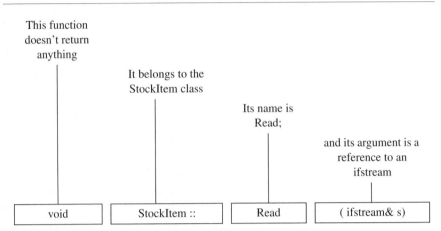

Putting it all together: we're defining a void function (one that doesn't return a value), called Read, which belongs to class StockItem. This function takes an argument named s that's a reference to an ifstream. That is, the argument s is another name for the ifstream passed to us by the caller, not a copy of the caller's ifstream. As you probably have guessed, Susan had some questions about this whole concept.

Susan: How does Read make Shopinfo go get data?

Steve: Well, the argument s is a reference to the ifstream object provided by the caller; in this case, the ifstream object to which s refers is Shopinfo. That ifstream is connected to the file shop2.in.

Susan: How does Read do the reading? How come you are using >> without a cin statement?

Steve: cin isn't a statement, but a stream that is created automatically whenever we #include iostream.h in our source file. Therefore, we can read from it without connecting it to a file. In this case, we're reading from a different stream, namely s.

Susan: How come this is a void type? I would think it would return data being read from a file.

Steve: You would think so, wouldn't you? I love it when you're logical. However, what it actually does is to read data from a file into the object for which it was called. Therefore, it doesn't need a return value.

Susan: So the ifstream object is a transfer mechanism? That is, ifstream s; would read data from a file named s?

Steve: Yes, it's a transfer mechanism. However, ifstream s; would create an ifstream called s, that was not connected to any file; the file could be specified later. If we wanted to create an ifstream called s that was connected to a file called xyz, then we would write ifstream s("xyz");

Susan: Okay. An ifstream just reads data from a file. It doesn't care which file, until you specify it?

Steve: Right.

Susan: What does this mean without cin? Is it just the same thing, only you can't call it cin because cin is for native use and this is a class? How come the >> is preceded by the argument s?

Steve: The s takes the place of cin, because we want to read from the stream s, not the stream cin.

Susan: Tell me what you mean by "just a stream".

Steve: Think of it like a real stream, and the bytes are little barges that float downstream. Isn't that poetic? Anyway, there are three predefined streams that we get automatically when we #include <iostream.h>: cin, cout, and cerr. The first two we've already seen, and the last one is intended for use in displaying error messages.

There is one point that we haven't examined yet, though: how this routine determines that it's finished reading from the input file. With keyboard input, we process each line separately when it's typed in, but that won't do the job with a file, where we want to read all the items in until we get to the end of the file. We actually handle this detail in the main program itemtst2.cc, by asking ShopInfo whether there is any data left in the file; to be more precise, we call the ifstream member function fail() to ask the ShopInfo ifstream whether we have tried to read past the end of the file. If we have, then the result of that call to ShopInfo.fail() will be nonzero (which signifies true). If we haven't yet tried to read past the end of the file, then the result of that call will be 0 (which signifies false). How do we use this information?

We use it to decide whether to execute a break statement. This is a loop control device that interrupts processing of a loop whenever it is executed. The flow of control passes to the next statement after the end of the controlled block of the for statement.[11]

The loop will terminate in one of two ways. Either 100 records have been read, in which case i will be 100; or the end of the file is reached, in which case i is the number of records that have been read successfully.

Susan had some questions about the implementation of this program.

Susan: What is fail()?

Steve: It's a member function of the ifstream class.

Susan: Where did it come from?

Steve: From the library that defines that class.

---

11. The break statement can also terminate execution of a while loop, as well as another type of control mechanism that we'll cover in Chapter 11.

Susan: But it could be used in other classes, right?

Steve: Not unless they define it as well.[12]

Susan: How does all the data having been read translate into "nonzero"? What makes a "nonzero" value true?

Steve: That's a convention used by that function.

Susan: So anything other than 0 is considered true?

Steve: Yes.

Susan: Where did break come from?

Steve: It's another keyword like for; it means to terminate the loop that is in progress.

Susan: I do not understand what is actually happening with the program at this time. When is break implemented? Is it just to end the reading of the entire file?

Steve: We have to stop reading data when there is no more data in the file. The break statement allows us to terminate the loop when that occurs.

Susan: What do you mean that the loop will terminate either by 100 records being read or when the end of the file is reached? Isn't that the same thing?

Steve: It's the same thing only if there are exactly 100 records in the file.

---

12. Actually, this isn't quite true. As we'll see in Chapter 9, there are mechanisms in C++ that will allow us to reuse functionality from existing classes when we create our own new classes.

Susan: So you mean when there are no more records to be read? So that the loop won't continue on till the end with nothing to do?

Steve: Exactly.

Susan: So does i just represent the number of records in the file?

Steve: Actually, it's the number of records that we've read.

Susan: Does this library have a card catalogue? I would like to know what else is in there.

Steve: There is a library reference manual for most libraries. If you get a library with a commercial compiler, that manual comes with the compiler documentation; otherwise, it's usually an on-line reference (that is, a help file).

Susan: A novice would not know this. Put it in the book.

Steve: Done.

Susan: Well, the program sounded like that indeed there were 100 records in the file. However, I see that in practice that might change, and why you would therefore need to have a break.

Steve: You obviously understand this.

Whether there are 100 records in the file or fewer than that number, obviously the number of items in the vector is equal to the current value of i. Or is it?

Don't Fence Me In

Let's examine this a bit more closely. You might be surprised at how easy it is to make a mistake in counting objects when writing a program. The most common error of this type is thinking you have one more or one less than the actual number of objects. In fact, this error is common enough to have a couple of widely known nicknames: *off by one error* and *fencepost error*. The former name should be fairly evident, but the latter name may require some explanation. First, let's try it as a "word problem". If you have to put up a fence 100 feet long, and each section of the fence is 10 feet long, how many sections of fence do you need? Obviously, the answer is 10. Now how many fenceposts do you need? 11. The confusion caused by counting fenceposts when you should be counting segments of the fence (or vice-versa) is the cause of a fencepost error.

That's fine as a general rule, but what about the specific example of counting records in our file? Well, let's start out by supposing that we have an empty file, so the sequence of events in the upper loop is as follows:

1. Set i to 0.

2. Is i less than 100? If not, exit. If so, continue.

3. Use the Read function to try to read a record into the ith element of the AllItems vector.

4. Call ShopInfo.fail() to find out whether we've tried to read past the end of the file.

5. If so, execute the break statement to exit the loop.

The answer to the question in step 4 is that in fact nothing was read, so we do execute the break and leave the loop. The value of i is clearly 0 here, because we never went back to the top of the loop; since we haven't read any records, setting InventoryCount to i works in this case.

Now let's try the same thing, but this time assuming that there is one record in the file. Here's the sequence of events:

1. Set i to 0.

2. Is i less than 100? If not, exit. If so, continue.

3. Use the Read function to try to read a record into the ith element of the AllItems vector.

4. Call ShopInfo.fail() to find out whether we've tried to read past the end of the file.

5. If so, execute the break statement to exit the loop. In this case, we haven't run off the end of the file, so we go back to the top of the loop, and continue as follows:

6. Increment i to 1.

7. Is i less than 100? If not, exit. If so, continue.

8. Call Read to try to read a record into the AllItems vector.

9. Call ShopInfo.fail() to find out whether we've tried to read past the end of the file.

10. If so, execute the break statement to exit the loop.

The second time through, we execute the break. Since i is 1, and the number of elements read was also 1, it's correct to set the count of elements to i.

It should be pretty clear that this same logic applies to all the possible numbers of elements up to 99. But what if we have 100 elements in the file? Relax, I'm not going to go through these steps 100 times, but I think we should start out from the situation that would exist after reading 99 elements, and see if we get the right answer in this case too. After the 99th element has been read, i will be 99; we know this from our previous analysis that indicates that whenever we start executing the statements in the controlled block of the loop, i is always equal to the number of elements previously read. So here's the 100th iteration of the loop:

1. Call Read to try to read a record into the AllItems array.

2. Call ShopInfo.fail() to find out whether we've tried to read past the end of the file.

3. If so, execute the break statement to exit the loop.

4. Otherwise, increment i to 100.

5. Is i less than 100? If not, exit. If so, continue.

6. Since i is not less than 100, we exit.

At this point, we've read 100 records and i is 100, so these two numbers are still the same. Therefore, we can conclude that setting InventoryCount equal to i when the loop is finished is correct; we have no fencepost error here.

Susan wasn't sure why I was hammering this fencepost thing into the ground:

> **Susan:** Why are you always saying that "it's correct to set the count of elements to i"?

> **Steve:** Because I'm showing how to tell whether or not we have a fencepost error. That requires a lot of analysis.

Actually, this whole procedure we've just been through reminds me of the professor who claimed that some point he was making was obvious. This was questioned by a student, so the professor spent 10 minutes absorbed in calculation and finally emerged triumphantly with the news that it was indeed obvious.

Assuming that you've installed the software from the CD-ROM in the back of this book, you can try out this program. First, you have to compile it by changing to the code subdirectory under the main directory where you installed the software, and typing RHIDE itemtst2, then using the "Make" command from the "Compile" menu. Then exit back to DOS and type itemtst2 to run the program. You'll see that it indeed prints out each StockItem object read from the file.

To run it under the debugger, make sure you are in the code subdirectory, and then type RHIDE itemtst2. Again, do *not* add the ".cc" to the end of the file name. Once RHIDE has started up, you can step through the program by hitting F8, which will treat any function

call as one statement, or by hitting F7, which will step into any function call. Any time you want to see the display that the user would see when running the program normally, hit ALT-F5, then ENTER to get back to the debugger.

Can I Help You?

Of course, this isn't all we want to do with the items in the store's inventory. Since we have a working means of reading and displaying the items, let's see what else we might want to do with them. Here are a few possible transactions at the grocery store:

1. George comes in and buys 3 bags of marshmallows. We have to adjust the inventory for the sale.

2. Sam wants to know the price of a can of string beans.

3. Judy comes in looking for chunky chicken soup; there's none on the shelf where it should be, so we have to check the inventory to see if we're supposed to have any.

All of these scenarios require the ability to find a StockItem object given some information about it. Let's start with the first example, which we might state as a programming task in the following manner: "Given the UPC from the bag of marshmallows, and the number of bags purchased, adjust the inventory by subtracting the number purchased from the previous quantity on hand". Figure 6.15 is a program intended to solve this problem.

FIGURE 6.15. First attempt to update inventory of StockItems
(code\itemtst3.cc)

```
#include <iostream.h>
#include <fstream.h>
#include "vector.h"
#include "string6.h"
#include "item2.h"
```

```
int main()
{
   ifstream ShopInfo("shop2.in");
   vector<StockItem> AllItems(100);
   short i;
   short InventoryCount;
   string PurchaseUPC;
   short PurchaseCount;
   bool Found;

   for (i = 0; i < 100; i ++)
      {
      AllItems[i].Read(ShopInfo);
      if (ShopInfo.fail() != 0)
         break;
      }

   InventoryCount = i;

   cout << "What is the UPC of the item?" << endl;
   cin >> PurchaseUPC;
   cout << "How many items were sold?" << endl;
   cin >> PurchaseCount;

   Found = false;
   for (i = 0; i < InventoryCount; i ++)
      {
      if (PurchaseUPC == AllItems[i].m_UPC)
         {
         Found = true;
         break;
         }
      }

   if (Found == true)
      {
      AllItems[i].m_InStock -= PurchaseCount;
      cout << "The inventory has been updated." << endl;
```

```
        }
    else
        cout << "Can't find that item. Please check UPC" << endl;

    return 0;
}
```

Here is a more detailed analysis of the steps that the program in Figure 6.15 is intended to perform:

1. Take the UPC from the item.

2. For every item in the inventory list, check whether its UPC is the same as the one from the item.

3. If it doesn't match, go back to step 2.

4. If it does match, subtract the number purchased from the inventory.

There's nothing really new here except for the bool variable type, which we'll get to in a moment, and the -= operator that the program uses to adjust the inventory; -= is just like +=, except that it subtracts the right-hand value from the left-hand variable, while += adds.

The bool variable type is a relatively new addition to C++. Expressions and variables of this type are limited to the two values true and false.[13] This is a new data type that was added to C++ in the process of developing the standard, and is available on any compiler that conforms to the standard. We've been using the terms true and false to refer to the result of a logical expression such as if (x < y); similarly, a bool variable or function return value can be either true or false.

---

13. The type bool is short for "boolean", which means "either true or false". The derivation of the term "boolean" is interesting but not relevant here.

Access Denied

If you compile the program in Figure 6.15, you'll find that it is not valid. The problem is the lines:

```
if (PurchaseUPC == AllItems[i].m_UPC)
```

and

```
AllItems[i].m_InStock -= PurchaseCount;
```

The first of these lines could be translated into English as follows:

"if the input UPC is the same as the value of the m_UPC member variable of the object stored in the ith element of the AllItems vector, then..."

while the second of these lines could be translated as:

"subtract the number of items purchased from the value of the m_InStock member variable of the object stored in the ith element of the AllItems vector".

While both of these lines are quite understandable to the compiler, they are also illegal, because they are trying to access private member variables of the StockItem class, namely m_UPC and m_InStock, from function main. Since main is not a member function of StockItem, this is not allowed. The error message from the compiler should look something like Figure 6.16.

FIGURE 6.16. Unauthorized access prohibited

```
itemtst3.cc: In function 'int main()':
itemtst3.cc:34: member 'm_UPC' is a private member of class 'StockItem'
itemtst3.cc:43: member 'm_InStock' is a private member of class 'StockItem'
```

Does this mean that we can't accomplish our goal of updating the inventory? Not at all. It merely means that we have to do things "by the book" rather than going in directly and reading or changing member variables that belong to the StockItem class. Of course, we could theoretically "solve" this access problem by simply making these member variables public rather than private. However, this would allow anyone to mess around with the internal variables in our StockItem objects, which would defeat one of the main purposes of using class objects in the first place: that they behave like native types as far as their users are concerned. We want the users of this class to ignore the internal workings of its objects and merely use them according to their externally defined interface; the implementation of the class is our responsibility, not theirs.

This notion of implementation being separated from interface led to an excellent question from Susan:

> **Susan:** Please explain to me why you needed to list those member variables as private in the interface of StockItem. Actually, why do they even need to be there at all? Well, I guess you are telling the compiler that whenever it sees the member variables that they will always have to be treated privately?

> **Steve:** They have to be there so that the compiler can figure out how large an object of that class is. Many people, including myself, consider this a flaw in the language design, because private variables should really be private, not exposed to the class user.

Obviously, she'd lost her true novice status by this point. Six months after finding out what a compiler is, she was questioning the design decisions made by the inventor of C++; what is more, her objections were quite well founded.

As it happens, we can easily solve our access problem without exposing the implementation of our class to the user. All we have to do is to add a couple of new member functions called CheckUPC and DeductSaleFromInventory to the StockItem class; the first of these allows us to check whether a given UPC belongs to a given StockItem, and the second allows us to adjust the inventory level of an item.

Susan had another suggestion as to how to solve this problem, as well as a question about why I hadn't anticipated it in the first place:

Susan: Hey, wouldn't it be easier to write a special main that is a member function to get around this?

Steve: That's an interesting idea, but it wouldn't work. For one thing, main is never a member function; this is reasonable when you consider that you generally have quite a few classes in a program. Which one would main be a member function of?

Susan: So then all these new member functions do is to act as a gobetween linking the StockItem class and the inventory update program to compare data that is privately held in the StockItem class?

Steve: Yes, the new entries in the interface are designed to make the private data available in a safe manner. I think that's the same as what you're saying.

Susan: If you wanted to change the program, why didn't you just do it in the first place instead of breaking it down in parts like this?

Steve: Because that's not the way it actually happens in real life.

Susan: Do you think it less confusing to do that, and also does this act as an example of how you can modify a program as you see the need to do it?

Steve: Right on both counts.

Figure 6.17 shows the new, improved interface definition.

FIGURE 6.17. An enhanced interface for the StockItem class **(code\item4.h)**

```
class StockItem
{
public:
    StockItem();

    StockItem(string Name, short InStock, short Price,
    string Distributor, string UPC);

    void Display();
    void Read(ifstream& s);

    bool CheckUPC(string ItemUPC);
    void DeductSaleFromInventory(short QuantitySold);
    short GetInventory();
    string GetName();

private:
    short m_InStock;
    short m_Price;
    string m_Name;
    string m_Distributor;
    string m_UPC;
};
```

I strongly recommend that you print out the files that contain this interface and its implementation, as well as the test program, for reference as you are going through this part of the chapter; those files are item4.h, item4.cc, and itemtst4.cc, respectively. The declarations of the two new functions CheckUPC and DeductSaleFromInventory should be pretty easy to figure out: CheckUPC takes the UPC that we want to find and compares it to the UPC in its StockItem, then returns true if they match and false if they don't. Here's another good use for the bool data type; the only possible results of the   CheckUPC function are that the UPC in the StockItem matches the one we've supplied (in which case we return true) or it doesn't match (in which case we return false). DeductSaleFromInventory takes the number of items sold and subtracts it from the previous inventory. But where did GetInventory and GetName come from?

The Customer Is Always Right

I added those functions because I noticed that the itemtst program wasn't very user-friendly. Originally it followed these steps:

1. Ask for the UPC.

2. Ask for the number of items purchased.

3. Search through the list to see whether the UPC is legitimate.

4. If so, adjust the inventory.

5. If not, give an error message.

6. Exit.

What's wrong with this picture? Well, for one thing, why should the program make me type in the number of items sold if the UPC is no good? Also, it never told me the new inventory or even what the name of the item was. It may have known these things, but it never bothered to inform me. So I changed the program to work as follows:

1. Ask for the UPC.

2. Search through the list to see whether the UPC was legitimate.

3. If not, give an error message and exit.

4. If the UPC was okay, then

   a. Display the name of the item and the number in stock.

   b. Ask for the number of items purchased.

c. Adjust the inventory.

d. Display a message with the name of the item and number of remaining units in inventory.

5. Exit.

To do this, I needed those two new functions GetInventory and GetName, so as you've seen I added them to the class declaration. Figure 6.18 shows the implementation of all of these new functions.

FIGURE 6.18. Some new functions for the StockItem class **(from code\item4.cc)**

```cpp
bool StockItem::CheckUPC (string ItemUPC)
{
  if (m_UPC == ItemUPC)
    return true;

  return false;
}

void StockItem::DeductSaleFromInventory(short QuantitySold)
{
  m_InStock -= QuantitySold;
}

short StockItem::GetInventory()
{
  return m_InStock;
}

string StockItem::GetName()
{
  return m_Name;
}
```

Our current itemtst example is getting to be enough like a real program that I'm going to start using the term *application program* (or equivalently, *application*) to refer to it sometimes. As is generally true of C++ programs, the responsibility for doing the user's work is divided up into a main program (or application program) and a set of classes (sometimes called *infrastructure*) used in the application. In this case, itemtst4.cc is the main program, or application program, whereas the other two files (item4.h and item4.cc) are the infrastructure. Figure 6.19 shows the new, improved version of our application, which updates the inventory and actually tells the user what it's doing.

FIGURE 6.19. **Updating** StockItem **inventory (code\itemtst4.cc)**

```
#include <iostream.h>
#include <fstream.h>
#include "vector.h"
#include "string6.h"
#include "item4.h"

int main()
{
    ifstream ShopInfo("shop2.in");
    vector<StockItem> AllItems(100);
    short i;
    short InventoryCount;
    short OldInventory;
    short NewInventory;
    string PurchaseUPC;
    string ItemName;
    short PurchaseCount;
    bool Found;

    for (i = 0; i < 100; i ++)
        {
        AllItems[i].Read(ShopInfo);
        if (ShopInfo.fail() != 0)
```

```
        break;
      }

    InventoryCount = i;
    cout << "What is the UPC of the item? ";
    cin >> PurchaseUPC;
    Found = false;

    for (i = 0; i < InventoryCount; i ++)
       {
       if (AllItems[i].CheckUPC(PurchaseUPC) == true)
          {
          Found = true;
          break;
          }
       }

    if (Found == true)
       {
       OldInventory = AllItems[i].GetInventory();
       ItemName = AllItems[i].GetName();

       cout << "There are currently " << OldInventory << " units of "
       << ItemName << " in stock." << endl;
       cout << "How many items were sold? ";
       cin >> PurchaseCount;

       AllItems[i].DeductSaleFromInventory(PurchaseCount);
       cout << "The inventory has been updated." << endl;

       NewInventory = AllItems[i].GetInventory();
       cout << "There are now " << NewInventory << " units of "
       << ItemName << " in stock." << endl;
       }
    else
       cout << "Can't find that item. Please check UPC" << endl;

    return 0;
  }
```

This code should be pretty easy to follow; it simply implements the first item purchase scenario I outlined in the list on page . Assuming that you've installed the software from the CD-ROM in the back of this book, you can try out this program. First, you have to compile it by changing to the code subdirectory under the main directory where you installed the software, and typing RHIDE itemtst4, then using the "Make" command from the "Compile" menu. Then exit back to DOS and type itemtst4 to run the program.

To run it under the debugger, make sure you are in the code subdirectory, and then type RHIDE itemtst4. Again, do *not* add the ".cc" to the end of the file name. Once RHIDE has started up, you can step through the program by hitting F8, which will treat any function call as one statement, or by hitting F7, which will step into any function call. Any time you want to see the display that the user would see when running the program normally, hit ALT-F5, then ENTER to get back to the debugger.

In either case, the program will start up and ask you for the UPC; you can use 7904886261, which is the (made-up) UPC for "antihistamines". Type in that number and hit ENTER.[14]

Next Customer, Please?

Now let's consider what might be needed to handle some of the other possibilities, starting with the second scenario in that same list. To refresh your memory, here it is again: "Sam wants to know the price of a can of string beans". A possible way to express this as a programming task is "Given a UPC, look up the price of the item in the inventory".

Here is a set of steps to solve this problem:

1. Ask for the UPC.

2. Search through the list to see whether the UPC is legitimate.

---

14. The Found variable will be shown as 0 (false) and 1 (true) in the debugger.

3. If not, give an error message and exit.

4. If the UPC is okay, then display the name and price of the item.

5. Exit.

Have you noticed that this solution is very similar to the solution to the first problem? For example, the search for an item with a given UPC is exactly the same. It seems wasteful to duplicate code rather than using the same code again, and in fact we've seen how to avoid code duplication by using a function. Now that we're doing "object-oriented" programming, perhaps this new function should be a member function instead of a global one.

This is a good idea, except that the search function can't be a member function of StockItem, because we don't have the right StockItem yet; if we did, we wouldn't need to search for it. Therefore, we have to create a new class that contains a member variable that is a vector of StockItems and write the search routine as a member function of this new class; the new member function would look through its vector to find the StockItem we want. Then we can use the member functions of StockItem to do the rest. Figure 6.20 shows the interface (class declaration) for this new class, called Inventory.

FIGURE 6.20. Interface of Inventory class **(code\invent1.h)**

```
#include "vector.h"

class Inventory
{
public:
    Inventory();

    short LoadInventory(ifstream& is);
    StockItem FindItem(string UPC);
    bool UpdateItem(StockItem Item);

    private:
```

```
    vector<StockItem> m_Stock;
    short m_StockCount;
};
```

I strongly recommend that you print out the files that contain this interface and its implementation, as well as the test program, for reference as you are going through this chapter; those files are invent1.h, invent1.cc, and itemtst5.cc, respectively.

Susan was somewhat surprised that I would even consider writing a global function to find a StockItem:

Susan: What do you mean by making this a member function instead of a global function? When was it ever a global function?

Steve: It wasn't any kind of function before; we were just duplicating code. However, making it a function would make sense; the question is what kind of function, global or member?

Susan: I am not sure if I truly understand the problem as to why you can't search StockItem as a member function.

Steve: A member function of StockItem always accesses a particular StockItem. However, our problem is that we don't know which StockItem we want; therefore, a member function, which must apply to a particular StockItem, won't solve our problem.

Susan: Okay, Stevie, here is the deal. Why would you even consider making this a global function? Of course it is a member function. We are doing object oriented programming, aren't we?

Steve: Aren't we knowledgeable all of a sudden? Who was that person who knew nothing about programming eight months ago?

Susan: You've got me there. But seriously, what would be the advantage of making it a global function rather than a member function? This is what has me bothered about the whole thing.

Steve: There wouldn't be any advantage. I just wanted to point out that it clearly can't be a member function of StockItem, and indicate the possible alternatives.

Susan: Oh, then so far that is all our program is able to do? It is unable to locate one item of all possible items and display it just from the UPC code? In fact that is what we are trying to accomplish, right?

Steve: Exactly.

Susan also wasn't sure why we needed LoadInventory.

Susan: What does the code short LoadInventory (ifstream& is); do? Does it just give you an object named LoadInventory that reads a file that has a reference argument named is? I don't get this.

Steve: That's quite close. The line you're referring to is the declaration of a function named LoadInventory, which takes a reference to an ifstream. The implementation of the function, as you'll see shortly, reads StockItem records from the file connected to the ifstream.

Once that was cleared up, she had some questions about the way the FindItem function works, including its interface.

Susan: Is the argument UPC to the FindItem function a string because it is returning the name of a stock item?

Steve: That argument is the input to the FindItem function, not its output; therefore, it's not "returning" anything. FindItem returns the StockItem that it finds. Or did I misunderstand your question?

Susan: Let's see if I even know what I was asking here. Okay, how about this: I wanted to know why UPC was a string and not a short, since a UPC is usually a number. In this case, it will be returning a name of a "found item" so that is why it is a string, right?

Steve: No, it's because the UPC won't fit in any of the types of numbers we have available. Thus, the most sensible way to store it is as a **string**. Since we don't use it in calculations anyway, the fact that you can't calculate with **string** variables isn't much of a restriction.

Susan: Oh, okay. So a **string** is more useful for storing numbers that are somewhat lengthy as long as you don't calculate with those numbers. They are nothing more than "numerical words"?

Steve: Exactly.

Most of this should be fairly self-explanatory by this point. We start out with the default constructor which makes an empty Inventory.[15] Figure 6.21 has the implementation for the default constructor.

FIGURE 6.21. Default constructor for Inventory class **(from code\invent1.cc)**

```
Inventory:: Inventory ()
: m_Stock (vector<StockItem>(100)),
m_StockCount(0)
{
}
```

There's nothing complex here; we're using the member initialization list to initialize the m_Stock variable to a newly constructed vector of 100 StockItems and the number of active StockItems to 0. The latter, of course, is because we haven't yet read any data in from the file.

Then we have a couple of handy functions. The first is LoadInventory, which will take data from an ifstream and store it in its Inventory object, just as we did with the AllItems vector in our application itemtst4.cc.

---

15. As before, we can count on the compiler to supply the other three standard member functions needed for a concrete data type: the copy constructor, the assignment operator =, and the destructor.

Susan had a question about this:

Susan: How did you know that you were going to need to use an ifstream again?

Steve: Because we're reading data from a file into a vector of StockItems, and reading data from a file is what ifstreams are for.

Figure 6.22 shows the implementation of LoadInventory.

FIGURE 6.22. LoadInventory **function for** Inventory class **(from code\invent1.cc)**

```
short Inventory:: LoadInventory (ifstream& is)
{
  short i;

  for (i = 0; i < 100; i ++)
    {
    m_Stock[i].Read(is);
    if (is.fail() != 0)
    break;
    }

  m_StockCount = i;
  return m_StockCount;
}
```

Now we come to the FindItem member function. Its declaration is pretty simple: It takes an argument of type string which contains the UPC that we're looking for. Its implementation should be pretty simple, too: It will search the Inventory object for the StockItem that has that UPC and return a copy of that StockItem, which can then be interrogated to find the price or whatever other information we need.

However, there's a serious design issue here: What should this function return if the UPC doesn't match the UPC in any of the StockItem entries in the Inventory object? The application program has to be able to determine whether or not the UPC is found. In the original program this was no problem, because the main program maintained that information itself. But in this case, the member function FindItem has to communicate success or failure to the caller somehow.

Of course, we could use a return value of true or false to indicate whether the UPC is found, but we're already using the return value to return the StockItem to the calling function. We could add a reference argument to the FindItem function and use it to set the value of a variable in the caller's code, but that's very nonintuitive; functions that don't modify their arguments are easier to use and less likely to cause surprises.

Nothing Ventured, Nothing Gained

There's one more possibility. We can return a **null object** of the StockItem class; that is, an object that exists solely to serve as a placeholder, representing the desired object that we couldn't find.

I like this solution, because when the member function terminates, the application program has to test something anyway to see if the desired StockItem was found; why not test whether the returned object is a null StockItem? This solution, while quite simple, requires a minor change to our implementation of StockItem: We have to add an IsNull member function to our StockItem class so that we can tell whether the returned StockItem is a null StockItem or a "normal" one. We have to add the line bool IsNull(); to the class interface and provide the implementation as shown in Figure 6.23. I strongly recommend that you print out the files that contain this interface and its implementation, as well as the test program, for reference as you are going through this part of the chapter; those files are item5.h, item5.cc, and itemtst5.cc, respectively.

FIGURE 6.23. The implementation of IsNull (from code\item5.cc)

```
bool StockItem:: IsNull ()
{
  if (m_UPC == "")
    return true;

  return false;
}
```

As you can see, not much rocket science is involved in this member function: all we do is check whether the UPC in the item is the null string "". If it is, we return true; otherwise, we return false. Since no real item can have a UPC of "", this should work well. Let's hear from Susan on the topic of this function (and function return values in general).

Susan: This is something I have not thought about before: When you call a function where does the return value go?

Steve: Wherever you put it. If you say x = sum(weight);, then the return value goes into x. If you just say sum(weight);, then it is discarded.

Susan: Why is it discarded?

Steve: Because you didn't use it; therefore, the compiler assumes you have no further use for it.

Susan: So the return value can be used in only one place?

Steve: Yes, unless you save it in a variable, in which case you can use it however you like.

Figure 6.24 shows the implementation of FindItem, which uses CheckUPC to check whether the requested UPC is the one in the current item and returns a null StockItem if the desired UPC isn't found in the inventory list.

FIGURE 6.24. FindItem **function for** Inventory class **(from code\invent1.cc)**

```
StockItem Inventory:: FindItem (string UPC)
{
  short i;
  bool Found = false;

  for (i = 0; i < m_StockCount; i ++)
    {
    if (m_Stock[i].CheckUPC(UPC) == true)
      {
      Found = true;
      break;
      }
    }

  if (Found == true)
    return m_Stock[i];

  return StockItem();
}
```

Here's my interchange with Susan on how we're using CheckUPC:

Susan: About the first if statement in this CheckUPC function, if (m_Stock[i].CheckUPC(UPC) == true): does that mean if you find the UPC you are looking for then the program breaks and you don't need to continue looking? In that case, what does the statement Found = true; do? It looks as if you are setting Found to the value true.

Steve: That's right. If we've actually found the item we're looking for, then Found will have been set to true, so we'll return the real item; otherwise, we'll return a null StockItem to indicate that we couldn't find the one requested.

After we get a copy of the correct StockItem and update its inventory via DeductSaleFromInventory, we're not quite done; we still have to update the "real" StockItem in the Inventory object. This is the task of the last function in our Inventory class: UpdateItem. Figure 6.25 shows its implementation.

FIGURE 6.25. UpdateItem **function for** Inventory class (**from code\invent1.cc**)

```
bool Inventory:: UpdateItem (StockItem Item)
{
  string UPC = Item.GetUPC();

  short i;
  bool Found = false;

  for (i = 0; i < m_StockCount; i ++)
    {
    if (m_Stock[i].CheckUPC(UPC) == true)
      {
      Found = true;
      break;
      }
    }

  if (Found == true)
    m_Stock[i] = Item;

  return Found;
}
```

Why do we need this function? Because we are no longer operating on the "real" StockItem, as we had been when we accessed the inventory vector directly in the previous version of the application program. Instead, we are getting a copy of the StockItem from the Inventory object and changing that copy; thus, to have the final result put back into the Inventory object, we need to use the UpdateItem member function of Inventory, which overwrites the original StockItem with our changed version.

This function needs another function in the StockItem class to get the UPC from a StockItem object, so that UpdateItem can tell which object in the m_Stock vector is the one that needs to be updated. This additional function, GetUPC, is shown in Figure 6.26.

FIGURE 6.26. The implementation of GetUPC **(from code\item5.cc)**

```
string StockItem:: GetUPC ()
{
  return m_UPC;
}
```

The application program also needs one more function, GetPrice(), to be added to the interface of StockItem, to retrieve the price from the object once we have found it. This is shown in Figure 6.27.

FIGURE 6.27. The implementation of GetPrice **(from code\item5.cc)**

```
short StockItem:: GetPrice ()
{
  return m_Price;
}
```

We're almost ready to examine the revised test program. First, though, let's pause for another look at all of the interfaces and implementations of the StockItem and Inventory classes. The interface for the Inventory class is in Figure 6.28.

FIGURE 6.28. Current interface for Inventory class **(code\invent1.h)**

```
#include "vector.h"

class Inventory
{
public:
    Inventory();

    short LoadInventory(ifstream& is);
    StockItem FindItem(string UPC);
    bool UpdateItem(StockItem Item);

private:
    vector<StockItem> m_Stock;
    short m_StockCount;
};
```

Figure 6.29 contains the implementation for Inventory.

FIGURE 6.29. Current implementation for Inventory class **(code\invent1.cc)**

```
#include <iostream.h>
#include <fstream.h>
#include "vector.h"
#include "string6.h"
#include "item5.h"
#include "invent1.h"

Inventory::Inventory()
: m_Stock (vector<StockItem>(100)),
  m_StockCount(0)
{
}

short Inventory::LoadInventory(ifstream& is)
{
    short i;
```

```
for (i = 0; i < 100; i ++)
   {
   m_Stock[i].Read(is);
   if (is.fail() != 0)
      break;
   }

m_StockCount = i;
return m_StockCount;
}

StockItem Inventory::FindItem(string UPC)
{
   short i;
   bool Found = false;

   for (i = 0; i < m_StockCount; i ++)
      {
      if (m_Stock[i].CheckUPC(UPC) == true)
         {
         Found = true;
         break;
         }
      }

   if (Found == true)
      return m_Stock[i];

   return StockItem();
}

bool Inventory::UpdateItem(StockItem Item)
{
   string UPC = Item.GetUPC();

   short i;
   bool Found = false;
```

```
for (i = 0; i < m_StockCount; i ++)
  {
  if (m_Stock[i].CheckUPC(UPC) == true)
    {
    Found = true;
    break;
    }
  }

if (Found == true)
  m_Stock[i] = Item;

return Found;
}
```

Figure 6.30 shows the interface for StockItem.

FIGURE 6.30. Current interface for StockItem class **(code\item5.h)**

```
class StockItem
{
public:
  StockItem();

  StockItem(string Name, short InStock, short Price,
  string Distributor, string UPC);

  void Display();
  void Read(ifstream& s);

  bool CheckUPC(string ItemUPC);
  void DeductSaleFromInventory(short QuantitySold);
  short GetInventory();
  string GetName();
  bool IsNull();
  short GetPrice();
  string GetUPC();
```

```
private:
    short m_InStock;
    short m_Price;
    string m_Name;
    string m_Distributor;
    string m_UPC;
};
```

The implementation for StockItem is in Figure 6.31.

FIGURE 6.31. **Current implementation for** StockItem class **(code\item5.cc)**

```
#include <iostream.h>
#include <fstream.h>
#include "string6.h"
#include "item5.h"

StockItem::StockItem()
: m_InStock(0), m_Price(0), m_Name(),
  m_Distributor(), m_UPC()
{
}

StockItem::StockItem(string Name, short InStock,
short Price, string Distributor, string UPC)
: m_InStock(InStock), m_Price(Price), m_Name(Name),
  m_Distributor(Distributor), m_UPC(UPC)
{
}

void StockItem::Display()
{
    cout << "Name: ";
    cout << m_Name << endl;
    cout << "Number in stock: ";
    cout << m_InStock << endl;
    cout << "Price: ";
    cout << m_Price << endl;
    cout << "Distributor: ";
```

```
      cout << m_Distributor << endl;
      cout << "UPC: ";
      cout << m_UPC << endl;
      cout << endl;
}

void StockItem::Read(ifstream& s)
{
   s >> m_Name;
   s >> m_InStock;
   s >> m_Price;
   s >> m_Distributor;
   s >> m_UPC;
}

bool StockItem::CheckUPC(string ItemUPC)
{
   if (m_UPC == ItemUPC)
      return true;

   return false;
}

void StockItem::DeductSaleFromInventory(short QuantitySold)
{
   m_InStock -= QuantitySold;
}

short StockItem::GetInventory()
{
   return m_InStock;
}

string StockItem::GetName()
{
   return m_Name;
}
```

```
bool StockItem::IsNull()
{
   if (m_UPC == "")
      return true;

   return false;
}

short StockItem::GetPrice()
{
   return m_Price;
}

string StockItem::GetUPC()
{
   return m_UPC;
}
```

To finish this stage of the inventory control project, Figure 6.32 is the revised test program that uses the Inventory class rather than doing its own search through a vector of StockItems. This program can perform either of two operations, depending on what the user requests. Once the UPC has been typed in, the user is prompted to type either "C" for price check or "S" for sale. Then an if statement selects which of the two operations to perform. The code for the S (i.e., sale) operation is the same as it was in the previous version of this application, except that, of course, at that time it was the only possible operation so it wasn't controlled by an if statement. The code for the C (i.e., price check) operation is new, but it's very simple. It merely displays both the item name and the price.

FIGURE 6.32. Updated inventory application (code\itemtst5.cc)

```
#include <iostream.h>
#include <fstream.h>
#include "string6.h"
#include "item5.h"
```

```
#include "invent1.h"

int main()
{
    ifstream InputStream("shop2.in");
    string PurchaseUPC;
    short PurchaseCount;
    string ItemName;
    short OldInventory;
    short NewInventory;
    Inventory MyInventory;
    StockItem FoundItem;
    string TransactionCode;

    MyInventory.LoadInventory(InputStream);

    cout << "What is the UPC of the item? ";
    cin >> PurchaseUPC;

    FoundItem = MyInventory.FindItem(PurchaseUPC);
    if (FoundItem.IsNull() == true)
        {
        cout << "Can't find that item. Please check UPC." << endl;
        return 0;
        }

    OldInventory = FoundItem.GetInventory();
    ItemName = FoundItem.GetName();

    cout << "There are currently " << OldInventory << " units of "
        << ItemName << " in stock." << endl;

    cout << "Please enter transaction code as follows:\n";
    cout << "S (sale), C (price check): ";
    cin >> TransactionCode;

    if (TransactionCode == "C" || TransactionCode == "c")
        {
        cout << "The name of that item is: " << ItemName << endl;
```

```
        cout << "Its price is: " << FoundItem.GetPrice();
        }
    else if (TransactionCode == "S" || TransactionCode == "s")
        {
        cout << "How many items were sold? ";
        cin >> PurchaseCount;

        FoundItem.DeductSaleFromInventory(PurchaseCount);
        MyInventory.UpdateItem(FoundItem);

        cout << "The inventory has been updated." << endl;

        FoundItem = MyInventory.FindItem(PurchaseUPC);
        NewInventory = FoundItem.GetInventory();

        cout << "There are now " << NewInventory << " units of "
        << ItemName << " in stock." << endl;
        }

    return 0;
    }
```

The only part of the program that might not be obvious at this point is the expression in the if statement that determines whether the user wants to enter a price check or sale transaction. The first part of the test is if (TransactionCode == "C" || TransactionCode == "c"). The || is the "logical or" operator. An approximate translation of this expression is "if at least one of the two expressions on its right or left is true, then produce the result true; if they're both false, then produce the result false".[16] In this case, this means that the if statement will be

---

16. The reason it's only an approximate translation is that there is a special rule in C++ governing the execution of the || operator: if the expression on the left is true, then the expression on the right is not executed at all. The reason for this *short-circuit evaluation* rule is that in some cases you may want to write a right-hand expression that will only be legal if the left-hand expression is false.

true if the TransactionCode variable is either C or c. Why do we have to check for either a lower- or upper-case letter, when the instructions to the user clearly state that the choices are C or S?

This is good practice because users generally consider upper and lower case letters to be equivalent. Of course, as programmers, we know that the characters c and C are completely different; however, we should humor the users in this harmless delusion. After all, they're our customers!

Susan had a couple of questions about this program.

Susan: What do the following output statements mean: cout << S (sale); and cout << C (price check);? I am not clear as to what they are doing.

Steve: Nothing special; the prompts S (sale) and C (price check) are just to notify the user what his or her choices are.

Susan: Okay, so the line with the || is how you tell the computer to recognize upper case as well as lower case to have the same meaning?

Steve: Yes, that's what we're doing here.

Susan: So what do you call those || thingys?

Steve: They're called "vertical bars". The operator that is spelled || is called a "logical OR" operator, because it results in the value true if either the left-hand **or** the right-hand expression is true (or if both are true).

Susan: What do you mean by using else and if in the line else if (TransactionCode == "S" || TransactionCode == "s")? I don't believe I have seen them used together before.

Steve: I think you're right. Actually, it's not that mysterious: As always, the else means that we're specifying actions to be taken if the original if isn't true. The second if merely checks whether another condition is true and executes its controlled block if that is the case.

Assuming that you've installed the software from the CD-ROM in the back of this book, you can try out this program. First, you have to compile it by changing to the code subdirectory under the main directory where you installed the software, and typing RHIDE itemtst5, then using the "Make" command from the "Compile" menu. Then exit back to DOS and type itemtst5 to run the program. When the program asks for a UPC, you can use 7904886261, which is the (made-up) UPC for "antihistamines". When the program asks you for a transaction code, type S for "sale" or P for "price check", and then hit ENTER.

To run it under the debugger, make sure you are in the code subdirectory, and then type RHIDE itemtst5. Again, do *not* add the ".cc" to the end of the file name. Once RHIDE has started up, you can step through the program by hitting F8, which will treat any function call as one statement, or by hitting F7, which will step into any function call. Any time you want to see the display that the user would see when running the program normally, hit ALT-F5, then ENTER to get back to the debugger.

Paging Rosie Scenario

By this point, you very understandably might have gotten the notion that we have to make changes to our classes every time we need to do anything slightly different in our application program. In that case, where's the advantage of using classes instead of just writing the whole program in terms of shorts, chars, and so on?

Well, this is your lucky day. It just so happens that the next (and last) scenario we are going to examine requires no more member functions at all; in fact, we don't even have to change the application program. Here it is, for reference: "Judy comes in looking for chunky chicken soup; there's none on the shelf where it should be, so we have to check the inventory to see if we're supposed to have any".

The reason we don't have to do anything special for this scenario is that we're already displaying the name and inventory for the item as soon as we find it. Of course, if we hadn't already handled this issue, there are many other ways that we could solve this same problem. For example, we could use the Display member function of StockItem to display an item as soon as the UPC lookup succeeds, rather than waiting for the user to indicate what operation our application is supposed to perform.

For that matter, we'd have to consider a number of other factors in writing a real application program, even one that does such a simple task as this one. For example, what would happen if the user indicated that 200 units of a particular item had been sold when only 100 were in stock? Also, how would we find an item if the UPC isn't available? The item might very well be in inventory somewhere, but the current implementation of Inventory doesn't allow for the possibility of looking up an item by any information other than the UPC.

Although these topics and many others are essential to the work of a professional programmer, they would take us too far afield from our purpose here. We'll get into some similar issues later, when we discuss the topic of "software engineering" in Chapter 12. Now let's review what we've covered in this chapter.

Review

The most important concept in this chapter is the idea of creating user defined data types. In C++, this is done by defining a class for each such data type. Each class has both a class *interface*, which describes the behavior that the class displays to the "outside world" (i.e., other, unrelated functions), and a class *implementation*, which tells the compiler how to perform the behaviors promised in the interface definition. A variable of a class type is called an *object*. With proper attention to the interface and the details of implementation, it is possible to make objects behave just like native variables; that is, they can be initialized, assigned, compared, passed as function arguments, and returned as function return values.

Both the interface and the implementation of a class are described in terms of the functions and variables of which the class is composed; these are called *member functions* and *member variables*, because they belong to the class rather than being "free-floating" or localized to one function like the global functions and local variables we encountered earlier.

Of course, one obvious question is why we need to make up our own variable types. What's wrong with char, short, and the rest of the native types built into C++? The answer is that it's easier to write an inventory control program, for example, if we have data types representing items in the stock of a store, rather than having to express everything in terms of the native types. An analogy is the universal preference of professionals to use technical jargon rather than "plain English": Jargon conveys more information, more precisely, in less time.

Creating our own types of variables allows us to use objects rather than functions as the fundamental building blocks of programming, which is the basis of the "object-oriented programming" paradigm.[17]

Then we examined how creating classes differs from using classes, as we have been doing throughout the book. A fairly good analogy is that creating your own classes is to using classes as writing a program is to using a program.

Next, we went through the steps needed to actually create a new class; our example is the StockItem class, which is designed to allow

---

17. Purists may not approve of this use of the term *object-oriented programming*, as I'm not using this term in its strictest technical sense. However, since we are using objects and classes as our central organizing ideas, using the term *object-oriented* programming seems reasonable to me in this context. Chapters 9 and 10 will cover the other main concepts included in the strict definition of object-oriented programming.

tracking of inventory for a small grocery store. These steps include writing the interface definition, writing the implementation, writing the program that uses the class, compiling the implementation, compiling the program that uses the class, and linking the object files resulting from these compilation steps together with any needed libraries to produce the final executable program.

Then we moved from the general to the specific, analyzing the particular data and functions that the StockItem class needed to perform its duties in an application program. The member variables needed for each StockItem object included the name, count, distributor, price, and UPC. Of course, merely having these member variables doesn't make a StockItem object very useful, if it can't do anything with them. This led us to the topic of what member functions might be needed for such a class.

Rather than proceed immediately with the specialized member functions that pertain only to StockItem, however, we started by discussing the member functions that nearly every class needs to make its objects act like native variables. A class that has (at least) the capabilities of a native type is called a *concrete data type*. Such a class requires the following member functions:

1. A *default constructor*, which makes it possible to create an object of that class without supplying any initial data.

2. A *copy constructor*, which makes it possible to create a new object of this type with the same contents as an existing object of the same type.

3. An *assignment operator*, which copies the contents of one object of this type to another object of the same type.

4. A *destructor*, which performs whatever cleanup is needed when an object of this type "dies".

Since these member functions are so important to the proper functioning of a class, the compiler will create a version of each of them for us if we don't write them ourselves. In the case of StockItem, these compiler-generated member functions are perfectly acceptable, with the exception of the default constructor. The compiler-generated default constructor doesn't initialize a new StockItem object to a valid state, so we had to write that constructor ourselves to be sure of what a newly created StockItem contains. Next, we looked at the first version of a class interface specification for StockItem (Figure 6.3), which tells the user (and the compiler) exactly what functions objects of this class can perform. Some items of note in this construct are these:

1. The *access specifiers* public and private, which control access to the implementation of a class by functions not in the class (*nonmember functions*). Member variables and functions in the public section are available for use by nonmember functions, whereas member variables and functions in the private section are usable only by member functions.

2. The declarations of the *constructor* functions, which construct a new object of the class. The first noteworthy point about constructors is that they have the same name as the class, which is how the compiler identifies them as constructors. The second point of note is that there can be more than one constructor for a given class; all constructors have the same name, and are distinguished by their argument lists. This facility, called *function overloading*, is applicable to C++ functions in general, not just constructors. That is, you can have any number of functions with the same name as long as they have different argument lists; the difference in argument lists is enough to make the compiler treat them as different functions. In this case, we have written two constructors: the default constructor, which is used to create a StockItem when we don't specify an initial value, and a constructor that has arguments to specify values for all of the member variables.[18]

3. The declaration of a "normal" member function (that is, not a constructor or other predefined function) named Display, which as its name indicates, is used to display a StockItem on the screen.

4. The declarations of the member variables of StockItem, which are used to keep track of the information for a given object of the StockItem class.

Once we'd defined the class interface, we started on the class implementation by writing the default constructor for the StockItem class: StockItem::StockItem(). The reason for the doubled name is that when we write the implementation of a member function, we have to specify what class that member function belongs to; in this example, the first StockItem is the name of the class, whereas the second StockItem is the name of the function, which, as always with constructors, has the same name as the class. By contrast, we didn't have to specify the class name when declaring member functions in the interface definition, because all functions defined there are automatically member functions of that class. During this discussion, we saw that the preferred way to set the values of member variables is by using a member initialization list.

The next topic we visited was the scope of member variables, which is class scope. Each object of a given class has one set of member variables, which live as long as the object does. These member variables can be accessed from any member function as though they were global variables.

Then we examined how the default constructor was actually used in the example program, discovering that the line StockItem soup; was enough to cause it to be called. This is appropriate because one of the design goals of C++ was to allow a class object to be as easy to use as a native variable. Since a native variable can be created simply by

---

18. The compiler has also supplied a copy constructor for us, so that we can use StockItem objects as function arguments and return values. In this case, the compiler-generate copy constructor does exactly what we want, so we don't have to write our own. As we'll see in the rest of the book, these compiler-generated functions don't always behave properly, especially with more complicated classes than the StockItem class, where the compiler can't figure out how to copy or assign objects correctly without more help from us.

specifying its type and name, the same should be true of a class object.

This led to a discussion of the fact that the person who writes a class isn't always the person who uses it. One reason for this is that the skills required to write a program using a class are not necessarily the same as those required to create the class in the first place.

Next, we covered the other constructor we wrote for the StockItem class. This one has arguments specifying the values for all of the member variables that make up the data part of the class.

Then we got to the final function of the first version of the StockItem class: the Display function, which as its name indicates is used to display the contents of a StockItem on the screen. This function uses the pre-existing ability of << to display shorts and strings, including those that hold the contents of a StockItem. The return type of this function is a type we hadn't seen before, void, which simply means that there is no return value from this function. We don't need a return value from the Display function because we call it solely for its *side effect*: displaying the value of its StockItem on the screen.

Next, we took up the private part of the StockItem class definition, which contains the member variables. We covered two reasons why it is a good idea to keep the member variables private: First, it makes debugging easier, because only the member functions can modify the member variables; second, we can change the names or types of our member variables or delete them from the class definition much more easily if we don't have to worry about what other functions might be relying on them. While we were on the subject of the member variables of StockItem, I also explained how we could use a short to store a price: By expressing the price in cents, rather than dollars and cents, any price up to $327.67 could be stored in such a variable.

As we continued with the analysis of how the StockItem objects would be used, we discovered that our example program actually needed a vector of such objects, one for each different item in the stock. We also needed some way to read the information for these StockItem objects from a disk file, so we wouldn't have to type it in every time we started the program up. So the next program we examined provided this function via a C++ library class we hadn't seen before: ifstream (for input from a file). We also added a new function called Read to use this new class to read information for a StockItem from the file containing that information.

While looking at the implementation of the new Read member function, we ran into the idea of a *reference argument*, which is an argument that is another name for the caller's variable, rather than a copy of that variable (a *value argument*). This makes it possible to change the caller's variable by changing the value of the argument in the function. In most cases, we don't want to be able to change the caller's variable, but it is essential when reading from a stream, because otherwise we'd get the same data every time we read something from the stream. Therefore, we have to use a reference argument in this case, so that the stream's internal state will be updated correctly when we retrieve data from it.

Then we got to the question of how we could tell when there were no data left in the input file; the answer was to call the ifstream member function fail, which returns zero if some data remain in the stream, and nonzero if we have tried to read past the end of the file. We used a nonzero return value from fail to trigger a break statement, which terminates whatever loop contains the break. In this case, the loop was the one that read data from the input file, so the loop would stop whenever we got to the end of the input file or when we had read 100 records, whichever came first.

This led to a detailed investigation of whether the number of records read was always calculated correctly. The problem under discussion was the potential for a *fencepost error*, also known as an *off by one error*. After careful consideration, I concluded that the code as written was correct.

Having cleared up that question, we proceeded to some other scenarios that might occur in the grocery store for which this program theoretically was being written. All of the scenarios we looked at had a common requirement: to be able to look up a StockItem, given some information about it. We first tried to handle this requirement by reading the UPC directly from each StockItem object in the vector. When we found the correct StockItem, we would display and update the inventory for that StockItem. However, this didn't compile, because we were trying to access private member variables of a StockItem object from a nonmember function, which is illegal. While we could have changed those variables from private to public, that would directly contradict the reason that we made them private in the first place; that is, to prevent external functions from interfering in the inner workings of our StockItem objects. Therefore, we solved the problem by adding some new member functions (CheckUPC and DeductSaleFromInventory) to check the UPC of a StockItem and manipulate the inventory information for each StockItem, respectively. At the same time, we examined a new data type, bool, which is limited to the two values true and false; it is handy for keeping track of information such as whether we have found the StockItem object we are looking for, and communicating such information back to a calling function.

While I was making these changes, I noticed that the original version of the test program wasn't very helpful to its user; it didn't tell the user whether the UPC was any good, the name of the item, or how much inventory was available for sale. So I added some more member functions (GetInventory and GetName) to allow this more "user-friendly" information to be displayed.

Then we progressed to the second of the grocery store scenarios, in which the task was to find the price of an item, given its UPC. This turned out to be very similar to the previous problem of finding an item to update its inventory. Therefore, it was a pretty obvious step to try to make a function out of the "find an item by UPC" operation, rather than writing the code for the search over again. Since we're doing "object-oriented" programming, such a function should probably be a member function. The question was "of which class?" It couldn't be a member function of StockItem, because the whole idea of this function was to locate a StockItem. A member function of StockItem needs a StockItem object to work on, but we didn't have the StockItem object yet.

The solution was to make another class, called Inventory, which had member functions to load the inventory information in from the disk file (LoadInventory) and search it for a particular StockItem (FindItem). Most of this class was pretty simple, but we did run into an interesting design question: What should the FindItem function return if the UPC didn't match anything in the inventory? After some consideration, I decided to use a *null object* of the class StockItem; that is, one that exists solely to serve as a placeholder representing a non-existent object. This solution required adding an IsNull member function to the StockItem class, so that the user of FindItem could determine whether the returned object was "real" or just an indication of an incorrect UPC.

Then we updated the test program to use this new means of locating a StockItem. Since the new version of the test program could perform either of two functions (price check or sale), we also added some output and input statements to ask the user what he wanted to do. To make this process more flexible, we allowed the user to type in either an upper- or lowercase letter to select which function to perform. This brought up the use of the "logical OR" operator || to allow the controlled block of an if statement to be executed if either (or both) of two expressions is true. We also saw how to combine an else with a following if statement, when we wanted to select among more than two alternatives.

We needed two more functions to make this new version of the application program work correctly: one to update the item in the inventory (Inventory::UpdateItem(StockItem item)) and one to get the UPC of a StockItem (StockItem::GetUPC()). The reason that we had to add these new functions to the interfaces of Inventory and StockItem, respectively, is that we were no longer operating on the "real" StockItem, as we had been when we accessed the inventory vector directly in the previous version of the application program. Instead, we were getting a copy of the StockItem from the Inventory object and changing that copy; thus, to have the final result put back into the Inventory object, we had to add the UpdateItem member function of Inventory, which overwrote the original StockItem with our changed version. The GetUPC function's role in all this was to allow the UpdateItem function to look up the correct StockItem to be replaced without the main program having to pass the UPC in explicitly; instead, the GetUPC function allowed the UpdateItem function to retrieve the correct UPC from the updated object provided by the main program.

This brought us to the final scenario, which required us to look up the inventory for an item, given its UPC. As it happened, we had already solved that problem by the simple expedient of displaying the name and inventory of the StockItem as soon as it was located.

Finally, I mentioned a few other factors, such as alternative means of looking up an item without knowing its UPC, that would be important in writing a real application program and noted that we couldn't go into them here due to space limitations, but that we would deal with similar issues later in the book.

Exercises

1. In a real inventory control program, we would need to do more than merely read the inventory information in from a disk file, as we have done in this chapter. We'd also want to be able to write the updated inventory back to the disk file via an ofstream object, which is exactly like an ifstream object except that it allows us to write to a file rather than reading from one. Modify the header files item5.h and invent1.h to include the declarations of the new functions StockItem::Write and Inventory::StoreInventory, needed to support this new ability.

2. Implement the new functions that you declared in exercise 1. Then update the test program to write the changed inventory to a new file. To connect an ofstream called OutputStream to a file named "test.out", you could use the line:

ofstream OutputStream("test.out");

Conclusion

In this chapter, we've delved into the concepts and implementations of classes and objects, which are the constructs that make C++ an object-oriented language. Of course, we have only scratched the surface of these powerful topics; in fact, we'll spend much of the rest of this book on the fundamentals of classes and objects. Unfortunately, it's impossible to cover these constructs in every detail in any one book, no matter how long or detailed it may be, and I'm not going to try to do that. Instead, we'll continue with our in-depth examination of the basics of object-oriented programming. In the next chapter, we'll start on the task of creating a string class like the one that we've been using so far in this book.

Answers to Exercises

1. Here is the new function declaration that needs to be added to the StockItem interface definition (from code\item6.h):

    void Write(ofstream& s);

    and the one to be added to the Inventory interface definition, (from code\invent2.h):

    void StoreInventory(ofstream& OutputStream);

2. Figure 6.33 shows the implementation of the Write member function for StockItem, and Figure 6.34 is the implementation of the StoreInventory member function of the Inventory class. As you

can see, neither of these functions is tremendously complex or, for that matter, very different from its counterpart used to read the data in from the file in the first place.

FIGURE 6.33. The Write **member function for the** StockItem class **(from code\item6.cc)**

```
void StockItem::Write(ofstream& s)
{
  s << m_Name << endl;
  s << m_InStock << endl;
  s << m_Price << endl;
  s << m_Distributor << endl;
  s << m_UPC << endl;
}
```

FIGURE 6.34. The StoreInventory **member function for the** Inventory class **(from code\invent2.cc)**

```
void Inventory:: StoreInventory (ofstream& os)
{
  short i;

  for (i = 0; i < m_StockCount; i ++)
    m_Stock[i].Write(os);

  return;
}
```

Finally, Figure 6.35 shows the changes needed to the application program to write the updated inventory back to a new file.

FIGURE 6.35. The changes to the application program (from code\itemtst6.cc)

```
ofstream OutputStream("shop2.out");
MyInventory.StoreInventory(OutputStream);
```

Of course, in a real program, it would probably be better to write the updated inventory back to the original file, so that the next time we ran the program, the updated inventory would be used. However, in the case of a test application, it's simpler to avoid modifying the input file so we can run the same test again if necessary.

Assuming that you've installed the software from the CD-ROM in the back of this book, you can try out my solution to these exercises. First, you have to compile it by changing to the code subdirectory under the main directory where you installed the software, and typing RHIDE itemtst6, then using the "Make" command from the "Compile" menu. Then exit back to DOS and type itemtst6 to run the program. When the program asks for a UPC, you can use 7904886261, which is the (made-up) UPC for "antihistamines".

CHAPTER 7   *Stringing Along*

You may recall the discussion near the beginning of Chapter 6 of *native* vs. *user defined* variable types. I provided a list of native C++ variable types; namely, char, short, long, float, double, bool, and int. We've already created several classes for our inventory control project, and now it's time to apply what we've learned to a more generally useful type, the string. We've been using strings for a long time, and now it's time to see exactly how to implement the string class we've been using.

Objectives of This Chapter

By the end of this chapter, you should

1. Understand how variables of the string class are created, destroyed, and assigned to one another.

2. Understand how to assign memory to variables where the amount of memory needed is not known until the program is running.

3. Understand how literal C strings can be used to initialize variables of the string class.

Playing out the string

Susan had some questions about these objectives. Here's the discussion.

Susan: What is the difference between literal C strings and variables of the string class?

Steve: A variable of the string class is what you've been using to store variable-length alphanumeric data. You can copy them, input them from the keyboard, assign values to them, and the like. By contrast, a literal C string is just a bunch of characters in a row; all you can do with it is display it or assign it to a string variable.

Susan: Okay, then you are saying that variables of the string class are what I am used to working with, but I just didn't know that they were part of a class because you were *keeping this all a big secret*. On the other hand, a literal C string is just some nonsense that you want me to learn to assign to something that might make sense? Okay, this is great; sure, this is logical. Hey, a literal C string must be a part of the native language?

Steve: Right all the way along.

Susan: Yes, but why would something so basic as string not be part of the native language? This is what I don't understand. And vectors too; even though they are gross, I can see that they are a very necessary evil. So tell me why those basic things would not be part of the native language?

Steve: That's a very good question. That decision was made to keep the C++ language itself as simple as possible.[1] In fact, versions of both strings and vectors are part of the "standard library" defined in the C++ standard, which was approved in 1998. This means that as soon as the compiler vendors manage to implement the standard fully, the user will be able to count on them being available without having to make them up himself, even though they aren't built into the compiler itself.

Before we get into how to create the string class we've been using in this book, I should expand on the answer I gave Susan as to why string isn't a native type in the first place. One of the design goals of C++, as of C, was to allow the language to be moved, or **ported**, from one machine type to another as easily as possible. Since strings, vectors, and so on can be written in C++ (i.e., created out of the more elementary parts of the language), they don't have to be built in. This reduces the amount of effort needed to port C++. In addition, some applications don't need and can't afford anything but the barest essentials; "embedded" CPUs such as those in cameras, VCRs, elevators, or microwave ovens, are probably the most important examples of such applications, and such devices are much more common than "real" computers. However, this still leaves the question of why these data types haven't been in a standard library that can be used when necessary. Bjarne says in his book *Design and Evolution of C++* that it might very well have been a mistake to have released C++ to the general public without this library; I tend to agree. In any event, this situation will be remedied when the C++ standard is actually implemented by compiler vendors; as of June 2000, this process is still not complete.

Even though strings aren't native, we've been using them for some time already without realizing that they're not native variables, so it should be fairly obvious that this class provides the facilities of a concrete data type; that is, one whose objects can be created, copied,

---

1. Which isn't very simple, unfortunately for compiler makers.

assigned, and destroyed as though they were native variables. You may recall from the discussion starting in the section entitled "Common Behavior" on page 316 that such data types need a default constructor, a copy constructor, an assignment operator, and a destructor. To refresh your memory, here's the description of each of these member functions:

1. A *default constructor* creates an object when there is no initial value specified for the object.

2. A *copy constructor* makes a new object with the same contents as an existing object of the same type.

3. An *assignment operator* sets an existing object to the value of another object of the same type.

4. A *destructor* cleans up when an object expires; for a local object, this occurs at the end of the block where it was created.

In our StockItem and Inventory class definitions, the compiler-generated versions of these functions were fine for all but the default constructor. In the case of the string class, though, we're going to have to create our own versions of all four of these functions, for reasons that will become apparent as we examine their implementations in this chapter and the next one.

Before we can implement these member functions for our string class, though, we have to define exactly what a string is. The string class is a data type that gives us the following capabilities in addition to those facilities that every concrete data type provides:

1. We can set a string to a literal value like "abc".

2. We can display a string on the screen with the << operator.

3. We can read a string in from the keyboard with the >> operator.

4. We can compare two strings to find out whether they are equal.

5. We can compare two strings to find out which is "less than" the other; that is, which one would come first in the dictionary.

We'll see how all of these capabilities work sometime in this chapter or the next one, but for now let's start with Figure 7.1, a simplified version of the interface specification for the string class, which includes the specification of the four member functions needed for a concrete data type, as well as a special constructor that is specific to the string class. I strongly recommend that you print out the files that contain this interface and its implementation, as well as the test program, for reference as you are going through this part of the chapter; those files are string1.h, string1.cc, and strtst1.cc, respectively.

FIGURE 7.1. The string class interface, initial version (code\string1.h)

```
class string
{
public:
    string();
    string(const string& Str);
    string& operator = (const string& Str);
    ~string();

    string(char* p);

private:
    short m_Length;
    char* m_Data;
};
```

The first four member functions in that interface are the standard concrete data type functions. In order, they are

1. The *default constructor.*

2. The *copy constructor.*

3. The *assignment operator*, operator =.

4. The *destructor.*

I've been instructed by Susan to let you see all of the code that implements this initial version of our string class at once before we start to analyze it. Of course, I've done so, and Figure 7.2 is the result.

FIGURE 7.2. The initial implementation for the string class **(code\string1.cc)**

```
#include <string.h>
#include "string1.h"

string::string()
: m_Length(1),
  m_Data(new char [m_Length])
{
    memcpy(m_Data,"",m_Length);
}

string::string(const string& Str)
: m_Length(Str.m_Length),
  m_Data(new char [m_Length])
{
    memcpy(m_Data,Str.m_Data,m_Length);
}

string::string(char* p)
: m_Length(strlen(p) + 1),
  m_Data(new char [m_Length])
{
    memcpy(m_Data,p,m_Length);
}

string& string::operator = (const string& Str)
{
  if (&Str != this)
  {
  delete [ ] m_Data;
  m_Length = Str.m_Length;
  m_Data = new char [m_Length];
  memcpy(m_Data,Str.m_Data,m_Length);
```

```
    }
    return *this;
}

string::~string()
{
    delete [ ] m_Data;
}
```

Now let's start by looking at the default constructor. Figure 7.3 shows its implementation.

FIGURE 7.3. The default constructor for the string class **(from code\string1.cc)**

```
string:: string ()
: m_Length(1),
  m_Data(new char [m_Length])
{
  memcpy(m_Data,"",m_Length);
}
```

The member initialization list in this constructor contains two expressions. The first of them, m_Length(1), isn't very complicated at all. It simply sets the length of our new string to 1. However, this may seem a bit odd: Why do we need any characters at all for a string that has no value? The answer to this riddle is quite simple: To make our strings as compatible as possible with pre-existing C functions that work on C strings, we need to include the null byte that terminates all C strings, so we need to reserve one more byte of memory for a string's data than are needed to hold the characters that we actually want to store. In the current case of a zero-character string, this means that we need one byte of storage for the null byte.

It's important to note that this is an example where the order of execution of member initializer expressions is important: we definitely want m_Length to be initialized before m_Data, because the amount of data being assigned to m_Data depends on the value of m_Length. As you may remember from Chapter 6, the order in which the initialization expressions are executed is dependent **not** on the order in which they are written in the list, but on the order in which the member variables being initialized are declared in the class interface definition. Therefore, it's important to make sure that the order in which those member variables are declared is correct. In this case, it is, because m_Length is declared before m_Data in string1.h.

Before proceeding to the next member initialization expression, let's take a look at the characteristics of the variables that we're using here. The scope of these variables, as we know from our previous discussion of the StockItem class, is class scope; therefore, each object of the string class has its own set of these variables, and they are accessible from any member functions of the class as though they were global variables.

However, an equally important characteristic of each of these variables is its data type. The type of m_Length is short, which is a type we've encountered before, a 16-bit integer variable that can hold a number between -32768 and 32767. But what about the type of the other member variable, m_Data, which is listed in Figure 7.1 as char*? We know what a char is, but what does that * mean?

Passing Along a Few Pointers

The star means **pointer**, which is just another term for a memory address. In particular, char* (pronounced "char star") means "pointer to a char".[2] This is considered one of the most difficult concepts for beginning programmers to grasp, but you shouldn't have any trouble understanding its definition if you've been following the discussion so far: A pointer is the address of some data item in memory. That is, to say "a variable points to a memory location" is almost exactly the same as saying "a variable's value is the address of a memory

---

2. By the way, char* can also be written as char *, but I find it clearer to attach the * to the data type being pointed to.

location". In the specific case of a variable x of type char*, for example, to say "x points to a C string" is exactly the same as saying "x contains the address of the first byte of the C string."[3] The m_Data variable is used to hold the address of the first char of the data that a string contains; the rest of the characters follow the first character at consecutively higher locations in memory.

If this sounds familiar, it should; a literal C string like "hello" (Chapter 3) consists of a number of chars in consecutive memory locations; it should come as no surprise then when I tell you that a literal C string has the type char*.

As you might infer from these cases, our use of one char* to refer to multiple chars isn't an isolated example. Actually, it's quite a widespread practice in C++, which brings up an important point: A char*, or any other type of pointer for that matter, has two different possible meanings in C++.[4] One of these meanings is the obvious one of signifying the address of a single item of the type the pointer points to. In the case of a char*, that means the address of a char. However, in the case of a literal C string, as well in the case of our m_Data member variable, we use a char* to indicate the address of the first char of an indeterminate number of chars; any chars after the first one occupy consecutively higher addresses in memory. Most of the time, this distinction has little effect on the way we write programs, but sometimes we have to be sensitive to this "multiple personality" of pointers; we'll run across one of these cases later in this chapter.

Susan had some questions (and I had some answers) on this topic of the true meaning of a char*:

---

3. C programmers are likely to object that a pointer has some properties that differ from those of a memory address. Technically, they're right, but in the specific case of char* the differences between a pointer and a memory address will never matter to us.

4. As this implies, it's possible to have a pointer to any type of variable, not just to a char. For example, a pointer to a short would have the type short*, and similarly for pointers to any other data type, including user-defined types. As we will see in Chapter 10, pointers to user-defined types are very important in some circumstances, but we don't need to worry about them right now.

Susan: What I get from this is that char* points to a char address either singularly or as the beginning of a string of multiple addresses. Is that right?

Steve: Yes, except that it's a string of several characters, not addresses.

Susan: Oh, here we go again; this is so confusing. So if I use a string "my name is" then char* points to the address that holds the string of all those letters. But if the number of letters exceeds what the address can hold, won't it take up the next available address in memory and char* point to it after it points to the first address?

Steve: Each memory address can hold 1 byte; in the case of a string, that byte is the value of one char of the string's data. So a char*, as we use it, will always point to the first char of the chars that hold our string's value; the other chars follow that one immediately in memory.

Susan: Let me ask this: When you show an example of a string with the value "Test" (Figure 7.10), the pointer at address 12340002 containing the address 1234febc is really pointing at the T as that would be the first char and the rest of the letters will actually be in the other immediately following bytes of memory?

Steve: Absolutely correct.

While we're on the subject of that earlier discussion of literal C strings, you may recall that I bemoaned the fact that such literal C strings use a 0 byte to mark the end of the literal value, rather than keeping track of the length separately. Nothing can be done about that decision now, at least as it applies to literal C strings. In the case of the string class, however, the implementation is under our control rather than the language designer's; therefore, I've decided to use a length variable (m_Length) along with the variable that holds the address of the first char of the data (m_Data).

To recap, what we're doing in this chapter and the next one is synthesizing a new data type called string. A string needs a length and a set of characters to represent the actual data in the string. The short named m_Length is used in the string class to keep track of the number of characters in the data part of the string; the char* named m_Data is used to hold the address of the first character of the data part of the string.

The next member initialization expression, m_Data(new char [m_Length]), takes us on another of our side trips. This one has to do with the dreaded topic of dynamic memory allocation.

The Dynamic Duo, new *and* delete

So far, we've encountered two storage classes: static and auto. As you might recall from the discussion in Chapter 5, static variables are allocated memory when the program is linked, while the memory for auto variables is assigned to them at entry to the block where they are defined. However, both mechanisms have a major limitation: The amount of memory needed is fixed when the program is compiled. In the case of a string, we need to allocate an amount of memory that in general cannot be known until the program is executed, so we need another storage class.

As you will be happy to learn, there is indeed another storage class called **dynamic storage** that enables us to decide the amount of memory to allocate at run time.[5] To allocate memory dynamically, we use the new operator, specifying the data type of the memory to be allocated and the number of elements that we need. In our example member initialization expression, m_Data(new char [m_Length]), the

---

5. This terminology doesn't exactly match the official nomenclature used by Bjarne Stroustrup to describe dynamic memory allocation. However, every C and C++ programmer will understand you if you talk about dynamic storage, and I believe that this terminology is easier to understand than the official terminology.

type is char and the count is m_Length. The result of calling new is a *pointer* to the specified data type; in this case, since we want to store chars, the result of calling new is a pointer to a char, that is, a char*. This is a good thing, because char* is the type of the variable m_Data that we're initializing to the address that is returned from new. So the result of the member initialization expression we're examining is to set m_Data to the value returned from calling new; that value is the address of a newly assigned block of memory that can hold m_Length chars. In the case of the default constructor, we've asked for a block of 1 byte, which is just what we need to hold the contents of the zero-length C string that represents the value of our empty string.

It may not be obvious why we need to call new to get the address where we will store our data. Doesn't a char* always point to a byte in memory? Yes, it does; the problem is *which* byte. We can't use static (link time) or auto (function entry time) allocation for our string class, because each string can have a different number of characters. Therefore, we have to assign the memory after we find out how many characters we need to store the value of the string. The new operator reserves some memory and returns the address of the beginning of that memory. In this case, we assign that address to our char* variable called m_Data. An important point to note here is that in addition to giving us the address of a section of memory, new also gives us the right to use that memory for our own purposes. That same memory area will not be made available for any other use until we say we're done with it by calling another operator called delete.

Susan had some questions about how (and why) we use new. Here's the discussion:

> **Susan:** Okay, so all Figure 7.3 does is lay the foundation to be able to acquire memory to store the C string "" and then copy that information that will go into m_Data that starts at a certain location in memory?

> **Steve:** Right; Figure 7.6 is the code for the constructor that accomplishes that task.

Susan: When you say that "the amount of memory needed is fixed when the program is compiled" that bothers me. I don't understand that in terms of auto variables, or is this because that type is known such as a short?

Steve: Right. As long as the types and the quantity of the data items in a class definition are known at compile time, as is the case with auto and static variables, the compiler can figure out the amount of memory they need. The addresses of auto variables aren't known at compile time, but how much space they will take up is.

Susan: Okay, I understand the types of the data items. However, I am not sure what you mean by the quantity; can you give me an example?

Steve: Sure. You might have three chars and four shorts in a particular class definition; in that case, the compiler would add up three times the length of a char and four times the length of a short and allocate that much memory (more or less). Actually, some other considerations affect the size of a class object that aren't relevant to the discussion here, but they can all be handled at compile time and therefore still allow the compiler to figure out the amount of memory needed to store an object of any class.

The statement inside the {} in the default constructor, memcpy(m_Data,"",m_Length); is responsible for copying the null byte from the C string "" to our newly allocated area of memory. The function memcpy (short for "memory copy") is one of the C *standard library* functions for C string and memory manipulation. As you can see, it takes three arguments. The first argument is a pointer to the destination, that is, the address that will receive the data. The second argument is a pointer to the source of the data; this, of course, is the address that we're copying from (i.e., the address of the null byte in the "", in our example). The last argument is the number of bytes to copy.

In other words, memcpy reads the bytes that starts at the address specified by its input argument (in this case, "") and writes a copy of those bytes to addresses starting at the address specified by its output argument (in this case, m_Data). The amount copied is specified by the length argument (in this case, m_Length). Effectively, therefore, memcpy copies a certain amount of data from one place in memory to another; in this case, it copies 1 byte (which happens to be a null byte) from the address of the literal C string "" to the address pointed to by m_Data (that is, the place where we're storing the data that make up the value of our string).

This notion of dynamic allocation was the subject of some more discussion with Susan.

> **Susan:** This stuff with operator new: I have no idea what you are talking about. I am totally gone, left in the dust. *What* is this stuff? Why do you need new to point to memory locations? I thought that is what char* did?

> **Steve:** You're right that char* points to a memory location. But which one? The purpose of new is to get some memory for us from the operating system and return the address of the first byte of that memory. In this case, we assign that address to our char* variable called m_Data. Afterward, we can store data at that address.

> **Susan:** I am not getting this because I just don't get the purpose of char*, and don't just tell me that it points to an address in memory. I want to know why we need it to point to a specific address in memory rather than let it take on just any random address in memory.

> **Steve:** Because then there would be no way of guaranteeing that the memory that it points to won't be used by some other part of the program or indeed some other program entirely in a multitasking system like Windows. We need to claim ownership of some memory by calling new before we can use it.

Susan: I think I understand now why we need to use new, but why should the result of calling new be a pointer? I am missing this completely. How does new result in char*? Some steps are not obvious here.

Steve: Because that's how new is defined: it gives you an address (pointer) to a place where you can store some chars (or whatever type you requested).

Susan: Okay, but in the statement m_Data = new char [m_Length], why is char in this statement not char*? I am getting so confused on this.

Steve: Because you're asking for an address (pointer) to a place where you can store a bunch of chars.

Susan: But then wouldn't it be necessary to specify char* rather than char in the statement?

Steve: I admit that I find that syntax unclear as well. Yes, in my opinion, the type should be stated as char*, but apparently Bjarne thought otherwise.

Susan: Okay, so then m_Data is the pointer address where new (memory from the heap) is going to store char data of m_Length. Right?

Steve: Almost right. The value assigned to m_Data in the constructor is the value returned from operator new; this value is the address of an area of memory allocated to this use. The area of memory is of length m_Length.

Susan: Well, I thought that the address stored in m_Data was the first place where you stored your chars. So is new just what goes and gets that memory to put the address in m_Data?

Steve: Exactly.

Susan: Here's what I understand about the purpose of char*. It functions as a pointer to a specific memory address. We need to do that because the computer is stupid and doesn't know where to put the char data, therefore we need char* to say "hey you, computer, look over here, this is where we are going to put the data for you to find and use".

Steve: That's fine.

Susan: We need to use char* for variable length memory. This is because we don't know how much memory we will need until it is used. For this we need the variable m_Data to hold the first address in memory for our char data. Then we need the variable m_Length that we have set to the length of the C string that will be used to get the initial data for the string. Then we have to have that nifty little helper guy new to get some memory from the heap for the memory of our C string data.

Steve: Sounds good to me.

Susan: Now about memcpy: This appears to be the same thing as initializing the variable. I am so confused.

Steve: That's exactly correct. Maybe you shouldn't get unconfused!

As the call to memcpy is the only statement in the constructor proper, it's time to see what we have accomplished. The constructor has initialized a string by:

1. Setting the length of the string to the effective length of a null C string, "", including the terminating null byte (i.e., 1 byte).

2. Allocating memory for a null C string.

3. Copying the contents of a null C string to the allocated memory.

Now let's continue with our examination of the string::string() constructor. Its final result is a string with the value "", whose memory layout might look like Figure 7.4.[6]

FIGURE 7.4. An empty string **in memory**

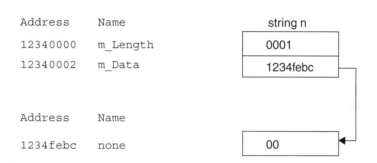

Using the default constructor is considerably easier than defining it. As we have seen in Chapter 6, the default constructor is called whenever we declare an object without specifying any data to initialize it with; for example, in the line string s; in Figure 7.5. Although this program doesn't do anything useful, it does illustrate how we can use the member functions of the string class, so you should pay attention to it.

FIGURE 7.5. Our first test program for the string class **(code\strtst1.cc)**

```
#include "string1.h"

int main()
{
    string s;
    string n("Test");
```

6. The reason for the different numbers of digits in the representations of m_Length, m_Data, and the data for the null C string is to indicate how long those data items are.

```
string x;

s = n;
n = "My name is: ";

x = n;
return 0;
}
```

I should point out here that the only file that the compiler needs to figure out how to compile the line string s; is the header file, string1.h. The actual implementation of the string class in string1.cc isn't required, because all the compiler cares about when compiling a program using classes is the contract between the class implementer and the user; that is, the header file. The actual implementation in string1.cc that fulfills this contract isn't needed until the program is linked to make an executable; at that point, the linker will complain if it can't find an implementation of any function that we've referred to.

Caution: Construction Area

Now that we've disposed of the default constructor, let's take a look at the line in the string interface definition (Figure 7.1) that says string(char* p);.[7] This is the declaration for another constructor; unlike the default constructor we've examined, this one has an argument, char* p.[8]

As we saw in Chapter 6, the combination of the function name and argument types is called the *signature* of a function. Two

---

7. I know we've skipped the copy constructor, the assignment operator, and the destructor. Don't worry, we'll get to them later.

8. There's nothing magical about the name p for a pointer. You could call it George if you wanted to, but it would just confuse people. The letter p is often used for pointers, especially by programmers who can't type, which unfortunately is fairly common.

functions that have the same name but differ in the type of at least one argument are distinct functions, and the compiler will use the difference(s) in the type(s) of the argument(s) to figure out which function with a given name should be called in any particular case. Of course, this leads to the question of why we would need more than one string constructor; they all make strings, don't they?

Yes, they do, but not from the same "raw material". It's true that every constructor in the string class makes a string, but each constructor has a unique argument list, which determines exactly how the new string will be constructed. The default constructor always makes an empty string (like the C string ""), whereas the constructor string(char* p) takes a C string as an argument and makes a string that has the same value as that argument.

Susan wasn't going to accept this without a struggle.

Susan: I don't get "whereas the string(char* p) constructor takes a C string and makes a string that has the same value as the C string does."

Steve: Well, when the compiler looks at the statement string n("Test"); it has to follow some steps to figure it out.

1. The compiler knows that you want to create a string because you've defined a variable called n with the type string; that's what string n means.

2. Therefore, since string is not a native data type, the compiler looks for a function called string::string, which would create a string.

3. However, there can be several functions named string::string, with different argument lists, because there are several possible ways to get the initial data for the string you're creating. In this case, you are supplying data in the form of a literal C string, whose type is char*; therefore, a constructor with the signature string::string(char*) will match.

4. Since a function with the signature string::string(char*) has been declared in the header file, the line string n("Test"); is translated to a call to that function.

Susan: So string(char* p) is just there in case you need it for "any given situation"; what situation is this?

Steve: It depends on what kind of data (if any) we're supplying to the constructor. If we don't supply any data, then the default constructor is used. If we supply a C string (such as a literal C string), then the constructor that takes a char* is used, because the type of a C string is char*.

Susan: So string s; is the default constructor in case you need something that uses uninitialized objects?

Steve: Not quite; the default constructor for the string class is string::string(), which doesn't need any arguments, because it constructs an empty string.

Susan: And the string n ("Test"); is a constructor that finally gets around to telling us what we are trying to accomplish here?

Steve: Again, not quite. The line string n("Test"); causes a string with the value "Test" to be created, by calling the constructor string::string(char* p);.

Susan: See, you are talking first about string n("Test"); in Figure 7.5 and then you get all excited that you just happen to have string::string(char* p) hanging around which is way over in Figure 7.1.

Steve: Now that you know that a literal C string such as "Test" has the data type char*, does this make sense?

Susan: Okay, I think this helped. I understand it better. Only now that I do, it raises other questions that I accepted before but now don't make sense due to what I do understand. Does that make sense to you? I didn't think so.

Steve: Sure, why not? You've reached a higher level of understanding, so you can now see confusions that were obscured before.

Susan: So this is just the constructor part? What about the default constructor, what happened to it?

Steve: We can't use it here, because we have some data to assign to the string when the string is created. A default constructor is used only when there is no initial value for a variable.

Susan: So was the whole point of discussion about default constructors just to let us know that they exist even though you aren't really using them here?

Steve: We are using them to create strings with no initial value, as discussed before.

Susan wasn't clear on why the C string "Test" would be of type char*, which is understandable because that's anything but obvious. Here's the discussion we entered into on this point.

Susan: When you say "Test" is a literal C string of type char* and that the compiler happily finds that declaration, that is fine. But see, it is not obvious to me that it is type char*; I can see char but not char*. Something is missing here so that I would be able to follow the jump from char to char*.

Steve: A literal C string isn't a single char, but a bunch of chars. Therefore, we need to get the address of the first one; that gives us the addresses of the ones after it.

Now that the reason why a literal C string is of type char* is a bit clearer, Figure 7.6 shows the implementation for the constructor that takes a char* argument.

FIGURE 7.6. The char* constructor for the string class **(from code\string1.cc)**

```
string:: string (char* p)
: m_Length(strlen(p) + 1),
  m_Data(new char [m_Length])
{
  memcpy(m_Data,p,m_Length);
}
```

You should be able to decode the header string::string(char* p): This function is a constructor for class string (because its class is string and its name is also string); its argument, named p, is of type char*. The first member initialization expression is m_Length(strlen(p) + 1). This is obviously initializing the string's length (m_Length) to something, but what?

As you may recall, C strings are stored as a series of characters terminated by a null byte (i.e., one with a 0 value). Therefore, unlike the case with our strings, where the length is available by looking at a member variable (m_Length), the only way to find the length of a C string is to search from the beginning of the C string until you get to a null byte. Since this is such a common operation in C, the C *standard library* (which is a subset of the C++ standard library) provides the function strlen (short for "string length") for this purpose; it returns a result indicating the number of characters in the C string, *not* including the null byte.[9] So the statement m_Length = strlen(p) + 1; sets our member variable m_Length to the length of the C string p, which we compute as the length reported by strlen (not including the terminating null byte) + 1 for the terminating null byte. So the member initialization expression m_Length(strlen(p) + 1), initializes our member variable m_Length to the length of the C string p, which we compute as the length reported by strlen (which doesn't include the terminating null byte) + 1 for the terminating null byte. We need this information because we've decided to store the length explicitly in our string class rather than relying solely on a null byte to mark the end of the string, as is done in C.[10]

Susan had some questions about the implementation of this function, and I supplied some answers.

Susan: What is strlen?

Steve: A function left over from C; it tells us how long a C string is.

Susan: Where did it come from?

Steve: It's from the standard C library, which is part of the C++ standard library.

Susan: What are you using it for here?

---

9.   This is probably a good place to clear up any confusion you might have about whether there are native and user defined functions; there is no such distinction. However, the reason might not be what you expect; rather than there being no user defined functions, it's just the opposite. That is, functions are never native in the way that variables are: built into the language. Quite a few functions such as strlen and memcpy come *with* the language; that is, they are supplied in the standard libraries that you get when you buy the compiler. However, these functions are not privileged relative to the functions you can write yourself, unlike the case with native variables in C. In other words, you can write a *function* in C or C++ that looks and behaves exactly like one in the library, whereas it's impossible in C to add a type of *variable* that has the same appearance and behavior as the native types; the knowledge of the native variable types is built into the C compiler and cannot be changed by the programmer.

But *why* aren't there any native functions? Because the language was designed to be easy to move (or **port**) from one machine to another. This is easier if the compiler is simpler; hence, most of the functionality of the language is provided by functions that can be written in the "base language" the compiler knows about. This includes basic functions such as strlen and memcpy, which can be written in C. For purposes of performance, they are often written in assembly language instead, but that's not necessary to get the language running on a new machine.

Steve: Finding out how long the C string is that we're supposed to copy into our string.

Susan: Is this C or C++?

Steve: Both.

Susan: Why is char* so special that it deserves a pointer? What makes it different?

Steve: The * means "pointer". In C++, char* means "pointer to a char".

Susan: I just don't understand the need for the pointer in char. See when we were using it (char) before, it didn't have a pointer, so why now? Well, I guess it was because I thought it was native back then when I didn't know that there was any other way. So why don't you have a pointer to strings then? Are all variables in classes going to have to be pointed to? I guess that is what I am asking.

Steve: We need pointers whenever we want to allocate an amount of memory that isn't known until the program is executing. If we wanted to have a rule that all strings could be only 10 characters in length (for example), then we could allocate the space for those characters in the string. However, we want to be able to handle strings of any length, so we have to decide how much space to allocate for the data when the constructor string::string(char* p) is called; the only way to do that is to use a pointer to memory that is

---

10. You may wonder why we even need to include the null byte if we're going to store the length also. Isn't this redundant? Yes, it is, but if we want to be able to use the debugger to look at our strings, we have to include that null byte at the end. Otherwise, the debugger won't know how to display them in an intelligible format.
    Also, there may be occasions when we will want to use C library functions with our strings; those functions won't work if we don't have a null byte at the end of the string.

allocated at run time, namely m_Data. Then we can use that memory to hold a copy of the C string pointed to by the parameter p.

Susan: Oh, no! Here we go again. Is m_Data a pointer? I thought it was just a variable that held an address.

Steve: Those are equivalent statements.

Susan: Why does it point? (Do you know how much I am beginning to hate that word?) I think you are going to have to clarify this.

Steve: It "points" in a metaphorical sense, but one that is second nature to programmers in languages like C. In fact, it merely holds the address of some memory location. Is that clearer?

Susan: So the purpose of m_Data is just a starting off point in memory?

Steve: Right. It's the address of the first char used to store the value of the string.

Susan: So the purpose of m_Length is to allot the length of memory that starts at the location where m_Data is?

Steve: Close; actually, it's to keep track of the amount of memory that has been allocated for the data.

Susan: But I see here that you are setting m_Length to strlen, so that in effect makes m_Length do the same thing?

Steve: Right; m_Length is the length of the string because it is set to the result returned by strlen (after adding 1 for the null byte at the end of the C string).

Susan: Why would you want a string with no data, anyway? What purpose does that serve?

Steve: So you can define a string before knowing what value it will eventually have. For example, the statement string s; defines a string with no data; the value can be assigned to the string later.

Susan: Oh yeah, just as you would have short x;. I forgot.

Steve: Yep.

Susan: Anyway, the first thing that helped me understand the need for pointers is variable-length data. I am sure that you mentioned this somewhere, but I certainly missed it. So this is a highlight. Once the need for it is understood then the rest falls in place. Well, almost; it is still hard to visualize, but I can.

Steve: I'll make sure to stress that point until it screams for mercy.

Susan: I think you might be able to take this information and draw a schematic for it. That would help. And show the code next to each of the steps involved.

Steve: Don't worry, we'll see lots of diagrams later.

Susan: So strlen is a function like any member function?

Steve: Yes, except that it is a global function rather than a member function belonging to a particular class. That's because it's a leftover from C, which doesn't have classes.

Susan: So it is what I can consider as a native function? Now I am getting confused again. I thought that just variables can be either made up (classes) or native. Why are we talking about functions in the same way? But then I remember that, in a backward way, functions belong to variables in classes rather than the other way around. This is just so crazy.

Steve: Functions are never native in the way that variables are; that is, built into the language. A lot of functions come with the language, in the form of the libraries, but they have no special characteristics that make them "better" than ones you write yourself. However, this is not true of variables in C, because C doesn't provide the necessary facilities for the programmer to add variable types that have the appearance and behavior of the native types.

Susan: You see I think it is hard for me to imagine a function as one word, because I am so used to main() with a bunch of code following it and I think of that as the whole function; see where I am getting confused?

Steve: When we call a function like strlen, that's not the whole function, it's just the name of the function. This is exactly like the situation where we wrote Average and then called it later to average some numbers.

Susan: A function has to "do something", so you will have to define what the function does; then when we use the function, we just call the name and that sets the action in gear?

Steve: Exactly.

Susan: Now, about this char* thing. . . (don't go ballistic, please) . . . exactly what is it? I mean it is a pointer to char, so what is *? Is it like an assignment operator? How is it classified?

Steve: After a type name, * means "pointer to the type preceding". So char* means "pointer to char", short* means "pointer to short", and so on.

Susan: So that would be fowithr a short with variable-length data? And that would be a different kind of short than a native short?

Steve: Almost, but not quite, correct. It would be for variable-length data consisting of one or more shorts, just as a literal C string is variable-length data consisting of one or more chars.

Susan: So it would be variable by virtue of the number of shorts?

Steve: Actually, by virtue of the *possibility* of having a number of shorts other than exactly one. If you *might* need two or three (or 100, for that matter) shorts (or any other type), and you don't know how many when the program is compiled, then you pretty much have to use a pointer.

Susan: Okay, yes, you said that about * and what it means to use a char*, but I thought it would work only with char so I didn't know I would be seeing it again with other variable types. I can't wait.

Steve: When we use pointers to other types, they will be to user-defined types, and we'll be using them for a different purpose than we are using char*. That won't be necessary until Chapter 10, so you have a reprieve for the time being.

The next member initialization expression in the constructor, m_Data(new char [m_Length]), is the same as the corresponding expression in the default constructor; in this case, of course, the amount of memory being allocated is equal to the length of the input C string (including its terminating null byte), rather than the fixed value 1.

Now that we have the address of some memory that belongs to us, we can use it to hold the characters that make up the value of our string. The literal value that our test program uses to call this constructor is "Test", which is four characters long, not counting the null byte at the end; since we have to make room for that null byte, the total is 5 bytes, so that's what we'd ask for from new. Assuming that the return value from new was 1234febc, Figure 7.7 illustrates what our new string looks like at this point.

FIGURE 7.7. string n **during construction**

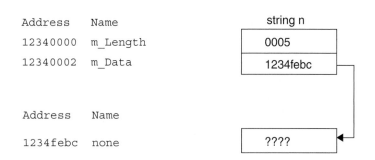

The reason for the ???? is that we haven't set the data at that location to any value yet, so we don't know what it contains. Actually, this brings up a point we've skipped so far: where new gets the memory it allocates. The answer is that all of the "free" memory in your machine (i.e., memory that isn't used to store the operating system, the code for your program, statically allocated variables, and the stack) is lumped into a large area called the *heap*, which is where dynamically allocated memory "lives".[11] That's a loose way of stating what actually happens, which is that new cordons off part of the heap as being "in use" and returns a pointer to that portion.

It's possible that the idea of a variable that holds a memory address but which is itself stored in memory isn't that obvious. It wasn't to Susan:

Susan: I don't get this stuff about a pointer being stored in a memory address and having a memory address in it. So what's the deal?

Steve: Here's an analogy that might help. Have you ever seen a set of mailboxes for an apartment building? The regular mailboxes are

---

11. I'm assuming that you are using an operating system that can access all of the memory in your computer. If not, the heap may be much smaller than this suggests.

pretty small, but what do they do when you get something that is too big to fit into your regular mailbox? One solution is to put the larger object into one of a few large mailboxes, and leave the key to the larger mailbox in your regular mailbox.

So at this point, we have allocated m_Length bytes of memory, which start at the address in the pointer variable m_Data. Now we need to copy the current value of the input C string (pointed to by p) into that newly allocated area of memory. This is the job of the sole statement inside the brackets of the constructor proper,

```
memcpy(m_Data, p, m_Length);
```

which copies the data from the C string pointed to by p to our newly allocated memory.

The final result is that we have made (constructed) a string variable and set it to a value specified by a C string. To see what our string might look like in memory, see Figure 7.10. But how would this string::string(char* p) constructor operate in a program? To answer that question, Figure 7.8 gives us another look at our sample program.

FIGURE 7.8. A simple test program for the string class **(code\strtst1.cc)**

```
#include "string1.h"

int main()
{
    string s;
    string n("Test");
    string x;

    s = n;
    n = "My name is: ";

    x = n;
    return 0;
}
```

Constructive Criticism?

How does the compiler interpret the line string n("Test");? First, it determines that string is the name of a class. A function with the name of a class, as we have already seen, is always a constructor for that class. The question is which constructor to call; the answer is determined by the type(s) of the argument(s). In this case, the argument is a literal C string, which has the type char*; therefore, the compiler looks for a constructor for class string that has an argument of type char*. Since there is such a constructor, the one we have just examined, the compiler generates a call to it. Figure 7.9 shows it again for reference while we analyze it.

FIGURE 7.9. The char* constructor for the string class, **again (from code\string1.cc)**

```
string:: string (char* p)
: m_Length(strlen(p) + 1),
  m_Data(new char [m_Length])
{
  memcpy(m_Data,p,m_Length);
}
```

When the program executes, string::string(char* p) is called with the argument "Test". Let's trace the execution of the constructor, remembering that member initialization expressions are executed in the order in which the member variables being initialized are listed in the class interface, not necessarily in the order in which they are written in the member initialization list.

1. The first member initialization expression is m_Length(strlen(p) + 1). This initializes the member variable m_Length to the length of the C string whose address is in p, including the null byte that terminates the string. In this case, the C string is "Test", and its length, including the null byte, is 5.

2. Next, the member initialization expression m_Data(new char [m_Length]) is executed. This allocates m_Length (5, in this case) bytes of memory from the heap and initializes the variable m_Data to the address of that memory.

3. Finally, the statement memcpy(m_Data,p,m_Length); copies m_Length bytes (5, in this case) of data from the C string pointed to by p to the memory pointed to by m_Data.

When the constructor is finished, the string variable n has a length, 5, and contents, "Test", as shown in Figure 7.10. It's now ready for use in the rest of the program. After all the discussion, Susan provided this rendition of the char* constructor for the string class.

> **Susan:** So first we define a class. This means that we will have to have one or more constructors, which are functions with the same name as the class, used to create objects of that class. The char* constructor we're dealing with here goes through three steps, as follows: Step 1 sets the length of the string; step 2 gets the memory to store the data, and provides the address of that memory; step 3 does the work; it copies what you want.

> **Steve:** Right.

Tricky Assignment

Now, let's look at the next line: s = n;. That looks harmless enough; it just copies one string, n, to another string, s.[12] But wait a second; how does the compiler know how to assign a value to a variable of a type we've made up?

---

12. By the way, in case you're wondering what useful function this statement serves in the sample program, the answer is "none". It's just to illustrate how operator = works.

Just as the compiler will generate a version of the default constructor if we don't define one, because every object has to be initialized somehow, the ability to assign one value of a given type to a variable of the same type is essential to being a data type; therefore, the compiler will supply a version of operator =, the *assignment operator*, if we don't define one ourselves. In Chapter 6, we were able to rely on the compiler-generated operator =, which simply copies every member variable from the source object to the target object. That was perfectly fine for our StockItem and Inventory objects, so wouldn't it do the job here? Unfortunately, no. The reason is that the member variable m_Data isn't really the data for the string; it's a pointer to (i.e., the address of) the data. The compiler-generated =, however, wouldn't be able to figure out how we're using m_Data, so it would copy the pointer rather than the data. In our example, s = n;, the member variable m_Data in s would end up pointing to the same place in memory as the member variable m_Data in n. Thus, if either s or n did something to change "its" data, both strings would have their values changed, which isn't how we expect variables to behave.

To make this more concrete, let's suppose that our string object n looks like Figure 7.10 in memory. So far, we have an object of type string that contains a length and a pointer to dynamically allocated memory where its actual data are stored. However, if we use the compiler-generated operator = to execute the statement s = n;, the result looks like Figure 7.11.

FIGURE 7.10. string **n in memory**

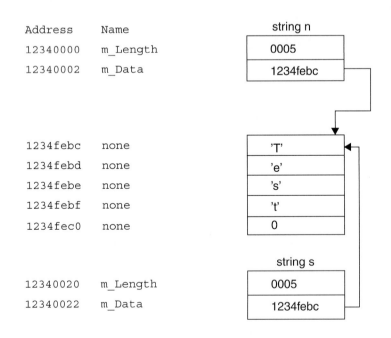

FIGURE 7.11. strings n **and** s **in memory after compiler-generated** =

In other words, the two strings s and n are like Siamese twins; whatever affects one of them affects the other, since they share one copy of the data "Test". What we really want is two strings that are independent of one another, so that we can change the contents of one without affecting the other one. Very shortly, we'll see how to accomplish this.

As you might suspect, Susan didn't think the need for us to define our own operator = was obvious at all. Here's how I started talking her into it.

Susan: I have a little note to you off to the side in the margins about this operator =, it says "If it was good enough for native data then why not class data?" I think that is a very good question, and I don't care about that pointy thing. I don't understand why m_Data isn't really data for the string.

Steve: It isn't the data itself but the address where the data starts.

Susan: Actually, looking at these figures makes this whole idea more understandable. Yes, I see somewhat your meaning in Figure 7.11; that pointy thing is pointing all over the place. Oh no, I don't want to see how to make two independent strings! Just eliminate the pointy thing and it will be all better. Okay?

Steve: Sorry, that isn't possible. You'll just have to bear with me until I can explain it to you better.

Susan: Well, let me ask you this: Is the whole point of writing the statement s=n just to sneak your way into this conversation about this use of operator =? Otherwise, I don't see where it would make sense for the sample program.

Steve: Yes, that's correct.

Susan: And the chief reason for creating a new = is that the new one makes a copy of the data using a new memory address off the heap, rather than having the pointer pointing to the same address while using the compiler-generated operator =? If so, why? Getting a little fuzzy around that point. With StockItem, the compiler-generated operator = was good enough. Why not now?

Steve: Yes, that's why we need to create our own operator =. We didn't need one before because the components of a StockItem are all concrete data types, we don't have to worry about "sharing" the data as we do with the string class, which contains a char*.

Susan: So when you use char* or anything with a pointer, that is outside the realm of concrete data types?

Steve: Right. However, the reason that we can't allow pointers to be copied as with the compiler-generated operator = isn't that they aren't concrete data types, but that they aren't the actual data of the strings. They're the *address* of the actual data; therefore, if we copy the pointer in the process of copying a variable, both pointers hold the same address. This means that changes to one of the variables affects the other one, which is not how concrete data types behave.

Susan: I think I actually understand this now. At least, I'm not as confused as I was before.

Steve: Good; it's working.

Assignment of Responsibility

Although it's actually possible to get the effect of two independent strings without the extra work of allocating memory and copying data every time an assignment is done, the mechanisms needed to do that are beyond the scope of this book.[13] By far the easiest way to have

---

13. We'll see how to implement a similar feature in another context when we get back to the discussion of inventory control later in the book.

the effect of two independent strings is to actually make another copy of a string's data whenever we copy the string, and that's how we'll do it here. The results will be as indicated in Figure 7.12.

FIGURE 7.12. strings n **and** s **in memory after custom** =

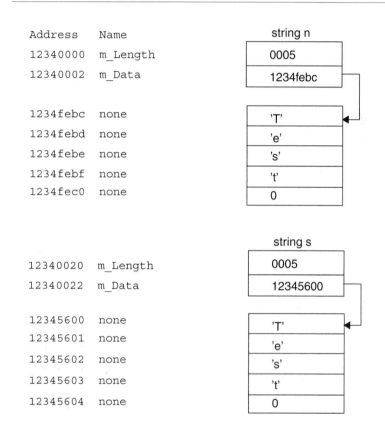

With this arrangement, a change to one of the string variables will leave the other one unaffected, as the user would expect. To make this happen, we have to implement our own operator =, which will copy the data rather than just the pointer to the data. That's the operator declared in Figure 7.1 by the line:

```
string& operator = (const string& Str);
```

What exactly does this mean? Well, as with all function declarations, the first part of the function declaration indicates the return type of the function. In this case, we're going to return a reference to the string to which we're assigning a value; that is, the string on the left of the = sign in an assignment statement. While this may seem reasonable at first glance, actually it's not at all obvious why we should return anything from operator =. After all, if we say a = b;, after a has been set to the same value as b, we're done; that operation is performed by the = operator, so no return value is needed after the assignment is completed.

However, there are two reasons why assignment of native types returns a value, which is equal to the value that was assigned to the left hand argument of =. First, it allows us to write an if statement such as if (a = b), when we really meant if (a == b); of course, this will cause a bug in the program, since these two statements don't have the same meaning. The first one sets a to b and returns the value of a; if a isn't 0, then the if condition is considered true. The latter statement, of course, compares a and b for equality and makes the if condition true if they are equal. To help prevent the error of substituting = for == in this situation, many compilers have a warning that indicates your use of, say, if (a = b); unfortunately, this is a legal construction with native types, and so cannot generate a compiler error. As it happens, using = in this way is an illegal operation with class objects, so even if you want to use this error-prone construction, you can't. Since I never use that construction with native variables, I don't mind not having it for class objects.

The other potential use of the return value from operator = is to allow statements such as a = b = c; where the current value of c is assigned to b and the return value from that assignment is assigned to a. Although I don't use that construction either, since I find it more confusing than useful, I have been told that this return value is required to use some of the library facilities specified in the C++ standard. Therefore, it is my obligation to teach you the "right" way to write assignment operators so that you will be able to use these standard facilities with your classes.

Now we're up to the mysterious looking construct operator =. This portion of the function declaration tells the compiler the name of the function we're defining; namely, operator =. The operator keyword lets the compiler know that the "name" of this function is actually an operator name, rather than a "normal" function name. We have to say operator = rather than merely =, for two reasons. First, because normal function names can't have a = character in them, but are limited to upper and lower case letters, numbers, and the underscore (_). Second, because when we're redefining *any* operator, even one (like new) whose name is made of characters allowed in identifiers, we have to tell the compiler that we're doing that on purpose. Otherwise, we'll get an error telling us that we're trying to define a function or variable with the same name as a keyword.[14]

We're ready to look at the argument to this function, specified by the text inside the parentheses, const string& Str. We've already seen in Chapter 6 that & in this context means that the argument to which it refers is a *reference argument* rather than a *value argument*.[15] In other words, the variable Str is actually just another name for the argument provided by the caller of this function, rather than being a separate local variable with the same value as the caller's argument. However, there is a new keyword in this expression: const, which is short for

14. As this explanation may suggest, we can't make up our own operators with strange names by prefixing those names with operator; we're limited to those operators that already exist in the C++ language.

15. In this section, you're going to see a lot of hedging of the form "in this context, *x* means *y*". The reason is that C and C++ both reuse keywords and symbols in many different situations, often with different meanings in each situation. In my opinion, this is a flaw in the design of these languages, as it makes learning them more difficult. The reason for this reuse is that every time a keyword is added to the language, it's possible that formerly working code that contains a variable or function with the same name as the keyword will fail to compile. Personally, I think this is an overrated problem compared to the problems caused by overuse of the same keywords; however, I don't have a lot of old C or C++ code to maintain, so maybe I'm biased.

"constant". In this context, it means that we promise that this function will not modify the argument to which const refers, namely string& Str. This is essential in the current situation, but it will take some discussion to explain why.

References Required

As you may recall from Chapter 5, when you call a function using a *value argument*, the argument that you supply in the calling function isn't the one that the called function receives. Instead, a copy is made of the calling function's argument, and the called function works on the copy. While this is fine most of the time, in this case it won't work properly, for reasons that will be apparent shortly; instead, we have to use a reference argument. As we saw in the discussion of reference arguments in Chapter 6, such an argument is *not* a copy of the caller's argument, but another name for the actual argument provided by the caller. This has a number of consequences. First, it's often more efficient than a "normal" argument, because the usual processing time needed to make a copy for the called function isn't required. Second, any changes made to the reference argument change the caller's argument as well. The use of this mechanism should be limited to those cases where it is really necessary, since it can confuse the readers of the calling function. There's no way to tell just by looking at the calling function that some of its variables can be changed by calling another function.

In this case, however, we have no intention of changing the input argument. All we want to do is to copy its length and data into the output string, the one for which operator = was called. Therefore, we tell the compiler, by using the const modifier, that we aren't going to change the input argument. This removes the drawback of non-const reference arguments: that they can change variables in the calling function with no indication of that possibility in the calling function. Therefore, using const reference arguments is quite a useful and safe way to reduce the number of time-consuming copying operations needed to make function calls.

The use of a const reference argument in this case is more than just efficient, however; as we'll see in the discussion starting under the heading "This sequence of events also holds the key to understanding why the argument of string::operator = must be a const string& (that is, a constant reference to a string) rather than just a string& (that is, a reference to a string) if we want to allow automatic conversion from a C string to a string. You see, if we declared the function string::operator = to have a string& argument rather than a const string& argument, then it would be possible for that function to change the value of the argument. However, any attempt to change the caller's argument wouldn't work properly if, as in the current example, the argument turned out to be a temporary string constructed from the original argument (the char* value "My name is: "); clearly, changing the temporary string would have no effect on the original argument. Therefore, if the argument to string::operator = were a string&, the line n = "My name is: "; would produce a compiler warning to the effect that we might be trying to alter an argument that was a temporary value. The reason that we don't get this warning is that the compiler knows that we aren't going to try to modify the value of an argument that has the specification const string&; therefore, constructing a temporary value and passing it to string::operator = is guaranteed to have the behavior that we want." on page 486 in Chapter 8, such an argument allows us to assign a C string (i.e., bytes pointed to by a char*) to one of our string variables without having to write a special operator = for that purpose.

You might be surprised to hear that Susan didn't have too much trouble accepting all this stuff about const reference arguments. Obviously her resistance to new ideas was weakening by this point.

> **Susan:** Okay, so the reference operator just renames the argument and doesn't make a copy of it; that is why it is important to promise not to change it?

Steve: Right. A non-const reference argument can be changed in the called function, because unlike a "regular" (i.e., value) argument, which is really a copy of the calling function's variable, a reference argument is just another name for the caller's variable. Therefore, if we change the reference argument, we're really changing the caller's variable, which is generally not a good idea.

Susan: Okay. But in this case since we are going to want to change the meaning of = in all strings it is okay?

Steve: Not quite. Every time we define an operator we're changing the meaning of that operator for all objects of that class. The question is whether we're intending to change the value of the caller's variable that is referred to by the reference argument. If we are, then we can't use const to qualify the reference; if not, we can use const. Does that answer your question?

Susan: Well, yes and no. I think I have it now: When you write that code it is for that class only and won't affect other classes that you may have written, because it is contained within that particular class code. Right?

Steve: Correct.

Susan: So we don't want to change the input argument because we are basically defining a new = for this class, right?

Steve: Right. The input argument is where we get the data to copy to the string we're assigning to. We don't want to change the input argument, just the string we're assigning to.

Back to the discussion of the function declaration, we now have enough information to decode the function declaration

```
string& string::operator = (const string& Str)
```

as illustrated in Figure 7.13.

FIGURE 7.13. **The declaration of** operator = **for the** string class

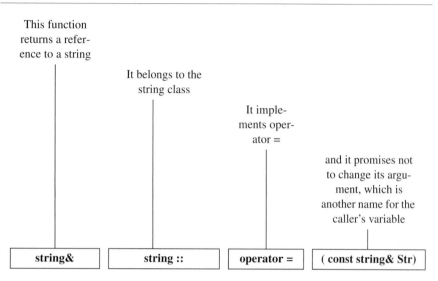

Putting it all together, we're defining a function belonging to class string that returns a reference to a string. This function implements operator = and takes an argument named Str that's a constant reference to a string. That is, the argument Str is another name for the string passed to us by the caller, not a copy of the caller's string. Furthermore, we're vowing not to use this argument to change the caller's variable.

Hello, operator?

Now that we've dissected the header into its atomic components, the actual implementation of the function should be trivial by comparison. But first there's a loose end to be tied up. That is, why was this function named string::operator = called in the first place? The line that caused the call was very simple: s = n;. There's no explicit mention of string or operator.

This is another of the ways in which C++ supports classes. Because you can use the = operator to assign one variable of a native type to another variable of the same type, C++ provides the same syntax for user defined variable types. Similar reasoning applies to operators like >, <, and so on, for classes where these operators make sense.

When the compiler sees the statement s = n;, it proceeds as follows:

1. The variable s is an object of class string.

2. The statement appears to be an assignment statement (i.e., an invocation of the C++ operator named operator =) setting s equal to the value of another string value named n.

3. Is there a definition of a member function of class string that implements operator = and takes one argument of class string?

4. Yes, there is. Therefore, translate the statement s = n; into a call to operator = for class string.

5. Compile that statement as though it were the one in the program.

Susan was appreciative of the reminder that we started out discussing the statement s = n;.

> **Susan:** Oh, my gosh, I totally forgot about s = n; thanks for the reminder. We did digress a bit, didn't we? Are you saying you have to go through the same thing to define other operators in classes?

> **Steve:** Yes.

> **Susan:** So are you saying that when you write the simple statement s = n; that the = calls the function that we just went through?

> **Steve:** Right.

Following this procedure, the correspondence between the *tokens*[16] in the original program and the call to the member function should be fairly obvious, as we see them in Figure 7.14.

FIGURE 7.14. Calling the operator = **implementation**

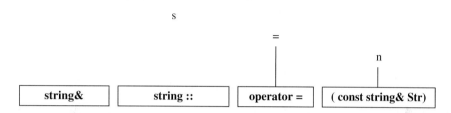

But we've left out something. What does the string s correspond to in the function call to operator =?

What Is the Meaning of this*?*

The string s corresponds to a hidden argument whose name is the keyword this. Such an argument is automatically included in every call to a member function in C++.[17] Its type is always a constant pointer to an object of the class that a member function belongs to. In this case its type is const string*; that is, a constant pointer to a string; the const means that we can't change the value of this by assigning a new value to it. The value of this is the address of the class object for which the member function call was made. In this case, the statement

---

16. A **token** is the smallest part of a program that the compiler treats as a separate unit; it's analogous to a word in English, with a statement being more like a sentence. For example, string is a token, as are :: and (. On the other hand, x = 5; is a statement.

17. Actually, there is another kind of member function called a static member function that doesn't get a this pointer passed to it. We'll discuss this type of member function later, starting in Chapter 9.

---

s = n; was translated into s.operator = (n); by the compiler; therefore, when the statement s = n; is being executed, the value of this is the address of the string s.

To see why we need to be concerned about this, let's start analyzing the implementation of operator =. Figure 7.15 shows the code for that function.

FIGURE 7.15. The assignment operator (operator =) **for the** string class **(from code\string1.cc)**

```
string& string:: operator = (const string& Str)
{
  if (&Str != this)
  {
  delete [] m_Data;
  m_Length = Str.m_Length;
  m_Data = new char [m_Length];
  memcpy(m_Data,Str.m_Data,m_Length);
  }
  return *this;
}
```

Equality Now!

In the case of the string class, as in most cases, the only reasons why we have to worry about this are to be able to determine whether two objects that are referred to by different names are actually the same object and to return a reference to the left-hand object in an assignment statement. You can see both uses of this in the code for string::operator = (const string& Str). The first use is illustrated by the following line:

```
if (&Str != this)
```

Most of this statement should be familiar by now. Like other if statements, it tests a condition for truth or falsity. The != is the comparison operator that tests for "not equal", and we've just seen that this is the address of the variable for which the operator = function was called; in the expression s = n, this would be the address of the variable s. However, that still leaves the expression &Str.

Unfortunately, & is one of the tokens that is used in several different ways depending on context; when it precedes the name of a variable without itself being preceded by a data type like string, it means "the address of the following variable". In this case, &Str means "the address of Str". The variable Str is the argument passed to us by the caller; remember, as a reference argument, Str is another name for the caller's variable, rather than a copy of it. Therefore, &Str is the address of the caller's variable (n, in our example).

Clearly, then, the expression if (&Str != this) is comparing the address of the caller's string (i.e., &Str) to this. As we just saw, this represents the address of the object that we're operating on; in the case of operator =, it's the address of (i.e., a pointer to) the string that is going to be changed by operator =. Therefore, this if statement is checking whether the string that was passed to us by the caller is a different string from the one to which the assignment is supposed to be made. For example, if the source line that caused operator = to be called was a = a; then the if statement would be false and therefore the block controlled by the if wouldn't be executed. Of course, there's no reason to do anything other than return the value of a in that case. However, there are good reasons besides efficiency to check for the attempt to assign a string to itself; those reasons are the subject of one of the exercises in this chapter. For now, let's continue with the contents of the block controlled by the if, assuming that the two strings are actually distinct.

The first statement in the controlled block of the if statement is delete [] m_Data;. This corresponds to the new statement that we used to allocate memory for a string in the constructor string::string(char* p) (Figure 7.6).[18] That is, the delete operator returns the memory to the available pool called the *heap*. There are actually two versions of the delete operator: One version frees memory for a single data item, and the other frees memory for a group of items that are stored consecutively in memory. Here, we're using the version of the delete operator that frees a group of items rather than a single item, which we indicate by means of the [] after the keyword delete; the version of delete that frees only one item doesn't have the [].[19] So after this statement is executed, the memory that was allocated in the constructor to hold the characters in our string has been handed back to the memory allocation routines for possible reuse at a later time.

Susan had a few minor questions about this topic, but nothing too alarming.

Susan: So delete just takes out the memory new allocated for m_Data?

Steve: Right.

Susan: What do you mean by "frees a group of items"?

Steve: It returns the memory to the heap, so it can be used for some other purpose.

Susan: Is that all the addresses in memory that contain the length of the string?

---

18. Or any other constructor that allocates memory in which to store characters. I'm just referring to the char* constructor because we've already analyzed that one.

19. By the way, this is one of the previously mentioned times when we have to explicitly deal with the difference between a pointer used as "the address of an item" and one used as "the address of some number of items"; the [] after delete tells the compiler that the latter is the current situation. The C++ standard specifies that any memory that was allocated via a new expression containing [] must be deleted via delete []. Unfortunately, the compiler probably can't check this. If you get it wrong, your program probably won't work as intended, and you may have a great deal of difficulty figuring out why. This is just another reason why it's important to use pointers only inside class implementations, where you have some chance of using them correctly.

Steve: Not the length of the string, but the data for the string, such as "Test".

Please delete *Me, Let Me Go*

A point that we should not overlook is the possibility of calling delete for a pointer that has never been assigned a value. Calling delete on a pointer that doesn't point to a valid block of memory allocated by new will cause the system to malfunction in some bizarre way, usually at a time considerably after the improper call to delete.[20] This occurs because the dynamic memory allocation system will try to reclaim the "allocated" memory pointed to by the invalid pointer by adding it back to the heap. Eventually, some other function will come along, ask for some memory, and be handed a pointer to this "available" block that is actually nothing of the sort. The result of trying to use this area of memory depends on which of three cases the erroneous address falls into: The first is that the memory at that address is nonexistent, the second is that the memory is already in use for some other purpose, and the third is that the invalid address points to data that is already in the heap. In the first case, the function that tries to store its data in this nonexistent area of memory will cause a system crash or error message, depending on the system's ability and willingness to check for such errors; the "General Protection Fault" message so familiar to Windows users is caused by this sort of error. In the second case, the function that is the "legal" owner of the memory will find its stored values changed mysteriously and will misbehave as a result. In the third case, the heap management routines would probably get confused and start handing out wrong

---

20. There's an exception to this rule: Calling delete for a pointer with the value 0 will not cause any untoward effects, as such a pointer is recognized as "pointing to nowhere".

addresses. Errors of this kind are common (and are extremely difficult to find) in programs that use pointers heavily in uncontrolled ways.[21]

Susan was interested in this topic of errors in memory allocation, so we discussed it.

Susan: Can you give me an example of what an "invalid pointer" would be? Would it be an address in memory that is in use for something else rather than something that can be returned to the heap?

Steve: That's one kind of invalid pointer. The other type would be an address that doesn't exist at all; that is, one that is past the end of the possible legal addresses.

Susan: Oh, wait, so it would be returned to the heap but later if it is allocated to something else, it will cause just a tiny little problem because it is actually in use somewhere else?

Steve: You bet.

Susan: Is this a crash?

Steve: This is a major cause of crashes.

Susan: Oh yeah, this is cool, this is exciting. So this is what really happens when a crash occurs?

Steve: Do you know what a GPF (General Protection Fault) is? It's the operating system detecting the attempt by a program to access memory that doesn't belong to it.

---

21. If you are going to develop commercial software someday, you'll discover that you need a utility to help you find these problems, especially if you have to use software designed and written by people who don't realize that pointers are dangerous. I've had pretty good luck with one called Purify, which is a product of Rational Software.

Susan: I like this. So when there is no memory address allocated you get a error message?

Steve: Yes, or if it belongs to someone else. Of course, you'll be lucky to get anything other than a hard crash if it's a DOS program; at least in Windows you'll probably get a GPF instead.

Another way to go wrong with dynamic memory allocation is the opposite one. Instead of trying to delete something that was never dynamically allocated, you can forget to delete something that has been dynamically allocated. This is called a **memory leak**; it's very insidious, because the program appears to work correctly when tested casually. The usual way to find these errors is to notice that the program runs apparently correctly for a (possibly long) time and then fails due to running out of available memory. I should mention here how we can tell that we've run out of memory: The new operator, rather than returning a value, will "throw an *exception*" if there is no free memory left. This will cause the program to terminate if we don't do anything to handle it.

Given all of the ways to misuse dynamic memory allocation, we'll use it only when its benefits clearly outweigh the risks. To be exact, we'll restrict its use to controlled circumstances inside class implementations, to reduce the probability of such errors.

Susan had some questions about the idea of new "throwing an exception" if no memory is left.

Susan: What is "throwing an exception"?

Steve: That's what new does when it doesn't have anything to give you. It causes your program to be interrupted rather than continuing along without noticing anything has happened.

Susan: How does a real program check for this?

Steve: By code that looks something like Figure 7.16.

FIGURE 7.16. **Running on empty**

```
try
  {
  p = new char[1000];
  }
catch (...)
  {
  cout << "You're hosed!" << endl;
  exit(1);
  }
```

The try keyword means "try to execute the following statements (called a try block)", and "catch (...)"a means "if any of the statements in the previous try block generated an exception, execute the following statements". If the statements in the try block don't cause an exception to be generated, then the catch block is ignored and execution continues at the next statement after the end of the catch block.

Finally, exit means "bail out of the program right now, without returning to the calling function, if any". The argument to exit is reported back to DOS as the return value from the program; 0 means okay, anything else means some sort of error. Of course, it's better to take some other action besides just quitting when you run into an exception, if possible, but that would take us too far afield from the discussion here.

The error prone nature of dynamic memory allocation is ironic, since it would be entirely possible for the library implementers who write the functions that are used by new and delete to prevent or at least detect the problem of deleting something you haven't allocated or failing to delete something that you have allocated. After all, those routines handle all of the memory allocation and deallocation for a C++ program, so there's no reason that they couldn't keep track of what has been allocated and released.[22]

Of course, an ounce of prevention is worth a pound of cure, so avoiding these problems by proper design is the best solution. Luckily, it is possible to write programs so that this type of error is much less likely; basically, this approach requires keeping all dynamic memory allocation inside class implementations, rather than exposing it to the application programmer. We're following this approach with our string class, and it can also be applied to other situations where it is less straightforward, as we'll see when we get back to the inventory control application later in this book.

Susan was intrigued by the possible results of forgetting to deallocate resources such as memory. Here's the resulting discussion:

> **Susan:** So when programs leak system resources, is that the result of just forgetting to delete something that is dynamically allocated?
>
> **Steve:** Yes.
>
> **Susan:** Then that would be basically a programming error or at least sloppiness on the part of the programmer?
>
> **Steve:** Yes.

The Next Assignment

Having discussed some of the possible problems with dynamic allocation, let's continue with the code for operator = (Figure 7.15). The next statement is m_Length = Str.m_Length;. This is the first time we've used the . operator to access a member variable of an object other than the object for which the member function was called. Up

---

22. Actually, most compilers now give you the option of being informed at the end of execution of your program whether you have had any memory leaks, if you are running under a debugger. However, as far as I know, there aren't any that warn you of deleting memory that you haven't allocated. If you want to find out about that sort of error, you'll need to use a utility such as the one I mentioned before.

until now, we've been satisfied to refer to a member variable such as m_Length just by that simple name, as we would with a local or global variable. The name m_Length is called an **unqualified name** because it doesn't specify which object we're referring to. The expression m_Length by itself refers to the occurrence of the member variable m_Length in the object for which the current function was called; i.e., the string whose address is this (the string s in our example line s = n;). If you think about it, this is a good default, because member functions refer to member variables of their "own" object more than any other kinds of variables. Therefore, to reduce the amount of typing the programmer has to do, whenever we refer to a member variable without specifying the object to which it belongs, the compiler will assume that we mean the variable that belongs to the object for which the member variable was called (i.e, the one whose address is the current value of this). However, when we want to refer to a member variable of an object other than the one pointed to by this, we have to indicate which object we're referring to, which we do by using the . operator. This operator means that we want to access the member variable (or function) whose name is on the right of the . for the object whose name is on the left of the ".". Hence, the expression Str.m_Length specifies that we're talking about the occurrence of m_Length that's in the variable Str, and the whole statement m_Length = Str.m_Length; means that we want to set the length of "our" string (i.e., the one pointed to by this) to the length of the argument string Str.

Susan had some questions about this issue of accessing variables of another string and how that relates to operator =.

Susan: I still don't get the . thingy.

Steve: All . does is separate the object (on the left) from the member variable or function (on the right). So s.operator=(n); might be roughly translated as "apply the operator = to the object s, with the argument n".

Susan: So wait: the . does more than separate; it allows access to other string member variables?

Steve: It separates an object's name from the particular variable or function that we're accessing for that object. In other words, Str.m_Length means "the instance of m_Length that is part of the object Str."

Susan: So in the statement m_Length = Str.m_Length; what we are doing is creating a new m_Length equal to the length of Str's m_Length for the = operator?

Steve: What we're doing is setting the value of the length (m_Length) for the string being assigned to (the left-hand string) to the same value as the length of the string being copied from (the right-hand string).

Susan: But it is going to be specific for this string?

Steve: If I understand your question, the value of m_Length will be set for the particular string that we're assigning a new value to.

Susan: When we say Str, does that mean that we are not using the variable pointed to by this? I am now officially lost.

Steve: Yes, that's what it means. In a member function, if we don't specify the class object we are talking about, it's the one pointed to by this; of course, if we do specify which variable we mean, then we get the one we specify.

Next, we use the statement m_Data = new char [m_Length]; to acquire the address of some memory that we will use to store our new copy of the data from Str; along with the address, new gives us the right to use that memory until we free it with delete.

Then we use memcpy to copy the data from Str (i.e., the group of characters starting at the address stored in Str.m_Data) to our newly allocated memory, which of course is pointed to by m_Data (i.e., the occurrence of m_Data in the string being assigned to). Now our target string is a fully independent entity with the same value as the string that was passed in.

Finally, we return *this, which means "the object to which this points", i.e., a reference to the string whose value we have just set, so that it can be used in further operations.

Although the individual statements weren't too much of a problem, Susan didn't get the big picture. Here's how I explained it:

> **Susan:** I don't get this whole code thing for Figure 7.15, now that I think about it. Why does this stuff make a new operator =? This is weird.

> **Steve:** Well, what does operator = do? It makes the object on the left side have the same value as the object on the right side. In the case of a string, this means that the left-hand string should have the same length as the one on the right, and all the chars used to store the data for the right-hand string need to be copied to the address pointed to by m_Data for the left-hand string. That's what our custom = does.

> **Susan:** Let's see. First we have to get some new memory for the new m_Data; then we have to make a copy. . . So then the entire purpose of writing a new operator = is to make sure that variables of that class can be made into separate entities when using the = sign rather than sharing the same memory address for their data?

> **Steve:** Right.

> **Susan:** I forget now why we did that.

> **Steve:** We did it so that we could change the value of one of the variables without affecting the other one.

Before we move on to the next member function, I should mention that Susan and I had quite a lengthy correspondence about the notion of this. Here are the highlights of that discussion.

Susan: I don't understand this.

Steve: this refers to the object that a member function is being called for. For example, in the statement xyz.Read();, when the function named Read is called, the value of this will be the address of the object xyz.

Susan: Okay, then, is this the result of calling a function? Or the address of the result?

Steve: Not quite either of those; this is the address of the object for which a class function is called.

Susan: Now that I have really paid attention to this and tried to commit it to memory it makes more sense. I think that what is so mysterious is that it is a hidden argument. When I think of an argument I think of something in (), as an input argument.

Steve: It actually is being passed as though it were specified in every call to a member function. The reason it is hidden is not to make it mysterious, but to reduce the amount of work the programmer has to do. Since almost every member function needs to access something via this, supplying it automatically is a serious convenience.

Susan: Now as far as my understanding of the meaning of this, it is the address of the object whose value is the result of calling a member function.

Steve: Almost exactly right; this is the address of the object for which a member function is called. Is this merely a semantic difference?

Susan: Not quite. Is there not a value to the object? Other than that we are speaking the same language. We usually do.

Steve: Yes, the object has a value. However, this is merely the address of the object, not its value.

Susan: How about writing this as if it were not hidden and was in the argument list; then show me how it would look. See what I mean? Show me what you think it would look like if you were to write it out and not hide it.

Steve: Okay, that sounds good. I was thinking of doing that anyway.

Figure 7.17 shows what the code for operator = might look like if the this pointer weren't supplied automatically, both in the function declaration and as a qualifier for the member variable names.[23]

FIGURE 7.17. A hypothetical assignment operator (operator =) **for the** string class **with explicit** this

```
string& string:: operator = (const string* this, const string& Str)
{
  if (&Str != this)
    {
    delete [] this->m_Data;
    this->m_Length = Str.m_Length;
```

---

23. By the way, I've introduced another new notation here: the operator ->, which is the "pointer member access" operator. It separates a pointer to an object or variable name, on its left, from the member variable or member function on its right. In other words, -> does the same thing for pointer variables that . does for objects. That is, if the token on the right of -> is a member variable, that token refers to the specific member variable belonging to the object pointed to by the pointer on the left of ->; if the token on the right of -> is a member function, then it is called for the object pointed to by the pointer on the left of ->. For example, this->m_Data means "the m_Data that belongs to the object pointed to by this".

```
   this->m_Data = new char [this->m_Length];
   memcpy(this->m_Data,Str.m_Data,this->m_Length);
   }
  return *this;
}
```

Note that every reference to a member variable of the current object would have to specify this. That would actually be more significant in writing the code than the fact that we would have to supply this in the call. Of course, how we would actually supply this when calling the operator = function is also a good question. Clearly the necessity of passing this explicitly would make for a messier syntax than just s = n;.

The Terminator

Now that we have seen how operator = works in detail, let's look at the next member function in the initial version of our string class, the *destructor*.[24] A destructor is the opposite of a constructor; that is, it is responsible for deallocating any memory allocated by the constructor and performing whatever other functions have to be done before a variable dies. It's quite rare to call the destructor for a variable explicitly; as a rule, the destructor is called automatically when the variable goes out of scope. As we've seen, the most common way for this to happen is that a function returns to its calling function; at that time, destructors are called for all local variables that have destructors, whereas local variables that don't have destructors, such

---

24. Susan has suggested that the constructor, the destructor, and the assignment operator would make good action figures: perhaps Saturday morning cartoons would be a good outlet for getting children interested in programming?

as those of native types, just disappear silently.[25]   Susan had some questions about how variables are allocated and deallocated. Here's the discussion that ensued.

> **Susan:** I remember we talked about the stack pointer and how it refers to addresses in memory but I don't remember deallocating anything. What is that?

> **Steve:** Deallocating variables on the stack merely means that the same memory locations can be reused for different local variables. Remember the function mess?

> **Susan:** Oh, that is right, the data stays in the memory locations until the location is used by something else. It really isn't meaningful after it has been used unless it is initialized, right?

> **Steve:** Yes, that's right.

> **Susan:** When I first read about the destructor my reaction was, "well, what is the difference between this and delete?" But basically it just is a function that makes delete go into auto-pilot?

> **Steve:** Basically correct.

> **Susan:** How does it know you are done with the variable, so that it can put the memory back?

> **Steve:** By definition, when the destructor is called, the variable is history. This happens automatically when it goes out of scope. For an auto variable, whether of native type or class type, this occurs at the end of the block where the variable was defined.

---

25. If we use new to allocate memory for a variable that has a destructor, then the destructor is called when that variable is freed by delete. We'll discuss this when we get back to the inventory control application later in this book.

Susan: I don't understand this. I reread your explanation of "going out of scope" and it is unclear to me what is happening and what the alternatives are. How does a scope "disappear"?

Steve: The scope doesn't disappear, but the execution of the program leaves it. For example, when a function terminates, the local variables (which have local scope), go out of scope and disappear. That is, they no longer have memory locations assigned to them, until and unless the function starts execution again.

Susan: What if you need the variable again?

Steve: Then don't let it go out of scope.

Because destructors are almost always called automatically when a variable goes out of scope, rather than by an explicit statement written by the programmer, the only information guaranteed to be available to a destructor is the address of the variable to be destroyed. For this reason, the C++ language specifies that a destructor cannot have arguments. This in turn means that there can be only one destructor for any class, since there can be at most one function in a given class with a given name and the same type(s) of argument(s) (or, as in this case, no arguments).

As with the constructor(s), the destructor has a special name to identify it to the compiler. In this case, it's the name of the class with the token ~ (the tilde) prefixed to it, so the destructor for class string is named ~string.[26] The declaration of this function is the next line in Figure 7.1, ~string();. Its implementation looks like Figure 7.18.

---

26. In case you're wondering, this somewhat obscure notation was chosen because the tilde is used to indicate logical negation; that is, if some expression x has the logical value true, then ~x will have the logical value false, and vice-versa.

FIGURE 7.18. **The destructor for the** string class **(from code/string1.cc)**

```
string:: ~string ()
{
  delete [ ] m_Data;
}
```

This function doesn't use any new constructs; we've already seen that the delete [ ] operator frees the memory allocated to the pointer variable it operates on.[27] In this case, that variable is m_Data, which holds the address of the first one of the group of characters that make up the actual data contained by the string.

Now that we've covered nearly all of the member functions in the initial version of the string class, it's time for some review.

Review

We've almost finished building a concrete data type called the string class, which provides a means of storing and processing a group of characters in a more convenient form than a *C string*. The fact that string is a concrete data type means that a string that is defined as a local variable in a block should be created when the block starts up and automatically deleted when the block ends. Another requirement for this data type is to be able to copy a string to another string and have the two copies behave like independent variables, not linked together in the manner of Siamese twins.

The creation of an object is performed by a special member function called a *constructor*. Any class can have several constructors, one for each possible way that a newly created object

---

27. By the way, in case you were wondering what happened to the old values of the m_Data and m_Length member variables, we don't have to worry about those because the string being destroyed won't ever be used again.

can be initialized. So far, we've examined the interface and implementation of the *default constructor*, which takes no arguments, and a constructor that takes a char* argument. The former is needed to create a string that doesn't have an initial value, while the latter allows us to create a string that has the same contents as a C string. The default constructor is one of the required member functions in a concrete data type.

We've also seen that in the case of our string constructors, we need to know the order in which the member initialization expressions are executed; since this is dependent on the order of declaration of member variables, we have to make sure that those member variables are declared in the correct order for our member initialization expressions to work properly.

Continuing with the requirements for a concrete data type, we've implemented our own version of operator =, which can set one string to the same value as another string while leaving them independent of one another.

We've also created one other required member function for a concrete data type, the *destructor*, which is used to clean up after a string when it expires. This member function is called automatically for an auto variable at the end of the block where that variable is defined.

We're still short a *copy constructor*, which can create a string that has the same value as another pre-existing string. This may sound just like operator =, but it's not exactly the same. While operator = is used to set a string that already exists to the same value as another extant string, the *copy constructor* creates a brand-new string with the same value as one that already exists. We'll see how this works in the next chapter; in the meantime, let's take a look at some exercises intended to test your understanding of this material.

Exercises

1. What would happen if we compiled the program in Figure 7.19? Why?

FIGURE 7.19. Exercise 1 (code\strex1.cc)

```
class string
{
public:
    string();
    string(const string& Str);
    string(char* p);
    string& operator = (const string& Str);
    ~string();
private:
    short m_Length;
    char* m_Data;
};

int main()
{
    string s;
    string n("Test");
    string x;
    short Length;

    Length = n.m_Length;

    s = n;
    n = "My name is: ";

    x = n;
    return 0;
}
```

2. What would happen if we compiled the program in Figure 7.20? Why?

FIGURE 7.20. Exercise 2 (code\strex2.cc)

```
class string
{
public:
    string(const string& Str);
    string(char* p);
    string& operator=(const string& Str);
    ~string();
private:
    string();
    short m_Length;
    char* m_Data;
};

int main()
{
    string s("Test");
    string n;

    n = s;

    return 0;
}
```

3. What would happen if we compiled the program in Figure 7.21? Why?

FIGURE 7.21. Exercise 3 (code\strex3.cc)

```
class string
{
public:
    string();
```

```
        string(const string& Str);
        string(char* p);
        string& operator=(const string& Str);
    private:
        ~string();
        short m_Length;
        char* m_Data;
};

int main()
{
    string s("Test");

    return 0;
}
```

4. What would happen if a user of our string class wrote an expression that tried to set a string variable to itself (e.g., a = a;) and we hadn't bothered to check for that situation in our operator = (Figure 7.15)?

Conclusion

We've covered a lot of material about how a real, generally useful class such as string works in this chapter. In the next chapter, we'll continue with the saga of the string class, finishing up the additional functionality needed to turn it into a full-fledged concrete data type. We'll put this new functionality to the test in a modified version of the sorting algorithm from the early chapters that sorts strings rather than numeric values.

Answers to Exercises

1. The output of the compiler should look something like this:

```
strex1.cc: In function 'int main()':
strex1.cc:21: member 'm_Length' is a private member of class 'string'
```

This one is simple; since m_Length is a private member variable of string, a nonmember function such as main can't access it.

2. The output of the compiler should look something like this:

```
strex2.cc: In function 'int main()':
strex2.cc:9: constructor 'string::string()' is private
strex2.cc:17: within this context
strex2.cc:17: in base initialization for class 'string'
```

This is also pretty simple. Since the default constructor string::string() is in the private area, it's impossible for a nonmember function such as main to use it. Notice that there was no error message about string::string(char* p); that constructor is in the public area, so main is permitted to create a string from a C string. It's just the default constructor that's inaccessible.

3. The output of the compiler should look something like this:

```
strex3.cc:12: warning: 'class string' only defines a private destructor
and has no friends[28]
strex3.cc: In function 'int main()':
strex3.cc:16: destructor for type 'string' is private in this scope
```

This answer is considerably less obvious than the previous ones. To be sure, the destructor is private and can't be called from main, but that doesn't explain why main is trying to call the destructor in the first place. The reason is that every auto variable of a type that has a destructor must have its destructor called at the end of that function. That's part of the mechanism that makes our objects act like "normal" variables, which also lose their values at the end of the function where they are declared.[29] In the case of a user

---

28. In case you're wondering what a friend is, it's a class or a function that has special access to the internal workings of another class. We'll get into that mechanism in Chapter 8.

defined variable, though, more cleanup may be required; this is certainly true for strings, which have to deallocate the memory that they allocated to store their character data.

Therefore, you cannot create an object of a class whose destructor is private as an auto variable, as the automatic call of the destructor at the end of the scope would be illegal.

Susan didn't get this one exactly right, but she was obviously in the ballpark.

> **Susan:** I have a note here that this program would not work because the ~string () thingy should be public and that, if this were to run, it would cause a memory leak. Am I on the right track?

> **Steve:** Yes, you're close. Actually, what would happen is that the compiler would refuse to compile this program because it wouldn't be able to call ~string at the end of the function, since ~string is private. If the compiler were willing to compile this program without calling the destructor, there would indeed be a memory leak.

4. Let's take a look at the sequence of events that would have transpired if the user had typed a = a; and we hadn't taken the precaution of checking for that situation in the operator = code. The first statement to be executed would be delete [] m_Data;. This gives the memory that had been allocated to store characters in string a back to the operating system.

The second statement to be executed would be m_Length = Str.m_Length;. Since m_Length and Str.m_Length are actually the same memory location in this case, this statement wouldn't do anything.

---

29. To be more precise, the destructor is called at the end of the *scope* in which the variable was defined. It's possible for a variable to have scope smaller than an entire function; in that case, the variable is destroyed when its scope expires.

The third statement to be executed would be m_Data = new char [m_Length];. This would allocate memory for the target string, and assign it to the member variable m_Data.

The fourth statement to be executed would be memcpy(m_Data,Str.m_Data,m_Length);. This would copy m_Length bytes of data to the address stored in m_Data, which points to the newly allocated piece of memory, from the address stored in Str.m_Data, which points to. . . the same address. Remember, if this and &Str are the same, as they are in this case, then m_Data and Str.m_Data are two names for the same memory location. Therefore, this operation will have no effect. Furthermore, the preceding step has assigned the address of the newly allocated memory to m_Data, overwriting the previous contents of m_Data, that is, the address of the original contents of the string a. Therefore, the original value of a, which was pointed to by m_Data when we started, is no longer accessible. Even if we had a copy of that address, we couldn't use it because the memory to which it refers to has already been returned to the operating system and no longer belongs to us.

The net result of all of this is that the m_Data member variable of string a would point to uninitialized data.For a further explanation of this, you might want to take a look at the discussion I had with Susan. The topic is the if statement "if (&Str != this)", which checks whether the source string is the same as the destination string:

Susan: I don't get the purpose of this if statement. Do we want the two strings to be the same or to be different?

Steve: We want them to be the same *after* we do the copy; if they're the same *before* the copy, we don't need (or want) to do anything. This may not be completely obvious, so here's a more detailed explanation:

1. If the two strings are different when the if statement is executed, then we can safely execute the code controlled by the if statement, because executing delete on the old contents of the string on the left-hand side of the = sign won't affect the string on the right-hand side.

2. If the two strings are actually the same string, then the delete call will deallocate the memory that was used to hold the string's data; therefore, the memcpy will be copying from a pointer that is no longer valid. Even if this code would work, there's no reason to execute it if the two strings are already the same at the beginning of the code for the assignment statement.

Susan: Okay, so if the two strings are the same then the if statement won't go into effect, but if they are different, then it will; it is important that they are different otherwise you would be deleting the original address of the caller?

Steve: Right, with one very small modification: It's the data at the original address of the string that would get freed prematurely.

CHAPTER 8

Down the Garden Path

Objectives of This Chapter

By the end of this chapter, you should

1. Understand how to implement all the concrete data type functions for a class that uses pointers, namely the string class.

2. Understand in detail the operation and structure of a string class that is useful in some real programming situations.

3. Understand how to write appropriate input and output functions (operator >> and operator <<) for the objects of our string class.

4. Understand how to use some additional C library functions such as memcmp and memset.

5. Understand the (dreaded) C data type, the *array*, and some of the reasons why it is hazardous to use.

6. Understand the friend declaration, which allows access to private members by selected nonmember functions.

For Reference Only

Now we're finally ready to examine exactly why the code for our operator = needs a *reference argument* rather than a *value argument*. I've drawn two diagrams that illustrate the difference between a value argument and a reference argument. First, Figure 8.1 illustrates what happens when we call a function with a value argument of type string using the compiler-generated copy constructor.[1]

FIGURE 8.1. Call by value ("normal argument") using the compiler-generated copy constructor

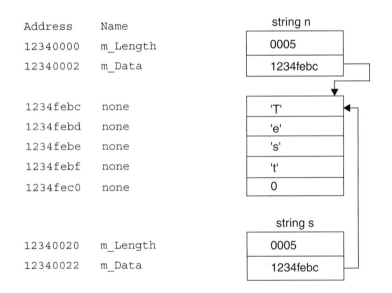

In other words, with a value argument, the called routine makes a copy of the argument on its stack. This won't work properly with a string argument; instead, it will destroy the value of the caller's variable upon return to the calling function. Why is this?

---

1. In case this diagram looks familiar, it's the same as the one illustrating the problem with the compiler-generated operator =, in Figure 7.11.

Unfair Copy

The problem occurs when the destructor is called at the end of a function's execution to dispose of the copy of the input argument made at entry. Since the copy points to the same data as the caller's original variable, the destruction of the copy causes the memory allocated to the caller's variable to be freed prematurely.

This is due to the way in which a variable is copied in C++ by the compiler-generated *copy constructor*. This constructor, like the compiler-generated operator =, makes a copy of all of the parts of the variable (a so-called *memberwise copy*). In the case of our string variable, this results in copying only the length m_Length and the pointer m_Data, and not the data that m_Data points to. That is, both the original and the copy refer to the same data, as indicated by Figure 8.1. If we were to implement our operator = with a string argument rather than a string&, then the following sequence of events would take place during the execution of the statement s = n;:

1. A default copy like the one illustrated by Figure 8.1 would be made of the input argument n, causingthe variable Str in the operator = code to point to the same data as the caller's variable n.

2. The Str variable would be used in the operator = code.

3. The Str variable would be destroyed at the end of the operator = function. During this process, the destructor would free the memory that Str.m_Data points to by calling delete [].

Since Str.m_Data holds the same address as the caller's variable n.m_Data, the latter now points to memory that has been freed and may be overwritten or assigned to some other use at any time. This is a bug in the program caused by the string destructor being called for a temporary copy of a string that shares data with a caller's variable. When we use a reference argument, however, the variable in the called function is nothing more (and nothing less) than another name

for the caller's variable. No copy is made on entry to the operator =
code; therefore, the destructor is not called on exit. This allows the
caller's variable n to remain unmolested after operator = terminates.

That may sound good, but Susan wanted some more explanation.

Susan: I don't get why a value argument makes a copy and a
reference argument doesn't. Help.

Steve: The reason is that a value argument is actually a new auto
variable, just like a regular auto variable, except that it is initialized
to the value of the caller's actual argument. Therefore, it has to be
destroyed when the called function ends. On the other hand, a
reference argument just renames the caller's variable; since the
compiler hasn't created a new auto variable when the called routine
starts, it doesn't need to call the destructor to destroy that variable at
the end of the routine.

Figure 8.2 helped her out a bit by illustrating the same call as in
Figure 8.1, using a reference argument instead of a value argument.

FIGURE 8.2. **Call by reference**

Address	Name	Caller's string n and called routine's string Str
12340000	m_Length	0005
12340002	m_Data	1234febc
1234febc	none	'T'
1234febd	none	'e'
1234febe	none	's'
1234febf	none	't'
1234fec0	none	0

Finally, we're finished examining the intricacies that result from the
apparently simple statement s = n; in our test program (Figure 8.3).

FIGURE 8.3. Our first test program for the string class (code\strtst1.cc)

```
#include "string1.h"

int main()
{
    string s;
    string n("Test");
    string x;

    s = n;
    n = "My name is: ";

    x = n;
    return 0;
}
```

Now let's take a look at the next statement in that test program, n = "My name is: ";. The type of the expression "My name is: " is char*; that is, the compiler stores the character data somewhere and provides a pointer to it. In other words, this line is attempting to assign a char* to a string. Although the compiler has no built-in knowledge of how to do this, we don't have to write any more code to handle this situation, because the code we've already written is sufficient. That's because if we supply a value of type char* where a string is needed, the constructor string::string(char*) is automatically invoked, much as the default constructor is invoked when we create a string with no arguments. Such automatic conversion is another of the features of C++ that makes our user defined types more like native types.[2]

The sequence of events during compilation of the line n = "My name is: "; is something like this:

---

2.   There are situations, however, where this usually helpful feature is undesirable; for this reason, C++ provides a way of preventing the compiler from supplying such conversions automatically. We'll see how to do that in Chapter 12.

1. The compiler sees a string on the left of an =, which it interprets as a call to some version of string::operator =.

2. It looks at the expression on the right of the = and sees that it is not a string, but a char*.

3. Have we defined a function with the signature string::operator = (char*)? If so, use it.

4. In this case, we have not defined such an operator. Therefore, the compiler checks to see whether we have defined a constructor with the signature string::string(char*) for the string class.

5. Yes, there is such a constructor. Therefore, the compiler interprets the statement as n.operator = (string("My name is: "));. If there were no such constructor, then the line would be flagged as an error.

So the actual interpretation of n = "My name is: "; is n.operator = (string("My name is: "));. What exactly does this do?

Figure 8.4 is a picture intended to illuminate the compiler's "thoughts" in this situation; that is, when we assign a C string with the value My name is: " to a string called n via the constructor string::string(char*).[3]

Temporary Help Wanted

Let's go over Figure 8.4, step by step. The first thing that the compiler does is to call the constructor string::string(char*) to create a *temporary* (jargon for **temporary variable**) of type string, having the value "My name is: ". This temporary is then used as the argument to the function string::operator = (const string& Str) (see Figure 7.15).

---

3. Rather than showing each byte address of the characters in the strings and C strings as I've done in previous diagrams, I'm just showing the address of the first character in each group, so that the figure will fit on one page.

FIGURE 8.4. Assigning a C string to a string **via** string::string(char*)

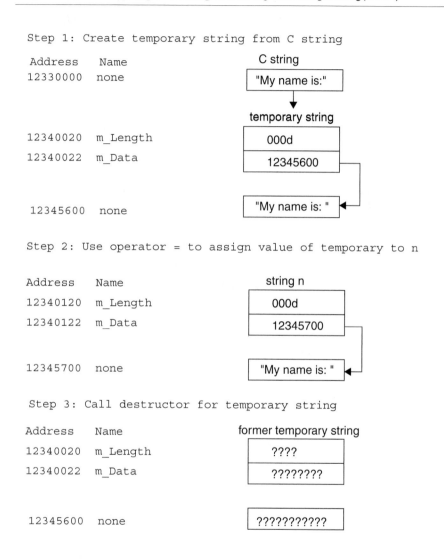

Step 1: Create temporary string from C string

Address	Name	C string
12330000	none	"My name is:"

temporary string

| 12340020 | m_Length | 000d |
| 12340022 | m_Data | 12345600 |

| 12345600 | none | "My name is: " |

Step 2: Use operator = to assign value of temporary to n

Address	Name	string n
12340120	m_Length	000d
12340122	m_Data	12345700

| 12345700 | none | "My name is: " |

Step 3: Call destructor for temporary string

Address	Name	former temporary string
12340020	m_Length	????
12340022	m_Data	????????

| 12345600 | none | ??????????? |

Since the argument is a reference, no copy is made of the temporary; the variable Str in the operator = code actually refers to the (unnamed) temporary variable. When the operator = code is finished executing, the string n has been set to the same value as the temporary (i.e., "My name is: "). Upon return from the operator = code, the temporary is automatically destroyed by a destructor call inserted by the compiler.

This sequence of events also holds the key to understanding why the argument of string::operator = must be a const string& (that is, a constant reference to a string) rather than just a string& (that is, a reference to a string) if we want to allow automatic conversion from a C string to a string. You see, if we declared the function string::operator = to have a string& argument rather than a const string& argument, then it would be possible for that function to change the value of the argument. However, any attempt to change the caller's argument wouldn't work properly if, as in the current example, the argument turned out to be a temporary string constructed from the original argument (the char* value "My name is: "); clearly, changing the temporary string would have no effect on the original argument. Therefore, if the argument to string::operator = were a string&, the line n = "My name is: "; would produce a compiler warning to the effect that we might be trying to alter an argument that was a temporary value. The reason that we don't get this warning is that the compiler knows that we aren't going to try to modify the value of an argument that has the specification const string&; therefore, constructing a temporary value and passing it to string::operator = is guaranteed to have the behavior that we want.[4]

This example is anything but intuitively obvious and, as you might imagine, led to an extended discussion with Susan.

> **Susan:** So no copy of the argument is made, but the temporary is a copy of the variable to that argument?

---

4. By the way, the compiler doesn't just take our word that our operator = function isn't going to modify an argument with the const specifier; if we wrote an operator = (or any other function) with a const argument that tried to modify such an argument, it wouldn't compile.

Steve: The temporary is an unnamed string created from the C string that was passed to operator = by the statement n = "My name is: ";.

Susan: Okay. But tell me this: Is the use of a temporary the result of specifying a reference argument? If so, then why don't you discuss this when you first discuss reference arguments?

Steve: It's not exactly because we're using a reference argument. When a function is called with the "wrong" type of argument but a constructor is available to make the "right" type of argument from the "wrong" one that was supplied, then the compiler will supply the conversion automatically. In the case of calling operator = with a char* rather than a string, there is a constructor that can make a string from a char*; so, the compiler will use that constructor to make a temporary string out of the supplied char* and use that temporary string as the actual argument to the function operator =. However, if the argument type were specified as a string& rather than a const string&, then the compiler would warn us that we might be trying to change the temporary string that it had constructed; since we have a const string& argument, the compiler knows that we won't try to change that temporary string, so it doesn't need to warn us about this possibility.

Susan: Well, I never looked at it that way, I just felt that if there is a constructor for the argument then it is an OK argument.

Steve: As long as the actual argument matches the type that the constructor expects, there is no problem.

Susan: So, if the argument type were a string& and we changed the temporary argument, what would happen? I don't see the problem with changing something that was temporary; I see that it would be a problem for the original argument but not the temporary.

Steve: The reason why generating a temporary is acceptable in this situation is that the argument is a const reference. If we didn't add the const in front of the argument specifier, then the compiler would warn us about our possibly trying to modify the temporary. Since we have a const reference, the compiler knows that we won't try to modify the argument, and thus it's safe for the compiler to generate the temporary value.

Susan: Okay, then the temporary is created any time you call a reference argument? I thought that the whole point of a temporary was so you could modify it and not the original argument and the purpose of the const was to ensure that would be the case.

Steve: The point is precisely that nothing would happen to the original argument if we changed the copy. Since one of the reasons that reference arguments are available is to allow changing of the caller's argument, the compiler warns us if we appear to be interested in doing that (a non-const reference argument) in a situation where such a change would have no effect because the actual argument is a temporary.

Susan: So, if we have a non-const string& argument specification with an actual argument of type char* then a temporary is made that can be changed (without affecting the original argument). If the argument is specified as a const string& and the actual argument is of type char* then a temporary is made that cannot be changed.

Steve: You've correctly covered the cases where a temporary is necessary, but haven't mentioned the other cases. Here is the whole truth and nothing but the truth:

1. If we specify the argument type as string& *and* a temporary has to be created because the actual argument is a char* rather than a string, then the compiler will warn us that changes to that temporary would not affect the original argument.

2. If we specify the argument type as const string& *and* a temporary has to be created because the actual argument is a char*, then the compiler won't warn us that our (hypothetical) change would be ineffective, because it knows that we aren't going to make such a change.

3. However, if the actual argument is a string, then no temporary needs to be made in either of these cases (string& or const string&. Therefore, the argument that we see in the function is actually the real argument, not a temporary, and the compiler won't warn us about trying to change a (nonexistent) temporary.

Susan: Okay, this clears up another confusion I believe, because I was getting confused with the notion of creating a temporary that is basically a copy but I remember that you said that a reference argument doesn't make a copy; it just renames the original argument. So that would be the case in 3 here, but the temporary is called into action only when you have a situation such as in 1 or 2, where a reference to a string is specified as the argument type in the function declaration, while the actual argument is a char*.

Steve: Right.

Copy Cat

Assuming you've followed this so far, you might have noticed one loose end. What if we want to pass a string as a value argument to a function? As we have seen, with the current setup bad things will happen, since the compiler-generated copy constructor doesn't copy strings correctly. Well, you'll be relieved to learn that this, too, can be fixed. The answer is to implement our own version of the *copy constructor*, created precisely to solve the problem of copying variables of a given class, in this case string. Let's take another look at the header file, now in Figure 8.5.

FIGURE 8.5. The string class **interface (code\string1.h)**

```
class string
{
public:
```

```
        string();
        string(const string& Str);
        string& operator = (const string& Str);
        ~string();

        string(char* p);

    private:
        short m_Length;
        char* m_Data;
    };
```

The line we're interested in here is string(const string& Str);. This is a constructor, since its name is the class name string. It takes one argument, which is a const string&, that is, a reference to a constant string. This means that we're not going to change the argument's value "through" the reference, as we could do via a non-const reference. The code in Figure 8.6 implements this new constructor.

FIGURE 8.6. The copy constructor for the string class

```
string::string(const string& Str)
: m_Length(Str.m_Length),
  m_Data(new char [m_Length])
{
  memcpy(m_Data,Str.m_Data,m_Length);
}
```

This function's job is similar to that of operator =, which makes sense because since both of these functions are in the copying business. However, there are also some differences; otherwise, we wouldn't need two separate functions.

Of course, the first difference is that because a copy constructor is a constructor, we can use a member initialization list to initialize the member variables; this convenience is not available to operator =, as it is not a constructor.

The next difference is that we don't have to check whether the argument refers to the same string as this. That's because a constructor always creates a new, never before seen, object of whatever class it's a constructor for. There's no equivalent of the statement a = a; that can cause trouble for operator = without special handling.

Finally, we don't have to delete any previously held storage that might have been assigned to m_Data. Of course, this is also because we're building a new string, not reusing one that already exists. Therefore, we know that m_Data has never had any storage assigned to it previously.

One fine point that might have slipped past you is why we can't use a value argument rather than a reference argument to our copy constructor. The reason is that using a value argument of a class type requires a copy of the actual argument to be made, using ... the copy constructor! Obviously this won't work when we're writing the copy constructor for that type, and the compiler will let us know if we try to do this accidentally.

Now that we have a correct copy constructor, we can use a string as a value argument to a function, and the copy that's made by the compiler when execution of the function starts will be an independent string, not connected to the caller's variable. When this copy is destroyed at the end of the function, it will go away quietly and the caller's original variable won't be disturbed. This is all very well in theory, but it's time to see some practice. Let's write a function that we can call with a string to do some useful work, like displaying the characters in the string on the screen.

Screen Test

As I hope you remember from the previous chapters, we can send output to the screen via cout, a predefined output destination. For example, to write the character 'a' to the screen we could use the statement cout << 'a';. Although we have previously used cout and << to display string variables, our current version of the string class doesn't support them. If we want this ability, we'll have to provide it ourselves. Since variables that can't be displayed are limited in usefulness, we're going to start to do just that right now. Figure 8.7 is the updated header file.

I strongly recommend that you print out the files that contain this interface and its implementation, as well as the test program, for reference as you are going through this part of the chapter; those files are string3.h, string3.cc, and strtst3.cc, respectively.

FIGURE 8.7. The string class **interface, with** Display **function (code\string3.h)**

```
class string
{
public:
    string();
    string(const string& Str);
    string& operator = (const string& Str);
    ~string();

    string(char* p);
    void Display();

private:
    short m_Length;
    char* m_Data;
};
```

As you can see, the new function is declared as void Display();. This means that it returns no value, its name is Display, and it takes no arguments. This last characteristic may seem odd at first, because surely Display needs to know which string we want to display. However, as we've already seen, each object has its own copy of all of the variables defined in the class interface. In this case, the data that are to be displayed are the characters pointed to by m_Data.

Figure 8.8 is an example of how Display can be used.

FIGURE 8.8. The string class **test program, using the** Display **function (code\strtst3.cc)**

```
#include <iostream.h>
#include "string3.h"

int main()
{
    string s;
    string n("Test");
    string x;

    s = n;
    n = "My name is: ";

    n.Display();

    return 0;
}
```

See the line that says, n.Display();? That is how our new Display function is called. Remember, it's a member function, so it is always called with respect to a particular string variable; in this case, that variable is n.

As is often the case, Susan thought she didn't understand this idea, but actually did.

Susan: This Display stuff. . . I don't get it. Are you having to write also the information that the classes need to display information on the screen?

Steve: Yes.

Now let's look at the implementation of this new member function, in Figure 8.9.

FIGURE 8.9. The string class **implementation of the** Display **function**

```
void string::Display()
{
  short i;

  for (i = 0; i < m_Length-1; i ++)
    cout << m_Data[i];
}
```

This should be looking almost sensible by now; here's the play by play. We start out with the function declaration, which says we're defining a void function (i.e., one that returns no value) that is a member function of the class string. This function is named Display, and it takes no arguments. Then we define a short called i. The main part of the function is a for loop, which is executed with the index starting at 0 and continuing while the index is less than the number of displayable characters that we use to store the value of our string; of course, we don't need to display the null byte at the end of the string. So far, so good. Now comes the tricky part. The next statement, which is the controlled block of the for loop, says to send something to cout; that is, display it on the screen. This makes sense, because after all that's the purpose of this function. But what is it that is being sent to cout?

A Character Study

It's just a char but that may not be obvious from the way it's written. This expression m_Data[i] looks just like a vector element, doesn't it? In fact, m_Data[i] is an element, but not of a vector. Instead, it's an element of an *array*, the C equivalent of a C++ vector. What's an array? Well, it's a bunch of data items (elements) of the same type; in this case, it's an array of chars. The array name, m_Data in this case, corresponds to the address of the first of these elements; the other elements follow the first one immediately in memory. If this sounds familiar, it should; it's very much like Susan's old nemesis, a pointer. However, like a vector, we can also refer to the individual elements by their indexes; so, m_Data[i] refers to the ith element of the array, which in the case of a char array is, oddly enough, a char.

So now it should be clear that each time through the loop, we're sending out the ith element of the array of chars where we stored our string data.

Susan and I had quite a discussion about this topic, and here it is.

Susan: And if this is an array or a vector (I can't tell which), how does the class know about it if you haven't written a constructor for it?

Steve: Arrays are a native feature of C++, left over from C. Thus, we don't have to (and can't) create a constructor and the like for them.

Susan: The best I can figure out from this discussion is that an array is like a vector but instead of numbers it indexes char data and uses a pointer to do it?

Steve: Very close. It's just like a vector except that it's missing some rather important features of a vector. The most important one from our perspective is that an array doesn't have any error-checking; if you give it a silly index, you'll get something back, but exactly what is hard to determine.

Susan: If it is just like a vector and it is not as useful as a real vector, then why use it? What can it do that a vector can't?

Steve: A vector isn't a native data type, whereas an array is. Therefore, you can use arrays to make vectors, which is in fact how I did it. We also wouldn't want to use vectors to hold our string data because they're much more "expensive" (i.e., large and slow) to use. I'm trying to illustrate how we could make a string class that would resemble one that would actually be usable in a real program, and although simplicity is important, I didn't want to go off the deep end in hiding arrays from the reader.

Susan: So when you say that "we're sending out the ith element of the array of chars where we stored our value." does that mean that the "ith" element would be the pointer to some memory address where char data is stored?

Steve: No, the ith element of the array is just like the ith element of a vector. If we had a vector of four chars called x, we'd declare it as follows:

vector<char> x(4);

Then we could refer to the individual chars in that vector as x[0], x[1], x[2], or x[3]. It's much the same for an array. If we had an array of four chars called y, we'd declare it as follows:

char y[4];

Then we could refer to the individual chars in that array as y[0], y[1], y[2], or y[3].

That's all very well, but where did that array come from? We defined m_Data as a char*, which is a pointer to (i.e., the address of) a char. As is common in C and C++, this particular char* is the first of a bunch of chars one after the other in memory.

Array of Hope?

Brace yourself for this one. In C++, a pointer and the address of an array are for almost all purposes the same thing. You can treat an array address as a pointer and a pointer as an array address, pretty much as you please. This is a holdover from C, necessary for compatibility with C programs. People who like C will tell you how "flexible" the equivalence of pointers and arrays in C is. That's true, but it's also extremely dangerous, because arrays have no error checking whatsoever. You can use whatever index you feel like, and whatever happens to be at the address that that index would have corresponded to will be your target of opportunity. The program in Figure 8.10 is an example of what can go wrong when using arrays.

FIGURE 8.10. **Dangerous** characters (code\dangchar.cc)

```cpp
#include <iostream.h>

int main()
{
    char High[10];
    char Middle[10];
    char Low[10];
    char* Alias;
    short i;

    for (i = 0; i < 10; i ++)
        {
        Middle[i] = 'A' + i;
        High[i] = '0';
        Low[i] ='1';
        }

    Alias = Middle;

    for (i = 10; i < 20; i ++)
        {
        Alias[i] = 'a' + i;
        }

    cout << "Low: ";
    for (i = 0; i < 10; i ++)
        cout << Low[i];

    cout << endl;
```

```
        cout << "Middle: ";
        for (i = 0; i < 10; i ++)
            cout << Middle[i];

        cout << endl;

        cout << "Alias: ";
        for (i = 0; i < 10; i ++)
            cout << Alias[i];

        cout << endl;

        cout << "High: ";
        for (i = 0; i < 10; i ++)
            cout << High[i];

        cout << endl;
    }
```

Let's look at what this program does when it's executed. First, we define three variables High, Middle, and Low, each as an array of 10 chars. Then we define a variable Alias as a char*; as you may recall, this is how we specify a pointer to a char. Such a pointer is essentially equivalent to a plain old memory address.

In the next part of the program, we use a for loop to set each element of the arrays High, Middle, and Low to a value. So far, so good, except that the statement Middle[i] = 'A' + i; may look a bit odd. How can we add a char value like 'A' and a short value such as i?

A Slippery Character

Let us return to those thrilling days of yesteryear, or at least Chapter 3. Since then, we've been using chars to hold ASCII values, which is their most common use. However, every char variable actually has a "double life"; it can also be thought of as a "really short" numeric variable, which can take on any of 256 values. Thus, we can add and subtract chars and shorts, as long as we're careful not to try to use a char to hold a number greater than 255 (or greater than 127, for a signed char). In this case, there's no problem with the magnitude of the result, since we're starting out with the value *A* and adding a number between 0 and 9 to it; the highest possible result is *J*, which is still well below the maximum value that can be stored in a char.

With that detail taken care of, let's proceed with the analysis of this program. The next statement after the end of the first for loop is the seemingly simple line alias = middle;. This is obviously an assignment statement, but what is being assigned?

The value that Alias receives is the address of the first element of the array Middle. That is, after the assignment statement is executed, Alias is effectively another name for Middle. Therefore, the next loop, which assigns values to elements 10 through 19 of the "array" Alias, actually operates on the array Middle, setting those elements to the values *k* through *t*.

The rest of the program is pretty simple. It just displays the characters from each of the Low, Middle, Alias, and High arrays. Of course, Alias isn't really an array, but it acts just like one; to be precise, it acts just like Middle, since it points to the first character in Middle. Therefore, the Alias and Middle loops will display the same characters. Then the final loop displays the values in the High array.

Overwrought

That's pretty simple, isn't it? Not quite as simple as it looks. If you've been following along closely, you're probably thinking I've gone off the deep end. First, I said that the array Middle had 10 elements (which are numbered 0 through 9, as always in C++); now I'm assigning values to elements numbered 10 through 19. Am I nuts?

No, but the program is. When you run it, you'll discover that it produces output similar to Figure 8.11.

FIGURE 8.11. **Reaping the whirlwind**

Low: 1111111111
Middle: ABCDEFGHIJ
Alias: ABCDEFGHIJ
High: mnopqrst00

Most of these results are pretty reasonable: Low is just as it was when we initialized it, and Middle and Alias have the expected portion of the alphabet. But look at High. Shouldn't it be all 0s?

Yes, it should. However, we have broken the rules by writing "past the end" of an array, and the result is that we have overwritten some other data in our program, which in this case turned out to be the original values of High. You may wonder why we didn't get an error message, as we did when we tried to write to a nonexistent vector element in an earlier chapter. The reason is that, in C, the name of an array is translated into the address of the first element of a number of elements stored consecutively in memory. In other words, an array acts just like a pointer, except that the address of the first element it refers to can't be changed at run time.

In case this equivalence of arrays and pointers isn't immediately obvious, you're not alone; it wasn't obvious to Susan, either.

> **Susan:** And when you say that "that is, a pointer (i.e., the address of) a char, which may be the first of a bunch of chars one after another in memory", does that mean the char* points to the first address and then the second and then the third individually, and an array will point at all of them at the same time?

> **Steve:** No, the char* points to the first char, but we can figure out the addresses of the other chars because they follow the first char sequentially in memory. The same is true of the array; the array name refers to the address of the first char, and the other chars in the array can be addressed with the index added to the array name. In other words, y[2] in the example means "the char that is 2 bytes past the beginning of the array called y".

As suggested by this near-identity between pointers and arrays, the compiler does not and cannot keep track of how many elements are in an array. To the compiler, keeping track of such information makes no sense, any more than it can tell how many elements there are "in a pointer". This is why pointers and (equivalently) arrays are the single most error-prone construct in C (and C++, when they're used recklessly). It's also why we're not going to use either of these constructs except when there's no other reasonable way to accomplish our goals; even then, we'll confine them to tightly controlled circumstances in the implementation of a user defined data type. For example, we don't have to worry about going "off the end" of the array in our Display function, because we know exactly how many characters we've stored (m_Length), and we've written the function to send exactly that many characters to the screen via cout. In fact, all of the member functions of our string class are carefully designed to allocate, use, and dispose of the memory pointed to by m_Data so that the user of this class doesn't have to worry about pointers or arrays, or the problems they can cause. After all, one of the main benefits of using C++ is that the users of a class don't have to concern themselves with the way it works, just with what it does.

Assuming that you've installed the software from the CD-ROM in the back of this book, you can try out this program. First, you have to compile it by changing to the code subdirectory under the main directory where you installed the software, and typing RHIDE dangchar, then using the "Make" command from the "Compile" menu. Then exit back to DOS and type dangchar to run the program. To run it under the debugger, make sure you are in the code subdirectory, and then type RHIDE dangchar. Again, do *not* add the ".cc" to the end of the file name. Once RHIDE has started up, you can step through the program by hitting F8, which will treat any function call as one statement, or by hitting F7, which will step into any function call. Any time you want to see the display that the user would see when running the program normally, hit ALT-F5, then ENTER to get back to the debugger.

Susan and I had quite a discussion about this program:

Susan: It is still not clear to me why you assigned values to elements numbered 10–19. Was that for demonstration purposes to force "writing past the end"?

Steve: Yes.

Susan: So by doing this to Middle then it alters the place the pointer is going to point for High?

Steve: No, it actually uses some of the same addresses that High uses, with the result being. . . well, do you remember the function mess?

Susan: Oh, don't remind me. So then when High runs there isn't any memory to put its results in? Why does Middle overwrite High instead of High overwrite Middle? But it was Alias that took up high's memory?

Steve: Actually High is filled up with the correct values, but then they're overwritten by the loop that stores via Alias, which is just another name for Middle. I'll explain that in detail.

Susan: Is that why High took on the lower case letters? Because Middle took the first loop and then Alias is the same as middle, so that is why it also has the upper case letters but then when High looped it picked up the pointer where Alias left off and that is why it is in lower case? But how did it manage two zeros at the end? I better stop talking, this is getting too weird. You are going to think I am nuts.

Steve: No. You're not nuts, but the program is. We're breaking the rules by writing "past the end" of the array Middle, using the pointer Alias to do so. We could have gotten the same result by storing data into elements 10 through 20 of Middle, but I wanted to show the equivalence of pointers and arrays.

Susan: Oops, I got ahead of myself, and yes, I was just going to ask if Middle alone would have been sufficient to do the job.

Steve: Yes, it would have been. However, it would not have made the point that arrays and pointers are almost identical in C++.

Susan: I am confused as to why the lower case letters are in High and why k and l are missing and two zeros made their way in. You never told me why those zeros were there.

Steve: Because the end of one array isn't necessarily immediately followed by the beginning of the next array; this depends on the sizes of the arrays and on how the compiler allocates local variables on the stack. What we're doing here is breaking the rules of the language, so it shouldn't be a surprise that the result isn't very sensible.

Susan: Okay, so if you are breaking the rules you can't predict an outcome? Here I was trying to figure out what was going on by looking at the results even knowing it was erroneous. Ugh.

Steve: Indeed.

private *Property: Keep Out!*

Now that we have disposed of the correspondence between arrays and pointers, it's time to return to our discussion of the private access specifier that we've used to control access to the member variables of the class. First of all, let me refresh your memory as to what this access specifier means: only member functions of the string class can refer to variables or functions marked private. As a rule, no member variables of a class should be public, for reasons that we'll get into later. By contrast, most member functions are public, because such functions provide the interface that is used by programmers who need the facilities of the class being defined. However, non-public member functions are sometimes useful for handling implementation details that aren't of interest or use to the "outside world" beyond the class boundaries, as we'll see later in this book.

Now that I've clarified the role of these access specifiers, let's take a look at the program in Figure 8.12, which won't compile because it tries to refer to m_Length, a private member variable of string.

FIGURE 8.12. **Attempted privacy violation (code\strtst3a.cc)**

```
#include <iostream.h>
#include "string3.h"

int main()
{
    string n("Test");

    n.m_Length = 12;

    n.Display();

    return 0;
}
```

Here's the result of trying to compile this program:

```
strtst3a.cc: In function 'int main()':
strtst3a.cc:8: member 'm_Length' is a private member of class 'string'
```

As discussed previously, the reason that we want to prevent access to a member variable is that public member variables have problems similar to those of global variables. To begin with, we want to guarantee consistent, safe behavior of our strings, which is impossible if a nonmember function outside our control can change one of our variables. In the example program, assigning a new value to the m_Length member variable would trick our Display member function into trying to display 12 characters, when our string contains only four characters of displayable data. Similar bad results would occur if a nonmember function were to change the value of m_Data; we wouldn't have any idea of what it was pointing to or whether we should call delete in the destructor to allow the memory formerly used for our string data to be reused.

Of course, Susan had some questions about access restrictions.

Susan: Now let me see if I get the problem here with this Figure 8.12. When you originally wrote m_Length, it was placed in a private area, so it couldn't be accessed through this program?

Steve: Right.

Susan: I am confused on your use of the term *nonmember function*. Does that mean a nonmember of a particular class or something that is native?

Steve: A nonmember function is any function that is not a member of the class in question.

Susan: A simple concept but easy to forget for some reason.

Steve: Probably because it's stated negatively.

While this may be a convincing argument against letting nonmember functions change our member variables, what about letting them at least retrieve the values of member variables?

Maintenance Required

Unfortunately this would be hazardous too. The problem here is akin to the other difficulty with global variables: Removing or changing the type of a global variable can cause repercussions everywhere in the program. If we decide to implement our string class by a different mechanism than a char* and a short, or even change the names of the member variables from m_Data and m_Length, any programs that rely on those types or names would have to be changed. If our string class were to become popular, this might amount to dozens or even hundreds of programs that would need to be changed if we were to make the slightest change in our member variables. Therefore, allowing nonmember functions even to retrieve the values of member variables in a class makes it harder to maintain that class.

However, it is sometimes useful for a program that is using an object to find out something about the object's internal state. For example, a user of a string variable might very well want to know how many characters it is storing at the moment, for example when formatting a report. Each string might require a different amount of padding to make the columns on the report line up, depending on the number of visible characters in the string; however, we don't want the length the user sees to include the null byte, which doesn't take up any space on the page. Susan wanted to know how we could allow the user to determine the string's length.

> **Susan:** So how would you "fix" this so that it would run? If you don't want to change m_Length to something public, then would you have to rewrite another string class for this program?
>
> **Steve:** No, you would generally fix this by writing a member function that returns the length of the string; the GetLength function to be implemented in Figure 8.14 is an example of that.
>
> **Susan:** Oh, so m_Length stays private but GetLength is public?
>
> **Steve:** Exactly.

As I've just mentioned to Susan, it is indeed possible to provide such a service without compromising the safety or maintainability of our class by writing a function that tells the user how long the string is. Figure 8.13 has the new interface definition that includes the GetLength function.

I strongly recommend that you print out the files that contain this interface and its implementation, as well as the test program, for reference as you are going through this part of the chapter; those files are string4.h, string4.cc, and strtst4.cc, respectively.

FIGURE 8.13. Yet another version of the string class **interface (code\string4.h)**

```
class string
{
public:
    string();
    string(const string& Str);
    string& operator = (const string& Str);
    ~string();

    string(char* p);
    void Display();
    short GetLength();

private:
    short m_Length;
    char* m_Data;
};
```

As you can see, all we have to do here is to add the declaration of the new function, GetLength. The implementation in Figure 8.14 is extremely simple: it merely returns the number of chars in the string, deducting 1 for the null byte at the end.

FIGURE 8.14. The string class **implementation of the** GetLength **function (from code\string4.cc)**

```
short string::GetLength()
{
  return m_Length-1;
}
```

This solves the problem of letting the user of a string variable find out how long the string is without allowing functions outside the class to become dependent on our implementation. It's also a good example of how we can provide the right information to the user more easily by creating an access function rather than letting the user get at our member variables directly; after all, we know that m_Length includes the null byte at the end of the string's data, which is irrelevant to the user of the string, so we can adjust our return value to indicate the "visible length" rather than the actual one.

With this mechanism in place, we can make whatever changes we like in how we store the length of our string;[5] as long as we don't change the name or return type of GetLength, no function outside the string class would be affected.[6] The example program in Figure 8.15 illustrates how to use this new function.

FIGURE 8.15. Using the GetLength **function in the** string class **(code\strtst4.cc)**

```
#include <iostream.h>
#include "string4.h"

int main()
{
    short len;
    string n("Test");

    len = n.GetLength();
```

5. For example, we could eliminate our m_Length member variable and just have the GetLength call strlen to figure out the length. Because we're not giving access to our member variable, the user's source code wouldn't have to be changed just because we changed the way we keep track of the length.

6. Of course, if we were to allow strings longer than 32767 bytes, we would have to change the return type of GetLength to something more capacious than an short. However, we still have a lot more leeway to make changes in the implementation than we would have if we allowed direct access to our member variables.

```
    cout << "The string has " << len << " characters." << endl;

    return 0;
}
```

First Review

After finishing most of the requirements to make the string class a concrete data type in the previous chapter, we went back to look at why the operator = needs a *reference argument* rather than a *value argument*. When we use a value argument, a copy of the argument is made. In the case of a user-defined data type, this copy is made via the copy constructor defined for that type. If we don't define our own copy constructor, the compiler will generate one for us, which will use *memberwise copy*; that is, simply copying all of the member variables in the object. While a memberwise copy is fine for simple objects whose data are wholly contained with themselves, it isn't sufficient for objects that contain pointers to data stored in other places, because copying a pointer from one object to another results in the two objects sharing the same actual data. Since our string class does contain such a pointer, the result of this simple(minded) copy is that the newly created string points to the same data as the caller's string. Therefore, when the newly created local string expires at the end of the operator = function, the destructor for that string frees the memory that the caller's string was using to store its data.

    This problem is very similar to the reason why we had to write our own operator = in the first place; the compiler-generated operator = just copies the member variables from the source to the destination object, which causes similar havoc when one of the two "twinned" strings is changed. In the case of our operator =, we can solve the twinning problem by using a reference argument rather than a value argument. A reference argument is actually another name for the caller's variable rather than a copy of the value in that variable, so no destructor is called for a reference argument when the function exits; therefore, the caller's variable is left unmolested.

Next, we examined how it was possible to assign a C string to one of our string variables. This didn't require us to write any more code because we already had a constructor that could create a string from a C string, and an operator = that could assign one string to another one. The compiler helps us out here by employing a rule that can be translated roughly as follows: If we need an object of type A (string, in this case) and we have an object of type B (char*, in this case), and there is a constructor that constructs an A and requires exactly one argument, which is of type B, then invoke that constructor automatically. The example code is as follows:

```
n = "My name is: ";
```

where n is a string, and "My name is" is a C string, whose type is char*. We have an operator = with the declaration:

```
string& string::operator = (const string& Str);
```

that takes a string reference argument, and we have a constructor of the form:

```
string::string(char* p);
```

that takes a char* argument and creates a new string. So we have a char*, "My name is: ", and we need a string. Since we have a constructor string::string(char*), the compiler will use that constructor to make a temporary string with the same value as the char*, and then use the assignment operator string::operator = (const string& Str) to assign the value of that temporary string to the string n. The fact that the temporary is created also provides the clue as to why the argument to string::operator = (const string& Str) should be a const reference, rather than just a (non-const) reference, to a string. The temporary string having the value "My name is: " created during the execution of the statement n = "My name is: "; disappears after operator = is executed, taking with it any changes that operator = might have wanted to apply to the original value. With a const reference argument, the compiler knows that operator = doesn't wish to change that argument, and therefore doesn't give us a warning that we might be changing a temporary value.

At this point, we've taken care of operator =. However, to create a concrete data type, we still have to allow our string variables to be passed as value arguments. Unfortunately, the compiler-generated copy constructor suffers from the same drawback as the compiler-generated operator =; namely, it copies the pointer to the actual data of the string, rather than the data itself. Logically, therefore, the solution to this problem is quite similar to the solution for operator =: We write our own copy constructor that allocates space for the character data to be stored in the newly created string and then copies the data from the old string to the new string.

However, we still can't use a value argument to our copy constructor, because a value argument needs a copy constructor to make the copy. This obviously won't work, and will be caught by the compiler. Therefore, as in the case of operator =, we have to use a reference argument; since this is actually just another name for the caller's variable rather than a copy of it, no destructor for the reference argument is called at exit from our copy constructor. Since we are not going to change the caller's argument, we specify a constant reference argument of type string, or a const string& in C++ terms.

At that point in the chapter, we had met the requirements for a concrete data type, but such a type is of limited usefulness as long as we can't get the values displayed on the screen. Therefore, the next order of business was to add a Display member function that takes care of this task. This function isn't particularly complicated, but it does require us to deal with the notion of a C legacy type, the *array*. Since the compiler treats an array in almost the same way as a pointer, we can use array notation to extract each character that needs to be sent out to the screen. Continuing with our example of the

Display function's use, the next topic was a discussion of how chars can be treated as numeric variables.

Then we saw a demonstration of how easy it is to misuse an array so that you destroy data that belong to some other variable. This is an important warning of the dangers of uncontrolled use of pointers and arrays; these are the most error-prone constructs in both C and C++, when not kept under tight rein.

We continued by revisiting the topic of access control and why it is advantageous to keep member variables out of the public section of the class definition. The reasons are similar to those of using global variables; it's too hard to keep track of where the value of a public member variable is being referenced and therefore to update all the affected areas of the code when changing the class definition. However, it is sometimes useful to allow external functions access to some information about a class object. We saw how to do this by adding a GetLength member function to our string class.

A String of Wins

At this point, we have a fairly minimal string class. We can create a string, assign it a literal value in the form of a C string, and copy the value of one string to another; we can even pass a string as a value argument. Now we'll use the techniques that we've already covered (along with others that we find necessary in the process) to improve the facilities that the string class provides.

To make this goal more concrete, let's suppose that we want to modify the sorting program of Chapter 4 to sort strings, rather than shorts. To use the sorting algorithm from that program, we'll need to be able to compare two strings to see which would come after the other in the dictionary, as we can compare two shorts to see which is greater. We also want to be able to use cout and << to display strings on the screen, and cin and >> to read them from the keyboard, just as we can with native types.

Before we go into the changes needed in the string class to allow us to write a string sorting program, Figure 8.16 shows our goal: The selection sort algorithm adapted to sort a vector of strings rather than shorts.

Assuming that you've installed the software from the CD-ROM in the back of this book, you can try out this program. First, you have to compile it by changing to the code subdirectory under the main directory where you installed the software, and typing RHIDE strsort1, then using the "Make" command from the "Compile" menu. Then exit back to DOS and type strsort1 to run the program.

To run it under the debugger, make sure you are in the code subdirectory, and then type RHIDE strsort1. Again, do *not* add the ".cc" to the end of the file name. Once RHIDE has started up, you can step through the program by hitting F8, which will treat any function call as one statement, or by hitting F7, which will step into any function call. Any time you want to see the display that the user would see when running the program normally, hit ALT-F5, then ENTER to get back to the debugger.

FIGURE 8.16. **Sorting a** vector **of** strings (**code\strsort1.cc**)

```cpp
#include <iostream.h>
#include "string6.h"
#include "vector.h"

int main()
{
    vector<string> Name(5);
    vector<string> SortedName(5);
    string FirstName;
    short FirstIndex;
    short i;
    short k;
    string HighestName = "zzzzzzzz";

    cout << "I'm going to ask you to type in five last names." << endl;
```

```
for (i = 0; i < 5; i ++)
  {
  cout << "Please type in name #" << i+1 << ": ";
  cin >> Name[i];
  }

for (i = 0; i < 5; i ++)
   {
   FirstName = HighestName;
   FirstIndex = 0;
   for (k = 0; k < 5; k ++)
      {
      if (Name[k] < FirstName)
         {
         FirstName = Name[k];
         FirstIndex = k;
         }
      }
   SortedName[i] = FirstName;
   Name[FirstIndex] = HighestName;
   }

cout << "Here are the names, in alphabetical order: " << endl;
for (i = 0; i < 5; i ++)
   cout << SortedName[i] << endl;

return 0;
}
```

Susan had a couple of comments and questions about this program:

Susan: Okay, I have this figured out now. I mentioned to you a long time ago that I was confused with the code here when you ask for last names but you are using a variable FirstName. This is a little confusing to a novice because it seems that you don't know what you are asking for. Now I get it: you are asking for the first one of the *last* names.

Steve: Actually, FirstName is the "lowest" name that we've found so far in the current pass, sort of like HighestWeight in the original program. I think we're saying the same thing here.

Susan: Why aren't you using caps when you initiate your variable of HighestName; I don't understand why you use "zzzzzzzzzz" instead of "ZZZZZZZZZZ"? Are you going to fix this later so that caps will work the same way as lower case letters?

Steve: If I were to make that change, the program wouldn't work correctly if someone typed their name in lower case letters, because lower case letters are higher in ASCII value than upper case letters. That is, "abc" is higher than "ZZZ". Thus, if someone typed in their name in lower case, the program would fail to find their name as the lowest name. Actually, the way the string sorting function works, "ABC" is completely different from "abc"; they won't be next to one another in the sorted list. We could fix this by using a different method of comparing the strings that would effectively convert everything to upper case before sorting it, if that were necessary.

As you can see, this program looks very similar to the code that sorts short values, which is good because that's what we wanted to achieve. Let's take a look at the differences between this program and the original one in Figure 4.6.

1. One difference is that we're sorting the names in ascending alphabetical order, rather than descending order of weight as with the original program. This means that we have to start out by finding the name that would come first in the dictionary (the "lowest" name). By contrast, in the original program we were looking for the highest weight, not the lowest one; therefore, we have to do the sort "backward" from the previous example.

2. The next difference is that the vectors Name and SortedName are collections of strings, rather than the corresponding vectors of shorts in the first program: Weight and SortedWeight.

3. The final difference is that we've added a new variable called HighestName, which plays the role of the value 0 that was used to initialize HighestWeight in the original program; that is, it is used to initialize the variable FirstName to a value that will certainly be replaced by the first name we find, just as 0 was used to initialize the variable HighestWeight to a value that had to be lower than the first weight we would find. The reason why we need a "really high" name rather than a "really low" one is because we're sorting the "lowest" name to the front, rather than sorting the "highest" weight to the front as we did originally.

You may think these changes to the program aren't very significant. That's a correct conclusion; we'll spend much more time on the changes we have to make to our string class before this program will run, or even compile. The advantage of making up our own data types (like strings) is that we can make them behave in any way we like. Of course, the corresponding disadvantage is that we have to provide the code to implement that behavior and give the compiler enough information to use that code to perform the operations we request. In this case, we'll need to tell the compiler how to compare strings, read them in via >> and write them out via <<. Let's start with Figure 8.17, which shows the new interface specification of the string class, including all of the new member functions needed to implement the comparison and I/O operators, as well as operator ==, which we'll implement later in the chapter.

FIGURE 8.17. The updated string class **interface, including comparison and I/O operators (code\string5.h)**

```
class string
{
friend ostream& operator << (ostream& s, const string& Str);
friend istream& operator >> (istream& s, string& Str);

public:
    string();
```

```
          string(const string& Str);
          string& operator = (const string& Str);
          ~string();

          string(char* p);
          short GetLength();
          bool operator < (const string& Str);
          bool operator == (const string& Str);

    private:
          short m_Length;
          char* m_Data;
    };
```

I strongly recommend that you print out the files that contain this interface and its implementation, as well as the test program, for reference as you are going through this part of the chapter; those files are string5.h, string5.cc, and strtst5.cc, respectively.

Let's start by implementing operator < (the "less than" operator) so that we can use the selection sort to arrange strings by their dictionary order. The signature of this operator is similar to that of operator =, except that rather than defining what it means to say x = y; for two strings x and y, we are defining what it means to say x < y. Of course, we want our operator < to act analogously to the < operator for short values; that is, our operator will compare two strings and return true if the first string would come before the second string in the dictionary and false otherwise, as needed for the selection sort.

Less Than Obvious

All right, then, how do we actually implement this undoubtedly useful facility? Let's start by examining the function declaration bool string::operator < (const string& Str); a little more closely. This means that we're declaring a function that returns a bool and is a member function of class string; its name is operator <, and it takes a constant reference to a string as its argument. As we've seen before, operators don't look the same when we use them as when we define them. In the sorting program in Figure 8.16, the line if (Name[k] < FirstName) actually means if (Name[k].operator < (FirstName)). In other words, if the return value from the call to operator < is false, then the if expression will also be considered false and the controlled block after the if won't be executed. On the other hand, if the return value from the call to operator < is true, then the if expression will also be considered true and the controlled block of the if will be executed. To make this work correctly, our version of operator < will return the value true if the first string is less than the second and false otherwise.

Now that we've seen how the compiler will use our new function, let's look at its implementation, which follows these steps:

1. Determine the length of the shorter of the two strings.

2. Compare a character from the first string with the corresponding character from the second string.

3. If the character from the first string is less than the character from the second string, then we know that the first string precedes the second in the dictionary, so we're done and the result is true.

4. If the character from the first string is greater than the character from the second string, then we know that the first string follows the second in the dictionary, so we're done and the result is false.

5. If the two characters are the same, and we haven't come to the end of the shorter string, then move to the next character in each string, and go back to step 2.

6. When we run out of characters to compare, if the strings are the same length, then the answer is that they are identical, so we're done and the result is false.

7. On the other hand, if the strings are different in length, and if we run out of characters in the shorter string before finding a difference between the two strings, then the longer string follows the shorter one in the dictionary. In this case, the result is true if the second string is longer and false if the first string is longer.

One question that might occur to you on looking over the preceding explanation is why we care whether two strings differ in length. Wouldn't it be simpler just to compare up to the length of the longer string?

Down for the Count

As it happens, that approach would work properly so long as both of the strings we're comparing had a null byte at their ends *and* neither of them had a null byte anywhere else. To see the reason for the limitation of that approach, let's look at what the memory layout might look like for two string variables x and y, with the contents "post" and "poster" respectively. In Figure 8.18, the letters in the box labeled "string contents" represent themselves, while the 0s represent the null byte, not the digit 0.

If we were to compare the strings up to the longer of the two lengths with this memory layout, the sequence of events would be:

1. Get character *p* from location 12345600.

2. Get character *p* from location 12345607.

3. They are the same, so continue.

4. Get character *o* from location 12345601.

5. Get character *o* from location 12345608.

6. They are the same, so continue.

7. Get character *s* from location 12345602.

8. Get character *s* from location 12345609.

9. They are the same, so continue.

10. Get character *t* from location 12345603.

11. Get character *t* from location 1234560a.

12. They are the same, so continue.

13. Get character *e* from location 12345604.

14. Get a null byte from location 1234560b.

15. The character *e* from the first string is higher than the null byte from the second string, so we conclude (correctly) that the first string comes after the second one.

This works because the null byte, having an ASCII code of 0, in fact is less than whatever non-null byte in the corresponding position of the other string.

FIGURE 8.18. strings x **and** y **in memory**

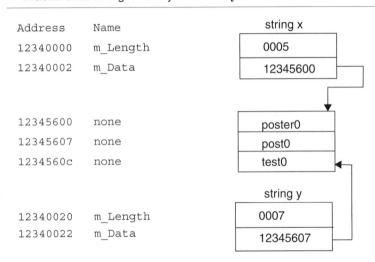

Address	Name		string x
12340000	m_Length		0005
12340002	m_Data		12345600
12345600	none		poster0
12345607	none		post0
1234560c	none		test0
			string y
12340020	m_Length		0007
12340022	m_Data		12345607

However, this plan wouldn't work reliably if we had a string with a null byte in the middle. To see why, let's change the memory layout slightly to stick a null byte in the middle of string y. Figure 8.19 shows the modified layout.

You may reasonably object that we don't have any way to create a string with a null byte in it. That's true at the moment, but one reason we're storing the actual length of the string rather than relying on the null byte to mark the end of a string, as is done with C strings, is that keeping the length separately makes it possible to have a string that has any characters whatever in it, even nulls. For example, we could add a string constructor that takes an array of bytes and a length and copies the specified number of bytes from the array.

FIGURE 8.19. strings x and y **in memory, with an embedded null byte**

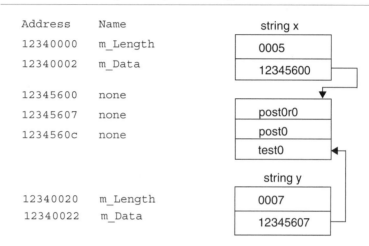

Since an array of bytes can contain any characters in it, including nulls, that new constructor would obviously allow us to create a string with a null in the middle of it; if we tried to use the preceding comparison mechanism, it wouldn't work reliably, as shown in the following analysis.

1. Get character *p* from location 12345600.

2. Get character *p* from location 12345607.

3. They are the same, so continue.

4. Get character *o* from location 12345601.

5. Get character *o* from location 12345608.

6. They are the same, so continue.

7. Get character *s* from location 12345602.

8. Get character *s* from location 12345609.

9. They are the same, so continue.

10. Get character *t* from location 12345603.

11. Get character *t* from location 1234560a.

12. They are the same, so continue.

13. Get a null byte from location 12345604.

14. Get a null byte from location 1234560b.

15. They are the same, so continue.

16. Get character *r* from location 12345605.

17. Get character *t* from location 1234560c.

18. The character *r* from the first string is less than the character *t* from the second string, so we conclude that the first string comes before the second one.

Unfortunately, this conclusion is incorrect; what we have actually done is run off the end of the second string and started retrieving data from the next location in memory. Since we want to be able to handle the situation where one of the strings has one or more embedded nulls, we have to stop the comparison as soon as we get to the end of the shorter string; whatever happens to be past the end of that string's data, it's not anything relevant to our comparison of the two strings.

Let's listen in on the discussion Susan and I had on this topic.

Susan: Why is the return value from operator < a bool?

Steve: Because it has to return a value indicating whether the first string is less than the second string. An if statement using this operator < will work properly if the result of this function is false for "not less than" and true for "less than". Thus, a bool is appropriate for this use.

Susan: Again I am not seeing where we're using string::operator < (const string& Str); in the sorting program.

Steve: That's because all you have to say is a < b, just as with operator =; the compiler knows that a < b, where a and b are strings, means string::operator < (const string&).

Susan: Why are you bringing up this stuff about what the operator looks like and the way it is defined? Do you mean that is what is really happening even though it looks like built in code?

Steve: Yes.

Susan: Who puts those null bytes into memory?

Steve: The compiler supplies a null byte automatically at the end of every literal string, such as "abc".

Susan: I don't get where you are not using a null byte when storing the length; it looks to me that you are. This is confusing. Ugh.

Steve: I understand why that's confusing, I think. I am including the null byte at the end of a string when we create it from a literal C string, so that we can mix our strings with C strings more readily; however, because we store the length separately, it's possible to construct a string that has null bytes in the middle of it as well as at the end. This is not possible with a C string, because that has no explicit length stored with it; instead, the routines that operate on C strings assume that the first null byte means the C string is finished.

Susan: Why do you jump from a null byte to a *t*? Didn't it run out of letters? Is this what you mean by retrieving data from the next location in memory? Why was a *t* there?

Steve: Yes, this is an example of retrieving random information from the next location in memory. We got a *t* because that just happened to be there. The problem is that since we're using an explicit length rather than a null byte to indicate the end of our strings, we can't count on a null byte stopping the comparison correctly. Thus, we have to worry about handling the case where there is a null byte in the middle of a string.

Now that we've examined why the algorithm for operator < works the way it does, it will probably be easier to understand the code if we follow an example of how it is used. I've written a program called strtst5x.cc for this purpose; Figure 8.20 has the code for that program.

FIGURE 8.20. **Using** operator < **for** strings (**code\strtst5x.cc**)

```
#include <iostream.h>
#include "string5.h"

int main()
{
    string x;
    string y;

    x = "ape";
    y = "axes";

    if (x < y)
      cout << x << " comes before " << y << endl;
    else
      cout << x << " doesn't come before " << y << endl;

    return 0;
}
```

You can see that in this program the two strings being compared are "ape" and "axes", which are assigned to strings x and y respectively. As we've already discussed, the compiler translates a comparison between two strings into a call to the function string::operator <(const string& Str); in this case, the line that does that comparison is if (x < y).

Now that we've seen how to use this comparison operator, Figure 8.21 shows one way to implement it.

FIGURE 8.21. **The implementation of** operator < **for strings (from code\string5a.cc)**

```cpp
bool string::operator < (const string& Str)
{
  short i;
  bool Result;
  bool ResultFound;
  short CompareLength;

  if (Str.m_Length < m_Length)
    CompareLength = Str.m_Length;
  else
    CompareLength = m_Length;

  ResultFound = false;
  for (i = 0; (i < CompareLength) && (ResultFound == false); i ++)
    {
    if (m_Data[i] < Str.m_Data[i])
      {
      Result = true;
      ResultFound = true;
      }
    else
      {
      if (m_Data[i] > Str.m_Data[i])
        {
        Result = false;
        ResultFound = true;
        }
      }
    }

  if (ResultFound == false)
    {
    if (m_Length < Str.m_Length)
      Result = true;
    else
      Result = false;
```

```
    }

  return Result;
}
```

The variables we'll use in this function are:

1. i, which is used as a loop counter in the for loop that steps through all of the characters to be compared.

2. Result, which is used to hold the true or false value that we'll return to the caller.

3. ResultFound, which we'll use to keep track of whether we've found the result yet.

4. CompareLength, which we'll use to determine the number of characters to compare in the two strings.

After defining variables, the next four lines of the code determine how many characters from each string we actually have to compare; the value of CompareLength is set to the lesser of the lengths of our string and the string referred to by Str. In this case, that value is 4, the length of our string (including the terminating null byte).

Now we're ready to do the comparison. This takes the form of a for loop that steps through all of the characters to be compared in each string. The header of the for loop is for (i = 0; (i < CompareLength) && (ResultFound == false); i ++). The first and last parts of the expression controlling the for loop should be familiar by now; they initialize and increment the loop control variable. But what about the continuation expression (i < CompareLength) && (ResultFound == false)?

For Better or Worse?

That expression states a two-part condition for continuing the loop. The first part, (i < CompareLength), is the usual condition that allows the program to execute the loop as long as the index variable is within the correct range. The second part, (ResultFound == false) should also be fairly clear; we want to test whether we've already found the result we're looking for, and continue only as long as that isn't the case (i.e., ResultFound is still false). The () around each of these expressions are used to tell the compiler that we want to evaluate each of these expressions first, before the && is applied to their results. That leaves the && symbol as the only mystery.

It's really not too mysterious. The && operator is the symbol for the "logical AND" operation, which means that we want to combine the truth or falsity of two expressions each of which has a logical value of true or false. The result of using && to combine the results of these two expressions will also be a logical value. Here is the way the value of that expression is determined:

1. If both of the expressions connected by the && are true, then the value of the expression containing the && is also true;

2. Otherwise, the value of the expression containing the && is false.

If you think about it for a minute, this should makes sense. We want to continue the loop as long as both of the conditions are true; that is,

1. i is less than CompareLength; *and*

2. ResultFound is false (we haven't found what we're looking for).

That's why the && operator is called *logical AND*; it checks whether condition 1 *and* condition 2 are both true. If either is false, we want to stop the loop, and this continuation expression will do just that.[7]

Now let's trace the path of execution through the for loop in Figure 8.21. On the first time through the loop, the index i is 0 and ResultFound is false. Therefore, the continuation expression allows us

---

7.   This operator follows a rule analogous to the one for ||: if the expression on the left is false, then the answer must be false and the expression on the right is not executed at all. The reason for this "short-circuit evaluation rule" is that in some cases you may want to write a right-hand expression that will only be legal if the left-hand expression is true.

to execute the statements in the loop, where we test whether the current character in the current string, m_Data[i], is less than the corresponding character from the string Str, Str.m_Data[i].

By the way, in case the expression in the if statement doesn't make sense immediately, perhaps I should remind you that the array notation m_Data[i] means the ith character of the data pointed to by m_Data; an index value of 0 means the first element, as is always the case when using an array. We've already covered this starting with the section entitled "Array of Hope?" on page 496; you should go back and reread that section if you're not comfortable with the equivalence between pointers and arrays.

The code in Figure 8.22 compares characters from the two strings.

FIGURE 8.22. Is our character less than the other one? (from code\string5a.cc)

```
if (m_Data[i] < Str.m_Data[i])
  {
  Result = true;
  ResultFound = true;
  }
```

In the event that the current character in our string is indeed less than the corresponding character in Str, we have our answer: Our string is less than the other string. If that were the case, we would set Result to true and ResultFound to true, and we would be finished with this execution of the for loop.

As it happens, in our current example both m_Data[0] and Str.m_Data[0] are equal to 'a', so they're equal to each other as well. What happens when the character from our string is the same as the one from the string Str?

In that case, the first if, whose condition is stated as if (m_Data[i] < Str.m_Data[i]), is false. So we continue with the else clause of that if statement, which looks like Figure 8.23.

FIGURE 8.23. The else clause in the comparison loop (from code\string5a.cc)

```
else
  {
  if (m_Data[i] > Str.m_Data[i])
    {
    Result = false;
    ResultFound = true;
    }
  }
```

This clause contains another if statement that compares the character from our string to the one from Str. Since the two characters are the same, this if also comes out false, so the controlled block of the if isn't executed. After this if statement, we've reached the end of the controlled block of the for statement. The next iteration of the for loop starts by incrementing i to 1. Then the continuation expression is evaluated again; i is still less than CompareLength, and ResultFound is still false, so we execute the controlled block of the loop again with i equal to 1.

On this pass through the for loop, m_Data[1], the character from our string, is 'p', and Str.m_Data[1], the character from the other string, is 'x'. Therefore, the condition in the first if statement (that the character from our string is less than the character from the other string) is true, so we execute the controlled block of the if statement; this sets Result to true, and ResultFound also to true, as you can see in Figure 8.22.

We're now at the end of the for loop, so we return to the for statement to continue execution. First, i is incremented again, to 2. Then the continuation expression (i < CompareLength) && (ResultFound == false) is evaluated. The first part of the condition, i < CompareLength is true, since i is 2 and CompareLength is 4. However, the second part of the condition, ResultFound == false, is false, because we've just set ResultFound to true. Since the result of the && operator is true only when both subconditions are true, the for loop terminates, passing control to the next statement after the controlled block of the loop (Figure 8.24).

FIGURE 8.24. **Handling the return value (from code\string5a.cc)**

```
if (ResultFound == false)
  {
  if (m_Length < Str.m_Length)
    Result = true;
  else
    Result = false;
  }
```

In the current scenario, ResultFound is true because we have found a character from m_Data that differs from the corresponding character from Str.m_Data; therefore, the condition in the first if is false, and we proceed to the next statement after the end of the if statement, return Result;. This shouldn't come as too much of a surprise; we know the answer to the comparison, namely, that our string is less than the other string, so we're ready to tell the caller the information that he requested by calling our routine.

A Greater Cause

The path of execution is almost exactly the same if, the first time we find a mismatch between the two strings, the character from our string is greater than the character from the other string. The only difference is that the if statement that handles this scenario sets Result to false rather than true (Figure 8.23), because our string is not less than the other string; of course, it still sets ResultFound to true, since we know the result that will be returned.

There's only one other possibility: That the two strings are the same up to the length of the shorter one (e.g., "post" and "poster"). In that case, the for loop will expire of natural causes when i gets to be greater than or equal to CompareLength. Then the final if statement shown in Figure 8.24 will evaluate to true, because ResultFound is still false. In this case, if the length of our string is less than the length of the other string, we will set Result to true, because a shorter string will precede a longer one in the dictionary if the two strings are the same up to the length of the shorter one.

Otherwise, we'll set Result to false, because our string is at least as long as the other one; since they're equal up to the length of the shorter one, our string can't precede the other string. In this case, either they're identical, or our string is longer than the other one and therefore should follow it. Either of these two conditions means that the result of operator < is false, so that's what we tell the caller via our return value.

Simple Pleasures

This implementation of operator < for strings definitely works. However, there's a much simpler way to do it. Figure 8.25 shows the code.

FIGURE 8.25. **Implementing** operator < **for strings (from code\string5.cc)**

```
bool string::operator < (const string& Str)
{
  short Result;
  short CompareLength;

  if (Str.m_Length < m_Length)
    CompareLength = Str.m_Length;
  else
    CompareLength = m_Length;

  Result = memcmp(m_Data,Str.m_Data,CompareLength);

  if (Result < 0)
    return true;
```

```
    if (Result > 0)
      return false;

    if (m_Length < Str.m_Length)
      return true;

    return false;
  }
```

This starts out in the same way as our previous version, by figuring out how much of the two strings we actually need to compare character by character. Right after that calculation, though, the code is very different; where's that big for loop?

It's contained in the standard library function memcmp, a carryover from C, which does exactly what that for loop did for us. Although C doesn't have the kind of strings that we're implementing here, it does have primitive facilities for dealing with arrays of characters, including comparing one array with another, character by character. One type of character array supported by C is the C string, which we've already encountered. However, C strings have a serious drawback for our purposes here: They use a null byte to mark the end of a group of characters. This isn't suitable for our strings, whose length is explicitly stored; as noted previously, our strings could theoretically have null bytes in them. There are several C functions that compare C strings, but they rely on the null byte for their proper operation, so we can't use them.

However, these limitations of C strings are so evident that the library writers have supplied another set of functions that act almost identically to the ones used for C strings, except that they don't rely on null bytes to determine how much data to process. Instead, whenever you use one of these functions, you have to tell it how many characters to manipulate. In this case, we're calling memcmp, which compares two arrays of characters up to a specified length. The first argument is the first array to be compared (corresponding to our string), the second argument is the second array to be compared (corresponding to the string Str), and the third argument is the length for which the two arrays are to be compared. The return value from memcmp is calculated by the following rules:

1. It's less than 0 if the first array would precede the second in the dictionary;

2. It's 0 if they are the same up to the length specified;

3. It's greater than 0 if the first array would follow the second in the dictionary.

This is very convenient for us, because if the return value from memcmp is less than 0, we know that our result will be true, while if the return value from memcmp is greater than 0, then our result will be false. The only complication, which isn't very complicated, is that if the return value from memcmp is 0, meaning that the two arrays are the same up to the length of the shorter character array, we have to see which is longer. If the first one is shorter, then it precedes the second one; therefore, our result is true. Otherwise, it's false.

Susan had some questions about this version of operator <, including why we had to go through the previous exercise, if we could just use memcmp.

> **Susan:** What is this? I suppose there was a purpose to all the confusing prior discussion if you have an easier way of defining operator <? UGH! This new stuff just pops up out of the blue! What is going on? Please explain the reason for the earlier torture.

> **Steve:** I thought we should examine the character-by-character version of operator < before taking the shortcut. That should make it easier to follow the explanation of the "string overrun" problem, as each character comparison shows up in the code.

> **Susan:** So, memcmp is another library function, and does it stand for memory compare? Also, are the return values are built into memcmp? This is very confusing, because you have return values in the code.

Steve: Yes, memcmp stands for "memory compare". As for return values: yes, it has them, but they aren't exactly the ones that we want. We have to return the value true for "less than" and false for "not less than", which aren't the values that memcmp returns. Also, memcmp doesn't do the whole job when the strings aren't the same length; in that case, we have to handle the trailing part of the longer string manually.

One small point that shouldn't be overlooked is that in this version of the operator < code, we have more than one return statement; in fact, we have four! That's perfectly legal and should be clear to a reader of this function. It's usually not a good idea to scatter return statements around in a large function, because it's easy to overlook them when trying to follow the flow of control through the function. In this case, though, that's not likely to be a problem; any reasonably fluent reader of C++ code will find this organization easy to understand.

Equalization of Opportunity

Although our current task requires only operator <, another comparison operator, operator ==, will make an interesting contrast in implementation; in addition, a concrete data type that allows comparisons should really implement more than just operator <. Since we've just finished one comparison operator, we might as well knock this one off now (Figure 8.26).

This function is considerably simpler than the previous one. Why is this, since they have almost the same purpose? It's because in this case we don't care which of the two strings is greater than the other, just whether they're the same or different. Therefore, we don't have to worry about comparing the two char arrays if they're of different lengths. Two arrays of different lengths can't be the same, so we can just return false. Once we have determined that the two arrays are the same length, we do the comparison via memcmp. This gives us the answer directly, because if Result is 0, then the two strings are equal; otherwise, they're different.

FIGURE 8.26. **Implementing** operator == **for** strings **(from code\string5.cc)**

```
bool string::operator == (const string& Str)
{
  short Result;

  if (m_Length != Str.m_Length)
    return false;

  Result = memcmp(m_Data,Str.m_Data,m_Length);

  if (Result == 0)
    return true;

  return false;
}
```

Even though this function is simpler than operator <, it's not simple enough to avoid Susan's probing eye:

Susan: Does == only check to see if the lengths of the arrays are the same? Can it not ever be used for a value?

Steve: It compares the values in the arrays, but only if they are the same length. Since all it cares about is whether they are equal, and arrays of different length can't be equal, it doesn't have to compare the character data unless the arrays are of the same length.

Displaying Expertise

Before moving on to see how we will display a string on the screen via operator <<, I should bring up a couple of points here, because otherwise they might pass you by. First, we didn't have to change our interface header file string5.h (Figure 8.17) just because we changed the implementation of operator <. Since the *signature* of this function didn't change, neither the header file nor the user program had to change. Second, we didn't even implement operator == in the string5a.cc version of the string library and yet our test program still compiled without difficulty. How can this be?

In C++, you can declare all of the functions you want to, whether they are member functions or global functions, without actually defining them. As long as no one tries to actually use the functions, everything will work fine. In fact, the compiler doesn't even care whether any functions you *do* refer to are available; that's up to the linker to worry about. This is very handy when you know that you're going to add functions in a later revision of a class, as was the case here. Of course, you should warn your class users if you have listed functions in the interface header file that aren't available. It's true that they'll find out about the missing functions the first time they try to link a program that uses one of these functions, because the linker will report that it can't find the function; however, if they've spent a lot of time writing a program using one of these functions, they're likely to get mad at you for misleading them. So let them know what's actually implemented and what's "for later".

Now let's continue with our extensions to the string class, by looking at how we send a string out to the screen.

Down by the Old cout *Stream*

We've been using cout and its operator << for awhile, but have taken them for granted. Now we have to look under the hood a bit.

The first question is what type of object cout is. The answer is that it's an ostream (short for "output stream"), which is an object that you can use to send characters to some output device. I'm not sure of the origin of this term, but you can imagine that you push the characters out into a "stream" that leads to the output device.

As you may recall from our uses of cout, you can chain a bunch of << expressions together in one statement, as in Figure 8.27. If you compile and execute that program, it will display:

On test #1, your mark is: A

Notice that it displays the short as a number and the char as a letter, just as we want it to do. This desirable event occurs because there's a separate version of << for each type of data that can be displayed; in other words, operator << uses function overloading, just like the constructors for the StockItem class and the string class. We'll also use function overloading to add support for our string class to the I/O facilities supplied by the iostreams library.

FIGURE 8.27. Chaining several operator << **expressions together (code\cout1.cc)**

```
#include <iostream.h>

int main()
{
    short x;
    char y;

    x = 1;
    y = 'A';

    cout << "On test #" << x << ", your mark is: " << y << endl;

    return 0;
}
```

Gently Down the Stream

Before we examine how to accomplish this goal, though, we'll have to go into some detail about how the pre-existing output functions behave. Let's start with a simple case using a version of operator << supplied by the iostream.h header file. The simplest possible use of ostream's operator <<, of course, uses only one occurrence of the operator. Here's an example where the value is a char:

```
cout << 'a';
```

As you may remember, using an operator such as << on an object is always equivalent to a "normal" function call. This particular example is equivalent to the following:

```
cout.operator << ('a');
```

which calls ostream::operator << (char) (i.e., the version of the operator << member function of the iostream class that takes a char as its input) for the predefined destination cout, which writes the char on the screen.

That takes care of the single occurrence of operator <<. However, as we've already seen, it's possible to string together any number of occurrences of operator <<, with the output of each successive occurrence following the output created by the one to its left. We want our string output function to behave just like the ones predefined in iostream.h, so let's look next at an example that illustrates multiple uses of operator <<, taking a char and a C string:

```
cout << 'a' << " string";
```

This is equivalent to

```
(cout.operator << ('a')).operator << (" string");
```

What does this mean? Well, since an expression in parentheses is evaluated before one outside the parentheses, the first thing that happens is that ostream::operator << (char) is called for the predefined destination cout, which writes the 'a' to the screen. Now here's the tricky part: the return value from every version of ostream::operator << is a reference to the ostream that it operates on (cout, in this case). Therefore, after the 'a' has been written on the screen, the rest of the expression reduces to this:

```
cout.operator << (" string");
```

That is, the next output operation behaves exactly like the first one. In this case, ostream::operator << (char*) is the function called, because char* is the type of the argument to be written out. It too returns a reference to the ostream for which it was called, so that any further << calls can add their data to that same ostream. It should be fairly obvious how the same process can be extended to handle any number of items to be displayed.

Friends of Global Progress

That illustrates how the designers of ostream could create member functions that would behave in this convenient way. However, we can't use the same mechanism that they did; we can't modify the definition of the ostream class in the library, because we didn't write it in the first place and don't have access to its source code.[8] Is there some way to give our strings convenient input and output facilities?

In fact, there is. To do this, we create a *global* function called operator << that accepts an ostream& (that is, a reference to an ostream), adds the contents of our string to the ostream, and then returns a reference to the same ostream. This will support multiple occurrences of operator << to be chained together in one statement, just as with the operator << member functions from the iostreams library. The implementation of this function is shown in Figure 8.28.

As usual, we should first examine the function declaration; in this case, a couple of points are worth noting. We've already seen that the first argument is an ostream&, to which we will add the characters from the string that's the second argument. Also notice that the second argument is a const string&, that is, a reference to a constant

---

8. Even if we did have the source code to the ostream class, we wouldn't want to modify it, for a number of reasons. One excellent reason is that every time a new version of the library came out, we'd have to make our changes again. Also, there are other ways to reuse the code from the library for our own purposes, using mechanisms that we'll get to later in this book, although we won't use them with the iostream classes.

string. This is the best way to declare this argument because we aren't going to change the argument, and there's no reason to make a copy of it.

FIGURE 8.28. An operator << **function to output a** string **(from code\string5.cc)**

```
ostream& operator << (ostream& s, const string& Str)
{
  short i;
  for (i=0; i < Str.m_Length-1; i ++)
  s << Str.m_Data[i];

  return s;
}
```

But possibly the most important point about the function declaration is that this operator << is *not* a member function of the string class, which explains why it isn't called string::operator <<. It's a global function that can be called anywhere in a program that needs to use it, so long as that program has included the header file that defines it. Its operation is pretty simple: It simply calls ostream::operator << (char) to write out each character from the array called m_Data that we use to store the data for our string. Since there is no ostream function to write out a specified number of characters from a char array, we have to call ostream::operator << (char) for each character in the array.[9] After all the characters have been written to the ostream, we return it so that the next operator << call in the line can continue producing output.

However, there's a loose end here. How can a global function, which by definition isn't a member function of class string, get at the internal workings of a string? We declared that m_Length and m_Data

---

9. In case it's not obvious that we're calling ostream::operator <<(char) here, it's because s is an ostream&, which is just another name for the ostream that is the first argument to this function.

were private, so that they wouldn't be accessible to just any old function that wandered along to look at them. Is nothing sacred?

Members and Friends Only

In fact, private data aren't accessible to just any function. However, operator << (ostream&, const string&) isn't just any function. Take a look at string5.h in Figure 8.17 to see why. The line we're interested in here is this one:

```
friend ostream& operator << (ostream& s, const string& Str);
```

The key word here is friend. We're telling the compiler that a function with the signature ostream& operator << (ostream&, const string&) is permitted to access the information normally reserved for member functions of the string class; that is, anything that isn't marked public. It's possible to make an entire class a friend to another class; here, we're specifying one function that is a friend to this class.[10]

You probably won't be surprised to learn that Susan had some questions about this operator. Let's see how the discussion went:

Susan: Let's start with friend. . . what is that?

Steve: A friend is a function or class that is allowed to access internals of this class, as though the friend were a member function. In other words, the private access specifier doesn't have any effect on friends.

Susan: What is an ostream?

---

10. The signature of the function is important here, as elsewhere in C++; this friend declaration would not permit a function with the same name and a different signature, for example ostream& operator << (ostream&, int) to access non-public members of string.

Steve: An ostream is a stream that is used for output; streams can be either input (istream) or output (ostream).

Susan: This stream character seems to have a lot of relatives.

Steve: You're right; there are lots of classes in the stream family, including istream, ostream, ifstream, and ofstream. And it really is a family, in the C++ sense at least; these classes are related by *inheritance*, which we'll get to in Chapter 9.

That explains why this global function can access our non-public data. But why did we have to create a global function in the first place, rather than just adding a member function to our string class?

Because a member function of a class has to be called for an object of that class, whose address then becomes the this pointer; in the case of the << operator, the class of the object is ostream, not string. Figure 8.29 is an example.

FIGURE 8.29. **Why we need a global function for** operator <<

```
string x = "this is it";
cout << x;
```

The line cout << x; is the same as cout.operator << (x);. Notice that the object to which the operator << call is applied is cout, not x. Since cout is an ostream, not a string, we can't use a member function of string to do our output, but a global function is perfectly suitable.

Before we move on to our next topic, I think one small point in the implementation of operator << for strings could use some additional explanation: Why do we have to subtract 1than from the string length in the loop continuation expression i < Str.m_Length-1? The reason is that the stored length of the string (m_Length) includes the added null byte at the end of the string; thus, if we write out all the bytes indicated by the length, we'll include the null byte as well. This would work all right if we were writing the data out to the screen, because we can't read the data back from the screen, and the null byte doesn't take up any room on the screen. However, it would cause trouble if we wrote the data to a file and then tried to reread the data later, as we did in the StockItem class (see the discussion under the heading "Vectoring In" on page 350). Therefore, we have to be careful to avoid writing the null byte.

Of course, if we had a way to make a string that had null bytes inside it rather than just at the end, then we'd really have to deal with the problem of handling null bytes during input and output. However, in that case we would presumably have to deal with all the other ramifications of such strings, and this would be just another detail to handle. For now, it's best to avoid it in the interest of simplicity.

Reader and Advisor

Now that we have an output function that will write our string variables out to an ostream like cout, it would be very handy to have an input function that could read a string in from an istream like cin. You might expect that this would be pretty simple now that we've worked through the previous exercise, and you'd be mostly right. As usual, though, there are a few twists in the path. Let's start by looking at the code in Figure 8.30.

FIGURE 8.30. An operator >> **function to input a** string **(from code\string 5.cc)**

```
istream& operator >> (istream& s, string& Str)
{
  const short BUFLEN = 256;

  char Buf[BUFLEN];
  memset(Buf,0,BUFLEN);

  if (s.peek() == '\n')
    s.ignore();
```

```
    s.getline(Buf,BUFLEN,'\n');
    Str = Buf;

    return s;
}
```

The header is pretty similar to the one from the operator << function, which is reasonable, since they're complementary functions. In this case, we're defining a global function with the signature istream& operator >> (istream& s, string& Str). In other words, this function, called operator >>, has a first argument that is a reference to an istream, which is just like an ostream except that we read data from it rather than writing data to it. One significant difference between this function signature and the one for operator << is that the second argument is a **non**-const reference, rather than a const reference, to the string into which we want to read the data from the istream. That's because the whole purpose of this function is to modify the string passed in as the second argument; to be exact, we're going to fill it in with the characters taken out of the istream.

Continuing with the analysis of the function declaration, the return value is another istream reference, which is passed to the next operator >> function to the right, if there is one; otherwise it will just be discarded.

After decoding the header, let's move to the first line in the function body, const short BUFLEN = 256;. While we've encountered const before, specifying that we aren't going to change an argument passed to us, that can't be the meaning here. What does const mean in this context?

It specifies that the item being defined, which in this case is short BUFLEN, isn't a variable, but a constant, or const value.[11] That is, its

---

11. In case you were wondering how I came up with the name BUFLEN, it's short for "buffer length". Also, I should mention the reason that it is all caps rather than mixed case or all lower case: An old C convention (carried over into C++) specifies that named constants should be named in all caps to enable the reader to distinguish them from variables at a glance.

value can't be changed. Of course, a logical question is how we can use a const, if we can't set its value.

Initial Here

This is another of the places where it's important to differentiate between *initialization* and *assignment*. We can't assign a value to a const, but we can initialize it; in fact, because an uninitialized const is useless, the attempt to define a const without specifying its initial value is a compile-time error. In this case, we're initializing it to the value 256; if we just wrote const short BUFLEN;, we'd get an error something like the one in Figure 8.31 when we tried to compile it.

FIGURE 8.31. **Error from an uninitialized** const **(code\string5x.out)**

```
gcc -c -I. -g string5x.cc
string5x.cc: In function 'class istream & operator >>(class istream &, class string &)':
string5x.cc:84: uninitialized const 'short int BUFLEN'
```

Susan wanted some further explanation.

Susan: I still don't get why const is used here.

Steve: This is a different use of const than we've seen before; in this case, it's an instruction to the compiler meaning "the following 'variable' isn't really variable, but constant. Don't allow it to be modified." This allows us to use it where we would otherwise have to use a literal constant, like 256 itself. The reason that using a const is better than using a literal constant is that it makes it easier to change all the occurrences of that value. In the present case, for example, we use BUFLEN three times after its definition; if we used the literal constant 256 in all of those places, we'd have to change all of them if we decided to make the buffer larger or smaller. As it is, however, we only have to change the definition of

BUFLEN, and all of the places where it's used will use the new value automatically.

Susan: Okay, I think I have it now.

Now that we've disposed of that detail, let's continue with our examination of the implementation of operator >>. The next nonblank line is char Buf[BUFLEN];. This is a little different from any variable definition we've seen before; however, you might be able to guess something about it from its appearance. It seems to be defining a variable called Buf[12] whose type is related in some way to char. But what about the [BUFLEN] part?

This is a definition of a variable of that dreaded type, the *array*; specifically, we're defining an array called Buf, which contains BUFLEN chars. As you may recall, this is somewhat like the vector type that we've used before, except that it has absolutely no error checking; if we try to access a char that is past the end of the array, something will happen, but not anything good.[13] In this case, as in our previous use of pointers, we'll use this dangerous construct only in a very small part of our code, under controlled circumstances; the user of our string class won't be exposed to the array. We'll see how it's used in this function.

First, though, I should point out that C++ has a rule that the number of elements of an array must be known at compile time. That is, the program in Figure 8.32 isn't legal C++.

FIGURE 8.32. Use of a non-const array size (code\string5y.cc)

```
int main()
{
    short BUFLEN = 256;
```

---

12. This is another common C practice; using "buf" as shorthand for "buffer", or "place to store stuff while we're working on it".

13. See the discussion startung under "A Character Study" on page 494.

```
    char ch;

    char Buf[BUFLEN];

    ch = Buf[0];
}
```

I'll admit that I don't understand exactly *why* using a non-const array size is illegal; a C++ compiler has enough information to create and access an array whose length is known at run time.[14] In fact, the DJGPP compiler supplied with this book by default does accept this construct: You have to set a special *warning option* (*pedantic-errors*) to treat this as an error. I've added this option to the settings in RHIDE. Figure 8.33 shows the output that you would get if you used RHIDE to compile the program in Figure 8.32 with that setting in force.

FIGURE 8.33. Trying to compile a program with a non-const array size (code\string5y.out)

```
gcc -o string5y.o -c -I. -g string5y.cc -pedantic-errors
string5y.cc: In function 'class istream & operator >>(class istream &, class string &)':
string5y.cc:9: ANSI C++ forbids variable-size array 'Buf'
```

Although the ability to declare an array whose size isn't known until run time is sometimes very convenient and is provided by the DJGPP compiler, you should avoid it. No other compiler I'm familiar with will accept this construct; it also isn't part of the C++ standard, so when standard-conforming compilers are available, they won't accept it either.

Therefore, we'll use the const value BUFLEN to specify the number of chars in the array Buf in the statement char Buf[BUFLEN];.

---

14. According to Eric Raymond, a well-known historian of programming and the author of *The New Hacker's Dictionary*, there is no good reason for this limitation; it's a historical artifact.

Pointers and Setters

Now we're up to the first line of the executable part of the operator >> function in Figure 8.30: memset(Buf,0,BUFLEN);. This is a call to a function called memset, which is in the standard C library. You may be able to guess from its name that it is related to the function memcmp that we used to compare two arrays of chars. If so, your guess would be correct; memset is C-talk for "set all the bytes in an area of memory to the same value". The first argument is the address of the area of memory to be set to the value, the second argument is the char value to be used, and the third argument is the number of characters to be set to that value, starting at the address given in the first argument. In other words, we're setting all of the characters in the array called Buf to 0. This is important because we're going to treat that array as a C string later. As you may recall, a C string is terminated by a null byte, so we want to make sure that the array Buf doesn't contain any junk that might be misinterpreted as part of the data we're reading in from the istream.

Next, we have an if statement controlling a function called ignore:

```
if (s.peek() == '\n')
  s.ignore();
```

What exactly does this sequence do? It solves a problem with reading C string data from a file; namely, where do we stop reading? With a numeric variable, that's easy; the answer is "whenever we see a character that doesn't look like part of a number". However, with a data type that can take just about any characters as part of its value, this is more difficult. The solution I've adopted is to stop reading when we get to a newline ('\n') character; that is, an end-of-line character. This is no problem when reading from the keyboard, as long as each data item is on its own line, but what about reading from a file?

When we read a C string from a file, the newline at the end of the line is discarded, so the next C string to be read in starts at the beginning of the next line of the file, as we wish. This approach to handling newline characters works well as long as all of the variables being read in are strings. However, in the case of the StockItem class, we needed to be able to mix shorts and strings in the file. In that case, reading a value for a short stops at the newline, because that character isn't a valid part of a numeric value. This is okay as long as the next variable to be read is also a short, because spaces and newlines at the beginning of a line are ignored when we're reading a numeric value. However, when the next variable to be read is a string, the leftover newline from the previous read is interpreted as the beginning of the data for the string, which messes up everything. Therefore, we have to check whether the next available char in the input stream is a newline, in which case we have to skip it. On the other hand, if the next character to be read in is something other than a newline, we want to keep it as the first character of our string. That's what the if statement does: First, the s.peek() function call returns the next character in the input stream without removing it from the stream; then, if it turns out to be a newline, we tell the input stream to ignore it, so it won't mess up our reading of the actual data in the next line.

You won't be surprised to hear that Susan had a couple of questions about this function.

Susan: Where do peek and ignore come from?

Steve: They're defined in the iostreams header file iostream.h.

Susan: How did you know that they were available?

Steve: By reading a book called *C++ IOstreams Handbook* by Steve Teale.

Now that we've dealt with that detail, we're ready to read the data for our string. That's the job of the next line in the function: s.getline(Buf,BUFLEN,'\n');. Since s is an istream, this is a member function of istream. To be precise, it's the member function that reads a number of characters into a char array. The arguments are as follows:

1. The array into which to read characters.

2. The number of characters that the array can contain.

3. The "terminating character", where getline should stop reading characters.

This function will read characters into the array (in this case Buf) until one of two events occurs:

1. The size of the array is reached.

2. The "terminating character" is the next character to be read.

Note that the terminating character is not read into the array.

Before continuing with the rest of the code for operator >>, let's take a closer look at the following two lines, so we can see why it's a bad idea to use the C string and memory manipulation library any more than we have to. The lines in question are

```
memset(Buf,0,BUFLEN);
s.getline(Buf,BUFLEN,'\n');
```

The problem is that we have to specify the length of the array Buf explicitly (as BUFLEN, in this case). In this small function, we can keep track of that length without much effort, but in a large program with many references to Buf, it would be all too easy to make a mistake in specifying its length. As we've already seen, the result of specifying a length that is greater than the actual length of the array would be a serious error in the functioning of the program; namely, some memory belonging to some other variable would be overwritten. Whenever we use the mem functions in the C library, we're liable to run into such problems. That's an excellent reason to avoid them except in strictly controlled situations, such as the present one, where the definition of the array is in the same small function as the uses of the array. By no coincidence, this is the same problem caused by the indiscriminate use of pointers; the difficulty with the C memory manipulation functions is that they use pointers (or arrays, which are essentially interchangeable with pointers), with all of the hazards that such use entails.

Now that I've nagged you sufficiently about the dangers of arrays, let's look at the rest of the operator >> code. The next statement is Str = Buf;, which sets the argument Str to the contents of the array Buf. Buf is the address of the first char in an array of chars, so its type is char*; Str, on the other hand, is a string. Therefore, this apparently innocent assignment statement actually calls string::string(char*) to make a temporary string, and then calls string::operator=(const string&) to copy that temporary string to Str. Because Str is a reference argument, this causes the string that the caller provided on the right of the >> to be set to the value of the temporary string that was just created.

Finally, we have the statement return s;. This simply returns the same istream that we got as an argument, so that the next input operator in the same statement can continue reading from the istream where we left off. Now our strings can be read in from an input stream (such as cin) and written out to an output stream (such as cout), so our program that sorts strings can do some useful work.[15]

---

15. The implementation of operator << will also work for any other output destination, such as a file; however, our current implementation of operator >> isn't really suitable for reading a string in from an arbitrary input source. The reason is that we're counting on the input data being able to fit into the Buf array, which is 256 bytes in length. This is fine for input from the keyboard, at least under DOS, because the maximum line length in that situation is 128 characters. It will also work for our inventory file, because the lines in that file are shorter than 256 bytes. However, there's no way to limit the length of lines in any arbitrary data file we might want to read from, so this won't do as a general solution. Of course, increasing the size of the Buf array wouldn't solve the problem; no matter how large we make it, we couldn't be sure that a line from a file wouldn't be too long. The solution would be to handle long lines in sections, which we will do when we upgrade the string class further in Chapter 12.

Assuming that you've installed the software from the CD-ROM in the back of this book, you can try out this program. First, you have to compile it by changing to the code subdirectory under the main directory where you installed the software, and typing RHIDE strsort1, then using the "Make" command from the "Compile" menu. Then exit back to DOS and type strsort1 to run the program.

To run it under the debugger, make sure you are in the code subdirectory, and then type RHIDE strsort1. Again, do *not* add the ".cc" to the end of the file name. Once RHIDE has started up, you can step through the program by hitting F8, which will treat any function call as one statement, or by hitting F7, which will step into any function call. Any time you want to see the display that the user would see when running the program normally, hit ALT-F5, then ENTER to get back to the debugger.

Now that we've finished our current set of improvements to the string class, it's time to look back at what we've covered since our first review in this chapter.

Second Review

After finishing up the requirements to make the string class a concrete data type, we continued to add more facilities to the string class; to be precise, we wanted to make it possible to modify the sorting program of Chapter 4 to handle strings rather than shorts. To do this, we had to be able to compare two strings to determine which of the two would come first in the dictionary and to read strings from an input stream (like cin) and write them to an output stream (like cout). Although the Display function provided a primitive mechanism for writing a string to cout, it's much nicer to be able to use the standard >> and << operators that can handle all of the native types, so we resolved to make those available for strings as well.

We started out by implementing the < operator so that we could compare two strings x and y to see which would come before the other in the dictionary, simply by writing if (x < y). The implementation of this function turned out to be a bit complicated because of the possibility of "running off the end" of one of the strings, when the strings are of different lengths.

Once we worked out the appropriate handling for this situation, we examined two implementations of the algorithm for operator <. The first compared characters from the two strings one at a time, while the second used memcmp, a C function that compares two sets of bytes and returns a different value depending on whether the first one is "less than", "equal to", or "greater than" the second one, using dictionary ordering to make this determination.

Then we developed an implementation of operator == for strings, which turned out to be considerably simpler than the second version of operator <, even though both functions used memcmp to do most of the work; the reason is that we have to compare the contents of the strings only if they are of the same length, because strings of different lengths cannot be equal.

Then we started looking beneath the covers of the output functions <<, starting with the predefined versions of << that handle char and C string arguments. The simplest case of using this operator, of course, is to display one expression on the screen via cout. Next, we examined the mechanism by which several uses of this operator can be chained together to allow the displaying of a number of expressions with one statement.

The next question was: How could we provide these handy facilities for the users of our string class? Would we have to modify the ostream classes to add support for strings? Luckily, the designers of the stream classes were foresightful enough to enable us to add support for our own data types without having to modify their code. The key is to create a *global* function that can add the contents of our string to an existing ostream variable and pass that ostream variable on to the next possible user, just as in the chaining mentioned previously for native types.

The implementation of this function wasn't terribly complicated; it merely wrote each char of the string's data to the output stream. The unusual part of this function was that it wasn't a member function of string, but a global function, as is needed to maintain the same syntax as the output of native types. We used the friend specifier to allow this version of operator << access to private members of string such as m_Length and m_Data.

After we finished the examination of our version of operator << for sending strings to an ostream, we went through the parallel exercise of creating a version of operator >> to read strings from an istream. This turned out to be a bit more complicated, since we had to make room for the incoming data, which limited the maximum length of string that we could read in. In the process of defining this maximum length, we also encountered a new construct, the const value. This is a data item that is declared just like a variable, except that its value is initialized once and cannot be changed, which makes it ideal for specifying a constant size for an array, a constant loop limit, or other value that doesn't change from one execution of the program to the next. Next, we used this const value to declare an *array* of chars to hold the input data to be stored in the string, and filled the array with null bytes, by calling the C function memset. We followed this by using some member functions of the istream class to eliminate any newline ('\n') character that might have been left over from a previous input operation.

Finally, we were ready to read the data into the array of chars, in preparation for assigning it to our string. After doing that assignment, we returned the original istream to the caller, to allow chaining of operations as is standard with operator << and operator >>.

That completes the review of this chapter. Now let's do some exercises to help it all sink in.

Exercises

1. What would happen if we compiled the program in Figure 8.34? Why?

FIGURE 8.34. Exercise 1 (code\strex5.cc)

```
class string
{
public:
    string(const string& Str);
    string(char* p);
    string& operator = (const string& Str);
    ~string();
private:
    string();
    short m_Length;
    char* m_Data;
};

int main()
{
    string n("Test");
    string x = n;

    n = "My name is: ";

    return 0;
}
```

2. What would happen if we compiled the program in Figure 8.35? Why?

FIGURE 8.35. Exercise 2 (code\strex6.cc)

```
class string
{
public:
    string();
    string& operator = (const string& Str);
private:
    string(char* p);
    short m_Length;
```

```
      char* m_Data;
};

int main()
{
    string n;

    n = "My name is: ";

    return 0;
}
```

3. We have already implemented operator < and operator ==. However, a concrete data type that allows for ordered comparisons such as < should really implement all six of the comparison operators. The other four of these operators are >, >=, <=, and != ("greater than", "greater than or equal to", "less than or equal to", and "not equal to", respectively). Add the declarations of each of these operators to the string interface definition.

4. Implement the four comparison operators that you declared in the previous exercise.

5. Write a test program to verify that all of the comparison operators work. This program should test that each of the operators returns the value true when its condition is true; equally important, it should test that each of the operators returns the value false when the condition is *not* true.

Conclusion

In this chapter, we have significantly improved the string class, learning some generally useful techniques and lessons in the process. In the next chapter, we'll return to our inventory control example, which we'll extend with some techniques that we haven't seen before. First, though you should finish doing the exercises.[16]

Answers to Exercises

1. This one was a little tricky. I'll bet you thought that making the default constructor private would keep this from compiling, but it turns out that we're not using the default constructor. That should be obvious in the line string n("Test");, which clearly uses string::string(char* p), but what does the compiler do with the line string x = n;? You might think that it calls the default constructor to make x and then uses operator = to copy the value of n into it. If that were true, the private status of the default constructor would prevent the program from compiling. However, what actually happens is that the copy constructor string::string(const string&) is used to make a brand new string called x with the same value as n. So, in this case, the private access specifier on the default constructor doesn't get in the way.

2. The output of the compiler should look something like this:

    ```
    strex6.cc: In function 'int main()':
    strex6.cc:9: constructor 'string::string(char *)' is private
    strex6.cc:21: within this context
    strex6.cc:6: in passing argument 1 of 'string::operator =(const string &)'
    ```

    This one is a bit tricky. The actual problem is that making the constructor string::string(char*) private prevents the automatic conversion from char* to string required for the string::operator = (const string&) assignment operator to work. As long as there is an accessible string::string(char*) constructor, the compiler will use that constructor to build a temporary string from a char* argument on the right side of an =. This temporary string will then be used by string::operator = (const string&) as the source of data to modify the

---

16. You have been doing the exercises, haven't you? If not, you should definitely go back and do them. If you can get all of the answers right, including the reasons *why* the answers are the way they are, then you'll be ready to continue learning some of the more advanced concepts of C++ in the rest of this book.

string on the left of the =. However, this is not possible if the constructor that makes a string from a char* isn't accessible where it is needed.[17]

3. The new class interface is shown in Figure 8.36.

FIGURE 8.36. The string class **interface file (from code\string6.h)**

```
class string
{
friend ostream& operator << (ostream& s, const string& Str);
friend istream& operator >> (istream& s, string& Str);

public:
  string();
  string(const string& Str);
  string& operator = (const string& Str);
  ~string();
  string(char* p);
  short GetLength();
  bool operator < (const string& Str);
  bool operator == (const string& Str);
  bool operator > (const string& Str);
  bool operator >= (const string& Str);
  bool operator <= (const string& Str);
  bool operator != (const string& Str);

private:
  short m_Length;
  char* m_Data;
};
```

---

17. By the way, in case you're wondering what char * means, it's the same as char*. As I've mentioned previously, I prefer the latter as being easier to understand, but they mean the same to the compiler.

4. The implementations of the comparison operators are shown in Figure 8.37 through Figure 8.40.

FIGURE 8.37. The string class **implementation of** operator >

```cpp
bool string::operator > (const string& Str)
{
  short Result;
  short CompareLength;

  if (Str.m_Length < m_Length)
    CompareLength = Str.m_Length;
  else
    CompareLength = m_Length;

  Result = memcmp(m_Data,Str.m_Data,CompareLength);

  if (Result > 0)
    return true;

  if (Result < 0)
    return false;

  if (m_Length > Str.m_Length)
    return true;

  return false;
}
```

FIGURE 8.38. The string class **implementation of** operator >=

```cpp
bool string::operator >= (const string& Str)
{
  short Result;
  short CompareLength;

  if (Str.m_Length < m_Length)
    CompareLength = Str.m_Length;
```

```
  else
    CompareLength = m_Length;

  Result = memcmp(m_Data,Str.m_Data,CompareLength);

  if (Result > 0)
    return true;

  if (Result < 0)
    return false;

  if (m_Length >= Str.m_Length)
    return true;

  return false;
}
```

FIGURE 8.39. **The** string class **implementation of** operator != **(from code\string6.cc)**

```
bool string::operator != (const string& Str)
{
  short Result;

  if (m_Length != Str.m_Length)
    return true;

  Result = memcmp(m_Data,Str.m_Data,m_Length);

  if (Result == 0)
    return false;

  return true;
}
```

FIGURE 8.40. **The** string class **implementation of** operator <= **(from code\string6.cc)**

```
bool string::operator <= (const string& Str)
{
  short Result;
  short CompareLength;

  if (Str.m_Length < m_Length)
    CompareLength = Str.m_Length;
  else
    CompareLength = m_Length;

  Result = memcmp(m_Data,Str.m_Data,CompareLength);

  if (Result < 0)
    return true;

  if (Result > 0)
    return false;

  if (m_Length <= Str.m_Length)
    return true;

  return false;
}
```

5. The test program appears in Figure 8.41.

FIGURE 8.41. **The test program for the comparison operators of the** string class **(code\strcmp.cc)**

```
#include <iostream.h>
#include "string6.h"

int main()
{
  string x = "x";
```

```
    string xx = "xx";
    string y = "y";
    string yy = "yy";

// testing <
  if (x < x)
     cout << "ERROR: x < x" << endl;
  else
     cout << "OKAY: x NOT < x" << endl;
  if (x < xx)
     cout << "OKAY: x < xx" << endl;
  else
     cout << "ERROR: x NOT < xx" << endl;
  if (x < y)
     cout << "OKAY: x < y" << endl;
  else
     cout << "ERROR: x NOT < y" << endl;

// testing <=
  if (x <= x)
     cout << "OKAY: x <= x" << endl;
  else
     cout << "ERROR: x NOT <= x" << endl;
  if (x <= xx)
     cout << "OKAY: x <= xx" << endl;
  else
     cout << "ERROR: x NOT <= xx" << endl;
  if (x <= y)
     cout << "OKAY: x <= y" << endl;
  else
     cout << "ERROR: x NOT <= y" << endl;

// testing >
  if (y > y)
     cout << "ERROR: y > y" << endl;
  else
     cout << "OKAY: y NOT > y" << endl;
  if (yy > y)
     cout << "OKAY: yy > y" << endl;
```

```
      else
         cout << "ERROR: yy NOT > y" << endl;
      if (y > x)
         cout << "OKAY: y > x" << endl;
      else
         cout << "ERROR: y NOT > x" << endl;

   // testing >=
      if (y >= y)
         cout << "OKAY: y >= y" << endl;
      else
         cout << "ERROR: y NOT >= y" << endl;
      if (yy >= y)
         cout << "OKAY: yy >= y" << endl;
      else
         cout << "ERROR: yy NOT >= y" << endl;
      if (y >= x)
         cout << "OKAY: y >= x" << endl;
      else
         cout << "ERROR: y NOT >= x" << endl;

   // testing ==
      if (x == x)
         cout << "OKAY: x == x" << endl;
      else
         cout << "ERROR: x NOT == x" << endl;
      if (x == xx)
         cout << "ERROR: x == xx" << endl;
      else
         cout << "OKAY: x NOT == xx" << endl;
      if (x == y)
         cout << "ERROR: x == y" << endl;
      else
         cout << "OKAY: x NOT == y" << endl;

   // testing !=
      if (x != x)
         cout << "ERROR: x != x" << endl;
      else
```

```
        cout << "OKAY: x NOT != x" << endl;
if (x != xx)
    cout << "OKAY: x != xx" << endl;
else
    cout << "ERROR: x NOT != xx" << endl;
if (x != y)
    cout << "OKAY: x != y" << endl;
else
    cout << "ERROR: x NOT != y" << endl;

return 0;
}
```

CHAPTER 9

Stocking Up

We're going to continue our investigation of C++ concepts and practices by revisiting the inventory control example from Chapter 6. We'll build on the StockItem class that we created there by using one of the primary organizing principles of C++ that we haven't encountered before: **inheritance**. First, let's define this term and a few others that we'll be using in this chapter; then we'll take a look at the objectives.

Definitions

Inheritance is the definition of one class as a more specific version of another class that has been previously defined. The newly defined class is called the *derived* (or sometimes *child*) class, and the previously defined class is called the *base* (or sometimes *parent*) class. In this book, we will use the terms *base* and *derived*. The derived class inherits all of the member variables and *regular member functions* from the base class. Inheritance is one of the primary organizing principles of object-oriented programming.

A **regular member function** is a member function that is *not* in any of the following categories:

1. constructor,

2. destructor,

3. assignment operator (i.e., operator =).

A member function in a derived class is said to **override** a base class member function if the derived class function has the same *signature* (name and argument types) as that of the base class member function. The derived class member function will be called instead of the base class member function when the member function is referred to via an object of the derived class. A member function in a derived class with the same name but a different signature from that of a member function in the base class does *not* override the base class member function. Instead, it "hides" that base class member function, which is no longer accessible as a member function in the derived class.

For example, the function Reorder(ostream &) may be defined in a base class (StockItem) and in a derived class (DatedStockItem). When Reorder is called via an object of the base class StockItem, the base class version of Reorder will be called; when Reorder is called via an object of the derived class DatedStockItem, the derived class version of Reorder will be called. This behavior of C++ allows a derived class to supply the same functionality as a base class but implement that functionality in a different way.

A **manipulator** is a special type of member function of one of the iostreams classes. Such a function controls how output will be formatted without itself necessarily producing any output.

A **static member function** is a member function of a class that can be called without reference to an object of that class. Such a function has no this pointer passed to it on entry, and therefore it cannot refer to member variables of the class.

Buffering is the use of a *buffer* to store or retrieve information.

A **normal constructor** is a constructor whose arguments supply enough information to initialize all of the member fields in the object being created.

Objectives of This Chapter

By the end of this chapter, you should

1. understand how we can use inheritance to create a new class by extending an existing class, and

2. understand how to use manipulators to control the format of iostreams output.

Under Control

Before we return to the detailed examination of our inventory control classes, StockItem and its companion class Inventory, let's expand a bit on the first objective as it applies to this case.

There are two reasons to use inheritance. The first is to create a new class that has all of the capabilities of an existing class while adding capabilities that are unique to the new class. In such a case, objects of the new class are clearly not equivalent to objects of the existing class, which means that the user[1] of these classes has to know which class any given object belongs to so that he or she can tell which operations that object can perform. In such a case, it does not make sense to be able to substitute objects of the derived class for objects of the base class. We could call this use of inheritance "inheritance for extension". It's illustrated by one of the Employee class exercises in this chapter.

In the current case, however, we'll be using inheritance to create a new class called DatedStockItem that will be exactly like the StockItem class except that its items will have expiration dates. As a result, the user of these classes will be able to treat objects of the new DatedStockItem class in the same way as those of the base class. Of course, to create an object of this new class, the expiration date for the object must be provided, but once such an object exists, its user can view it exactly as if it were an object of the base class, which makes this an example of "inheritance for reimplementation". In such a case, it is reasonable to be able to substitute objects of the derived class for those of the base class, and we will see how to do that in the next chapter.

Before we can do that, though, we'll need to learn how to create a new class by derivation from an existing class. In this case, we're going to start with a version of our previous StockItem class that has been extended slightly to include a Reorder function that generates a reordering report when we get low on an item, as well as some new input and output facilities. We'll also need to improve on our companion Inventory class, which, as before, we'll use to keep track of all the StockItems in the store.

Now let's get to the details of how this version of the StockItem class works. Figure 9.1 shows the header file for that class.

Here's a rundown on the various member functions of the StockItem class, including those that we've already seen:

1. StockItem(); is the default constructor.

---

1. As elsewhere in this book, when I speak of the "user" of a class, I mean the application programmer, who is using objects of the class to perform work in his or her program, not the "end user", who is using the finished program.

2. StockItem(string Name, written short InStock, short Price, short MinimumStock, short MinimumReorder, string Distributor, string UPC); is the normal constructor, which has a couple of new arguments, MinimumStock and MinimumReorder, that are needed for the reordering function.

3. void FormattedDisplay(ostream& os); displays the member variables of a StockItem object with labels so that you can tell which value is for which member variable.

4. bool CheckUPC(string ItemUPC); returns true if its argument is the same as the UPC (i.e., the m_UPC member variable) of its StockItem.

5. void DeductSaleFromInventory(short QuantitySold); reduces the inventory (i.e., the value of the m_InStock member variable) by the value of its argument.

6. short GetInventory(); returns the number of items in stock for this StockItem (i.e., the value of the m_InStock member variable).

7. string GetName(); returns the name of the StockItem (i.e., the value of the m_Name member variable).

8. string GetUPC(); returns the UPC of the StockItem (i.e., the value of the m_UPC member variable).

9. bool IsNull(); returns true if this is a "null StockItem". This can happen, for example, when a StockItem is returned as a "not found" value by a search.

10. short GetPrice(); returns the price of the StockItem (i.e., the value of the m_Price member variable).

11. void Reorder(ostream& os); generates a reorder report based on the relationship of the number in stock (m_InStock) versus the minimum desired stock (m_MinimumStock), taking the minimum reorder quantity (m_MinimumReorder) into account.

FIGURE 9.1. The next StockItem **header file (code\item20.h)**

```
class StockItem
{
friend ostream& operator << (ostream& os,
  const StockItem& Item);

friend istream& operator >> (istream& is, StockItem& Item);

public:
  StockItem();

  StockItem(string Name, short InStock,
  short Price, short MinimumStock,
  short MinimumReorder, string Distributor, string UPC);

  void FormattedDisplay(ostream& os);
  bool CheckUPC(string ItemUPC);
  void DeductSaleFromInventory(short QuantitySold);
  short GetInventory();
  string GetName();
  string GetUPC();
  bool IsNull();
  short GetPrice();

  void Reorder(ostream& os);

private:
  short m_InStock;
  short m_Price;
  short m_MinimumStock;
  short m_MinimumReorder;
  string m_Name;
  string m_Distributor;
  string m_UPC;
};
```

Here's a brief description of the input/output operators for this class, which will allow us to read and write its objects in much the same way as we can with the built-in types and the string class we've created earlier in the book:

1. friend ostream& operator << (ostream& os, const StockItem& Item); sends a human-readable version of the state of a StockItem object to the ostream specified as the left-hand argument to <<. This is analogous to the use of operator << for output of the built-in types.

2. friend istream& operator >> (istream& is, StockItem& Item); creates a StockItem object by reading a human-readable version of the state of the object from the istream specified as the left-hand argument to >>. This is analogous to the use of operator >> for input of the built-in types.

Susan wanted to know why we needed the FormattedDisplay function.

> **Susan:** Do we need the FormattedDisplay to make the data appear on the screen the way we want it? I mean, does the FormattedDisplay function do something that we can't do by just using operator <<?

> **Steve:** Yes. It puts labels on the data members so that you can tell what they are.

Figure 9.2 shows the implementation of the StockItem class that we will start our inheritance exercise from.

FIGURE 9.2. The next implementation of StockItem (code\item20.cc)

```
#include <iostream.h>
#include <string.h>
#include "string6.h"
#include "item20.h"

StockItem::StockItem()
```

```
          : m_InStock(0), m_Price(0), m_MinimumStock(0),
            m_MinimumReorder(0), m_Name(), m_Distributor(),
            m_UPC()
          {
          }

          StockItem::StockItem(string Name, short InStock,
          short Price, short MinimumStock,
          short MinimumReorder, string Distributor, string UPC)
          : m_InStock(InStock), m_Price(Price),
            m_MinimumStock(MinimumStock),
            m_MinimumReorder(MinimumReorder), m_Name(Name),
            m_Distributor(Distributor), m_UPC(UPC)
          {
          }

          void StockItem::FormattedDisplay(ostream& os)
          {
           os << "Name: ";
           os << m_Name << endl;
           os << "Number in stock: ";
           os << m_InStock << endl;
           os << "Price: ";
           os << m_Price << endl;
           os << "Minimum stock: ";
           os << m_MinimumStock << endl;
           os << "Minimum Reorder quantity: ";
           os << m_MinimumReorder << endl;
           os << "Distributor: ";
           os << m_Distributor << endl;
           os << "UPC: ";
           os << m_UPC << endl;
          }

          ostream& operator << (ostream& os, const StockItem& Item)
          {
           os << Item.m_Name << endl;
           os << Item.m_InStock << endl;
           os << Item.m_Price << endl;
```

```cpp
  os << Item.m_MinimumStock << endl;
  os << Item.m_MinimumReorder << endl;
  os << Item.m_Distributor << endl;
  os << Item.m_UPC << endl;

  return os;
}

istream& operator >> (istream& is, StockItem& Item)
{
  is >> Item.m_Name;
  is >> Item.m_InStock;
  is >> Item.m_Price;
  is >> Item.m_MinimumStock;
  is >> Item.m_MinimumReorder;
  is >> Item.m_Distributor;
  is >> Item.m_UPC;

  return is;
}

bool StockItem::CheckUPC(string ItemUPC)
{
  if (m_UPC == ItemUPC)
    return true;

  return false;
}

void StockItem::DeductSaleFromInventory(short QuantitySold)
{
  m_InStock -= QuantitySold;
}

short StockItem::GetInventory()
{
  return m_InStock;
}
```

```
string StockItem::GetName()
{
  return m_Name;
}

string StockItem::GetUPC()
{
  return m_UPC;
}

bool StockItem::IsNull()
{
  if (m_UPC == "")
    return true;

  return false;
}

short StockItem::GetPrice()
{
  return m_Price;
}

void StockItem::Reorder(ostream& os)
{
  short ActualReorderQuantity;

  if (m_InStock < m_MinimumStock)
    {
    ActualReorderQuantity = m_MinimumStock - m_InStock;
    if (m_MinimumReorder > ActualReorderQuantity)
      ActualReorderQuantity = m_MinimumReorder;
    os << "Reorder " << ActualReorderQuantity;
    os <<  " units of " << m_Name;
    os << " with UPC " << m_UPC;
    os << " from " << m_Distributor << endl;
    }
}
```

Susan had a lot of questions about the operator << and operator >> functions for this class as well as about streams in general.

Susan: Why do you have to define these functions again?

Steve: They have to be defined for every class of objects we want to be able to use them for. After all, every class of objects has different data items in it; how is a stream supposed to know how to read or write some object that we've made up, unless we tell it how to?

Susan: What's "is" again? I forgot.

Steve: The istream that we're using to get the data for the StockItem.

Susan: So, it's just a file? Is it always called is?

Steve: No, it's not a file; it's an istream, which is an object connected to a file that allows us to read from the file using >>.

Susan: Do you mean any file that has >> or <<? If it is like an istream where does the data end up? Just how does it work? When does the istream, start flowing and at what point does the data jump in and get out? What is the istream doing when there is no data to be transported? Where is it flowing? If it is not a file, then where is it stored? So, whenever you read something from an istream, is it always called "is"?

Steve: Obviously streams are going to take a lot more explaining, with pictures. We'll get to it later in this chapter.[2]

---

2. See "stream of Consciousness" on page 621.

Taking Inventory

The StockItem class is designed to keep track of an individual item in the inventory, but we also need a way to keep track of all the StockItems in the store. So let's take a look at the next version of the class that serves that purpose in the inventory control application, Inventory. Figure 9.3 shows the header file for this version of that class, which is essentially identical to the last one from Chapter 6, except that we have added a ReorderItems function to allow us to generate a reorder report for all of the items in stock.

FIGURE 9.3. The next header file for the Inventory class (**code\invent20.h**)

```
class Inventory
{
public:
    Inventory();

    short LoadInventory(istream& is);

    void StoreInventory(ostream& os);

    StockItem FindItem(string UPC);
    bool UpdateItem(StockItem Item);
    void ReorderItems(ostream& os);

private:
    vector<StockItem> m_Stock;
    short m_StockCount;
};
```

Besides the default constructor, this class has several other member functions that we should discuss briefly, including those that we have already discussed in Chapter 6.

1. LoadInventory reads data from an istream to create StockItem objects for the inventory.

2. StoreInventory writes the current StockItem data out to an ostream to save it for posterity.

3. FindItem locates an item in the inventory by its UPC.

4. UpdateItem updates the data for an item in the inventory.

5. ReorderItems calls each item in the inventory and asks it to generate a line for the reordering report, which tells the user how many of each item need to be reordered from the distributor.

Susan had some questions about the arguments to LoadInventory and StoreInventory:

Susan: What are is and os? Why didn't you talk about them?

Steve: They're just the names of the reference arguments of type istream and ostream, respectively, as indicated in the header file.

Claiming an Inheritance

Now let's examine the details of the part of this inventory control program that calculates how much of each item has to be ordered to refill the stock. As I mentioned previously, I've chosen the imaginative name ReorderItems for the member function in the Inventory class that will perform this operation. The ReorderItems function is pretty simple. Its behavior can be described as follows:

'For each element in the StockItem vector in the Inventory object, call its member function Reorder to generate an order if that StockItem object needs to be reordered.'

Of course, this algorithm is much simpler than what we would need in the real world; however, it's realistic enough to be useful in illustrating important issues in program design and implementation, which is how we will use it.

Figure 9.4 shows the version of the inventory test program that uses the versions of those classes that we will use as the starting point for our inheritance exercise.

FIGURE 9.4. The StockItem **test program for the base** StockItem **class (code\itmtst20.cc)**

```
#include <iostream.h>
#include <fstream.h>
#include "vector.h"
#include "string6.h"
#include "item20.h"
#include "invent20.h"

int main()
{
  ifstream ShopInfo("shop20.in");
  ofstream ReorderInfo("shop20.reo");

  Inventory MyInventory;

  MyInventory.LoadInventory(ShopInfo);

  MyInventory.ReorderItems(ReorderInfo);

  return 0;
}
```

This shouldn't be too hard to follow. We start by creating an ifstream (i.e., an input stream that can be connected to a file) and an ofstream (i.e., an output stream that can be connected to a file). Then we create an inventory object called MyInventory, load items into it from the ifstream, and call the ReorderItems function to create the reorder report, which is written to the ofstream. Finally, we return 0 to indicate successful completion. If you want to see how this program runs, you can compile and step through it using RHIDE. To do this, change to the \shcppg\code directory and type RHIDE itmtst20. When

RHIDE starts up, hit F9 to compile the program; then you can use F8 to step through each line of itmtst20. If you want to see how any particular line works, you can use F7 to step into the code that executes that line. When the program terminates, you can look at its output file, shop20.reo, to see what the reorder report looks like.

Now let's take a look at how the Inventory class does its work (Figure 9.5).

FIGURE 9.5. **The implementation of the** Inventory class **(code\invent20.cc)**

```
#include <iostream.h>
#include <fstream.h>
#include "vector.h"
#include "string6.h"
#include "item20.h"
#include "invent20.h"

Inventory::Inventory()
: m_Stock (vector<StockItem>(100)),
  m_StockCount(0)
{
}

short Inventory::LoadInventory(istream& is)
{
  short i;

  for (i = 0; i < 100; i ++)
    {
    is >> m_Stock[i];
    if (is.fail())
      break;
    }

  m_StockCount = i;
  return m_StockCount;
}
```

```
StockItem Inventory::FindItem(string UPC)
{
  short i;
  bool Found = false;

  for (i = 0; i < m_StockCount; i ++)
    {
    if (m_Stock[i].GetUPC() == UPC)
      {
      Found = true;
      break;
      }
    }

  if (Found == true)
    return m_Stock[i];

  return StockItem();
}

bool Inventory::UpdateItem(StockItem Item)
{
  string UPC = Item.GetUPC();

  short i;
  bool Found = false;

  for (i = 0; i < m_StockCount; i ++)
    {
    if (m_Stock[i].GetUPC() == UPC)
      {
      Found = true;
      break;
      }
    }

  if (Found == true)
    m_Stock[i] = Item;
```

```
    return Found;

  }

  void Inventory::StoreInventory(ostream& os)
  {
    short i;

    for (i = 0; i < m_StockCount; i ++)
      os << m_Stock[i];
  }

  void Inventory::ReorderItems(ostream& os)
  {
    short i;

    for (i = 0; i < m_StockCount; i ++)
      m_Stock[i].Reorder(os);
  }
```

The ReorderItems function can hardly be much simpler: as you can see, it merely tells each StockItem element in the m_Stock vector to execute its Reorder function. Now let's see what that function, whose full name is void StockItem::Reorder(ostream&), needs to do:

1. Check to see if the current stock of that item is less than the desired minimum.

2. If we are below the desired stock minimum, order the amount needed to bring us back to the stock minimum, unless that order amount is less than the minimum allowable quantity from the distributor. In the latter case, order the minimum allowable reorder quantity.

3. If we are not below the desired stock minimum, do nothing.

To support this Reorder function, StockItem uses the data items m_MinimumStock and m_MinimumReorder to calculate the number of units of the current StockItem object that have to be reordered. Figure 9.6 shows the code for the Reorder function.

FIGURE 9.6. The Reorder **function for the** StockItem class **(from code\item20.cc)**

```
void StockItem::Reorder(ostream& os)
{
  short ActualReorderQuantity;

  if (m_InStock < m_MinimumStock)
    {
    ActualReorderQuantity = m_MinimumStock - m_InStock;
    if (m_MinimumReorder > ActualReorderQuantity)
      ActualReorderQuantity = m_MinimumReorder;
    os << "Reorder " << ActualReorderQuantity;
    os << " units of " << m_Name;
    os << " with UPC " << m_UPC;
    os << " from " << m_Distributor << endl;
    }
}
```

Here's the translation of this code:

1. If the number of units in stock is less than the minimum number desired, we calculate the number needed to bring the inventory back to the minimum.

2. However, the number we want to order may be less than the minimum we are allowed to order; the latter quantity is specified by the variable m_MinimumReorder.

3. If the value of m_MinimumReorder is more than we actually needed, we have to substitute the minimum quantity for that previously calculated number.

4. Finally, we display the order for the item. Of course, if we already have enough units in stock, we don't have to reorder anything, so we don't display anything.

Susan had a question about the implementation of this function:

Susan: So, are you ordering more than needed in some cases?

Steve: Yes, if that's the minimum number that can be ordered.

She also had a question about the type of the argument that the test program supplies to ReorderItems:

Susan: In the test program, ReorderInfo, which is an ofstream, is passed as an argument to the ReorderItems member function in the Inventory class. But the ReorderItems(ostream&) function in the Inventory class expects a reference to an ostream as an argument. I understand the code of both functions, but I don't see how you can pass an ofstream as an ostream. As far as I know, we use fstreams to write to and read from files and istream and ostream to read from the keyboard and write to the screen. So, can you mix these when you pass them on as arguments?

Steve: Yes. As we'll see later, this is legal because of the relationship between the ofstream and ostream classes.[3]

A Dated Approach

Now we want to add one wrinkle to this algorithm: handling items that have expiration dates. This actually applies to a fair number of items in a typical grocery store, including dairy products, meats, and even dry cereals. To keep things as simple as possible, we'll assume

---

3. See the discussion under the heading "class Interests" on page 614.

that whenever we buy a batch of some item with an expiration date, all of the items of that type have the same date. When we get to the expiration date of a given StockItem, we send back all of the items and reorder as though we had no items in stock.

The first question to answer is how to store the expiration date. My first inclination was to use a short to store each date as a number representing the number of days from (for example) January 1, 1990, to the date in question. Since there are approximately 365.25 days in a year, the range of minus 32768 to 32767 days should hold us roughly until the year 2080, which should be good enough for our purposes. Perhaps by that year, we'll all be eating food pills that don't spoil.

However, storing a date as a number of days since a "base date" such as January 1, 1990, does require a means of translating a human-readable date format like "September 4, 1995" into a number of days from the base date, and vice versa. Owing to the peculiarities of our Gregorian calendar (primarily the different numbers of days in different months and the complication of leap years), this is not a trivial matter and is a distraction from our goal here.

However, if we represent a date as a string of the form YYYYMMDD, where YYYY is the year, MM is the month, and DD is the day within the month, we can use the string comparison functions to tell us which of two dates is later than the other one.[4] Here's the analysis:

1. Of two dates with different year numbers, whichever has the higher year number is the later date.

2. Of two dates with the same year number but different month numbers, whichever has the higher month number is the later date.

---

4. In case you're wondering why I allocated 4 digits for the year, it was to ensure that the program will work both before and after 1999. Unfortunately, not all programmers have been so considerate. Many programs use a 2-digit number to represent the year portion of a date in the form YYMMDD and, as a result, have behaved oddly during the transition from 1999 to 2000.

3. Of two dates having the same year and month numbers, whichever has the higher day number is the later date.

Because the string comparison operators compare bytes from left to right and stop when a mismatch is detected, as is needed for alphabetical sorting, it should be clear that dates using the representation YYYYMMDD will have their year numbers compared first, followed by the month numbers if needed, followed by the day numbers if needed. Thus, comparing two strings via string::operator > will produce the result true if the "date string" on the left represents a date later than the "date string" on the right, exactly as we would wish.

Now that we've figured out that we can store the expiration date as a string, how do we arrange for it to be included in the StockItem object? One obvious solution is to make up a new class called, say, DatedStockItem by copying the interface and implementation from StockItem, adding a new member variable m_Expires, and modifying the copied Reorder member function to take the expiration date into account. However, doing this would create a maintenance problem when we had to make a change that would affect both of these classes, as we'd have to make such a change in two places. Just multiply this nuisance ten or twenty times, and you'll get a pretty good idea of how program maintenance has acquired its reputation as difficult and tedious work.

Susan had some questions about this notion of program maintenance:

> **Susan:** What kind of change would you want to make? What is maintenance? What is a typical thing you would want to do to some code?

> **Steve:** For our purposes here, maintenance includes any kind of change to a program.[5] For example, if we decide that a short isn't the right type of variable to hold the price, then we have to change its definition to some other type.

Since one of the purposes of object-oriented programming is to reduce the difficulty of maintaining programs, surely there must be a better way to create a new class "just like" StockItem but with an added member variable and a modified member function to use it.

Ancestor Worship

Yes, there is; it's called *inheritance*. We can define our new class called DatedStockItem with a notation that it inherits (or derives) from StockItem. This makes StockItem the *base* class (sometimes referred to as the *parent* class) and our new DatedStockItem class the *derived* class (sometimes referred to as the *child* class). By doing this, we are specifying that a DatedStockItem includes every data member and regular member function that a StockItem has. Since DatedStockItem is a separate class from StockItem, when we define DatedStockItem, we can also add whatever other functions and data we need to handle the differences between StockItem and DatedStockItem.

Susan wanted to clarify some terms:

Susan: Are inheritance and derivation the same thing?

Steve: Yes. To say that B inherits from A is the same as saying that B is derived from A.

She also had some questions about the relationship between the notions of friend and inheritance.

Susan: How about a little reminder about friend here, and how about explaining the difference between friend and inheritance, other than inheritance being an entirely different class. They kinda do the same thing.

---

5. In other contexts, people use "maintenance" to mean fixing bugs rather than adding new features, but that distinction is irrelevant here; all we care about is that the program is being changed.

Steve: Sure. When, in a class definition, you make a function or class a friend of the one you're defining, the friend function or class has access to all members of the class you are defining, disregarding their access specifiers; however, the friend has no other relationship to the class being defined. That is, making class B a friend to class A does *not* make a B object a substitute for an A object.

On the other hand, if B is (publicly) derived from A, then a B object can be used wherever an A object can be used.

I think a picture might help here. Let's start with a simplified version of the StockItem and DatedStockItem classes, whose interface is shown in Figure 9.7. I recommend that you print out the file that contains these interfaces (code\itema.h) for reference as you go through this section of the chapter.

FIGURE 9.7. Simplified interface for StockItem **and** DatedStockItem **classes (code\itema.h)**

```cpp
#include "string6.h"

class StockItem
{
public:
  StockItem(string Name, short InStock,
    short MinimumStock);

  void Reorder(ostream& s);

protected:
  string m_Name;
  short m_InStock;
  short m_MinimumStock;
};

class DatedStockItem: public StockItem // deriving a new class
{
```

```
public:
  DatedStockItem(string Name, short InStock, short MinimumStock,
  string Expires);

  void Reorder(ostream& s);

protected:
  static string Today();

protected:
  string m_Expires;
};
```

Given these definitions, a StockItem object might look as depicted in Figure 9.8.[6]

FIGURE 9.8. A simplified StockItem object

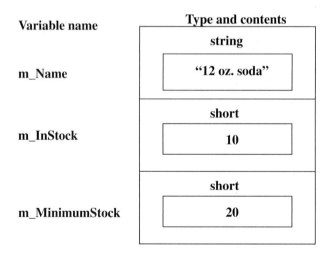

6.   I'm simplifying by leaving out the internal structure of a string, which affects
     the actual layout of the object; this detail isn't relevant here.

588   *Learning to Program in C++*

And a DatedStockItem object might look as depicted in Figure 9.9.

FIGURE 9.9. A DatedStockItem **object**

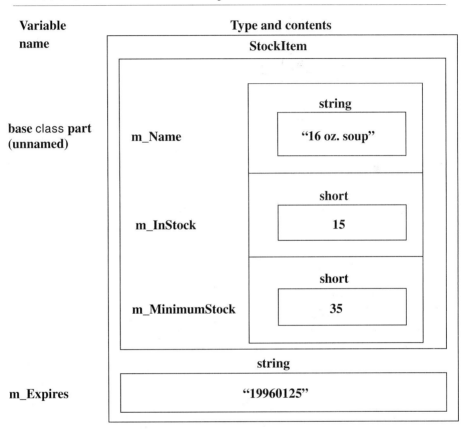

As you can see, an object of the new DatedStockItem class contains a StockItem as part of its data. In this case, that *base class part* accounts for most of the data of a DatedStockItem; all we've added is a data member called m_Expires. In fact, a derived class object always contains all of the variables and "regular" member functions in the base class because the derived class object effectively has an object of the base class embedded in it, as indicated in Figure 9.9. We can access those member variables and functions that are part of the base class part of our derived class object exactly as though they were defined in the derived class, so long as their access specifiers are either public or protected. Although the public and private access specifiers have been part of our arsenal of tools for some time, this is our first encounter with the protected access specifier. We'll see shortly that the sole purpose of the protected access specifier is to allow derived class member functions to use member functions and variables of the base class part of an object of that derived class, while protecting those member functions and variables from use by unrelated classes.

Susan had some interesting comments and questions about the notion of the base class part of a derived class object.

Susan: When I look at , I get the feeling that every DatedStockitem object contains a StockItem object; is this the "base class part of the derived class object"?

Steve: Yes.

Susan: The word "derived" is confusing: if a DatedStockItem is derived from a StockItem, one tends to take a linear approach as in a family tree, which isn't quite right. It would be better to think of DatedStockItem as a fruit like a plum, with the pit being the StockItem, which is the core of the object.

Steve: Or maybe an onion, where all the layers are edible, rather than making the distinction between the flesh of the fruit and an inedible pit.

Susan: But if so, every member function of the derived class could access every member variable of the base class because "They occur as the base class part of a derived class object".

Steve: No, as we'll see, even though private members are actually present in the derived class object, they are not accessible to derived class functions. That's why we need protected.

Of course, as noted before, we don't have to rely solely on the facilities we inherit from our base class; we can also add whatever new functions or variables needed to provide the new functionality of the new class. As you will see, we don't want or need to add any public member functions in the present case because our eventual goal is to allow the application programmer to treat objects of the new DatedStockItem class as equivalent to objects of the StockItem class. To reach this goal, these two classes must have the same class interface, i.e., the same public member functions.[7]

Instead of adding new public member functions, we will *override* the base class version of Reorder by writing a new version of Reorder for our DatedStockItem class. Our new function, which has the same signature as that of the base class Reorder function, will use the new data member m_Expires. Since the StockItem::Reorder has been overridden by DatedStockItem::Reorder, the latter function will be called whenever the user's program calls the Reorder function of a DatedStockItem.

Susan wasn't sure about the meaning of "overriding" a base class function rather than writing an entirely new one. That discussion led to a more general one about the whole idea of inheritance.

> **Susan:** Why is the term "override" used here? The derived class member function is called for an object of the derived class, so I don't see how it "overrides" the base class member function with the same signature.

---

7. By the way, it's not enough just to have the same names for the member functions in the derived class; they have to have the same meanings as well. That is, the user shouldn't be surprised by the behavior of a derived class function if he or she knows how the base class function behaves. For example, if the DatedStockItem Reorder function were to rearrange the items in the inventory rather than generate a reorder report, as the StockItem version does, the user would get very confused! The solution to this problem is simple: make sure that your derived class functions do the "same thing" as the corresponding base class functions, differing only in how they do it.

Steve: What would happen if we didn't write the derived class function? The base class function would be called. Therefore, the derived class function is overriding the previously existing base class function.

Susan: But why do you write a new version of Reorder instead of adding a new public member function?

Steve: Precisely because our eventual goal is to allow the user to use stock items with and without dates interchangeably. If StockItem and DatedStockItem had different names for their reordering function, the user would have to call a different function depending on which type the object really was, which would defeat our attempt to make them interchangeable.

Susan: But if they (the two versions of Reorder) were exactly the same, couldn't you just declare them public?

Steve: If they were *exactly* the same, we wouldn't need two functions in the first place. Reordering works slightly differently for dated than for undated items, so we need two different functions to do the "same" thing in two different ways.

Susan: Yes, but if the names were the same couldn't they be used anywhere just by making them public? I thought this was the whole idea: not to have to rewrite these things.

Steve: They are public. The point is that StockItem::Reorder and DatedStockItem::Reorder accomplish the same result in different ways, so the user of these classes should be able to just call Reorder and get the correct function executed without having to worry about which one that is.

Susan: So is it the expiration date that makes it necessary (?) to make a derived class?

Steve: Yes.

Susan: Is it impossible to extend our old class so it can handle objects both with and without expiration dates rather than making a new class?

Steve: Yes. We need two different classes to handle these two different kinds of objects.

Susan: Why can't we just add some new member functions and member variables to a class instead of making a derived class? Are you using inheritance here just to make a point, or is it vital to achieve what we want to achieve?

Steve: If you added more functions, then StockItem would not be StockItem as it is and needs to be. You could copy the code for StockItem and then change the copy to handle expiration dates, but that would cause serious maintenance problems later if (when) you had to change the code, because you would have to make the changes in both places. Avoiding such problems was one of the main reasons that C++ was invented.

Susan: Okay, so that explains why we shouldn't add more functions to StockItem, but not why we shouldn't add any functions to DatedStockItem.

Steve: Because a DatedStockItem should act just like a StockItem but won't if we add new functions.[8] Instead, we'll write new versions of the ones we already have, like Reorder.

Susan: I still don't understand why you have to write a new version of Reorder. A DatedStockItem is supposed to act just like a StockItem.

---

8. Actually, this is not strictly true. We can add functions to a derived class without affecting how it appears to users, so long as the functions that we add are either private or protected. We'll see some examples of this later.

Steve: Yes, it is supposed to act "just like" a StockItem. However, that means that it has to do the "same" things differently; in particular, reordering items is different when you have to send things back because their expiration dates have passed. However, this difference in implementation isn't important to the application program, which can treat DatedStockItems just like StockItems.

Before we get into the details of the Reorder function in the DatedStockItem class, I should explain what I mean by "regular member function". A regular member function is one that is *not* in any of the following categories:

1. constructor,

2. destructor,

3. assignment operator (*operator* =).

When we write a derived class (in this case DatedStockItem), it inherits only the regular member functions, not the constructor, destructor, or operator = functions, from the base class (in this case StockItem). Instead, we have to write our own derived class versions of these functions if we don't want to rely on the compiler-generated versions in the derived class.

It may not be obvious why we have to write our own versions of these functions. It wasn't to Susan:

Susan: So in this case our derived class DatedStockitem doesn't inherit the constructor, destructor, and assignment operator because it takes an object of the Stockitem class and combines it with a new member variable m_Expires to make an object of the derived DatedStockItem class. But if the only differences between the two classes are in the implementation of the "regular member functions", then the default constructor, after the inheritance of the base class, should have no problem making a new derived class object because it won't contain any new member variables.

Steve: You're right: that would be possible in such a case, but it's not the way the language works. However, the code in the base class functions isn't wasted because the base class constructor, destructor, and operator = functions are used automatically in the implementation of the corresponding derived class functions.

Susan: But what if they are similar to the derived class functions that do the same thing? Can't you use them then?

Steve: In the case of the base class constructor and destructor, you actually do use them indirectly; the compiler will always call a base class constructor when a derived class constructor is executed, and it will always call the base class destructor when the derived class destructor is executed.[9] Similarly, the derived class assignment operator will call the base class assignment operator to copy the base class part of the derived class object. However, any new member variables added to the derived class will have to be handled in the derived class functions.

Susan: So, anything not derived that is added to a derived class has to be handled as a separate entity from the stuff in the base class part of the derived class? UGH!

Steve: Yes, but just the newly added data has to be handled separately; the inherited data from the base class is handled by the base class functions. *Someone* has to write the code to handle the new member variables; the compiler can't read our minds!

We won't be wasting any effort when writing the derived class versions of the constructors, destructor, and assignment operator, because the base class versions of these functions are called automatically to construct, destroy, and assign the base class part of

---

9. When we write a derived class constructor, the base class default constructor is called to initialize the base class part of this class if we don't say which base class constructor we want; however, we can tell the compiler explicitly to call a different base class constructor.

the derived class object. Therefore, we can concentrate on the newly added parts of that class. We'll see exactly how and when these base class functions are called as we go through the corresponding derived class functions.[10]

For the moment, we won't have to define any of these derived class functions, except two new constructors. Since the member variables and the base class part of DatedStockItem are all concrete data types, the compiler-generated versions of the destructor and assignment operator, which call the destructors and assignment operators for those member variables (and the base class part), work perfectly well.

Susan didn't let this "compiler-generated" stuff slip by without a bit of an argument:

> **Susan:** About this statement that "compiler-generated versions of the destructor and assignment operators work perfectly well": Since when were destructors compiler-generated? I thought only assignment operators could be compiler-generated. You are holding out on me.

> **Steve:** Every class, by default, has a default constructor, copy constructor, assignment operator, and destructor. Any of these that we don't mention in our interface will be generated by the compiler.

She also had some questions about concrete data types:

> **Susan:** Aren't the member variables of a class always concrete data types (i.e., variables that act like native data types)? I thought a

---

10. It may seem that this automatic calling of base class functions for the constructor, destructor, and assignment operator is a type of inheritance. However, it really isn't because those functions are applied to the base class part of the derived class object, not to the derived class object itself. In the same way, you can refer to base class functions explicitly by qualifying the function name with the class name. This is also not a case of inheritance because these functions are applied only to the base class part.

concrete data type was "a class whose objects behave like native data types".

Steve: Well, if every class defined a concrete data type, we wouldn't need a separate name for that concept, would we? As this suggests, it's entirely possible to have member variables that aren't concrete data types. In particular, *pointers* aren't concrete data types, because copying them doesn't actually copy their data, only the address of the data to which they refer. That's part of what makes them so tricky to work with.

Before we can use StockItem as a base class, however, there is one change we're going to make to our previous definition of StockItem to make it work properly in that application; namely, we have to change the access specifier for its member variables from private to protected. By this point, you should be familiar with the meaning of private: Any member variables or member functions that are marked private can be referred to only by member functions of the same class; all other functions are denied access to them. On the other hand, when we mark member functions or member data of a class as public, we are specifying that any function, whether or not a member function of the class in question, can access them. That seems to take care of all the possibilities, so what is protected good for? I hope the following definitions will help clear this up.

More Definitions

The **base class part** of a derived class object is an unnamed component of the derived class object whose member variables and functions are accessible as though they were defined in the derived class so long as they are either public or protected.

The keyword **protected** is an access specifier. When present in a base class definition, it allows derived class functions access to members in the base class part of a derived class object while preventing access by other functions outside the base class.

Protection Racket

Member variables and member functions that are listed in a protected section of the interface definition are both treated as though they were private, with one important exception: Member functions of derived classes can access them when they occur as the base class part of a derived class object.

In the current case, we've seen that a DatedStockItem is "just like" a StockItem with one additional member variable and some other additions and changes that aren't relevant here. The important point is that every DatedStockItem contains everything that a StockItem contains. For example, every DatedStockItem has an m_MinimumStock member variable because the StockItem class has an m_MinimumStock member variable, and we're defining DatedStockItem as being derived from StockItem. Logically, therefore, we should be able to access the value of the m_MinimumStock member variable in our DatedStockItem. However, if that member variable is declared as private, we can't. The private access specifier doesn't care about inheritance; since DatedStockItem is a different class from StockItem, any private member variables and functions that StockItem might contain wouldn't be accessible to member functions of DatedStockItem, even though the member variables of StockItem are actually present in every DatedStockItem! That's why we have to make those variables protected rather than private.

Susan had some questions about this new concept of protected members:

Susan: I don't understand why, if DatedStockItem has those member variables, it wouldn't be able to access them if they were specified as private in the base class.

Steve: Because the compiler wouldn't let DatedStockItem member functions access them; private variables are private to the class where they are defined (and its friends, if any) even if they are part of the base class part of a derived class object. That's why protected was invented.

Susan: Well, friend lets a class or a function access something in another class, so what's the main difference between protected and friend?

Steve: They're used in different situations. You can use friend when you know exactly what other class or function you want to allow to access your private or protected members. On the other hand, if all you know is that a derived class will need to access these members, you make them protected.

In other words, a protected variable or function is automatically available to any derived class, as it applies to the base class part of the derived class object. To make a class or function a friend to a class being defined, you have to name the friend class or friend function explicitly.

Susan: What do you mean by "base class part of the derived object"? I'm fuzzy here.

Steve: Every DatedStockItem (derived class) object contains a StockItem (base class) object and can use all of the non-private member functions of StockItem, because DatedStockItem is derived from StockItem. This is what allows us to avoid having to rewrite all the code from the base class in the derived class.

Susan: I don't get this. I need some pictures to clear up these base class and derived class things.

Steve: Okay, I'll give it a shot. Take a look at Figure 9.10, where I've used a dashed-dotted line around the base class, StockItem, to indicate its boundaries as a base class part. I've also used different line types to indicate the level of access to member variables and functions: a solid box to indicate private members, a dashed box to indicate protected members, and a dotted box to indicate public members.

As I told Susan, Figure 9.10 illustrates a hypothetical DatedStockItem class. Here, class, m_Name, m_Price, and m_InStock are protected base class member variables, whereas m_UPC is a private member variable and GetPrice() is a public member function.[11]

According to this scenario, the derived class member functions can access m_Name, m_Price, and m_InStock. Of course, any member function can access any public member of any other class, so GetPrice is accessible to DatedStockItem member functions as well. However, with this setup, member functions of DatedStockItem cannot access m_UPC, even though this member variable is actually present in the base class part of a DatedStockItem.

Now that we've cleared up that point (I hope), we have to consider the question of when to use protected versus private variables. The private member variables of the base class cannot be accessed directly by derived class member functions. This means that when we define the base class, we have to decide whether we want to allow any derived classes direct access to some of the member variables of the base class part of the derived object. If we do, we have to use the protected access specifier for those member variables. If we make them private and later discover that we need access to those variables in a derived class, we then have to change the definition of the base class so that the variables are protected rather than private. Such changes are not too much trouble when we have

---

11. Of course, because m_Expires is a member of DatedStockItem, all DatedStockItem member functions can access it freely regardless of its access specifier.

written all of the classes involved, but they can be extremely difficult or even impossible when we try to derive new classes from previously existing classes written by someone else.

FIGURE 9.10. A derived class object with its base class part

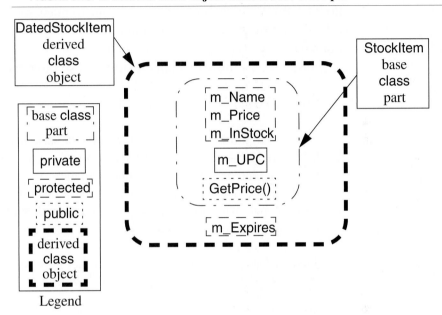

However, protected members (especially protected variables) have some of the drawbacks of public variables and functions. Anyone can define a new derived class that uses those variables or functions, and any changes to those base class variables or functions will cause the code in the derived class to break. Hence, making everything protected isn't a panacea.

Analogous to our earlier discussion of public member variables versus public member functions, the drawbacks of protected variables are more serious than those of protected member functions, which at least don't commit you to specific implementation details. In the present case, I doubt that there would be any significant difference in maintainability between these two approaches, as we are designing both the base and derived classes, but in a larger project, it might very well be better to use protected member functions to allow access to private member variables in the base class rather than to use protected member variables for the same purpose.

The moral of the story is that it's easier to design classes for our own use and derivation than for the use of others. Even though we can go back and change our class definitions to make them more flexible, that alternative may not be available to others. The result may be that our classes will not meet others' needs.

Susan didn't think this conclusion was so obvious.

Susan: I don't get your moral of the story. Sorry.

Steve: The moral is that when designing classes that may be used by others as base classes, we have to know whether those others will ever need access to our member variables. If we are in charge of all of the classes, we can change the access specifiers easily enough, but that's not a very good solution if someone else is deriving new classes from our classes.

Susan: Okay, I guess. But what does that have to do with using protected variables or private ones with protected member functions?

Steve: Only that if we used private variables with protected member functions to access them, we could allow the derived class to use the member variables in our base class in a controlled way rather than an uncontrolled one, and therefore could keep some say in how they are used. Unfortunately, this solution still requires us to figure out how the derived class member functions may want to use our member variables, so it isn't a "silver bullet".

Susan: I still don't understand why we need to worry about who else is going to use our classes; who are these other people?

Steve: One of the main advantages claimed for object-oriented programming is that it allows "division of labor"; that is, some programmers can specialize in building classes while others can specialize in writing application programs. This can increase productivity greatly, just as it does in medicine (e.g., general practitioners, specialists, nurses, and lab technicians).

Susan: Okay, but what does that have to do with access specifiers? Why don't we just make everything public and avoid all this stuff?

Steve: If we are going to let others use our classes, we have to design them to be easy to use correctly and hard to use incorrectly. That's one of the main reasons we use private and protected: so we can determine where in our program an error might be caused. If we notice that one of our private member variables is being changed when it shouldn't be, we know where to look: in the code that implements the class. Because the member variable is private, we don't have to worry that it's being changed somewhere else. This is not the case with a public member variable, which can be modified anywhere in the program. If you'd ever had to try to find out where a variable is being modified in a gigantic program in C or another language that doesn't have private variables, you would know exactly what I mean!

Stock Footage

After that excursion into the use of the protected access specifier and its impact on class design, let's look at the revised test program in Figure 9.11.

FIGURE 9.11. **The next version of the inventory control test program** (code\itmtst21.cc)

```
#include <iostream.h>
#include <fstream.h>
#include "vector.h"
#include "string6.h"
#include "item21.h"
#include "invent21.h"
```

```
int main()
{
ifstream ShopInfo("shop21.in");
ofstream ReorderInfo("shop21.reo");

Inventory MyInventory;

MyInventory.LoadInventory(ShopInfo);

MyInventory.ReorderItems(ReorderInfo);

return 0;
}
```

The new test program, Itmtst21.cc, is exactly the same as its predecessor, itmtst20.cc, except that it #includes the new header files item21.h (shown in Figures 9.12) and invent21.h and uses different input and output file names.[12] If you want to see how this program runs, you can compile it and step through it using RHIDE. To do this, change to the \shcppg\code directory and type RHIDE itmtst21. When RHIDE starts up, hit F9 to compile the program; then you can use F8 to step through each line of itmtst21. If you want to see how any particular line works, you can use F7 to step into the code that executes that line. When the program terminates, you can look at its output file, shop21.reo, to see what the reorder report looks like; if you do, you will see that it includes instructions to return some expired items.

Now that we've seen the results of using the new versions of our inventory control classes, let's take a look at the interface definitions of StockItem and DatedStockItem (Figure 9.12) as well as the implementation of those classes (Figure 9.13). I strongly recommend

---

12. The reason that I am not listing either the header file or the implementation file for invent21 (the new version of the inventory class) is that they are essentially identical to the previous versions except that they use DatedStockItem rather than StockItem to keep track of the inventory items.

that you print out the files that contain these interfaces and their implementation for reference as you go through this section of the chapter; those files are code\item21.h and code\item21.cc, respectively.[13]

Susan had some questions about where the new class interface and implementation were defined:

> **Susan:** So you just write your new class right there? I mean you don't start over with a new page or something; shouldn't it be a different file or coded off all by itself somewhere? How come it is where it is?

> **Steve:** We could put it in another file, but in this case, the classes are intended to be used interchangeably in the application program, so it's not unreasonable to have them in the same file. In other circumstances, it's more common to have the derived class in a separate file. Of course, sometimes you don't have any choice, such as when you're deriving a new class from a class that you didn't create in the first place and may not even have the source code for; in that case, you *have* to create a separate file for the derived class.

FIGURE 9.12. Full interface for StockItem **and** DatedStockItem **(code\item21.h)**

```
class StockItem
{
friend ostream& operator << (ostream& s,
  const StockItem& Item);

friend istream& operator >> (istream& s, StockItem& Item);
```

13. After looking at the interface file, you may wonder why I have two protected access specifiers in the DatedStockItem class. The reason is that I like to explicitly state the access specifiers for functions and for data separately to clarify what I'm doing. This duplication doesn't mean anything to the compiler, but it makes my intention clearer to the next programmer.

```
public:
  StockItem();
  StockItem(string Name, short InStock,
  short Price, short MinimumStock,
  short MinimumReorder, string Distributor, string UPC);
  bool CheckUPC(string ItemUPC);
  void DeductSaleFromInventory(short QuantitySold);
  short GetInventory();
  string GetName();
  string GetUPC();
  bool IsNull();
  short GetPrice();
  void Reorder(ostream& s);
  void FormattedDisplay(ostream& s);

protected:
  short m_InStock;
  short m_Price;
  short m_MinimumStock;
  short m_MinimumReorder;
  string m_Name;
  string m_Distributor;
  string m_UPC;
};

class DatedStockItem: public StockItem
{
friend ostream& operator << (ostream& s,
  const DatedStockItem& Item);

friend istream& operator >> (istream& s, DatedStockItem& Item);

public:
  DatedStockItem();
  DatedStockItem(string Name, short InStock, short Price,
  short MinimumStock, short MinimumReorder,
  string Distributor, string UPC, string Expires);
  void FormattedDisplay(ostream& s);
  void Reorder(ostream& s);
```

```
protected:
static string Today();

protected:
  string m_Expires;
};
```

FIGURE 9.13. Latest implementation of StockItem class **and first implementation of** DatedStockItem class **(code\item21.h)**

```
#include <iostream.h>
#include <iomanip.h>
#include <strstream.h>
#include <string.h>
#include "string6.h"
#include "item21.h"
#include <dos.h>

StockItem::StockItem()
: m_InStock(0), m_Price(0), m_MinimumStock(0),
  m_MinimumReorder(0), m_Name(), m_Distributor(),
  m_UPC()
{
}

StockItem::StockItem(string Name, short InStock,
  short Price, short MinimumStock, short MinimumReorder,
  string Distributor, string UPC)
: m_InStock(InStock), m_Price(Price),
  m_MinimumStock(MinimumStock),
  m_MinimumReorder(MinimumReorder), m_Name(Name),
  m_Distributor(Distributor), m_UPC(UPC)
{
}

void StockItem::FormattedDisplay(ostream& os)
{
  os << "Name: ";
```

```
  os << m_Name << endl;
  os << "Number in stock: ";
  os << m_InStock << endl;
  os << "Price: ";
  os << m_Price << endl;
  os << "Minimum stock: ";
  os << m_MinimumStock << endl;
  os << "Minimum Reorder quantity: ";
  os << m_MinimumReorder << endl;
  os << "Distributor: ";
  os << m_Distributor << endl;
  os << "UPC: ";
  os << m_UPC << endl;
}

ostream& operator << (ostream& os, const StockItem& Item)
{
  os << Item.m_Name << endl;
  os << Item.m_InStock << endl;
  os << Item.m_Price << endl;
  os << Item.m_MinimumStock << endl;
  os << Item.m_MinimumReorder << endl;
  os << Item.m_Distributor << endl;
  os << Item.m_UPC << endl;

  return os;
}

istream& operator >> (istream& is, StockItem& Item)
{
  is >> Item.m_Name;
  is >> Item.m_InStock;
  is >> Item.m_Price;
  is >> Item.m_MinimumStock;
  is >> Item.m_MinimumReorder;
  is >> Item.m_Distributor;
  is >> Item.m_UPC;

  return is;
```

```
}

bool StockItem::CheckUPC(string ItemUPC)
{
  if (m_UPC == ItemUPC)
    return true;

  return false;
}

void StockItem::DeductSaleFromInventory(short QuantitySold)
{
  m_InStock -= QuantitySold;
}

short StockItem::GetInventory()
{
  return m_InStock;
}

string StockItem::GetName()
{
  return m_Name;
}

string StockItem::GetUPC()
{
  return m_UPC;
}

bool StockItem::IsNull()
{
  if (m_UPC == "")
    return true;

  return false;
}

short StockItem::GetPrice()
```

```
{
  return m_Price;
}

void StockItem::Reorder(ostream& os)
{
  short ActualReorderQuantity;

  if (m_InStock < m_MinimumStock)
    {
    ActualReorderQuantity = m_MinimumStock - m_InStock;
    if (m_MinimumReorder > ActualReorderQuantity)
      ActualReorderQuantity = m_MinimumReorder;
    os << "Reorder " << ActualReorderQuantity;
    os <<  " units of " << m_Name;
    os << " with UPC " << m_UPC;
    os << " from " << m_Distributor << endl;
    }
}

DatedStockItem::DatedStockItem()
: m_Expires()
{
}

string DatedStockItem::Today()
{
  date d;
  short year;
  char day;
  char month;
  string TodaysDate;
  strstream FormatStream;

  getdate(&d);
  year = d.da_year;
  day = d.da_day;
  month = d.da_mon;
```

```
FormatStream << setfill('0') << setw(4) << year <<
  setw(2) << month << setw(2) << day;
FormatStream >> TodaysDate;

return TodaysDate;
}

DatedStockItem::DatedStockItem(string Name, short InStock,
  short Price, short MinimumStock, short MinimumReorder,
  string Distributor, string UPC, string Expires)
: StockItem(Name, InStock, Price, MinimumStock,
  MinimumReorder, Distributor, UPC),
  m_Expires(Expires)
{
}

void DatedStockItem::Reorder(ostream& os)
{
  if (m_Expires < Today())
    {
    os << "Return " << m_InStock;
    os << " units of " << m_Name;
    os << " with UPC " << m_UPC;
    os << " to " << m_Distributor << endl;
    m_InStock = 0;
    }

  StockItem::Reorder(os);
}

void DatedStockItem::FormattedDisplay(ostream& os)
{
  os << "Expiration Date: ";
  os << m_Expires << endl;
  StockItem::FormattedDisplay(os);
}

ostream& operator << (ostream& os, const DatedStockItem& Item)
{
```

```
      os << Item.m_Expires << endl;
      os << Item.m_Name << endl;
      os << Item.m_InStock << endl;
      os << Item.m_Price << endl;
      os << Item.m_MinimumStock << endl;
      os << Item.m_MinimumReorder << endl;
      os << Item.m_Distributor << endl;
      os << Item.m_UPC << endl;

      return os;
    }

    istream& operator >> (istream& is, DatedStockItem& Item)
    {
      is >> Item.m_Expires;
      is >> Item.m_Name;
      is >> Item.m_InStock;
      is >> Item.m_Price;
      is >> Item.m_MinimumStock;
      is >> Item.m_MinimumReorder;
      is >> Item.m_Distributor;
      is >> Item.m_UPC;

      return is;
    }
```

Before we get to the new implementation for these classes in item21.cc, I should mention the new header file #included in item21.cc: dos.h. This header file defines a data type needed by the Today function, which we'll get to in a little while.

If you're writing programs to run under another operating system, such as Unix™, I should warn you that dos.h, as its name suggests, is specific to MS-DOS™. Therefore, this program won't compile in its current form under other operating systems. While this is a soluble problem, the solution is outside the scope of this book.

Now let's get to the interface definition for DatedStockItem. Most of this should be pretty simple to follow by now. We have to declare new versions of operator << and operator >>, which will allow us to write and read objects of the DatedStockItem class as we can already do with the normal StockItem. As before, the friend specifiers are needed to allow these global input and output functions to access the internal variables of our class.

Susan wanted to know why we had to write new operators << and >> for the DatedStockItem class when we had already written them for its base class, StockItem.

> **Susan:** Why can't DatedStockItem use the same >> and << that StockItem uses? If it's derived from StockItem, it should be able to use the same ones. I don't get it.

> **Steve:** It can't use the same ones because a DatedStockItem has a new member variable that the StockItem I/O operators don't know about.

> **Susan:** But why can't the compiler do it for us?

> **Steve:** Because the compiler doesn't know how we want to display the data. Should it put an endl after each member variable or run them all together on one line? Should it even display all of the member variables? Maybe there are some that the user of the class doesn't care about. In some cases, the real data for the class isn't even contained in its objects, as we'll see in Chapter 10. Therefore, we have to write operator << ourselves.

Then we have the default constructor, DatedStockItem(), and the "normal" constructor that supplies values for all of the member variables. We also have to declare the Reorder function we are writing for this class.

Although all of the preceding function declarations should be old hat by now, there are a couple of constructs here that we haven't seen before. The first one is in the class header: DatedStockItem: public StockItem. I'm referring specifically to the expression : public StockItem, which states that the new class being defined, in this case DatedStockItem, is publicly derived from StockItem. We have discussed the fact that deriving a new class from an old one means that the new class has everything in it that the old class had in it. But what does the public keyword mean here?

class *Interests*

It means that we are going to allow a DatedStockItem to be treated as a StockItem; that is, any function that takes a StockItem as a parameter will accept a DatedStockItem in its place. As this implies, all of the public member functions and public data items (if there were any) in the base class (StockItem in this case) are publicly accessible in an object of the derived class (DatedStockItem in this case) object as well. This is called, imaginatively enough, public inheritance.

The relationship between a base class and a publicly derived class is commonly expressed by saying that the derived class "isA" base class object.[14]

private *Bequest*

You might be wondering whether there are other types of inheritance besides public. The answer is that there is one that is sometimes useful: private. If we wrote : private StockItem rather than : public StockItem as the base class specification for DatedStockItem, DatedStockItem member functions would still be able to use the protected and public member variables and member functions of StockItem in their implementation, just as with public inheritance. However, the fact that DatedStockItem is derived from StockItem would not be apparent to any outside function. That is, if we specified

---

14. By the way, this is the reason it's all right to provide an ofstream variable where an ostream is expected, as I told Susan in the discussion on page 583. Because ofstream is publicly derived from ostream, an ofstream "isAn" ostream. This means that you can provide an ofstream wherever an ostream is specified as an argument or return type.

private rather than public inheritance, a DatedStockItem would not be an acceptable substitute for a StockItem; alternatively, we could say that DatedStockItem would not have an "isA" relationship with StockItem. The primary use for private inheritance is to reuse the implementation of an existing class while being able to modify some of its behavior.[15] We won't be using private inheritance in this book.

Susan had a number of questions about the uses of inheritance.

Susan: I don't understand this idea of substituting one type of object for another. Why don't you decide which kind of object you want and use that one?

Steve: The StockItem and DatedStockItem classes are a good example of why we would want to be able to substitute one type of object for another: To the user of these classes, they appear the same, except that DatedStockItem requires one more item of information (the expiration date) and produces a slightly different reordering report. Therefore, being able to treat them in the same way makes it much easier to write a program using these two classes, because the user doesn't need a lot of code saying, "if it's a DatedStockItem, do this; if it's a StockItem, do something else".

Susan: Okay, but if you use : private StockItem, then how come it can use the protected and public parts of StockItem and not just the private parts? I just don't get this at all.

Steve: That's understandable because this is another confusing case of C++ keyword abuse: The private keyword in the class declaration line means something different from its meaning in the class definition. In the class declaration line, it means that no user of the class can treat an object of the derived class being declared as a substitute for a base class object. In other words, what is private is the inheritance from the base class, not the variables in

---

15. This is most useful when we are using inheritance to extend the facilities provided by an existing class in "inheritance for extension".

the base class. It's sort of like an unrecognized child; the derived class has the DNA of the base class, but can't claim parentage in public.

This substitutability of an object of a publicly derived class (e.g., a DatedStockItem) for an object of its base class (e.g., StockItem) extends to areas where its value is somewhat questionable. In particular, a derived class object can be assigned to a base class object; for example, if x is a StockItem and y is a DatedStockItem, the statement x = y; is legal. The result will be that any member variables that exist in the derived class object but not in the base class object will be lost in the assignment. In our example, after the statement x = y;, x will contain all the member variables of y except for m_Expires, which is not present in the base class. This "partial assignment" is called *slicing*, and it can be a serious annoyance because the compiler won't warn you that it's taking place. After all, since a DatedStockItem "isA" StockItem, it's perfectly legal to assign an object of the former class to an object of the latter class, even if that isn't what you had in mind. However, you shouldn't worry about this problem too much; as we'll see in the next chapter, we can solve it by using more advanced techniques.

Before we get into the implementation of the DatedStockItem class, let's take a look at the other new construct in its interface: a static member function. I'll give you a hint as to its meaning: In the grand old C/C++ tradition of keyword abuse, the meaning of static here is almost but not quite entirely unlike its meaning for either local or global variables.

Getting static

Give up? Okay. When we declare a member function to be static, we don't have to specify an object when we call the member function. Thus, we can refer to the static member function Today by just its name followed by empty parentheses to indicate a function call. Within DatedStockItem member functions, writing "Today();" is sufficient. Of course, if Today were public, and we wanted to call it from a nonmember function, we would have to refer to it by its full name: DatedStockItem::Today. Either of these calls differs from the normal use of a member function, where we specify the function along with the object to which it applies—for example, in the expression "soup.GetInventory();".

That explains what the static modifier does, but why would we want to use it? Because some member functions don't apply to any particular object, it is convenient to be able to call such a function without needing an object to call it for. In the case of the Today function, the value of today's date is not dependent on any DatedStockItem object; therefore, it makes sense to be able to call Today without referring to any object of the DatedStockItem class.

At this point, Susan had a cognition about the utility of static member functions:

Susan: I just realized that this way of writing functions is sort of like writing a path; it tells the compiler where to go to find things — is that right?

Steve: Right. The reason that we make this a member function is to control access to it and to allow it to be used by this class, not because it works on a particular class object (as is the case with non-static member functions).

Susan: So, is using this static thing like making it a default?

Steve: Sort of, because you don't have to specify an object for the function to act on.

Of course, we could also avoid having to pass an object to the Today function by making it a global function. However, the advantages of using a static protected member function rather than a global one are much the same as the advantages of using private rather than public member variables. First, we can change the interface of this function more easily than that of a global function, as we know that it can be accessed only by member functions of DatedStockItem and any possible derived classes of that class, not by any function anywhere. Second, we don't have to worry that someone else might want to define a different function with the same signature, which could be a problem with a global function. The full name of this function, DatedStockItem::Today, is sufficient to distinguish it from any other Today functions that belong to other classes, or even from a global function of that name, should another programmer be so inconsiderate as to write one!

There's one other thing here that we haven't seen before: Today is a protected member function, which means that it is accessible only to member functions of DatedStockItem and its descendants, just as a protected member variable is. We want to keep this function from being called by application programs for the same reason that we protect member variables by restricting access: to reserve the right to change its name, return value, or argument types. Application code can't access this function and therefore can't depend on its interface.

Susan had some questions about changing the Today function as well as about the more general idea of many programmers working on the same program.

> **Susan:** Why would we want to change the Today function? It seems like it would work fine the way it is.

> **Steve:** Well, we might decide to make it return a number rather than a string, if we changed the way we implemented our date comparisons. But the point is more general: The fewer people who know about a particular function, the easier it will be to make changes to its interface.

> **Susan:** Who are these other people you're always talking about? I thought a programmer wrote his own programs.

> **Steve:** That all depends. Some small projects are done by a single programmer, which might seem to make access specifiers redundant. But they really aren't, even in that case, because a lone

programmer puts on different "hats" while writing a significant program. Sometimes he's a class designer and sometimes an application programmer.

But where these design considerations are *really* important is in big projects, which may be written by dozens or even hundreds of programmers. In such cases, the result of letting everyone access every variable or function can be summed up in one word: chaos. Such free-for-alls have led to a lot of buggy software.

Figure 9.14 is the implementation of the protected static member function DatedStockItem::Today.

FIGURE 9.14. DatedStockItem::Today() **(from code\item21.cc)**

```
string DatedStockItem::Today()
{
  date d;
  short year;
  char day;
  char month;
  string TodaysDate;
  strstream FormatStream;

  getdate(&d);
  year = d.da_year;
  day = d.da_day;
  month = d.da_mon;

  FormatStream << setfill('0') << setw(4) << year <<
    setw(2) << month << setw(2) << day;
  FormatStream >> TodaysDate;

  return TodaysDate;
}
```

Here's where we use the date type defined in the line #include <dos.h> in Figure 9.13. As its name suggests, a date is used to store the components of a date (i.e., its month, day, and year). Now that we've gotten that detail out of the way, let's look at this Today function. First, we have to call the getdate function (whose declaration is also in dos.h) to ascertain the current date; getdate handles this request by filling in the member variables in a variable of type date. Note that the argument to the getdate function is the address of the date variable (i.e., &d) rather than the variable itself. This is necessary because the getdate function is left over from C, which doesn't have reference variables. Since all C arguments are value arguments, a C function can't change any of its arguments. C handles this limitation by giving the called function the address of the variable to be modified; then the called function uses that address as a pointer to the actual variable. Happily, we don't have to concern ourselves about this in any more detail than what I've just mentioned.

By the way, this is a good example of the difference between calling a member function and calling a nonmember function: We have to specify the address of the date variable d as an argument when calling getdate because getdate isn't a member function of the date type, for the excellent reason that C doesn't have member functions. Of course, with a member function, the compiler automatically supplies the this pointer to every (non-static) member function as a hidden argument, so we don't have to worry about it.

After we call getdate, the current year is left in the da_year member variable of the date variable d, and the current day and month are left in the other two member variables, da_day and da_mon. Now that we have the current year, month, and day, the next step is to produce a string that has all of these data items in the correct order and format. To do this, we use some functions from the iostreams library that we haven't seen before. While these functions are very convenient, we can't call them unless we have a stream of some sort for them to work with.

So far, we've used istream and ostream objects, but neither of those will do the job here. We don't really want to do any input or output at all; we just want to use the formatting functions that streams provide. Since this is a fairly common requirement, the inventors of the iostreams library have anticipated it by supplying strstream.

A strstream is a stream that exists entirely in memory rather than as a conduit to read or write data. In this case, we've declared a strstream called FormatStream, to which we'll write our data. When done, we'll read the formatted data back from FormatStream.

This discussion assumes that you're completely comfortable with the notion of a stream, which may not be true. It certainly wasn't for Susan, as the following indicates:

> **Susan:** I don't understand your definition for strstream. What does the str part stand for? Why is FormatStream a part of strstream instead of just from the iostream library? When does it exist in memory? When is it called to work? How is it different from the "conduit" type of streams? I am *not* understanding this because I told you that I don't understand what a stream really is. So what does strstream really do?

Let's see if we can answer her (and possibly your) questions by taking a closer look at streams.

stream *of Consciousness*

A stream is a facility that allows us to use various input and output devices more or less uniformly. There are a number of variants of this data type, which are related by inheritance so that we can substitute a more highly specialized variant for a more basic one. So far we've encountered istream, ostream, ifstream, ofstream, and of course most recently strstream. The best place to start a further investigation of this family of classes is with one of the simplest types, an ostream. We've used a predefined object of this type, namely cout, quite a few times already. To see a little bit more about how this works, take a look at the program in Figure 9.15.

FIGURE 9.15. A simple stream **example (code\stream1.cc)**

```
#include <iostream.h>

int main()
{
    short x;
    char y;

    x = 1;
    y = 'A';

    cout << "Test " << x;
    cout << " grade: " << y;
    cout << endl;

    return 0;
}
```

When the program starts, cout looks something like Figure 9.16.

FIGURE 9.16. An empty ostream **object**

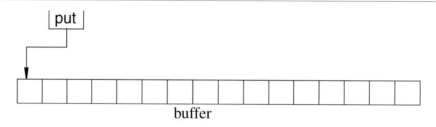

buffer

What is the purpose of the buffer and the put pointer?[16] Here's a breakdown:

---

16. Please note that the type of the put pointer is irrelevant to us, as we cannot ever access it directly. However, you won't go far wrong if you think of it as the address of the next available byte in the buffer.

1. The buffer is the area of memory where the characters put into the ostream are stored.

2. The put pointer holds the address of the next byte in the output area of the ostream—that is, where the next byte will be stored if we use << to write data into the ostream.

At this point, we haven't put anything into the ostream yet, so the put pointer is pointing to the beginning of the buffer. Now, let's execute the line cout << "Test " << x;. After that line is executed, the contents of the ostream looks something like Figure 9.17.

FIGURE 9.17. An ostream **object with some data**

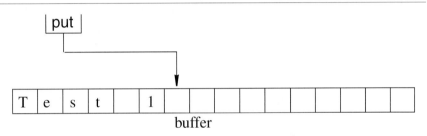

buffer

As you can see, the data from the first output line has been put into the ostream buffer. After the next statement, cout << " grade: " << y;, is executed, the ostream looks like Figure 9.18.

FIGURE 9.18. An ostream **object with some more data**

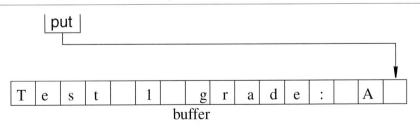

buffer

Now we're ready for the final output statement, cout << endl;. Once this statement is executed, the ostream looks like Figure 9.19.

FIGURE 9.19. **An empty** ostream **object**

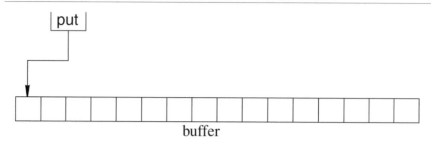

buffer

By now, you're probably wondering what happened to all the data we stored in the ostream. It went out to the screen because that's what endl does (after sticking a newline character on the end of the buffer). Once the data has been sent to the screen, we can't access it anymore in our program, so the space that it took up in the buffer is made available for further use.

We All stream *for* strstream

Now it's time to get back to our discussion of strstream. A strstream (short for *string stream*) allows us to write data to its buffer and then read the resulting data back into a variable. An example is the program shown in Figure 9.20, which uses a strstream object to combine a year, month, and day number to make one string containing all of those values.

FIGURE 9.20. **A** strstream **formatting example (code\stream2.cc)**

```
#include <iostream.h>
#include <strstream.h>
#include "string6.h"

int main()
{
```

```
        strstream FormatStream;
        string date;

        short year = 1996;
        short month = 7;
        short day = 28;

        FormatStream << year;
        FormatStream << month;
        FormatStream << day;

        FormatStream >> date;

        cout << "date: " << date << endl;

        return 0;
    }
```

A strstream is very similar to an ostream, except that once we have written data to a strstream, we can read it from the strstream into a variable just as though we were reading from a file or the keyboard. Figure 9.21 shows what an empty strstream looks like.

FIGURE 9.21. **An empty** strstream **object**

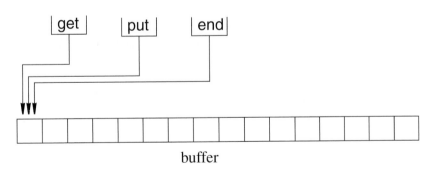

buffer

We've discussed the put pointer and the buffer, but what about the get and end pointers? Here's what they're for:

1. The get pointer holds the address of the next byte in the input area of the stream, or the next byte we get if we use >> to read data from the strstream.

2. The end pointer indicates the end of the strstream. Attempting to read anything at or after this position will cause the read to fail because there is nothing else to read.

You probably won't be surprised to learn that Susan wasn't that thrilled with all these new kinds of pointers, or with streams in general for that matter.

> **Susan:** The only thing that can be worse than pointers is different kinds of pointers. How are get and end different from other kinds of pointers? Ick.

> **Steve:** They are effectively the addresses of the current places in the buffer where characters will be read and written, respectively. Since they are not directly accessible to the programmer, their actual representation is irrelevant; all that matters is how they work.

> **Susan:** You just have no idea how much trouble this stream stuff is to me. It's all just a vague mess that I have to trust is doing something. I just don't get it.

> **Steve:** Why is it any more vague than cout? It's just the same, except that the actual destination may vary.

> **Susan:** No, there is no cout word when we're using these other streams.

> **Steve:** Yes, but that's the only difference between writing to a strstream and writing to cout, which never bothered you before.

> **Susan:** But I can see the screen; I can't see these other things.

Steve: Yes, but you can't see the stream in either case. Anyway, I drew all those diagrams so you could "see" the stream. Don't they help?

Susan: Yes, they help but it still isn't the same thing as cout. Anyway, I'm not really sure at any given time exactly where the data really is; it just seems to be in some area of memory that is somewhat vague. Where are these put, get, and end pointers stored?

Steve: They're stored in the strstream object as part of its member data, just as m_Name and the other member variables are stored in a StockItem object.

Susan: Okay, but what about the buffer?

Steve: That's in an area of memory allocated for that purpose by the strstream member functions. The streams classes use the get and put pointers to keep track of the exact position of the data in the buffer, so we don't have to worry about it.

Susan: I still don't like it. It's not like cout.

Steve: Yes, but cout is just an ostream, and a strstream is just like an ostream and an istream combined; you can write to it just like an ostream and then read back from it just like an istream.

Susan: I still think streams are going to be my downfall. They're just too vague and there seem to be so many of them. I know you say that they are good, and I believe you, but they are still a little mysterious. This is not going to be the last you've heard of this.

Steve: It seems to me that you've managed to survive lots of other new concepts pretty well. I suspect streams won't be any exception.

After the statement FormatStream << year;, the strstream might look like Figure 9.22.

FIGURE 9.22. A strstream **object with some contents**

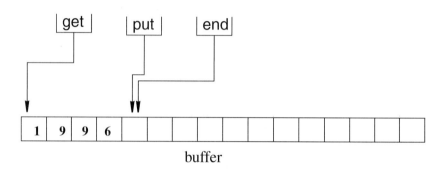

buffer

The put pointer has moved to the next free byte in the strstream, but the get pointer hasn't moved because we haven't gotten anything from the strstream.

The next statement is FormatStream << month;, which leaves the strstream looking like Figure 9.23.

FIGURE 9.23. A strstream **object with some more contents**

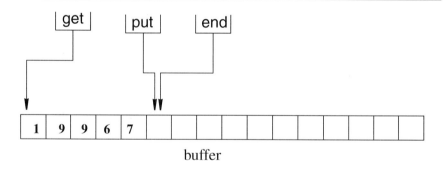

buffer

After we execute the statement FormatStream << day;, the strstream looks like Figure 9.24.

FIGURE 9.24. A strstream **object with even more contents**

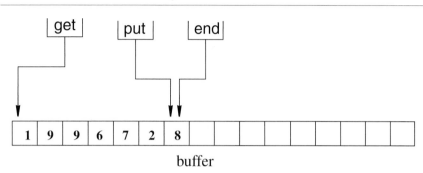

buffer

Now it's time to get back what we put into the strstream. That's the job of the next statement, FormatStream >> date;. Afterward, the variable date has the value "1996728" and the strstream looks like Figure 9.25.

FIGURE 9.25. A strstream **object after reading its contents**

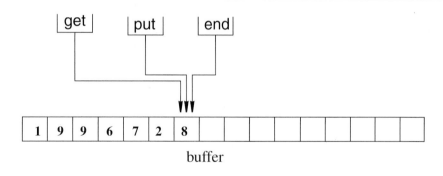

buffer

In other words, we've read to the end of the strstream, so we can't read from it again until we "reset" it. This shouldn't seem too strange, as it is exactly analogous to what happens when we've read all of the data in a file through an ifstream, which causes the next read to "fail".[17]

---

17.   This is covered in the section called "References Required" in Chapter 6.

In these diagrams, the end and put pointers always point to the same place, so why do we need both? Because we can reset the put pointer to any place in the strstream before the current end pointer and write over the data already written. We don't make use of that facility in this book, but it's there when needed.

Use It or Lose It

Now let's get back to the problem of converting a date to a string so that we can compare it with another date. You might think that all we have to do is write each data item out to the strstream and then read the resulting formatted data back in, as in the program in Figure 9.20. However, it's a bit more complicated than that because in order to compare two of these values correctly, we need to control the exact format in which the data will be written. To see why this is necessary, consider the program shown in Figure 9.26.

FIGURE 9.26. **Default formatting example (code\coutdef1.cc)**

```
#include <iostream.h>
#include <strstream.h>
#include "string6.h"

int main()
{
    strstream FormatStream1;
    strstream FormatStream2;
    string date1;
    string date2;

    short year1 = 1996;
    short month1 = 12;
    short day1 = 28;

    short year2 = 1996;
    short month2 = 7;
```

```
    short day2 = 28;

    FormatStream1 << year1 << month1 << day1;
    FormatStream1 >> date1;

    FormatStream2 << year2 << month2 << day2;
    FormatStream2 >> date2;

    cout << "date1: " << date1 << ", date2: " << date2 << endl;

    if (date1 < date2)
        cout << "date1 is less than date2" << endl;
    else if (date1 == date2)
        cout << "date1 is the same as date2" << endl;
    else
        cout << "date1 is greater than date2" << endl;

    return 0;
}
```

The output of that program is shown in Figure 9.27.

FIGURE 9.27. Output of default formatting example (code\coutdef1.out)

```
date1: 19961228, date2: 1996728
date1 is less than date2
```

What's wrong with this picture? Well, the string comparison of the first value with the second shows that the first is less than the second. Clearly, this is wrong, since the date the first string represents is later than the date the second string represents. The problem is that we're not formatting the output correctly; what we have to do is make month numbers less than 10 come out with a leading 0 (e.g., July as 07 rather than 7). The same consideration applies to the day number; we want it to be two digits in every case. Of course, if we knew that a particular number was only one digit, we could just add a leading 0 to it explicitly, but that wouldn't work correctly if the month or day number already had two digits.

To make sure the output is correct without worrying about how many digits the value has, we can use iostreams member functions called *manipulators*, which are defined not in iostream.h but in another header file called iomanip.h. This header file defines setfill, setw, and a number of other manipulators that we don't need to worry about at the moment. These manipulators operate on fields; a field can be defined as the result of one << operator. In this case, we use the setw manipulator to specify the width of each field to be formatted, and the setfill manipulator to set the character to be used to fill in the otherwise empty places in each field.

Susan had some questions about why we're using manipulators here.

> **Susan:** Why are manipulators needed? Why can't you just add the 0 where it is needed?

> **Steve:** Well, to determine that, we'd have to test each value to see whether it was large enough to fill its field. It's a lot easier just to use setw and setfill to do the work for us.

Let's change our example program to produce the output we want, as shown in Figure 9.28.

FIGURE 9.28. Output of controlled formatting example (code\coutdef2.out)

```
date1: 19961228, date2: 19960728
date1 is greater than date2
```

Manipulative Behavior

The new program is shown in Figure 9.29. Let's go over how it works. To start with, setfill takes an argument specifying the char that will be used to fill in any otherwise unused positions in an output field. We want those unused positions to be filled with 0 characters so that our output strings will consist entirely of numeric digits.[18]

FIGURE 9.29. **Controlled formatting example (code\coutdef2.cc)**

```
#include <iostream.h>
#include <strstream.h>
#include <iomanip.h>
#include "string6.h"

int main()
{
    strstream FormatStream1;
    strstream FormatStream2;
    string date1;
    string date2;

    short year1 = 1996;
    short month1 = 12;
    short day1 = 28;

    short year2 = 1996;
    short month2 = 7;
    short day2 = 28;

    FormatStream1 << setfill('0') << setw(4) <<
    year1 << setw(2) << month1 << setw(2) << day1;
```

18. Actually, our comparison functions would work correctly even if we left the fill character at its default value of "space", but the date strings would contain spaces instead of zeroes for day and month numbers less than 10, and they would look silly that way!

```
FormatStream1 >> date1;

FormatStream2 << setfill('0') << setw(4) <<
year2 << setw(2) << month2 << setw(2) << day2;

FormatStream2 >> date2;

cout << "date1: " << date1 << ", date2: " << date2 << endl;

if (date1 < date2)
  cout << "date1 is less than date2" << endl;
else if (date1 == date2)
  cout << "date1 is the same as date2" << endl;
else
  cout << "date1 is greater than date2" << endl;

return 0;
}
```

The setfill manipulator is "sticky"; that is, it applies to all of the fields that follow it in the same output statement. However, this is not true of setw, which sets the minimum width (i.e., the minimum number of characters) of the next field. Hence, we need three setw manipulators, one for each field in the output. The year field is four digits, while the month and day fields are two digits each.

Now let's get back to our DatedStockItem::Today function. Once we understand the manipulators we're using, it should be obvious how we can produce a formatted value on our strstream, but how do we get it back?

That turns out to be easy. Since the get pointer is still pointing to the beginning of the strstream, the statement FormatStream >> TodaysDate; reads data from the strstream into a string called TodaysDate just as if we were reading data from cin or a file.

Susan had a question about the statement that reads the data back from the strstream.

Susan: How do you know that FormatStream >> TodaysDate will get your data back?

Steve: Because that's how strstreams work. You write data to them just like you write to a regular ostream, then read from them just like you read from a regular istream. They're really our friends!

Baseless Accusations?

Now that we've taken care of the new function, Today, let's take a look at some of the other functions of the DatedStockItem class that differ significantly from their counterparts in the base class StockItem, the constructors, and the Reorder function.[19]

We'll start with the default constructor, which of course is called DatedStockItem::DatedStockItem() (Figure 9.30). It's a very short function, but there's a bit more here than meets the eye.

FIGURE 9.30. Default constructor for DatedStockItem **(from code\item21.cc)**

```
DatedStockItem::DatedStockItem()
: m_Expires()
{
}
```

A very good question here is what happens to the base class part of the object. This is taken care of by the default constructor of the StockItem class, which will be invoked by default to initialize that part of this object.

Susan had some questions about this notion of constructing the base class part of an object:

---

19. There are other functions whose implementation in DatedStockItem is different from the versions in StockItem, but we'll wait until later to discuss them. These are the input and output functions FormattedDisplay, operator >> and operator <<.

Susan: I don't understand your good question. What do you mean by base class part?

Steve: The base class part is the embedded base class object in the derived class object.

Susan: So derived classes use the default constructor from the base classes?

Steve: They always use *some* base class constructor to construct the base class part of a derived class object. By default, they use the default constructor for the base class object, but you can specify which base class constructor you want to use.

Susan: If that is so, then why are you writing a constructor for DatedStockItem?

Steve: Because the base class constructor only constructs the base class part of a derived class object (such as DatedStockItem). The rest of the derived class object has to be constructed too, and that job is handled by the derived class constructor.

The following is a general rule: Any base class part of a derived class object will automatically be initialized when the derived object is created at run time, by a base class constructor. By default, the default base class constructor will be called when we don't specify which base class constructor we want to execute. In other words, the code in Figure 9.30 is translated by the compiler as though it were the code in Figure 9.31.

The line : StockItem(), specifies which base class constructor we want to use to initialize the base class part of the DatedStockItem object. This is a construct called a *base class initializer*, which is the only permissible type of expression in a *member initialization list* other than a member initialization expression. In this case, we're calling the default constructor for the base class, StockItem.

FIGURE 9.31. Specifying the base class **constructor for a derived** class **object**

```
DatedStockItem::DatedStockItem()
: StockItem(),
  m_Expires()
{
}
```

Susan wanted a refresher on the idea of a member initialization list.

Susan: What's a member initialization list again? I forget.

Steve: It's a set of expressions that you can specify before the opening { of a constructor. These expressions are used to initialize the member variables of the object being constructed. A member initialization list has much the same effect as a list of variable declaration statements that initialize the variables has, except that it applies only to member variables and (in the case of a derived class object) the base class part of the object. If we weren't going to use a base class initializer, we could achieve much the same effect by including a list of statements in the constructor to initialize the member variables, but using a member initialization list is more efficient and therefore preferable even in that case.

After clearing that up, Susan wanted to make sure that she understood the reason for the base class initializer, which led to the following exchange:

Susan: Okay, let me see if I can get this straight. The derived class will use the base class default constructor unless you specify otherwise.

Steve: Correct so far.

Susan: But to specify it, you have to use a base class initializer?

Steve: Right. If you don't want the base class part to be initialized with the base class default constructor, you have to use a base class initializer to specify which base class constructor you want to use. *Some* base class constructor will always be called to initialize the base class part; the only question is which one.

Susan: It just doesn't "know" to go to the base class as a default unless you tell it to?

Steve: No, it always goes to the base class whether or not you tell it to; the question is which base class constructor is called.

Susan: Okay, then say that the base class initializer is necessary to let the derived class know which constructor you are using. This is not clear.

Steve: Hopefully, we've clarified it by now.

Whether we allow the compiler to call the default base class constructor automatically, as in Figure 9.30, or explicitly specify that base class constructor, as in Figure 9.31, the path of execution for the default DatedStockItem constructor is as illustrated in Figure 9.32.

At step 1, the DatedStockItem constructor calls the default constructor for StockItem, which starts in step 2 by initializing all the variables in the StockItem class to their default values. Once the default constructor for StockItem is finished, in step 3, it returns to the DatedStockItem constructor. In step 4, that constructor finishes the initialization of the DatedStockItem object by initializing m_Expires to the default string value (which happens to be "").

This is fine as long as the base class default constructor does the job for us. However, if it doesn't do what we want, we can specify which base constructor we wish to call, as shown in the "normal" constructor for the DatedStockItem class (Figure 9.33).

FIGURE 9.32. Constructing a default DatedStockItem **object**

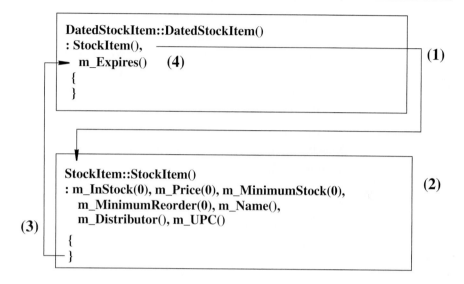

DatedStockItem::DatedStockItem()
: StockItem(), ────────────────── **(1)**
── **m_Expires()** **(4)**
{
}

StockItem::StockItem() **(2)**
: m_InStock(0), m_Price(0), m_MinimumStock(0),
m_MinimumReorder(0), m_Name(),
m_Distributor(), m_UPC()
(3)
{
}

FIGURE 9.33. Normal constructor for DatedStockItem **(from code\item21.cc)**

```
DatedStockItem::DatedStockItem(string Name, short InStock,
    short Price, short MinimumStock, short MinimumReorder,
    string Distributor, string UPC, string Expires)
  : StockItem(Name, InStock, Price, MinimumStock,
    MinimumReorder, Distributor, UPC),
    m_Expires(Expires)
{
}
```

The member initialization expression "StockItem(Name, InStock, Price, MinimumStock, MinimumReorder, Distributor, UPC)" specifies which base class constructor will be used to initialize the base class part of the DatedStockItem object. This base class initializer specifies that we want to call the "normal" constructor for the base class, StockItem. Thus, the StockItem part of the DatedStockItem object will be initialized exactly as though it were being created by the corresponding constructor for StockItem. Figure 9.34 illustrates how this works.

At step 1, the DatedStockItem constructor calls the "normal" constructor for StockItem, which starts in step 2 by initializing all the variables in the StockItem class to the values specified in the argument list to the constructor. Once the "normal" constructor for StockItem is finished, in step 3, it returns to the DatedStockItem constructor. In step 4, that constructor finishes the initialization of the DatedStockItem object by initializing m_Expires to the value of the argument Expires.

As you can see by these examples, using a base class initializer allows us to use an appropriate base class constructor to initialize the base class part of an object, which in turn means that our derived class constructor won't have to keep track of the details of the base class. This is an example of one of the main benefits claimed for object-oriented programming: We can confine the details of a class to the internals of that class, which simplifies maintenance efforts. In this case, after specifying the base class initializer the only remaining task for the DatedStockItem constructor is to initialize the member variable m_Expires.

Susan wasn't overwhelmed by the simplicity of this notion:

Susan: How does all the information of step 3 get into step 4? And exactly what part of the code here is the base class initializer? I don't see which part it is.

Steve: The information from 3 gets into the derived class DatedStockItem object in the upper part of the diagram because the DatedStockItem object contains a base class part consisting of a StockItem object. That's the object being initialized by the call to the base class constructor caused by the base class initializer, which consists of the following two lines:

```
: StockItem(Name,InStock,Price,MinimumStock,
MinimumReorder, Distributor,UPC)
```

FIGURE 9.34. Constructing a DatedStockItem object

```
DatedStockItem::DatedStockItem(
string Name,
short InStock,
short Price,
short MinimumStock,
short MinimumReorder,
string Distributor,
string UPC,
string Expires)
: StockItem(Name, InStock, Price, MinimumStock,
  MinimumReorder, Distributor, UPC),
  m_Expires(Expires)    (4)
{
}
```
(1)

```
StockItem::StockItem(
string Name,
short InStock,
short Price,
short MinimumStock,
short MinimumReorder,
string Distributor
string UPC)
: m_InStock(InStock), m_Price(Price),
m_MinimumStock(MinimumStock),
m_MinimumReorder(MinimumReorder),
m_Name(Name),
m_Distributor(Distributor), m_UPC(UPC)
}
{
```
(2)

(3)

There's another reason besides simplicity for using a base class initializer rather than trying to initialize the member variables of the base class part of our object directly: It's much safer. If we initialized the base class variables ourselves, and if the base class definition were later changed to include some new variables initialized according to arguments to the normal constructor, we might very well neglect to modify our derived class code to initialize the new variables. On the other hand, if we used a base class initializer, and its arguments changed (as they presumably would if new variables needed to be initialized), a derived class constructor that called that initializer would no longer compile. That would alert us to the change we'd have to make.

Reordering Priorities

Now that we have dealt with the constructors, let's take a look at the Reorder function (Figure 9.35).

FIGURE 9.35. Reorder **function for** DatedStockItem **(from code\item21.cc)**

```
void DatedStockItem::Reorder(ostream& os)
{
  if (m_Expires < Today())
    {
    os << "Return " << m_InStock;
    os << " units of " << m_Name;
    os << " with UPC " << m_UPC;
    os << " to " << m_Distributor << endl;
    m_InStock = 0;
    }

  StockItem::Reorder(os);
}
```

We have added a new piece of code that checks whether the expiration date on the current batch of product is before today's date; if that is the case, we create an output line indicating the product to be returned. But what about the "normal" case already dealt with in the base class Reorder function? That's taken care of by the line

StockItem::Reorder(os);, which calls the StockItem::Reorder function, using the class name with the membership operator :: to specify the exact Reorder function we want to use. If we just wrote Reorder(os), that would call the function we're currently executing, a process known as *recursion*. Recursion has its uses in certain complex programming situations, but in this case, of course, it would not do what we wanted, as we have already handled the possibility of expired items. We need to deal with the "normal" case of running low on stock, which is handled very nicely by the base class Reorder function.

We shouldn't pass by this function without noting one more point: The only reason that we can access m_InStock and the other member variables of the StockItem base class part of our object is that those member variables are protected rather than private. If they were private, we wouldn't be able to access them in our DatedStockItem functions, even though every DatedStockItem object would still have such member variables.

Susan didn't care for that last statement, but I think I talked her into accepting it.

> **Susan:** I can't picture the statement "even though every DatedStockItem object would still have such member variables."

> **Steve:** Well, every DatedStockItem has a StockItem base class part, and that base class part contributes its member variables to the DatedStockItem. Even if we can't access them because they're private, they're still there.

Now we have a good solution to the creation of stock items with dates. Unfortunately, it's not possible to have a vector of dissimilar types—that is, our current solution can't handle a combination of StockItem and DatedStockItem objects. On the other hand, it is possible to have a vector of pointers that can refer to either StockItem or DatedStockItem objects, by making use of the characteristic of C++ that a pointer to a base class object can point to a derived class object.

However, using a vector of StockItem*s to point to a mixture of StockItem and DatedStockItem objects won't give us the results we want with the current definitions of these classes. To be precise, if we call Reorder through a StockItem*, the wrong version of Reorder will be called for DatedStockItem objects. To help explain why this is so, I've drawn a number of diagrams that show how C++ determines which function is called for a given type of pointer.

Before we get to the first diagram, there's one new construct that I should explain: the use of operator new for an object of a class type. The first example of this usage is the statement SIPtr = new StockItem("beans",40,110);. In this statement, we're creating a StockItem via the expression new StockItem("beans",40,110)[20] and then assigning the address returned by new to the variable SIPtr (whose name is supposed to represent "StockItem pointer"). It should be fairly obvious why we have to use operator new here: to allocate memory for the newly constructed object, just as we did when we used operator new to allocate memory for an array of chars when creating an object of our string class.[21] The only difference from that usage is that when we use operator new with a class object, we have to choose a constructor to create the object. Here we're specifying the arguments for the name, price, and number in stock. Since the "normal" constructor will accept such types of arguments, it's the one that will be called. On the other hand, if we hadn't supplied any arguments—for example, by writing SIPtr = new StockItem;—we'd get the default constructor.

Now that I've explained this use of new, let's look at Figure 9.36, which shows how a normal function call works when Reorder is called for a StockItem object through a StockItem pointer.

---

20. The examples in this section use simplified versions of the StockItem and DatedStockItem classes to make the diagrams smaller; the principles are the same as with the full versions of these classes.

21. This was covered in Chapter 7.

FIGURE 9.36. Calling Reorder **through a** StockItem **pointer, part 1**

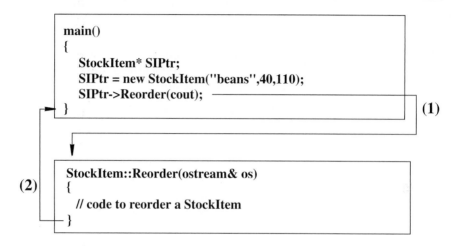

Step 1 calls StockItem::Reorder via the StockItem* variable named SIPtr. When StockItem::Reorder finishes execution, it returns to the main program (step 2); since there isn't anything else to do in the main program, the program ends at that point.

Susan had a question about the syntax of the line SIPtr->Reorder(cout);.

Susan: What does that -> thing do?

Steve: It separates a pointer to an object (on its left) from a member variable or function (on its right). In this case, it separates the pointer SIPtr from the function Reorder, so that line says that we want to call the function Reorder for whatever object SIPtr is pointing to. In other words, it does for pointers exactly what "." does for objects.

So far, so good. Now let's see what happens when we call Reorder for a DatedStockItem object through a DatedStockItem pointer (Figure 9.37).

FIGURE 9.37. **Calling** Reorder **through a** DatedStockItem **pointer**

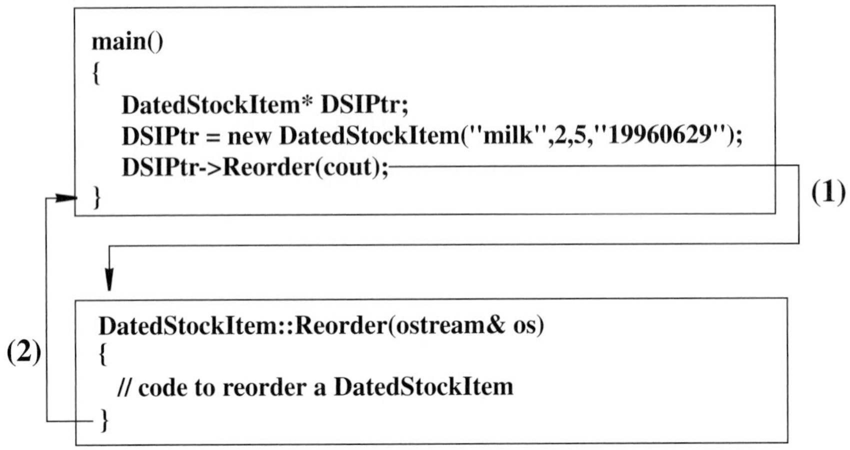

```
main()
{
    DatedStockItem* DSIPtr;
    DSIPtr = new DatedStockItem("milk",2,5,"19960629");
    DSIPtr->Reorder(cout);
}                                                                    (1)


        DatedStockItem::Reorder(ostream& os)
(2)     {
            // code to reorder a DatedStockItem
        }
```

In Figure 9.37, step 1 calls DatedStockItem::Reorder via DSIPtr, a variable of type DatedStockItem*. When DatedStockItem::Reorder finishes execution, it returns to the main program (step 2); again; since there isn't anything else to do in the main program, the program ends at that point. That looks okay, too. But what happens if we call Reorder for a DatedStockItem object through a StockItem pointer, as in Figure 9.38?

Unfortunately, step 1 in Figure 9.38 is incorrect because the line SIPtr->Reorder(cout) calls StockItem::Reorder whereas we wanted it to call DatedStockItem::Reorder. This problem arises because when we call a normal member function through a pointer, the compiler uses the declared type of the pointer to decide which actual function will be called. In this case, we've declared SIPtr to be a pointer to a StockItem, so even though the actual data type of the object it points to is DatedStockItem, the compiler thinks it's a StockItem. Therefore, the line SIPtr->Reorder(cout) results in a call to StockItem::Reorder.

FIGURE 9.38. **Calling** Reorder **through a** StockItem **pointer, part 2**

```
main()
{
    StockItem* SIPtr;
    SIPtr = new DatedStockItem("milk",2,5,"19960629");
    SIPtr->Reorder(cout);
}                                                               (1)


    StockItem::Reorder(ostream& os)
(2) {
        // code to reorder a StockItem
    }
```

Before we see how to fix this problem, we should look at a test program that actually uses these versions of the Reorder functions with the simplified versions of our StockItem and DatedStockItem classes we've been using for this discussion. Figure 9.39 shows the test program, Figure 9.40 shows the output of the test program, and Figure 9.41 shows the implementation of the classes.[22] (You may very well want to print out the files that contain this interface and its implementation, as well as the test program. Those files are code\itema.h, code\itema.cc, and code\nvirtual.cc, respectively.).

FIGURE 9.39. **Function call example (code\nvirtual.cc)**

```
#include <iostream.h>
#include "itema.h"

int main()
{
```

_____

22. The interface for these simplified StockItem and DatedStockItem classes was shown in Figure 9.7.

```
    StockItem StockItemObject("soup",32,100);
    StockItem* StockItemPointer;
    DatedStockItem DatedStockItemObject("milk",
      10,15,"19950110");

    DatedStockItem* DatedStockItemPointer;

    StockItemObject.Reorder(cout);
    cout << endl;
    DatedStockItemObject.Reorder(cout);
    cout << endl;

    StockItemPointer = new StockItem("beans",40,110);
    StockItemPointer->Reorder(cout);
    cout << endl;

    DatedStockItemPointer = new DatedStockItem("ham",
      22,30,"19970110");
    DatedStockItemPointer->Reorder(cout);
    cout << endl;

    StockItemPointer = new DatedStockItem("steak",
      90,95,"19960110");
    StockItemPointer->Reorder(cout);
    cout << endl;
}
```

FIGURE 9.40. Function call example output (code\nvirtual.out)

```
StockItem::Reorder says:
Reorder 68 units of soup

DatedStockItem::Reorder says:
Return 10 units of milk
StockItem::Reorder says:
Reorder 15 units of milk

StockItem::Reorder says:
Reorder 70 units of beans
```

StockItem::Reorder says:
Reorder 8 units of ham

StockItem::Reorder says:
Reorder 5 units of steak

FIGURE 9.41. Simplified implementation for StockItem **and** DatedStockItem **classes (code\itema.cc)**

```
#include <iostream.h>
#include <iomanip.h>
#include <strstream.h>
#include <string.h>
#include "itema.h"
#include <dos.h>

StockItem::StockItem(string Name, short InStock,
short MinimumStock)
: m_InStock(InStock), m_Name(Name),
  m_MinimumStock(MinimumStock)
{
}

void StockItem::Reorder(ostream& s)
{
short ActualReorderQuantity;

if (m_InStock < m_MinimumStock)
{
ActualReorderQuantity = m_MinimumStock - m_InStock;
s << "StockItem::Reorder says:" << endl;
s << "Reorder " << ActualReorderQuantity << " units of ";
s << m_Name << endl;
}
}

string DatedStockItem::Today()
{
```

```
        struct date d;
        unsigned short year;
        unsigned short day;
        unsigned short month;
        string TodaysDate;
        strstream FormatStream;

        getdate(&d);
        year = d.da_year;
        day = d.da_day;
        month = d.da_mon;

        FormatStream << setfill('0') << setw(4) << year <<
          setw(2) << month << setw(2) << day;
        FormatStream >> TodaysDate;

        return TodaysDate;
    }

    void DatedStockItem::Reorder(ostream& s)
    {
    short ReturnQuantity = 0;

    if (m_Expires < Today())
    {
    s << "DatedStockItem::Reorder says:" << endl;
    ReturnQuantity = m_InStock;
    m_InStock = 0;
    s << "Return " << ReturnQuantity <<  " units of ";
    s << m_Name << endl;
    }

    StockItem::Reorder(s);
    }

    DatedStockItem::DatedStockItem(string Name, short InStock,
    short MinimumStock, string Expires)
    : StockItem(Name, InStock,MinimumStock),
      m_Expires(Expires)
    {
    }
```

There shouldn't be anything too surprising in this program. When we call the Reorder function for an object, we get the function for that type of object, and when we call the Reorder function through a pointer to an object, we get the function for that type of pointer. However, what we really want is to have the DatedStockItem version of Reorder called if the object in question is a DatedStockItem, even if the pointer is of type StockItem*. We'll see how to solve that problem in the next chapter.

Review

We started the chapter with a simple inventory control example that used a StockItem class and an Inventory class, including a function called ReorderItem that can be called for an Inventory object to produce a reordering report. This function calls a Reorder function for each StockItem in its StockItem vector to calculate the quantity of that StockItem to be ordered based on the desired and current stock.

Then we built on that StockItem class by adding an expiration date. Rather than copying all of the old code and class definitions, we made use of a concept that is essential to the full use of C++ for object-oriented programming—*inheritance*. Inheritance is a method of constructing one class (the derived class) by specifying how it differs from another class (the base class) rather than writing it from scratch. We used inheritance to create a new DatedStockItem class that had all of the capabilities of the StockItem class, adding the ability to handle items with expiration dates.

In the process, we wrote a new Reorder function with the same signature as that of the base class function of the same name. This is called *overriding* the base class function. When the function with that signature is called via an object of the base class, the base class function will be called. On the other hand, when the function with that signature is called via an object of the derived class, the derived class function will be called. This allows a derived class to supply the same functionality as that of a base class but to implement it in a different way.

A derived class object can do anything that a base class object can do because a derived class object actually contains an object of the base class, called the base class part of the derived class object. This base class part is very similar to a member variable in the derived class, but it is not the same for two reasons:

1. A member variable always has a name, whereas the base class part does not.

2. The base class definition can give derived class member functions privileged access to some member variables and functions of the base class part of an object of the derived class, by marking those member variables and functions protected.

In the process of writing the new Reorder function for the DatedStockItem class, we saw how we could store a date as a string that allowed comparison of two dates to see which was later. This required us to create a formatted string representing the date as YYYYMMDD—that is, a four-digit year number, a two-digit month number, and a two-digit day number. Getting the current date wasn't too hard; we used the date variable type along with its associated getdate function to retrieve the year, month, and day of the current date. However, once we had this information, we still had to combine the parts of the date into a formatted string. One way to do this is to use the strstream data type, which is a stream that exists only in memory as a formatting aid. This topic led to a discussion of how we can specify the formatting of data rather than accept the default formatting, as we did previously; it also led to the related discussion of using the strstream class to generate formatted output.

After delving into the general topic of streams in more detail, we returned to the more specific issue of strstreams, which allowed us to solve our formatting problem by combining the << operator with the *manipulators* setw and setfill to control the width and *fill characters* of the data we wrote to the strstream.

Once we had used << to write the data to the strstream in the required YYYYMMDD format, we used >> to read it back into a string for comparison with the expiration date stored in a DatedStockItem object (see Figures 9.28 and 9.29).

After discussing the formatting of the date string, we continued by examining the default constructor of the DatedStockItem class. While this is an extremely short function, having only one member initialization expression and no code in the constructor proper, there is more to it than meets the eye. The default constructor deals only with the newly added member variable, m_Expires, but behind the scenes, the base class part of the DatedStockItem object is being initialized by the default constructor of the base class—StockItem::StockItem(). The rule is that a base class constructor will always be called for the base class part of a derived class object. If we don't specify which base class constructor we want, the default constructor for the base class will be used. To select the constructor for the base class part, we can use a construct known as a base class initializer in the member initializer list in the derived class constructor. In our "normal" constructor for DatedStockItem, we used this construct to call the corresponding constructor for the base class (see Figures 9.33 and 9.34).

Then we looked at the Reorder function for the DatedStockItem class, which includes code to request the return of any items that are past their expiration date and calls the base class Reorder function to handle the rest of the job.

At that point, we had a working DatedStockItem class, but we still couldn't mix StockItem and DatedStockItem objects in the same vector. However, it was possible to create a vector of pointers to StockItems; once we did that, we could make any of those pointers point to a DatedStockItem, employing the C++ feature that a base class pointer can also point to an object of a derived class. After seeing how to use operator new to allocate StockItem and DatedStockItem variables, we discovered that just using a base class pointer doesn't do what we wanted. As these classes are currently defined, the version of the Reorder function called through a

StockItem pointer is always the base class version, rather than the correct version for the actual type of the object the pointer refers to.

Exercises

1. Suppose that the store using our inventory control program adds a new pharmacy department. Most of their items are nonprescription medications that can be handled with the DatedStockItem class we already created, but their prescription drug items need to be handled more carefully. This means that the DeductSaleFromInventory member function has to ask for a password before allowing the sale to take place. Create a new DrugStockItem class that enforces this new rule without using inheritance.

2. The store also needs some way to keep track of its employees' hours so it can calculate their pay. We'll assume that the employees are paid their gross wages, ignoring taxes. These wages are calculated as follows:

   a. Managers are paid a flat amount per week, calculated as their hourly rate multiplied by 40 hours.

   b. Hourly employees are paid a certain amount per hour no matter how many hours they work (i.e., overtime is not paid at a higher rate).

   Write an Employee class that allows the creation of Employee objects with a specified hourly wage level and either "manager" or "hourly" salary rules. The pay for each object is to be calculated via a CalculatePay member function that uses the "manager" or "hourly" category specified when the object was created. Use the double data type to keep track of the pay rate and the total pay.[23]

3. Rewrite the DrugStockItem class from Exercise 1 using inheritance from the DatedStockItem class.

4. Rewrite the Employee class from Exercise 2 as two classes: the base Exempt class and an Hourly class derived from the base class. The CalculatePay member function for each of these classes should use the appropriate method of calculating the pay for each class. In particular, this member function doesn't need an argument specifying the number of hours worked for the Exempt class, while the corresponding member function in the Hourly class does need such an argument.

5. Rewrite the Employee class that you wrote in Exercise 2 as two classes: the base Exempt class and an Hourly class derived from the base class. To maintain the same interface for these two classes, the CalculatePay member function in both classes should have an argument specifying the number of hours worked. The implementation of the Exempt class will ignore this argument, while the Hourly implementation will use it.

6. Write an essay comparing the advantages and disadvantages of the two approaches to inheritance in the previous two exercises.[24]

7. Reimplement the DatedStockItem class to use a long variable of the form YYYYMMDD, rather than a string, to store the date.[25] Is this a better approach than using a string? Why or why not?

8. Rewrite the operator << functions for DatedStockItem and StockItem so that the former function uses the latter to display the common data items for the two classes, rather than display all the data items itself.

---

23. This data type is just like a short, except that it can handle larger numbers, including those with fractional parts. See the Glossary for details on this data type.

24. If you'll e-mail this essay to me, I might put it on my WWW page!

25. A long is just like a short, except that it can hold larger numbers. See the Glossary for details on this type.

Conclusion

In this chapter, we defined a StockItem class and then extended the functionality provided in that class by deriving a new class, DatedStockItem, based on StockItem.

However, we have not yet seen how objects of these two classes can be used interchangeably. Although we can use base class pointers to point to objects of both base and derived types, we can't yet arrange for the correct function to be called based on the actual type of the object to which the pointer refers. In Chapter 10, we will see how to overcome this barrier.

Pretty Poly

By the end of the previous chapter, we had created a DatedStockItem class by inheritance from the StockItem class, adding an expiration date field. This was a fine solution to the problem of creating a new class based on the existing StockItem class without rewriting all of the already functioning code in that class. Unfortunately, however, it didn't allow us to mix objects of the original StockItem class in the same vector with those of the new DatedStockItem class and still have the correct Reorder function called for the derived class object. So far, we've been using the first two major organizing principles of object-oriented programming: *encapsulation* and *inheritance*. Now our requirement of mixing base and derived class objects leads us to the third and final major organizing principle: *polymorphism*. Once we have defined some terms, we'll get right to using polymorphism to solve our problem of freely interchanging StockItems and DatedStockItems in our application programs.

Definitions

Static typing means determining the exact type of a variable when the program is compiled. It is the default typing mechanism in C++. Note that this has no particular relation to the keyword static.

Dynamic typing means delaying the determination of the exact type of a variable until run time rather than fixing that type at compile time, as in static typing.

Polymorphism, one of the major organizing principles in C++, allows us to implement several classes with the same interface and treat objects of all these classes as though they were of the same class. Polymorphism is a variety of *dynamic typing* that maintains the safety factor of *static type-checking*, because the compiler can determine at compile time whether a function call is legal even if it does not know the exact type of the object that will receive that function call at run time. *Polymorphism* is derived from the Greek *poly*, meaning "many", and *morph*, meaning "form". In other words, the same behavior is implemented in different forms.

Declaring a function to be **virtual** means that it is a member of a set of functions having the same *signatures* and belonging to classes related by *inheritance*. The actual function to be executed as the result of a given function call is selected from this set of functions dynamically (i.e., at run time) based on the actual type of an object referred to via a base class pointer (or base class reference). This is the C++ *dynamic typing* mechanism used to implement polymorphism, in contrast to the *static typing* used for nonvirtual functions, which are selected at compile time.

Reference counting is a mechanism that allows one copy of an object to be shared among a number of users while arranging for the automatic disposal of that object as soon as no one is using it.

Objectives of This Chapter

By the end of this chapter, you should

1. Understand how we can use polymorphism to allow objects of different classes to be treated interchangeably by the user of these classes,

2. Understand how to create a *polymorphic object* that allows polymorphism to be used safely in application programs without exposing the class user to the hazards of pointers, and

3. Understand how to use *reference counting* to allow one data item to be safely shared among several users.

Polymorphism

To select the correct function to be called based on the actual type of an object at run time, we have to use polymorphism. Polymorphic behavior of our StockItem and DatedStockItem classes means that we can (for example) mix StockItem and DatedStockItem objects in a vector and have the right Reorder function executed for each object in the vector.

Susan had a question about the relationship between base and derived classes:

> **Susan:** What do the base and derived classes share besides an interface?

> **Steve:** The derived class contains all of the member variables of the base class and can call any of the member functions of the base class. Of course, the derived class can also add whatever new member functions and member variables it needs.

Susan also had a question about this idea of mixing objects of two different types:

> **Susan:** Why would you want to handle several different types of data as though they were the same type?

> **Steve:** Because the objects of these two classes perform the same operation, although in a slightly different way, which is why they can have the same interface. In our example, a DatedStockItem acts just like a StockItem except that it has an additional data field and produces different reordering information. Ideally, we would be able to mix these two types in the application program without having to worry about which class each object belongs to except when creating an individual item (at which time we have to know whether the item has an expiration date).

However, there is a serious complication in using polymorphism: We have to refer to the objects via a pointer rather than directly.[1] While C++ does have a "native" means of doing this, it exposes us to all the dangers of pointers, both those that you're already acquainted with and others that we'll get to later in this chapter.

Susan wanted more details on why pointers are dangerous; here's the first installment of our discussion of this point.

> **Susan:** You keep saying that pointers are dangerous; what do they do that is so dangerous?

> **Steve:** It's not what they do but what their users do: mostly, create memory leaks and dangling pointers (which point to memory that has already been freed).

---

1. We could also use a reference, as we'll see in the implementation of the << and >> operators. However, that still wouldn't provide the flexibility of using real objects.

Susan: So pointers are dangerous because it is just too easy to make mistakes when you use them?

Steve: Yes.

The ideal solution to this problem is to confine pointers to the interior of classes we design so that we can keep track of them ourselves and let the application programmer worry about getting the job done. As it happens, this is possible; thus, we can obtain the benefits of polymorphism without exposing the application programmer (as opposed to the class designers; i.e., us) to the hazards of pointers. We'll see how to do that later in this chapter.

But before investigating that more sophisticated method of providing polymorphism, we need to understand the workings of the native polymorphism mechanism in C++. As we saw in Chapter 9, the address of a derived class object can be assigned to a pointer declared to be a pointer to a base class of that derived class. While this does not by itself solve the problem of calling the correct function in these circumstances, there is a way to get the behavior we want. If we define a special kind of function called a virtual function and refer to it through a pointer (or a reference) to an object, the version of that function to be executed will be determined by the actual type of the object to which the pointer (or reference) refers, rather than by the declared type of the pointer (or reference). This implies that if we declare a function to be virtual, when a function with that signature is called via a base class pointer, the actual function to be called is selected at run time rather than at compile time, as happens with nonvirtual functions. Clearly, if the actual run-time type of the object determines which version of the function is called, the compiler can't select the function at compile time.

Because the determination of the function to be called is delayed until run time, the compiler has to add code to each function call to make that determination. This code uses a construct called a vtable to keep track of the locations of all the functions for a given type of object so that the compiler-generated code can find the right function when the call is about to be executed.

As you might imagine, Susan had some questions about this notion of virtual function calls.

> **Susan:** I don't understand how the function to be executed is selected.

> **Steve:** The mechanism depends on whether it is a virtual function. If not, the linker can figure out the exact address of the function when it is linking the program, because the type of the pointer (which is known at compile time) is used. On the other hand, with a virtual function declaration, the function to be executed depends on the actual type of the object pointed to rather than the type of the pointer to the object; since that information can't be known at compile time, the linker can't do it. Therefore, in such cases the compiler sticks code in the executable program that figures it out at run time by consulting the vtable for the particular type of object the base class pointer refers to.

virtual *Certainty*

But exactly how does this help us with our Reorder function? Let's see how a virtual function affects the behavior of our final example program from Chapter 9 (nvirtual.cc, Figure 9.39). Figure 10.1 shows the same interface as before, except that StockItem::Reorder is declared to be virtual.[2] Because the current test program (virtual.cc) and implementation file (itemb.cc) are almost identical to the final test

---

2. You will notice that the virtual declaration for Reorder is repeated in DatedStockItem—this is optional. Even if you don't write virtual again in the derived class declaration of Reorder, it's still a virtual function in that class; the rule is "once virtual, always virtual". Even so, I think it's clearer to specify that the derived class function is virtual, so that's how I will show it in this book.

program (nvirtual.cc) and implementation file (itema.cc) in Chapter 9, differing only in that the new ones #include itemb.h rather than itema.h, I haven't reproduced the new versions of those files here.

If you printed out the corresponding files from the previous chapter, you might just want to mark them up to indicate these changes. Otherwise, I strongly recommend that you print out the files that contain this interface and its implementation, as well as the test program, for reference as you go through this section of the chapter; those files are itemb.h, itemb.cc, and virtual.cc, respectively.

FIGURE 10.1. Dangerous polymorphism: Interfaces of StockItem **and** DatedStockItem **with** virtual Reorder **function (code\itemb.h)**

```
// itemb.h

#include "string6.h"

class StockItem
{
public:
StockItem(string Name, short InStock, short MinimumStock);
virtual void Reorder(ostream& s);

protected:
string m_Name;
short m_InStock;
short m_MinimumStock;
};

class DatedStockItem: public StockItem // deriving a new class
{
public:
DatedStockItem(string Name, short InStock, short MinimumStock,
string Expires);

virtual void Reorder(ostream& s);

protected:
static string Today();
```

```
protected:
string m_Expires;
};
```

Figure 10.2 shows the output of the new test program.

FIGURE 10.2. virtual **function call example output (code\virtual.out)**

```
StockItem::Reorder says:
Reorder 68 units of soup

DatedStockItem::Reorder says:
Return 10 units of milk
StockItem::Reorder says:
Reorder 15 units of milk

StockItem::Reorder says:
Reorder 70 units of beans

StockItem::Reorder says:
Reorder 8 units of ham

DatedStockItem::Reorder says:
Return 90 units of steak
StockItem::Reorder says:
Reorder 95 units of steak
```

Notice that the output of this program is exactly the same as the output of the previous test program except for the last entry. With the nonvirtual Reorder function in the previous program, we got the following output:

```
StockItem::Reorder says:
Reorder 5 units of steak
```

whereas with our virtual Reorder function, we get this output:

DatedStockItem::Reorder says:
Return 90 units of steak

StockItem::Reorder says:
Reorder 95 units of steak

According to our rules, the correct answer is 95 units of steak because the stock has expired, so the program that uses the virtual Reorder function works correctly while the previous one didn't. Why is this? Because when we call a virtual function through a base class pointer, the function executed is the one defined in the class of the actual object to which the pointer points, not the one defined in the class of the pointer.

To see how this works, let's start by looking at the way in which the layout of an object with virtual functions differs from that of a "normal" object. First, Figure 10.3 shows a possible memory representation of a simplified StockItem without virtual functions.

FIGURE 10.3. A simplified StockItem **object without** virtual **functions**

Address   Name

12340000 m_Name	"soup"
12340004 m_InStock	0005
12340006 m_MinimumStock	0008

StockItem member functions

12350000 StockItem(string, short, short)
12351000 Reorder(ostream&)

One of the interesting points about this figure is that there is no connection at run time between the StockItem object and its functions. Such a connection is unnecessary because the compiler can tell exactly which function will be called whenever a function is referenced for this object, whether directly or through a pointer.

The situation is different if we have virtual functions. In that case, the compiler can't decide exactly which functions will be called for an object pointed to by a StockItem* because the actual object may be a descendant of StockItem rather than an actual StockItem. If so, we want the function defined in the derived class (e.g., DatedStockItem) to be called even though the pointer is declared to point to an object of the base class (e.g., StockItem).

Since the actual type of the object for which we want to call the function isn't available at compile time, another way must be found to determine which function should be called. The most logical place to store this information is in the object itself because, after all, we need to know where the object is in order to call the function for it. In fact, an object of a class for which any virtual functions are declared does have an extra data item in it for exactly this purpose. So whenever a call to a virtual function is compiled, the compiler translates that call into instructions that use the information in the object to determine at run time which version of the virtual function will be called.

As you might imagine, virtual functions were a major point of discussion with Susan. Here's the first installment of that discussion:

Susan: So, is a virtual function polymorphism?

Steve: No. You need virtual functions to implement polymorphism in C++, but they're not the same thing.

Susan: Where in the definition of Reorder does it say it's virtual? The implementation file is the same as it was before.

Steve: It's in the declaration of Reorder in the interface of the StockItem class in the itemb.h header file: virtual void Reorder(ostream& os);. I've also repeated it in the derived class function declaration even though that's not strictly necessary. After a function is declared as virtual in a base class, we don't have to say it's virtual in the derived class or classes; the rule is "once virtual, always virtual".

If every object needed to contain the addresses of all its virtual functions, objects might be a lot larger than they would otherwise have to be. However, this is not necessary because all objects of the same class have the same virtual functions. Therefore, the addresses of all of the virtual functions for a given class are stored in a virtual function address table, or vtable for short, and every object of that class contains the address of the vtable for that class.

Given this description of the vtable, if we make the Reorder function virtual, a StockItem object will look like Figure 10.4.[3]

FIGURE 10.4. Dangerous polymorphism: A simplified StockItem **object with a** virtual **function**

Address	Name	StockItem
12400000	(vtable address)	12410000
12400004	m_Name	"beans"
12400008	m_InStock	0040
1240000a	m_MinimumStock	0110

StockItem vtable

12410000	Reorder address	12419000

StockItem member functions

12418000 StockItem(string, short, short)
12419000 Reorder(ostream&)

On the other hand, a DatedStockItem will resemble Figure 10.5.

---

3. Please note that the layout of this figure and other similar figures has been simplified by the omission of the details of the m_Name field, which actually contains a pointer to the data of the string value of that field.

FIGURE 10.5. Dangerous polymorphism: A simplified DatedStockItem
object with a virtual **function**

DatedStockItem

12500000	(vtable address)	12510000
12500004	m_Name	"milk"
12500008	m_InStock	0005
1250000a	m_MinimumStock	0008
1250000c	m_Expires	"19960629"

DatedStockItem vtable

12510000	Reorder address	12519000

DatedStockItem member functions

Address   Name

12518000 DatedStockItem(string, short, short, string)
12519000 Reorder(ostream&)

Susan had some more questions about vtables, and I had some more
answers:

Susan: Are vtables customized for each class?

Steve: Yes.

Susan: Where do they come from, how are they created, and how
do they do what they do?

Steve: The linker creates them based on instructions from the
compiler after the compiler examines the class definition. All they
do is store the addresses of the virtual functions for that class so that

the compiler can generate code that will select the correct function for the object being referred to at run time.

Susan: How is this stuff different from derivation?

Steve: It's part of making derivation work correctly when we want to use pointers to the base class and mix base and derived class objects in our program.

Susan: I don't get this vtable stuff. Does it just point the Reorder function in the proper direction at run time?

Steve: Exactly!

Susan: This stuff is beyond "UGH!". It is just outrageous, and I can't believe that you understand this stuff.

Steve: It wasn't that easy for me either. Acquiring a full understanding of virtual functions is one of the major milestones in learning C++, even for programmers with substantial experience in other languages.

Now that we have declared Reorder as a virtual function, let's see how this affects the operation of the function call examples we saw in Chapter 9 (Figures 9.36 through 9.38). First, Figure 10.6 shows how a virtual (i.e., dynamically determined) function call works when Reorder is called for a StockItem object through a StockItem pointer such as SIPtr.

Next, Figure 10.7 shows how a virtual (i.e., dynamically determined) function call works when Reorder is called for a DatedStockItem object through a DatedStockItem pointer.

Finally, Figure 10.8 shows how a virtual (i.e., dynamically determined) function call works when Reorder is called for a DatedStockItem object through a StockItem pointer.

FIGURE 10.6. **Dangerous polymorphism: Calling a** virtual Reorder **function through a** StockItem **pointer to a** StockItem **object**

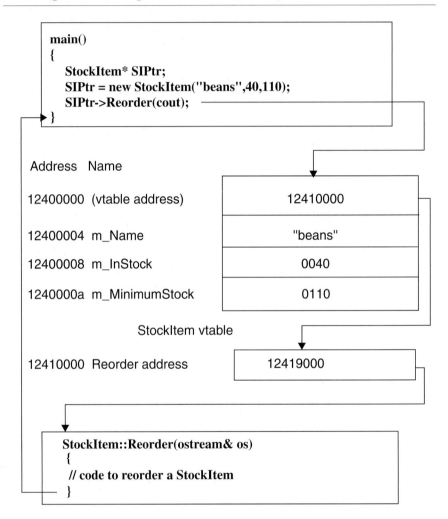

The net result of the call illustrated in Figure 10.6 is the same as that illustrated in Figure 9.36: StockItem::Reorder is called. As before, this is what we want in this situation.

FIGURE 10.7. Dangerous polymorphism: Calling a virtual Reorder **function through a** DatedStockItem **pointer to a** DatedStockItem **object**

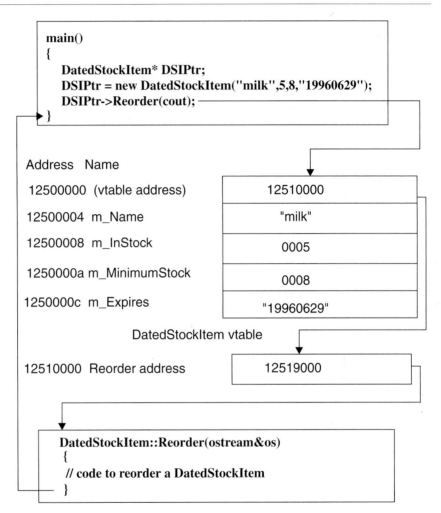

Again, the net result of the call illustrated in Figure 10.7 is the same as that illustrated in Figure 9.37: DatedStockItem::Reorder is called. This is correct in this situation.

FIGURE 10.8. **Dangerous polymorphism: Calling a** virtual Reorder **function through a** StockItem **pointer to a** DatedStockItem **object**

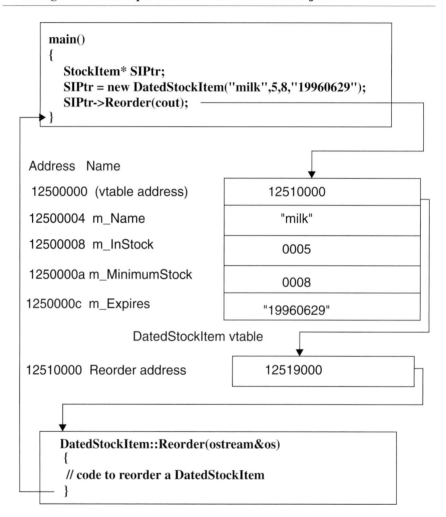

Figure 10.8 is where the virtual function pays off. The correct function, DatedStockItem::Reorder, is called even though the type of the pointer through which it is called is StockItem*. This is in contrast

to the result of that same call with the non-virtual function, illustrated in Figure 9.38. In that case, StockItem::Reorder rather than DatedStockItem::Reorder was called.

What happens if we add another virtual function, say Write, to the StockItem class after the Reorder function? The new virtual function will be added to the vtables for both the StockItem and DatedStockItem classes. Then the situation for a StockItem object might look like Figure 10.9.

FIGURE 10.9. Dangerous polymorphism: A simplified StockItem **object with two** virtual **functions**

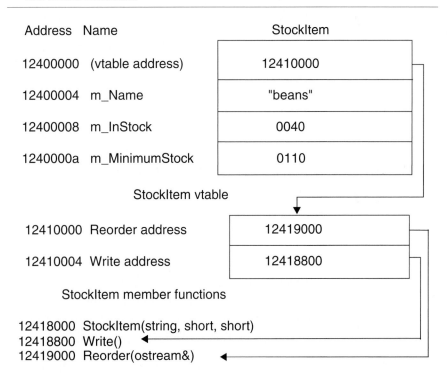

And the situation for a DatedStockItem might look like Figure 10.10.

FIGURE 10.10. **Dangerous polymorphism: A simplified** DatedStockItem **with two** virtual **functions**

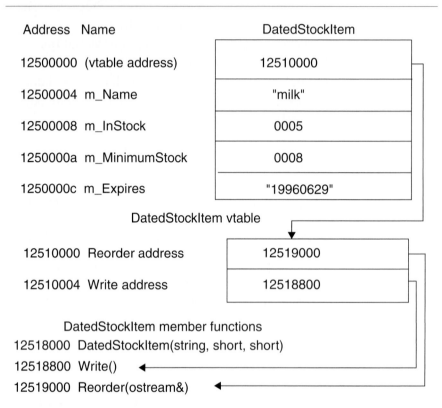

As you can see, the new function has been added to both vtables, so a call to Write through a base class pointer will call the correct function.

To translate this virtual function mechanism into what I hope is understandable English, we can express the call to the virtual function Write in the line SIPtr->Write(cout); as follows:

1. Get the vtable address from the object whose address is in SIPtr.

2. Since we are calling Write through a StockItem*, and Write is the second defined virtual function in the StockItem class, retrieve the address of the Write function from the second function address slot in the vtable for the actual object that the StockItem* points to.

3. Execute the function at that address.

By following this sequence, you can see that while both versions of Write are referred to via the same relative position in both the StockItem and the DatedStockItem vtables, the particular version of Write executed depends on which vtable the object refers to. Since all objects of the same class have the same member functions, all StockItem objects point to the same StockItem vtable and all DatedStockItem objects point to the same DatedStockItem vtable.

Susan had some questions about adding a new virtual function:

Susan: What do you mean by "added to both vtables"? Do StockItem and DatedStockItem each have their own?

Steve: Yes.

Susan: How does the vtable get the address for the new StockItems?

Steve: It's the other way around. Each StockItem, when it's created by the constructor, has its vtable address filled in by the compiler automatically.

A Pointed Reminder

Unfortunately, it's not quite as simple to make polymorphism work for us as this might suggest. As is so often the case, the culprit is the use of pointers. To see how pointers cause trouble with polymorphism, let's start by adding the standard I/O functions, operator << and operator >>, to our simplified interface for the StockItem and DatedStockItem classes. Figure 10.11 shows a test program illustrating how we can use these new functions, Figure 10.12 shows the output of the test program, and Figure 10.13 shows the new version of the interface. I strongly recommend that you print out that header file and the test program for reference as you leaf through this section of the chapter; the latter file is polyioa.cc.

FIGURE 10.11. Dangerous polymorphism: Using operator << **with a** StockItem* **(code\polyioa.cc)**

```
#include <iostream.h>
#include "vector.h"
#include "itemc.h"

int main()
{
    vector <StockItem*> x(2);

    x[0] = new StockItem("3-ounce cups",71,78);

    x[1] = new DatedStockItem("milk",76,87,"19970719");

    cout << "A StockItem: " << endl;
    cout << x[0] << endl;

    cout << "A DatedStockItem: " << endl;
    cout << x[1] << endl;

    delete x[0];
    delete x[1];

    return 0;
}
```

FIGURE 10.12. Result of using operator << **with a** StockItem* **(code\polyioa.out)**

```
A StockItem:
0
3-ounce cups
71
```

78

A DatedStockItem:
19970719
milk
76
87

FIGURE 10.13. Dangerous polymorphism: StockItem **interface with** operator << **and** operator >> **(code\itemc.h)**

```cpp
#include "string6.h"

class StockItem
{
friend ostream& operator << (ostream& os, StockItem* Item);
friend istream& operator >> (istream& is, StockItem*& Item);

public:
    StockItem(string Name, short InStock, short MinimumStock);
virtual ~StockItem();

virtual void Reorder(ostream& os);
virtual void Write(ostream& os);

protected:
    string m_Name;
    short m_InStock;
    short m_MinimumStock;
};

class DatedStockItem: public StockItem
{
public:
    DatedStockItem(string Name, short InStock,
      short MinimumStock, string Expires);

virtual void Reorder(ostream& os);
virtual void Write(ostream& os);
```

```
protected:
static string Today();

protected:
    string m_Expires;
};
```

Susan had some questions about the StockItem::~StockItem destructor declared in this latest version of the interface.

Susan: Why do we need a destructor for StockItem now, when we didn't need one before?

Steve: The reason we haven't needed a destructor for the StockItem class until now is that the compiler-generated destructor works fine as long as two conditions are both present. First, the member variables of the class must all be of concrete data types (which they are here). Second, the class must have no virtual functions, which of course isn't true for StockItem anymore. We've discussed the reason for the first condition: If we have member variables that aren't of concrete data types (e.g., pointers), they won't clean up after themselves properly. We'll find out exactly why the second condition is important as soon as we get through looking at the output of the sample program.

Susan: Okay, I'm sure I can wait. But why is it virtual?

Steve: We'll cover that at the same time.

The first item of note in the test program in Figure 10.11 is that we can create a vector of StockItem*s to hold the addresses of any mixture of StockItems and DatedStockItems, because we can assign the addresses of variables of either of those types to a base class pointer (i.e., a StockItem*). Once we have the vector of StockItem*s, we use operator new to acquire the memory for whichever type of object we're creating. This allows us to access these objects via pointers rather than directly and thus to use polymorphism. Once we finish using the objects, we have to make sure they are properly disposed of by calling operator delete at the end of the program; otherwise, a memory leak results.

The calls to delete in Figure 10.11 also hold the key to Susan's question about why we needed to write a destructor for this new version of the StockItem class. You see, when we call operator delete for an object of class type, delete calls the destructor for that object to do whatever cleanup is necessary at the end of the object's lifespan. For this reason, it is very important that the correct destructor is called. If a base class destructor instead of a derived class destructor were called, the cleanup of the fields defined in the derived class wouldn't occur. However, when we delete a derived class object through a base class pointer, as we are doing in the current example program, the compiler can't tell at compile time which destructor it should call when the program executes. What do we do when we need to delay the determination of a function call until run time? We use a virtual function. Therefore, whenever we want to call delete on an object through a base class pointer, we need to make the destructor for that object virtual.[4]

But that still doesn't explain exactly why we need a virtual destructor whenever we have any other virtual functions. The reason for that rule is that there isn't much point in referring to an object through a base class pointer if it doesn't have any virtual functions, because the correct function will never be called in that case! Therefore, although the strict rule is "the destructor must be virtual if there are any calls to delete through a base class pointer", that amounts to the same thing as "the destructor must be virtual if there are any other virtual functions in the class", and that's easier to remember and follow.

---

4. There's one more fine point that I should address here: If a base class destructor is virtual, the destructors in all classes derived from that class will also automatically be virtual, so we don't have to make them virtual explicitly.

Now let's take a look at the new implementation of the StockItem class, which is shown in Figure 10.14. This code is in code\itemc.cc if you want to print it out for reference.

FIGURE 10.14. Dangerous polymorphism: StockItem **implementation with** operator << **and** operator >> **(code\itemc.cc)**

```cpp
#include <iostream.h>
#include <iomanip.h>
#include <strstream.h>
#include <string.h>
#include "itemc.h"
#include <dos.h>

StockItem::StockItem(string Name, short InStock,
short MinimumStock)
: m_InStock(InStock), m_Name(Name),
  m_MinimumStock(MinimumStock)
{
}

StockItem::~StockItem()
{
}

void StockItem::Reorder(ostream& os)
{
  short ReorderAmount;

  if (m_InStock < m_MinimumStock)
    {
    ReorderAmount = m_MinimumStock-m_InStock;
    os << "Reorder " << ReorderAmount << " units of " << m_Name;
    }
}

ostream& operator << (ostream& os, StockItem* Item)
{
    Item->Write(os);
```

```
      return os;
   }

   void StockItem::Write(ostream& os)
   {
      os << 0 << endl;
      os << m_Name << endl;
      os << m_InStock << endl;
      os << m_MinimumStock << endl;
   }

   istream& operator >> (istream& is, StockItem*& Item)
   {
      string Expires;
      short InStock;
      short MinimumStock;
      string Name;

      is >> Expires;
      is >> Name;
      is >> InStock;
      is >> MinimumStock;

      if (Expires == "0")
         Item = new StockItem(Name,InStock,MinimumStock);
      else
         Item = new DatedStockItem(Name,InStock,
         MinimumStock,Expires);

      return is;
   }

   void DatedStockItem::Reorder(ostream& os)
   {
      if (m_Expires < Today())
         {
         os << "DatedStockItem::Reorder says:" << endl;
         os << "Return " << m_InStock <<  " units of ";
         os << m_Name << endl;
```

```
        m_InStock = 0;
        }

    StockItem::Reorder(os);
}

string DatedStockItem::Today()
{
  struct date d;
  unsigned short year;
  unsigned short day;
  unsigned short month;
  string TodaysDate;
  strstream FormatStream;

  getdate(&d);
  year = d.da_year;
  day = d.da_day;
  month = d.da_mon;

  FormatStream << setfill('0') << setw(4) << year <<
    setw(2) << month << setw(2) << day;
  FormatStream >> TodaysDate;

  return TodaysDate;
}

DatedStockItem::DatedStockItem(string Name, short InStock,
short MinimumStock, string Expires)
: StockItem(Name, InStock,MinimumStock),
  m_Expires(Expires)
{
}

void DatedStockItem::Write(ostream& os)
{
  os << m_Expires << endl;
  os << m_Name << endl;
  os << m_InStock << endl;
```

```
    os << m_MinimumStock << endl;
}
```

Susan had some questions about the test program and how it relates to the implementation.

Susan: Why do you need the same headers in the test program as you do in the implementations?

Steve: Because otherwise the compiler doesn't know how to allocate memory for a StockItem or what functions it can perform.

Susan: I didn't know that the use of headers also allocates memory.

Steve: It doesn't. However, the compiler needs the headers to figure out how large every object is so it can allocate storage for each object.

Susan: How does it figure that out?

Steve: It adds up the sizes of all the components in the object you're defining. For example, if you've defined a StockItem to contain three shorts and two strings, then the size of a StockItem object will be equal to the size of three shorts plus the size of two strings, with possibly some additional space for other stuff the compiler knows about, such as a vtable pointer.

Susan: Why do you have to allocate storage anyway? I mean, why can't you just tell the compiler how much memory you have left and let it use as much as it wants until the memory is used up? Then you know you're done.

Steve: It does use as much memory as it needs, but it has to know how much of the memory to set aside for each object that you create.

Susan: So, if you have a string class in the implementation of a program and you intend to use it in the interface, then it has to be included in both because they both get compiled separately?

Steve: Sort of. An interface (i.e., a header file) doesn't get compiled separately; it's #included wherever it's needed.

Susan: Yes, but why does it need to be in both places? Why isn't one place good enough?

Steve: Because each .cc file is compiled separately; when the compiler is handling any particular .cc file, it doesn't know about any header file that isn't mentioned in that file. Therefore, we have to mention every header in every .cc file that uses objects defined in that header.

Susan: So they are compiled separately. How are they ever connected, and if they do become connected, why is it necessary to write them twice?

Steve: They are connected only by the linker.

Susan: If they are included in the implementations, aren't they included in the test programs?

Steve: No, because the test program is compiled separately from the implementations. In fact, the writer of the test program may not even have the source code for the implementations.

Susan: And if they are needed, then why aren't the other header files needed in the test programs or any other programs for that matter?

Steve: You only have to include those header files that the compiler needs to figure out the size and functions of any object you use.

Susan: Yes, but then if they're necessary for the implementation, then they should be needed for the test programs, I would think. I still don't get it.

Steve: Each header file is needed only in source files that refer to the objects whose classes are defined in that header file.

Susan: Well, if you're writing an implementation for a program, then I think that every source file that uses the class needs to include all the header files, no?

Steve: Yes, except that sometimes you have objects that are used only inside the implementation of a class, as we'll see later in this chapter.

Let's start our analysis of the new versions of the I/O functions with the declaration of operator <<, which is friend ostream& operator << (ostream& os, StockItem* Item);. The second argument to this function is a StockItem* rather than a StockItem because we have to refer to our StockItem and DatedStockItem objects through a base class pointer (i.e., a StockItem*) to get the benefits of polymorphism. Although operator << isn't a virtual function (since it's not a member function at all), we will see that it still makes use of polymorphism.

Susan wanted to know why we needed new I/O functions again:

Susan: Why are you explaining >> and << again? Why won't the old ones do?

Steve: Because the old ones can use StockItems directly, whereas the new ones have to operate on StockItem*s instead. This is part of what is wrong with the standard method of using virtual functions to achieve polymorphism.

Susan: Why aren't you showing how polymorphism is done with real data instead of these >> and << things again?

Steve: This *is* how polymorphism is done with real data, if we expose the pointers to the application program.

Susan: Do you have to write *everything* that you see in your classes? Do you even have to define your periods?

Steve: No, as a matter of fact, the "." operator is (unfortunately) one of the few operators that can't be redefined.

The next point worthy of discussion is that we can use the same operator << to display either a StockItem or a DatedStockItem even though the display functions for those two types are actually different. Let's look at the implementation of this version of operator <<, shown in Figure 10.15.

FIGURE 10.15. Dangerous polymorphism: The implementation of operator << with a StockItem* (from code\itemc.cc)

```
ostream& operator << (ostream& os, StockItem* Item)
{
   Item->Write(os);
   return os;
}
```

This implementation looks pretty simple, as it merely calls a function called Write to do the actual work. In fact, this code looks too simple: How does it decide whether to display a StockItem or a DatedStockItem?

The Old Switcheroo

This is an application of polymorphism: operator << doesn't have to decide whether to call the version of Write in the StockItem class or the one in the DatedStockItem class because that decision is made automatically at run time. Write is a virtual function declared in the

StockItem class; therefore, the exact version of Write called through a StockItem* is determined by the run-time type of the object that the StockItem* actually points to.

To complete the explanation of how operator << works, we'll need to examine Write. Let's look at its implementation for the simplified versions of our StockItem (Figure 10.16) and DatedStockItem (Figure 10.17) classes.

FIGURE 10.16. Dangerous polymorphism: StockItem::Write **(from code\itemc.cc)**

```
void StockItem::Write(ostream& os)
{
    os << 0 << endl;
    os << m_Name << endl;
    os << m_InStock << endl;
    os << m_MinimumStock << endl;
}
```

FIGURE 10.17. Dangerous polymorphism: DatedStockItem::Write **(from code\itemc.cc)**

```
void DatedStockItem::Write(ostream& os)
{
    os << m_Expires << endl;
    os << m_Name << endl;
    os << m_InStock << endl;
    os << m_MinimumStock << endl;
}
```

The only thing that might not be obvious about these functions is why StockItem::Write writes the "0" out as its first action. We know that there's no date for a StockItem, so why not just write out the data that it does have? The reason is that if we want to read the data back in, we need some way to distinguish between a StockItem and a DatedStockItem. Since "0" is not a valid date, we can use it as an indicator meaning "the following data belongs to a StockItem, not to a

DatedStockItem". In other words, when we read data from the inventory file to create our StockItem and DatedStockItem objects, any set of data that starts with a "0" will produce a StockItem while any set that starts with a valid date will produce a DatedStockItem.[5]

If this still isn't perfectly clear, don't worry. The next section, which covers operator >>, should clear it up.

It's Not Polite to Point

First, let's examine the header of the operator >> function:

```
istream& operator >> (istream& is, StockItem*& Item)
```

Most of this should be familiar by now, but there is one oddity: The declaration of the second argument to this function is StockItem*&. What does that mean?

It's a reference to a pointer. Now, before you decide to throw in the towel, recall that we use a reference argument when we need to modify a variable in the calling function. In this case, that variable is a StockItem* (a pointer to a StockItem or one of its derived classes), and we are going to have to change it by assigning the address of a newly created StockItem or DatedStockItem to it. Hence, our argument has to be a reference to the variable in the calling function; since that variable is a StockItem*, our argument has to be declared as a reference to a StockItem*, which we write as StockItem*&.

Having cleared up that point, let's look at how we would use this new function (Figure 10.18). In case you want to print out the file containing this code, it is polyiob.cc.

Susan had a question about the argument to the ifstream constructor:

---

5. By the way, the use of "0" to mean "never" is safe because "0" is easily distinguishable from any real date, unlike actual dates in the year 1999, which have been used to signify "never" in old programs written in the last 30 years.

Susan: What is polyiob.in?

Steve: It's the data file we're going to read the data from.

FIGURE 10.18. Dangerous polymorphism: Using operator >> **and** operator << **with a** StockItem* **(code\polyiob.cc)**

```
// polyiob.cc

#include <iostream.h>
#include <fstream.h>
#include "vector.h"
#include "itemc.h"

int main()
{
    StockItem* x;
    StockItem* y;

    ifstream ShopInfo("polyiob.in");

    ShopInfo >> x;

    ShopInfo >> y;

    cout << "A StockItem: " << endl;
    cout << x;

    cout << endl;

    cout << "A DatedStockItem: " << endl;
    cout << y;

    delete x;
    delete y;

    return 0;
}
```

Before we continue to analyze this program, look at Figure 10.19, which shows the output it produces.

FIGURE 10.19. Dangerous polymorphism: The results of using operator >> **and** operator << **with a** StockItem* **(code\polyiob.out)**

A StockItem:
0
3-ounce cups
71
78

A DatedStockItem:
19970719
milk
76
87

Now let's get back to the code. You alert readers will have noticed something odd here: How can we assign a value to a variable such as x or y without allocating any memory for it? For that matter, how can we call operator delete for a pointer variable that hasn't had memory assigned to it? These aren't errors but consequences of the way we have to implement operator >> with the tools we have so far. To see why this is so, take a look at that implementation, in Figure 10.20.

This starts out reasonably enough by declaring variables to hold the expiration date (Expires), number in stock (InStock), minimum number desired in stock (MinimumStock), and the name of the item (Name). Then we read values for these variables from the istream supplied as the left-hand argument in the operator >> call, which in the case of our example program is ShopInfo. Next, we examine the variable Expires, which was the first variable to be read in from the istream. If the value of Expires is "0", meaning "not a date", we create a new StockItem by calling the normal constructor for that class and assigning memory to that new object via operator new. If the Expires value isn't "0", we assume it's a date and create a new

DatedStockItem by calling the constructor for DatedStockItem and assigning memory for the new object via operator new. Finally, we return the istream so it can be used in further operator >> calls.

The fact that we have to create a different type of object in these two cases is the key to why we have to allocate the memory in the operator >> function rather than in the calling program. The actual type of the object isn't known until we read the data from the file, so we can't allocate memory for the object until that time. This isn't necessarily a bad thing in itself; the trouble is that we can't free the memory automatically because the calling program owns the vector of StockItem pointers and has to call delete to free the memory allocated to those pointers when the objects are no longer needed.

FIGURE 10.20. Dangerous polymorphism: The implementation of operator >> **(from code\itemc.cc)**

```
istream& operator >> (istream& is, StockItem*& Item)
{
    string Expires;
    short InStock;
    short MinimumStock;
    string Name;

    is >> Expires;
    is >> Name;
    is >> InStock;
    is >> MinimumStock;

    if (Expires == "0")
        Item = new StockItem(Name,InStock,MinimumStock);
    else
        Item = new DatedStockItem(Name,InStock,
        MinimumStock,Expires);

    return is;
}
```

While it is legal (and very common) to write programs in which memory is allocated and freed in this way, it isn't a good idea. The likelihood of error in any large program that uses this method of memory management is approximately 100%. Besides the problem of forgetting to free memory or using memory that has already been freed, we also have the problem that copying pointers leaves two pointers pointing to the same data, which makes it even more likely that the data will either be freed prematurely or not freed at all when it is no longer in use.

Susan had some questions about the dangers of pointers:

Susan: So the programmer forgets to free memory?

Steve: Yes.

Susan: Can't you just write the code to free the memory once?

Steve: Yes, unless you ever change the program.

Susan: Or can these bad things happen on their own even if the program is written properly?

Steve: Yes, that can happen under certain circumstances, but luckily we won't run into any of those circumstances in this book.

We'll begin to solve these problems right after some exercises.

Exercises, First Set

1. Rewrite the DrugStockItem class that you wrote in Chapter 9 as a derived class of DatedStockItem, using virtual functions to allow DrugStockItem objects to be used in place of StockItem objects or DatedStockItem objects, just as you can use DatedStockItem objects in place of StockItem objects.

2. Rewrite the Employee class that you wrote in Chapter 9 as three classes: a base Employee class, an Exempt class, and an Hourly class. The latter two classes will be derived from the base class. The virtual CalculatePay member function for each of these derived classes should use the appropriate method of calculating the pay for each class so that an Exempt object or an Hourly object can be substituted for an Employee class object. The Employee class CalculatePay function should display an error message, as that class does not have a method of calculating pay. Note that unlike the first Employee exercise in Chapter 9, you *must* maintain the same interface for the CalculatePay function in these classes because you are using a base class pointer to derived class objects.

Pretty Polly Morphic

As we have just seen, the "standard" method of adding polymorphism to our programs is, to use a technical term, *ugly*; that is, it is error prone and virtually impossible to maintain. After a few more definitions, we're going to see how to fix these problems with an advanced technique I refer to as *polymorphic objects*.

More Definitions

A **polymorphic object** is a C++ object that presents the appearance of a simple object while behaving polymorphically, but without the hazards of exposing the user of the polymorphic object to the pointers used within its implementation. The user does not have to know about any of the details of the implementation, but merely instantiates an object of the single visible class (the *manager* class). That object does what the user wants with the help of an object of a *worker* class, which is derived from the manager class.

The **manager/worker idiom** is a mechanism that allows the effective type of an object to be determined at run time without requiring the user of the object to be concerned with pointers.[6]

The **reference-counting idiom** is a mechanism that allows one object (the reference-counted object) to be shared by several other objects (the client objects); thus, a copy needn't be made for each of the client objects.

Paging Miss Management

You may be wondering what an "idiom" is in programming. Well, in English or any other natural language, an idiom is a phrase whose meaning can't be derived directly from the meanings of its individual words. An example would be "to make good time", which actually means "to proceed rapidly". Similarly, the manager/worker idiom used to implement polymorphic objects has effects that aren't at all obvious from a casual inspection of its components.

I should tell you that many, if not most, professional C++ programmers don't know about this method of making polymorphism safe and easy to use for the application programmer. Why then am I including it in a book for relatively inexperienced programmers?

Because I believe it is the best solution to the very serious problems caused by dynamic memory allocation when using polymorphism. For that reason, every serious C++ programmer should know this idiom and understand how to apply it to real-life problems.

---

6. *Manager/worker* is my name for what James Coplien calls the *envelope/letter idiom* in his book, *Advanced C++: Programming Styles and Idioms* (Addison-Wesley Publishing Company, Reading, Mass., 1992). Warning: As its title indicates, his is not an easy book; however, it does merit study by those who have a solid grasp of C++ fundamentals.

At this point, Susan was ready to give this new idea a shot, as the following exchange indicates:

Susan: Okay, I feel I have followed you fairly well up to the point of the big thing you're going to do here with the polymorphic objects. I think that stuff is going to take some real thinking time. I hope it goes well.

Steve: I hope so too. Otherwise, we'll see lots of "ughs".

Assuming that I have impressed the importance of this technique on you, how does it work? The most elementary answer is that it involves creating a set of classes that work as a team to present the appearance of a simple object that has the desired polymorphic behavior. The user of the class (i.e., the application programmer) doesn't have to know about any of the details of this idiom; he or she merely defines an object of the single visible class, and that object does what the user wants with the help of an object of another class. James Coplien calls these two kinds of classes *envelope* and *letter*, respectively, but I'm going to call them *manager* and *worker*. I think these names are easier to remember because the outside world sees only objects of the manager class, which take credit for everything done by the polymorphic object even though most of the work is actually done by objects of the worker classes.

As usual, all of the intricacies of the implementation are the responsibility of the class designers (us). However, before we get into the details of how a polymorphic object works, let's see how it affects the way we use the StockItem class. For reference, Figure 10.21 shows the way we used the old StockItem class in Chapter 9, and Figure 10.22 shows how we will use the new StockItem class; note the lack of deletes and the fact that the variables in Figure 10.22 are StockItems rather than StockItem pointers.[7]

FIGURE 10.21. Dangerous polymorphism: Using operator >> **and** operator << **with a** StockItem* **(code\polyiob.cc)**

```
// polyiob.cc

#include <iostream.h>
#include <fstream.h>
#include "vector.h"
#include "itemc.h"

int main()
{
    StockItem* x;
    StockItem* y;

    ifstream ShopInfo("polyiob.in");

    ShopInfo >> x;

    ShopInfo >> y;

    cout << "A StockItem: " << endl;
    cout << x;

    cout << endl;

    cout << "A DatedStockItem: " << endl;
    cout << y;

    delete x;
    delete y;

    return 0;
}
```

7. If you were wondering why the file name is different in these two figures, it's because the program in Figure 10.22 is using the "real" version of the StockItem class rather than the simplified one used by the program in Figure 10.21. Therefore, it needs more input to fill in the extra member variables.

FIGURE 10.22. Safe polymorphism: Using operator >> **and** operator << **with a polymorphic** StockItem **(code\polyioc.cc)**

```cpp
#include <iostream.h>
#include <fstream.h>
#include "vector.h"
#include "itemp.h"

int main()
{
    StockItem x;
    StockItem y;

    ifstream ShopInfo("shop22.in");

    ShopInfo >> x;

    ShopInfo >> y;

    cout << "A StockItem: " << endl;
    cout << x;

    cout << endl;

    cout << "A DatedStockItem: " << endl;
    cout << y;

    return 0;
}
```

I strongly recommend that you print out the files that contain the interface and the implementation of the polymorphic object version of StockItem, as well as the test program, to refer to as you go through this section of the chapter. Those files are itemp.h (StockItem interface in Figure 10.23), itempi.h (UndatedStockItem and DatedStockItem interfaces in Figure 10.24), itemp.cc (UndatedStockItem and DatedStockItem implementation in Figure 10.25), and polyioc.cc (test program in Figure 10.22). By the way, the line class string; at the beginning of itemp.h merely tells the compiler that string is the name of a class, so that it won't complain when we try to use string as an argument type in our function declarations for the StockItem class.

You must be happy to see that we've eliminated the visible pointers in the new version of the example program, but how does it work? Let's start by looking at Figure 10.23, which shows the interface for the manager class StockItem. As we've discussed, this is the class of the objects that are visible to the user of the polymorphic object.

FIGURE 10.23. Safe polymorphism: The polymorphic object version of the StockItem **interface (code\itemp.h)**

```
// itemp.h

class string;

class StockItem
{
friend ostream& operator << (ostream& os,
  const StockItem& Item);

friend istream& operator >> (istream& is, StockItem& Item);

public:
  StockItem();
  StockItem(const StockItem& Item);
  StockItem& operator = (const StockItem& Item);
virtual ~StockItem();

  StockItem(string Name, short InStock,
  short Price, short MinimumStock,
  short MinimumReorder, string Distributor, string UPC);

  StockItem(string Name, short InStock,
  short Price, short MinimumStock,
  short MinimumReorder, string Distributor, string UPC,
```

```
    string Expires);

    virtual bool CheckUPC(string UPC);
    virtual void DeductSaleFromInventory(short QuantitySold);
    virtual short GetInventory();
    virtual string GetName();

    virtual void Reorder(ostream& os);
    virtual void FormattedDisplay(ostream& os);
    virtual void Write(ostream& os);

    protected:
      StockItem(int);

    protected:
      StockItem* m_Worker;
      short m_Count;
    };
```

Unlike the classes we've dealt with before, where the member functions deserved most of our attention, possibly the most interesting point about this new version of the StockItem class is its member variables, especially the variable named m_Worker. It's a pointer, which isn't all that strange; the question is, what type of pointer?

It's a pointer to a StockItem—that is, a pointer to the same type of object that we're defining! Assuming that is useful, is it even legal?

We'll Manage Somehow

Yes, it is legal, because the compiler can figure out how to allocate storage for a pointer to any type whether or not it knows the full definition of that type. However, this doesn't answer the question of why we would want a pointer to a StockItem in our StockItem class in the first place. The answer is that, as we saw in the discussion of polymorphism earlier in this chapter, a pointer to a StockItem can actually point to an object of any class derived from StockItem via public inheritance. We're going to make use of this fact to implement the bulk of the functionality of our StockItem objects in the classes UndatedStockItem and DatedStockItem, which are derived from StockItem.

Susan didn't think this use of a pointer to refer to a worker object was very obvious. Here's the discussion we had about it.

> **Susan:** Ugh. What is m_Worker? Where did it come from, and why is it suddenly so popular? Don't tell me it's a pointer. I want to know exactly what it does.

> **Steve:** It points to the "worker" object that actually does the work for the StockItem, which is why it is called m_Worker.

In essence, we're renaming the old StockItem class to UndatedStockItem and creating a new StockItem class that will handle interaction with the application programmer. Objects of this new StockItem class will pass the actual class-specific operations to an object of the UndatedStockItem or DatedStockItem class as needed.

Now that we have an overview of the structure of the classes we're designing, Figure 10.24 shows the interfaces for the worker classes UndatedStockItem and DatedStockItem.

FIGURE 10.24. Safe polymorphism: The UndatedStockItem **and** DatedStockItem **interfaces for the polymorphic version of** StockItem **(code\itempi.h)**

```
class UndatedStockItem : public StockItem
{
public:
  UndatedStockItem();

  UndatedStockItem(string Name, short InStock,
    short Price, short MinimumStock, short ReorderQuantity,
    string Distributor, string UPC);
```

```
virtual bool CheckUPC(string UPC);
virtual void DeductSaleFromInventory(short QuantitySold);
virtual short GetInventory();
virtual string GetName();

virtual void Reorder(ostream& os);
virtual void FormattedDisplay(ostream& os);
virtual ostream& Write(ostream& os);

protected:
  short m_InStock;
  short m_Price;
  short m_MinimumStock;
  short m_MinimumReorder;
  string m_Name;
  string m_Distributor;
  string m_UPC;
};

class DatedStockItem : public UndatedStockItem
{
public:

  DatedStockItem(string Name, short InStock,
    short Price, short MinimumStock, short MinimumReorder,
    string Distributor, string UPC, string Expires);

virtual void Reorder(ostream& os);
virtual void FormattedDisplay(ostream& os);
virtual ostream& Write(ostream& os);

protected:
static string Today();

protected:
  string m_Expires;
};
```

And Figure 10.25 shows the implementation of these classes.

FIGURE 10.25. Safe polymorphism: The implementation of the
UndatedStockItem **and** DatedStockItem classes **(code\itemp.cc)**

```cpp
#include <iostream.h>
    #include <iomanip.h>
    #include <strstrea.h>
    #include <string.h>
    #include "string6.h"
    #include "itemp.h"
    #include "itempi.h"
    #include <dos.h>


    //friend functions of StockItem

    ostream& operator << (ostream& os, const StockItem& Item)
    {
      return Item.m_Worker->Write(os);
    }

    istream& operator >> (istream& is, StockItem& Item)
    {
      string Expires;
      string Name;
      short InStock;
      short Price;
      short MinimumStock;
      short MinimumReorder;
      string Distributor;
      string UPC;

      is >> Expires;
      is >> Name;
      is >> InStock;
      is >> Price;
      is >> MinimumStock;
      is >> MinimumReorder;
      is >> Distributor;
      is >> UPC;
```

```
  if (Expires == "0")
    {
    Item = StockItem(Name, InStock, Price, MinimumStock,
        MinimumReorder, Distributor, UPC);
    }
  else
    {
    Item = StockItem(Name, InStock, Price, MinimumStock,
        MinimumReorder, Distributor, UPC, Expires);
    }

  return is;

}


// StockItem member functions

StockItem::StockItem()
: m_Count(0), m_Worker(new UndatedStockItem)
{
  m_Worker->m_Count = 1;
}

StockItem::StockItem(const StockItem& Item)
: m_Count(0), m_Worker(Item.m_Worker)
{
  m_Worker->m_Count ++;
}

StockItem& StockItem::operator = (const StockItem& Item)
{
  if (&Item != this)
    {
    m_Worker->m_Count --;
    if (m_Worker->m_Count <= 0)
      delete m_Worker;
    m_Worker = Item.m_Worker;
```

```
        m_Worker->m_Count ++;
        }
    return *this;
}

StockItem::~StockItem()
{
  if (m_Worker == 0)
    return;

  m_Worker->m_Count --;
  if (m_Worker->m_Count <= 0)
    delete m_Worker;
}

StockItem::StockItem(string Name, short InStock, // Undated
    short Price, short MinimumStock, short MinimumReorder,
    string Distributor, string UPC)
: m_Count(0),
  m_Worker(new UndatedStockItem(Name, InStock, Price,
  MinimumStock, MinimumReorder, Distributor, UPC))
{
  m_Worker->m_Count = 1;
}

StockItem::StockItem(int)
: m_Worker(0)
{
}

StockItem::StockItem(string Name, short InStock, // Dated
    short Price, short MinimumStock, short MinimumReorder,
    string Distributor, string UPC, string Expires)
: m_Count(0),
  m_Worker(new DatedStockItem(Name, InStock, Price,
  MinimumStock, MinimumReorder, Distributor, UPC, Expires))
{
  m_Worker->m_Count = 1;
}
```

```
bool StockItem::CheckUPC(string UPC)
{
  return m_Worker->CheckUPC(UPC);
}

short StockItem::GetInventory()
{
  return m_Worker->GetInventory();
}

void StockItem::DeductSaleFromInventory(short QuantitySold)
{
  m_Worker->DeductSaleFromInventory(QuantitySold);
}

string StockItem::GetName()
{
  return m_Worker->GetName();
}

ostream& StockItem::Write(ostream& os)
{
  exit(1); // should never get here
}

void StockItem::Reorder(ostream& os)
{
  m_Worker->Reorder(os);
}


void StockItem::FormattedDisplay(ostream& os)
{
  m_Worker->FormattedDisplay(os);
}


// UndatedStockItem member functions
```

```
UndatedStockItem::UndatedStockItem()
: StockItem(1),
  m_InStock(0),
  m_Price(0),
  m_MinimumStock(0),
  m_MinimumReorder(0),
  m_Name(),
  m_Distributor(),
  m_UPC()
{
}

UndatedStockItem::UndatedStockItem(string Name,
  short InStock, short Price, short MinimumStock,
  short MinimumReorder, string Distributor, string UPC)
: StockItem(1),
  m_InStock(InStock),
  m_Price(Price),
  m_MinimumStock(MinimumStock),
  m_MinimumReorder(MinimumReorder),
  m_Name(Name),
  m_Distributor(Distributor),
  m_UPC(UPC)
{
}

void UndatedStockItem::FormattedDisplay(ostream& os)
{
  os << "Name: ";
  os << m_Name << endl;
  os << "Number in stock: ";
  os << m_InStock << endl;
  os << "Price: ";
  os << m_Price << endl;
  os << "Minimum stock: ";
  os << m_MinimumStock << endl;
  os << "Reorder quantity: ";
  os << m_MinimumReorder << endl;
```

```
  os << "Distributor: ";
  os << m_Distributor << endl;
  os << "UPC: ";
  os << m_UPC << endl;
  os << endl;
}

ostream& UndatedStockItem::Write(ostream& os)
{
  os << 0 << endl;
  os << m_Name << endl;
  os << m_InStock << endl;
  os << m_Price << endl;
  os << m_MinimumStock << endl;
  os << m_MinimumReorder << endl;
  os << m_Distributor << endl;
  os << m_UPC << endl;

  return os;
}

void UndatedStockItem::Reorder(ostream& os)
{
  short ReorderAmount;

  if (m_InStock < m_MinimumStock)
    {
    ReorderAmount = m_MinimumStock-m_InStock;
     if (ReorderAmount < m_MinimumReorder)
       ReorderAmount = m_MinimumReorder;
    os << "Reorder " << ReorderAmount;
    os << " units of " << m_Name << " with UPC ";
    os << m_UPC << " from " << m_Distributor << endl;
    }
}

bool UndatedStockItem::CheckUPC(string UPC)
{
  return (UPC == m_UPC);
```

```
}

short UndatedStockItem::GetInventory()
{
  return m_InStock;
}

void UndatedStockItem::DeductSaleFromInventory(
short QuantitySold)
{
  m_InStock -= QuantitySold;
}

string UndatedStockItem::GetName()
{
  return m_Name;
}


// DatedStockItem member functions

DatedStockItem::DatedStockItem(string Name, short InStock,
short Price, short MinimumStock, short MinimumReorder,
string Distributor, string UPC, string Expires)
: UndatedStockItem(Name,InStock,Price,MinimumStock,
  MinimumReorder,Distributor,UPC),
  m_Expires(Expires)
{
}

ostream& DatedStockItem::Write(ostream& os)
{
  os << m_Expires << endl;
  os << m_Name << endl;
  os << m_InStock << endl;
  os << m_Price << endl;
  os << m_MinimumStock << endl;
  os << m_MinimumReorder << endl;
  os << m_Distributor << endl;
```

```
  os << m_UPC << endl;

  return os;
}

void DatedStockItem::FormattedDisplay(ostream& os)
{
  os << "Expiration date: ";
  os << m_Expires << endl;
  os << "Name: ";
  os << m_Name << endl;
  os << "Number in stock: ";
  os << m_InStock << endl;
  os << "Price: ";
  os << m_Price << endl;
  os << "Minimum stock: ";
  os << m_MinimumStock << endl;
  os << "Reorder quantity: ";
  os << m_MinimumReorder << endl;
  os << "Distributor: ";
  os << m_Distributor << endl;
  os << "UPC: ";
  os << m_UPC << endl;
  os << endl;
}

string DatedStockItem::Today()
{
  struct date d;
  unsigned short year;
  unsigned short day;
  unsigned short month;
  string TodaysDate;
  strstream FormatStream;

  getdate(&d);
  year = d.da_year;
  day = d.da_day;
  month = d.da_mon;
```

```
      FormatStream << setfill('0') << setw(4) << year <<
        setw(2) << month << setw(2) << day;
      FormatStream.seekg(0);
      FormatStream >> TodaysDate;

      return TodaysDate;
    }

    void DatedStockItem::Reorder(ostream& os)
    {
      if (m_Expires < Today())
        {
        os << "Return " << m_InStock << " units of " << m_Name;
        os << " with UPC " << m_UPC;
        os << " to " << m_Distributor << endl;
        m_InStock = 0;
        }

      UndatedStockItem::Reorder(os);
    }
```

Let's start our examination of this new StockItem class by looking at the implementation of operator << in Figure 10.26.

FIGURE 10.26. Safe polymorphism: The implementation of operator << **for a polymorphic** StockItem **(from code\itemp.cc)**

```
    ostream& operator << (ostream& os, const StockItem& Item)
    {
      return Item.m_Worker->Write(os);
    }
```

At first glance, this isn't particularly complicated. It just calls a function named Write via the StockItem* member variable m_Worker and returns the result from Write to its caller. But what does that m_Worker pointer point to?

This is the key to the implementation of polymorphic objects: The pointer m_Worker points to either an UndatedStockItem or a DatedStockItem depending on whether the object was created with or without an expiration date. Since the type of object that m_Worker points to is determined during program execution rather than when the program is compiled, the actual version of the Write function called by operator << varies accordingly, as it does with any type of polymorphism. The difference between this version of StockItem and the one described earlier in this chapter is that the pointer is used only in the implementation of StockItem rather than being accessible to the user of the class. This allows us to prevent the plague of memory allocation errors associated with pointer manipulation in the application program.

Susan had a question about the syntax of the call to the Write function.

Susan: What does the -> mean in that line?

Steve: It means to call the function on the right of the -> for the object pointed to by the pointer on the left of the ->. It's exactly like the . operator, except that operator has an object on its left instead of a pointer.

Before we get into the details of creating an object of this new version of StockItem, we'll look at a couple of diagrams of the StockItem variables from the example program in Figure 10.22 to see exactly how this "internal polymorphism" works. First, Figure 10.27 shows a possible layout of the StockItem object, x, which is the argument to operator << in the statement cout << x;.

FIGURE 10.27. Safe polymorphism: A polymorphic StockItem object with no date

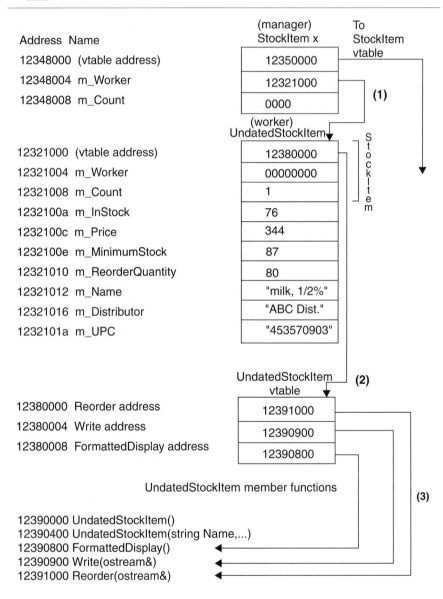

Let's trace the execution of the statement return Item.m_Worker->Write(s); from operator << (Figure 10.26) when it is executed to display the value of the StockItem x (as a result of the statement cout << x; in the example program in Figure 10.22). In step 1, the pointer m_Worker is followed to location 12321000, the address of the beginning of the UndatedStockItem worker object that will handle the operations of the StockItem manager class object. This location contains the address of the vtable for the worker object. In this case, the worker object is an UndatedStockItem object, so the vtable is the one for the UndatedStockItem class.

In our diagram, that vtable is at location 12380000, so in step 2 we follow the vtable pointer to find the address of the Write function. The diagram makes the assumption that the Write function is the second virtual function defined in the StockItem class, so in step 3 we fetch the contents of the second entry in the vtable, which is 12390900. That is the address of the Write function that will be executed here.

Figure 10.28 shows a possible layout of the StockItem object y that is the argument to operator << in the statement cout << y;.

Susan had a number of questions about Figure 10.28.

Susan: What in Figure 10.28 is the StockItem? I can't tell exactly what it is supposed to be, just the vtable address, m_Worker, and m_Count? That's it, huh?

Steve: Yes.

Susan: What are all those member functions in step 3 supposed to be? I don't know where they're coming from.

Steve: They're from the class interface for the new version of StockItem, which is listed in Figure 10.23.

Susan: Why is there an UndatedStockItem listed along the side of the DatedStockItem thingy?

FIGURE 10.28. Safe polymorphism: A polymorphic StockItem object with a date

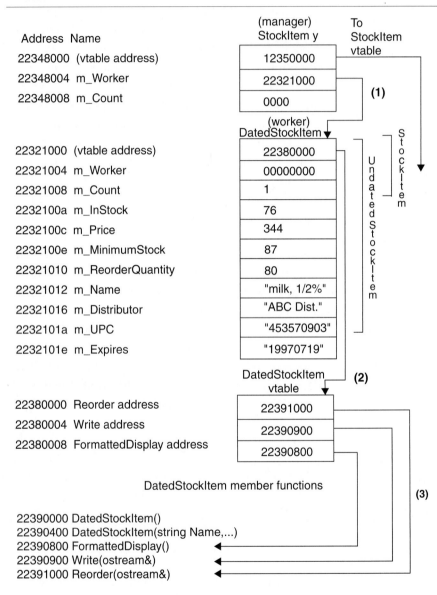

Steve: Since DatedStockItem is derived from UndatedStockItem, every DatedStockItem has an UndatedStockItem in it, just as every UndatedStockItem has a StockItem in it because UndatedStockItem is derived from StockItem.

Susan: Where is the UndatedStockItem now?

Steve: The only UndatedStockItem in Figure 10.28 is the base class part of the DatedStockItem worker object.

Susan: I still can't see how these objects look.

Steve: I think we need a diagram here. Take a look at Figure 10.29 and let me know if that helps.

Susan: Yes, it does.

Now that we've cleared that up, let's trace how the line return Item.m_Worker->Write(s); is executed to display the value of the StockItem y (as a result of the statement cout << y; in the example program in Figure 10.22). In step 1, the pointer m_Worker is followed to location 22321000, the address of the worker object that will handle the operations of the StockItem manager class object. This location contains the address of the vtable for the worker object. In this case, the worker object is a DatedStockItem object, so the vtable is the one for the DatedStockItem class. In our diagram, that vtable is at location 22380000, so in step 2 we follow the vtable pointer to find the address of the Write function. As before, the diagram makes the assumption that the Write function is the second virtual function defined in the StockItem class, so in step 3 we fetch the contents of the second entry in the vtable, which is 22390900. That is the address of the Write function that will be executed in this case.

FIGURE 10.29. A simplified version of the structure of a DatedStockItem object

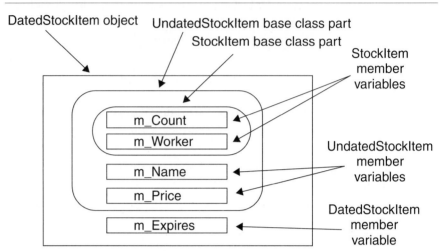

Setting the Standard

We have seen how a polymorphic object works once it is set up, so let's continue our examination of the StockItem class by looking at the "standard" member functions; that is, the ones that are necessary to make it a concrete data type. As you may remember, these are the default constructor, the copy constructor, the assignment operator (operator =), and the destructor.

It may occur to you to wonder why we have to rewrite all these functions; what's wrong with the ones we've already written for StockItem? The answer is that these functions create, copy, and destroy objects of a given class. Now that we have changed the way we want to use the StockItem class and the way it works, we have to rewrite these functions to do the right thing in the new situation.

Susan wanted to make sure she understood where we were going with this:

Susan: Okay, then this is the new StockItem, not the old one. This is your manager StockItem that tells the worker what to do; the DatedStockItem is the worker, right?

Steve: Yes, this is the new type of StockItem. By the way, besides a DatedStockItem, an UndatedStockItem can also be a worker.

Let's start with the default constructor for this new StockItem class, shown in Figure 10.30.

FIGURE 10.30. Safe polymorphism: The default constructor for the polymorphic StockItem **class (from code\itemp.cc)**

```
StockItem::StockItem()
: m_Count(0), m_Worker(new UndatedStockItem)
{
  m_Worker->m_Count = 1;
}
```

The first member initialization expression in this function merely initializes m_Count to 0. We won't actually be using this variable in a StockItem object, but I don't like leaving variables uninitialized.

The second member initialization expression, however, looks a bit odd. Why are we creating an UndatedStockItem object here when we have no data to put in it? Because we need some worker object to perform the work of a default-constructed StockItem. For example, if the user asks for the contents of the StockItem to be displayed on the screen with labels (by calling FormattedDisplay), we want the default values displayed with the appropriate labels, which can only be done by an object that has a working FormattedDisplay function. The StockItem class itself doesn't have any data except for the StockItem* and the m_Count variable (which we'll get to later). Therefore, all of the functionality of a StockItem has to be handed off to the worker object, which in this case is the newly created UndatedStockItem.

Let's see what a default-constructed StockItem might look like (Figure 10.31).

FIGURE 10.31. Safe polymorphism: A default-constructed polymorphic StockItem **object**

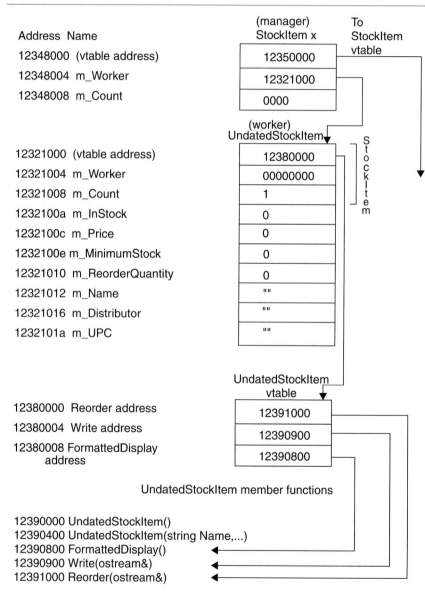

Susan didn't think the need for a valid object as the worker object in a default-constructed manager object was intuitively obvious.

> **Susan:** I don't get why you say that we can only call the FormattedDisplay function with an object that has a working version of that function. That doesn't mean anything to me.

> **Steve:** Well, what would happen if we called FormattedDisplay via a pointer that didn't point to anything? It wouldn't work, that's for sure.
>
> In particular, any attempt by the user to call a virtual function through a pointer to a nonexistent object will fail because there won't be a valid vtable address in that missing object. The most likely result will be a crash when the code tries to use a vtable entry that contains random garbage.

I still haven't explained exactly what the member initialization expression, m_Worker(new UndatedStockItem), actually does. On the surface, it's pretty simple: It creates a new UndatedStockItem object via the default constructor of that class and uses the address of the resulting object to initialize m_Worker.

However, there are some tricks in the implementation of the constructor of a worker class, and now is the time to see how such a constructor actually works. Figure 10.32 shows the code for the default constructor for the UndatedStockItem class.

FIGURE 10.32. Safe polymorphism: The default constructor for the UndatedStockItem class **(from code\itemp.cc)**

```
UndatedStockItem::UndatedStockItem()
: StockItem(1),
  m_InStock(0),
  m_Price(0),
  m_MinimumStock(0),
  m_MinimumReorder(0),
  m_Name(),
  m_Distributor(),
```

```
  m_UPC()
{
}
```

Most of the code in this constructor is standard: All we're doing is initializing the values of the member variables to reasonable default values. But there's something a bit unusual about that base class initializer, StockItem(1). Before we get into exactly what the argument 1 means, it's important to understand why we *must* specify a base class initializer here.

As we saw in Chapter 9 in the discussion of Figure 9.33, we use a base class initializer when we want to specify which base class constructor will initialize the base class part of a derived class object. If we don't specify any particular base class initializer, the base class part will be initialized with the default constructor for that base class. In the example in Chapter 9, we needed to call a specific base class constructor to fill in the fields in the base class part of the UndatedStockItem object, which should seem reasonable enough. But that can't be the reason we need to specify a base class constructor here, because the StockItem object doesn't have any data fields that need to be initialized in our UndatedStockItem constructor. So why can't we just let the compiler use the default constructor for the base class part of an UndatedStockItem?

Base Instincts

We can't do that because the default constructor for StockItem calls the default constructor for UndatedStockItem; that is, the function that we're examining right now. Therefore, if we allow the StockItem default constructor to initialize the StockItem part of an UndatedStockItem, that default constructor will call our UndatedStockItem default constructor again, which will call the StockItem default constructor again, and the program will eventually use up all the stack space and die.

To avoid this problem, we have to make a special constructor for StockItem that doesn't create an UndatedStockItem object and therefore avoids an indefinitely long chain of constructor calls. As no one outside the implementation of the StockItem polymorphic object knows anything about classes in this idiom other than StockItem, they don't need to call this constructor. As a result, we can make it protected.

Susan didn't see why we need a special constructor in this case, so I explained it to her some more:

> **Susan:** So, how many default constructors are you going to need for StockItem? How do you know when or which one is going to be used? This is confusing.

> **Steve:** There is only one default constructor for each class. In this case, StockItem has one, DatedStockItem has one, and UndatedStockItem has one. The question is how to prevent the StockItem default constructor from being called from the UndatedStockItem one, which would be a big booboo, since the UndatedStockItem default constructor was called from the StockItem default constructor. This would be like having two mirrors facing one another, where you see endless reflections going off into the distance.

Okay, so how do we declare a special constructor for this purpose? As was shown in Figure 10.23, all we have to do is to put the line StockItem(int); in a protected section of the class definition. The implementation of this function is shown in Figure 10.33.

FIGURE 10.33. Safe polymorphism: Implementing a special protected **constructor for** StockItem **(from code\itemp.cc)**

```
StockItem::StockItem(int)
: m_Worker(0)
{
}
```

How can a function that doesn't have any code inside its { } be complicated? In fact, this apparently simple function raises three questions. First, why do we need any entries in the argument list when the function doesn't use any arguments? Second, why does the list contain just a type and no argument name instead of a name and type for each argument, as we had in the past? And third, why are we initializing m_Worker to the value 0? We'll examine the first two of these questions now and put off the third until we discuss the destructor for the StockItem class.

The answers to the first two questions are related: The reason we don't need to specify a name for the argument is that we aren't going to use the argument in the function. The only reason to specify an argument list here is to make use of the *function overloading* mechanism, which allows the compiler to distinguish between functions with the same name but different argument types. In this case, even though all the constructors for the StockItem class have the same name—StockItem::StockItem—the compiler can tell them apart so long as they have different argument types. Therefore, we're supplying an argument we don't need to allow the compiler to pick this function when we want to use it. Here, when we call the function from the worker object's constructor, we supply the value 1, which will be ignored in the function itself but will tell the compiler that we want to call this constructor rather than any of the other constructors.

Susan wanted to know exactly where the 1 was going to come from and how I decided to use that value in the first place:

Susan: Where are you supplying the 1 value?

Steve: In the base class initializer in the default constructor for UndatedStockItem. This is needed to prevent the infinite regress mentioned just above.

Susan: But why 1? Why not any other number, like 0?

Steve: Actually, the value 1 is fairly arbitrary; any number would work. However, it's a good idea to avoid using 0 where you just need some number, because 0 is a "magic number" in C++; it's a legal value for any type of built-in variable as well as any type of pointer. This "multiple identity" of 0 can be a bountiful source of confusion and error in C++, which it's best to avoid whenever possible.

Of course, there's nothing to stop us from giving the argument a name even though we aren't going to use it in the constructor. It's better not to do this, however, to avoid confusing both the compiler and the next programmer to look at this function. The compiler may give us a warning message if we don't use an argument we've declared, while the next programmer to look at this function may think we forgot to use that argument. We can solve both of these problems by not giving it a name, which makes it clear that we weren't planning to use it in the first place.

So now we've followed the chain of events down to the initialization of the base class part of the UndatedStockItem object that was created as the worker object inside the default constructor for StockItem. The rest of Figure 10.32 is pretty simple. It merely initializes the data for the UndatedStockItem class itself. When that's done, we're ready to execute the lone statement inside the {} in Figure 10.30, which is m_Worker->m_Count = 1;. Clearly, this sets the value of m_Count in the newly created UndatedStockItem object to 1, but what might not be as clear is *why* we need to do this.

References Count

The reason we have to set m_Count to 1 in the UndatedStockItem variable pointed to by m_Worker is that we're going to keep track of the number of StockItems that are using that UndatedStockItem worker object, rather than copy the worker object every time we copy a StockItem that points to it. This is called *reference counting*.

The general idea of reference counting is fairly simple, as most great ideas are (after you understand them, at least). It's inefficient to copy a lot of data whenever we set one variable to the same value as that of another; copying a pointer to the data is much easier. Even so, we have to consider how we will know when we can delete the data being pointed to, which will be when no one needs the data anymore. If we don't take care of this requirement, we'll have a serious problem with memory management—when one of the StockItem objects that refers to the worker object goes out of scope and is destroyed, the destructor can do either of the following, neither of which is correct:

1. free the memory where the data is kept, via delete,

2. fail to free the memory.

The first of these is incorrect because there may be other StockItems that still want to use the data in question, and they will now be referring to memory that is no longer allocated to that data. Therefore, at any time the data in that area of memory may be overwritten by new data. The second is also incorrect because when the last StockItem that was using the shared data goes away, a memory leak results. In other words, although the data used by the StockItem can no longer be accessed, the memory it occupies cannot be used for other purposes because it has not been released back to the system via operator delete.[8]

The correct way to share data in such a situation is to write the constructor(s), destructor, and assignment operator to keep track of the number of objects using a particular set of data, and, when that set of data has no more users, to free the memory it occupies.[9] Let's see how reference counting works with our StockItem class.

---

8. This is the same problem we saw with the compiler-generated copy constructor and the compiler-generated assignment operator for the string class we created earlier in this book. See Chapter 8, starting with the section "For Reference Only".

Learning to Program in C++

Starring Sharon Sharalike

Suppose that we have the example program in Figure 10.34 (which is contained in the file refcnt1.cc if you want to print it out).

FIGURE 10.34. Safe polymorphism: An example program for reference-counting with StockItems **(code\refcnt1.cc)**

```
#include <iostream.h>
#include "string6.h"
#include "itemp.h"

int main()
{
    StockItem item1("cups",32,129,10,5,"Bob's Dist.",
        "2895657951"); // create an undated object

    StockItem item2("Hot Chicken",48,158,15,12,"Joe's Dist.",
        "987654321", "19960824"); // create a dated object

    StockItem item3 = item1; // copy constructor
    item1 = item2; // assignment operator

    item1.FormattedDisplay(cout); // display an object with labels

    return 0;
}
```

This program doesn't do anything very useful, except to illustrate the constructors and assignment operator, as follows. First, it creates two StockItems, item1 and item2, with specified contents (via the

---

9. There is actually another requirement for correct sharing of data in this situation: We mustn't make changes to the data in a shared worker object that has more than one user. In the current application, we don't have that problem, but it's something we'll have to deal with in Chapter 11, when we develop a polymorphic object type whose objects can be changed after creation.

"normal" constructors for undated and dated items, respectively). Then it creates another StockItem, item3, with the same value as that of item1, via the copy constructor. Then it assigns the value of item2 to item1 using the assignment operator.

The line StockItem item1("cups",32,129,10,5,"Bob's Dist.", "2895657951"); calls the constructor illustrated in Figure 10.35 to create a StockItem whose m_Worker points to an UndatedStockItem, because the arguments "cups", 32, 129, 10, 5, "Bob's Dist.", and "2895657951" match the argument list for that constructor.

FIGURE 10.35. Safe polymorphism: A normal constructor to create a StockItem without a date (from code\itemp.cc)

```
StockItem::StockItem(string Name, short InStock,
  short Price, short MinimumStock, short MinimumReorder,
  string Distributor, string UPC)
: m_Count(0),
  m_Worker(new UndatedStockItem(Name, InStock, Price,
  MinimumStock, MinimumReorder, Distributor, UPC))
{
  m_Worker->m_Count = 1;
}
```

Susan had some comments about this normal constructor for the new version of the StockItem class as well as about the other normal constructor (in Figure 10.37):

Susan: I don't get how this can be a normal constructor if it has m_Worker in it. The normal ones are the ones you wrote before this. I am confused. Same thing with Figure 10.37; these are not normal constructors for StockItem.

Steve: The implementation of the constructor doesn't determine whether it is "normal". A "normal" constructor is one that creates an object with specified data in it, as opposed to a default constructor (Figure 10.32) or a copy constructor (Figure 10.39).

Immediately after the execution of the line StockItem item1("cups",32,129,10,5,"Bob's Dist.","2895657951");, the newly constructed StockItem object and its UndatedStockItem worker object look something like the diagram in Figure 10.36.[10]

FIGURE 10.36. Safe polymorphism: A polymorphic StockItem **object with an** UndatedStockItem **worker**

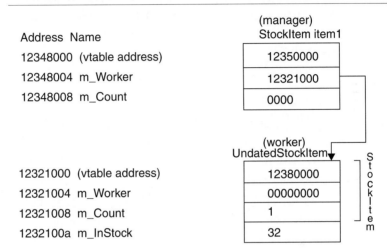

The next line in Figure 10.34 on page 725, StockItem item2("Hot Chicken", 48, 15, 12, "Joe's Dist.","987654321", "19960824");, calls the constructor shown in Figure 10.37, which creates a StockItem whose m_Worker member variable points to a DatedStockItem. As you can see, this is almost identical to the previous constructor, except, of course, that it creates a DatedStockItem as the worker object rather than an UndatedStockItem.

After the statement StockItem item2("Hot Chicken", 48, 158, 15, 12, "Joe's Dist.", "987654321", "19960824"); is executed, the newly constructed StockItem object and its DatedStockItem worker object looks something like the diagram in Figure 10.38.

---

10. In this and the following diagrams, I've omitted a number of the data elements to make the figure fit on the page.

FIGURE 10.37. Safe polymorphism: A normal constructor that constructs a
StockItem **having a date (from code\itemp.cc)**

```
StockItem::StockItem(string Name, short InStock,
  short Price, short MinimumStock, short MinimumReorder,
  string Distributor, string UPC, string Expires)
: m_Count(0),
  m_Worker(new DatedStockItem(Name, InStock, Price,
  MinimumStock, MinimumReorder, Distributor, UPC, Expires))
{
  m_Worker->m_Count = 1;
}
```

FIGURE 10.38. Safe polymorphism: A polymorphic StockItem **object with a**
DatedStockItem **worker**

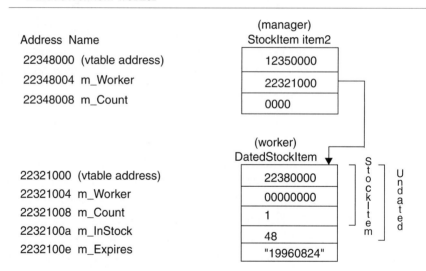

Now let's take a look at what happens when we execute the next statement in Figure 10.34 on page 725, StockItem item3 = item1;. Since we are creating a new StockItem with the same contents as an existing StockItem, this statement calls the copy constructor, which is shown in Figure 10.39.

FIGURE 10.39. Safe polymorphism: The copy constructor for StockItem
(from code\itemp.cc)

```
StockItem::StockItem(const StockItem& Item)
: m_Count(0), m_Worker(Item.m_Worker)
{
  m_Worker->m_Count ++;
}
```

Susan wanted to know why we would want to create a new StockItem
with the same contents as an existing one.

Susan: Why would you want to create a new StockItem just like
an old one? Why not just use the old one again?

Steve: The most common use for the copy constructor is when we
pass an argument by value or return a value from a function. In
either of these cases, the copy constructor is used to make a new
object with the same contents as an existing one.

Susan: I still don't see why we need to make copies rather than
using the original objects.

Steve: In the case of a value argument, this is necessary because
we don't want to change the value of the caller's variable if we
change the local variable.

In the case of a return value, it's necessary to make a copy because
an object that is created inside the called function will cease to exist
at the end of the function, before the calling function can use it.
Therefore, when we return an object by value we are actually
asking the compiler to make a copy of the object; the copy is
guaranteed to last long enough for the calling function to use it.

This copy constructor uses the pointer from the existing StockItem
object (Item.m_Worker) to initialize the newly created StockItem
object's pointer, m_Worker, so that the new and existing StockItem

objects will share a worker object. Then we initialize the value of m_Count in the new object to 0 so that it has a known value. Finally, we increment the m_Count variable in the worker object because it has one more user than it had before.

After this operation, the variables item1 and item3, together with their shared worker object, look something like Figure 10.40.

FIGURE 10.40. Safe polymorphism: Two polymorphic StockItem **objects sharing the same** UndatedStockItem **worker object**

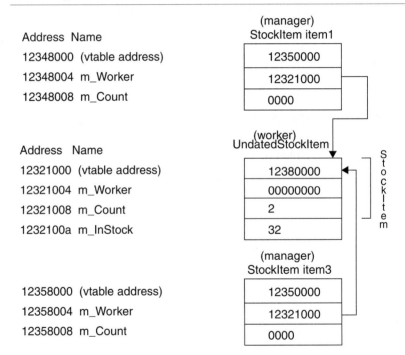

Why is it all right to share data in this situation? Because we have the m_Count variable to keep track of the number of users of the worker object so that our StockItem destructor will know when it is time to delete that object. This should be abundantly clear when we get to the end of the program and see what happens when the destructor is called for the StockItem variables.

Now let's continue by looking at the next statement in Figure 10.34 on page 725: item1 = item2;. As you may have figured out already, this is actually a call to the assignment operator (operator =) for the StockItem class.

In case that wasn't obvious to you, don't despair; it wasn't to Susan either:

> **Susan:** No, I didn't figure out that this is a call to the assignment operator. It seems to me that you are setting item2 to item1. I see that operator = has to be called to do this, but I don't see how the program is intentionally calling it.

> **Steve:** Whenever we assign the value of one object to another existing object of the same class, we are calling the assignment operator of that class. That's what "=" means for objects.

The code for that operator is shown in Figure 10.41.

FIGURE 10.41. Safe polymorphism: The assignment operator (operator =) **for** StockItem **(from code\itemp.cc)**

```
StockItem& StockItem::operator = (const StockItem& Item)
{
  if (&Item != this)
    {
    m_Worker->m_Count --;
    if (m_Worker->m_Count <= 0)
      delete m_Worker;
    m_Worker = Item.m_Worker;
    m_Worker->m_Count ++;
    }
  return *this;
}
```

This function starts out with the line if (&Item != this), which implements the standard test to see if the source object and the target object are actually the same object, in which case it doesn't have to (and doesn't) do anything. In the example program, the source object is item2 and the target object is item1, which are different objects. So we continue with the next statement in the code for operator =, m_Worker->m_Count--;, which decrements the count in the worker object pointed to by the target object (item1). If you look at Figure 10.40, you'll see that the previous value of that variable was 2, so it is now 1, meaning that there is one StockItem that is still using that worker object. Therefore, the condition in the next line, if (m_Worker->m_Count <= 0), is false, which means that the controlled statement of the if statement—delete m_Worker;—is not executed. This is correct because as long as there is at least one user of the worker object, it cannot be deleted.

The next statement in the code for operator = is m_Worker = Item.m_Worker;, which sets the worker object pointer in the target object (item1) equal to the pointer in the source object (item2), which was the main point of the whole operation in the first place. Now item1 and item2 are sharing a worker object, so they are effectively the same. Then the statement m_Worker->m_Count ++; increments the count of users of the shared worker object (in this case to 2). Again, this is necessary so that we know when it's safe and appropriate to delete the worker object and reclaim the memory it occupies. Finally, as is standard with assignment operators, we return to the calling function by the statement return *this;, which returns the object to which we have assigned a new value.

When all this has been done, item1 and item2 will share a DatedStockItem, while item3 will have its own UndatedStockItem. The manager variables item1 and item2, together with their shared worker object, look something like Figure 10.42, and item3 looks pretty much as shown in Figure 10.43.

FIGURE 10.42. Safe polymorphism: Two polymorphic StockItem **objects sharing the same** DatedStockItem **worker object**

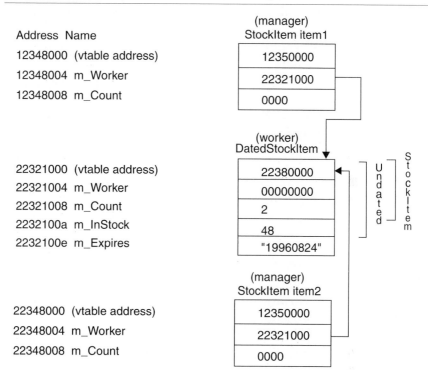

You should note that item1 has effectively changed its type from UndatedStockItem to DatedStockItem as a result of the assignment statement. This is one of the benefits of using polymorphic objects: The effective type of an object can vary not only when it is created, but also at any time thereafter. Therefore, we don't have to be locked in to a particular type when we create an object, but can adjust the type as necessary according to circumstances. By the way, this ability to change the effective type of an object at run time also solves the *slicing* problem referred to in Chapter 9, where we assigned an object of a derived class to a base class object with the result that the extra fields from the derived class object were lost.

FIGURE 10.43. Safe polymorphism: A polymorphic StockItem object

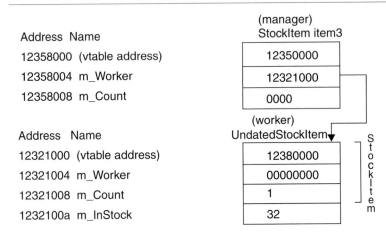

	(manager) StockItem item3
Address Name	
12358000 (vtable address)	12350000
12358004 m_Worker	12321000
12358008 m_Count	0000
	(worker) UndatedStockItem
Address Name	
12321000 (vtable address)	12380000
12321004 m_Worker	00000000
12321008 m_Count	1
1232100a m_InStock	32

Susan and I had quite a discussion about the implementation of this version of operator =:

> **Susan:** If this is an assignment operator, then how come it has the code for reference counting in it?

> **Steve:** It needs code for reference counting because it has to keep track of how many users of its worker object (pointed to by m_Worker) still remain. The following line does that:

```
m_Worker->m_Count --;
```

> If there aren't any more users of that worker object, then it can (and indeed must) be deleted. That's the purpose of the lines:

```
if (m_Worker->m_Count <= 0)
  delete m_Worker;
```

> Then it has to copy the pointer to the worker object from "Item", like so:

```
m_Worker = Item.m_Worker;
```

Susan: Wait a minute. I don't understand what this part does.

Steve: It makes the current object (the one pointed to by this) share a "worker" object with the manager object on the right of the =, which we refer to here as Item.

Susan: Okay.

Steve: Finally, it has to increment the number of users of the worker object from "Item", since that worker object is now being used by "our" object (i.e., the one pointed to by this). That's taken care of by the line:

```
m_Worker->m_Count ++;
```

Susan: So, do we have pointers pointing to pointers here?

Steve: Not exactly: We have one object containing a pointer to another object.

The Last Shall Be First

Now let's take a look at what happens when the StockItem objects are destroyed at the end of the main program. As the C++ language specifies for the destruction of auto variables, the last to be created will be the first to be destroyed. Thus, item3 will be destroyed first, followed by item2, and finally item1. Figure 10.44 shows the code for the destructor for StockItem.

FIGURE 10.44. Safe polymorphism: The destructor for the StockItem class **(from code\itemp.cc)**

```
StockItem::~StockItem()
{
  if (m_Worker == 0)
    return;
```

```
    m_Worker->m_Count --;
    if (m_Worker->m_Count <= 0)
      delete m_Worker;
  }
```

Before we get into the details of this code, I should mention that whenever any object is destroyed, all of its constituent elements that have destructors are automatically destroyed as well. In the case of a StockItem, the string variables are automatically destroyed during the destruction of the StockItem.

Susan had some questions about the destructor. Here's the first installment:

Susan: Why are you doing reference counting again in the destructor? Is that where it belongs? So, you have to reference-count twice, once for when something is added and again, with different code for when something is subtracted?

Steve: Close. Actually, it's a bit more general: Every time a worker object acquires another user, we have to increment its count, and every time it loses one of its users, we have to decrement its count. That way, when the count gets to 0, we know there aren't any more users, and we can therefore use **delete** to free the memory occupied by the worker object.

Susan: So with this reference counting, the whole point is to know when to use **delete**?

Steve: Yes.

Susan: How does the **delete** operator automatically call the destructor for that variable?

Steve: That's a rule in C++: Calling **delete** for a variable that has a destructor always calls the destructor for that variable.

The first if statement in the destructor, if (m_Worker == 0), provides a clue as to why our special StockItem constructor (Figure 10.33 on page 721) had to set the m_Worker variable to 0. We'll see exactly how that comes into play shortly. For now, we know that the value of m_Worker in item3 is not 0, as it points to an UndatedStockItem (see Figure 10.43 on page 734), so the condition in the first if statement is false. Therefore, we move to the next statement, which is m_Worker->m_Count--;. Since, according to Figure 10.43, the value of m_Count in the UndatedStockItem to which m_Worker points is 1, this statement reduces the value of that variable to 0, making the condition in the statement if (m_Worker->m_Count <= 0) true. This means that the controlled statement of the if statement, delete m_Worker;, is executed. Since the value of m_Count is 0, no other StockItem variables are currently using the UndatedStockItem pointed to by m_Worker. Therefore, we want that UndatedStockItem to go away so that its memory can be reclaimed, and we use the delete operator to accomplish that goal.

Susan had a question about why I used <= as the condition in the if statement.

Susan: Why did you say <= 0? How could the count ever be less than 0?

Steve: If the program is working correctly, it can't. This is a case of "defensive programming": I wanted to make sure that if, by some error, the count got below 0, the program wouldn't hang onto the memory for the worker object forever. In a production program, it would probably be a good idea to record such an "impossible" condition somewhere so the maintenance programmer could take a look at it.

This is not quite as simple as it may seem, however, because before the memory used by a UndatedStockItem can be reclaimed, the destructor for that UndatedStockItem must be called to allow all of its constituent parts (especially the string variables it contains) to expire properly. As I've mentioned, when we call the delete operator for a variable that has a destructor, it automatically calls the destructor for that variable. Therefore, the next function called is the destructor for the UndatedStockItem being deleted.

Before going into the details of this function, I should explain why it is called in the first place. Remember, we're using StockItem*'s to refer to either DatedStockItem or UndatedStockItem objects. How does the compiler know to call the right destructor?

Just as it does with other functions in the same situation: We have to make the destructor virtual so that the correct destructor will be called, no matter what the type of the pointer through which the object is accessed. This answers the earlier question of why we had to define a destructor and declare it to be virtual in Figure 10.13. As a general rule, destructors should be virtual if there are any other virtual functions in the class, as we have to make sure that the right destructor will be called via a base class pointer. Otherwise, data elements that are defined in the derived class won't be destroyed properly, possibly resulting in memory leaks or other undesirable effects.

At this point, Susan had some questions on virtual destructors and the nature of reality (as it applies to C++, at least) :

Susan: How are destructors virtual? Do they have a vtable?

Steve: They're in the vtable if they're declared to be virtual, as the one in the final version of StockItem is.

Susan: With all this virtual stuff going on, what is really real? What is the driving force behind all this? It seems like this is a fun house of smoke and mirrors, and I can't tell any more what is really in control.

Steve: The StockItem object is the "manager", who takes credit for work done by a "worker" object; the worker is either a DatedStockItem or an UndatedStockItem. Hopefully, the rest of the discussion will clarify this.

We don't have to write a destructor for UndatedStockItem because the compiler-generated one does the job for us. But what exactly does that compiler-generated destructor do?

It calls the destructor for every member variable in the class that has a destructor. This is necessary to make sure that those member variables are properly cleaned up after their scope expires when the object they're in goes away. In addition, just as the constructor for a derived class always calls a constructor for its embedded base class object, so a destructor for a derived class always calls the destructor for the base class part of the derived class object. There are two differences between these situations, however:

1. The constructor for the base class part of the object is called *before* any of the code in the derived class constructor is executed; the base class destructor is called *after* the code in the derived class destructor is executed. Here, of course, this distinction is irrelevant because we haven't written any code in the derived class destructor.

2. There is only one destructor for a given class.

This second difference between constructors and destructors means that we can't use a trick similar to the "special base class constructor" trick used to prevent the base class constructor from calling the derived class constructor again. Instead, we have to arrange a way for the base class destructor to determine whether it's being asked to destroy a "real" base class object (a StockItem) or the embedded base class part of a derived class object (the StockItem base class part of an UndatedStockItem or DatedStockItem). In the latter case, the destructor should exit immediately, since the StockItem base class part of either of those classes contains nothing that needs special handling by the destructor. The special constructor called by the UndatedStockItem constructor to initialize its StockItem part (Figure 10.33 on page 721) works with the first if statement in the StockItem destructor (Figure 10.44 on page 735) to solve this problem. The special StockItem constructor sets m_Worker to 0, which cannot be the address of any object, during the initialization of the base class part of an UndatedStockItem. When the destructor for StockItem is executed, a 0 value for m_Worker is the indicator of a StockItem that is the base class part of a derived class object. This allows the StockItem destructor to distinguish between a real StockItem and the base class part of an object of a class derived from StockItem by examining the value of m_Worker and bailing out immediately if it is the reserved value of 0.

Going, Going, Gone

Now it's time to go into detail about what happens when item3, item2, and item1 are destroyed. They go away in that order because the last object to be constructed on the stack in a given scope is the first to be destroyed, as you might expect when dealing with stacks.

Figure 10.45 is another listing of the destructor for the StockItem class (StockItem::~StockItem()), for reference as we trace its execution.

FIGURE 10.45. Safe polymorphism: The destructor for the StockItem class **(from code\itemp.cc)**

```
StockItem::~StockItem()
{
  if (m_Worker == 0)
    return;

  m_Worker->m_Count --;
  if (m_Worker->m_Count <= 0)
    delete m_Worker;
}
```

At the end of the main program, item3 (Figure 10.43 on page 734), which was the last StockItem to be created, is the first to go out of scope. At that point, the StockItem destructor is automatically invoked to clean up. Since the value of m_Worker in item3 isn't 0, the statement controlled by the first if statement isn't executed. Next, we execute the statement m_Worker->m_Count--;, which reduces the value of the variable m_Count in the UndatedStockItem pointed to by m_Worker to 0. Since this makes that variable 0, the condition in the second if statement is true, so its controlled statement, delete m_Worker;, is executed. As we've seen, this eliminates the object pointed to by m_Worker, calling the UndatedStockItem destructor in the process.

As before, calling this destructor does nothing other than destroy the member variable that has a destructor (namely, the m_Expires member variable, which is a string), followed by the mandatory call to the base class destructor.

At that point, the first if statement in StockItem::~StockItem comes into play along with its controlled statement. These two statements are

```
if (m_Worker == 0)
    return;
```

Remember the special base class constructor StockItem(int) (Figure 10.33 on page 721)? That constructor, which is called from our UndatedStockItem default and normal constructors, initializes m_Worker to 0. Thus, we know that m_Worker will be 0 for any object that is actually an UndatedStockItem or a DatedStockItem, because all of the constructors for DatedStockItem call one of those two constructors for UndatedStockItem to initialize their UndatedStockItem base class part. Therefore, this if statement will be true for the base class part of all UndatedStockItem and DatedStockItem objects. Since the current object being destroyed is in fact an UndatedStockItem object, the if is true, and so, the destructor exits immediately, ending the destruction of the UndatedStockItem object. Then the destructor for item3 finishes by freeing the storage associated with that object.

Next, the StockItem destructor is called for item2 (Figure 10.42 on page 733). Since m_Worker is not 0, the condition in the first if in

Figure 10.45 on page 740 is false, so we proceed to the next statement, m_Worker->m_Count--;. As you can see by looking back at Figure 10.42, the previous value of that variable was 2, so it is now 1. As a result, the condition in the next if statement, if (m_Worker->m_Count <= 0), is also false. Thus, the controlled statement that uses delete to get rid of the DatedStockItem pointed to by m_Worker is not executed. Then the destructor for item2 finishes by freeing the storage associated with that object.

Finally, item1 (Figure 10.42 on page 733) dies at the end of its scope. When it does, the StockItem destructor is called to clean up its act. As before, m_Worker isn't 0, so the controlled statement of the first if statement in Figure 10.45 on page 740 isn't executed. Next, we execute the statement m_Worker->m_Count--;, which reduces the value of the variable m_Count in the DatedStockItem pointed to by m_Worker to 0. This time, the condition in the next if statement is true, so its controlled statement, delete m_Worker;, is executed. We've seen that this eliminates the object pointed to by m_Worker, calling the appropriate destructor for the worker object, which in this case is DatedStockItem::~DatedStockItem. As with the UndatedStockItem destructor, the compiler-generated destructor for DatedStockItem calls all the destructors for the member variables and base class part, which in this case is an UndatedStockItem. Therefore, we don't have to write this destructor ourselves.

Lastly, the call to the StockItem destructor occurs exactly as it did in the destruction of item3, except that there is an additional step because the base class of DatedStockItem is UndatedStockItem, and the destructor for that class in turn calls the destructor for its base class part, which is a StockItem. Once we get to the destructor for StockItem, the value of m_Worker is 0, so that destructor simply returns to the destructor for UndatedStockItem, which returns to the destructor for DatedStockItem. Then the destructor for item1 finishes by freeing the storage associated with that object.

If you find the above explanation clear, congratulations. Susan didn't:

Learning to Program in C++

Susan: How do you know that the m_Worker can never be 0 in a real StockItem and is always 0 in a StockItem that is a base class part of a derived class object?

Steve: Because I set m_Worker to 0 in the special StockItem constructor called from the base class initializer in the default and normal constructors for UndatedStockItem. Therefore, that special constructor is always used to set up the base class part of an UndatedStockItem, and since DatedStockItem derives from UndatedStockItem, the same will be true of a DatedStockItem.

For the Benefit of Posterity

Now it's time to clear up a point we've glossed over so far. We have already seen that the member initialization expression m_Count(0), present in the constructors for the StockItem object, is there just to make sure we don't have an uninitialized variable in the StockItem object—even though we won't be using m_Count in a StockItem object. While this is true as far as it goes, it doesn't answer the question of why we need this variable at all if we're not using it in the StockItem class. The clue to the answer is that we are using that member variable in the object pointed to by m_Worker (i.e., m_Worker->m_Count). But why don't we just add the m_Count variable when we create the UndatedStockItem class rather than carry along extra baggage in the StockItem class?

The answer is that m_Worker is not an UndatedStockItem* but a StockItem*. Remember, the compiler doesn't know the actual type of the object being pointed to at compile time; all it knows is the declared type of the pointer, which in this case is StockItem*. It must therefore use that declared type to determine what operations are permissible through that pointer. Hence, if there's no m_Count variable in a StockItem, the compiler won't let us refer to that variable through a StockItem*.

Susan wasn't sure of what I was trying to say here:

Susan: What do you mean, if there were no m_Count variable in a StockItem, we wouldn't be able to access it through a StockItem pointer?

Steve: The only member variables and member functions that you can access through a pointer are ones that exist in the class it's a pointer to, no matter what type the pointer may really be pointing to. This is a consequence of C++'s "static type checking"; if we were allowed to refer to a member variable or function that might theoretically not be present in an object at run time, the compiler would have no way of knowing whether what we were trying to do was legal. Therefore, if we want to access a member variable called m_Count through a StockItem*, there has to be a member variable called m_Count in the StockItem class, even if we don't need it until we get to a class derived from StockItem.

This also brings up another point that may or may not be obvious to you: The workings of the polymorphic StockItem object don't depend on the fact that the DatedStockItem class is derived from UndatedStockItem. So long as both the UndatedStockItem and DatedStockItem classes are derived directly or indirectly from StockItem, we can use a StockItem* to refer to an object of either of these classes, UndatedStockItem or DatedStockItem, which is all that we need to make the idiom work.

Review

We started this chapter with the DatedStockItem class from Chapter 9, which extended the StockItem class by adding an expiration date field to the member variables that DatedStockItem inherited from the StockItem class. While this was a fine solution to the problem of creating a class based on the StockItem class without having to rewrite all the functioning code in the latter class, it didn't solve the bigger problem: how to create a vector of objects that might or might not have expiration dates. That is, we wanted to be able to mix StockItem objects with DatedStockItem objects in the same vector, which can't be done directly in C++.

Part of this difficulty was solved easily enough by making a vector of StockItem*s (i.e., pointers to StockItems), rather than StockItems, to take advantage of the fact that C++ allows us to assign the address of an object of a derived type to a pointer of its base class (e.g., to assign the address of a DatedStockItem to a pointer of type StockItem*). Creating such a vector of StockItem*s allowed us to create both StockItems and DatedStockItems and to assign the addresses of these objects to various elements of that vector. Even so, this didn't solve the problem completely: When we called the Reorder function through a StockItem pointer, the function that was executed was always StockItem::Reorder. This result may seem reasonable, but it doesn't meet our needs. When we call the Reorder function for an object, we want to execute the correct Reorder function for the actual type of the object the pointer is referring to even though the pointer is declared as a StockItem*.

The reason the StockItem function is always called in this situation is precisely that when we make a base class pointer (e.g., a StockItem*) refer to a derived class object (e.g., a DatedStockItem), the compiler doesn't know what the actual type of the object is at compile time. By default, the compiler determines exactly which function will be called at compile time, and the only information the compiler has about the type of an object pointed to by a StockItem* is that it's either a StockItem or an object of a class derived from StockItem. In this situation, the compiler defaults to the base class function.

The solution to this problem is to make the Reorder function virtual. This means that when the compiler sees a call to the Reorder function, it generates code that will call the appropriate version of that function for the actual type of the object referred to. In this case, StockItem::Reorder is called if the actual object being referred to through a StockItem* is a StockItem, while DatedStockItem::Reorder is called if the actual object being referred to through a StockItem* is a

DatedStockItem. This is exactly the behavior we need to make our StockItem and DatedStockItem objects do the right thing when we refer to them through a StockItem*.

To make this run-time determination of which function will be called, the compiler has to add something to every object that contains at least one virtual function. What it adds is a pointer to a vtable (virtual function table), which contains the addresses of all the virtual functions defined in the class of that object or in any of its ancestral classes. The code the compiler generates for a virtual function call uses this table to look up the actual address of the function to be called at run time.

After going over the use of virtual functions, we looked at the implementation of the usual I/O functions, operator << and operator >>. Even though these can't be virtual functions, as they aren't member functions at all, they can still use the virtual mechanism indirectly by calling virtual functions that provide the correct behavior for each class. However, while this solves most of the problems with operator <<, the implementation of operator >> is still pretty tricky. It has to allocate the memory for the object it is creating because the actual type of that object isn't known until the data for the object has been read. The real problem here, though, is not that operator >> has to allocate that memory, or even that it has to use a reference to a pointer to notify the calling function of the address of the allocated memory. The big difficulty is that after operator >> allocates the memory, the calling function has to free the memory when it is done with the object. Getting a program written this way to work properly is very difficult; keeping it working properly after later changes is virtually impossible. Unfortunately, there's no solution to this problem as long as we require the user program to use a vector of StockItem*s to get the benefits of polymorphism.

As is often the case in C++, though, there is a way to remove that requirement. We can hide the pointers and the consequent memory allocation problems from the user by creating a *polymorphic object* using the *manager/worker idiom*. With these idioms, the user sees only a base class object, within which the pointers are hidden. The base class is the manager class, which uses an object of one of the worker classes to do the actual work.

Possibly the most unusual aspect of the manager/worker idiom is that the type of the pointer inside the manager object is the same as the type of the manager class. In the current case, each StockItem object contains a StockItem* called m_Worker as its main data member. This may seem peculiar, but it makes sense. The actual type of the object being referred to is always one of the worker classes, which in this case means either UndatedStockItem or DatedStockItem. Since we know that a StockItem* can refer to an object of any of the derived classes of StockItem, and because we want the interface of the StockItem class to be the same as that of any of its derived classes, declaring the pointer to the worker object as a StockItem* is quite appropriate.

We started our examination of this new StockItem class with operator <<, whose header indicates one of the advantages of this new implementation of StockItem. Rather than taking a StockItem*, as the previous version of operator << did, it takes a const reference to a StockItem. The implementation of this function consists of a call to a virtual function called Write. Since Write is virtual, the exact function that will be called here depends on the actual type of the object pointed to by m_Worker, which is exactly the behavior we want.

After going into more detail on how this "internal polymorphism" works, we looked at how such a polymorphic object comes into existence in the first place, starting with the default constructor for StockItem. This constructor is a bit more complicated than it seems at first. When it creates an empty UndatedStockItem to perform the duties of a default-constructed StockItem, that newly constructed UndatedStockItem has to initialize its base class part, as is required for all derived class objects. That may not seem too unusual, but keep in mind that the base class for UndatedStockItem is StockItem; therefore, the constructor for UndatedStockItem will necessarily call a constructor for StockItem. We have to make sure that it doesn't call the default constructor for StockItem, as that is where the

UndatedStockItem constructor was called from in the first place! The result of such a call would be a further call to the default constructor for UndatedStockItem, then to the default constructor for StockItem, and so on forever (or at least until we had run out of stack space). The solution is simple enough: We have to create a special constructor for StockItem, StockItem::StockItem(int), that we call explicitly via a base class initializer in the default and normal constructors for UndatedStockItem. This special constructor doesn't do anything but initialize m_Worker to 0, for reasons we'll get to later, and then return to its caller. Since it doesn't call any other functions, we avoid the potential disaster of an infinite regress.

This simple function, StockItem::StockItem(int), does have a couple of other interesting features. First, I declared it protected so that it couldn't be called by anyone other than our member functions and those of our derived classes. This is sensible because, after all, we don't want a user to be able to create a StockItem with just an int argument. In fact, we are using that argument only to allow the compiler to tell which constructor we mean via the *function overloading* facility. This also means that we don't need to provide a name for that argument, since we're not using it. Leaving the name out tells the compiler that we didn't accidentally forget to use the argument, so we won't get "unused argument" warnings when we compile this code. Any programmers who may have to work on our code in the future will also appreciate this indication that we weren't planning to use the argument.

Then we examined the use of *reference-counting* to keep track of the number of users of a given DatedStockItem or UndatedStockItem object, rather than copying those objects whenever we copied their manager objects. As long as we keep track of how many users there are, we can safely delete the DatedStockItem or UndatedStockItem as soon as there are no more users left. To keep track of the number of users, we use the m_Count member variable in the StockItem class.

To see how this works in practice, we went through the actions that occur when StockItem objects are created, copied, and destroyed. This involves the implementation of the assignment operator, which copies the pointer to the worker object contained in the manager object. We can do this because we are using the *reference-counting idiom* to keep track of the number of users of each object, so memory is freed correctly when the objects are destroyed at the end of the function where they are created.

The destructor for the StockItem class has a number of new features. First, it is virtual, which is necessary because the derived class object pointed to by the StockItem object must be destroyed when it no longer has any users, but the type of the pointer through which it is accessed is StockItem*. To allow the compiler to call the correct destructor—the one for the derived class object—we must declare the base class destructor virtual. This is the same rule that applies to all other functions that have to be resolved according to the run-time type of the object for which they are called.

Second, the StockItem destructor has to check whether it has been called to destroy the base class part of a derived class object. Just as in the case of the constructor for StockItem, we have to prevent an infinite regress in which the destructor for StockItem calls the destructor for DatedStockItem, which calls the destructor for StockItem, which calls the destructor for DatedStockItem again, and so on. In fact, in this case we can't avoid the first "round trip" because the destructor for DatedStockItem must call the destructor for StockItem; we don't have any control over that. However, the first if statement in the StockItem destructor cuts off the regress right there, as m_Worker will be 0 in the base class part of a derived class object. That's why we initialized m_Worker to 0 in the special constructor for StockItem that was used to construct the base class part of an object of a class derived from StockItem.

We finished by examining the exact sequence of events that occurs when the objects in the example program are destroyed. We also determined the reason that we had to include m_Count in the base class when it was never used there: The type of the pointer we use to access m_Count is a StockItem*, so there has to be an m_Count variable in a StockItem. If there were no such variable in the StockItem class, the compiler couldn't guarantee that it would exist in the object pointed to by a StockItem pointer and therefore wouldn't let us access it through such a pointer.

Exercises, Second Set

3. Rewrite the DrugStockItem class that you wrote earlier in this chapter as a derived class of DatedStockItem, adding the new class to the polymorphic object implementation based on the StockItem class. The Reorder member function of the DrugStockItem class will be inherited from DatedStockItem, and the member function DeductSaleFromInventory will have to be made a virtual function in StockItem so that the correct version will be called via the StockItem* in the StockItem class. The resulting set of classes will allow the effective type of a StockItem object to be any of UndatedStockItem, DatedStockItem, or DrugStockItem.

4. Rewrite the Employee, Exempt, and Hourly classes that you wrote earlier in this chapter as a set of classes implementing a polymorphic object type. The base class will be Employee, with an Exempt class and an Hourly class derived from the base class. The resulting set of classes will allow the effective type of an Employee object to be either Exempt or Hourly, with the CalculatePay function producing the correct result for either type. To distinguish the effective types, you will need to write two different versions of the constructor for the Employee class. Do this by adding an additional argument of type float in the constructor that creates an Hourly worker object, specifying the multiplier used to calculate overtime pay. For example, a value of 1.5 specifies the standard "time-and-a-half for overtime" multiplier. Note that you *must* maintain the same interface for the CalculatePay function in these classes because you are using a base class pointer to access derived class objects.

Conclusion

Now that we have enough tools to work with, it's time to tackle a more realistic project. That's what we'll do in the next chapter, where we start to develop a home inventory system.

CHAPTER 11

The Home Inventory Project

Now that we have enough tools to start working on a somewhat more realistic project, what sort of project should that be? I've spent some time thinking that question over and have come up with what I think is a good way to hone our skills as well as advance them: a "home inventory program" to keep track of the myriad objects, technically known as "stuff", that we have lying around in our houses or apartments. When you consider that insurance companies are a lot happier and quicker to pay after a loss if you have an up-to-date list of your possessions, with any luck this program may actually be useful as well as instructive! Of course, before we start we need to define some terms and establish some objectives for this chapter.

Definitions

Aliasing is the practice of referring to one object by more than one "name"; in C++ these names are actually pointers.

The **aliasing problem** is a name for the difficulties caused by altering a shared object.

An **enum** is a way to define a number of unchangeable values, which are quite similar to consts. The value of each successive name in an enum is automatically incremented from the value of the previous name (if you don't specify another value explicitly). The term enum is short for "enumeration", which is a list of numbers.

The **switch** statement is functionally equivalent to a number of if/else statements in a row, but is easier to read and modify. The keyword switch is followed by a *selection expression* (in parentheses), which specifies an expression used to select an alternative section of code. The various alternatives to be considered are enclosed in a set of curly braces following the selection expressions and are marked off by the keyword case followed by the (constant) value to be matched and a colon.

An **array initialization list** is a list of values that are used to initialize the elements of an *array*. The ability to specify a list of values for an array is built into the C++ language and is not available for user-defined data types such as the vector.

Objectives of This Chapter

By the end of this chapter, you should

1. Understand how to create a more realistic application using the tools we already have,

2. Know how to use the switch statement to select among a number of alternatives,

3. Know how to use the enum data type to give names to constant values that will be used to refer to items in a list,

4. Understand the advantages of creating variables at the point of use rather than at the beginning of a function,

5. Know how to find or change the size of a vector dynamically when necessary, and

6. Understand how to use virtual functions for implementation purposes within a polymorphic class hierarchy.

Homing In

What information will we need to store for the various types of objects in our home inventory? No matter what type of object we are recording, we will want to store the following data:

1. type of object,

2. date of acquisition,

3. price,

4. description,

5. category (e.g., office furniture, kitchen appliance).

While we'll have to maintain the above data for every object, we'll also need to keep track of other infomation on some types of objects. Of course, the exact form of that extra information will depend on each object's type. After some thought, I have come up with the following types of objects that we might want to keep track of (in no particular order):

1. "Basic" objects, for which the above data are sufficient;

2. "Music" objects (e.g., CDs, LPs, cassettes);

3. computer hardware;

4. computer software;

5. other electric and electronic appliances;

6. books;

7. kitchen items such as plates and flatware;

8. clothes and shoes.

Of course, each of these types has different additional information, which is why we need the individual types in the first place.

Undoubtedly you can think of a number of other kinds of objects that don't fit exactly into one of the listed types. However, I think most of these other kinds are close enough to one of the above types that we can use one of those listed without too much strain. For example, what about jewelry and art objects? It seems to me that the "Basic" type is fine for both of these, as we have to keep track of the basic information needed for all objects (value, date of acquisition, description, and category) and not much else.

What It Is, Mama!

This brings us to a very important point in the design of any program, especially an object-oriented one: deciding how to fit the nearly infinite possibilities of real-world entities into a necessarily limited number of categories in the program. I wish there were a hard-and-fast rule I could give you so you wouldn't have to make this decision for every program you write; unfortunately, however, this isn't possible, precisely because there are so many possibilities in the real world. The best I can do is give guidelines and examples.

Consider the example of LP records or cassette tapes. In this case, I think it's pretty obvious that an LP or a cassette tape is similar enough to a CD that using the "Music" type for either of these other types of sound recording is appropriate.[1] How did I make this determination?

1. The *purpose* of a CD is to contain music or speech. This is also the purpose of an LP or cassette.

2. The *information* that we might want to store about a CD includes artist, title, and track names. These are also appropriate for an LP or cassette.

Note that the storage medium and other surface similarities among objects aren't significant in this analysis. In fact, a CD-ROM, which uses exactly the same storage medium as a music CD does, is a completely different type of object from a music CD, and needs to be categorized under "computer software". That's because the purpose of the objects and the information we need to store about these two different kinds of CDs are completely different.[2]

What about rare coins or stamps? If you had only a couple of either of these objects, you might very well use the "Basic" type to keep track of them. However, if you had an extensive collection, you probably would want to keep track of their condition, year of minting or printing, denomination, and other data of interest to collectors. To handle this extra information, you would add a "Coin/Stamp" type or even two separate types, if you happened to collect both. This merely illustrates the rule that the handling of data has to be based on the use to which it will be put, not on its intrinsic characteristics alone.

---

1. Of course, if you still have 8-track tapes, you probably also need a "lava lamp" category.

2. This is an oversimplification because both music CDs and CD-ROMs can be stored in the same "CD holder", whereas cassettes and LPs each need their own type of holders. Therefore, for purposes of figuring out how much storage you need for each type of object, the physical form of the object is indeed important. As always, the question is how you will use the information, not merely what information is available.

Now that we've developed a general outline of these classes and the data that they need to keep track of, let's start designing the interface they will present to the application program that uses them.

Interface R Us

Why do I say "the interface" rather than "the interfaces"? Because we're going to implement these classes to give the appearance of a single type of object that can change its behavior; in other words, we're going to use the *manager/worker idiom* again to implement another type of *polymorphic object*. This will enable us to write a main program that allows access to an object of any of these types in a uniform manner. Of course, the implementation of the member functions will be somewhat different in each class, to take account of the peculiarities of each class, but the structure of the program will be essentially the same for any number of types once we've made provisions to handle more than one. For this reason, we'll use just the "Basic" and "Music" types in the text; handling other types will be left as an exercise. Figure 11.1 shows the initial HomeItem interface.

FIGURE 11.1. **The initial interface for the** HomeItem **manager class (code/ hmit1.h)**

```
// hmit1.h

#include "string6.h"
#include "vector.h"

class HomeItem
{
friend ostream& operator << (ostream& os,
  const HomeItem& Item);

friend istream& operator >> (istream& is, HomeItem& Item);
```

```
public:
  HomeItem();
  HomeItem(const HomeItem& Item);
  HomeItem& operator = (const HomeItem& Item);
virtual ~HomeItem();

// Basic: Art objects, furniture, jewelry, etc.
  HomeItem(string Name, double PurchasePrice,
  long PurchaseDate, string Description, string Category);

// Music: CDs, LPs, cassettes, etc.
  HomeItem(string Name, double PurchasePrice,
  long PurchaseDate, string Description, string Category,
  string Artist, vector<string> Track);

virtual void Write(ostream& os);

protected:
  HomeItem(int);

protected:
  HomeItem* m_Worker;
  short m_Count;
};
```

If you think this looks familiar, you're right. It's almost exactly the same as the polymorphic object version of the StockItem interface we saw in Chapter 10. This is not a coincidence: Every polymorphic object interface is going to look very similar to every other one. Why is this?

Deja Vu All Over Again

They all look alike because the objects of every polymorphic object manager class do very similar things: managing the "real" objects of classes derived from the manager class. The only differences between the interfaces of two polymorphic object types are in the member functions that the user of the polymorphic objects sees. In this case, we don't have a Reorder function as we did in the StockItem class, for the very simple reason that we don't have to figure out how many HomeItem objects to reorder from our distributors.

Before we get into the worker classes for the HomeItem polymorphic object, let's go over the similarities and differences between the StockItem and HomeItem interfaces.

1. The operators << and >>, as well as the default constructors, copy constructors, assignment operators, and destructors, have exactly the same interfaces in the StockItem class and the HomeItem class except, of course, for their names and the types of their arguments (if applicable). This also applies to the "special" constructor used to prevent an infinite loop during construction of a worker object and to the Write function used to create a human-readable version of the data for an object.

2. The "normal" constructors that create objects for which the initial state is known are the same in these two classes except, of course, for the exact arguments, which depend on the data needed by each object. One point we'll cover later is the use of a vector as an argument to the second "normal" constructor.

3. The GetName, GetPrice, and other class-specific member functions of StockItem don't exist in HomeItem because it is a different class with different requirements from those of StockItem.[3]

4. The member data items for the two classes are the same except, again, for the type of m_Worker, which is a pointer to a HomeItem rather than to a StockItem.

---

3. As we'll see, HomeItem will eventually have its own version of GetName. Many classes need the ability to retrieve the name of an item; using a function called something like GetName is a fairly common way to handle this requirement.

Of course, this class doesn't really do anything by itself; as with all polymorphic objects, we also need the worker classes to get the job done. Figure 11.2 shows the interfaces for HomeItemBasic and HomeItemMusic.

FIGURE 11.2. The initial interface for the HomeItemBasic **and** HomeItemMusic **worker** classes **(code\hmiti1.h)**

```
// hmiti1.h

class HomeItemBasic : public HomeItem
{
public:
  HomeItemBasic();

  HomeItemBasic(string Name, double PurchasePrice,
    long PurchaseDate, string Description, string Category);

  virtual void Write(ostream& s);

  virtual string GetType();

protected:
  string m_Name;
  double m_PurchasePrice;
  long m_PurchaseDate;
  string m_Description;
  string m_Category;
};

class HomeItemMusic : public HomeItemBasic
{
public:

  HomeItemMusic(string Name, double PurchasePrice,
    long PurchaseDate, string Description, string Category,
    string Artist, vector<string> Track);
```

```
virtual void Write(ostream& s);

virtual string GetType();

protected:
  string m_Artist;
  vector<string> m_Track;
};
```

Susan had a question about having two interface files.

Susan: Why do we need two different interface files again?

Steve: The first one (hmit1.h) is for the user of these classes; the second one (hmiti1.h) is only for our use as class implementers. The user never sees this second interface file, which means that we can change it if we need to without forcing the user to recompile everything.

As we did with the manager classes, let's take a look at the similarities and differences between the HomeItem and StockItem worker classes.

1. The default constructors, copy constructors, assignment operators, and destructors have exactly the same interfaces in the StockItem worker classes and the HomeItem worker classes except, of course, for their names and the types of their arguments (if applicable). This also applies to the Write function used to create a human-readable version of the data for an object.[4]

2. The "normal" constructors that create objects for which the initial state is known are the same in all of these classes except, of course, for the exact arguments, which depend on the data needed

---

4. In case you were wondering, we don't have to state that the destructors are virtual because that is guaranteed by the fact that the base class destructor is virtual. I've added the virtual keyword to the declaration of the derived class destructors solely for clarity.

by each object. Again, we'll go into what it means to have a vector argument when we cover the implementation of the "normal" constructor for the HomeItemMusic class.

3. The HomeItem worker classes have a GetType member function that the StockItem class doesn't have. The purpose of this function is to allow the proper storage and display of objects of various types. In the StockItem class, we depended on the value of the expiration date ("0" or a real date) to give us this information.

4. The GetName, GetPrice, and other class-specific member functions of the StockItem worker classes don't exist in the HomeItem worker classes, as explained above.

5. The member data items for the HomeItem worker classes are as needed for these classes, as is the case with the HomeItem worker classes.

6. We are using the long data type for the m_PurchaseDate member variable rather than the string data type that we used for a similar field in DatedStockItem.

7. We are using the double data type for the m_PurchasePrice member variable rather than the short data type that we used for price information in the StockItem classes.

The first of the differences between the StockItem worker classes and the HomeItem worker classes that needs additional explanation is the GetType virtual function first declared in HomeItemBasic. Since I have claimed that all the classes that participate in a polymorphic object implementation must have the same interface (so the user can treat them all the same), why am I declaring a new function in one of the worker classes that wasn't present in the base class?

What They Don't Know Won't Hurt Them

That rule applies only to functions that are to be used by the user of the polymorphic object. The GetType function is intended for use only in the implementation of the polymorphic object, not by its users; therefore, it is not only possible but desirable to keep it "hidden" by declaring it inside one of the worker classes. Because the user never creates an object of any of the worker classes directly, declaring a function in one of those classes has much the same effect as making it a private member function. As we have already seen, hiding as many implementation details as possible helps to improve the robustness of our programs.

I should also mention the different data types for member variables in the HomeItem classes that have similar functions to those in the StockItem classes. In HomeItemBasic, we are using a long to hold a date, where we used a string in the DatedStockItem class. A sufficient reason for this change is that in the current class, we are getting the date from the user, so we don't have the problem of converting the system date to a storable value as we did with the implementation of the former class.[5] As for the double we're using to store the price information, that's a more sensible data type than short for numbers that may have decimal parts. I avoided using it in the earlier example only to simplify the presentation, but at this point I don't think it should cause you any trouble.

Aside from these details, this polymorphic object's definition is very similar to the one for the StockItem polymorphic object. The similarity between the interfaces (and corresponding similarity of implementations) of polymorphic objects is good news because it makes generating a new polymorphic object interface and basic implementation quite easy. It took me only a couple of hours to write

---

5.   There's another reason as well. After I finished developing the StockItem class, I decided that it was more sensible to use a long anyway. That's why I added an exercise in Chapter 9 to replace the string date with a long.

the initial version of the HomeItem classes using StockItem as a starting point. What is even more amazing is that the test program (Figure 11.3) worked the very first time I ran it![6]

FIGURE 11.3. The initial test program for the HomeItem classes **(code\hmtst1.cc)**

```
// hmtst1.cc

#include <iostream.h>
#include <fstream.h>
#include "vector.h"
#include "hmit1.h"

int main()
{
    HomeItem x;
    HomeItem y;

    ifstream HomeInfo("home1.in");

    HomeInfo >> x;

    HomeInfo >> y;

    cout << "A basic HomeItem: " << endl;
    cout << x;

    cout << endl;

    cout << "A music HomeItem: " << endl;
    cout << y;
```

---

6. It took quite a few compiles before I actually had an executable, but that was mostly because I started writing this chapter and the HomeItem program on my laptop while on a trip away from home. Because I had a relatively small screen to work on and no printer, it was faster to use the compiler to tell me about statements that I needed to change.

}

I don't think that program needs much explanation. It is exactly the same as the corresponding StockItem test program in Figure 10.22 on page 697, with the obvious exception of the types of the objects and the name of the ifstream used to read the data. Figure 11.4 shows the result of running the above program.

FIGURE 11.4. Results of running the first HomeItem **test program (code\hmit1.out)**

A basic HomeItem:
Basic
Living room sofa
1600
19970105
Our living room sofa
Furniture

A music HomeItem:
Music
Relish
12.95
19950601
Our first album
CD
Joan Osborne
2
Right Hand Man
Ladder

Now that we've gone over the interfaces for the classes that cooperate to make a polymorphic HomeItem object, as well as the first test program and its output, we can see the initial implementation in Figure 11.5.

FIGURE 11.5. Initial implementation of HomeItem **manager and worker classes (code\hmit1.cc)**

```
// hmit1.cc

#include <iostream.h>
#include <iomanip.h>
#include <strstream.h>
#include <string.h>
#include <dos.h>
#include "string6.h"
#include "hmit1.h"
#include "hmiti1.h"


//friend functions of HomeItem

ostream& operator << (ostream& os, const HomeItem& Item)
{
  Item.m_Worker->Write(os);
  return os;
}

istream& operator >> (istream& is, HomeItem& Item)
{
  string Type;
  string Name;
  double PurchasePrice;
  long PurchaseDate;
  string Description;
  string Category;

  while (Type == "")
    {
    is >> Type;
    if (is.fail() != 0)
      {
      Item = HomeItem();
      return is;
```

```
            }
          }

        is >> Name;
        is >> PurchasePrice;
        is >> PurchaseDate;
        is >> Description;
        is >> Category;

        if (Type == "Basic")
          {
          Item = HomeItem(Name, PurchasePrice, PurchaseDate,
                Description, Category);
          }
        else if (Type == "Music")
          {
          string Artist;
          short TrackCount;
          is >> Artist;
          is >> TrackCount;
          vector<string> Track(TrackCount);
          for (short i = 0; i < TrackCount; i ++)
            {
            is >> Track[i];
            }
          Item = HomeItem(Name, PurchasePrice, PurchaseDate,
                Description, Category, Artist, Track);
          }
        else
          {
          cout << "Can't create object of type " << Type << endl;
          exit(0);
          }

        return is;
      }


    // HomeItem member functions
```

```
HomeItem::HomeItem()
: m_Count(0), m_Worker(new HomeItemBasic)
{
  m_Worker->m_Count = 1;
}


HomeItem::HomeItem(const HomeItem& Item)
: m_Count(0), m_Worker(Item.m_Worker)
{
  m_Worker->m_Count ++;
}

HomeItem& HomeItem::operator = (const HomeItem& Item)
{
  if (&Item != this)
    {
    m_Worker->m_Count --;
    if (m_Worker->m_Count <= 0)
     delete m_Worker;
    m_Worker = Item.m_Worker;
    m_Worker->m_Count ++;
    }
  return *this;
}


HomeItem::~HomeItem()
{
  if (m_Worker == 0)
    return;

  m_Worker->m_Count --;
  if (m_Worker->m_Count <= 0)
    delete m_Worker;
}

HomeItem::HomeItem(string Name, double PurchasePrice,
long PurchaseDate, string Description,
string Category)
```

```
: m_Count(0),
  m_Worker(new HomeItemBasic(Name, PurchasePrice,
  PurchaseDate, Description, Category))
{
  m_Worker->m_Count = 1;
}

HomeItem::HomeItem(int)
: m_Worker(0)
{
}

HomeItem::HomeItem(string Name, double PurchasePrice,
long PurchaseDate, string Description,
string Category, string Artist,
vector<string> Track)
: m_Count(0),
  m_Worker(new HomeItemMusic(Name, PurchasePrice,
  PurchaseDate, Description, Category, Artist, Track))
{
  m_Worker->m_Count = 1;
}


void HomeItem::Write(ostream& os)
{
  exit(1); // error
}

// HomeItemBasic member functions

HomeItemBasic::HomeItemBasic()
: HomeItem(1),
  m_Name(),
  m_PurchasePrice(0),
  m_PurchaseDate(0),
  m_Description(),
  m_Category()
{
```

```
}

HomeItemBasic::HomeItemBasic(string Name,
double PurchasePrice, long PurchaseDate,
string Description, string Category)
: HomeItem(1),
  m_Name(Name),
  m_PurchasePrice(PurchasePrice),
  m_PurchaseDate(PurchaseDate),
  m_Description(Description),
  m_Category(Category)
{
}

void HomeItemBasic::Write(ostream& os)
{
  os << GetType() << endl;
  os << m_Name << endl;
  os << m_PurchasePrice << endl;
  os << m_PurchaseDate << endl;
  os << m_Description << endl;
  os << m_Category << endl;
}

string HomeItemBasic::GetType()
{
  return "Basic";
}


// HomeItemMusic member functions

HomeItemMusic::HomeItemMusic(string Name,
double PurchasePrice, long PurchaseDate,
string Description, string Category,
string Artist, vector<string> Track)
: HomeItemBasic(Name,PurchasePrice,PurchaseDate,
  Description, Category),
  m_Artist(Artist),
```

```
        m_Track(Track)
        {
        }

        void HomeItemMusic::Write(ostream& os)
        {
          HomeItemBasic::Write(os);

          os << m_Artist << endl;

          int TrackCount = m_Track.size();
          os << TrackCount << endl;
          for (short i = 0; i < TrackCount; i ++)
            os << m_Track[i] << endl;
        }

        string HomeItemMusic::GetType()
        {
          return "Music";
        }
```

What does this first version of HomeItem do for us? Not too much; it merely allows us to read HomeItem objects from a file, display them, and write them out to a file. Although we've seen the implementation of similar functions in the StockItem class, it should still be worthwhile to discuss how these are similar to and different from the corresponding functions in the HomeItem classes. However, to avoid too much repetition, we'll skip the functions that are essentially identical in these two cases, including the following functions for the base class, HomeItem:

1. operator <<;

2. the copy constructor;

3. the default constructor;

4. operator =;

5. the destructor;

6. the normal constructors that create worker objects with known initial data;

7. the "special" constructor that prevents an infinite regress when creating a worker object.

Here's a list of the functions we'll skip for the HomeItemBasic and HomeItemMusic classes:

1. the default constructor;

2. the copy constructor;

3. operator =;

4. the normal constructor;

5. the destructor.

The first HomeItem function we'll discuss is Write, shown in Figure 11.6.

FIGURE 11.6. HomeItem::Write **(from code\hmit1.cc)**

```
void HomeItem::Write(ostream& os)
{
  exit(1); // error
}
```

Calling this function is an error and will cause the program to exit. In case you're wondering why this is an error, you may be happy to know that Susan had the same question.

Susan: Why is calling HomeItem::Write an error?

Steve: Because this function exists solely for use by operator << in writing out the data for a derived class object. Therefore, if it is ever called for a HomeItem base class object, we know that someone has used the function incorrectly, and we leave the program before any more incorrect processing can occur.

The next function we need to look at is operator >>, shown in Figure 11.7.

FIGURE 11.7. The HomeItem **implementation of** operator >> **(from code\hmit1.cc)**

```
istream& operator >> (istream& is, HomeItem& Item)
{
  string Type;
  string Name;
  double PurchasePrice;
  long PurchaseDate;
  string Description;
  string Category;

  while (Type == "")
    {
    is >> Type;
    if (is.fail() != 0)
      {
      Item = HomeItem();
      return is;
      }
    }

  is >> Name;
  is >> PurchasePrice;
  is >> PurchaseDate;
  is >> Description;
  is >> Category;

  if (Type == "Basic")
    {
    Item = HomeItem(Name, PurchasePrice, PurchaseDate,
        Description, Category);
```

```
      }
    else if (Type == "Music")
      {
      string Artist;
      short TrackCount;
      is >> Artist;
      is >> TrackCount;
      vector<string> Track(TrackCount);
      for (short i = 0; i < TrackCount; i ++)
        {
        is >> Track[i];
        }
      Item = HomeItem(Name, PurchasePrice, PurchaseDate,
          Description, Category, Artist, Track);
      }
    else
      {
      cout << "Can't create object of type " << Type << endl;
      exit(0);
      }

    return is;
  }
```

This is quite similar in outline to the corresponding function in StockItem in that it reads data from an input source and creates a worker object of the correct type based on the value of one of the fields. However, this function does have a few noticeable differences from the StockItem version:

1. This function skips any empty lines that may be in the input file before reading the type of the object.

2. The type is specified explicitly as an extra field ("Basic" or "Music" in the current cases), rather than by the use of a special "0" value for the expiration date field, as in the DatedStockItem input file.

3. This function calls istream::fail to determine whether the program has attempted to read more information from the input file than it contains (or if any other error has occurred when trying to read from the input file). If such an error occurs, the operator >> function assigns a default-constructed HomeItem to the reference argument Item and returns to the calling function immediately.

4. The local variables Artist, TrackCount, and Track are created only when the function needs them (for a "Music" object) rather than at the beginning of the function as has been our practice until now.

5. In the case of a "Music" object, one of those local variables is a vector of strings.

6. The index variable i is also created only when it is needed, at the beginning of the for loop.

Susan had a question about the first of these differences.

> **Susan:** Why would you want to put blank lines in the input file?

> **Steve:** To make it easier to read. Because our StockItem input file couldn't have any blank lines in it, the data for each item started right after the end of the data for the previous item, which makes it hard for a human being to tell what the entries in the input file mean. Of course, the program doesn't care, but sometimes it's necessary for a person to look at the input file, especially when there's something wrong with it!

The reason for the second difference from the StockItem version of operator >> is fairly simple: All of the types of HomeItems share the basic data in the HomeItemBasic class, so we don't have any otherwise unused field that we can use to indicate which actual type the object belongs to; thus, we have to add another field to explicitly specify that type.

However, the other differences are a bit more interesting. First, part of the reason that we have to check for the input stream terminating (or "failing") here, when we didn't have to do that in the StockItem case, is that we're trying to skip blank lines between the data for successive objects. This means that when we reach the end of the file, we will have blank lines that we might try to read while looking for the next set of data; if there isn't any more data, we might run off the end of the file. I added this "blank line skipping" feature of operator >> to make the input files easier to read and write for human beings, but the way I originally implemented it had an unexpected side effect: The program looped forever if I gave it a bad file name. In fact, it always did this at the end of the file! Figure 11.8 is my original implementation; see if you can tell what's wrong with it.

FIGURE 11.8. The (incorrect) while **loop in the original implementation of** operator >>

```
while (Type == "")
  {
  s >> Type;
  }
```

This won't work if the file tied to s doesn't exist or if we've already reached the end of that file, because the line s >> Type; won't change the value of Type in either of those cases. Therefore, Type will retain its original value, which is "" (the empty string). Since the loop continues as long as s is the empty string, it becomes an endless loop and the program will "hang" (run forever). The solution is simple enough: Use fail to check if the stream is still working before trying to read something else from it.

Of course, if the stream isn't still working, we can't get any data to put into a HomeItem object; in that case, we set the reference argument Item to the value of a default-constructed HomeItem (so that the calling function can tell that it hasn't received a valid HomeItem) and return immediately.

Now that we've cleared that up, let's examine why it is more than just a convenience to be able to create new local variables at any point in a function.

Making All Local Stops

There are a couple of reasons to create the local variable Track only after we detect that we're dealing with a "Music" object. First, it's relatively time-consuming to create a vector, especially one of a nonnative data type like strings, because each of those strings has to be created and placed in the vector before it can be used. But a more significant reason is that we don't know how large the vector needs to be until we have read the "track count" from the file. As you'll see later, it's possible (and even sometimes necessary) to change the size of a vector after it has been created, but that takes extra work that we should avoid if we can. Therefore, it is much more sensible to wait until we have read the count so that we can create the vector with a size that is just right to hold all of the track names for the CD, LP, or cassette.

Susan had a question about reading the track names in from the file.

> **Susan:** I don't get how the code works to read in the track names from the file when there can be different numbers of tracks for each album.

> **Steve:** That's what these lines are for:

```
s >> TrackCount;
vector<string> Track(TrackCount);
for (short i = 0; i < TrackCount; i ++)
  {
  s >> Track[i];
  }
```

> First, we read the number of tracks from the file into the variable TrackCount. Next, we create a vector to hold that many strings (the track names). Finally, we use the loop to read all of the track names into the vector.

Susan: Okay, I get it.

The final reason to wait as long as possible before creating the vector of strings to hold the track names is that we don't need it at all if we're not creating a "Music" object, so any effort to create it in any other case would be a complete waste. Although we don't have to be fanatical about saving computer time, doing work that doesn't need to be done is just silly.

What Have i Started?

The creation of an index variable such as i during the initialization of a for loop is also a bit more significant than it looks, because the meaning of this operation changed recently. Earlier versions of C++ had an inadvertent "feature" that was fixed in the final standard: A variable created in the initialization section of a for loop used to exist from that point until the end of the block enclosing the for loop, not just during the for loop's execution. This old rule was replaced by the more logical rule that the scope of a variable created in the initialization section of a for loop consists of the for loop's header and the controlled block of the for loop. Thus, the program in Figure 11.9 was illegal under the old rule because you can't have two local variables named i in the same scope and, under the old rule, the scopes of the two i's were overlapping. However, it is perfectly legal under the new rule because the scopes of the two i's are separate.[7]

Susan had a question about creating a variable in the header of a for loop.

Susan: What does "for (short i=0" mean that is different from just "for (i=0"?

---

7. Unfortunately, as of this writing, not all compilers support this new feature, including some compilers that claim to be compliant with the standard. If you want your programs to compile under both the old and new rules, you will have to define your loop variables outside the loop headers.

Learning to Program in C++

Steve: The former phrase means that we're creating a new variable called i that will exist only during the execution of the for loop; the latter one means that we're using a preexisting variable called i for our loop index.

Susan: Why would you want to use one of these phrases rather than the other?

Steve: You would generally use the first one because it's a good idea to limit the scope of a variable as much as possible. However, sometimes you need to know the last value that the loop index had after the loop terminates; in that case, you have to use the latter method so that i is still around after the end of the for loop.

FIGURE 11.9. A legal program (code\fortest.cc)

```cpp
#include <iostream.h>

int main()
{
  for (short i = 0; i < 10; i ++)
    {
    cout << i << endl;
    }

  cout << endl;

  for (short i = 0; i < 10; i ++)
    {
    cout << 2 * i << endl;
    }
}
```

Stereo Typing

Before we get to the derived class member functions that have significant changes from the StockItem versions, I want to point out one of the oddities of using the value 0 in C++. Figure 11.10 shows an incorrect version of the HomeItemBasic default constructor.

FIGURE 11.10. **An incorrect default constructor for the** HomeItemBasic class

```
HomeItemBasic::HomeItemBasic()
 : HomeItem(1),
   m_Name(),
   m_PurchasePrice(0),
   m_PurchaseDate(0),
   m_Description(0),
   m_Category(0)
 {
 }
```

What's wrong with this picture? The 0 values in the m_Description and m_Category member variable initializers. These are string variables, so how can they be set to the value 0?

The answer is that, as we've discussed briefly in Chapter 10, 0 is a "magic number" in C++. In this case, the problem is that 0 is a legal value for any type of pointer, including char*. Because the string class has a constructor that makes a string out of a char*, the compiler will accept a 0 as the value in a string variable initializer. Unfortunately, the results of specifying a 0 in such a case are undesirable; whatever data happens to be at address 0 will be taken as the initial data for the string. Therefore, we have to be very careful not to supply a 0 as the initial value for a string variable.

It's all very well to say "be careful", but that doesn't answer the question of how I found this problem in the first place. We'll cover that in Chapter 13, in the section "Nothing Ventured, Nothing Gained" on page 892.

Now that I've warned you about that problem, let's take a look at the other functions pertaining to the HomeItem manager and worker classes that differ from those in the StockItem classes. The first two of these functions are HomeItemBasic::GetType (Figure 11.11) and HomeItemMusic::GetType (Figure 11.12). Each of these functions returns a string representing the type of the object to which it is applied, which in this case is either "Basic" or "Music".

FIGURE 11.11. HomeItemBasic::GetType **(from code\hmit1.cc)**

```
string HomeItemBasic::GetType()
{
  return "Basic";
}
```

FIGURE 11.12. HomeItemMusic::GetType **(from code\hmit1.cc)**

```
string HomeItemMusic::GetType()
{
  return "Music";
}
```

In case it's not obvious why we need these functions, the explanation of the Write functions for the two worker classes should clear it up. Let's start with HomeItemBasic::Write (Figure 11.13).

FIGURE 11.13. HomeItemBasic::Write **(from code\hmit1.cc)**

```
void HomeItemBasic::Write(ostream& os)
{
  os << GetType() << endl;
  os << m_Name << endl;
  os << m_PurchasePrice << endl;
  os << m_PurchaseDate << endl;
  os << m_Description << endl;
```

```
    os << m_Category << endl;
}
```

This function writes out all the data for the object it was called for, which isn't too unusual. But what about that first output line, os << GetType() << endl;, which gets the type of the object to be written via the GetType function? Isn't the object in question obviously a HomeItemBasic?

Virtual Reality

In fact, it may be an object of any of the HomeItem classes—say, a HomeItemMusic object—because the HomeItemBasic::Write function is designed to be called from the Write functions of other HomeItem worker classes. For example, it is called from HomeItemMusic::Write, as you can see in Figure 11.14.

FIGURE 11.14. HomeItemMusic::Write **(from code\hmit1.cc)**

```
void HomeItemMusic::Write(ostream& os)
{
  HomeItemBasic::Write(os);

  os << m_Artist << endl;

  int TrackCount = m_Track.size();
  os << TrackCount << endl;
  for (short i = 0; i < TrackCount; i ++)
    os << m_Track[i] << endl;
}
```

It would be redundant to make the HomeItemMusic::Write function display all the data in a HomeItemBasic object. After all, the HomeItemBasic version of Write already does that.

Susan wasn't convinced that reusing HomeItemBasic::Write was that important.

Susan: So who cares if we have to duplicate the code in HomeItemBasic::Write? It's only a few lines of code anyway.

Steve: Yes, but duplicated code is a prescription for maintenance problems later. What if we add another five or six data types derived from HomeItemBasic? Should we duplicate those few lines in every one of their Write functions? If so, we'll have a wonderful time tracking down all of those sets of duplicated code when we have to make a change to the data in the base class part!

Assuming this has convinced you of the benefit of code reuse in this particular case, we still have to make sure of one detail before we can reuse the code from HomeItemBasic::Write: The correct type of the object has to be written out to the file.

Remember, to read a HomeItem object from a file, we have to know the appropriate type of HomeItem worker object, which is determined by the type indicator (currently "Basic" or "Music") in the first line of the data for each object in the input file. Therefore, when we write the data for a HomeItem object out to the file, we have to specify the correct type so that we can reconstruct the object properly when we read it back in later. That's why we use the GetType function to get the type from the object in the HomeItemBasic::Write function: If the HomeItemBasic::Write function always wrote "Basic" as the type, the data written to the file wouldn't be correct when we called HomeItemBasic::Write to write out the common parts of any HomeItem worker object. As it is, however, when HomeItemBasic::Write is called from HomeItemMusic::Write, the type is correctly written out as "Music" rather than as "Basic", because the GetType function will return "Music" in that case.

The key to the successful operation of this mechanism, of course, is that GetType is a virtual function. Therefore, when we call GetType from HomeItemBasic::Write, we are actually calling the appropriate GetType function for the HomeItem worker object for which HomeItemBasic::Write was called (i.e., the object pointed to by this). Because each of the HomeItemBasic worker object types has its own version of GetType, the call to GetType will retrieve the correct type indicator.

By this point, Susan was apparently convinced that using HomeItemBasic::Write to handle the common parts of any HomeItem object was a good idea, but that led to the following exchange.

Susan: Why didn't we do this with the StockItem classes?

Steve: Because I wrote separate Write functions for the different StockItem classes.

Susan: You should have done it this way.

Steve: Yes, you're right, but I didn't think of it then. I guess that proves that you can always improve your designs!

After we account for this important characteristic of the Write functions, the rest of HomeItemMusic::Write is pretty simple, except for one function that we haven't seen before: size, which is a member function of vector.[8] This function returns the number of elements of the vector, which we can then write out to the output file so that when we read the data back in for this object, we'll know how big to make the vector of track information.

We have covered the member functions of the first version of our HomeItem polymorphic classes, so now let's add a few more features. Obviously, it would be useful to be able to search through all of the items of a given type to find one that matches a particular description. For example, we might want to find a HomeItemMusic object (such as a CD) that has a particular track on it.

Susan had a question about our handling of different types of objects.

---

8. Actually, there is a different size for each different type of vector—vectors of strings, vectors of shorts, vectors of StockItems, and so on, all have their own size member functions. However, this is handled automatically by the compiler, so it doesn't affect our use of the size function.

Susan: I thought we weren't supposed to have to know whether we were dealing with a HomeItemMusic or a HomeItemBasic object.

Steve: Well, that depends on the context. The application program shouldn't have to treat these two types differently when the difference doesn't matter (e.g., when loading them from a disk file), but the user definitely will need to be able to distinguish them sometimes (e.g., when looking for an album that has a particular track on it). The idea is to confine the knowledge of these differences to situations where they matter rather than having to worry about them throughout the program.

As we saw in the StockItem situation, it's not feasible to have a member function of HomeItem that looks for a particular HomeItem, because a member function needs an object of its class to work on and we don't know which object that is when we're doing the search; if we did, we wouldn't be searching!

For that reason, we have to create another class we'll call HomeInventory. This class contains a vector of HomeItems, which the search functions examine whenever we look for a particular HomeItem.

Why do I say "search functions" rather than "search function"? Because there are several ways that we might want to specify the HomeItem we're looking for. One way, of course, would be by its name, which presumably would be distinct for each HomeItem in our list.[9] However, we might also want to find all the HomeItems in the Furniture category, or even all the HomeItems in the Furniture category that have the color "red" in their description, for interior decorating purposes.

To implement these various searches, we will need several search functions. A good place to start is with the simplest one, which searches for a HomeItem with a given name. We'll call this function

---

9. For the moment, I'm going to assume that each name that the user types in for a new object is unique. We'll add code to check this in one of the exercises.

FindItemByName. Let's take a look at the first version of the interface of the HomeInventory class, which includes this member function (Figure 11.15).

FIGURE 11.15. The initial HomeInventory class **interface (code\hmin2.h)**

```
#include "vector.h"

class HomeInventory
{
public:
  HomeInventory();

  short LoadInventory(ifstream& is);
  HomeItem FindItemByName(string Name);

private:
  vector<HomeItem> m_Home;
};
```

This is a pretty simple interface because it doesn't allow us to do anything other than load the inventory from a disk file into the vector called m_Home (LoadInventory) and find an item in that vector given the name of the item(FindItemByName). However, the implementation is a little less obvious, as suggested by the fact that there is no member data item to keep track of the number of elements in the m_Home vector. To see how this works, let's take a look at the implementation of the HomeInventory class (Figure 11.16).

FIGURE 11.16. The initial implementation of HomeInventory **(code\hmin2.cc)**

```
#include <iostream.h>
  #include <fstream.h>
  #include "vector.h"
  #include "string6.h"
  #include "hmit2.h"
```

```
#include "hmin2.h"

HomeInventory::HomeInventory()
: m_Home (vector<HomeItem>(0))
{
}

short HomeInventory::LoadInventory(ifstream& is)
{
   short i;

   for (i = 0; ; i ++)
     {
     m_Home.resize(i+1);

      is >> m_Home[i];
      if (is.fail() != 0)
        break;
      }

   m_Home.resize(i);
   return i;
}

HomeItem HomeInventory::FindItemByName(string Name)
{
   short i;
   bool Found = false;
   short ItemCount = m_Home.size();

   for (i = 0; i < ItemCount; i ++)
     {
     if (m_Home[i].GetName() == Name)
       {
       Found = true;
       break;
       }
     }
```

```
      if (Found == true)
        return m_Home[i];

      return HomeItem();
    }
```

The first clue to how a HomeInventory object keeps track of the number of HomeItems it contains is the size we specify for the m_Home vector in the HomeInventory constructor: 0 elements. Clearly, this can't be the final size because we almost certainly want to keep track of more than zero items!

The question, of course, is how many items we are going to have. The way the input file is currently laid out, there isn't any way to know how many items we will have initially until we've read them all from the input file. For that matter, even after we have read them all, we may still want to add items at some other point in the program. Therefore, we have two choices when designing a class like this:

1. Establish a vector containing a fixed number of elements and keep track of how many of them are in use.

2. Resize the vector as needed to hold as many elements as we need, using the size member function to keep track of how large it is.

Until this point, we've taken option 1, mainly because it's easier to explain. However, I think it's time to learn how we can take advantage of the more flexible second option, including some of the considerations that make it a bit complicated to use properly.

We will go over the LoadInventory function (shown in Figure 11.16) in some detail to see how this dynamic sizing works (and how it can lead to inefficiencies) as soon as we have dealt with another question Susan had about how we decide whether to declare loop index variables in the loop or before it starts.

Susan: Why are we saying short i; at the beginning of the function here instead of in the for loop?

Steve: Because we will need the value of i after the end of the loop to tell us how many items we've read from the file. If we declared i in the for loop header, we wouldn't be able to use it after the end of the loop.

With that cleared up, let's start with the first statement in the loop, m_Home.resize(i+1);. This sets the size of the vector m_Home to one more than the current value of the loop index i. Because i starts at 0, on the first time through the loop the size of m_Home is set to 1. Then the statement is >> m_Home[i]; reads a HomeItem from the input file into element i of the m_Home vector; the first time through the loop, that element is m_Home[0].

Actually, I oversimplified a little bit when I said that the line we just discussed "reads a HomeItem from the input file". To be more precise, it *attempts* to read a HomeItem from the input file. As we saw in our analysis of the operator >> function that we wrote to read HomeItems from a file, that operator can fail to return anything; in fact, failure is guaranteed when we try to read another HomeItem from the file when there aren't any left. Therefore, the next two lines

```
if (is.fail() != 0)
    break;
```

check for this possibility. When we do run out of data in the file, which will happen eventually, the break statement terminates the loop. Finally, the two lines

```
m_Home.resize(i);
return i;
```

reset the number of elements in the vector to the exact number that we've read successfully and return the result to the calling program in case it wants to know.

Susan had some questions about this process.

Susan: So, what we're doing here is setting aside memory for the HomeItem objects?

Steve: Yes, and we're also loading them from the file at the same time. These two things are connected because we don't know how much memory to allocate for the items before we've read all of them from the file.

Waste Not, Want Not

This is definitely a legal way to fill up a vector with a number of data elements when we don't know in advance how many we'll have, but it isn't very efficient. The problem is in the way we are using the innocent-looking resize function: to resize the vector every time we want to add another element. Every time we resize a vector, it has to call new to allocate enough memory to hold the number of elements of its new size; it also has to call delete to release the memory it was using before. Thus, if we resize a vector 100 times (for example) to store 100 elements, we are doing 100 news and 100 deletes. This is a very slow operation compared to other common programming tasks such as arithmetic, looping, and comparison, so it is best to avoid unnecessary memory reallocations.

Susan had some questions about reallocating memory.

Susan: I don't understand this idea of reallocating memory.

Steve: When we create a vector, we have to say how many elements it can hold so that the code that implements the vector type knows how much room to allocate for the information it keeps about each of those elements. When we increase the number of elements in the vector, the resize member function has to increase the size of the area it uses to store the information about the elements. The resize member function handles this by allocating another piece of memory big enough to hold the information for all of the elements in the new size, copying all the information it previously held into that new space, and then freeing the original piece of memory. Therefore, every time we change the size of a vector, the resize function has to do an allocation, a copy, and a deallocation. This adds up to a lot of extra work that is best avoided if we don't have to do it all the time.

Susan: Okay. Does this reallocation occur every time the user tries to look something up in the inventory?

Steve: No, just when we're adding an item or reading items from the file.

You Can Get What You Need

As long as we don't know how many elements we will need until we read them all in, we can't get rid of reallocations entirely. However, we can reduce them significantly by doing them every so often rather than every time we read one element from the file. For example, we could resize the m_Home vector before reading every fifth element rather than before every element, producing the code in Figure 11.17.

FIGURE 11.17. Another possible implementation of LoadInventory **(from code\hmin2a.cc)**

```
short HomeInventory::LoadInventory(ifstream& is)
{
    short i;

    for (i = 0; ; i ++)
        {
        if (i % 5 == 0)
          m_Home.resize(i+5);

        is >> m_Home[i];
        if (is.fail() != 0)
          break;
        }
```

```
    m_Home.resize(i);
    return i;
}
```

There's only one change between the previous version of this function and the current one: The two lines

```
if (i % 5 == 0)
  m_Home.resize(i + 5);
```

replace the following line in the previous version:

```
m_Home.resize(i + 1);
```

First, let's look at the meaning of the % symbol in the line if (i % 5 == 0). This is the *modulus operator*, which produces the remainder of a division operation. In this case, we are dividing i by 5 and taking the remainder; if that remainder is 0 (i.e., i is evenly divisible by 5), then the if statement will be true, so the next statement, m_Home.resize(i + 5);, will allocate five additional elements to the vector m_Home.

Let's analyze how these statements work in more detail. If i is 0, the remainder will be 0, so we will execute the call to resize, setting the size of m_Home to 0 + 5, or 5. When i has a value between 1 and 4, its remainder after division by 5 won't be 0, so we won't execute the resizing line. When i becomes 5 on the sixth time through the loop, the if statement will compute the remainder of dividing 5 by 5, which of course is 0, so the call to resize will be executed again. This time, it will set the number of elements of the vector to 5 + 5, or 10 altogether. Continuing in this way, we can see that the result will be to expand the vector by five elements every fifth time through the loop, as desired.

As clever as this might be, there is a much better solution to reducing the number of allocations, which we've already employed in a slightly different part of this program. If you'd like to try to figure it out yourself, stop here and think about it.

A Smith and Wesson Beats Four Aces

Give up? Okay, here it is: When we create the file that contains the data for the HomeItem objects, we can start by writing the number of elements as the first line of the file. This is the solution we used to preallocate the m_Track vector that holds the track names for a "Music" HomeItem. The disadvantage of this solution is that it is harder to apply when the input file is generated directly by a human being, who is likely to make a mistake in counting the elements. However, this is not much of a drawback when we consider that the most common way to generate such a file in the real world is to create, edit, and delete items via a program. This program will read any pre-existing data file, allow modifications to the items from the file, and write out the updated data to the file so that it will be there the next time we start the program. Of course, such a program provides other facilities such as producing reports and searching for individual items, but as long as we're maintaining the whole database in memory, those functions don't have to worry about the structure of the file.

Susan had some questions about the inventory file.

Susan: What file are you talking about?

Steve: The file that holds the information about all of the HomeItem objects in the inventory.

Susan: How was that file created?

Steve: Either by writing it with a text editor or by adding objects using the AddItem function and then telling the program to write it out.

Susan: How does the program know where the data for each item starts?

Steve: Our implementation of operator >> knows how many fields there are for each object; when the data for one object is finished, the data for the next object must be coming up next in the file.

Figure 11.18 is the version of the LoadInventory function that uses a preset count of items at the beginning of the file.

FIGURE 11.18. Yet another implementation of LoadInventory **(from code\hmin3.cc)**

```
short HomeInventory::LoadInventory(ifstream& is)
{
    short i;
    short ElementCount;

    is >> ElementCount;

    m_Home.resize(ElementCount+1);

    for (i = 0; ; i ++)
      {
      is >> m_Home[i];

      if (is.fail() != 0)
        break;
      }

    if (i < ElementCount)
      {
      cerr << "Not enough items in input file" << endl;
      exit(1);
      }

    m_Home.resize(ElementCount);

    return i;
}
```

The first part of this should be fairly obvious: We are reading the number of elements from the file into a variable called ElementCount. However, the next statement might not be so obvious: It sets the size of the vector to one more than the number of items that we expect to read. Why do we need an extra element in the vector?

Everything Is More Complicated Than It Looks

If we were to allocate exactly enough elements to store the data that we read from the file, we wouldn't be able to try to read one more element so that we could tell that we had reached the end of the file. The problem is that an attempt to use a vector element that doesn't exist produces an "invalid element number" error from the vector code, so we would never reach the statement that calls fail to find out that we are at the end of the file. For this reason, I've added one element to the number of items that we actually expect so that we can tell if we have reached the end of file on schedule.

Of course, after we have finished reading all the data and have reached the end of the file, we must make sure that we have read the number of items we expected. If we're short one or more items, we display an error and exit from the program; on the other hand, if the number of items is correct, we reset the size of the m_Home vector to that number and return to the calling function.

Susan had a question about the way the error message was displayed.

Susan: What's cerr?

Steve: That's another automatically created ostream object, like cout. The difference is that you can make the output from cout go to a different file in a number of ways, both in the program and outside it. However, doing that doesn't affect where cerr sends its data. In other words, even if you change where the "normal" output goes, cerr will still send its data to the screen where the user can see the messages.

So that explains how the error message for a short file is displayed. However, we still need to consider the other possibility: having more items in the file than were supposed to be there. Why is this important? Because if there were actually more items in the file and we continued processing the data without telling the user about this problem, the information for those remaining items would be lost when we rewrote the file at the end of the program; obviously, that would be a serious mistake. It's almost always better to program "defensively" when possible rather than to assume that everything is as it is supposed to be and that no one has made any errors in the data.

So what will happen if there are more items in the file than there were supposed to be? We get an error from the vector code, because we try to read into an element of the vector that doesn't exist. Therefore, that possibility is covered.

Ignoring the possibility of errors in the data is just one way to produce a system that is overly susceptible to errors originating outside the code. Such errors can also result from the program being used in unexpected ways or even from the seemingly positive situation of a program with an unexpectedly long service life, as has occurred in some cases when the century part of the date changed from "19" to "20" (i.e., the "Year 2000 problem").

Back to the Future

After that discussion of "errors, their cause and cure", let's get back to our regularly scheduled discussion. The next thing we will need, as I've suggested previously, is a way for the user to enter, modify, and delete information for home inventory items without having to manually create or edit a data file.

Susan thought I had something against data files. I cleared up her confusion with the following discussion.

Susan: What's wrong with data files?

Steve: Nothing's wrong with them. What's wrong is making the user type everything in using a text editor; instead, we're going to give the user the ability to create the data file with a data entry function designed for that purpose.

Susan: Oh, so we're creating a database?

Steve: You could say that. Its current implementation is pretty primitive, but could be upgraded to handle virtually any number of items if that turned out to be necessary.

Let's start with the ability to enter data for a new object, as that is probably the first operation a new user will want to perform.

Figure 11.19 shows the new header file for the HomeInventory class, which includes the new AddItem member function.

FIGURE 11.19. The next interface for the HomeInventory class **(code\hmin4.h)**

```
#include "vector.h"

class HomeInventory
{
public:
    HomeInventory();

    short LoadInventory(ifstream& is);
    HomeItem FindItemByName(string Name);
    HomeItem AddItem();

private:
    vector<HomeItem> m_Home;
};
```

How did I decide on the signature of the AddItem member function? Well, it seems to me that the result of this function should be the HomeItem that it creates. As for the arguments (or lack thereof), the data for the new item is going to come from the user of the program via the keyboard (i.e., cin), so it doesn't seem necessary to provide any other data to the function when it is called in the program.

Susan wanted to make sure she knew what "user" meant in this context.

Susan: Is that the end user or the user of the HomeItem class?

Steve: Good question. In this case, it's the end user.

The implementation of this new function is shown in Figure 11.20.

FIGURE 11.20. The AddItem **member function of** HomeInventory **(from code\hmin4.cc)**

```
HomeItem HomeInventory::AddItem()
{
    HomeItem TempItem = HomeItem::NewItem();

    short OldCount = m_Home.size();

    m_Home.resize(OldCount + 1);

    m_Home[OldCount] = TempItem;

    return TempItem;
}
```

The first statement of this function, HomeItem TempItem = HomeItem::NewItem();, creates a new HomeItem object called TempItem.

Susan had some questions about that statement.

Susan: Why is TempItem a HomeItem?

Steve: Because that's the type of object we use to keep track of the items in our home inventory.

Susan: I don't get how HomeItem is a type. It should be an object.

Steve: A class defines a new type of object. A type like HomeItem could be compared to a common noun like "dog", whereas the objects of that type resemble proper nouns like "Spot". You wouldn't say that you have "dog", but you might say that you have "a dog named Spot". Similarly, you wouldn't say that your program has HomeItem, but that it has a HomeItem called (in this case) TempItem.

The initial value for TempItem is the return value of the call to HomeItem::NewItem();. The reason we have to specify the class of this function (HomeItem) is that it is a member function of the HomeItem class, not of the HomeInventory class. But what kind of function call is HomeItem::NewItem()? It obviously isn't a normal member function call because there's no object in front of the function name NewItem.

This is a static member function call. You may recall from Chapter 9 that a static member function is one for which we don't need an object. Our previous use of this type of function was in the Today function, which returns today's date; clearly, today's date doesn't vary between objects. However, this type of member function is also convenient in cases such as the present one, where we are creating an object from keyboard input and therefore don't have the object available for use yet.

Before we get started on the implementation of the static member function called NewItem, let's take a look at the new interface for the HomeItem class, which is shown in Figure 11.21.

FIGURE 11.21. **The new interface for** HomeItem **(code\hmit4.h)**

```
// hmit4.h

#include "string6.h"
#include "vector.h"

class HomeItem
```

```
{
friend ostream& operator << (ostream& os, const HomeItem& Item);
friend istream& operator >> (istream& is, HomeItem& Item);

public:
  HomeItem();
  HomeItem(const HomeItem& Item);
  HomeItem& operator = (const HomeItem& Item);
virtual ~HomeItem();

// Basic: Art objects, furniture, jewelry, etc.
  HomeItem(string Name, double PurchasePrice,
  long PurchaseDate, string Description, string Category);

// Music: CDs, LPs, cassettes, etc.
  HomeItem(string Name, double PurchasePrice,
  long PurchaseDate, string Description, string Category,
  string Artist, vector<string> Track);

virtual void Write(ostream& os);
virtual void FormattedDisplay(ostream& os);
virtual string GetName();

static HomeItem NewItem();

protected:
  HomeItem(int);

protected:
  HomeItem* m_Worker;
  short m_Count;
};
```

We'll get to some of the changes between the previous interface and this one as soon as we get through with the changes in the implementation needed to allow data input from the keyboard. The first part of this implementation is the code for HomeItem::NewItem(), which is shown in Figure 11.22.

FIGURE 11.22. **The implementation of** HomeItem::NewItem() **(from code\hmit4.cc)**

```
HomeItem HomeItem::NewItem()
{
  HomeItem TempItem;

  cin >> TempItem;

  return TempItem;
}
```

As you can see, this is a very simple function, as it calls operator >> to do all the real work; however, I had to modify operator >> to make this possible. Susan wanted to know what was wrong with the old version of operator >>.

> **Susan:** Why do we need another new version of operator >>? What was wrong with the old one?

> **Steve:** The previous version of that operator wasn't very friendly to the user who was supposed to be typing data at the keyboard. The main problem is that it didn't tell the user what to enter or when to enter it; it merely waited for the user to type in the correct data.

I fixed this problem by changing the implementation of operator >> to the one shown in Figure 11.23.

FIGURE 11.23. **The new version of** operator >> **(from code\hmit4.cc)**

```
istream& operator >> (istream& is, HomeItem& Item)
{
  string Type;
  string Name;
  double PurchasePrice;
  long PurchaseDate;
  string Description;
```

```
string Category;
bool Interactive = (&is == &cin);

while (Type == "")
  {
  if (Interactive)
    cout << "Type (Basic, Music) ";
  is >> Type;
  if (is.fail() != 0)
    {
    Item = HomeItem();
    return is;
    }
  }

if (Interactive)
  cout << "Name ";
is >> Name;

if (Interactive)
  cout << "Purchase Price ";
is >> PurchasePrice;

if (Interactive)
  cout << "Purchase Date ";
is >> PurchaseDate;

if (Interactive)
  cout << "Description ";
is >> Description;

if (Interactive)
  cout << "Category ";
is >> Category;

if (Type == "Basic")
  {
  Item = HomeItem(Name, PurchasePrice, PurchaseDate,
       Description, Category);
```

```
        }
      else if (Type == "Music")
       {
       string Artist;
       short TrackCount;

       if (Interactive)
         cout << "Artist ";
       is >> Artist;

       if (Interactive)
         cout << "TrackCount ";
       is >> TrackCount;

       vector<string> Track(TrackCount);
       for (short i = 0; i < TrackCount; i ++)
         {
         if (Interactive)
           cout << "Track # " << i + 1 << ": ";
         is >> Track[i];
         }
       Item = HomeItem(Name, PurchasePrice, PurchaseDate,
           Description, Category, Artist, Track);
       }
      else
       {
       cout << "Can't create object of type " << Type << endl;
       exit(0);
       }

      return is;
     }
```

I think most of the changes to this function should be fairly obvious. Assuming that we are reading data from the keyboard (i.e., Interactive is true), we have to let the user know what item we want typed in by displaying a prompt message such as "Name: " or "Category: ".

Susan had an excellent question about the implementation of this function.

Susan: How does it know whether input is from a file or the keyboard?

Steve: By testing whether the istream that we're reading from is the same as cin.

This test is performed by the statement

```
bool Interactive = (&is == &cin);
```

which defines a variable of type bool called Interactive that is initialized to the value of the expression (&is == &cin). What is the value of that expression going to be?

Strong Like bool

The value is the result of applying the comparison operator, ==, to the arguments &is and &cin. As always with comparison operators, the type of this result is bool, which is why the type of the variable Interactive is bool as well. As for the value of the result, in this case the items being compared are the addresses of the variables cin and is. If you look back at the header for operator >>, you'll see that is is a reference argument that is actually just another name for the istream being supplied as the left-hand argument to the operator >> function. Therefore, what we are testing is whether the istream that is the left-hand argument to operator >> has the same address as cin has (i.e., whether they are different names for the same variable); if so, we are reading data from the keyboard and need to let the user know what we want. Otherwise, we assume the data is from a file, so there is no need to prompt the user.[10] Once that bit of code is clear, the rest of the changes should be pretty obvious, as they consist of the code needed to display prompts when necessary. For example, the sequence:

```
if (Interactive)
    cout << "Type (Basic, Music) ";
```

writes the line "Type (Basic, Music)" to the screen if and only if the input is from cin—that is, if the user is typing at the keyboard. The other similar sequences do the same thing for the other data items that need to be typed in.

Susan still wasn't convinced of the necessity to rewrite operator >>, but I think I won her over.

> **Susan:** But why should we have to change operator >> in the first place? Why not just write a separate function to read the data from the keyboard and leave operator >> as it was? Isn't object-oriented programming designed to allow us to reuse existing functions rather than modify them?

> **Steve:** Yes, but it's also important to try to minimize the number of functions that do essentially the same function for the same data type. In the current case, my first impulse was to write a separate function so that I wouldn't have to add all those if statements to operator >>. However, I changed that plan when I realized that such a new function would have to duplicate all of the data input operations in operator >>. This means that I would have to change both operator >> and this new function every time I changed the data for any of the HomeItem classes. Since this would cause a maintenance problem in future updates of this program, I decided that I would just have to put up with the if statements.

---

10. You may wonder why we have to compare the addresses of these two variables and not simply their contents—that is, why we have to write (is == cin) instead of (&is == &cin). The reason is that the expression (is == cin) compares whether the two streams is and cin are in the same "state"; i.e., whether both (or neither) are available for use, not whether they are the same stream. If this isn't obvious to you, you're not alone. Not only did I not figure it out right away but when I asked a C++ programmer with over 20 years experience in the language, he took two tries to decipher it.

Susan: Why would this cause a maintenance problem?

Steve: If we have more than one function that shares the same information, we have to locate all such functions and change them whenever that shared information changes. In this case, the shared information is embodied in the code that reads values from an istream and uses those values to create a HomeItem object. Therefore, if we were to change the information needed to create a HomeItem object, we would have to find and change every function that created such an object. In a large program, just finding the functions that were affected could be a significant task.

Another reason to use the same function for both keyboard and file input is that it makes the program easier to read if we use the same function (e.g., operator >>) for similar operations.

Besides changing operator >>, I've added a couple of new functions to the interface for HomeItem—namely, FormattedDisplay and GetName. The first of these functions, as usual for virtual functions declared in the interface of a polymorphic object, simply uses the virtual function mechanism to call the "real" FormattedDisplay function in the object pointed to by m_Worker. The code in the versions of this function in the HomeItemBasic and HomeItemMusic classes is almost identical to the code for Write, except that it adds an indication of what each piece of data represents. Knowing that, you shouldn't have any trouble following either of these functions, so I'm going to list them without comment in Figures 11.24 and 11.25.

FIGURE 11.24. HomeItemBasic::FormattedDisplay **(from code\hmit4.cc)**

```cpp
void HomeItemBasic::FormattedDisplay(ostream& os)
{
  os << "Type: ";
  os << GetType() << endl;
  os << "Name: ";
  os << m_Name << endl;
```

```
    os << "Purchase price: ";
    os << m_PurchasePrice << endl;
    os << "Purchase date: ";
    os << m_PurchaseDate << endl;
    os << "Description: ";
    os << m_Description << endl;
    os << "Category: ";
    os << m_Category << endl;
}
```

FIGURE 11.25. HomeItemMusic::FormattedDisplay **(from code\hmit4.cc)**

```
void HomeItemMusic::FormattedDisplay(ostream& os)
{
    HomeItemBasic::FormattedDisplay(os);

    os << "Artist: ";
    os << m_Artist << endl;
    os << "Tracks: ";

    int TrackCount = m_Track.size();
    os << TrackCount << endl;
    for (short i = 0; i < TrackCount; i ++)
        os << m_Track[i] << endl;
}
```

Now that we've looked at FormattedDisplay, what about GetName? You might think that this is about as simple as a function can get, as its sole purpose is to return the value of the m_Name member variable. We'll see shortly how this function is used in the test program. Before we look at that, though, you should note that this function has a characteristic that we haven't run across before: It is a virtual function implemented in HomeItem and HomeItemBasic but not in HomeItemMusic. Why is this, and how does it work?

Leaving Well Enough Alone

The answer is that, just as with a non-virtual function, if we don't write a new version for a derived class (in this case, HomeItemMusic), the compiler will assume that we are satisfied with the version in the base class (in this case, HomeItemBasic). Since the correct behavior of GetName (returning the value of m_Name) is exactly the same in both of these cases, there's no reason to write a new version of GetName for HomeItemMusic, and therefore we won't.

Figure 11.26 shows how we can use these functions to add an item from the keyboard. After adding the item to the inventory, this test program retrieves its name via the GetName function, uses FindItemByName to look it up by its name, and displays it. Just to make sure our new operator >> still works for file input, this test program also loads the inventory from an input file and displays one of the elements read from that file, as the previous test program did. Making sure we haven't broken something that used to work is called *regression testing*, and it's a very important part of program maintenance.[11]

FIGURE 11.26. **The test program for adding a** HomeItem **interactively (hmtst4.cc)**

```
#include <iostream.h>
#include <fstream.h>
#include "vector.h"
#include "string6.h"
#include "hmit4.h"
#include "hmin4.h"

int main()
```

---

11. In fact, operator >> did *not* work correctly for file input the first time I tried it because I had made the mistake of testing the equality of the istreams is and cin rather than the equality of their addresses, as mentioned previously. So it's a good thing I thought to check that use of operator >>!

```
{
    ifstream HomeInfo("home3.in");
    HomeInventory MyInventory;
    HomeItem TempItem;
    string Name;

    MyInventory.LoadInventory(HomeInfo);

    TempItem = MyInventory.AddItem();
    Name = TempItem.GetName();
    HomeItem test2 = MyInventory.FindItemByName(Name);
    cout << endl << "Here is the item you added" << endl;
    test2.FormattedDisplay(cout);

    HomeItem test1 = MyInventory.FindItemByName("Relish");
    cout << endl << "Here is an item from the file" << endl;
    test1.FormattedDisplay(cout);

    return 0;
}
```

Now we can add a new item and retrieve it, so what feature should we add next? A good candidate would be a way to make changes to data that we've already entered. We will call this new function of the Inventory class EditItem, to correspond to our AddItem function. Let's look at the new interface of the HomeInventory class, which is shown in Figure 11.27.

FIGURE 11.27. The next version of the interface for HomeInventory **(code\hmin5.h)**

```
//hmin5.h

#include "vector.h"

class HomeInventory
{
public:
```

```
HomeInventory();

short LoadInventory(ifstream& is);
void DumpInventory();
HomeItem FindItemByName(string Name);
HomeItem AddItem();
short LocateItemByName(string Name);
HomeItem EditItem(string Name);

private:
    vector<HomeItem> m_Home;
};
```

You may have noticed that I've added a couple of other support functions besides the new EditItem function. These are DumpInventory, which just lists all of the elements in the m_Home vector (useful in debugging the program), and LocateItemByName, which we'll cover in the discussion of EditItem.

Susan had a question about the first of these support functions.

Susan: Why do we want to get rid of items with DumpInventory?

Steve: We don't want to. "Dump" is programming slang for "display without worrying about formatting". In other words, a dump function is one that gives "just the facts".

Figure 11.28 shows the test program for this new version of the home inventory application.

FIGURE 11.28. The next version of the HomeInventory **test program (code\hmtst5.cc)**

```
#include <iostream.h>
#include <fstream.h>
#include "vector.h"
#include "string6.h"
#include "hmit5.h"
```

```
#include "hmin5.h"

int main()
{
    ifstream HomeInfo("home3.in");
    HomeInventory MyInventory;
    HomeItem TempItem;
    string Name;

    MyInventory.LoadInventory(HomeInfo);

    TempItem = MyInventory.FindItemByName("Relish");
    cout << endl;

    TempItem.Edit();
    cout << endl;

    TempItem.FormattedDisplay(cout);
    cout << endl;

    return 0;
}
```

The test program hasn't gotten much more complicated, as you can see; it loads the inventory, uses the new EditItem function to modify one of the items, and then displays the changed item.

Susan had a couple of good questions about this program and some comments about software development issues.

> **Susan:** What happens if the program can't find the object that it's trying to look up?

> **Steve:** That's a very good question. In the present case, that should never happen because the input file does have a record whose name is "Relish". However, we should handle that possibility anyway by checking whether the returned item is null. We'll do so in a later version of the test program; the discussion of that issue is on page 892.

Susan: I don't see why we need to write a whole new function called LocateItemByName. What's wrong with the one we already have, FindItemByName?

Steve: Because FindItemByName returns a copy of the object but doesn't tell us where it came from in the m_Home vector. Therefore, if we used that function we wouldn't be able to put the object back when we were finished editing it.

Susan: Why can't we leave the classes alone? It's annoying to have to keep changing them all the time.

Steve: I'm afraid that's the way software development works. Of course, I could make it more realistic by playing the role of a pointy-haired manager hovering over you while you're working.

Susan: No, thanks. I believe you.

Steve: Okay, we'll save that for our future management book, *Programmers Are from Neptune, Managers Are from Uranus.*

Susan: I can't wait.

After that bit of comic relief, let's take a look at the implementation of the new EditItem function, shown in Figure 11.29.

FIGURE 11.29. The EditItem **function of** HomeInventory **(from code\hmin5.cc)**

```
HomeItem HomeInventory::EditItem(string Name)
{
    short ItemNumber = LocateItemByName(Name);

    HomeItem TempItem = m_Home[ItemNumber];

    TempItem.Edit();
```

```
m_Home[ItemNumber] = TempItem;

return TempItem;
}
```

As you can see, this function isn't too complicated either. It calls LocateItemByName to find the element number of the HomeItem to be edited, copies that HomeItem from the m_Home vector into a temporary HomeItem called TempItem, calls the Edit function (which we'll get to shortly) for that temporary HomeItem, and then copies the edited HomeItem back into the same position in the m_Home vector. If you compare this function with AddItem (Figure 11.20 on page 799), you will notice a couple of differences. First, this function calls LocateItemByName rather than FindItemByName. These two functions are exactly the same, except that LocateItemByName returns the element number of the found HomeItem in the m_Home vector rather than the HomeItem itself. This allows us to update the m_Home vector with the edited HomeItem when we are through editing it. Second, the call to Edit in this function is different from the call to NewItem in AddItem because Edit has an object to operate on whereas NewItem had to create a previously nonexistent object. Therefore, Edit is a normal (non-static) member function rather than a static member function like AddItem.

What about the implementation of this new Edit function? I have good news and bad news. The good news: Using it is pretty simple. The bad news: Implementing it led to a fairly extensive revision of the HomeItem classes. I think the results are worth the trouble; hopefully, you will come to the same conclusion when we are done. Let's start with the new interface for the HomeItem class.

'Tis a Gift to Be Simple

Figure 11.30 is the latest, greatest version of the interface for the HomeItem class.

FIGURE 11.30. **The latest version of the** Homeitem class **interface (code\hmit5.h)**

```cpp
// hmit5.h

#include "string6.h"
#include "vector.h"

class HomeItem
{
friend ostream& operator << (ostream& os,
  const HomeItem& Item);

friend istream& operator >> (istream& is, HomeItem& Item);

public:
  HomeItem();
  HomeItem(const HomeItem& Item);
  HomeItem& operator = (const HomeItem& Item);
virtual ~HomeItem();

// Basic: Art objects, furniture, jewelry, etc.
  HomeItem(string Name, double PurchasePrice,
    long PurchaseDate, string Description, string Category);

// Music: CDs, LPs, cassettes, etc.
  HomeItem(string Name, double PurchasePrice,
    long PurchaseDate, string Description, string Category,
    string Artist, vector<string> Track);

virtual void Write(ostream& os);
virtual short FormattedDisplay(ostream& os);
virtual string GetName();
static HomeItem NewItem();

virtual void Read(istream& is);
virtual void Edit();

protected:
```

```
    HomeItem(int);
    virtual HomeItem* CopyData();

    protected:
     HomeItem* m_Worker;
     short m_Count;
    };
```

If you compare this interface with the previous version in Figure 11.21, you'll notice that I've added a few new member functions—namely, Edit, CopyData, and Read. We'll get to Read in due time, but we're going to start with HomeItem::Edit. Unlike a "normal" function in a polymorphic object, where the base class version simply passes the buck to the appropriate worker object, the base class version of Edit (Figure 11.31) is a bit more involved.

FIGURE 11.31. HomeItem::Edit **(from code\hmit5.cc)**

```
    void HomeItem::Edit()
    {
      if (m_Worker->m_Count > 1)
        {
        m_Worker->m_Count --;
        m_Worker = m_Worker->CopyData();
        m_Worker->m_Count = 1;
        }

      m_Worker->Edit();
    }
```

The reason that HomeItem::Edit is different from most of the base class functions is that it has to deal with the *aliasing* problem: the possibility of altering a shared object, which arises when we use *reference counting* to share one copy of a worker object among a possibly large number of manager objects. This is much more efficient than copying the worker object whenever we copy the manager object, but it has one drawback: If more than one manager object is pointing to the same worker object, and any of those manager objects changes the contents of "its" worker object, all of the other manager objects will also have "their" worker objects changed without their advice or consent. This can cause chaos in a large system.

Luckily, it's not that difficult to prevent, as the example of HomeItem::Edit shows. This function starts by executing the statement if (m_Worker->m_Count > 1), which checks whether this object has more than one manager. If it has only one, we can change it without causing difficulty for its other manager objects; therefore, we skip the code in the {} and proceed directly to the worker class Edit function. On the other hand, if this worker object does have more than one manager, we have to "unhook" it from its other managers. We do this by executing the three statements in the controlled block of the if statement.

First, the statement m_Worker->m_Count --; subtracts 1 from the count in the current worker object to account for the fact that this manager object is going to use a different worker object. Then the next statement, m_Worker = m_Worker->CopyData();, creates a new worker object with the same data as the previous worker object and assigns its address to m_Worker so that it is now the current worker object for this manager object. Finally, the statement m_Worker->m_Count = 1; sets the count of managers in this new worker object to 1 so that the reference-counting mechanism will be able to tell when this worker object can be deleted.

After these housekeeping chores are finished, we call the Edit function of the new worker object to update its contents.

Now let's take a look at the CopyData helper function. The first oddity is in its declaration: It's a protected virtual function. The reason that it has to be virtual should be fairly obvious: Copying the data for a HomeItem derived class object depends on the exact type of the object, so CopyData has to be virtual. However, that doesn't explain why it is protected.

The explanation is that we don't want users of HomeItem objects to call this function. In fact, the only classes that should be able to use

CopyData are those in the implementation of HomeItem. Therefore, we make CopyData protected so that the only functions that can access it are those in HomeItem and its derived classes.

The only remaining question that we have to answer about editing a HomeItem object is how the CopyData function works. Because CopyData is inaccessible to outside functions and is always called for a worker class object within the implementation of HomeItem, the base class version of CopyData should never be called and therefore consists of an exit statement. Let's continue by examining the code for HomeItemBasic::CopyData ().

FIGURE 11.32. HomeItemBasic::CopyData()

```
HomeItem* HomeItemBasic::CopyData()
{
  HomeItem* TempItem = new HomeItemBasic(*this);
  return TempItem;
}
```

This isn't a terribly complicated function, but it does have one new construct: the use of *this as an argument. Because *this is C++ speak for "the object for which this function was called", the phrase new HomeItemBasic(*this); allocates memory for a HomeItemBasic object and then calls the copy constructor for the HomeItemBasic class to create that object and initialize it as a copy of the object for which CopyData was called. Next, the address of the resulting HomeItemBasic object is assigned to the HomeItem pointer called TempItem. Finally, TempItem is returned to the calling function, where it is used as the new value of m_Worker for a manager object.

Of course, HomeItemMusic::CopyData is identical to HomeItemBasic::CopyData except for the type of the new object being created, so I won't bother explaining it again.

Better Read Than Dead

Now that we've cleared up the potential problem with changing the value of a shared worker object, we can proceed to the new version of operator >> (Figure 11.33), which uses Read to fill in the data in an empty HomeItem.

FIGURE 11.33. **The latest version of** operator >> **(from code\hmit5.cc)**

```cpp
istream& operator >> (istream& is, HomeItem& Item)
{
  string Type;
  bool Interactive = (&is == &cin);

  while (Type == "")
    {
    if (Interactive)
      cout << "Type (Basic, Music) ";
    is >> Type;
    if (is.fail() != 0)
      {
      Item = HomeItem();
      return is;
      }
    }

  if (Type == "Basic")
    {
    // create empty Basic object to be filled in
    HomeItem Temp("",0.0,0,"","");
    Temp.Read(is);
    Item = Temp;
    }
  else if (Type == "Music")
    {
    // create an empty Music object to be filled in
    HomeItem Temp("",0.0,0,"","","",vector<string>(0));
    Temp.Read(is);
```

```
    Item = Temp;
    }
  else
    {
    cerr << "Can't create object of type " << Type << endl;
    exit(0);
    }

  return is;
  }
```

The first part of this function, where we determine the type of the object to be created, is just as it was in the previous version (Figure 11.23). However, once we figure out the type, everything changes: Rather than read the data directly from the file or the user, we create an empty object of the correct type and then call a function called Read to get the data for us.

Susan had some questions about the constructor calls that create the empty HomeItemBasic and HomeItemMusic objects.

Susan: Why do you have a period in the middle of one of the numbers when you're making a HomeItemMusic object?

Steve: That's the initial value of the price field, which is a floating-point variable, so I've set the value to 0.0 to indicate that.

Susan: What's a floating-point variable?

Steve: One that can hold a number that has a fractional part as well as a number that has only a whole part.

Susan: Okay, but why do you need all those null things (0 and "") in the constructor calls?

Steve: Because the compiler needs the arguments to be able to figure out which constructor we want it to call. If we just said HomeItem Temp();, we would get a default-constructed HomeItem object that would have a HomeItemBasic worker object, but we want to specify whether the worker object is actually a HomeItemBasic or a HomeItemMusic. If the arguments match the argument list of the constructor that makes a HomeItem object with a HomeItemBasic worker object, then that's what the compiler will do; if they match the argument list of the constructor that makes a HomeItemMusic, it will make a HomeItem manager object with a HomeItemMusic worker object instead. That's how we make sure that we get the right type of empty object for the Read method to fill in.

One question not answered in this dialogue is what was wrong with the old method of filling in the fields in the object being created. That's the topic of the next section.

For Your Eyes Only

The old method of creating and initializing the object directly in the operator >> code was fine for entering and displaying items, but as soon as we want to edit them, it has one serious drawback: The knowledge of field names has to be duplicated in a number of places. As we saw in the discussion of our recent changes to operator >>, this is undesirable because it harms maintainability. For example, let's suppose we want to change the prompt "Name: " to "Item Name: ". If this were a large program, it would be a significant problem to find and change all the occurrences of that prompt. It would be much better to be able to change that prompt in one place and have the whole program use the new one, as the new version of the program will allow us to do.

Susan had a question about changing prompts.

Susan: Why would you want to change the prompts? Who cares if it says "Name" or "Item Name"?

Steve: Well, the users of the program might care. Also, what if we wanted to translate this program into another language, like

Spanish? In that case, it would be a lot more convenient if all of the prompts were in one place so we could change them all at once.

Before we get into the implementation of Read, however, we should look at the new version of the interface for the worker classes of HomeItem (Figure 11.34), which contains some new member functions as well as some constructs we haven't seen before.

FIGURE 11.34. **The latest version of the interface for the** HomeItem **worker** classes (code\hmiti5.h)

```
// hmiti5.h

class HomeItemBasic : public HomeItem
{

public:
  HomeItemBasic();

  HomeItemBasic(string Name, double PurchasePrice,
    long PurchaseDate, string Description, string Category);

virtual string GetName();
virtual void Read(istream& is);
virtual void Edit();

virtual void Write(ostream& os);
virtual string GetType();
virtual short FormattedDisplay(ostream& os);

virtual short ReadInteractive();
virtual short ReadFromFile(istream &is);
virtual bool EditField(short FieldNumber);

protected:
  enum FieldNum {e_Name = 1, e_PurchasePrice,
    e_PurchaseDate, e_Description, e_Category};
```

```cpp
  string GetFieldName(short FieldNumber);
virtual HomeItem* CopyData();

protected:
  string m_Name;
  double m_PurchasePrice;
  long m_PurchaseDate;
  string m_Description;
  string m_Category;
};

class HomeItemMusic : public HomeItemBasic
{
public:
  HomeItemMusic(string Name, double PurchasePrice,
  long PurchaseDate, string Description, string Category,
  string Artist, vector<string> Track);

HomeItemMusic& operator = (const HomeItemMusic& Item);

virtual void Write(ostream& os);
virtual string GetType();
virtual short FormattedDisplay(ostream& os);

virtual short ReadInteractive();
virtual short ReadFromFile(istream &is);
virtual bool EditField(short FieldNumber);

protected:
  enum FieldNum {e_Artist = HomeItemBasic::e_Category + 1,
  e_TrackCount, e_TrackNumber};

  string GetFieldName(short FieldNumber);
virtual HomeItem* CopyData();

protected:
  string m_Artist;
  vector<string> m_Track;
};
```

Before we get to the new functions, I should tell you about some details of the declaration and implementation of the concrete data type functions in this version of the HomeItem classes. As in previous header files for the worker classes of a polymorphic object, we don't have to declare the copy constructor, operator =, or the destructor for the first derived class, HomeItemBasic. Even so, we do have to declare and write the default constructor for this class so that we can specify the special base class constructor. This is necessary to avoid an infinite regress during the construction of a manager object. We also don't have to declare any of those functions or the default constructor for the second derived class, HomeItemMusic.

None of this is new. However, there is one oddity in the implementation of the HomeItemMusic class, which appears to result from a bug in the version of DJGPP that I'm using to compile the programs in this book. For some reason, if I don't define operator = for the HomeItemMusic class, I get a linker error telling me that there's an undefined reference to the compiler-generated operator = code. When I define my own version of HomeItemMusic::operator =, the linker error goes away. That's strange enough, but here's the really weird part: If I comment out the declaration of operator = in the interface file shown in Figure 11.34, the compiler doesn't complain about the fact that I'm implementing an undeclared function! I posted a message on a couple of Usenet newsgroups about this problem, but haven't had any responses. For the present, we'll just have to accept this as one of those mysterious problems that sometimes plague software development (and developers).

Another thing I should mention is that the functions ReadInteractive, ReadFromFile, and EditField are defined in HomeItemBasic and HomeItemMusic, rather than in HomeItem, because they are used only within the worker class implementations of Read and Edit rather than by the users of these classes. To be specific, the new functions ReadInteractive and ReadFromFile are used in the implementation of Read, and we'll discuss them when we look at Read, whereas the new EditField function is similarly used in the implementation of the Edit function. As in other cases where we've added functions that are not intended for use by the user of the HomeItem class, I have not defined them in the interface of HomeItem. This is an example of *information hiding*, similar in principle to making data and functions private or protected. Even though these functions are public, they are defined in classes that are accessible only to the implementers of the HomeItem polymorphic object—us.

There's also a new protected function called GetFieldName defined in HomeItemBasic and HomeItemMusic: It is used to encapsulate the knowledge of the field name prompts in connection with the information stored in the two versions of FieldNum. This latter is a new kind of construct called an enum. Of course, this leads to the obvious question: What's an enum?

U Pluribus enum

An enum is a way to define a number of unchangeable values, which are quite similar to consts. One of the differences between these two types of named values is relevant here: The value of each successive name in an enum is automatically incremented from the value of the previous name (if you don't specify another value explicitly). This is quite convenient for defining names for a set of values such as vector or array indexes for prompts, which is how we will use enums in our program.

Susan had some questions about enums, starting with the derivation of this keyword.

Susan: What does enum mean? Is it short for something?

Steve: Yes. An enum is called that because it gives names to an "enumeration", which is a list of numbers.

Susan: Are you going to put the prompts in a vector?

Steve: No, but you're close; they'll be in an array, for reasons that I'll explain at the appropriate point.

Let's start with the definition of HomeItemBasic::FieldNum, which is:

```
enum FieldNum {e_Name = 1, e_PurchasePrice,
e_PurchaseDate, e_Description, e_Category};
```

This defines an enum called FieldNum that consists of the named values e_Name, e_PurchasePrice, e_PurchaseDate, e_Description, and e_Category. The first of these is defined to have the value 1, and the others have consecutive values starting with 2 and continuing through 5. These values, by absolutely no coincidence, are the field numbers we are going to use to prompt the user for the values of the member variables m_Name, m_PurchasePrice, m_PurchaseDate, m_Description, and m_Category.

The definition of HomeItemMusic::FieldNum is similar, but the values could use some explanation. First, here's the definition:

```
enum FieldNum {e_Artist = e_Category + 1,
e_TrackCount, e_TrackNumber};
```

The only significant difference between this definition and the previous one (besides the names of the values) is in the way we set the value of the first data item: We define it as one more than the value of e_Category, which, as it happens, is the last named value in HomeItemBasic::FieldNum. We need to do this so that we can display the correct field numbers for a HomeItemMusic, which of course contains everything that a HomeItemBasic contains as well as its own added variables. The user of the program should be able to edit either of these types of variables without having to worry about which fields are in the derived or the base class part. Thus, we want to make sure that the field number prompts run smoothly from the end of the data entry for a HomeItemBasic to the beginning of the data entry for a

HomeItemMusic. If this isn't clear yet, don't worry. It will be by the time we get through the implementation of Read and the other data entry functions.

Now, what about those protected GetFieldName functions? All they do is to return the prompt corresponding to a particular field number. However, they deserve a bit of scrutiny because their implementation isn't quite so obvious as their function. Let's start with HomeItemBasic::GetFieldName, which is shown in Figure 11.35.

FIGURE 11.35. HomeItemBasic::GetFieldName **(from code\hmit5.cc)**

```
string HomeItemBasic::GetFieldName(short FieldNumber)
{
  static string Name[e_Category+1] = {"","Name",
    "Purchase Price","Purchase Date", "Description",
    "Category"};

  if ((FieldNumber > 0) && (FieldNumber <= e_Category))
    return Name[FieldNumber];

  return "";
}
```

This function contains a static array of strings, one for each field prompt and one extra null string at the beginning of the array. To set up the contents of the array, we use the construct {"","Name", "Purchase Price","Purchase Date", "Description", "Category"};, which is an *array initialization list* that supplies data for the elements in an array.

We need that null string ("") at the beginning of the initialization list to simplify the statement that returns the prompt for a particular field, because the field numbers that we display start at 1 rather than 0 (to avoid confusing the user of the program). Arrays always start at element 0 in C++, so if we want our field numbers to correspond to elements in the array, we need to start the prompts at the second element, which is how I've set it up. As a result, the statement that actually selects the prompt, return Name[FieldNumber], just uses the field number as an index into the array of strings and returns the appropriate one. For example, the prompt for e_Name is "1. Name: ", the prompt for e_PurchasePrice is "2. Purchase Price: ", and so on.

There are two questions I haven't answered yet about this function. First, why is the array static? Because it should be initialized only once, the first time this function is called, and that's what happens with static data. This is much more efficient than reinitializing the array with the same data every time this function is called, which is what would happen if we didn't add the static modifier to the definition of the Name array.

The second question is why we are using an array in the first place—aren't they dangerous? Yes, they are, but, unfortunately, in this situation we cannot use a vector as we normally would. The reason is that the ability to specify a list of values for an array is built into the C++ language and is not available for user-defined data types such as the vector. Therefore, if we want to use this very convenient method of initializing a multi-element data structure, we have to use an array instead.

This also explains why we need the if statement: to prevent the possibility of a caller trying to access an element of the array that doesn't exist. With a vector, we wouldn't have to worry that such an invalid access could cause havoc in the program; instead, we would get an error message from the index-checking code built into vector. However, arrays don't have any automatic checking for valid indexes, so we have to take care of that detail whenever we use them in a potentially hazardous situation like this one.

There's one more point I should mention here. I've already explained that when we define an enum such as HomeItemBasic::FieldNum, the named values in that enum (such as e_Name) are actually values of a defined data type. To be precise, e_Name is a value of type HomeItemBasic::FieldNum. That's not too weird in itself, but it does lead to some questions when we look at a statement such as if ((FieldNumber > 0) && (FieldNumber <= e_Category)). The problem is that we're comparing a short called

FieldNumber with a HomeItemBasic::FieldNum called e_Category. Is this legal, and if so, why?

Taking a shortcut

Yes, it is legal, because an enum value will automatically be converted to an integer value for purposes of arithmetic and comparison. For example, you can compare an enum with a value of any integer type, add an enum to an integer value, or assign an enum to an integer variable, without a peep from the compiler. While this is less than desirable from the point of view of strong type checking, it can be handy in circumstances like the present ones. By the way, this *automatic conversion* doesn't completely eliminate type checking for enums; you can't assign an integer variable to an enum without the compiler warning you that you're doing something questionable, so there is *some* real difference between enums and integer types![12]

Finally, we're ready for the implementation of Read. As with HomeItem::Edit, the base class version of this function has to handle the possibility that we're reading data into a shared worker object, as shown in Figure 11.36.

FIGURE 11.36. HomeItem::Read **(from code\hmit5.cc)**

```
void HomeItem::Read(istream& is)
{
  if (m_Worker->m_Count > 1)
    {
    m_Worker->m_Count --;
    m_Worker = m_Worker->CopyData();
    m_Worker->m_Count = 1;
    }
```

---

12. The subject of automatic conversions among the various built-in types in C++ is complex enough to require more coverage than I can provide here. Suffice it to say that it is a minefield of opportunities for subtle errors.

```
    m_Worker->Read(is);
  }
```

I won't bother going over the *anti-aliasing* code again, as it is identical to the corresponding code in HomeItem::Edit. Instead, let's move right along to Figure 11.37, which shows the worker version of this function, HomeItemBasic::Read. Before reading on, see if you can guess why we need only one worker version of this function rather than one for each worker class.

FIGURE 11.37. HomeItemBasic::Read **(from code\hmit5.cc)**

```
void HomeItemBasic::Read(istream& is)
{
  if (&is == &cin)
    ReadInteractive();
  else
    ReadFromFile(is);
}
```

The reason we need only one worker class version of this function is that its only job is to decide whether the input is going to be from the keyboard (cin) or from a file, and then to call a function to do the actual work. The class of the worker object doesn't affect the decision as to whether the input is from cin or a file, and the functions it calls are virtual, so the right function will be called for the type of the worker object. This means that the HomeItemMusic version of this function is identical, so we can rely on inheritance from HomeItemBasic to supply it and therefore don't have to write a new version for each derived class.

By the same token, the code for Read doesn't tell us much about how reading data for an object actually works; for that we'll have to look at the functions it calls, starting with Figure 11.38, which shows the code for HomeItemBasic::ReadInteractive.

FIGURE 11.38. HomeItemBasic::ReadInteractive **(from code\hmit5.cc)**

```
short HomeItemBasic::ReadInteractive()
{
  short FieldNumber = e_Name;

  cout << FieldNumber << ". ";
  cout << GetFieldName(FieldNumber) << ": ";
  FieldNumber ++;
  cin >> m_Name;

  cout << FieldNumber << ". ";
  cout << GetFieldName(FieldNumber) << ": ";
  FieldNumber ++;
  cin >> m_PurchasePrice;

  cout << FieldNumber << ". ";
  cout << GetFieldName(FieldNumber) << ": ";
  FieldNumber ++;
  cin >> m_PurchaseDate;

  cout << FieldNumber << ". ";
  cout << GetFieldName(FieldNumber) << ": ";
  FieldNumber ++;
  cin >> m_Description;

  cout << FieldNumber << ". ";
  cout << GetFieldName(FieldNumber) << ": ";
  FieldNumber ++;
  cin >> m_Category;

  *this = HomeItemBasic(m_Name, m_PurchasePrice,
  m_PurchaseDate, m_Description, m_Category);

  return FieldNumber;
}
```

This isn't too complicated, but there are a few tricky parts, starting with the statement short FieldNumber = e_Name;. Why are we using a short value (FieldNumber) to keep track of which field number we are using when we have an enum type called FieldNum that can apparently be used for this purpose?

We have to use a short for this purpose because, as I noted earlier, we can't assign an integer value to an enum without the compiler complaining. Although we aren't directly assigning an integer value to FieldNumber, we are incrementing it by using the ++ operator. This operator, as you may recall, is shorthand for "add one to the previous value of the variable and put the new value back in the variable". The first part of that operation is allowed with an enum variable because such a variable is automatically converted to an integer type when it is used for arithmetic. However, the second part prevents us from using an enum variable because it tries to assign the integer result of the addition back to the enum, and that violates the rule against assigning an enum an integer value.[13]

Susan had a question about the rules for using enums.

Susan: I understand that we can't do arithmetic operations on an enum. What I don't understand is *why*.

Steve: It's to try to prevent errors in using them. An enum consists of a number of named values. As long as we stick to the rules for using enum values, the compiler can tell whether we're using them correctly. For example, because e_TrackNumber is the highest value defined in the FieldNum enum, if we were to try to refer to the value e_TrackNumber + 1, the compiler could tell that we were doing something illegal. However, if we could add a number to an enum *variable*, the compiler wouldn't be able to tell if we were

---

13. Of course, it is theoretically possible simply to ignore the compiler warning and use the enum for arithmetic anyway, but I don't write programs that way. Once we start ignoring compiler warnings because "we know what we're doing", it's entirely too easy to ignore a warning that is really serious.

doing something illegal because the value of the variable wouldn't be known until run time.

Susan: I still don't get it. I need an example.

Steve: That's a reasonable request. Okay, let's suppose that we used an enum instead of a short and tried to add 1 to it. If we created a local variable of type FieldNum and tried to add 1 to it via the statement FieldNumber = FieldNumber + 1;, we would get a warning message something like the following:

```
In method 'short int HomeItemBasic::ReadInteractive()':
warning: conversion from 'int' to 'enum HomeItemBasic::FieldNum'
```

Susan: Okay, I guess that makes sense. So how do we get around this compiler warning stuff?

Steve: By using a short variable instead of an enum. We can use an enum value to initialize the short variable, then increment the short to keep track of the field number that we're on.

Now that we've presumably cleared up that point, most of the rest of this function is pretty simple; it consists primarily of a number of sequences that are all quite similar. Let's take a look at the first of these sequences, which handles the name of the object.

First, we display the field number for the current field via the statement cout << FieldNumber << ". ";. Next, we retrieve and display the field name for the current field via the next statement, cout << GetFieldName(FieldNumber) << ": ";. Then we increment the field number to set up for the next field via the statement "FieldNumber ++;". Finally, we request the value for the variable corresponding to the name of the object via the last statement in the sequence, cin >> m_Name;.

Of course, the sequences that handle the other fields are almost the same as this one, differing only in the name of the variable we're assigning the input value to. However, as simple as this may be, it raises another question: Why are we repeating almost the same code a number of times rather than using a function? The problem is that these sequences aren't similar enough to work as a function; to be exact, the type of the variable to which the data is being assigned is different according to which field we're working on. For example, m_Name is a string, m_PurchasePrice is a double, and m_PurchaseDate is a long. Therefore, we would need at least three different functions that were almost identical except for the type of data they returned, which wouldn't be worth the trouble. Instead, we'll just put up with the duplication.

The only other statement that will need significant study is the following one:

```
*this = HomeItemBasic(m_Name, m_PurchasePrice,
m_PurchaseDate, m_Description, m_Category);
```

What does this mean?

this Must Be the Place

There are two parts to that statement: the constructor call on the right of the = and the construct "*this" on the left of the =. The constructor call is easier to explain: It constructs a HomeItem object with the contents specified by the arguments to the constructor. In the present case, those arguments are the values that we've just read in from the keyboard. After that object is constructed, we assign it to ... what?

I hope you remember that "this" is the address of the object for which a member function was called. The purpose of this ReadInteractive function is to assign a new value to its object, which is accomplished by of this statement, so the appearance of this in the statement shouldn't be too surprising. The burning question, of course, is "What does * mean in this context?"

The answer is "The object pointed to by whatever is after the *". In this case, that means we can translate "*this" as "the object pointed to by this", which of course is just the object for which the current function was called. In other words, the statement we're analyzing assigns the result of the constructor call to the object for which this function (HomeItemBasic::ReadInteractive) was called. Since this is the purpose for which ReadInteractive was written, we must be almost done. In fact, we are; the only remaining statement is return FieldNumber;, which lets the calling function know what field number is the next to be handled. As we'll see, this return value is needed when this function is called from a derived class function such as HomeItemMusic::ReadInteractive to tell the calling function which fields it has to handle itself and which ones have been dealt with.

Susan didn't care for this idea very much, so we talked it over.

Susan: I hate this, and *this is even worse! What is it?

Steve: Remember, this is the address of the object for which the member function was called. The * before a pointer means "the object to which the following pointer points", so *this means "the object to which the this pointer points", which is the object for which the member function was called.

Susan: I still don't understand what this refers to.

Steve: Well, suppose we call the function ReadInteractive by the following statement: x.ReadInteractive();. In that case, what would be the value of *this during the execution of ReadInteractive?

Susan: Would it be x?

Steve: Exactly right!

Now let's take a look at HomeItemBasic::ReadFromFile (Figure 11.39), which, as its name suggests, reads data from a file and uses it to assign a value to a HomeItemBasic object.

FIGURE 11.39. HomeItemBasic::ReadFromFile **(from code\hmit5.cc)**

```
short HomeItemBasic::ReadFromFile(istream& is)
{
  is >> m_Name;
  is >> m_PurchasePrice;
  is >> m_PurchaseDate;
  is >> m_Description;
  is >> m_Category;

  *this = HomeItemBasic(m_Name, m_PurchasePrice,
  m_PurchaseDate, m_Description, m_Category);
}
```

As you can see, this is much simpler than the previous function. However, it does basically the same thing; the difference is merely that it deals with a file rather than a user, which makes its job much easier. This illustrates a maxim known to all professional programmers: Having to deal with users is the most difficult part of writing programs!

We've examined all the functions that make up the implementation of Read for the HomeItemBasic class. Now it's time to take a look at HomeItemBasic::Edit, which is the function called by HomeItem::Edit to edit existing data in a HomeItemBasic worker object. As in the case of Read, this function doesn't do anything class-specific, but hands all the dirty work over to virtual functions that will do the right thing for their objects. Therefore, we need only one version of Edit, which will call the appropriate functions depending on the type of the object we're actually editing. Figure 11.40 shows the code for this function, HomeItemBasic::Edit.

FIGURE 11.40. HomeItemBasic::Edit **(from code\hmit5.cc)**

```
void HomeItemBasic::Edit()
{
  short FieldNumber;
```

```
    FormattedDisplay(cout);
    cout << endl;

    cout << "Please enter field number to be changed: ";
    cin >> FieldNumber;
    cout << endl;

    EditField(FieldNumber);
}
```

There's nothing terribly complicated about this function, largely because it uses FormattedDisplay and EditField to do most of the work. First, it calls FormattedDisplay to display the current value of the object in question, then it asks for the number of the field to be changed, and finally it calls EditField to do the actual modification for that field.

Susan had a question about the field number.

Susan: Is the field number the element number in the vector of HomeItems?

Steve: No, it's the number of the individual field that we're going to change in the HomeItem that we're editing.

Let's start by looking at Figure 11.41, which shows the new version of HomeItemBasic::FormattedDisplay.

FIGURE 11.41. HomeItemBasic::FormattedDisplay (from code\hmit5.cc)

```
short HomeItemBasic::FormattedDisplay(ostream &os)
{
  short FieldNumber = e_Name;

  os << "Type: " << GetType() << endl;

  os << FieldNumber << ". ";
```

```
        os << GetFieldName(FieldNumber) << ": ";
        FieldNumber ++;
        os << m_Name << endl;

        os << FieldNumber << ". ";
        os << GetFieldName(FieldNumber) << ": ";
        FieldNumber ++;
        os << m_PurchasePrice << endl;

        os << FieldNumber << ". ";
        os << GetFieldName(FieldNumber) << ": ";
        FieldNumber ++;
        os << m_PurchaseDate << endl;

        os << FieldNumber << ". ";
        os << GetFieldName(FieldNumber) << ": ";
        FieldNumber ++;
        os << m_Description << endl;

        os << FieldNumber << ". ";
        os << GetFieldName(FieldNumber) << ": ";
        FieldNumber ++;
        os << m_Category << endl;

        return FieldNumber;
    }
```

This is almost identical to the HomeItemBasic version of ReadInteractive. The differences are these:

1. It writes its output to the ostream specified by its argument, os, rather than to cout, as HomeItemBasic::ReadInteractive does.

2. It doesn't prompt the user for input.

Now let's look at the code for the HomeItemBasic version of the EditField function (Figure 11.42).

FIGURE 11.42. HomeItemBasic::EditField **(from code\hmit5.cc)**

```cpp
bool HomeItemBasic::EditField(short FieldNumber)
{
  bool result = true;

  switch (FieldNumber)
    {
    case e_Name:
    cout << FieldNumber << ". ";
    cout << GetFieldName(FieldNumber) << ": ";
    cin >> m_Name;
    break;

    case e_PurchasePrice:
    cout << FieldNumber << ". ";
    cout << GetFieldName(FieldNumber) << ": ";
    cin >> m_PurchasePrice;
    break;

    case e_PurchaseDate:
    cout << FieldNumber << ". ";
    cout << GetFieldName(FieldNumber) << ": ";
    cin >> m_PurchaseDate;
    break;

    case e_Description:
    cout << FieldNumber << ". ";
    cout << GetFieldName(FieldNumber) << ": ";
    cin >> m_Description;
    break;

    case e_Category:
    cout << FieldNumber << ". ";
    cout << GetFieldName(FieldNumber) << ": ";
    cin >> m_Category;
    break;

    default:
```

```
        cout << "Sorry, that is not a valid field number." << endl;
        result = false;
        break;
        }

    return result;
    }
```

This code probably looks a little odd. Where are all the if statements needed to select the field to be modified based on its field number? That would be one way to code this function, but I've chosen to use a different construct designed specifically to select one of a number of alternatives: the switch statement. This statement is functionally equivalent to a number of if/else statements in a row, but is easier to read and modify. Its syntax consists of the keyword switch followed by a *selection expression* in parentheses that specifies the value that will determine the alternative to be selected. The various alternatives to be considered are enclosed in a set of curly braces and are marked off by the keyword case followed by the (constant) value to be matched and a colon. In the current situation, the selection expression is FieldNumber, whose value will be compared with the various *case labels* inside the curly brackets of the switch statement. For example, if the value of FieldNumber is equal to e_Name, the section of code following case e_Name: will be executed.

We use the break statement to indicate the end of the section of code to be executed for each case. We've already seen the break statement used to terminate a for loop, and it works in much the same way here: It breaks out of the curly braces containing the code for the switch statement. It's also possible to terminate the code to be executed for a given case by executing a return statement to exit from the function. If we have already accomplished the purpose of the function, this is often a convenient alternative.

There's one more item I should mention: the default keyword, which begins a section of code that should be executed in the event that the value of the selection expression doesn't match any of the individual cases. This is very handy to catch programming errors that result in an invalid value for the selection expression. If we don't use default, the switch statement will essentially be skipped if there is no matching case, and that probably isn't the right thing to do. Therefore, it's a good idea to use default to catch such an error whenever you use a switch statement.

In the current situation, we're using the default code to display an error message and return the value false to the calling function so that it will know that its attempt to edit the object didn't work.

However, if you have been following along very carefully, you'll notice that the function that calls this one, Edit, doesn't bother to check the return value from EditField, so it wouldn't notice if this error ever occurred. Such an omission doesn't cause any trouble here because the user has already been notified that his edit didn't work. Unfortunately, however, the very common problem of forgetting to check return values isn't always so benign. In fact, it's one of the main reasons for the introduction of *exception handling* to C++. However, we won't get a chance to discuss this important topic in this book, other than our brief discussion of what happens when operator new doesn't have any memory to give us.[14]

Facing the Music

We've now covered all the new member functions in HomeItemBasic, so it's time to take a look at the functions implemented in HomeItemMusic. Thankfully, there aren't as many of these. For one thing, GetName, Read, and Edit don't have to be overridden in HomeItemMusic because they do most of their work by calling virtual functions anyway. Two more functions in this class, Write and GetType, haven't changed since we first saw them in hmit1.cc, so we

---

14. That discussion starts on page 459.

don't have to go over them again. HomeItemMusic::FormattedDisplay, on the other hand, has changed since we examined it in hmit4.cc, so it would be a good idea to look it over quickly (Figure 11.43).

FIGURE 11.43. HomeItemMusic::FormattedDisplay **(from code\hmit5.cc)**

```
short HomeItemMusic::FormattedDisplay(ostream &os)
{
  short FieldNumber = HomeItemBasic::FormattedDisplay(os);

  short TrackCount = m_Track.size();

  os << FieldNumber << ". ";
  os << GetFieldName(FieldNumber) << ": ";
  FieldNumber ++;
  os << m_Artist << endl;

  os << FieldNumber << ". ";
  os << GetFieldName(FieldNumber) << ": ";
  FieldNumber ++;
  os << TrackCount << endl;

  for (short i = 0; i < TrackCount; i ++)
    {
    os << FieldNumber << ". ";
    os << GetFieldName(FieldNumber) << i + 1 << ": ";
    FieldNumber ++;
    os << m_Track[i] << endl;
    }

  return FieldNumber;
}
```

This function isn't very different from its counterpart in HomeItemBasic, but there are a couple of points worth mentioning. First, of course, it calls HomeItemBasic::FormattedDisplay to display the part of the data contained in the base class part of the object. Then it assigns the return value from that call to a local variable called

FieldNumber, which it uses to keep track of the current field it is displaying. Why do we want to use the return value from that function to initialize our current field variable rather than a const value, as we did in the base class?

Maintaining Our Position

We do this to reduce the difficulty of maintaining this program. If we use the return value from HomeItemBasic::FormattedDisplay, we won't have to make any changes in the derived class function if the HomeItemBasic class eventually has more data added to it; the starting field number in HomeItemMusic:FormattedDisplay will automatically be the right value as long as the modifications to the HomeItemBasic::FormattedDisplay function have been made correctly. Therefore, we have to make such a change only in one place rather than in two, as we would if we used a const value in the derived class function.

Susan wanted a bit more detail on this issue.

Susan: What kind of change would you make that might mess up the field numbers?

Steve: Let's suppose that we had six fields in the HomeItemBasic class, which of course would be numbered 1 through 6. In that case, the added fields in HomeItemMusic would start at 7. However, if we added another field to the HomeItemBasic class, then the number of the first field in the HomeItemMusic class would change to 8. All of this would have to be handled manually if we used a constant value to specify where we wanted to start in the HomeItemMusic class. However, as long as we use the return value from the HomeItemBasic version of FormattedDisplay, any such adjustments will happen automatically.

Susan: But the user might get confused if the field that used to be #5 suddenly became #6.

Steve: True, but there isn't much we can do about that, assuming that the new field was really necessary. All we can do is make sure that the numbers will still be in the right order with no gaps.

I should also mention that the field name prompt for track names is "Track #" followed by the track number. Because we don't want to confuse the user by starting at 0, we add 1 to the value of the loop index before we use it to construct the field name prompt. This ensures that the first track number displayed is 1, not 0. Remember, users don't normally count from 0, and we should humor them; without them, we wouldn't have anyone to use our programs!

Now let's take a look at HomeItemMusic::ReadInteractive (Figure 11.44).

FIGURE 11.44. HomeItemMusic::ReadInteractive **(from code\hmit5.cc)**

```cpp
short HomeItemMusic::ReadInteractive()
{
  short TrackCount;

  short FieldNumber = HomeItemBasic::ReadInteractive();

  cout << FieldNumber << ". ";
  cout << GetFieldName(FieldNumber) << ": ";
  FieldNumber ++;
  cin >> m_Artist;

  cout << FieldNumber << ". ";
  cout << GetFieldName(FieldNumber) << ": ";
  FieldNumber ++;
  cin >> TrackCount;
  m_Track.resize(TrackCount);

  vector<string> Track(TrackCount);
  for (short i = 0; i < TrackCount; i ++)
    {
    cout << FieldNumber << ". ";
```

```
    cout << GetFieldName(FieldNumber) << i + 1 << ": ";
    FieldNumber ++;
    cin >> Track[i];
    }

 *this = HomeItemMusic(m_Name, m_PurchasePrice,
 m_PurchaseDate, m_Description, m_Category, m_Artist,
 Track);

 return FieldNumber;
 }
```

Only one thing in this function might be a bit puzzling: Where do we get the values of the member variables m_Name through m_Category, which we use as arguments in the call to the constructor for HomeItemMusic near the end of the function? The answer is that they were input by the user during the execution of HomeItemBasic::ReadInteractive, which we called at the beginning of this function. Therefore, when we are ready to create the HomeItemMusic object containing all the data read from the user, we can combine all of those data items with the ones that we requested from the user in this function—namely, m_Artist and the track names in the local vector Track.

There are two more functions that we need to look at briefly. The first is HomeItemMusic::ReadFromFile, which is shown in Figure 11.45. Assuming that you understand the HomeItemBasic versions of ReadFromFile and ReadInteractive, this function should hold no secrets for you, so just take a look at it and make sure you understand it. Then let's move on.

FIGURE 11.45. HomeItemMusic::ReadFromFile (**from code\hmit5.cc**)

```
short HomeItemMusic::ReadFromFile(istream& is)
{
  short TrackCount;

  HomeItemBasic::ReadFromFile(is);
```

```
is >> m_Artist;
is >> TrackCount;

vector<string> Track(TrackCount);
for (short i = 0; i < TrackCount; i ++)
  {
  is >> Track[i];
  }

*this = HomeItemMusic(m_Name, m_PurchasePrice,
m_PurchaseDate, m_Description, m_Category, m_Artist, Track);
}
```

Finally, there's HomeItemMusic::EditField (Figure 11.46), which has a few points that we should consider before (finally!) ending this chapter.

FIGURE 11.46. HomeItemMusic::EditField **(from code\hmit5.cc)**

```
bool HomeItemMusic::EditField(short FieldNumber)
{
  if (FieldNumber < e_Artist)
    {
    return HomeItemBasic::EditField(FieldNumber);
    }

  short TrackCount = m_Track.size();

  switch (FieldNumber)
    {
    case e_Artist:
    cout << FieldNumber << ". ";
    cout << GetFieldName(FieldNumber) << ": ";
    cin >> m_Artist;
    return true;

    case e_TrackCount:
```

```
    cout << FieldNumber << ". ";
    cout << GetFieldName(FieldNumber) << ": ";
    cin >> TrackCount;
    m_Track.resize(TrackCount);
    return true;
    }

  if (FieldNumber > (e_TrackCount + TrackCount))
    {
    cout << "Sorry, that is not a valid field number." << endl;
    return false;
    }

  cout << FieldNumber << ". ";
  cout << GetFieldName(FieldNumber);
  cout << FieldNumber - e_TrackCount << ": ";

  cin >> m_Track[FieldNumber - e_TrackNumber];

  return true;
  }
```

Let's start at the beginning, where we figure out whether the field the user wants to edit is handled by this function or by HomeItemBasic::Edit. If the field number is less than e_Artist, we know that this function isn't responsible for editing it, so we pass the editing task on to the HomeItemBasic version of EditField and return the return value from that function to our caller.

But suppose we have to handle the editing chore for the user's field here. In that case, we need to execute the proper code for the field the user wants to edit. If that field happens to be either the artist's name or the number of tracks, we handle it in the switch statement and return the value true to indicate success. However, handling the other fields (i.e., the track names) isn't quite as simple. If you compare HomeItemBasic::EditField (Figure 11.42) with the current function you'll notice that the switch statement in HomeItemBasic::EditField has a default case to handle the possibility that the field number is invalid, whereas the HomeItemMusic switch statement doesn't. Why is this?

Because a HomeItemMusic object can contain a variable number of track names in its m_Track member variable. This means that we can't tell at compile time how many fields are in the object we're going to edit, which in turn means that we have to wait until run time to figure out whether a particular field number is valid for a particular object. That's the purpose of the if statement

```
if (FieldNumber > (e_TrackCount + TrackCount))
```

that adds the number of tracks to the field number for the track count itself and then compares the result to the field number the user typed in. Since the track name fields immediately follow the track count field, if the user's field number is greater than that total, the field number is invalid. For example, if there's only one track, the maximum field number is e_TrackCount + 1; if there are two tracks, it is e_TrackCount + 2; and so on. If the field number the user typed is beyond the legal range, the code in the if statement displays a warning and returns the value false to the calling function to indicate that it was unable to update the object.

Assuming that the user typed in a legal field number, we continue with the code that prompts the user to type in the new name for the selected track:

```
cout << FieldNumber << ". ";
cout << GetFieldName(FieldNumber);
cout << FieldNumber - e_TrackCount << ": ";
```

This starts out by displaying the field number for the track to be edited followed by its field name ("Track #" followed by its track number). For example, if the starting field number for the track names is 8, the prompt for track 5 is "12. Track #5: ". Then the line

```
cin >> m_Track[FieldNumber - e_TrackNumber];
```

accepts the new value of the track name and stores it in the correct place in the m_Track member variable. Finally, the function returns true to indicate success.

Review

We started out this chapter by considering the problem of keeping track of all the "stuff" that we accumulate in our homes. This happens to make a good project to illustrate the use of the C++ tools that we've already covered, as well as to introduce a few new tools along the way. It also has the fortunate characteristic that the finished program might actually be useful.

Once we selected a project, the next step was to figure out exactly what the program should do.[15] In this case, we wanted to be able to keep track of the type of object, date of acquisition, price, and description for every item in the home, as well as any additional information needed for specific types of objects. An example is the CD, for which the additional information is the name of the artist and those of the tracks.

This led to the more general question of how to divide the nearly infinite number of real-world objects that we might encounter into the categories represented by a necessarily limited number of possible types of program objects. For example, what should we do with LPs or cassette tapes? Because they are used for much the same purpose as music CDs are, I decided to put all of these objects in the same "Music" type. A CD-ROM, on the other hand, is probably best represented by a "software" type, even though it is physically identical to a music CD, because it is used differently and has

---

15. This may seem too simple even to mention, but the failure to define exactly what a particular program is supposed to do is a major cause of wasted money and effort, especially in large corporations.

different information associated with it. For example, a CD-ROM often has a serial number whereas a music CD doesn't.

Having made a decision on this matter, we were ready to start designing the interface that the user of the HomeItem classes will see, using the *manager/worker idiom* to implement a *polymorphic object* solution to our problem.

Once we looked at the first version of the interface for the HomeItem class, the most obvious observation was that it is very similar to the StockItem class from previous chapters. The main reason for that similarity is that both of these classes play the role of the manager class in a polymorphic object implementation. One manager class looks very much like any other because a manager object's main duties are to create, destroy, and otherwise handle its worker objects; those duties are similar no matter what the worker objects actually do.

For this reason, all of the "structural" functions in the manager classes for the StockItem and HomeItem types are almost identical except for the exact data types of arguments and return values. These structural functions include the operators << and >>, the default constructors, copy constructors, "normal" constructors, assignment operators, and destructors. They also include the "special" constructor used to prevent an infinite loop during construction of a worker object and the Write function used to create a human-readable version of the data for an object.

By contrast, the "regular" member functions of each of these manager classes are whatever is needed to allow the users of that class to get their work done. These functions differ signficantly from one polymorphic object implementation to another, as they are the most specific to the particular task of each class.

Upon examination, we saw that the same analogies apply to the worker classes for these two types as to the manager classes. The main difference between the StockItem worker classes and the first version of the HomeItem worker classes is that the HomeItem worker classes have a GetType member function that the StockItem worker classes don't have. This function allows the base class member data to be displayed with the correct tag indicating the exact type of the worker object being displayed, rather than requiring the duplication of code in the base and derived class output functions.[16]

Because this GetType function is used only within inside the implementation of the worker classes, it is first declared in HomeItemBasic rather than in HomeItem. This doesn't violate the principle that all objects of a polymorphic object type must have the same user interface, because GetType is not visible to the user of the HomeItem types and therefore doesn't change the user's view of these objects.

Next, we analyzed the first version of operator >> for the HomeItem classes. This function differs from the StockItem version of the same operator in a number of ways, the primary differences being its ability to skip blank lines in the input file, its deferred creation of variables until they are needed rather than all at the beginning of the function, and its use of an explicit type indicator ("Basic" or "Music") to determine the type of the worker object, rather than relying on the value of the expiration date field as the operator >> for StockItem did.

The most generally applicable of these differences is the deferred creation of variables, which is a good way to save execution time and make the program easier to follow. In this case, we didn't create a vector of track names until we had read the rest of the data for the object, including its type and track count; of course, a "Basic" object doesn't have the track count and track name fields anyway.

This implementation of operator >> also illustrates the new C++ feature that restricts the scope of a for index variable created in a for statement to the loop controlled by that for statement. Earlier versions of C++ allowed that variable to be accessed after the end of the for loop, an oversight that was corrected in the final C++ standard.

---

16. The use of a GetType member function to allow sharing of code for the base class member data display would probably have been a good idea for the StockItem classes as well, but I hadn't thought of it yet when I designed those classes.

Then we moved on to the HomeItemBasic::Write function, which uses the GetType function to determine which type of object it is writing to the ostream specified by its argument. The HomeItemBasic version of Write has to call GetType because the derived class function HomeItemMusic::Write calls this function to do most of the work; thus, the object for which HomeItemBasic::Write has been called may be a derived class object rather than a HomeItemBasic object. This means that HomeItemBasic::Write has to call the virtual function GetType to find out the actual type of the object being written so that it can write the correct type indicator to the output file along with the other data for the object. This is what makes it possible for us to reconstruct the object properly when we read the data back from the file.

When we got done with HomeItemBasic::Write, we continued by analyzing HomeItemMusic::Write. That function is pretty simple, except that it uses the size member function of the vector data type to find out how many tracks are in the vector so that it can write that track count, followed by all of the track names. This is necessary for us to reconstruct the "Music" object properly when we read its data from the file.

The next operation we undertook was to create a new HomeInventory class, which serves much the same function for HomeItems that the Inventory class does for StockItems: It allows us to create and keep track of a number of HomeItems and to search for a particular HomeItem.

The initial interface of this new HomeInventory class is also pretty simple, providing only the minimal set of operations we might want to use: loading the inventory from a disk file and searching for a particular item by name. After considering several ways to keep track of the number of elements in use, we decided on storing the number of elements in the input file and creating a vector of the correct size when we open the file. If we add new items to the vector, we keep track of that fact via its size member function.

This solution eliminates the waste of space or time of the other ways to determine the size of the vector when reading data from the input file, but it also has a twist of its own: the need to read the data into a temporary holding variable so we can detect the end of the input file without running off the end of the vector. This problem led to a discussion of the dangers of ignoring the possibility of errors in the data, as well as other sources of errors that lie outside the immediate scope of the code we write.

We continued by creating the ability for the user to enter data for a new object by adding an AddItem member function to the HomeInventory class and a NewItem static member function to the HomeItem class. The latter needs to be a static member function because it creates a new HomeItem object by reading data from the keyboard; it doesn't have an existing HomeItem object to work on, so it can't be a regular member function.

The implementation of HomeItem::NewItem is quite simple: It uses operator >> to read data from the keyboard into a newly created HomeItem object and then returns it to the caller. However, this works only because we changed operator >> to be usable for keyboard input by having it determine whether the user is typing at the keyboard according to the identity of the input stream. If that stream is cin, the function displays prompts before each input operation; if not, the input operations are performed as they were previously.

We had to change operator >> rather than using it as previously implemented because adding another function for keyboard input would have required require us to duplicate the code that reads the data, causing maintenance problems when any of those input operations had to be modified.

Then we added versions of FormattedDisplay to both HomeItemBasic and HomeItemMusic, which provide output virtually identical to the output of operator << for objects of those two types, except that FormattedDisplay also displays labels indicating what the data items represent.

The next order of business was to discuss GetName, whose only notable characteristic is that even though it is a virtual function, it is not implemented in HomeItemMusic because the implementation in HomeItemBasic will work perfectly for a HomeItemMusic object. As with a nonvirtual function, if we call a virtual function for a derived class object that hasn't been defined in that class, the result will be to call the function in the nearest base class that defines the function—in this case HomeItemBasic::GetName.

Next we analyzed the test program hmtst4.cc, which includes the new AddItem and GetName functions added since the last test program. We used these functions to add a new item and retrieve it, as well as to retrieve an item loaded from the file (just to make sure that that still worked after all the changes we'd made).

In the next step, we added a mechanism to edit an object that already exists, via a new function called EditItem in the Inventory class and a corresponding function called Edit in the HomeItem class. We also added a helper function called LocateItemByName to the Inventory class to help us find an existing HomeItem to be edited.

We didn't have to change the test program very much from the previous version to accommodate this new ability to edit an existing object. However, we did have to modify the HomeItem classes significantly so that we could avoid keeping track of the field names in more than one function: This was intended to simplify maintenance later. One modification was the addition of a Read function that could fill in the data for an existing object rather than create the object directly in operator >>, as we had done until that point.

This revamping of the input mechanism required several new functions, which I added to HomeItemBasic and HomeItemMusic rather than to HomeItem, because they are used only as aids to the implementation of the new Read function. Included among these functions are ReadInteractive, ReadFromFile, EditField, and GetFieldName.

The last of these, GetFieldName, is particularly interesting on several counts. First, it uses a new construct, the enum, which is a way to define a number of constant values that are appropriate for naming array or vector indexes. Second, it uses a static array of strings to hold the field names for use in prompts. This array is static so that it will be initialized only once, during the first call to GetFieldName, rather than every time the function is called. The reason we're using an array instead of a vector is that it is (unfortunately) impossible in C++ to initialize a vector from a list of values; this special C++ facility is available only for arrays. Because we're using an array, we have to check for the possibility of a bad index rather than rely on the safety checks built into a vector; the program would fail in some mysterious way if we tried to access a nonexistent array element.

After some discussion of the properties of enums, including their ability to be converted to an integer type automatically when needed for arithmetic purposes, we continued with the implementation of Read, which merely decides whether the input is interactive and then calls the appropriate subfunction, ReadInteractive or ReadFromFile, accordingly. ReadInteractive, as its name implies, prompts the user for each field to be entered, using GetFieldName to retrieve the appropriate prompt for that field. ReadFromFile reads the same data but without displaying any prompts.

As soon as we have read all the data for an item, either interactively or from a file, either of the Read subfunctions finishes by calling the appropriate constructor to create an object containing that data and assigning the newly created object to *this. The latter expression means "the object pointed to by the this pointer" (the object for which the Read subfunction was called).

The other new function added to the HomeItem interface, Edit, first calls the updated version of FormattedDisplay to display the current data for the object to be edited, using GetFieldName to determine the prompt for each field to be displayed, and then calls EditField to request the new value for the field being modified. To simplify the code, this function uses a new construct, switch. This is essentially equivalent to a number of if...else if statements that select one of a number of possible actions.

After finishing the changes to HomeItemBasic, we examined the corresponding functions in HomeItemMusic, which use the HomeItemBasic base class functions to do as much of the work as possible. For this reason, the new HomeItemMusic functions added no great complexity except for the necessity of handling a variable number of data elements in the track name vector.

Exercises

1. Implement the HomeItemComputer class as a derived class of HomeItemBasic to keep track of computers. The added fields should include serial number, amount of RAM, amount of disk space, a list of installed storage devices, and lists of installed ISA and PCI interface cards.

2. Implement the HomeItemSoftware class as a derived class of HomeItemBasic to keep track of computer software. The added fields should include the serial numbers of the software and computer on which it is installed. Can you devise a way to make sure that the latter serial number is the same as the serial number of a HomeItemComputer in the inventory?

3. Implement the HomeItemAppliance class as a derived class of HomeItemBasic to keep track of other electric and electronic appliances. The added fields should include the serial number of the appliance.

4. Can you think of a way to simplify the implementation of the classes in the above exercises by adding an additional class?

5. Implement the HomeItemBook class as a derived class of HomeItemBasic to keep track of books. The added fields should include author, publisher, publication date, number of pages, and ISBN (International Standard Book Number, a 10-character field that can contain the digits from 0 to 9 and the letter X).

6. Implement the HomeItemSet class as a derived class of HomeItemBasic to keep track of sets of identical items such as plates and flatware. The added fields should include the pattern name and number of items of each type.

7. Implement the HomeItemClothing class as a derived class of HomeItemBasic to keep track of clothes and shoes. The added fields should include owner's name and size.

8. Add code to the AddItem member function of the HomeInventory class to make sure that the new object being added has a name different from that of every object already in the inventory.

Conclusion

At this point, we have a working, if rudimentary, set of HomeItem classes along with the HomeInventory class that manages the objects of these classes. Next, we're going to add some more facilities to the string class so that we can improve our application program enough to actually use it for keeping track of all the "stuff" we collect in everyday life.

CHAPTER 12

Homeward Bound

In this chapter, we will begin to take the home inventory project to a stage where it will be a useful, if limited, application program that will allow you to keep track of your possessions. Of course, this doesn't mean that we will have completely finished this project; it's rare for a software application to be finished in the sense that nothing more can be done to improve it. In fact, the usual way to tell when you're done working on a project is that you have run out of time and have to put it into service, not that it does everything that you would like it to do. In this way, the home inventory project is quite representative of programming projects in general.

We'll get right to our improvements as soon as we get through some definitions as well as the objectives for the chapter.

Definitions

The **preprocessor** is a part of the C++ compiler that deals with the source code of a program before the rest of the compiler ever sees that source code; thus, the name "preprocessor".

A **preprocessor directive** is a command telling the preprocessor to handle the following source code in a special manner.

A **preprocessor symbol** is a constant value similar to a const but is known only to the preprocessor, not to the rest of the compiler. The rules for naming preprocessor symbols are the same as those for other identifiers, but it is customary to use all uppercase letters in preprocessor symbols so that they can be readily distinguished from other identifiers.

The **#ifndef** preprocessor directive tells the preprocessor to check whether a particular preprocessor symbol has been defined. If not, the following source code is treated normally; if it has been defined, the following source code is skipped by the rest of the compiler as though it were not present in the source file.

The **#define** preprocessor directive defines a preprocessor symbol.

The **#endif** preprocessor directive terminates a section of source code controlled by a #ifndef or other conditional preprocessor directive.

An **include guard** is a mechanism to prevent a class definition from being included in a source code file more than once.

A **default argument** is a method of specifying a value for an argument to a function when the user of the function hasn't supplied a value for that argument. The value of the default argument is specified in the declaration of the function.

Objectives of This Chapter

By the end of this chapter we will have

1. Improved the string class to make it easy to search for a partially matching string;

2. Learned how to use **include guards** to prevent a class interface from accidentally being defined more than once;

3. Learned about **default arguments**, which allow us to write one function that can take a varying number of arguments;

4. Learned about the **explicit** keyword, which gives us more control over how constructors will be used;

5. Defined a **concatenation** operator that "adds" one string to the end of another one;

6. Written a version of operator >> that can read a string of any length from the keyboard or a file;

7. Learned something about the hazards of the "magic" value 0;

8. Discovered just how difficult it is to anticipate how a program will be used, and how many bugs it contains;

9. Seen how a seemingly simple request for an added feature in a program can be extremely difficult to fulfill.

Super-string Theory

The strings we've been using in this book have been satisfactory for the uses we've made of them so far, but at this point we need some more functionality. Figure 12.1 shows the interface of the new string class that implements the new functions we'll need to finish our home inventory project.[1]

FIGURE 12.1. The new string class **interface (code\string7.h)**

```
#ifndef STRING7_H
#define STRING7_H

#include <iostream.h>
#include <string.h>

class string
{
friend ostream& operator << (ostream& os, const string& Str);
friend istream& operator >> (istream& is, string& Str);

public:
    string();
    string(const string& Str);
    string& operator = (const string& Str);
    ~string();

    string(char* p);
explicit string(short Length, char Ch=0);

    short GetLength();

    bool operator < (const string& Str);
    bool operator == (const string& Str);
    bool operator > (const string& Str);
    bool operator >= (const string& Str);
    bool operator <= (const string& Str);
    bool operator != (const string& Str);

    string operator + (const string& Str);
    short find_nocase(const string& Str);
    bool less_nocase (const string& Str);
```

---

1. This is an improved version of the string class we covered in Chapters 7 and
    8. You might want to review that discussion before proceeding with these
    improvements.

```
private:
    short m_Length;
    char* m_Data;
};
#endif
```

Batteries Not #included

The first change in this header file from the previous version, string6.h, doesn't have anything to do with adding new functionality to the string class. Instead, it is a means of preventing problems if we accidentally #include this header twice, using a mechanism generally referred to as an **include guard**. I'm referring to the two lines at the very beginning of the file and the last line at the end of the file. The first of these lines,

```
#ifndef STRING7_H
```

uses a **preprocessor directive** called #ifndef (short for "if not defined") to determine whether we've already defined a preprocessor symbol called STRING7_H. If this is the case, the compiler will ignore the rest of the file until it sees an #endif (which in this case is at the end of the file).

The next line,

```
#define STRING7_H
```

defines the same preprocessor symbol, STRING7_H, that we tested for in the previous line. Finally, the last line of the file,

```
#endif
```

ends the scope of the #ifndef directive.

Susan: I don't get it. What is a preprocessor directive? For that matter, what is a preprocessor?

Steve: The preprocessor used to be a separate program that was executed before the compiler itself, to prepare the source code for the compiler. Nowadays, the preprocessor is almost always part of the compiler, but it is still logically distinct. A preprocessor directive is a command to the preprocessor to manipulate the source code in some way.

Susan: Why do we need the preprocessor anyway?

Steve: We don't need it very much anymore. About the only functions it still serves are the processing of included header files (via the #include preprocessor directive) and the creation of the "include guard".

Susan: About the preprocessor symbol: Why would you want several things all equal to (for example) 123?

Steve: Because that makes the program easier to read than if you just said 123 everywhere you needed to use such a value. Giving a name to a number is now most commonly done via the const construct in C++, which replaces most of the old uses of preprocessor symbols, but we still need them to implement include guards so that we can prevent the C++ compiler itself from seeing the definition of a class more than once.

What is the point of all this? To solve a problem in writing large C++ programs: the possibility that we might #include the same header file more than once in the same source code file. This can happen because a source code file often uses #include to gain access to a number of interface definitions stored in several header files, more than one of which uses a common header file (like string7.h). If this were to happen without precautions such as an include guard, we would get an error when we tried to compile our program. The error message would say that we had defined the same class twice, which is not allowed. Therefore, any header file that might be used in a number of places should use an include guard to prevent such errors. Susan had some questions about this notion and why it should be needed in the first place.

Susan: Why should it be illegal to define the same class twice?

Steve: If we define the same class twice, which definition should the compiler use? The first one or the second one?

Susan: I see how that might cause a problem, but what if the two definitions are exactly the same? Why would the compiler care then?

Steve: For the compiler to handle that situation, it would have to keep track of every definition it sees for a class rather than just one. Because it's almost always an error to try to define the same class more than once, there's no reason to add that extra complexity to the compiler when we can prevent the problem in the first place.

Assuming that I've convinced you of the value of include guards, how do they work? Well, the #ifndef directive checks to see if a specific preprocessor symbol, in this case STRING7_H, has already been defined. If it has, then the rest of the #include file is essentially ignored. Let's suppose that STRING7_H hasn't been defined yet. In that case, we define that symbol in the next line and then allow the compiler to process the rest of the file.

So far this works exactly as it would if we hadn't added the include guard. But suppose that later, during the compilation of the same source file, another header file #includes string7.h again. In that case, the symbol STRING7_H would already be defined (because we defined it on the first access to string7.h). Therefore, the #ifndef would cause the compiler to skip the rest of the header file, preventing the string class from being redefined and causing an error.

Of course, the choice of the preprocessor symbol to be defined is more or less arbitrary, but there is a convention in C and C++ that the symbol should be derived from the name of the header file. This is intended to reduce the likelihood of two header files using the same preprocessor symbol in their include guards. If that happened and if both of these header files were #included in the same source file, the definitions in the second one to be #included would be ignored during compilation because the preprocessor symbol used by its include guard would already be defined. To prevent such problems, I'm following the (commonly used) convention of defining a preprocessor symbol whose name is a capitalized version of the header file's name, with the period changed to an underscore to make it a legal preprocessor symbol name. If everyone working on a project follows this convention (or a similar one), the likelihood of trouble will be minimized.

Construction Ahead

The next change to the interface of string is the addition of a new constructor, whose signature is specified in the interface file as explicit string(short Length, char Ch=0);. We'll get to the reason for adding this constructor as soon as I explain a few details: what the construct char Ch=0 means in a function declaration, what the **explicit** keyword means, and why we need to specify it here. Let's start with the meaning of char Ch=0 in this context.

Default Is Mine

This is another C++ feature that is new to us. It's called a *default argument*, and its purpose is to specify a value for an argument to a function when the user of the function doesn't supply a value for that argument. In this case, the construct "char ch=0" specifies that if the application programmer calls a string constructor with only a short argument, the string::string(short, char) constructor will be called, with the first argument set to the short value supplied in the constructor call and the second argument set to 0. On the other hand, if the application programmer calls a string constructor with two arguments, the first a short and the second a char, this string::string(short, char) constructor will also be called, but the first argument will be set to the short value supplied in the constructor call and the second argument will be set to the char value supplied in the constructor call.

We don't have to use default arguments if we don't want to; we can achieve the same effect by writing a separate function for each possible number of arguments supplied by the calling program. To see how this alternative works, let's start with Figure 12.2, which shows a simplified version of a string interface file that contains two overloaded string constructors that take the place of the one we're discussing.

FIGURE 12.2. A simplified interface file for a string class (**code\string7x.h**)

```
#ifndef STRING7X_H
#define STRING7X_H

#include <iostream.h>
#include <string.h>

class string
{
public:

  string(short Length);
  string(short Length, char Ch);

private:
  short m_Length;
  char* m_Data;
};

#endif
```

The implementation of the first constructor is shown in Figure 12.3.

FIGURE 12.3. An alternate string(short Length) **constructor (from code\string7x.cc)**

```
string::string(short Length)
: m_Length(Length + 1),
  m_Data(new char [m_Length])
{
    char Ch = 0;
    memset(m_Data,Ch,Length);
    m_Data[Length] = 0;
}
```

The implementation of the second constructor is the same as the implementation for the actual string::string(short Length, char Ch=0) constructor we are discussing (shown in Figure 12.5); the only difference is that the interface file doesn't specify a default value. As a result, we have to write two different functions to handle constructor calls with and without the second argument.

To recapitulate: Specifying the default argument as char Ch=0 for the second entry in the argument list of the constructor whose first argument is a short is exactly equivalent to writing two overloaded string constructors:

1. One with a single argument. This constructor, shown in Figure 12.3, uses a constant value 0 for the char value to be stored in the string, instead of the Ch argument.

2. One with two arguments of types short and char, neither having a default value. The code for this constructor is the same as the code for the constructor having a default value (Figure 12.5).

Warning: Explicit Material

I hope this explains the notion of a default argument. Now let's get to the explicit keyword, which was added to C++ to allow class designers to solve a problem with constructors that resulted from a (usually convenient) feature of the language called **implicit conversion**. Under the rules of implicit conversion, a constructor that takes one argument (or that takes more than one argument but has default arguments for all arguments after the first one) is also a **conversion function** that is called automatically (or *implicitly*) where an argument of a certain type is needed and an argument of another type is ofsupplied. In many cases, an implicit constructor call is very useful; for example, it's extremely handy to be able to supply a char* argument when a string (or a const string&) is specified as the actual argument type in a function declaration. The compiler allows this without complaint because we have a string constructor that takes a char* argument and can be called implicitly. However, sometimes we don't want the compiler to supply this automatic conversion because the results would be surprising to the user of the class. In some previous versions of C++, it wasn't possible to prevent the compiler from supplying the automatic conversion, but in standard C++what we can use the explicit keyword to tell the compiler, in essence, that we don't want it to use a particular constructor unless we explicitly ask for it.

To see how this affects the way we write a program using one of these constructors, take a look at Figure 12.4, which illustrates the difference between an implicit and an explicit constructor call.

FIGURE 12.4. An explicit **constructor call vs an implicit one (code\strtstx.cc)**

```
// strtstx.cc

#include <iostream.h>
#include "string7.h"

main()
{
    string a;
    string b = "Test";

    a = string(5); // legal
```

```
        a = 5;        // illegal

        cout << a << endl;
}
```

The reason that the line marked "legal" is legal, given the definitions in string7.h, is that we are explicitly stating that we want to construct a string by calling a constructor (which happens to be string(short, char), with the second argument using the default value 0). By contrast, the line marked "illegal" will be rejected by the compiler; for this line to be legal, the string class defined in string7.h would have to have a constructor that could be called implicitly to create a string from the literal value 5. Although that interface file does indeed define a string constructor that can be called with one argument of the short type, we've added the explicit keyword to its declaration to tell the compiler that this constructor doesn't accept implicit calls. This is a safety measure that prevents a user from accidentally calling the string(short, char) constructor by providing a short argument to a function that expects a string. Because the user is very unlikely to want a short value such as 5 silently converted to a string of 5 null bytes, as the string(short,char) constructor would do in this case, making this constructor explicit will reduce unpleasant surprises.

But why have we defined this string constructor at all? We'll get to that as soon as we take a look at its implementation, which is shown in Figure 12.5.[2]

FIGURE 12.5. The string(short, char) **constructor for the** string class **(from code\string7.cc)**

```
string::string(short Length, char Ch)
    : m_Length(Length + 1),
```

---

2. Please note that the default value for the second argument, or even the fact that it has a default value, is not visible in the implementation of this constructor. That information is present only in the interface file.

```
    m_Data(new char [m_Length])
{
    memset(m_Data,Ch,Length);
    m_Data[Length] = 0;
}
```

This function creates a new string that can hold a specified number of chars, then sets them all to the value of the second argument (or 0 if no second argument was supplied) via the memset function. Then it sets the last char to the null byte 0, as we always do when constructing a string so that the C string functions can recognize it as a valid C string (assuming that it contains no other null bytes). We need this new constructor for the next function we're defining, operator + (Figure 12.7).[3] But before we get into the implementation of the operator + function, perhaps we should consider what the meaning of + might be for a string in the first place.

Adding Insult to Injury

While the ability to read and write strings is very important, there are other operations that the string class needs to support if it is to be useful in the real world. One of these is **concatenation**, which is just a fancy word for "adding one string onto the end of another one". For example, if we have someone's first and last names as separate strings, it might be handy to be able to tack the last name to the end of the first name so we can store the entire name as one string. While we could use strstreams, that is a very inefficient way to accomplish a common operation. The reason we have to worry about this in the first place is that there isn't any built-in concatenation operation for strings C++ (mostly because the string class isn't a native type). However, this is a common enough operation that a convention has been developed to use the + sign to indicate it. This symbol is also

---

3. We'll also be using this constructor later to create strings of blanks for formatting item listings, in the section "Categorical Imperative" on page 964.

used in languages such as Java and Basic for the same operation, so C++ isn't too unusual in this regard. At any rate, it's time for us to see how we would use the + to concatenate strings in C++ (Figure 12.6).

FIGURE 12.6. Using operator + **for** string **concatenation (code\strtst7a.cc)**

```
#include <iostream.h>
#include "string7.h"

int main()
{
    string x;
    string y;

    cout << "Please enter your first name: ";
    cin >> x;

    cout << "Please enter your last name: ";
    cin >> y;

    z = x + " ";
    z = z + y;

    cout << "Hello, " << z;

    return 0;
}
```

This program asks the user to type in his or her first name and then last name. Once the first and last names have been typed in, the statement z = x + " "; uses the + to concatenate a space onto the end of the first name; then the statement z = z + y; uses another + to concatenate the last name onto the result of the first operation.[4] Finally, the program greets the user by saying "Hello, " followed by the user's name.

Now that we've seen how we can use this new operator, let's take a look at how it is implemented (Figure 12.7).

FIGURE 12.7. The implementation of operator + **for the** string class **(from code\string7.cc)**

```
string string::operator + (const string& Str)
{
    short length = m_Length - 1;
    short strlength = Str.m_Length - 1;

    string tempstring(length + strlength);

    memcpy(tempstring.m_Data, m_Data, length);

    memcpy(tempstring.m_Data+length, Str.m_Data, strlength);

    return tempstring;
}
```

This function starts by initializing a couple of variables called length and strlength. The value of length is initalized to the number of chars in the left-hand argument to operator + (i.e., the string pointed to by this, which is x in the expression "z + y"). Similarly, the value of strlength is initialized to the number of chars in the right-hand argument to operator + (i.e., the input argument Str, which is y in the expression "z + y"). In both cases, we exclude the trailing null byte from the count. Once these variables are initialized, the function creates a new string variable called tempstring having a length equal to

---

4. In case you were wondering whether we should also write a version of operator += for the string class, the answer is that such an operator could be quite useful. That's why I've made it an exercise.

the sum of these two lengths, which will be used to hold the concatenated value. All of the chars in tempstring are set to null bytes because it is created by the string(short,char) constructor with the second argument equal to 0 by default.

The next step is to use memcpy to copy the data from the left-hand argument (z in the expression "z + y") to the data area of this new string. The next line, memcpy(tempstring.m_Data+length, Str.m_Data, strlength);, copies the data from the right-hand argument (y in the expression "z + y") to the data area of tempstring beginning immediately after the end of the data from the left-hand argument. The result of all this is a string containing the original contents of the left-hand argument followed by the original contents of the right-hand argument to operator +.

Susan had some questions about the implementation of this function.

Susan: Why is the length –1?

Steve: Because we don't want to copy the null byte at the end of the data. The string constructor will add a null at the end of the new string.

Susan: What would happen if we left off the null byte at the end of a string?

Steve: All of our code would still work. The problem would be if we wanted to use some of the C string functions or look at our strings with a debugger. The debugger knows how to display C strings but not our own kind of strings; however, as long as we add the null byte at the end of the data area, the debugger can display the data as though it were a C string.

Susan: OK, I get that. Now I have a request. Please change the name of the length variable to left_length and the name of the other variable to right_length.

Steve: That might be a good idea, but it's too late; to be consistent, I'd have to change a lot of other places that use the same convention. With the explanation here, the readers should be able to figure out what the code means.

Inner Peace

While the ability to concatenate strings is useful in many applications, I have a specific reason to add it now: It's needed in the reimplementation of operator >> for the string class. The prior version of operator >> couldn't handle strings of more than 256 characters, which was adequate for our use with StockItem objects because they don't have any fields that are likely to grow beyond that length. However, it's entirely possible that a description field for a HomeItem object might be a whole paragraph, and having a fixed maximum size for string input would therefore be a hindrance to proper use of the HomeItem class.

> **Susan:** Why would anyone want to type in such a long description when they couldn't change it if they made a mistake?

> **Steve:** That's a very good point. The solution is to add the ability to edit an existing description field. We won't have time to do that in this book, but I can always add it as an exercise! Also, the old version of the operator >> wouldn't behave very well if it tried to read a string that was longer than 79 characters; it would just leave the extra characters in the input file without any notice of the error being given to the user. Therefore, it's important to fix this problem.

Even though it might not be convenient for the user of the program to use very long descriptions, I've improved the implementation of operator >> to be able to read strings containing any number of characters. Figure 12.8 shows this new implementation.

FIGURE 12.8. **The new implementation of** operator >> **(from code\string7.cc)**

```
istream& operator >> (istream& is, string& Str)
{
    const short BUFLEN = 80;

    char Buf[BUFLEN];
    string Str1;
    string Str2;

    if (is.peek() == '\n')
        is.ignore();
    memset(Buf,0,BUFLEN);
    is.get(Buf,BUFLEN,'\n');
    Str2 = Buf;

    while ((is.fail() == 0) && (is.peek() != '\n'))
        {
        Str1 = Str1 + Str2;
        memset(Buf,0,BUFLEN);
        is.get(Buf,BUFLEN,'\n');
        Str2 = Buf;
        }

    Str = Str1 + Str2;

    return is;
}
```

This function is complicated enough to deserve some detailed discussion. After defining some variables, including Buf (the buffer that will hold the chars being read from the input stream), we check to see if the first char is a newline. If so, we ignore it so that we can safely mix numeric and string input.[5] Next, we use memset to fill Buf

---

5.   This is explained in detail in the discussion of the original version of the string class in Chapters 7 and 8.

with null bytes before we read data into it so that we it will be able to determine where the data ends. Then we use the istream::get member function to read a maximum of BUFLEN–1 chars from the input istream into the buffer. To complete this part of the operation, we set the temporary string variable Str2 to the contents of Buf. At this point, we have a string called Str2 that contains the first part of the string, which will be the entirety of the string if all the chars to be read would fit into Buf (i.e., the string is less than 80 chars long).

Susan had some questions about this function.

Susan: Why do we need to fill the buffer with null bytes?

Steve: Because we don't know where it has been. That is, we don't know what data might be lying around in a buffer that we have allocated on the stack. Remember the uninitialized variable problems we had in the past?

Susan: Ugh. Don't remind me. Anyway, why do we need this function again?

Steve: To read data from a stream into a string so we can use it in our program.

Susan: Where you say "the string is less than 80 chars long", don't you mean "80 chars or less"?

Steve: That's very perceptive of you, but in fact the original statement is correct. The maximum number of characters is BUFLEN–1 (79) rather than BUFLEN (80) because the get function always adds a null byte to the end of whatever it reads, so the C string functions can be used on the data that has been read. Therefore, we can't read BUFLEN characters into the buffer, because that would leave no room for the null byte.

The while loop that makes up the next part of the code handles the situation where the string is at least 80 chars. The condition in the while is (is.fail() == 0 && is.peek() != '\n'). The first part of this expression, is.fail() == 0, will be true if we haven't reached the end of the input file. If we have reached the end of the file, we're obviously finished with the input. Assuming that the istream hasn't failed yet, the second part of the expression, is.peek() != '\n', will be false if the next char in the istream is a newline. If so, we are finished because our input is defined to stop when we reach the end of a line. If the next char to be read isn't a newline, we must continue reading data for our string. The first operation inside the loop is to concatenate the data we have just read, in Str2, to the previous contents of our other temporary variable, Str1, which contains all of the input that we've read in previous executions of the while loop. The first time we go through the loop, of course, Str1 starts out empty. Next, we use memset to clear Buf in preparation for reading some more data from the input istream, which we do in the next line. The last statement in the loop sets Str2 to the contents of Buf, which leaves us ready for the next iteration of the while loop.

Assuming that we haven't yet read all the chars for this string, the next execution of the while loop will start by adding the contents of Str2 (the data we read on the previous execution of the loop) to the contents of Str1 (the data we read before the previous execution of the loop). Then we execute the same steps as before to retrieve another part of the string's data.

Eventually, we will get to the end of the data for the string we are reading, at which time the while loop will terminate. At that point, Str1 and Str2 contain the final data for the string Str, so we concatenate Str2 to the end of Str1 and set Str to the result. Finally, we return the updated istream object to the caller for possible use in further input operations.

Location, Location, Location

Now we're ready to discuss the next new string member function in this version of the string class: find_nocase. We need this function to determine whether a given string contains a particular sequence of characters. For example, if we have a string containing the value "red, blue, and green", describing the colors of a sofa, we want to be able to determine whether the letters "b", "l", "u", and "e" appear consecutively in that string. If they do, it is sometimes also useful to know where that sequence of characters starts in the string. To allow us to obtain this information, we have to add a new member function to our string class. Because this function finds a sequence of chars in a string, its name should be something like find. Because it is going to be case-insensitive (e.g., RED, Red, and red will all be considered equal), we'll call it find_nocase.[6]

What do I mean by "case-insensitive"? That when this function looks for a sequence of chars within a string, it considers upper- and lower-case letters as equivalent. We will employ this function in the HomeInventory class functions that will enable us to, for example, search through the home inventory for all HomeItem objects containing the word "purple" in their description fields. Before we look at how this is implemented, let's see how it can be used (Figure 12.9).

FIGURE 12.9. Using string::find_nocase (**code\strtst7b.cc**)

```
#include <iostream.h>
#include "string7.h"

int main()
```

---

6. I made this function case-insensitive after watching Susan's attempt to use a version of the HomeInventory example program that used a case-sensitive searching function. This illustrates why it is absolutely necessary to watch a (hopefully representative) user of a program actually try it before making the assumption that it is "ready for prime time".

```
{
    string x = "purple";
    string y = "A purple couch";
    short where;

    where = y.find_nocase(x);
    cout << "The string " << x <<
        " can be found starting at position " <<
        where << " in the string " << endl;
    cout << y << "." << endl;

    where = x.find_nocase("rp");
    cout << "The string 'rp' can be found starting at position " <<
        where << " in the string " << x << "." << endl;

    where = x.find_nocase("rpx");
    cout << "The string 'rpx' can be found starting at position " <<
        where << " in the string " << x << "." << endl;

    return 0;
}
```

This program starts out by defining some string variables called x and y and initializing them to the values "purple" and "A purple couch", respectively. Then it defines a short value called where that will hold the result of each search for an included sequence of chars. The next line, where = y.find_nocase(x);, calls the find_nocase member function of the string class to locate an occurrence of the value "purple" in the string y, which has the value "A purple couch". The next three lines display the results of that search; as you can see, the return value of this function is equal to the position in string y where the string to be found, "purple", was indeed found.

The other two similar sequences search the same string value (in y) for the literal values "rp" and "rpx", respectively, and display the results of these searches. The first of these is very similar to the previous search for the word "purple", but serves to point out that we don't have to search for a word—any sequence of characters will do.

The last sequence, however, is somewhat different because we are searching for a literal value ("rpx") that is not present in the string we're examining ("A purple couch"). The question, of course, is what value the find_nocase function should return when this happens. Perhaps the most obvious possibility is 0, but that is unfortunately not appropriate because it violates the C and C++ convention that the first position of a string is considered position 0; that is, the return value 0 would signify that the string we were searching for was found at the beginning of the string we were searching in. Therefore, find_nocase returns the value −1 to indicate that the desired value has not been found in the string being examined.

Now that we've seen how to use it, let's take a look at the implementation of find_nocase, which is shown in Figure 12.10.

FIGURE 12.10. The implementation of string::find_nocase **(from code\string7.cc)**

```
short string::find_nocase(const string& Str)
{
   short i;
   short length = m_Length-1;
   short strlength = Str.m_Length-1;

   for (i = 0; i < length-strlength+1; i ++)
     {
     if (strnicmp(m_Data+i,Str.m_Data,strlength) == 0)
       return i;
     }

   return -1;
}
```

This starts out the same way as operator + does: by defining some variables called length and strlength to hold the actual number of chars in the string we're going to examine (i.e., the one pointed to by this) and in the argument string Str, which contains the text for which we're searching, respectively; in both cases the counts exclude the terminating null byte. To make the discussion simpler, let's call the string that might contain the desired value the *target string* and the argument string the *search string*.

Now we get to the heart of the function: the loop that uses strnicmp to compare each possible section of the target string with the search string we're looking for. We haven't discussed the strnicmp function yet, but it's quite similar to memcmp, with two differences:

1. strnicmp ignores case in its comparison, so that (for example) RED, Red, and red all compare as equal.

2. strnicmp is a C string function rather than a C memory manipulation function like memcmp, so it stops when it encounters a null byte.

The first of these characteristics of strnicmp is the reason that we have to use strnicmp rather than memcmp, which is case-sensitive. The second characteristic isn't an advantage when dealing with strings, which can theoretically contain null bytes. However, this isn't a problem in the find_nocase function, as that function applies only to ASCII text that doesn't contain null bytes anyway.

Now let's get back to the discussion of find_nocase. On the first time through the loop, the value of i is 0; therefore, the function call strnicmp(m_Data+i,Str.m_Data,strlength) compares strlength bytes from the beginning of the target string to the same number of bytes in the search string. If the two sets of bytes are equal, the result of the comparison is 0, in which case we have found what we were looking for, and so we exit the loop.

On the other hand, if the result of the comparison is not 0, we have to keep looking. The next step is to increment the value of the loop index i. The second time through the loop, the value of i is 1, so the expression strnicmp(m_Data+i,Str.m_Data,strlength) compares strlength bytes starting at the *second* byte of the target string with the same number of bytes starting at the beginning of the search string. If this comparison is successful, we stop and indicate success; if not, we continue executing the loop until we find a match or run out of data in the target string.

Let's look at an example in more detail. Suppose we are searching through the target string "A purple couch", looking for the search string "purple". The first time through the loop, we compare the first 6 bytes in the target string to the 6 bytes in the search string. Since the first byte of the target string is 'A' and the first byte of the search string is 'p', strnicmp returns a non-zero value to let us know that we haven't yet found a match. Therefore, we have to re-execute the loop. The second time through, we start the comparison at the second byte of the target string and the first byte of the search string; the second byte of the target string is a space, which isn't the same as the 'p' from the search string, so strnicmp returns a non-zero value to let us know that we still haven't found the search string. The third time through the loop, we start the comparison at the third byte of the target string and (as always) the first byte of the search string. Both of these have the value 'p', so strnicmp continues by comparing the fourth byte of the target string with the second byte of the search string. Those also match, so strnicmp continues to compare the rest of the bytes in the two strings until it gets to the end of the search string. This time they all match, so strnicmp returns 0 to let us know that we have found the search string.

Of course, the other possibility is that the search string isn't present in the target string. In that case, strnicmp won't return 0 on any of these passes through the loop, so eventually i will exceed its limit, causing the loop to stop executing. However, there's one thing I haven't explained yet: how we calculate the maximum number of times that we have to execute the loop. If we look at the for loop, we see that the continuation expression is i < length − strlength + 1. Is this the right limit for i, and if so, why?

Well, if the target string is the same length as the search string, then we know that we have to execute the loop only once because there's only one possible place to start comparing two strings of the same length — at the beginning of both strings. If we start i at 0 on the first time through the loop, it will be 1 at the beginning of the second time through the loop, so length − strlength + 1 gives the correct limit (of 1) if length and strlength have the same value. This demonstrates that the expression length − strlength + 1 is correct for the case where the search and target strings are the same length. Now, what about the case where the target string is 1 byte longer than the search string? In that case, there is one extra position in which the search string could be found—namely, starting at the second character of the target string. Continuing with this analysis, each additional character in the target string beyond the length of the search string adds one possible position in which the search string might be found in the target string, and therefore adds 1 to the number of times we might have to go through the loop. Since adding 1 to the value of length will add 1 to the value of the expression length − strlength + 1, that expression will produce the correct limit for any value of length and strlength.

There's one more function in the string class that we need to discuss: less_nocase. Its code is shown in Figure 12.11.

FIGURE 12.11. The less_nocase function (from code\string7.cc)

```
bool string::less_nocase(const string& Str)
{
    short Result;
    short CompareLength;

    if (Str.m_Length < m_Length)
        CompareLength = Str.m_Length;
    else
        CompareLength = m_Length;

    Result = strnicmp(m_Data,Str.m_Data,CompareLength);

    if (Result < 0)
        return true;

    if (Result > 0)
        return false;
```

```
        if (m_Length < Str.m_Length)
            return true;

        return false;
    }
```

This function is exactly the same as the normal operator < function in the string class, except that it uses the strnicmp function rather than the memcmp function used in operator <.[7]

Home, Sweet Home

Now that we have finished discussing our new, improved string class, let's get back to using it to add capabilities to our home inventory project. First on the list is the ability to find an item by searching for a sequence of chars in its description. Before we see how this is implemented, let's take a look at how it is used. Figure 12.12 shows the new application program that uses this feature.

FIGURE 12.12. **The latest home inventory application program (code\hmtst6.cc)**

```
#include <iostream.h>
#include <fstream.h>
#include "vector.h"
#include "string7.h"
#include "hmit6.h"
#include "hmin6.h"

int main()
{
```

---

7. As with the other pre-existing functions in the string class, we won't go over the implementation of the operator < function because it is covered in detail in Chapter 8.

```
        ifstream HomeInfo("home3.in");
        HomeInventory MyInventory;
        HomeItem TempItem;
        string Name;
        string Description;

        MyInventory.LoadInventory(HomeInfo);

        TempItem = MyInventory.FindItemByName("Relish");
        cout << endl;

        TempItem.Edit();
        cout << endl;

        TempItem.FormattedDisplay(cout);
        cout << endl;

        cout << "Please enter a search string: ";
        cin >> Description;

        TempItem = MyInventory.FindItemByDescription(Description);

        if (TempItem.IsNull())
          cout << "Sorry, I couldn't locate that item." << endl;
        else
          TempItem.FormattedDisplay(cout);
        cout << endl;

        return 0;
    }
```

This program starts out just as the previous one did, by loading the inventory from the home3.in input file, looking up the entry whose name is "Relish", and displaying it for editing. Once the user has finished editing the entry, we get to the new part: reading a search string from the user and searching for that item in the inventory by the new FindItemByDescription member function of HomeInventory. Let's go through the changes needed to implement this new feature, starting with the new version of the HomeInventory interface, shown in Figure 12.13.

FIGURE 12.13. The latest version of the HomeInventory **interface (hmin6.h)**

```
//hmin6.h

#include "vector.h"

class HomeInventory
{
public:
   HomeInventory();

   short LoadInventory(ifstream& is);
   void DumpInventory();
   HomeItem FindItemByName(const string& Name);
   HomeItem AddItem();
   short LocateItemByName(const string& Name);
   HomeItem EditItem(const string& Name);

   HomeItem FindItemByDescription(const string& Partial);
   short LocateItemByDescription(const string& Partial);

private:
   vector<HomeItem> m_Home;
};
```

The only new functions added to this interface since the last version (see Figure 11.27) are the two "ItemByDescription" functions that parallel the "ItemByName" functions we implemented previously. However, there's another modification in this and the other new interface files: I've changed all the value arguments of nonnative types to const references, because passing such arguments by const reference is more efficient than passing them by value but just as safe, since it's impossible to accidentally change the calling function's variables through a const reference. For this reason, this is usually the best method of passing arguments of user-defined types. Variables of native types, on the other hand, are most efficiently passed by value because they do not require copy constructors or other overhead when passed in that way, as objects of user-defined types do.

Susan had a question about passing arguments.

Susan: Why does it matter whether an argument is native or user-defined?

Steve: Passing a native variable by value (i.e., copying it) is efficient because it's a simple "bunch of bits"; there's no need to worry about pointers and the like. On the other hand, copying a user-defined variable requires a lot more work because the compiler has to call the copy constructor for that type of variable.

Now let's take a look at the first of the two new functions, HomeInventory::FindItemByDescription, shown in Figure 12.14.

FIGURE 12.14. HomeInventory::FindItemByDescription (**from code\hmin6.cc**)

```
HomeItem HomeInventory::FindItemByDescription(
  const string& Partial)
{
    short i;
    string Description;
    bool Found = false;
    short ItemCount = m_Home.size();

    for (i = 0; i < ItemCount; i ++)
      {
      Description = m_Home[i].GetDescription();
      if (Description.find_nocase(Partial) >= 0)
        {
        Found = true;
        break;
```

```
    }
  }

  if (Found == true)
    return m_Home[i];

  return HomeItem();
}
```

This function is very similar to FindItemByName, so I won't go over it in excruciating detail. The main difference between the two is that FindItemByDescription uses the new find_nocase function to locate an occurrence of a search string named Partial in the description of each HomeItem object in the m_Home vector. To do this, it retrieves the description from a HomeItem object, using the GetDescription member function, and stores it in a string called (imaginatively enough) Description. Then it calls find_nocase to see if there is an occurrence of Partial in the Description string. If so, it leaves the loop and returns the object whose description contained the contents of the Partial argument; otherwise, it executes the loop again. This continues until it either finds a match or runs out of items to examine. In the latter case, it returns a null HomeItem to indicate that it couldn't find what the user was looking for.

However, this latter possibility means that we need an IsNull member function in the HomeItem class so that the calling program can tell whether it has received a null HomeItem. To see this and the other (relatively minor) changes to the HomeItem interface, let's take a look at the new version of that interface, which is shown in Figure 12.15.

FIGURE 12.15. The new version of the HomeItem **interface (code\hmit6.h)**

```
// hmit6.h

#include "string7.h"
#include "vector.h"
```

```
class HomeItem
{
friend ostream& operator << (ostream& os,
  const HomeItem& Item);

friend istream& operator >> (istream& is, HomeItem& Item);

public:
  HomeItem();
  HomeItem(const HomeItem& Item);
  HomeItem& operator = (const HomeItem& Item);
virtual ~HomeItem();

// Basic: Art objects, furniture, jewelry, etc.
  HomeItem(const string& Name, double PurchasePrice,
  long PurchaseDate, const string& Description,
  const string& Category);

// Music: CDs, LPs, cassettes, etc.
  HomeItem(const string& Name, double PurchasePrice,
  long PurchaseDate, const string& Description,
  const string& Category, const string& Artist,
  const vector<string>& Track);

virtual void Write(ostream& os);
virtual short FormattedDisplay(ostream& os);
virtual string GetName();
virtual string GetDescription();
virtual bool IsNull();
static HomeItem NewItem();

virtual void Read(istream& is);
virtual void Edit();

protected:
  HomeItem(int);
virtual HomeItem* CopyData();
```

```
protected:
  HomeItem* m_Worker;
  short m_Count;
};
```

Susan had a couple of questions about this new version of the interface.

Susan: Why didn't you put the destructor at the end of the interface? After all, it is the last function to be executed.

Steve: I always put the "concrete data type" functions together at the beginning of the public section of the interface. That makes them easier to find.

Susan: Why aren't the constructors virtual if the destructor is?

Steve: Constructors can't be virtual, because the whole point of a virtual function is to allow the program to use the actual type of an object to determine which function is called. When we call a constructor to create an object, the object doesn't exist yet, so there would be no way to determine which virtual function should be called.

As with the HomeInventory class, I've changed all the string arguments to const string& to improve efficiency by preventing excessive copying. I've done the same with the Track argument to the HomeItemMusic normal constructor; it's now a const vector<string>& rather than a vector<string>, as in the previous version of the header. I've also added two new functions: GetDescription and IsNull. As usual, the HomeItem versions of these functions merely call the corresponding virtual function in the worker object and pass the results back to the calling function. As for the HomeItemBasic version of GetDescription, this function just returns the current value of the m_Description field in its object, so we don't have to bother analyzing it. IsNull is pretty simple too, but we should still take a look at its implementation, shown in Figure 12.16.

FIGURE 12.16. HomeItemBasic::IsNull **(from code\hmit6.cc)**

```
bool HomeItemBasic::IsNull()
{
  if (m_Name == "")
    return true;

  return false;
}
```

The idea here is that every actual HomeItem has to have a name, so any object that doesn't have one must be a null HomeItem. Therefore, we check whether the name is null. If so, we have a null item, so we return true; otherwise, it's a real item, so we return false to indicate that it's not null.

Of course, we don't have to reimplement IsNull in HomeItemMusic because we can use the HomeItemBasic version of this function should we need to check whether a HomeItemMusic object is "real" or null.

Nothing Ventured, Nothing Gained

There's only one more point I want to mention before we leave the HomeItemBasic code. After I started using the new version of the string class, I got a compiler error in the constructor for HomeItemBasic. This was hard to understand because surely I hadn't changed anything in the string class that should cause it to stop working in situations where it had previously been operating properly. The problem turned out to be a slight oddity in the coding of the member initialization list in a previous version of the HomeItemBasic code. We discussed this code in Chapter 11 in the section entitled "Stereo Typing" on page 781, but at that time I deferred the explanation of how I found the error. For reference, Figure 12.17 is another listing of the code that gave me the problem after I changed to the new string class.

FIGURE 12.17. A slightly odd default constructor for HomeItem **(from code\hmit2.cc)**

```
HomeItemBasic::HomeItemBasic()
: HomeItem(1),
  m_Name(),
  m_PurchasePrice(0),
  m_PurchaseDate(0),
  m_Description(0),
  m_Category(0)
{
}
```

As I mentioned previously, it's the 0 value for m_Description and m_Category that caused the problem. Those are string variables, but the compiler didn't complain when I initialized them with a value of 0. The reason is that 0 is a "magic number" in C and C++: Among its other special characteristics, it is an acceptable value for any type of pointer. In this example, the compiler considered it as a char*, so the string::string(char*) constructor was being called to initialize the strings m_Description and m_Category to the value of the "char*" 0. This would not work very well, as the data stored at address 0 is unlikely to be anything we want to use. Therefore, it's a good thing that the compiler caught this in hmit6.cc. But why did this error suddenly surface when I changed to the new string class, when the compiler was happy to take a 0 previously?

The trigger was the new constructor that we added to implement the string concatenation function—the one that makes a string from a short value. Because 0 is a legal short as well as a legal char*, the compiler couldn't tell which of these I wanted and therefore gave an error message for each occurrence of this mistake—one message for the description field and one for the category field. Figure 12.18 shows the error messages.

FIGURE 12.18. Error messages triggered by accidental use of 0 to initialize a string (code\hmit6a.err)

```
hmit6a.cc: In method 'HomeItemBasic::HomeItemBasic()':
hmit6a.cc:208: call of overloaded constructor 'string(int)' is ambiguous
string7.h:14: candidates are: string::string(const string &)
string7.h:18:           string::string(char *)
string7.h:19:           string::string(short int, char)
hmit6a.cc:208: in base initialization for class 'string'
hmit6a.cc:208: call of overloaded constructor 'string(int)' is ambiguous
string7.h:14: candidates are: string::string(const string &)
string7.h:18:           string::string(char *)
string7.h:19:           string::string(short int, char)
hmit6a.cc:208: in base initialization for class 'string'
```

What's the moral of this story? I'm not sure, other than "Watch out for 0".[8]

Putting It All Together

When first writing this part of this chapter, I thought that we had already covered everything needed to build a real application program that would allow the user to create, update, and find items in the database with reasonable ease and convenience. The main program

---

8. You may wonder why this error occurred even though we defined the string(short, char) constructor to be explicit, which means that it shouldn't be considered in an expression that seems to refer to it implicitly. The answer is that a member initialization expression is considered an explicit constructor call, and so even constructors that are labeled as explicit are considered as possible matches for such an expression.

for my first attempt at this was called hmtst7.cc. When Susan tried it out and then read the code, it had quite an effect on her, as indicated in this letter she wrote to her sister.

> **Susan:** I had another revelation over programming last night. After having read hundreds of pages of this book, Steve showed me the Home Inventory program that we are writing. Annie, it is the smallest little program that you can imagine. Just in DOS, and it is so simple. But I have just spent weeks tearing my hair out trying to understand how it all comes together, it is so complicated, and JUST SO HARD.
>
> Then Steve shows me the program [running] and IT LOOKS LIKE NOTHING! I could not believe it. I just see this little menu on the screen and yet I know what is behind it. At least 1500 lines of code including 7 different header files. If you saw this program [run] you would laugh. It is just so basic. But if you saw what went into it you would die. It is nothing less than pure genius. As I told Steve yesterday it is like having a steak dinner but having not to just cook the meat, but having to go kill the cow. He corrected me, it is like having to make the gun first to kill the cow and invent fire and a grill to cook it.
>
> You have to write everything, and I mean all of it. That includes the meaning for = and all the other operators. Unbelievable. Then I looked at Windows 95 and said, then "What is in this?" Steve said "About 5 million lines of code." Computers look like they are technological miracles. And they are. But behind them is nothing but sheer, old fashioned, genius of man. And it is all hard work. It looks like a miracle but there is no magic.

If you wish, you can try the program yourself, but I won't be reproducing the code here because it turned out that it was far from finished. You see, as stunned as Susan may have been by the complexity of this program, she wasn't too amazed to tell me what was wrong with it and how it could be improved. Here's her "wish list", along with my responses.

First Test Session: Change Requests and Problem Reports

1. Presenting the menu options in different colors.

   Can't be done with standard C++ input/output functions.

2. Showing the list of names below the menu rather than above.

3. Putting the menu in the center of the screen rather than at the top.

   These two changes became irrelevant after I redesigned the program to use the screen more efficiently.

4. Sorting the items by name rather than by the order in which they were originally entered.

   Done, via a new HomeInventory::SortInventoryByName member function (but see later comments on problems with this function).

5. Being able to move to the next matching item if there is more than one (on a partial field match).

   Wrote several HomeInventory member functions to assist in handling multiple matching entries (for more details, see "handling more entries than will fit on the screen", below).

6. Removing an item.

   Done.

7. Making a list of categories and displaying it when adding a new item.

   Not done, for reasons indicated below.

While watching Susan use the program, I came up with my own list of problems that needed to be fixed and some other improvements in addition to the ones she mentioned above.

8. The error message for an invalid entry is poorly formatted.

   Added functions for error reporting.

9. An error in entering a numeric value isn't handled properly.

   Same as above.

10. There's no indication to the user as to how the date or amount fields are supposed to be entered (YYYYMMDD and a number with a decimal point but no $ or comma, respectively).

    Added a note in the input prompt indicating proper data entry format.

11. An invalid date entry (i.e., other than a valid YYYYMMDD date) should be detected and reported to the user.

    Added code to check for this problem: The date must be at least 19000101 (but see later discussion of problems with this solution).

12. The user should be able to determine how many items are in the inventory.

    Added a line at the top of the menu indicating how many elements are currently in the inventory.

13. Allowing the user to select an item from a list of all items that meet some criterion (e.g., name, description).

    Added selection functions as noted above for this purpose.

14. Handling a list containing more entries than will fit on the screen at one time.

    Wrote a selection function in a new HomeUtility class to allow scrolling through any number of items.

15. Continuing rather than aborting when an error is detected.

Handled most of these problems by improved error checking in the code; further problems surfaced later and were noted where they occurred.

16. Saving the data during the execution of the program.

Not handled in this version of the program.

17. Backing up the old database before writing over it.

Not done; left as an exercise.

18. If the user asks to delete an item, the program should ask, "Are you sure?"

Done.

Amazingly, the hardest one of these turned out to be the "list of categories". In fact, I didn't implement this at all because it would have required a fairly significant reconstruction of the structure of classes in the program. The problem with this seemingly simple request is that the category list would have to be generated in the HomeInventory member function (because each HomeItem has only one category value out of all those in use, not the entire list). However, the list would need to be used in the HomeItem classes because that's where the user needs to specify the category. Getting the data from the HomeInventory object to the appropriate HomeItem object would be difficult because the existing HomeItem functions don't have any facilities for doing this. While there are ways to solve such problems, they would take us too far afield to be worth the trip in this particular case, since the category listing is not absolutely essential to the usability of the program.

After finishing the above revisions to the program, I renamed the main program hmtst8.cc, compiled all of the files to produce hmtst8.exe, and tested it myself until I was satisfied that it worked. Then I had Susan give it another test. I fully expected that she would be happy with the new functionality and would find the program pretty much bullet-proof. Here are my notes from that second test session, along with my determination of the cause of the problem or question.

Second Test Session: Change Requests and Problem Reports

1. Adding a new Music item with a bad date such as "1997/02/15" (instead of 19970215) caused the program to abort with a fatal error.

   This was caused by my forgetting to check the return value of the HomeItemBasic version of the input function when calling it from the corresponding HomeItemMusic function.

2. The sorting algorithm used to put the items into alphabetical order sorts lowercase letters after uppercase ones. It should ignore case.

   This problem was caused by the use of <, which is case-sensitive, to compare strings. I fixed this by adding a less_nocase function to the string class and using that function in the sorting algorithm instead of <.

3. If the user typed in an item number that was not valid, the program exited with an illegal vector element error message.

   I added code to check whether the item number was valid and to ignore an invalid number rather than end the program.

Susan had some other comments and questions after using this version of the program.

   Susan: The Music items should be listed separately from the other items.

Steve: What if you want to see all the items in your inventory? That may not seem to make sense with CDs and furniture, but what about when we add the clothing, appliance, and other types?

Susan: I don't want them jumbled together.

Steve: Well, we could add separate functions for showing things of each type, but I'm not sure how valuable the discussion of all those functions would be. I know, I'll make it an exercise!

Susan: Okay. Now, I noticed that if you type in something illegal (like a bad date) you have to start over again rather than being able to fix it right there.

Steve: Yes, that's true. It would make another good exercise to add the ability to continue entering data for the same item after an error. Thanks for the suggestion!

Susan: As long as I don't have to do it. I also have some other questions about the dates. What if I got something by inheritance and it was originally bought before 1900? Also, what if I don't know the date when I bought something? Can I type in ???????

Steve: I'll make the starting date 1800 rather than 1900. As for using question marks to mean "I don't know": that won't work because the input routine is checking for a numeric value. However, I'll change it so you can use 0 to mean "I don't know when I got it". How's that?

Susan: That's okay. However, I noticed one more thing. It would let me type 19931822 (the 22nd day of the 18th month of 1993). Shouldn't it check for legal dates?

Steve: Yes, that would be a good . . . exercise!

After making all these changes, I recompiled and tested the program, then gave it to Susan to see what she could do with (or to) it. Here are my notes of that trial along with how I handled the points that came up.

Third Test Session: Change Requests and Problem Reports

1. On a screen with only 25 lines, it was pretty easy to overflow the available space when editing a long item. This resulted in a very messy display.

   I changed the program to clear the screen before editing an item. Now the entire screen was available to display the item rather than the main menu being on the screen all the time.

2. If the user typed something other than just hitting the ENTER key after a message that said "ENTER to continue", the other keystrokes were interpreted as menu selections.

   I added code to ignore any keystrokes preceding an ENTER in that situation.

3. When the user typed an invalid item number, the program just ignored it rather than giving any indication of an error.

   I added code to display an "invalid item number" message in such a situation.

4. The routine that asked for an item number didn't handle backspaces correctly.

   I changed the routine to fix that problem.

5. If there weren't any items matching the user's selection criterion, the selection area was blank with no other indication of what had happened.

I added code to provide a "No items found" error message.

6. The "category" field was pretty useless, as it couldn't be used for selecting items.

I added a "select by category" menu item, which displays the category as well as the name of the item.

In addition to these changes, this version of the program also implemented a "crash protection" feature, which automatically saves the latest version of the database in a separate file every time a change is made to any item or an item is added or deleted. This might be a problem in terms of performance if the database gets to be very large, but I think it's worth it overall; without such a feature, the user could spend an hour or two typing in data and then have a power failure (or a program bug for that matter) and lose all that work.

Another item that might be useful (especially with long descriptions), but isn't essential in getting the program to work, is the ability to edit a text field without typing it all in again. That's the topic of another exercise at the end of this chapter.

After making all of these changes and testing them to make sure they seemed to work, I went back to the well one more time. Here are the results of this go-round.

Fourth Test Session: Change Requests and Problem Reports

1. If Susan typed in a category that didn't exist, the program aborted with a "virtual memory exceeded" error.

The problem here turned out to be my attempt to format the category listing header. If the header was longer than the actual category names, the code calculated a negative number of characters of padding. Then it tried to create a string of that number of spaces by calling the string constructor that takes a short number of characters. When this constructor called the new operator to allocate the space for the padding, it passed the negative number of characters along to new. However, new doesn't expect to get a negative argument as the number of objects to create, and so it interpreted that negative value as a very large positive number. When it tried to allocate that number of characters, the underlying memory allocation routines couldn't handle the request and terminated the program after giving that error message. I fixed this by correcting the formatting logic so that the program wouldn't ask for a negative amount of padding.

2. The code to display an error if there were no items found wasn't working.

   I changed the "wait for CR" code to fix this.

3. The name and category header wasn't lined up properly with the actual name and category entries for item numbers greater than 9 (i.e., more than one digit).

   I changed the formatting of the selection function to fix the width of the item number at 5 digits rather than as variable according to the size of the item number. This made it much easier to line the header up with the data.

Susan had another suggestion to make the program easier to use, as well as a question about the category listing function.

Susan: How about letting the user type the date in with the slashes, as YYYY/MM/DD?

Steve: That would make a good exercise too.

Susan: How does the category listing function know where to put the categories on the screen?

Steve: It goes through the items once to figure out how long the names are and once to do the formatting. Thus, by the time it does the formatting, it knows how long the longest item name is. We'll go over exactly how that works when we get to that function, SelectItemFromCategoryList (Figure 13.25 on page 964).

After making all the changes indicated above, I had Susan try it once more, with the following results.

Fifth Test Session: Change Requests and Problem Reports

1. There wasn't any way to cancel the "Add item" operation if the user decided not to do that after starting the operation.

   I added code to allow ENTER to cancel the "Add item" operation.

2. Susan wanted to know how she could use the "Find item by category" operation if she didn't remember which category she was looking for.

   Here is one of the rare times when a program has a desired feature that the programmer didn't think to add explicitly. As it happens, all you have to do is hit ENTER when you are asked for the category name, and it will include items from all categories. I changed the prompt to inform the user about this feature. Since this serendipitous feature also works when the user is asked for a description or name, I changed those prompts as well.

After all these changes, I finally had a program that seemed to work properly according to a representative user's expectations for it. We'll start our analysis of this final version of the home inventory program shortly, but first we should take a look at the development process that I've just described.

Round and Round We Go

Most books on programming present the software development process as a linear progression from the beginning to the end of a project with no detours on the way. However, this is a very misleading picture of what is actually an iterative process: Every actual project requires a lot of feedback from users. It also requires considerable time spent correcting errors that may have been overlooked in previous revisions or introduced while adding new features (or even fixing old bugs). The whole process often involves one step back (or sideways) for each several steps forward.

In fact, even the picture I just presented of the incremental implementation of the home inventory program up to this point is over-simplified. I left out a number of occasions on which designing and implementing a new feature took several attempts, including adding further infrastructure support (e.g., the less_nocase function in the string class).

This may seem odd. After all, programming is not a "soft" subject; for any given program, it should be fairly easy to decide whether it works or it doesn't.[9] The error in this analysis is that even relatively simple programs (such as the one we've spent so much time on) are complex constructs that display a wide range of behavior. Given this complexity, determining whether a given program "works" is anything but trivial; otherwise, I wouldn't have needed Susan to test the program after I finished my own testing. In fact, on virtually every occasion when I had her test a new version of the program in which I had made significant changes, she found some anomaly that necessitated further work. This is anything but unusual; in fact, some

---

9. Actually, this is not true in theory. It was proven many years ago that it is impossible in the general case even to determine whether a particular program will run forever or stop, given a particular set of input, by any mechanical means. This is the famous "halting problem" of Alan Turing. In practice, however, it is usually possible to determine whether a meaningful program works correctly, although this may be quite difficult to do.

large software companies send out thousands of copies of each of their major programs to be tested before they release them, in the hope of finding most of the bugs before the paying customers find them (and get upset). Of course, those programs are much more complicated than the little one we've been developing, but the principle is the same: If a program hasn't been tested, it will have bugs.[10]

Luckily, by using the techniques I've illustrated, it's possible to produce programs that should have fewer bugs, and bugs that are less difficult to find.[11] Hopefully, the program that we'll finish in the next chapter won't have many bugs left by the time we get through with it. First, though, it's time for some review of what we've done so far.

Review

We started this chapter by improving the string class that we created in Chapters 7 and 8, so that we could add some new functionality to the home inventory program. Before we added any new functions to this class, the first modification we made was to add an **include guard**, which is a means of preventing the C++ compiler from seeing the same class definition more than one time for a given source code file. Implementing the include guard required us to look at some very old parts of C++ dating back to the early days of C: the **preprocessor** and its **preprocessor symbols**. The preprocessor was originally a separate program that was executed before the compiler itself, but nowadays it is often physically part of the compiler. Most of its

---

10. According to a very well known principle called "Murphy's Law", even if a program has been tested, it will still have bugs.

11. By the way, if you find any bugs in this or any of the other sample programs, which is certainly possible despite my (and Susan's) testing, please let me know so that I can fix them for the next printing of this book.

features are no longer needed in C++, but we still need it to create an include guard as well as to handle included header files—its most common use these days.

Once we finished with that discussion, we examined another C++ feature that we hadn't seen before: the **default argument**. This gives us the ability to specify a value for an argument when the user of a function doesn't supply one. By using a default argument, we were able to write one constructor for the string class that could create a string of a specified number of characters, which would all be set to a given character value. If the user of this constructor did not specify the character value he or she wanted, the constructor would set all the characters to 0; if the user specified a particular character value, the constructor would of course use that one. Using default arguments is optional; we could have written two different constructors to accomplish the same goal, but it is less work to write one constructor. This also reduces the total amount of source code in the system, which should improve reliability.

The next topic of discussion was the **explicit** keyword, which allows us to specify that a particular constructor should be called only when we explicitly ask for it. Unless we specify this keyword when we create a constructor with only one required argument, that constructor can be called automatically whenever we specify an actual argument of one type and we need an argument of a different type. For example, if we have a non-explicit constructor for the string class that takes a short argument, then any place where a string is required as an argument, we can supply a short value instead—the constructor will be called automatically to convert the short to a string. While this can be a very handy facility (as in the case of supplying a char* argument where a string argument was expected), it can also be very hazardous where it does something that the user doesn't expect. In the case of the string(short) constructor, somehow I doubt that anyone would expect a value of 5, for example, to be converted to a string of five null bytes! To prevent this, we made that constructor explicit so that this would not occur without the user's being aware of it.

After dealing with that new keyword, we went over the implementation of the new constructor for the string class. Then we examined exactly why we needed it in the first place: to allow us to implement a concatenation operator for the string class. We used operator + as the notation for this new operation, which might seem odd at first sight. However, this is a very common way to express the idea of tacking one string onto the end of another, and has been adopted as such in the C++ standard library, so we might as well use it here too.

The next question we tackled was why we need the ability to concatenate strings at this point in the project. The reason is that it allows us to improve the implementation of operator >> for strings. The problem with the previous version of this operator was that it could not handle strings of arbitrary length but was limited to those of 79 characters or less. Because it was possible that some fields in the home inventory data (especially the description) might be quite long, it was important for us to improve this operator so that it could handle strings of any length. To do this, we needed the ability to concatenate two strings.

After analyzing the code in operator >> that handles long strings in a number of sections, we continued to the next new member function in the string class: find_nocase. This function looks for a sequence of chars within a particular string, an ability that we need to implement the functions that allow the user to find items whose descriptions or other fields contain a specified sequence of characters. During the discussion of this function, we ran across a new C library function called strnicmp, which compares two C strings without considering the case of the characters in them. This is an important feature to provide because the user may not remember the case of the word for which he or she is looking.

The next and final new member function in the string class is less_nocase. It is exactly like the normal operator < function in the string class, except that it uses the strnicmp function to do the comparison so that upper- and lower-case characters will be compared without regard to considering their case. This was necessary in the implementation of the sorting routine in SortInventoryByName.

After finishing the discussion of the find_nocase function, we looked at an example program that illustrates the use of one of the newly added "find" functions, FindItemByDescription, which, as its name suggests, searches for an item whose description field contains a particular sequence of characters. After a brief description of this new example program, we started to tackle the latest version of the HomeInventory class, hmin6.h. Besides adding the new member functions needed to support searching for items by name or description, I took this opportunity to change the argument-passing conventions of all of the member functions that previously used value arguments of user-defined types to use const references instead. This is usually the best way to pass arguments of user-defined types because it avoids the necessity of making a copy of the argument. Arguments of native types, on the other hand, typically are best passed by value, as copying them is not very expensive.

Next, we discussed FindItemByDescription, which is very similar to the previously defined FindItemByName, except that it uses the new find_nocase function to search for an item that matches the user's partial description.

At this point, we were ready to look at the next version of the HomeItem interface, hmit6.h, which differs from the previous version of this interface in a few minor ways. First, I changed all the arguments of user-defined types to use const references rather than pass-by-value, just as I did with the HomeInventory class. I also added two new functions, GetDescription and IsNull. Neither of these functions is at all complicated, so we passed over them quickly.

At this point, I mentioned a compile-time error that surfaced in the normal constructor for the HomeItemBasic class. I had a bit of trouble figuring out why I should get an error just from using a new version of the string class when I had merely added a couple of new functions to that class. It turned out that the constructor in question was written incorrectly; it was trying to initialize a string variable with the value 0. The compiler was willing to accept the value 0 as a char*, so it automatically applied the string constructor that creates a string from a char* value. Once we defined another constructor that accepted a short argument, however, the value 0 could be interpreted as either a char* or a short value, so the compiler complained that our initialization expression was ambiguous. This saved us from a potentially nasty bug because we certainly wouldn't want to try to use whatever random data might be at memory address 0 to initialize a string variable!

After dealing with that compiler issue, I fondly believed that I had all the pieces to complete the home inventory project. Therefore, I wrote what I thought would be the final version of the program and submitted it to my beta tester, Susan, for her approval. I was quite surprised to discover that we still had a long way to go. After she had taken a look at the program, both in execution and in source code, we embarked on a voyage of discovery to find and fix errors and inconveniences, and to find ways to improve the functioning of the program. The next 10 pages or so of the chapter consisted of a repeated cycle of the following steps:

1. Susan's trying the program while I watched;

2. My fixing the problems she discovered and adding new features that would make the program easier to use.

Most of the changes I made fell into three main categories: fixing errors (including improved error handling), cosmetic changes (such as position of items on the screen), and improvements to the functioning of the program (such as allowing the user to select items by category). There were also a few changes that I didn't make because they would have required effort out of proportion to their importance in the functioning of the program. Instead, I left them as exercises, which you will see at the end of the next chapter, after we have gone over the code of the final version of the program.

Exercises

1. Write a version of operator += for the string class. This function should concatenate its right-hand argument to its left-hand argument.

2. Draw a picture of the functioning of the concatenation operator for strings when it is concatenating the value "Steve" onto a string containing the value "Hello, ". Please note that there is a space before the second quotation mark in the latter value.

3. Draw a picture of the functioning of the operator >> function for strings when it is reading data for a string of 85 characters.

4. Draw a picture of the operation of the find_nocase function when it is searching for the value "purple" in a string with the value "A purple couch".

Conclusion

In this chapter, we brought our home inventory project from humble beginnings to the threshold of greatness. In the process, we learned about a number of features of C++ that we hadn't needed before. In the next chapter, we'll finish the job that we started so many pages ago.

CHAPTER 13

Stealing Home

In this chapter, we will take the home inventory program to the stage of actual usability. I hope that in this process you will develop a better notion of how much work it takes to create even a relatively simple program that solves its users' problems in a natural and convenient way. We'll get started as soon as we cover some definitions and objectives.

Definitions

A **cursor** is an abstract object that represents the position on the screen where input or output will occur next.

The **global name space** is a name for the set of identifiers that is visible to all functions without a class name being specified.

Objectives of This Chapter

By the end of this chapter you should have:

1. Learned how to use a class to group a number of functions together even if they don't have any associated data;

2. Learned how to write an "endless" loop to execute a section of code an indefinite number of times;

3. Learned how to check numeric input for validity and give the user a reasonable error message if that input is invalid;

4. Learned how to obtain keyboard input without having to wait for the user to hit the ENTER key;

5. Learned how to write output on the screen at a particular position;

6. Learned how to clear the screen or an individual line on the screen;

7. Learned how to display part of a list on the screen, scrolling the rest of the list on and off the screen as necessary;

8. Learned how to use the string concatenation operator to aid in the formatting of data;

9. Learned how to compare and sort string data without regard for case;

10. Learned how to print data on the printer, including the use of the "form feed" character to ensure that any further data sent to the printer will start on a new page;

11. Learned how to delete an item from a list kept in a vector;

12. Improved our home inventory program sufficiently that a user could employ it to keep track of his or her possessions.

The Final Voyage

Now let's get to the detailed analysis of the final version of the home inventory program. We'll start with the main() function of this program, which is shown in Figure 13.1.

FIGURE 13.1. The main() function of the final version of the home inventory main program (from code\hmtst8.cc)

```
int main()
{
  ifstream HomeInfo("home.inv");
  HomeInventory MyInventory;
  char option;
  string answer;

  MyInventory.LoadInventory(HomeInfo);

  for (;;)
    {
    option = GetMenuChoice(MyInventory);

    if (option == Exit)
      break;
    else
      ExecuteMenuChoice(option,MyInventory);
    }

  HomeInfo.close();

  for (;;)
    {
    cout << "Save the changes you have made? (Y/N) ";
    cin >> answer;

    if ((answer == "Y") || (answer == "y"))
      {
      ofstream NewHomeInfo("home.inv");
```

```
            MyInventory.StoreInventory(NewHomeInfo);
            cout << "Inventory updated" << endl;
            break;
            }
        else if ((answer == "N") || (answer == "n"))
            {
            cout << "Changes cancelled" << endl;
            break;
            }
        else
            clrscr();
        }

    return 0;
    }
```

This starts off much like the previous versions, by creating a HomeInventory object called MyInventory and loading it with data from an input file called home.inv. Then it enters an "endless" for loop that calls the GetMenuChoice function to find out what operation the user wants to perform, and finally then calls the ExecuteMenuChoice function to perform that operation.

We haven't yet used an "endless" loop, which is written as "for (;;)".[1] Since we haven't specified any initialization, modification, or continuation expression, such a loop will run until it is interrupted by a break or return statement. In this case, the break statement is executed when the user indicates that he or she is finished with the program by entering the code for "exit" in the GetMenuChoice function.

Once the user is done entering, modifying, and examining data, the second "endless" for loop asks the user whether any changes should be made permanent by being written out to the home.inv file. If the user answers "y" or "Y", the changes are written out; if the answer is "n" or "N", the changes aren't written out. In either case,

---

1. One possible pronunciation of this construct is "forever".

the "endless" loop is terminated, as is the program immediately afterward. If the user doesn't type a valid character, the program keeps asking the question until it gets an answer it likes.

So much for the bird's-eye view of the program. Now let's take a more detailed look at how it works. The first topic we'll examine is where that Exit value came from. This question is answered by the enum defined in Figure 13.2.

FIGURE 13.2. The MenuItem enum **(from code\hmtst8.cc)**

```
enum MenuItem {AddItem=1, SelectItemFromNameList,
    EditByPartialName, EditByDescription, EditByCategory,
    DeleteItemFromNameList, PrintNames, PrintAll, Exit
};
```

As you can see, this enum lists all of the possible menu choices from which the user can select. I've put it at the top of the hmtst8.cc source file because the values it defines are needed in more than one function in the main program, and that's the easiest way to make these values available to several functions.

Next, let's look at the GetMenuChoice function, shown in Figure 13.3.

FIGURE 13.3. The GetMenuChoice **function (from code\hmtst8.cc)**

```
char GetMenuChoice(HomeInventory& Inventory)
{
    short MenuColumn = 1;
    short MenuRow;
    short option;

    for (;;)
    {
        clrscr();

        cout << Inventory.GetCount() << " items in database." << endl;
```

```
cout << endl;

cout << AddItem << ". Add item" << endl;

cout << SelectItemFromNameList <<
  ". Select item name from list" << endl;

cout << EditByPartialName <<
  ". Edit item by partial name" << endl;

cout << EditByDescription <<
  ". Edit item by description" << endl;

cout << EditByCategory <<
  ". Edit item by category" << endl;

cout << DeleteItemFromNameList <<
  ". Delete item" << endl;

cout << PrintNames <<
  ". Print item names" << endl;

cout << PrintAll << ". Print data base" << endl;

cout << Exit << ". Exit" << endl;

cout << endl;

cout << "Please enter a number from " <<
  AddItem << " to " << Exit << ": ";

cin >> option;

if ((option >= AddItem) && (option <= Exit))
  break;
else
  HomeUtility::HandleError("Sorry, that's an invalid option.");
}
```

```
clrscr();

return option;
}
```

Most of this code is pretty simple, but there are a few new twists. To start with, we're using a screen control function that we haven't seen before: clrscr. This function clears the screen so that we can start writing text on it without worrying about what might already be there.

Once the screen has been cleared, we display each of the menu choices on the screen and ask the user to type in the number of the operation to be performed. Next, we check the entered number to make sure that it is one of the legal values. If it is, we break out of the "endless" loop, clear the screen again so that the function we're going to perform has a fresh canvas to paint on, and return the number of the operation the user selected. On the other hand, if the user has typed in an invalid value, we call a utility function called HomeUtility::HandleError that notifies the user of the error; then we continue in the "endless" loop until we get a valid answer to our question.[2]

Susan had some questions about this function, so we discussed it.

Susan: Is this GetMenuChoice function listing the choices on the screen?

Steve: Yes.

Susan: How does it know how to put the number of the selection in front of each one?

---

2.   We'll get to the purpose and implementation of the HomeUtility class member functions in the section "Utility Room" on page 926.

Steve: That's how enum values are displayed by operator <<. That's why each line begins with one of the values from the MenuItem enum.

Susan: How did you know to use the clrscr function to clear the screen?

Steve: I read the documentation for the compiler.

Susan: But how did you know there even was such a function?

Steve: Because I've used it before.

Susan: Well, what if it was the first time you ever needed it?

Steve: Then I would either have to read a book (like this one) or ask somebody. It's just like learning about anything else.

Once we know which operation the user wants to perform, main calls the final function in the main program, ExecuteMenuChoice (Figure 13.4).

FIGURE 13.4. ExecuteMenuChoice **(from code\hmtst8.cc)**

```
void ExecuteMenuChoice(char option, HomeInventory& Inventory)
{
  short itemno;
  ofstream Printer("lpt1");
  string Name;
  string Description;
  string Category;

  switch (option)
    {
    case AddItem:
      {
      cout << "Adding item" << endl << endl;
```

```
    Inventory.AddItem();
    ofstream SaveHomeInfo("home.$$$");
    Inventory.StoreInventory(SaveHomeInfo);
    }
break;

case SelectItemFromNameList:
  cout << "Selecting item from whole inventory";
  cout << endl << endl;
  itemno = Inventory.SelectItemFromNameList();
  if (itemno != -1)
    {
    Inventory.EditItem(itemno);
    ofstream SaveHomeInfo("home.$$$");
    Inventory.StoreInventory(SaveHomeInfo);
    }
break;

case EditByPartialName:
  cout << "Selecting item by partial name";
  cout << endl << endl;
  cout << "Please enter part of the name of the item ";
  cout << "(or ENTER for all items): ";
  cin >> Name;
  cout << endl;
  itemno = Inventory.SelectItemByPartialName(Name);
  if (itemno != -1)
    {
    Inventory.EditItem(itemno);
    ofstream SaveHomeInfo("home.$$$");
    Inventory.StoreInventory(SaveHomeInfo);
    }
break;

case EditByDescription:
  cout << "Selecting item by partial description";
  cout << endl << endl;
  cout << "Please enter part of the description of the item ";
  cout << "(or ENTER for all items): ";
```

```
    cin >> Description;
    cout << endl;

    itemno =
      Inventory.SelectItemFromDescriptionList(Description);

    if (itemno != -1)
      {
      Inventory.EditItem(itemno);
      ofstream SaveHomeInfo("home.$$$");
      Inventory.StoreInventory(SaveHomeInfo);
      }
  break;

  case EditByCategory:
    cout << "Selecting item by partial category";
    cout << endl << endl;
    cout << "Please enter part or all of the category name ";
    cout << "(or ENTER for all categories): ";
    cin >> Category;
    cout << endl;

    itemno =
      Inventory.SelectItemFromCategoryList(Category);

    if (itemno != -1)
      {
      Inventory.EditItem(itemno);
      ofstream SaveHomeInfo("home.$$$");
      Inventory.StoreInventory(SaveHomeInfo);
      }
  break;

  case DeleteItemFromNameList:
    cout << "Deleting item" << endl << endl;
    itemno = Inventory.SelectItemFromNameList();
    if (itemno != -1)
      {
      string Query;
```

```
            cout << "Are you sure you want to delete item ";
            cout << itemno + 1 << " (Y/N)? ";
            cin >> Query;
            if (Query.find_nocase("Y") == 0)
               {
               Inventory.DeleteItem(itemno);
               ofstream SaveHomeInfo("home.$$$");
               Inventory.StoreInventory(SaveHomeInfo);
               }
            }
         break;

         case PrintNames:
            Inventory.PrintNames(Printer);
         break;

         case PrintAll:
            Inventory.PrintAll(Printer);
         break;
         }
      }
```

While this function is fairly long, there's nothing terribly complex about it. After declaring some variables, the rest of the function consists of a switch statement. Each of the cases of the switch executes whatever operation the user selected during the execution of the GetMenuChoice function. Most of these are very similar, as you'll see.

As soon as we take care of an initial question from Susan, we'll take a look at each of these cases in order.

Susan: What's a case?

Steve: It's the part of a switch statement that executes the code for one of the possibilities. Basically, the switch and case statements are like a bunch of if/else statements but easier to read and modify. Take a look at Figure 13.4 on page 920 for an example of how it works.

1. The AddItem case displays a message telling the user what operation is being performed and calls the AddItem member function of the Inventory object to add the item. Finally, the (modified) inventory is saved to a "backup" file called home.$$$. The purpose of this file is to prevent disaster should the power fail or the system crash during a lengthy editing session. Because the inventory is written out to the home.$$$ file whenever any change is made, the user can recover the work that might otherwise be lost in case of any kind of system failure. After this is done, the processing for this step is complete, so the break statement exits from the switch statement and the ExecuteMenuChoice function returns to the main program.

2. The SelectItemFromNameList case displays a message telling the user what operation is being performed and calls the SelectItemFromNameList member function of the Inventory object to determine which inventory item the user wants to edit. If the user doesn't select an item to be edited, the result of this call will be the value –1, in which case the editing step is omitted and the ExecuteMenuChoice function returns to the main program. However, if the user does select an item to be edited, the EditItem member function of the Inventory object is called with the index of that item. When that function has finished execution, the inventory is saved as in AddItem.

Susan had some more questions at this point.

> **Susan:** Why is the result –1?

> **Steve:** Because 0 is a valid index; remember, we're programming in C++, and 0 is the index of the first item in the inventory list.

> **Susan:** How about using 99?<g>

> **Steve:** What an original idea! That would work fine until we had 99 items; unfortunately, then we would have an Item100 problem.

3. The EditByPartialName case displays a message telling the user what operation is being performed, asks the user to type in part of the name of the item to be edited, and calls the SelectItemByPartialName member function of the Inventory object to determine which inventory item the user wants to edit. The rest of this function is the same as the previous case, which makes sense because the only difference in the purpose of these two sections of code is how the user selects the item.

Susan, with her keen eye for detail, spotted a small discrepancy in this section of code, which led to the following discussion.

> **Susan:** Why is the name of the case different from the name of the function?

> **Steve:** That's a good question. It really should be the same, but I changed the program several times and forgot to resynchronize the two names. Because it doesn't affect the functioning of the program, I'm going to leave it as is.

4. The EditByDescription case is exactly the same as the previous case, except that it asks the user for part of the description rather than the name and calls SelectItemFromDescriptionList, rather than SelectItemByPartialName, to select the item to be edited.

5. The EditByCategory case is exactly the same as the previous two, except that it asks the user for the category name, rather than the item name or description, and calls SelectItemFromCategoryList to select the item to be edited.

6. The DeleteItemFromNameList case is a bit different from the previous cases. It starts by allowing the user to select the item to be deleted from the entire inventory. Then it asks the user to confirm the deletion of that item, just to be sure that nothing gets deleted accidentally. Then it calls the DeleteItem member function of the Inventory object to do the actual deletion. Finally, it writes the changed inventory to the backup file.

Susan had a couple of comments about this case and its corresponding function.

> **Susan:** You know, these long names look like German words: a whole bunch of words all strung together.

> **Steve:** I do believe you're right!

> **Susan:** Anyway, I like the confirmation. It's better to be safe rather than to accidentally delete an item when you didn't mean to.

> **Steve:** I agree. Of course, we don't have a "mass delete" option, so an accident can't do unlimited damage, but I'd rather be safe than sorry.

7. The PrintNames and PrintAll cases are much simpler than the previous ones because they don't allow the user to select which items will be included in the printed list. The user can print either the names of all the items in the inventory or all the data for all the items. Of course, even though the program is useful without a fancier printing capability, there might be occasions where printing data for part of the inventory would be very handy. Therefore, I've added an exercise to improve these facilities.

Utility Room

That takes care of the main program. Now let's take a look at the HomeUtility class, starting with its interface, shown in Figure 13.5.

FIGURE 13.5. The HomeUtility interface (code\hmutil1.h)

```
//hmutil1.h

#ifndef HMUTIL1_H
#define HMUTIL1_H
```

```
#include <iostream.h>
#include "vector.h"
#include "string7.h"

class HomeUtility
{
public:

static void IgnoreTillCR();
static void HandleError(const string& Message);
static bool CheckNumericInput();
static bool CheckDateInput(long Date);
static short GetNumberOrEnter(bool AllowArrows=false);
static void ClearRestOfScreen(short StartingRow);
static short SelectItem(vector<short>& Number,
  vector<string>& Name);
enum KeyValue {e_Return = -1, e_Up = -2, e_Down = -3};
};

#endif
```

This class is different from any of the others we've seen so far, as it consists entirely of public static member functions and a public enum. You may reasonably wonder why this is even a class at all; why not just make these functions global?

The reason is to avoid polluting the *global name space*. That is, it's entirely possible that another programmer might write a function called HandleError, and we want to make sure that the code we write can coexist with code that uses such common names. By creating a class to hold these functions that would otherwise be global, we are preventing clashes with other functions that might have the same names.[3]

How did I decide which functions should go into this class rather than anywhere else? My criterion was that the function could be used in more than one other class, so that it would most reasonably belong in a commonly accessible place such as a utility class.

You might not be surprised that Susan had some questions about this issue. Here is our discussion.

Susan: Why are you creating a class that doesn't have any data? I don't get it.

Steve: It's an ecological issue. If we create global functions, especially ones with names that other programmers might want to use, it's like dumping garbage in the ocean where it can affect others. In fact, the practice of creating global functions without a good reason is widely referred to as "polluting the global name space" because such functions interfere with other programmers' use of the same names. Remember, there can be only one global function with a given name and parameter list, so we should create such functions only when absolutely necessary.[4]

Susan: OK, but why should these functions be in this class? How did you decide which ones should be here?

Steve: A function belongs in the utility class if it is used in several other classes. We certainly don't want to copy it into each of those classes: that wouldn't be very object-oriented!

Now that we know why we need the functions in the HomeUtility class, let's take a look at the first one, IgnoreTillCR, which is shown in Figure 13.6.

---

3. Actually, we don't need to create a class just to segregate these functions from the global name space; there's a new C++ feature called namespaces for exactly that purpose. However, I'd rather avoid introducing yet another concept and matching syntax as long as it's not strictly necessary, which it isn't in this case.

4. By an interesting coincidence, after first writing this paragraph I had exactly this problem when trying to reuse some old code I had written. This old code defined global names that conflicted with another library that the user of this code also needed. I fixed this by changing the names, but having kept them out of the global name space would have prevented the problem in the first place.

FIGURE 13.6. HomeUtility::IgnoreTillCR **(from code\hmutil1.cc)**

```
void HomeUtility::IgnoreTillCR()
{
  cin.ignore(10000,'\n');
}
```

This is a simple function that just calls the ignore function of the istream class to ignore a maximum of 10,000 chars in cin or up to the first newline (or "carriage return") character, whichever comes first. In fact, it's so simple that you might wonder why I even bothered making it a function, since cin.ignore(10000,'\n'); is actually shorter than HomeUtility::IgnoreTillCR().

That is true, but the reason I made this a function wasn't to reduce typing but to localize the knowledge of how it works in one place. That way, if I decided to use a different mechanism to ignore excess data, I could change just this one function rather than trying to find every place that I had used the ignore function for that purpose.

Susan had some questions about this function.

Susan: Why do we need this function again?

Steve: It ignores any extra characters that the user might type in before hitting the ENTER key. Otherwise, those characters will be interpreted as commands after the ENTER is pressed.

Susan: OK, but why 10,000?

Steve: Why not? After all, they're free.

Next, we have HomeUtility::HandleError, which is the common error-handling function used in the rest of the program whenever we simply want to display an error message, wait for the user to hit ENTER, and then continue with the program. The code for HandleError is shown in Figure 13.7.

FIGURE 13.7. HomeUtility::HandleError **(from code\hmutil1.cc)**

```
void HomeUtility::HandleError(const string& Message)
{
  cout << endl;
  cout << Message << endl;
  cin.clear();
  IgnoreTillCR();
  cout << "Please hit ENTER to continue." << endl;
  cin.get();
}
```

This is a simple function too. It starts by moving the cursor to the next line on the screen (so the user can tell where the error message begins). Then it displays the message, using the cin.clear() function call to clean up any errors that might have occurred in the cin input stream and calling IgnoreTillCR() to ignore any random characters that might be left in cin from the user's last input. Next, it displays the message "Please hit ENTER to continue" and waits for the user to hit a key, which is accepted via the cin.get() function call.

Susan had a couple of comments and questions about this function:

Susan: So, you have to clean up the garbage in the input stream before you can use it again?

Steve: Yes, we have to reset the status of the stream before we can read from it again. This prevents a program from continuing to read garbage from the stream without realizing it.

Susan: What error message does this function display?

Steve: Whatever error message the calling function specifies.

Susan: Oh, I see. It's generic, not specific to a particular situation.

Steve: Yes, that's exactly right.

The next utility function is HomeUtility::CheckNumericInput, which is called after the user has typed in a numeric value. The code for this function is shown in Figure 13.8.

FIGURE 13.8. HomeUtility::CheckNumericInput **(from code\hmutil1.cc)**

```cpp
bool HomeUtility::CheckNumericInput()
{
  string garbage;
  bool result = true;

  if (cin.peek() != '\n')
    {
    cin.clear();
    cin >> garbage;
    string Message = "Illegal data in numeric value: ";
    Message = Message + garbage;
    HandleError(Message);
    result = false;
    }

  return result;
}
```

While this is a bit more complex than the functions we've looked at so far in this class, it's not really that hard to follow. After declaring some variables, the code starts by calling the peek function of cin to see whether the next character in that istream is a newline ('\n') character. If it is, we can tell that the user has typed in a valid number, so we don't have to deal with an error. How do we know this?

Number, Please

We know this because the versions of operator >> that read numeric (short, int, long, float, or double) values stop when they get to a character that doesn't belong in a number. In the current case, we've asked the user to type in a number, after which he or she is supposed to hit ENTER. If the user has indeed typed in a valid numeric value, all of the characters up to (but not including) the ENTER key will already have been used by operator >> in computing the new value of the numeric variable to the right of the >>. Therefore, the next character in the input stream should be the ENTER (which is represented in C and C++ by the newline character, '\n'). However, if the user has typed some character that doesn't belong in a number, that character will be the next character in the input stream after operator >> finishes reading the value for the numeric variable to its right. Therefore, if the next character isn't a newline, we know the user typed in something illegal.

If that happens, we should let the user know exactly what the illegal characters were. Therefore, after we call the clear function to clear the error status of the istream, the next statement, cin >> garbage, uses operator >> to read the rest of the characters in the input line into a string called garbage, which will end up holding everything from the first illegal character up to but not including a newline. Then we construct the whole error message by concatenating the illegal characters to the end of the message "Illegal data in numeric value: ". Finally, we call HandleError to display the message and wait for the user to press ENTER.

Susan wanted to go over this in more detail.

Susan: Let me see if I understand this. If the user typed in illegal characters, the input operation would stop at that point?

Steve: Right.

Susan: Would that cause an error message?

Steve: No, not by itself; it just sets an error condition in the input stream. It's up to us to produce the error message, and that's what we're doing here.

Susan: So the garbage characters have been left in cin?

Steve: Yes. That's why we have to call clear before we can use cin again.

Making a List, Checking It Twice

The next function is HomeUtility::CheckDateInput, which is shown in Figure 13.9.

FIGURE 13.9. HomeUtility::CheckDateInput **(from code\hmutil1.cc)**

```cpp
bool HomeUtility::CheckDateInput(long Date)
{
  bool result = CheckNumericInput();

  if (result == false)
    return false;

  if ((Date < 18000101) && (Date != 0))
    {
    string Message = "Date must be either 0 (if unknown)";
    Message = Message + " or a number in the form YYYYMMDD";
    Message = Message + "\n";
    Message = Message + "which is on or after 18000101";
    Message = Message + " (January 1st, 1800)";
    HandleError(Message);
    result = false;
    }

  return result;
}
```

This isn't a very complicated function either. It starts by calling CheckNumericInput to make sure that the "date" the user typed in is at least a numeric value. If the input value fails that test, CheckDateInput returns the bad news to the calling function in the form of a false return value. If the input value is a valid number, the second if statement checks whether it is in the range that I've decided to allow (after consultation with Susan): on or after January 1, 1800, or 0. The latter is needed to handle the very real possibility that Susan pointed out: The user may not know when the object was acquired. If the date fails this test, we return false to indicate that it's invalid; otherwise, the return value is true.

Even though I had discussed the range of legal dates with Susan, she had a couple of additional questions about this notion.

Susan: Why do we need a limit on the date at all?

Steve: For error reduction. The chance that the user has had the object for more than a couple of hundred years is smaller than the chance that the user typed the date in incorrectly. At least, that's the way I figure it.

Susan: What about collectors who have extremely old objects?

Steve: Well, that is certainly possible. However, the field we're discussing here represents the date that the user acquired the object, not how old the object is. That might very well be a useful piece of information, especially for collectibles, so I'll add an exercise to include such a field in a collectibles type.

Enter Here

The next function we're going to examine in the HomeUtility class, GetNumberOrEnter (Figure 13.10), is somewhat more complicated than the ones we've been looking at so far. That's because it deals with getting input from the user one keystroke at a time.

FIGURE 13.10. HomeUtility::GetNumberOrEnter **(from code\hmutil1.cc)**

```cpp
short HomeUtility::GetNumberOrEnter(bool AllowArrows)
{
  int key;
  char keychar;
  short FoundItemNumber;

  cout.flush();

  for (;;)
    {
    key = getkey();
    keychar = key;

    if (key == K_Return)
      return e_Return;

    if (AllowArrows)
      {
      if (key == K_Up)
        return e_Up;
      if (key == K_Down)
        return e_Down;
      }

    if ((key < '0') || (key > '9'))
      continue;

    cout << keychar;
    cout.flush();

    FoundItemNumber = key - '0';

    for (;;)
      {
      key = getkey();
      keychar = key;
```

```
        if (key == K_BackSpace)
          {
          cout << keychar;
          cout.flush();
          cout << ' ';
          cout << keychar;
          cout.flush();
          FoundItemNumber /= 10;
          continue;
          }

        if (key == K_Return)
          {
          cout << keychar;
          cout.flush();
          return FoundItemNumber;
          }

        if ((key < '0') || (key > '9'))
          continue;

        cout << keychar;
        cout.flush();

        FoundItemNumber = FoundItemNumber * 10 + (key - '0');
        }
      }
    }
```

The first thing to note about this function is its argument, which is a bool called AllowArrows. If you look at the definition of the interface for the HomeUtility class (Figure 13.5 on page 926), you'll notice that this argument has a default value, which is false. The purpose of this argument is to determine whether the up and down arrow keys will be accepted as valid inputs; if the argument is false, they will be ignored, whereas if the argument is true and the user presses one of these keys, the function will return a code indicating which one. As you'll see, accepting the arrow keys will be useful in the last member function in this class, SelectItem.

The function starts by declaring some variables called key, keychar, and FoundItemNumber. The first of these is an int, which is a type we haven't used very much because it varies in size from one compiler to another. However, in this case I'm going to use an int variable to hold the return value from a function called getkey, which is the function that returns the key code for a key that has been pressed by the user. Since getkey is defined to return an int value, that's the appropriate type for a variable that holds its return value.

This getkey function is a leftover from C, but it is very useful all the same because it allows us to get input from the user without having to wait for him for her to hit ENTER. Under most circumstances, it's much easier to use the >> operator to get input from the user via the keyboard, but that approach has a serious limitation: It prevents us from giving the user immediate feedback. Such feedback is essential if we are going to allow the user to access varying segments of a large quantity of information in an intuitive manner, as you'll see when you try the program. Forcing the user to hit ENTER before getting any feedback would be very inconvenient, and we have to worry about how easy our programs are to use if we want happy users. Therefore, I've written this GetNumberOrEnter function to allow the user to receive immediate gratification when using our home inventory program.

This might be a good time for you to try the program out for yourself so you can see what I'm talking about. To do this, first compile it by changing to the \shcppg\code directory and typing RHIDE hmtst8. When RHIDE starts up, hit Ctl-F9 to compile the program and start it running; once it is finished, you can hit ENTER to dismiss the ending message and use Alt-X to exit back to DOS. Try out the program for a while and see how you like it before coming back to the discussion. Pay special attention to the "select" and "edit" functions, which allow you to see some of the items in the list, and use the up and down arrows to see more of the list. That behavior is implemented partly by GetNumberOrEnter and partly by the SelectItem function.

Now that we've seen how this function is used, let's get back to its implementation; as I've already mentioned, this is a somewhat complicated function, because it has to deal with the intricacies of reading data from the keyboard one character at a time. First, we call flush to make sure that any characters that have been written to cout have actually been sent to the screen. Then we start the "endless" loop that will allow the user to type as many keys as necessary to enter the data item. Why do I say "data item" rather than "number"? Because the user can type keys that aren't numbers at all, including the up or down arrow to select a different entry in the list of items that appears on the screen.

Susan had a question about this flush function.

Susan: I don't remember seeing this flush function before. What does it do?

Steve: It makes sure that everything we were planning to display on the screen is written out before we ask for any input from the user. Ordinarily, characters that are written to a stream are not sent immediately to the output device to which the stream is attached, because that is extremely inefficient. Instead, the characters are collected in an output buffer until there are enough of them to be worth sending out; this technique is called *buffering*.[5] However, in this case we have to make sure that any characters that were supposed to be displayed have been displayed already, because we are going to be taking characters from the user and displaying them immediately. Any leftover characters would just confuse the user.

---

5. This buffering technique is also applied to input. Rather than read one character at a time from an input file, the operating system reads a number of characters at a time and gives them to the program when it asks for them. This greatly improves the efficiency of reading from a file; however, it is much less useful when reading data from the keyboard, as the user doesn't know what to type before we provide a prompt.

Now let's continue with the analysis of the code in this function. The first statement inside the "endless" loop is key = getkey();. This statement calls a C function called getkey, which waits for the user to type a key and then reads it. The value of the getkey function is the ASCII code for the key the user hit. Therefore, that statement should be relatively simple to understand.

Secret Decoder Ring Not Required

However, the same is not true of the statement keychar = key;. Why would we want to assign one variable the same value as that of another? Because of the way that getkey works. Unlike normal cin input, getkey input is "silent"; that is, keys that are pressed by the user do not produce any visible results by themselves, so we have to display each character on the screen as the user types it. But to display a character on the screen via cout, the variable or expression to be displayed must have the type char, whereas the variable key is an int. If we were to write the statement, cout << key;, the program would display the ASCII numeric value for the key the user pressed. Needless to say, this would not be what the user expected; therefore, we have to copy the key value from an int variable to a char variable before we display it so that the user sees something intelligible on the screen.

Susan thought such cryptic output might have some use. Also, she wanted to know what would happen if the key value wouldn't fit.

Susan: If we displayed the ASCII value instead of the character, it would be sort of a secret code, wouldn't it?

Steve: Sort of, although not a very secure one. However, it would be fairly effective at confusing the user, which wouldn't be good.

Susan: OK. Now, about copying the value from an int to a char: A char is smaller than an int, right? What if the value was too big?

Steve: The answer is that it would be chopped off. However, in this case we're safe because we know that any key the user types will fit in a char.

The next order of business in this function is to check whether the user has hit the ENTER key. If so, we simply return the enum value e_Return to the calling function to inform it that the user has hit the ENTER key without typing a value.

Assuming that the user has not hit the ENTER key so far, we check the AllowArrows argument to see whether the arrow keys are allowed at this time. If they are, we check to see if either the up arrow or the down arrow has been hit. If it has, we return the appropriate code to tell the calling function that this has occurred so it can scroll the display if necessary.

The next statement after the end of the arrow-handling code is an if statement that checks whether the key that we are handling is in the range '0' to '9'. If the key is outside that range, we use the continue statement to skip back to the beginning of the outer for loop, essentially ignoring any such key. However, if the key is within the numeric digit range, we proceed by using the operator << to send it to the screen. Then we use the flush function of the cout object to ensure that the key has actually been displayed on the screen.

By this point, we have seen the first digit of the value, so we continue by setting FoundItemNumber to the numeric value of that digit, which can be calculated as the ASCII value of the key minus the ASCII value of '0'.

The Rest of the Story

Now we're ready to enter the inner for loop that gathers all the rest of the numeric digits of the number. This starts with the same "endless" condition, (;;), as the outer loop because we don't know how many times it will have to be executed. Therefore, rather than specify the loop count in the for statement, we use a return statement to exit from the loop as soon as the user presses ENTER.

The first two statements in this inner loop are exactly the same as the first two statements in the outer loop, which should not be a surprise as they serve exactly the same function—to get the key from the user and copy it into a char variable for display. However, the next segment of code is different, because once the user has typed at least one digit, another possibility opens up—editing the value by using the backspace key to erase an erroneous digit. That's the task of the next part of the code, which was a bit more difficult to develop than you might think. The problem is that simply echoing the backspace key to the screen, as we do with other keys, does not work properly because it leaves the erroneous digit visible on the screen. Even after we solve this problem, however—by writing a space character on the screen to erase the erroneous digit and backing up again to position the cursor at the correct place for entering the new digit—we have another problem to deal with. Namely, we have to correct the value of the FoundItemNumber variable to account for the erased digit. This requires only that we divide the previous value of that variable by 10 because the remainder will be discarded automatically by the integer division process, effectively eliminating the contribution of the erased digit. Once we have taken care of these details, we are finished with this particular keystroke, so we use a continue statement to proceed to the next execution of the loop.

The next possibility to be handled is that of the ENTER key. When we see that key, we display it on the screen, which of course causes the cursor to move to the next line. Then we return the value of the FoundItemNumber variable to the calling function, which ends the execution of this function.

By this point in the function, we shouldn't be seeing anything but a digit key. Therefore, any key other than a digit is ignored, as we use the continue statement to skip further processing of such a key.

We're almost done. The last phase of processing is to display the digit key we have received and use it to modify the previous value of the FoundItemNumber variable. The new value of the FoundItemNumber is 10 times the previous value plus the value of the new digit, and that's exactly how the last statement in this function calculates the new value.

I Can See Clearly Now

I'm sure you'll be happy to hear that the next function we will discuss is a lot simpler than the one we just looked at. This is the ClearRestOfScreen function, which is shown in Figure 13.11. It is used in the final function in the HomeUtility class, SelectItem, to clear the part of the screen that function uses for its item display.

FIGURE 13.11. HomeUtility::ClearRestOfScreen **(from code\hmutil1.cc)**

```
void HomeUtility::ClearRestOfScreen(short StartingRow)
{
   short i;

   for (i = StartingRow; i < ScreenRows(); i ++)
      {
      gotoxy(1,i);
      clreol();
      }

   gotoxy(1,StartingRow);
}
```

This is the first function one we've seen that uses the screen-handling functions from the conio library. The first of these functions is the gotoxy function, which moves the cursor to the column (X) and row (Y) specified by its arguments. The first argument is the column number, which for some reason doesn't follow the standard C and C++ convention of starting with 0 but starts at 1. The same is true of the row number, which is the second argument to the function.

The second C library function that we haven't seen before is the clreol function, which erases everything on a given line of the screen from the cursor position to the end of the line. We call this function for each line from StartingRow to the end of the screen.

Before we can clear the screen one line at a time, however, we need to know when to stop. That's why we need to call the other C library function in this function: ScreenRows. As its name suggests, it returns the number of rows on the screen.

Susan had a few questions about this function.

Susan: What is conio?

Steve: It stands for "console I/O". Before PCs, it was common for programmers to use a terminal that consisted of a video display screen and a keyboard; this combination was referred to as a "console".

Susan: How do you pronounce gotoxy?

Steve: It's pronounced "go-to-X-Y".

Now that we've seen how ClearRestOfScreen works, I should tell you why we need it: to allow the SelectItem function to keep its working area clear of random characters. Of course, it could be used in other situations, but that's how we're using it here.

The Final Frontier

The final function in the HomeUtility class is SelectItem, whose code is shown in Figure 13.12.

FIGURE 13.12. **The** HomeUtility::SelectItem **function (from code\hmutil1.cc)**

```
short HomeUtility::SelectItem(vector<short>& Number,
  vector<string>& Name)
{
    short FoundItemNumber;
```

```
    int Row;
    int Column;
    int RowCount = ScreenRows();
    short ItemCount = Name.size();

    ScreenGetCursor(&Row,&Column);
    Row ++;

// Max number of rows in scroll area is 1/2 rows on screen

    int RowsAvail = RowCount / 2;

// For testing, max rows is 5
    RowsAvail = 5;
// End test code

    if (RowsAvail > ItemCount)
      RowsAvail = ItemCount;

    if (RowsAvail == 0)
      {
      HandleError("No items found.");
      return 0;
      }

    short offset = 0;
    for (;;)
      {
      ClearRestOfScreen(Row);

      for (short i = offset; i < offset + RowsAvail ; i++)
        cout << setw(5) << Number[i] + 1 << ".  " << Name[i] << endl;

      cout << endl;

      cout << "Type item number to select or ENTER to end." << endl;

      if (ItemCount > RowsAvail)
        cout << "Hit down arrow or up arrow to scroll." << endl;
```

```
      cout << endl;

      FoundItemNumber = GetNumberOrEnter(true);
      if (FoundItemNumber == e_Return)
        return 0;

      if (FoundItemNumber == e_Up)
        {
        if (ItemCount > RowsAvail)
          {
          offset --;
          if (offset < 0)
            offset = 0;
          }
        continue;
        }

      if (FoundItemNumber == e_Down)
        {
        if (ItemCount > RowsAvail)
          {
          offset ++;
          if (offset >= Name.size()-RowsAvail)
            offset = Name.size()-RowsAvail;
          }
        continue;
        }

      for (short i = 0; i < ItemCount; i ++)
        {
        if (FoundItemNumber == Number[i]+1)
          return FoundItemNumber;
        }

      IgnoreTillCR();
      cout << FoundItemNumber <<
        " is an invalid entry. Hit ENTER to continue." << endl;
      IgnoreTillCR();
```

```
        return 0;
        }
  }
```

This function, as its name indicates, is the heart of the item selection process. Its arguments are the Number vector, which contains the indexes into the inventory list of the particular items from which the user is selecting, and the Name vector, which contains the names of these items and sometimes other information about them (e.g., the category in which each item is found).

The first operation to be performed in this function is determining how many lines there are on the "screen"; I have put the word "screen" in quotes because what we are actually concerned with is only the DOS window in which our program is running, not the actual physical screen of the monitor. The reason that the number of lines on the screen is important is that we may want to calculate the number of items to be displayed in the "scroll area" (the area where we will be displaying all or part of the list of items) based on the amount of space available on the screen. For testing purposes, I have set the maximum number of items to be displayed to 5. I actually like it that way, but you can easily change it to see more items at one time.

Susan had some questions about the way we're handling the screen.

Susan: So, you even have to tell the program how big the screen is? Doesn't it know anything?

Steve: You have to realize that the same program may run on different machines that are set up differently. Even if everyone were running Windows 95, some people have their DOS windows set for 25 lines, some for 50 lines, and probably others I haven't seen. It's not very difficult to handle all these different possibilities just by calling the ScreenRows function.

Susan: OK. Now about changing the number of lines in the scroll area: How do you do that?

Steve: By deleting the line in the program that sets RowsAvail to 5 (and recompiling, of course), it will use half the screen for the scroll area.

Susan: Oh, I thought there was an option when you ran the program.

Steve: You're a programmer now. You can do that yourself.

The next operation is to determine the number of entries in the list of items we're going to display, which we can do by calling the size member function of the Name argument. Of course, we could just as well call the size member function of Number, because that argument has to have the same number of elements as Name has: If they have different numbers of elements, the calling function has made a serious error!

After finding out how many items we are going to handle, the next operation is to determine the current position of the cursor so that we can position the "scroll area" properly below the heading that was displayed by the calling function. To find the current position of the cursor, we call another C function, ScreenGetCursor. This function requires two arguments, both of which are addresses of variables. The first argument is the address of a variable (in this case Row) that will receive the current row number. The second is the address of a variable (in this case Column) that will receive the current column number.[6] As soon as we have determined the current cursor row, we increment the Row variable to skip a row between the heading and the beginning of the scroll area.

The next segment of code figures out how many items to display at one time; the current version of this function, as I've already mentioned, ignores this calculation and sets the number of items to 5.

6. The reason we have to pass addresses of variables to this function, rather than using reference arguments, is that this is a C function, and C does not have reference arguments.

This makes my (and Susan's) testing more effective because most of the complexity of this routine is in the code that deals with the possibility of having to scroll the items onto and off the screen. This code is used only when there are more items than will fit in the limited space allocated for listing them, so if we have fewer items than will fit on the screen, the code that scrolls the list is not used. As I've mentioned before, code that is never used is never tested and therefore must be assumed not to work.

Once we have decided how many items to list at once and have assigned the appropriate value to the RowsAvail variable, we then check whether the number of items we can display (as specified in that variable) is greater than the total number of items we need to display (as specified by the ItemCount variable). If this is the case, we set the total number to be displayed to the latter value.

If there are no items to be displayed, the user has requested a set of items that doesn't exist, so we call the HandleError routine to tell the user about this situation, and return to the calling function.

Assuming that we have some items to display, we are ready to start displaying them. First, we initialize a variable called offset, which keeps track of what part of the whole list is currently being displayed in the scroll area. It begins at 0 because we start by displaying the first portion of the list, which consists of the number of items that will fit in the scroll area. Of course, if all of the items fit in the scroll area, they will all be displayed.

Once we have initialized offset, we enter the "endless" for loop that displays the elements and asks the user for input until he or she selects something. This for loop begins by calling the ClearRestOfScreen function to clear everything on the screen beyond the current cursor location.

The next two lines of code constitute the for loop that displays the items that are currently in the scroll area. The formatting of this display is somewhat interesting, at least to me, because it took me several tries to get it right. The elements of the display line include the item number, which is one more than the index of the item being displayed (to account for the first index being 0) and the item name.

Initially, I simply accepted the default formatting for the item number and the name. However, as soon as the item numbers exceeded 9, I discovered that the names no longer lined up properly because the extra character in the two-digit item number pushed the name over one extra position. To solve this problem, I decided to use the setw manipulator to force the size of the item number to five digits; because the item number is a short, the program is limited to 32767 items, so five digits will be sufficient.

Susan was surprised to hear that I had overlooked this, which led to the following exchange.

> **Susan:** I thought you left bugs in the program on purpose so I would find them.

> **Steve:** No, as a matter of fact, I thought it was working every time I gave it to you to test (all five times). I suppose that illustrates the eternal optimism of software developers!

After displaying the items along with their corresponding item numbers, one on each line, we display the message "Type item number to select or ENTER to end." Then, if we have more items than will fit in the scroll area, we display another message telling the user about the availability of the up and down arrow keys for scrolling.

Next, we call the GetNumberOrEnter function to get the item number from the user. Note that the argument to that function is true, which means that we want the function to accept the up and down arrows so that the user can hit those keys to tell us to scroll the item list either up or down. Of course, if all the items fit in the scroll area, hitting either of those keys will have no visible effect on the list.

Once we have received the value returned by the GetNumberOrEnter function, we examine it. If it is the value e_Return, the user has decided not to select any of the items. Therefore, we return the value 0 to indicate this situation.

However, assuming that the user hit something more than just the ENTER key, we have to check what the exact return value was. If it was the value e_Up or e_Down, and if we have more items than will fit in the scroll area, we change the value of the offset variable accordingly. Of course, we have to be careful not to try to display items whose indexes are before the beginning or beyond the end of the Name vector; the code that handles both of the arrow keys ensures this doesn't happen.

Finally, if we get past the handling of the arrow keys, we must have gotten a numeric value from the user. Therefore, we check that the value the user typed is actually an entry in the Number vector. Assuming that this is the case, we return that value to the calling function.

However, if the user entered an item number that is not found in the Number vector, we create an error message and display it. Finally, we return the value 0 to indicate to the calling function that the user did not make a valid selection.

Checking the Inventory

That concludes our tour of the HomeUtility class. Now it's time to look at the changes to the next class, HomeInventory. We'll start with the latest version of the header file, hmin8.cc, shown in Figure 13.13.

FIGURE 13.13. The latest header file for the HomeInventory class **(code\hmin8.h)**

```
//hmin8.h

#include "vector.h"
#include "string7.h"

class HomeInventory
{
public:
    HomeInventory();
```

```
    short LoadInventory(ifstream& is);
    void DumpInventory();
    HomeItem AddItem();
    HomeItem EditItem(short Index);
    vector<short> LocateItemByDescription(const string& Partial);

    vector<short> LocateItemByCategory(const string& Partial);
    vector<short> LocateItemByPartialName(const string& Partial);
    void PrintNames(ostream &os);
    void PrintAll(ostream &os);
    void StoreInventory(ofstream& ofs);
    void DisplayItem(short Index);

    void SortInventoryByName();
    short GetCount();
    short SelectItemByPartialName(const string& Partial);
    short SelectItemFromNameList();
    short SelectItemFromDescriptionList(const string& Partial);
    short SelectItemFromCategoryList(const string& Partial);
    void DeleteItem(short Index);

private:
    vector<HomeItem> m_Home;
};
```

As you will see if you compare this version of the HomeInventory class interface to the previous one we examined (hmin6.h in Figure 12.13), I've deleted three functions from this interface—namely, FindItemByDescription, FindItemByName, and LocateItemByName. The first of these is no longer used in the application program, which instead uses its relative, LocateItemByDescription. The other two functions are no longer necessary because they have been superseded by the new LocateItemByPartialName, which can do everything that the old functions could do and a lot more besides.

This new version of the HomeInventory class also includes changes to existing functions. Let's take them in order of their appearance in the header file, starting with the LoadInventory function. The only difference between this version and the previous one is that the new version sorts the inventory by calling the new SortInventoryByName function after loading it. I'll provide a brief explanation of how the sort function works when we get to it. I haven't bothered to reproduce the LoadInventory function here just to show you the one added line.

The next function that was changed is the AddItem function, whose new implementation is shown in Figure 13.14.

FIGURE 13.14. The latest version of AddItem **(from code\hmin8.cc)**

```
HomeItem HomeInventory::AddItem()
{
    HomeItem TempItem = HomeItem::NewItem();

    if (TempItem.IsNull())
      return TempItem;

    short OldCount = m_Home.size();

    m_Home.resize(OldCount + 1);

    m_Home[OldCount] = TempItem;

    SortInventoryByName();

    return TempItem;
}
```

As you can see, this version of the function checks whether the newly created item is null, using the new IsNull member function of the HomeItem class. If that turns out to be the case, it returns that null item to the calling function rather than adding it to the inventory. This new version also sorts the inventory after adding an item, just as the new version of the LoadInventory function does.

Now we're up to the EditItem function, the new version of which is shown in Figure 13.15.

FIGURE 13.15. The new version of the EditItem **function (from code\hmin8.cc)**

```
HomeItem HomeInventory::EditItem(short Index)
{
    bool NameChanged = false;

    HomeItem TempItem = m_Home[Index];

    TempItem.Edit();

    if (TempItem.GetName() != m_Home[Index].GetName())
        NameChanged = true;

    m_Home[Index] = TempItem;

    if (NameChanged)
        SortInventoryByName();

    return TempItem;
}
```

The main difference between this version of EditItem and the previous version is that this one checks to see whether the name of the item has been changed. If this is the case, EditItem calls the SortInventoryByName function to ensure that the inventory list is still in order by the names of the items.

The next function we'll examine is LocateItemByDescription, whose new implementation is shown in Figure 13.16.

FIGURE 13.16. The latest implementation of LocateItemByDescription **(from code\hmin8.cc)**

```
vector<short> HomeInventory::LocateItemByDescription(
    const string& Partial)
{
    short ItemCount = m_Home.size();
    string Description;
```

```
short FoundCount = 0;

for (short i = 0; i < ItemCount; i ++)
  {
  Description = m_Home[i].GetDescription();
  if (Description.find_nocase(Partial) >= 0)
    FoundCount ++;
  }

vector<short> Found(FoundCount);

FoundCount = 0;

for (short i = 0; i < ItemCount; i ++)
  {
  Description = m_Home[i].GetDescription();
  if (Description.find_nocase(Partial) >= 0)
    Found[FoundCount++] = i;
  }

return Found;
}
```

This function is quite different from its previous incarnation; even its interface has changed. That's because it now locates all the items that match the description specified in its argument, not just the first one. Therefore, it must return a vector of indexes rather than only one. Also, because we don't know how many items will be found before we look through the list, we don't know how large the result vector will be on our first pass. I've solved that by using two passes, with the first pass devoted to finding the number of matching items and the second pass devoted to storing the indexes of those items in the result vector. One other construct that we haven't seen before is the use of the increment operator in the line Found[FoundCount++] = i;. When this operator is used inside another expression, its value is the old value of the variable being incremented. In this case, the value of the expression FoundCount++ is the value that the variable FoundCount had before being incremented. After that value is used, the variable is incremented so that it will be greater by one the next time it is referred to.

Besides modifying the previously noted functions, I've also added quite a few functions to this interface to implement all the new facilities this new version of the program provides. Let's take them one at a time, starting with LocateItemByCategory, which is shown in Figure 13.17.

FIGURE 13.17. HomeInventory::LocateItemByCategory **(from code\hmin8.cc)**

```
vector<short> HomeInventory::LocateItemByCategory(
  const string& Partial)
{
  short ItemCount = m_Home.size();
  string Category;
  short FoundCount = 0;

  for (short i = 0; i < ItemCount; i ++)
    {
    Category = m_Home[i].GetCategory();
    if (Category.find_nocase(Partial) >= 0)
      FoundCount ++;
    }

  vector<short> Found(FoundCount);

  FoundCount = 0;

  for (short i = 0; i < ItemCount; i ++)
    {
    Category = m_Home[i].GetCategory();
    if (Category.find_nocase(Partial) >= 0)
      Found[FoundCount++] = i;
    }

  return Found;
}
```

As you can see, this is almost identical to the function we've just examined, LocateItemByDescription. The only difference is that we're searching for items whose category matches the user's specification rather than items whose description matches that specification.

I'm not going to waste space by reproducing the code for the LocateItemByPartialName function, which is again almost identical to the two functions we've just looked at. The difference, of course, is that the field it examines for a match is the item's name rather than its description or category.

The next function we will examine is PrintNames, which is shown in Figure 13.18.

FIGURE 13.18. The PrintNames **function (from code\hmin8.cc)**

```
void HomeInventory::PrintNames(ostream& os)
{
   short ItemCount = m_Home.size();

   for (short i = 0; i < ItemCount; i ++)
     {
     os << m_Home[i].GetName() << endl;
     }

   os << '\f' << endl;
   os.flush();
}
```

This function merely steps through all the items in the inventory and sends the name of each one to the output stream. One minor point of interest is that to ensure that any further data sent to the printer starts on a new page, I've added a "form-feed" character, represented as '\f', to the end of the output data. After sending that character to the printer, the function ends with a call to the flush function of the ostream object we are sending the data to.

Susan had a couple of questions about this function.

Susan: What is a form-feed?

Steve: It is a character that makes the printer go to a new page. It's called that because in olden days printers used continuous-form paper. When you finished printing on one form, you had to send a "form-feed" character to the printer so that it would advance the paper to the beginning of the next form. Today, most printers use cut-sheet paper, but the name has stuck.

Susan: How do we know that the form-feed character has been sent to the printer? Isn't it buffered?

Steve: That's exactly why we have to call the flush function, which ensures that the form-feed has actually been sent to the printer.

The next function is PrintAll. This, as shown in Figure 13.19, is exactly like the previous function, except that it displays all the data for each item rather than just its name.

FIGURE 13.19. The PrintAll **function (from code\hmin8.cc)**

```
void HomeInventory::PrintAll(ostream& os)
{
    short ItemCount = m_Home.size();

    for (short i = 0; i < ItemCount; i ++)
      {
      os << m_Home[i] << endl;
      }

    os << '\f' << endl;
    os.flush();
}
```

Now we're up to the StoreInventory function, whose code is shown in Figure 13.20.

FIGURE 13.20. The StoreInventory **function (from code\hmin8.cc)**

```
void HomeInventory::StoreInventory(ofstream& ofs)
{
   short i;
   short ElementCount = m_Home.size();

   ofs << ElementCount << endl << endl;

   for (i = 0; i < ElementCount; i ++)
     {
     ofs << m_Home[i];
     ofs << endl;
     }
}
```

As you can see from the code in this function, it is almost identical to the code for the previous one. The main differences follow:

1. It writes the number of items to the file before starting to write the items (so that we can tell how many items are in the file when we read it back later).

2. It doesn't write a form-feed character to the file after all the items are written because we aren't printing the information.

The similarity between this function and PrintAll shouldn't come as too much of a surprise. After all, storing the inventory data is almost the same as printing it out; both of these operations take data currently stored in objects in memory and transfer it to an output device. The iostream classes are designed to allow us to concentrate on the input or output task to be performed rather than on the details of the output device on which the data is to be written, so the operations needed to write data to a file can be very similar to the operations needed to write data to the printer.

Susan had some questions about this function.

Susan: What is ofs?

Steve: It stands for output file stream, because we are writing the data for the items to a file via an ofstream object.

Susan: Why is it good that writing data to a file is like writing data to the printer?

Steve: This characteristic of C++, called *device independence*, makes it easier to write programs that use a number of different types of output (or input) device, as they all look more or less the same. Having to treat every device differently is a major annoyance to the programmer in languages that don't support device independence.

Now let's take a look at the next function, DisplayItem, whose code is shown in Figure 13.21.

FIGURE 13.21. The DisplayItem **function (from code\hmin8.cc)**

```
void HomeInventory::DisplayItem(short Index)
{
    m_Home[Index].FormattedDisplay(cout);
}
```

This is quite a simple function, as it calls the FormattedDisplay function of the HomeItem class to do all the work of displaying the data for a particular item in the inventory. As you can see, this function always writes the data to the screen.

A Better Sort of Function

The next function we will look at is SortInventoryByName, whose code is shown in Figure 13.22.

FIGURE 13.22. The SortInventoryByName **function (from code\hmin8.cc)**

```
void HomeInventory::SortInventoryByName()
{
    short ItemCount = m_Home.size();
    vector<HomeItem> m_HomeTemp = m_Home;
    vector<string> Name(ItemCount);
    string HighestName = "zzzzzzzz";
    string FirstName;
    short FirstIndex;

    for (int i = 0; i < ItemCount; i ++)
        Name[i] = m_Home[i].GetName();

    for (int i = 0; i < ItemCount; i ++)
        {
        FirstName = HighestName;
        FirstIndex = 0;
        for (int k = 0; k < ItemCount; k ++)
            {
            if (Name[k].less_nocase(FirstName))
                {
                FirstName = Name[k];
                FirstIndex = k;
                }
            }
        m_HomeTemp[i] = m_Home[FirstIndex];
        Name[FirstIndex] = HighestName;
        }

    m_Home = m_HomeTemp;
}
```

I won't go into detail on the "selection sort" algorithm used in this function because I've already explained it in gory detail in Chapters 4 and 8. The only difference between this implementation and those previous versions is that here we're using the less_nocase function rather than operator < to compare the string variables so that we can sort without regard to case. Briefly, the basic idea of this algorithm is that we go through the inventory looking for the item that has the "lowest" name (i.e., the name that would be earliest in the dictionary). When we find it, we copy it to an output list, and then mark it so that we won't pick it again. Then we repeat this process for each item in the original list of names. This is not a particularly efficient sorting algorithm, but it is sufficient for our purposes here.

The next function, GetCount, is extremely simple. Its sole purpose is to return the number of items in the inventory so that the main program can display this information on the screen, and its implementation consists of returning the value obtained from the size member function of the inventory object. Therefore, I won't waste space reproducing it here.

The next function in the header file, SelectItemByPartialName, is more interesting. Take a look at its implementation, which is shown in Figure 13.23.

FIGURE 13.23. The SelectItemByPartialName **function (from code\hmin8.cc)**

```
short HomeInventory::SelectItemByPartialName(
  const string& Partial)
{
  vector<short> Found = LocateItemByPartialName(Partial);

  vector<string> Name(Found.size());

  for (short i = 0; i < Found.size(); i ++)
    Name[i] = m_Home[Found[i]].GetName();

  short Result = HomeUtility::SelectItem(Found,Name) - 1;

  return Result;
}
```

This function starts by using the LocateItemByPartialName function to get a list of all the items whose names match the string specified by the calling function in the argument called Partial (the string the user typed in to select the items to be listed). Once LocateItemByPartialName has returned the vector of indexes of matching items, SelectItemByPartialName continues by extracting the names of those items and putting them in another vector called Name. Once the names and indexes have been gathered, we're ready to call HomeUtility::SelectItem, which will take care of the actual user interaction needed to find out which item the user really wants to edit. The result of the SelectItem function is an item number, which starts at 1^7; however, the result of the SelectItemByPartialName function is an index into the inventory list, which is zero-based, as usual in C++. Therefore, we have to subtract 1 from the result of the SelectItem function before returning it as the index into the inventory list.

By this point, Susan had become absorbed in the role of software developer, if the following exchange is any indication:

Susan: Why are we coddling the users? Let them start counting at 0 like we have to.

Steve: Many developers take exactly that approach. However, the users are our customers, and they will be a lot happier (and likely to buy more products from us) if we treat them well.

The next function we'll look at is SelectItemFromNameList, whose code is shown in Figure 13.24.

FIGURE 13.24. The SelectItemFromNameList **function (from code\hmin8.cc)**

```
short HomeInventory::SelectItemFromNameList()
{
```

---

7. Or the value 0, which means that the user didn't select anything. If the user didn't select anything, then this function will return -1, which will tell the calling function that nothing was selected.

```
short ItemCount = m_Home.size();

vector<short> Found(ItemCount);

for (int i = 0; i < ItemCount; i ++)
   Found[i] = i;

vector<string> Name(Found.size());

for (short i = 0; i < Found.size(); i ++)
   Name[i] = m_Home[i].GetName();

short Result = HomeUtility::SelectItem(Found,Name) - 1;

return Result;
}
```

This is very similar to the previous function, except that it allows the user to choose from the entire inventory, as there is no selection expression to reduce the number of items to be displayed. Therefore, instead of calling a function to determine which items should be included in the list that the user will pick from, this function makes a list of all of the indexes and item names in the inventory, then calls the SelectItem function to allow the user to pick an item from the whole inventory list.

The next member function listed in the hmin8.h header file is SelectItemFromDescriptionList. I won't reproduce it here because it is virtually identical to the SelectItemByPartialName function, except of course that it uses the description field rather than the item name field to determine which items will end up in the list the user selects from. This means that it calls LocateItemByDescription to find items, rather than LocateItemByPartialName, which the SelectItemByPartialName function uses for that same purpose.

Categorical Imperative

The next function in the header file, SelectItemFromCategoryList (Figure 13.25), is more interesting, if only because it does some relatively fancy formatting to get its display to line up properly.

FIGURE 13.25. The SelectItemFromCategoryList **function (from code\hmin8.cc)**

```
short HomeInventory::SelectItemFromCategoryList(
  const string& Partial)
{
  vector<short> Found = LocateItemByCategory(Partial);

  vector<string> Name(Found.size());
  vector<string> Category(Found.size());
  string Padding;
  short PaddingLength;

  short MaxLength = 0;

  for (short i = 0; i < Found.size(); i ++)
    {
    Category[i] = m_Home[Found[i]].GetCategory();
    Name[i] = m_Home[Found[i]].GetName();
    if (Name[i].GetLength() > MaxLength)
      MaxLength = Name[i].GetLength();
    }

  for (short i = 0; i < Found.size(); i ++)
    {
    PaddingLength = MaxLength - Name[i].GetLength();
    Padding = string(PaddingLength,' ');
    Name[i] = Name[i] + Padding + "   " + Category[i];
    }

  MaxLength += 7; // allow for item number in item display line
  string Heading = "Item #  Name";
```

```
short HeadingLength = Heading.GetLength();
if (MaxLength > HeadingLength)
   PaddingLength = MaxLength - HeadingLength;
else
   PaddingLength = 0;
Padding = string(PaddingLength,' ');
Heading = Heading + Padding + "     Category";
cout << Heading << endl << endl;

short Result = HomeUtility::SelectItem(Found,Name) - 1;

return Result;
}
```

This function starts out pretty much like the other "select" functions—calling a "locate" function to gather indexes of items that match a particular criterion, which in this case is the category of the item. However, once these indexes have been gathered, instead of simply collecting the names of the items into a vector, we also must determine the length of the longest name, so that when we display the category of each item after its name, the category names will line up evenly. To make this possible, we have to "pad" the shorter names to the same length as the longest name. The code to do this is in the two lines of the for loop that gathers the names and categories:

```
if (Name[i].GetLength() > MaxLength)
      MaxLength = Name[i].GetLength();
```

If the current name is longer than the longest name so far, we update that MaxLength variable to the length of the current name. By the time we reach the end of the list of names, MaxLength will be the length of the longest name.

In the next for loop, we calculate the amount of padding each name will require, based on the difference between its length and the length of the longest name. Then we use the string(short, char) constructor to create a string consisting of the number of spaces that will make the current name as long as the longest name. As soon as we have done that, we add the padding and the category name. Then we are finished with the preparation of the data for the SelectItem function.

However, we still have more work to do before we call that function because we want to display a heading on the screen to tell the user what he or she is looking at. That's the task of the next section of the code. It starts out by adding 7 to the MaxLength variable to account for the length of the item number field.[8]

Next, we start constructing the heading line, starting with the literal value "Item # Name". To make the category heading line up over the category names in the display, we have to pad the heading line to the length of the longest name, if necessary. This will be needed if the heading is shorter than the length of the longest name plus the allowance of 7 characters for the item name.[9] Once we have calculated the length of that padding (if any), we construct it and add it to the end of the heading so far. Then we add the "Category" heading to the heading line. Now the heading is finished, so we write it to cout. Finally, we call SelectItem to allow the user to select an item, and return the result of that call to the calling function.

This function was the stimulus for a discussion of software development issues between Susan and me.

---

8. I should mention here that it is not a good idea to use "magic" numbers in programs. These are numbers that do not have any obvious relationship to the rest of the code. A good general rule is that numbers other than 0, 1, or other self-evident values should be defined as const or enum values rather than as literal values like '7'. However, I have commented this value in the code, so the next programmer should not have too much trouble figuring out what it does.

9. By the way, neglecting the possibility that the heading is already long enough is what caused the "virtual memory exceeded" error message in an earlier version of this program. The problem was that the length of the padding was calculated as a negative value. However, operator new can't handle negative values, considering them to be very large positive values. Therefore, when I asked it to allocate (for example) -3 characters of memory, it tried to give me approximately 4 billion bytes. That exceeds the maximum amount this compiler can handle, so I got an error message.

Susan: That sure is a lot of work just to handle item names of different lengths. Wouldn't it be simpler to assume a certain maximum size?

Steve: We'd still have to pad all the names before tacking the category on; the only simplification would be in the creation of the header, so it wouldn't really make the function much simpler.

Susan: What would happen if we had such a long name or category that the line wouldn't fit on the screen?

Steve: That's a very good question. In that case, the display would be messed up. However, I don't think that's very likely because the user probably wouldn't want to type in such a long name or category.

Susan: Okay. Now I have another question. If we were printing a report of all these items and categories, would each page line up differently from the others if it had a longer or shorter name length?

Steve: Well, so far we haven't implemented a report like that. However, if we did, each page would line up the same on any particular report because we go through the whole list to find the longest name. On the other hand, if we ran the report several times down with different data, it is possible that the longest name would be of a different length in each report, so the columns wouldn't line up the same between reports.

Susan: So there really isn't any cut and dried way to make these decisions?

Steve: No, I'm afraid not. That's why they pay me the (relatively) big bucks as a software developer. I have to laugh whenever I see ads for "automatic bug-finder" software, especially when it claims to be able to find design flaws automatically. How does it know what problem I'm trying to solve?

The final function in this class is DeleteItem, whose code is shown in Figure 13.26.

FIGURE 13.26. **The** DeleteItem **function (from code\hmin8.cc)**

```
void HomeInventory::DeleteItem(short Index)
{
    short ItemCount = m_Home.size();

    for (short i = Index; i < ItemCount-1; i ++)
        m_Home[i] = m_Home[i+1];

    m_Home.resize(ItemCount-1);
}
```

This is another simple function. Starting at the item to be deleted, it moves all of the items after that point one position closer to the beginning of the inventory list and then reduces the size of the list by one. This effectively eliminates the selected item from the inventory.

Homing In

Now it's time to return to the HomeItem class. Luckily, the changes here are much smaller than the changes to the HomeInventory class. In fact, only one new function as been added to the HomeItem interface since the last version we looked at, hmit6.h. That function is GetCategory, whose base class version simply calls the derived class function of the same name, which merely returns the value of the m_Category variable in the item. We've seen enough of this type of function, so we won't bother going over it further.

However, some of the functions have changed in implementation, so we should take a look at them. We'll start with the only function declared in hmit6.h whose implementation has changed: operator >>, the code for which is shown in Figure 13.27.

FIGURE 13.27. The new operator **>> implementation (from code\hmit8.cc)**

```cpp
istream& operator >> (istream& is, HomeItem& Item)
{
  string Type;
  bool Interactive = (&is == &cin);
  HomeItem Temp;

  Item = HomeItem();

  while (Type == "")
    {
    if (Interactive)
      {
      cout << "Type (Basic(B), Music(M)) ";
      cout << "or hit ENTER to exit: ";
      is >> Type;
      if (Type == "")
        return is;
      }
    else
      is >> Type;

    if (is.fail() != 0)
      return is;
    }

  if (Type.find_nocase("B") == 0)
    {
    // set type of Temp to Basic object, to be filled in
    Temp = HomeItem("",0.0,0,"","");
    }
  else if (Type.find_nocase("M") == 0)
    {
    // set type of Temp to Music object, to be filled in
    Temp = HomeItem("",0.0,0,"","","",vector<string>(0));
    }
  else
    {
```

```
        string Message = "Bad object type: ";
        Message = Message + Type;
        HomeUtility::HandleError(Message);
        return is;
        }

    Temp.Read(is);
    Item = Temp;

    if (is.fail() != 0)
        HomeUtility::HandleError("Couldn't create object");

    return is;
    }
```

This function isn't too different from the last version we saw (Figure 11.33). The differences are as follows:

1. We are allowing the user to hit ENTER to exit from this function without having to define a new item. This is useful when the user decides not to create a new item after selecting the "Add Item" function.

2. We are requiring only the first letter of the type rather than the whole type name. We are also allowing either upper- or lower-case versions of the type letter.

3. We are using the HandleError function to display the error message indicating that the object type was invalid.

4. If the data for the object cannot be read from the input stream, we are displaying a message telling the user about that problem.

Now let's move on to the changes to the HomeItemMusic class implementation. We'll start with the Edit function, whose code is shown in Figure 13.28.

FIGURE 13.28. The latest version of the HomeItemBasic::Edit **function (from code\hmit8.cc)**

```
void HomeItemBasic::Edit()
{
  short FieldNumber;
  bool result;

  FormattedDisplay(cout);
  cout << endl;

  cout << "Please enter field number to be changed " <<
    "or ENTER for none: ";

  FieldNumber = HomeUtility::GetNumberOrEnter();

  cout << endl;

  if (FieldNumber == -1)
    return;

  EditField(FieldNumber);
}
```

This function differs from the previous version (Figure 11.40) only in its improved flexibility and error checking. Rather than simply asking the user to enter a field number and then assuming that the field number entered is valid, we use the GetNumberOrEnter function to allow the user to enter a field number or to just hit the ENTER key to indicate that he or she has decided not to edit a field after all. Once we have received the return value from the GetNumberOrEnter function, we check to see whether it is the special value -1, which indicates that the user has decided not to enter a number but has just hit the ENTER key. If this is the case, we simply return to the calling function without calling EditField to do the actual field modification. Otherwise, we call EditField to modify the selected field and return when it is finished.

The next function in the HomeItemBasic class we will cover is ReadInteractive, whose code is shown in Figure 13.29.

FIGURE 13.29. The newest version of HomeItemBasic::ReadInteractive **(from code\hmit8.cc)**

```
short HomeItemBasic::ReadInteractive()
{
  double PurchasePrice;
  long PurchaseDate;
  bool result;

  short FieldNumber = e_Name;

  cout << FieldNumber << ". ";
  cout << GetFieldName(FieldNumber) << ": ";
  FieldNumber ++;
  cin >> m_Name;

  cout << FieldNumber << ". ";
  cout << GetFieldName(FieldNumber) << " (xxx.xx with no $ or ,): ";
  FieldNumber ++;
  cin >> PurchasePrice;
  result = HomeUtility::CheckNumericInput();
  if (result == true)
    m_PurchasePrice = PurchasePrice;
  else
    {
    m_Name = "";
    return 0;
    }

  cout << FieldNumber << ". ";
  cout << GetFieldName(FieldNumber) << " (YYYYMMDD): ";
  FieldNumber ++;
  cin >> PurchaseDate;
  result = HomeUtility::CheckDateInput(PurchaseDate);
  if (result == true)
    m_PurchaseDate = PurchaseDate;
```

```
else
 {
 m_Name = "";
 return 0;
 }

cout << FieldNumber << ". ";
cout << GetFieldName(FieldNumber) << ": ";
FieldNumber ++;
cin >> m_Description;

cout << FieldNumber << ". ";
cout << GetFieldName(FieldNumber) << ": ";
FieldNumber ++;
cin >> m_Category;

*this = HomeItemBasic(m_Name, m_PurchasePrice,
m_PurchaseDate, m_Description, m_Category);

return FieldNumber;
}
```

The only difference between this version of the ReadInteractive function and the one in Figure 11.38 is its improved error checking and feedback to the user. In addition to checking the validity of numbers and dates entered by the user, this new version also tells the user what sort of input is expected. In particular, it tells the user to type in the purchase price without using a $ or comma—it's entirely possible that the user might not realize that using these symbols would cause a problem in interpreting the value. This version also tells the user to type the date in the form YYYYMMDD rather than in a more familiar format such as MM/DD/YY. After telling the user how to enter these data items, it tries to check that the values entered for those items are reasonable. This is a much safer approach than assuming that these values must be all right, as the previous version of the function did.

The changes to the next function we will cover, EditItem (Figure 13.30), are very similar to those in the previous function. To be precise, they consist of more error checking. These changes should be obvious enough that we don't have to discuss them.

FIGURE 13.30. The new version of the HomeItemBasic::EditItem **function (from code\hmit8.cc)**

```
bool HomeItemBasic::EditField(short FieldNumber)
{
  bool result = true;
  double PurchasePrice;
  long PurchaseDate;

  switch (FieldNumber)
   {
  case e_Name:
  cout << FieldNumber << ". ";
  cout << GetFieldName(FieldNumber) << ": ";
  cin >> m_Name;
  break;

  case e_PurchasePrice:
  cout << FieldNumber << ". ";
  cout << GetFieldName(FieldNumber) << ": ";
  cin >> PurchasePrice;
  result = HomeUtility::CheckNumericInput();
  if (result == true)
    m_PurchasePrice = PurchasePrice;
  break;

  case e_PurchaseDate:
  cout << FieldNumber << ". ";
  cout << GetFieldName(FieldNumber) << ": ";
  cin >> PurchaseDate;
  result = HomeUtility::CheckDateInput(PurchaseDate);
  if (result == true)
    m_PurchaseDate = PurchaseDate;
```

```
      break;

      case e_Description:
      cout << FieldNumber << ". ";
      cout << GetFieldName(FieldNumber) << ": ";
      cin >> m_Description;
      break;

      case e_Category:
      cout << FieldNumber << ". ";
      cout << GetFieldName(FieldNumber) << ": ";
      cin >> m_Category;
      break;

      default:
      cout << endl;
      HomeUtility::HandleError("Sorry, that is not a valid field number");
      result = false;
      break;
      }

   return result;
   }
```

The two functions in the HomeItemMusic class, ReadInteractive and EditField, that have changed from the previous versions follow the changes that we have just looked at very closely, so I will list them without further comment.

FIGURE 13.31. The latest version of HomeItemMusic::ReadInteractive **(from code\hmit8.cc)**

```
short HomeItemMusic::ReadInteractive()
{
  short TrackCount;
  bool result;

  short FieldNumber = HomeItemBasic::ReadInteractive();
```

```
// Check whether Basic input worked. If not, forget it.
if (FieldNumber == 0)
  return 0;

cout << FieldNumber << ". ";
cout << GetFieldName(FieldNumber) << ": ";
FieldNumber ++;
cin >> m_Artist;

cout << FieldNumber << ". ";
cout << GetFieldName(FieldNumber) << ": ";
FieldNumber ++;
cin >> TrackCount;
result = HomeUtility::CheckNumericInput();
if (result == true)
  m_Track.resize(TrackCount);
else
  {
  m_Name = "";
  return 0;
  }

vector<string> Track(TrackCount);
for (short i = 0; i < TrackCount; i ++)
  {
  cout << FieldNumber << ". ";
  cout << GetFieldName(FieldNumber) << i + 1 << ": ";
  FieldNumber ++;
  cin >> Track[i];
  }

*this = HomeItemMusic(m_Name, m_PurchasePrice,
m_PurchaseDate, m_Description, m_Category, m_Artist,
Track);

return FieldNumber;
}
```

FIGURE 13.32. The latest version of HomeItemMusic::EditField **(from code\hmit8.cc)**

```cpp
bool HomeItemMusic::EditField(short FieldNumber)
{
  if (FieldNumber < e_Artist)
    {
    return HomeItemBasic::EditField(FieldNumber);
    }

  bool result;

  short TrackCount = m_Track.size();

  switch (FieldNumber)
    {
    case e_Artist:
    cout << FieldNumber << ". ";
    cout << GetFieldName(FieldNumber) << ": ";
    cin >> m_Artist;
    return true;

    case e_TrackCount:
    cout << FieldNumber << ". ";
    cout << GetFieldName(FieldNumber) << ": ";
    cin >> TrackCount;
    result = HomeUtility::CheckNumericInput();
    if (result == true)
      m_Track.resize(TrackCount);
    return result;
    }

  if (FieldNumber > (e_TrackCount + TrackCount))
    {
    HomeUtility::HandleError("Sorry, that is not a valid field number");
    return false;
    }

  cout << FieldNumber << ". ";
```

```
cout << GetFieldName(FieldNumber);
cout << FieldNumber - e_TrackCount << ": ";

cin >> m_Track[FieldNumber - e_TrackNumber];

return true;
}
```

Are We Having Fun Yet?

If nothing else, I hope that this exercise has given you a better appreciation of the difficulty of programming a solution to even an apparently simple problem in the real world. After reviewing what we've covered in the chapter, we'll get to some exercises that will give you an even better idea of how much fun programming can be![10]

Review

We started this chapter with our work cut out for us: The program was performing as intended, so we just had to go over exactly how it worked. We started with the new main function, which consists of two consecutive "endless" loops (loops that execute until a particular criterion is met). The first loop keeps executing as long as the user is still entering, modifying, or examining the data in the inventory. When the user is finished, the only remaining question is whether he

---

10. I'm sure you're just brimming with excitement at that thought, but please try to hold yourself back until you have read the review, so you don't lose track of what we've already covered in this chapter.

or she wants to save the changes, so the code in the second loop is designed to find the answer to that question and either save or discard the changes as desired.

The main work of the program is done inside the first loop, which consists of a call to the GetMenuChoice function to find out which operation the user wants to perform, followed by a call to the ExecuteMenuChoice function to execute that operation. When the user selects the "exit" operation, this loop terminates and allows the second loop to start execution.

The GetMenuChoice function is fairly simple, but it uses some functions we hadn't seen previously, including the clrscr function, which clears the screen, the GetCount function, which returns the number of items in the inventory, and the HandleError function of the HomeUtility class.

Once the GetMenuChoice function has determined which operation the user wants to perform, the ExecuteMenuChoice function takes over to execute it. It does this with a switch statement that contains one case for each possible operation. All of these cases are fairly similar. The main task of each of them is to request any information that might be required from the user, to display a heading telling the user what operation is in progress, and then to call a function in the Inventory class to do the actual work. If the operation results in a change to the database, the resulting inventory is saved in a backup file so that it can be recovered in the event of a power failure or other crash. Because of the similarity of the code in each of these cases, we won't review them further. Instead, we will proceed to the functions of the HomeUtility class, starting with a very simple function, IgnoreTillCR. As its name suggests, this function ignores characters until it gets to a "carriage return"[11], which is generated when the ENTER key is struck. The next function is HandleError, which is used to display an error message and wait for the user to hit ENTER.

---

11. This character is also known as "newline".

The next function in this class is CheckNumericInput, which is intended to be called after every numeric input operation. It determines whether the previous input operation was successful by looking to see whether the next character waiting in the input stream is a newline. If so, all of the characters up to that point have been accepted by the input operator as part of a numeric value, which means that the user didn't type anything that shouldn't be in a number. In that case, the function returns the value true to its caller to indicate success. However, if the next character in the input stream isn't a newline, the user must have included some inappropriate character(s) in the input. In that case, this function displays the leftover characters and returns the value false to the calling function to inform it of the error.

The next function we discussed is HomeUtility::CheckDateInput, which first calls CheckNumericInput to make sure that the user hasn't inserted any odd characters into the date value being typed in. Then it checks the value of the date to make sure that it is believable: Our definition of that characteristic is on or after January 1st, 1800, or 0. Of course, 0 is not a valid date; however, we need some way for the user to say, "I don't know when I acquired this object", and 0 is as good a way as any to say that.

The next function in the HomeUtility class, GetNumberOrEnter, is considerably more complicated than the other functions in that class, as it has the more complex task of taking input from the user one keystroke at a time. This function actually has two "modes" of operation. In the first mode, it accepts only digits, ENTER, and the backspace key, which is used for correcting errors; in the second mode, it also accepts the up and down arrow keys—this mode is used when the user wants to select an item from a list via the SelectItem function. While going through this function, we ran into several new constructs, the most significant being the getkey function (left over from C) that allows us to read one key from the keyboard without having to wait for the user to hit the ENTER key, as is necessary when we use the standard C++ stream input functions. In addition to getkey, we also discussed the symbols that represent the special keys, such as backspace and newline; these keys have to be handled differently from the "normal" digit keys in this function. We also saw that it is necessary to copy the key value from an int to a char variable before displaying it on the screen if we want it to come out in the proper format. Sending an int to cout via operator << will display the numeric value of the int, which in this case would not be informative to the user who is expecting to see the key he or she just pressed!

After we covered the details of this GetNumberOrEnter function, including the way in which it handles the backspace key so that the user can back up and change the value of the number, we moved on to the relatively simple HomeUtility::ClearRestOfScreen function, which is used by SelectItem to erase the part of the screen it uses to display its list of items. Even though this ClearRestOfScreen function isn't very complicated, it deserved some discussion because it was the first one where we used several of the screen-handling functions from the conio (console I/O) library: gotoxy, clreol, and ScreenRows. The gotoxy function, as its name suggests, allows us to position the "cursor" (the place where the next character will be written on the screen) to a particular X and Y coordinate: X is the column number and Y is the row number. Unusually for C or C++, this function starts counting at 1; that is, the first row and first column are numbered 1 rather than 0. The clreol function erases some or all of the characters on the line where the cursor is currently located, from the cursor's position rightward to the end of the line. The ScreenRows function tells us the number of lines on the screen, which we need so we will know where to stop clearing lines.

HomeUtility::SelectItem, the next function we discussed, is responsible for allowing the user to select from a list of items. It has two arguments: Number, a vector of indexes into the inventory list of the items to be displayed, and Name, a vector of textual information about each of those items. The latter vector always includes the names of the items and sometimes contains additional information about them (e.g., the category under which each item is found).

The first thing we do in this function is determine the number of lines on the "screen" in the DOS window in which our program is running, as well as how many lines have already been used by the calling program. The former information is accessible via the GetScreenRows function, which we've already discussed; the latter information is available via the GetCursor function, which tells us the row and column where the cursor is currently positioned. We can use this information and the number of items to be displayed to determine how much screen area we will devote to the "scroll area", which is where we display the listing of data items from which the user selects an individual item to be edited.[12]

Once we have decided how many lines we will use for the scroll area, we check how many items the calling function has provided. If this is less than the number of lines allocated for the scroll area, we reduce the size of the scroll area to match. If there are no items in the input vector, we give an error message to the user telling him or her that information.

After we know how many items we will display at one time, we start by displaying the first part of the item list. Once we have cleared the portion of the screen where we will display the list, we display each of the elements in this part of the list, using fixed-width formatting for the item number to ensure that all of the item names line up correctly. After displaying the list, we ask the user to type in one of the listed item numbers, via GetNumberOrEnter. Besides an item number, the user can hit the up or down arrow to ask us to scroll the item list up or down. The user can also hit the ENTER key to end input or the backspace key to correct an erroneous entry. If the user simply hits ENTER, or erases all the digits that were typed in by using the backspace key, we get a return value from GetNumberOrEnter that indicates this. In that event, we return the value 0 to our calling function to indicate that the user hasn't selected an item.

---

12. In the version of the program on the CD at the back of the book, the maximum size of the scroll area is fixed at 5, as this makes debugging the program easier. However, you are free to change that so it will use more of the screen. Personally, I like it the way it is.

On the other hand, if the user hasn't simply hit ENTER, we have to check the return value from GetNumberOrEnter to see what the user has done. If that return value is one of the arrow keys, we adjust the portion of the list to be displayed and continue. Otherwise, we must have received an actual numeric value from the user. In that case, we check that this value is a valid entry in the list of item numbers from which the user was selecting. If so, we are finished, and we return that value to the calling function. If it is not an item number from the list, we tell the user about this error and return 0 to the calling function to indicate that the user has not made a valid selection.

After dealing with that final function in the HomeUtility class, we moved on to the changes in the HomeInventory class. These changes weren't too extensive, primarily consisting of better error checking and sorting of the inventory list by the name of the item. Other changes included the ability of the "locate" functions to return a vector of item indexes rather than just one, the addition of functions to locate items by their category fields, and the ability to print items or item names. The most complicated function in this new version of the class, besides the sorting function, is SelectItemFromCategoryList, because it uses some fairly fancy formatting to get the category information to line up correctly. The main complexity is caused by the necessity to pad the item names to a consistent length so that the category information will start in the same column on the screen for each item no matter how long its name may be. Because we don't know how long the longest name will be until we have examined all the names, we have to make two passes through the list. The first pass finds the length of the longest name, and the second pass pads each name to that length. Once we have done this, we add the category name for each item to the end of the entry for that item. After we have created and displayed the heading, we call the SelectItem function to allow the user to select one of the items.

The final function in the HomeInventory class that we discussed is DeleteItem, which deletes an item from the inventory list. Starting at the item to be deleted, it moves all of the items after that point one position closer to the beginning of the inventory list; then it reduces the size of the list by one. This effectively eliminates the selected item from the inventory.

The changes to the HomeItem class were relatively small. We modified the implementation of operator >> to allow the user to hit ENTER to avoid entering an item, to allow the user to enter only the first letter of the type rather than having to type "Basic" or "Music", and to improve error handling. The changes in the HomeItemBasic and HomeItemMusic classes consisted of simple improvements to error handling and flexibility in user input, so they didn't require any additional discussion.

Exercises

1. Add the ability to edit an existing description field. Which classes will have to be changed to do this?

2. Before writing over the old version of the data base at the conclusion of the program, copy that file to another name so that the user can go back to it if necessary.

3. At present, the ExecuteMenuChoice function always saves the inventory in the backup file after calling AddItem. This is not necessary if the user didn't actually add a new item. Fix the code so that this unnecessary operation is avoided.

4. Add the ability for the user to see only items of a given type, such as "Basic" or "Music", rather than having to see all types together in one list.

5. Change the data entry function so that the user can correct an entry and continue entering data for an item even after making an error.

6. Add validation of dates so that invalid dates such as 19970231 are not accepted.

7. Allow the user to type dates with or without slashes so that 1997/02/28 will be the same as 19970228.

8. Add the ability for the user to print selected items according to category, description, and the like.

9. Explain why hitting the ENTER key when asked for a category produces a list including all categories.

10. Implement the HomeItemCollectible class as a derived class of HomeItemBasic to keep track of objects such as coins or stamps. The added fields should include date of creation, condition, artist, and any other appropriate fields.

Conclusion

If you've made it this far, congratulations! You have truly begun to understand the complexities of C++ in particular and software development in general. At this point, you should be able to read almost any book on software development in C++ with profit and understanding.

Tying up Loose Ends

Now that you've reached the end of this book, some questions have probably occurred to you. For example:

1. Am I a programmer now?

2. What am I qualified to do?

3. Where do I go from here?

4. Is that all there is to C++?

Before we get to the answers to these questions, let's take care of some assorted topics that are likely to be covered in any other book that you might read on programming in C++, so that they aren't foreign to you when you encounter them in your future reading.

Operator Precedence

You may recall from high school arithmetic that an expression like 5 + 3 * 9, is calculated as though it were written 5 + (3 * 9), not (5 + 3) * 9; that is, you have to perform the * before the +, so that the correct result is 32, not 72, as it would be under the latter interpretation. The reason for performing the operations in the former order is that multiplication has a higher *precedence* than addition. Well, every operator in C++ also has a precedence that determines the order of application of each operator in an expression with more than one operator. This seems like a good idea at first glance, since after all, arithmetic does follow precedence rules like the one we just saw. Unfortunately, C++ is just a little more complicated than arithmetic, and so its precedence rules are not as simple and easy to remember as those of arithmetic. In fact, there are 17 different levels of precedence, which no one can remember. Therefore, everyone (or at least, everyone who is sensible) ends up using parentheses to specify what order was meant when the expression was written; of course, if we're going to have to use parentheses, then why do we need the precedence rules in the first place?

Another Native Data Type

We've used almost all the native data types, but there is one other native type that you might see in other programs and in other textbooks, so I should tell you about it now. By the way, I haven't avoided this type because it's particularly difficult to use; the reason is simply that it wasn't necessary to the task at hand, which was teaching you how to program, using C++. Now that we have accomplished that task, you might as well add it to your arsenal of tools. This other native type is float, which, like the double type we've already seen, is used to store values that can contain fractional parts, (so-called *floating-point* numbers). Why are there two of these types rather than only one? The main difference between float and double is that a float is 4 bytes long and a double is 8 bytes long; therefore, a double can store larger values and maintain higher accuracy. However, it also uses twice the amount of memory of a float, which may not be important when we're dealing with a few values but is quite important if we have a vector or array of thousands or tens of thousands of elements.

Wrapping Up

The answer to the first three questions at the beginning of this chapter, as usual with such open-ended topics, is "It all depends". Of course, I can give you some general answers. Let's start with questions 1 and 2.

If you have done all of the exercises in this book, you certainly have earned the right to call yourself a programmer—you've read quite a bit of code and have written some nontrivial programs. But, of course, this doesn't mean that you're a professional programmer. No book can turn a novice into a professional—in any field. That takes a lot of hard work, and although you've undoubtedly worked hard in understanding this book and applying your understanding to the exercises, you still have a lot to learn about programming.

Questions 3 and 4 are also closely related. You now have enough background that you should be able to get some benefit from a well-written book about C++ that assumes you are already acquainted with programming; that would be a good way to continue. As for whether we've covered everything about C++, the answer is unequivocal: absolutely not. I would estimate that you are now familiar with perhaps 10% of the very large, complicated, and powerful C++ language; however, that 10% is the foundation for the rest of your learning in this subject. Most books try to cover every aspect of the language and, as a result, cannot provide the deep coverage of fundamentals. I've worked very hard to ensure that you have the correct tools to continue your learning. Good luck!

Glossary

Special Characters

& has a number of distinct meanings. When it precedes the name of a variable without following a type name, it means "the address of the following variable". For example, &Str means "the address of the variable Str". When & follows a type name and precedes a variable name, it means that the variable being declared is a reference—that is, another name for a preexisting variable. In this book, references are used only in argument lists, where they indicate that the variable being defined is a new name for the caller's variable rather than a new local variable.

% is the "modulus" operator, which returns the remainder after dividing its left-hand argument by its right-hand argument.

< is the "less than" operator, which returns the value true if the expression on its left has a lower value than the expression on its right; otherwise, it returns the value false. Also see *operator* < in the index.

= is the assignment operator, which assigns the value on its right to the variable on its left. Also see *operator =* in the index.

> is the "greater than" operator, which returns the value true if the expression on its left has a greater value than the expression on its right; otherwise, it returns the value false. Also see *operator >* in the index.

[is the left square bracket; see *square brackets* for usage.

] is the right square bracket; see *square brackets* for usage.

{ is the left curly brace; see *curly braces* for usage.

} is the right curly brace; see *curly braces* for usage.

!= is the "not equals" operator, which returns the value true if the expression on its left has a value different from the expression on its right; otherwise, it returns the value false. Also see *operator !=* in the index.

&& is the "logical AND" operator. It produces the result true if the expressions on both its right and left are true; if either of those expressions is false, it produces the result false. However, this isn't the whole story. There is a special rule in C++ governing the execution of the && operator: If the expression on the left is false, then the answer must be false and the expression on the right is not executed at all. The reason for this *short-circuit evaluation rule* is that in some cases you may want to write a right-hand expression that will only be legal if the left-hand expression is true.

++ is the increment operator, which adds 1 to the variable to which it is affixed.

+= is the "add to variable" operator, which adds the value on its right to the variable on its left.

-= is the "subtract from variable" operator, which subtracts the value on its right from the variable on its left.

// is the comment operator; see *comment* for usage.

<< is the "stream output" operator, used to write data to an ostream. Also see *operator* << in the index.

<= is the "less than or equal to" operator, which returns the value true if the expression on its left has the same or a lower value than that of the expression on its right; otherwise, it returns the value false. Also see *operator* <= in the index.

== is the "equals" operator, which returns the value true if the expression on its left has the same value as that of the expression on its right; otherwise, it returns the value false. Also see *operator* == in the index.

>= is the "greater than or equal to" operator, which returns the value true if the expression on its left has the same or a greater value than that of the expression on its right; otherwise, it returns the value false. Also see *operator* >= in the index.

>> is the "stream input" operator, used to read data from an istream. Also see *operator* >> in the index.

[ ] is used after the delete operator to tell the compiler that the pointer for which delete was called refers to a group of elements rather than just one data item. This is one of the few times when we have to make that distinction explicitly rather than leaving it to context.

|| is the "logical OR" operator. It produces the result true if at least one of the two expressions on its right and left is true; if both expressions are false, it produces the result false. However, there is a special rule in C++ governing the execution of the || operator: If the expression on the left is true, then the answer must be true and the expression on the right is not executed at all. The reason for this *short-circuit evaluation* rule is that in some cases you may want to write a right-hand expression that will only be legal if the left-hand expression is false.

A **#define** statement is a *preprocessor directive* that defines a *preprocessor symbol*. While this statement can be used to define constant values for general use, it has been mostly superseded except as part of the *include guard* mechanism.

An **#endif** statement is a *preprocessor directive* that terminates a section of conditional code. It is used in this book as part of the *include guard* mechanism.

An **#ifdef** statement is a *preprocessor directive* that begins a section of conditional code.

An **#ifndef** statement is a *preprocessor directive* that tells the preprocessor to check whether a particular *preprocessor symbol* has been defined. If not, the following source code is treated normally. However, if the specified preprocessor symbol has been defined, the following source code is skipped by the rest of the compiler as though it were not present in the source file. The #ifndef statement is used in this book as part of the *include guard* mechanism.

An **#include** statement is a *preprocessor directive* that has the same effect as that of copying all of the code from a specified file into another file at the point where the #include statement is written. For example, if we wanted to use definitions contained in a file called iostream.h in the implementation file test.cc, we could insert the include statement #include <iostream.h> in test.cc rather than physically copying the lines from the file iostream.h into test.cc.

A

An **access specifier** controls the access of nonmember functions to the member functions and variables of a class. The C++ access specifiers are public, private, and protected. See *public*, *private*, and *protected* for details. Also see *friend*.

Access time is a measure of how long it takes to retrieve data from a storage device, such as a hard disk or RAM.

Address; see *memory address*.

An **algorithm** is a set of precisely defined steps guaranteed to arrive at an answer to a problem or set of problems. As this implies, a set of steps that might never end is not an algorithm.

Aliasing is the practice of referring to one object by more than one "name"; in C++, these names are actually pointers.

The **aliasing problem** is a name for the difficulties that are caused by altering a shared object.

An **application program** is a program that actually accomplishes some useful or interesting task. Examples include inventory control, payroll, and games.

An **application programmer** (or *class user*) is a programmer who uses native and class variables to write an application program. Also see *library designer*.

An **argument** is a value supplied by one function (the *calling function*) that wishes to make use of the services of another function (the *called function*). There are two main types of argument: *value arguments*, which are copies of the values from the calling function, and *reference arguments*, which are not copies but actually refer to variables in the calling function.

An **argument list** is a set of argument definitions specified in a function declaration. The argument list describes the types and names of all the variables the function receives when it is called by a calling function.

An **array** is a group of elements of the same type—for example, an array of chars. The array name corresponds to the address of the first of these elements; the other elements follow the first one immediately in memory. As with a vector, we can refer to the individual elements by their indexes. Thus, if we have an array of chars called m_Data, m_Data[i] refers to the ith char in the array. Also see *pointer*, and *vector*.

An **array initialization list** is a list of values used to initialize the elements of an *array*. The ability to specify a list of values for an array is built into the C++ language and is not available for user-defined data types such as the vector.

The **ASCII code** is a standardized representation of characters by binary or hexadecimal values. For example, the letter "A" is represented as a char with the hexadecimal value 41, and the digit 0 is represented as a char with the hexadecimal value 30. All other printable characters also have representations in the ASCII code.

An **assembler** is a program that translates *assembly language* instructions into *machine instructions*.

An **assembly language** instruction is the human-readable representation of a *machine instruction*.

Assignment is the operation of setting a variable to a value. The operator that indicates assignment is the equal sign, =. Also see *operator =* in the index.

An **assignment operator** is a function that sets a preexisting variable to a value of the same type. There are three varieties of assignment operators:

1. For a variable of a native type, the compiler supplies a native assignment operator.

2. For a variable of a class type, the compiler generates its own version of an assignment operator (a compiler-generated assignment operator) if the class writer does not write one.

3. The class writer can write a member function to do the assignment; see *operator =* in the index.

An **assignment statement** such as *x = 5;* is not an algebraic equality, no matter how much it may resemble one. It is a command telling the compiler to assign a value to a variable. In the example, the variable is *x* and the value is *5*.

The **auto storage class** is the default *storage class* for variables declared within C++ functions. When we define a variable of the auto storage class, its memory address is assigned automatically upon entry to the function where it is defined; the memory address is valid for the duration of that function.

Automatic conversion is a feature of C++ that allows an expression of one type to be used where another type is expected. For example, a short variable or expression can be provided when an int expression is expected, and the compiler will convert the type of the expression automatically.

B

Base class: see *inheritance*.

A **base class initializer** specifies which base class constructor we want to use to initialize the base class part of a derived class object. It is one of the two types of expression allowed in a *member initialization list*. Also see *inheritance*.

The **base class part** of a derived class object is an unnamed component of the derived class object whose member variables and functions are accessible as though they were defined in the derived class, so long as they are either public or protected.

A **batch file** is a text file that directs the execution of a number of programs, one after the other, without manual intervention. A similar facility is available in most operating systems.

A **binary** number system uses only two digits, 0 and 1.

A **bit** is the fundamental unit of storage in a modern computer; the word *bit* is derived from the phrase *binary digit*. Each bit, as this suggests, can have one of two states: 0 and 1.

A **block** is a group of statements considered as one logical statement. It is delimited by the curly braces, { and }. The first of these symbols starts a block, and the second one ends it. A block can be used anywhere that a statement can be used and is treated exactly as if it were one statement. For example, if a block is the controlled block of an if statement, all of the statements in the block are executed if the condition in the if is true, and none is executed if the condition in the if is false.

A **bool** (short for Boolean) is a type of variable whose range of values is limited to true or false. This is the most appropriate return type for a function that uses its *return value* to report whether some condition exists, such as operator <. In that particular case, the return value true indicates that the first argument is less than the second, while false indicates that the first argument is not less than the second.

Brace; see *curly braces*.

A **break statement** is a loop control device that interrupts the processing of a loop whenever it is executed within the controlled block of a loop control statement. When a break statement is executed, the flow of control passes to the next statement after the end of the controlled block.

A **buffer** is a temporary holding place where information is stored while it is being manipulated.

Buffering is the process of using a buffer to store or retrieve information.

A **byte** is the unit in which data capacities are stated, whether in RAM or on a disk. In modern computers, a byte consists of eight bits.

C

A **C function** is one that is inherited from the *C library*. Because C does not have a number of features that have been added in C++, such as *function overloading* and *reference arguments*, C functions must often be called in different ways from those we use when calling a C++ function.

The **C library** is a collection of functions that were originally written for users of the C programming language. Because C++ is a descendant of C, these functions are often still useful in C++ programs.

A **C string** is a literal value representing a variable number of characters. An example is "This is a test.". C strings are surrounded by double quotes ("). Please note that this is *not* the same as the C++ string class.

A **cache** is a small amount of fast memory where frequently used data is stored temporarily.

Call; see *function call* or *call instruction*.

A **call instruction** is an *assembly language* instruction used to implement a *function call*. It saves the *program counter* on the stack and then transfers execution from the *calling function* to the *called function*.

A **called function** is a function that starts execution as the result of a *function call*. Normally, it returns to the *calling function* via a *return statement* when finished.

A **calling function** is a function that suspends execution as a result of a *function call*; the *called function* begins execution at the point of the function call.

The **carriage return** character is used to signal the end of a line of text. Also see *newline* in the index.

A function is said to be **case-sensitive** if upper- and lower-case letters are considered to be distinct.

A function is said to be **case-insensitive** if upper- and lower-case letters are considered equivalent. See *less_nocase* in the index.

To **catch** an *exception* means to handle an interruption in the normal flow control of a program, usually due to an error condition. An exception is generated via a throw statement, and can be caught in a function that has directly or indirectly called the function that threw the exception. The catch keyword is used in conjunction with try, which specifies a block of code to which a specific catch statement or statements may be applicable. A catch can specify the type of exceptions that it will handle, or can use "..." to specify that it will handle any and all exceptions.

A **char** is an *integer variable* type that can represent either one character of text or a small whole number. Both signed and unsigned chars are available for use as "really short" *integer variables*; a signed char can represent a number from -128 to +127, whereas an unsigned char can represent a number from 0 to 255. (In case you were wondering, the most common pronunciation of char has an "a" as in "married", while the "ch" sounds like "k". Other pronunciations include the standard English pronunciation of "char" as in overcooking meat, and even "car" as in "automobile".)

A **char*** (pronounced "char star") is a pointer to (i.e., the memory address of) a char or the first of a group of chars.

Child class: see *inheritance*.

cin (pronounced "see in") is a predefined *istream*; it gets its characters from the keyboard.

A **class** is a user-defined type; for example, string is a class.

A **class designer** is a programmer who designs classes. Also see *application programmer*.

A **class implementation** tells the compiler how to implement the facilities defined in the *class interface*. It is usually found in a implementation file, which the compiler on the CD-ROM in the back of this book assumes has the extension .cc.

A **class interface** tells the user of the class what facilities the class provides by specifying the class's public member functions. It also tells the compiler what data elements are included in objects of the class, but this is not logically part of the interface. A class interface is usually found in a *header file*—that is, one with the extension .h.

The **class membership operator**, ::, indicates which class a function belongs to. For example, the full name of the default constructor for the string class is string::string().

class scope describes the visibility of *member variables*—that is, those defined within a class. These variables can be accessed by any *member function* of that class; their accessibility to other functions is controlled by the *access specifier* in effect when they were defined in the *class interface*.

A **comment** is a note to yourself or another programmer; it is ignored by the compiler. The symbol // marks the beginning of a comment; the comment continues until the end of the line containing the //. For those of you with BASIC experience, this is just like REM (the "remark" keyword)—anything after it on a line is ignored by the compiler.

Compilation is the process of translating source code into an object program, which is composed of machine instructions along with the data needed by those instructions. Virtually all of the software on your computer was created by this process.

A **compiler** is a program that performs compilation.

A **compiler-generated function** is supplied by the compiler because the existence of that function is fundamental to the notion of a *concrete data type*. The compiler will automatically generate its own version of any of the following functions if they are not provided by the creator of the class: the *assignment operator*, the *copy constructor*, the *default constructor*, and the *destructor*.

A **compiler warning** is a message from the compiler informing the programmer of a potentially erroneous construct. While a warning does not prevent the compiler from generating an *executable program*, a wise programmer will heed such warnings, as they often reveal hazardous coding practices.

Compile time means "while the compiler is compiling the source code of a program".

Concatenation is the operation of appending a string to the end of another string. Also see *operator +* in the index.

A **concrete data type** is a class whose objects behave like variables of native data types. That is, the class gives the compiler enough information that objects of that class can be created, copied, assigned, and automatically destroyed, just as native variables are.

The keyword **const** has two distinct meanings as employed in this book. The first is as a modifier to an argument of a function. In this context, it means that we are promising not to modify the value of that argument in the function. An example of this use might be the function declaration string& operator = (const string& Str);. The second use of const in this book is to define a data item similar to a variable, except that its value cannot be changed once it has been initialized. For this reason, it is mandatory to supply an initial value when creating a const. An example of this use is const short x = 5;.

A **constructor** is a *member function* that creates new objects of a (particular) class type. All constructors have the same name as that of the class for which they are constructors; for example, the constructors for the string class have the name string. A constructor that takes only one required argument is also a *conversion function*.

A **continuation expression** is the part of a for statement computed before every execution of the controlled block. The block controlled by the for will be executed if the result of the computation is true but not if it is false. See *for statement* for an example.

The **continue** keyword causes execution of a for loop to continue to the next iteration without executing any further statements in the current iteration.

A **controlled block** is a block under the control of a loop control statement or an if or else statement. The controlled block of a loop control statement can be executed a variable number of times, whereas the controlled block of an if or else statement is executed either once or not at all.

Controlled statement; see *controlled block*.

A **conversion function** is a *member function* that converts an object of its class to some other type, or vice versa. Also see *implicit conversion*.

A **copy constructor** makes a new object with the same contents as an existing object of the same type.

cout (pronounced "see out") is a predefined ostream; characters sent to it are displayed on the screen.

CPU is an abbreviation for Central Processing Unit. This is the "active" part of your computer, which executes all the *machine instructions* that make the computer do useful work.

The **curly braces { and }** are used to surround a *block*. The compiler treats the statements in the block as one statement.

A **cursor** is an abstract object that represents the position on the screen where input or output will occur next.

D

Data refers to the pieces of information that are operated on by programs. Originally, "data" was the plural of "datum"; however, the form "data" is now commonly used as both singular and plural.

A **day number** is an integer value representing the number of days between two dates.

A **debugger** is a program that controls the execution of another program so that you can see what the latter program is doing. The RHIDE development environment on the CD-ROM in the back of this book includes a debugger that will allow you to examine the execution of your programs.

A **dedicated register** is a register such as the *stack pointer* whose usage is predefined rather than determined by the programmer, as in the case of *general registers* such as eax.

A **default argument** is a method of specifying a value for an argument to a function when the user of the function doesn't supply a value for that argument. The value of the default argument is specified in the declaration of the function.

A **default constructor** is a *member function* that is used to create an object when no initial value is specified for that object. For example, string::string() is the default constructor for the string class.

The **default** keyword is used with the switch statement to specify an action to be performed when none of the case statements match the selection expression of the switch.

The **delete** operator is used to free memory previously used for variables of the *dynamic storage class*. This allows the memory to be reused for other variables.

Derived class: see *inheritance*.

A **destructor** is a *member function* that cleans up when an object expires; for an object of the auto storage class, the destructor is called automatically at the end of the function where that object is defined.

A **digit** is one of the characters used in any positional numbering system to represent all numbers starting at 0 and ending at one less than the base of the numbering system. In the decimal system, there are ten digits, '0' through '9', and in the hexadecimal system, there are sixteen digits, '0' through '9' and 'a' through 'f'.

DJGPP is a DOS C++ compiler derived by D. J. Delorie from the GNU Unix C++ compiler.

A **double** is a type of *floating-point variable* that can represent a range of positive and negative numbers, including fractional values. With most current C++ compilers, including DJGPP, these numbers can vary from approximately $4.940656e-324$ to approximately $1.79769e+308$ (and 0), with approximately 16 digits of precision.

Dynamic memory allocation is the practice of assigning memory locations to variables during execution of the program by explicit request of the programmer.

Variables of the **dynamic storage class** are assigned memory addresses at the programmer's explicit request. This storage class is often used for variables whose size is not known until run time.

Dynamic type checking refers to checking the correct usage of variables of different types during execution of a program rather than during compilation; see *type system* for further discussion.

Dynamic typing means delaying the determination of the exact type of a *variable* until *run time* rather than fixing that type at *compile time*, as in *static typing*. Please note that dynamic typing is not the same as *dynamic type checking*; C++ has the former but not the latter. See *type system* for further discussion.

E

An **element** is one of the variables that make up a *vector* or an *array*.

The keyword **else** causes its *controlled block* to be executed if the condition in its matching *if* statement turns out to be false at run time.

An **empty stack** is a stack that currently contains no values.

Encapsulation means hiding the details of a class inside the *implementation* of that class rather than exposing them in the *interface*. This is one of the primary organizing principles of *object-oriented programming*.

An **end user** is the person who actually uses an application program to perform some useful or interesting task. Also see *application programmer*, and *library designer*.

The ENTER key is the key that generates a *newline* character, which tells an *input* routine that the user has finished entering data.

Envelope class; see *manager/worker idiom*.

An **enum** is a way to define a number of unchangeable values, which are quite similar to *const*s. The value of each successive name in an enum is automatically incremented from the value of the previous name (if you don't specify another value explicitly). The term enum is short for "enumeration", which is a list of numbers.

An **exception** is an interruption in the normal flow of control in a program. When a function encounters an error condition, it can "throw an exception" to notify any calling function that wishes to handle this problem that it has occurred. If none of the calling functions handles the exception via a *catch* statement, the program will terminate.

Executable; see *executable program*.

An **executable program** is a program in a form suitable for running on a computer; it is composed of *machine instructions* along with data needed by those instructions.

The **explicit** keyword tells the compiler not to call a specified constructor unless that constructor has been called explicitly. This prevents such a constructor from being called to perform an *implicit conversion*.

F

The keyword **false** is a predefined value representing the result of a conditional expression whose condition is not satisfied. For example, in the conditional expression x < y, if x is not less than y, the result of the expression will be false. Also see bool.

A **fencepost error** is a logical error that causes a loop to be executed one more or one fewer time than the correct count. A common cause of this error is confusing the number of elements in a *vector* or *array* with the index of the last element. The derivation of this term is by analogy with the problem of calculating the number of fence sections and fenceposts that you need for a given fence. For example, if you have to put up a fence 100 feet long and each section of the fence is 10 feet long, how many sections of fence do you need? Obviously, the answer is 10. Now, how many fenceposts do you need? 11. The confusion caused by counting fenceposts when you should be counting segments of fence (and vice versa) is the cause of a fencepost error. To return to a programming example, if you have a vector with 11 elements, the index of the last element is 10, not 11. Confusing the number of elements with the highest index has much the same effect as that of the fencepost problem. This sort of problem is also known, less colorfully, as an *off-by-one error.*

Field; see *manipulator.*

A **float** is a type of *floating-point variable* that can represent a range of positive and negative numbers, including fractional values. With most current C++ compilers, including DJGPP, these numbers can vary from approximately 1.401298e−45 to approximately 3.40282e+38 (and 0), with approximately 6 digits of precision.

A **floating-point variable** is a C++ approximation of a mathematical "real number". Unlike mathematical real numbers, C++ floating-point variables have a limited range and precision depending on their types. See the individual types *float* and *double* for details.

A **for** statement is a *loop control statement* that causes its *controlled block* to be executed while a specified logical expression (the *continuation expression*) is true. It also provides for a *starting expression* to be executed before the first execution of the controlled block and for a *modification expression* to be executed after every execution of the controlled block. For example, in the for statement for (i = 0; i < 10; i ++), the initialization expression is i = 0, the continuation expression is i < 10, and the modification expression is i ++.

A **form-feed** character, when sent to a printer, causes the paper to be advanced to a new page.

The keyword **friend** allows access by a specified *class* or *function* to *private* or *protected* members of a particular class.

A **function** is a section of code having a name, optional *arguments*, and a *return type*. The name makes it possible for one function to start execution of another one via a *function call*. The arguments provide input for the function, and the return type allows the function to provide output to its *calling function* when the return statement causes the *calling function* to resume execution.

A **function call** (or *call* for short) causes execution to be transferred temporarily from the current function (the *calling function*) to the one named in the function call (the *called function*). Normally, when a called function is finished with its task, it returns to the calling function, which picks up execution at the statement after the function call.

A **function declaration** tells the compiler some vital statistics of the function: its name, its *arguments*, and its *return type*. Before we can use a function, the compiler must have already seen its function declaration. The most common way to arrange for this is to use a *#include* statement to insert the function declaration from a *header file* into an *implementation file*.

Function header; see *function declaration*.

Function overloading is the C++ facility that allows us to create more than one function with the same name. So long as all such functions have different *signatures*, we can write as many of them as we wish and the compiler will be able to figure out which one we mean.

G

A **general register** is a register whose usage is determined by the programmer, not predefined as with dedicated registers such as the *stack pointer*. On an Intel CPU such as the 486 or Pentium, the 16-bit general registers are ax, bx, cx, dx, si, di, and bp; the 32-bit general registers are eax, ebx, ecx, edx, esi, edi, and ebp.

A **get pointer** holds the address of the next byte in the input area of an *istream*—that is, where the next byte will be retrieved if we use >> to read data from the stream.

Global scope describes the visibility of variables defined outside any function; such variables can be accessed by code in any function. It also describes the visibility of functions defined outside any class.

The **global name space** is a name for the set of identifiers visible to all functions without a class name being specified. Adding identifiers to the global name space should be avoided when possible, as such identifiers can conflict with other similar identifiers defined by other programmers.

A **global function** is a function that has *global scope*.

A **global variable** is a variable that has *global scope*.

H

Hardware refers to the physical components of a computer — the ones you can touch. Examples include the keyboard, the monitor, and the printer.

A **header file** is a file that contains *class interface* definitions and/or *global* function declarations. By convention, header files have the extension .h.

The **heap** is the area of memory where variables of the *dynamic storage class* store their data.

Hex is an abbreviation for hexadecimal.

A **hexadecimal** number system has sixteen digits, '0' through '9' and 'a' through 'f'.

I

An **identifier** is a user-defined name; both function names and variable names are identifiers. Identifiers must not conflict with keywords such as if and for; for example, you cannot create a function or a variable with the name for.

An **if** statement is a statement that causes its *controlled block* to be executed if the logical expression specified in the if statement is true.

An **ifstream** (pronounced "i f stream") is a *stream* used for input from a file.

Implementation; see *class implementation*.

An **implementation file** contains *source code statements* that are turned into *executable code* by a *compiler*. In this book, implementation files have the extension .cc.

An **implicit conversion** is one that occurs without the programmer's explicit request. Also see *explicit*.

Include; see #include statement.

An **include guard** is a mechanism used to prevent the same class definition from being included in the same source code file more than once.

To **increment** a variable means to add 1 to its value. This can be done in C++ by using the increment operator, ++.

An **index** is an expression used to select one of a number of elements of a *vector* or an *array*. It is enclosed in square brackets ([ ]). For example, in the expression a[i+1], the index is the expression i+1.

An **index variable** is a variable used to hold an index into a *vector* or an *array*.

Inheritance is the definition of one class as a more specific version of another previously defined class. The newly defined class is called the *derived* (or sometimes the child) class, while the previously defined class is called the *base* (or sometimes the parent) class. In this book, we use the terms *base* and *derived*. The derived class inherits all of the *member variables* and *regular member functions* from the base class. Inheritance is one of the primary organizing principles of *object-oriented programming*.

Initialization is the process of setting the initial value of a *variable* or *const*. It is very similar to *assignment* but not identical. Initialization is done only when a variable or const is created, whereas a variable can be assigned to as many times as desired. A const, however, cannot be assigned to at all, so it must be initialized when it is created.

Input is the process of reading data into the computer from the outside world. A very commonly used source of input for simple programs is the keyboard.

Instruction; see *machine instruction*.

An **int** (short for *integer*) is a type of *integer variable*. While the C++ language definition requires only that an int be at least as long as a short and no longer than a long, with most current C++ compilers, this type is equivalent to either a short or a long, depending on the compiler you are using. A 16-bit compiler such as Borland C++ 3.1 has 16-bit (2-byte) ints that are the same size as shorts. A 32-bit compiler such as DJGPP (the compiler on the CD-ROM that comes with this book) has 32-bit (4-byte) ints that are the same size as longs.

An **integer variable** is a C++ representation of a whole number. Unlike mathematical integers, C++ integers have a limited range, which varies depending on their types. See the individual types char, short, int, and long for details. The type bool is sometimes also considered an integer variable type.

Interface; see *class interface*.

Interface file; see *header file*.

Internal polymorphism; see *polymorphic object*.

I/O is an abbreviation for "input/output". This refers to the process of getting information into and out of the computer. See *input* and *output* for more details.

iostream.h is the name of the *header file* that tells the compiler how to compile code that uses predefined stream variables like cout and cin and operators like << and >>.

An object of a *derived class* is said to have an "**isA**" relationship with its *base class* if the derived class object can be substituted for a base class object. In C++, objects of publicly derived classes have this relationship with their base classes.

An **istream** is a *stream* used for input. For example, cin is a predefined istream that reads characters from the keyboard.

K

A **keyword** is a word defined in the C++ language, such as if and for. It is illegal to define an *identifier* such as a variable or function name that conflicts with a keyword; for example, you cannot create a function or a variable with the name for.

L

Letter class; see *manager/worker idiom*.

A **library** (or library module) contains the object code generated from several *implementation files*, in a form that the *linker* can search when it needs to find general-purpose functions.

A **library designer** is a programmer who creates classes for *application programmers* to use in writing application programs.

The **linker** is a program that combines information from all of the *object files* for our program, along with some previously prepared files called *libraries*, to produce an *executable program*.

Linking is the process of creating an executable program from *object files* and *libraries*.

A **literal value** is a value that doesn't have a name, but instead represents itself in a literal manner. Some examples are 'x' (a char literal having the ASCII value that represents the letter "x") and 5 (a numeric literal with the value 5).

Local scope describes the visibility of variables defined within a function; such variables can be accessed only by code in that function.[1]

A **local variable** is a variable that has *local scope*.

A **logical expression** is an expression that takes on the value true or false rather than a numeric value. Some examples of such an expression are x > y (which will be true if x has a greater value than y and false otherwise) and a == b (which will be true if a has the same value as b, and false otherwise). Also see *bool*.

A **long** is a type of *integer variable* that can represent a whole number. With most current C++ compilers, including DJGPP, a long occupies 4 bytes of storage and therefore can represent a number in either the range —2147483648 to 2147483647 (if signed) or the range 0 to 4294967295 (if unsigned).

A **loop** is a means of executing a *controlled block* a variable number of times depending on some condition. The statement that controls the controlled block is called a loop control statement. This book covers the while and for loop control statements. See *while* and *for* for details.

A **loop control statement** is a statement that controls the *controlled block* in a loop.

---

1. In fact, a variable can be declared in any block, not just in a function. In that case, its scope is from the point where it is declared until the end of the block where it is defined. However, in this book all local variables have function scope, so omitting this distinction simplifies the discussion without invalidating the analysis.

M

Machine address; see *memory address*.

Machine code is the combination of *machine instructions* and the data they use. A synonym is *object code*.

A **machine instruction** is one of the fundamental operations that a *CPU* can perform. Some examples of these operations are addition, subtraction, or other arithmetic operations; other possibilities include operations that control what instruction will be executed next. All C++ programs must be converted into machine instructions before they can be executed by the CPU.

A **machine language program** is a program composed of *machine instructions*.

A **magic number** is a number that does not have any obvious relationship to the rest of the code. A good general rule is that numbers other than 0, 1, or other self-evident values should be defined as const or enum values rather than as literal values such as '7'.

Manager object; see *manager/worker idiom*, and *polymorphic objects*.

The **manager/worker idiom** (also known as the "envelope/letter idiom") is a mechanism that allows the effective type of an object to be determined at run time without requiring the user of the object to be concerned with pointers. It is used to implement *polymorphic objects* in C++.

A **manipulator** is a member function of one of the iostreams classes that controls how output will be formatted without necessarily producing any output of its own. Manipulators operate on *fields*; a field can be defined as the result of one << operator.

A **member function** is a function defined in a *class interface*. It is viewed as "belonging" to the class, which is the reason for the adjective "member".

A **member initialization expression** is the preferred method of specifying how a *member variable* is to be initialized in a *constructor*. Also see *inheritance*.

A **member initialization list** specifies how *member variables* are to be initialized in a *constructor*. It includes two types of expressions: *base class initializers* and *member initialization expressions*. Also see *inheritance*.

A **member variable** is a variable defined in a *class interface*. It is viewed as "belonging" to the class, which is the reason for the adjective "member".

Memberwise copy means to copy every *member variable* from the source object to the destination object. If we don't define our own *copy constructor* or *assignment operator* for a particular class, the *compiler-generated* versions will use memberwise copy.

A **memory address** is a unique number identifying a particular byte of *RAM*.

A **memory hierarchy** is the particular arrangement of the different kinds of storage devices in a given computer. The purpose of using storage devices having different performance characteristics is to provide the best overall performance at the lowest cost.

A **memory leak** is a programming error in which the programmer forgot to delete something that had been dynamically allocated. Such an error is very insidious because the program appears to work correctly when tested casually. The usual way to find these errors is to notice that the program runs apparently correctly for a (possibly long) time and then fails because it runs out of available memory.

A **modification expression** is the part of a for statement executed after every execution of the *controlled block*. It is often used to increment an *index variable* to refer to the next element of an *array* or vector; see *for statement* for an example.

Modulus operator; see %.

A **month number** is an integer value representing the number of months between two dates.

N

A **nanosecond** is one-billionth of a second.

A **native data type** is one defined in the C++ language, as opposed to a *user-defined data type* (class).

The **new operator** is used to allocate memory for variables of the *dynamic storage class*; these are usually variables whose storage requirements may not be known until the program is executing.

The **newline** character is the C++ character used to indicate the end of a line of text.

Nondisplay character; see *nonprinting character*.

A **nonmember function** is one that is not a member of a particular class being discussed, although it may be a *member function* of another class.

A **nonnumeric variable** is a variable that is not used in calculations like adding, multiplying, or subtracting. Such variables might represent names, addresses, telephone numbers, Social Security numbers, bank account numbers, or driver's license numbers. Note that even a data item referred to as a number and composed entirely of the digits 0 through 9 may be a nonnumeric variable by this definition; the question is how the item is used. No one adds, multiplies, or subtracts driver's license numbers, for example; these numbers serve solely as identifiers and could just as easily have letters in them, as indeed some of them do.

A **nonprinting character** is used to control the format of our displayed or printed information, rather than to represent a particular letter, digit, or other special character. The *space* is one of the more important nonprinting characters.

A **non-virtual** function is one that is not declared with the virtual keyword. This means that the compiler can decide at compile time the exact version of the function to be executed when it is referred to via a base class pointer or base class reference.

A **normal constructor** is a *constructor* whose arguments supply enough information to initialize all of the member fields in the object being created. Also see *constructor*.

A **null byte** is a byte with the value 0, commonly used to indicate the end of a *C string*. Note that this is not the same as the character "0", which is a normal printable character having the ASCII code 48.

A **null object** is an object of some (specified) class whose purpose is to indicate that a "real" object of that class does not exist. It is analogous to a *null pointer*. One common use for a null object is as a *return value* from a *member function* that is supposed to return an object with some specified properties but cannot find such an object. For example, a null StockItem object might be used to indicate that an item with a specified UPC cannot be found in the inventory of a store.

A **null pointer** is a *pointer* with the value 0. This value is particularly suited to indicate that a pointer isn't pointing to anything at the moment, because of some special treatment of zero-valued pointers built into the C++ language.

A **null string** is a string or *C string* with the value "".

A **numeric digit** is one of the digits 0 through 9.

A **numeric variable** is a variable that represents a quantity that can be expressed as a number, whether a whole number (an *integer variable*) or a number with a fractional part (a *floating-point variable*), and that can be used in calculations such as addition, subtraction, multiplication, or division. The integer variable types in C++ are char, short, int, and long. Each of these can be further subdivided into signed and unsigned versions. The signed versions can represent both negative and positive values (and 0), whereas the unsigned versions can represent only positive values (and 0) but provides greater ranges of positive values than the corresponding signed versions do. The floating-point variable types are float and double, which differ in their range and precision. Unlike the integer variable types, the floating-point types are not divided into signed and unsigned versions; all floating-point variables can represent either positive or negative numbers as well as 0. See *float* and *double* for details on range and precision.

O

An **object** is a variable of a class type, as distinct from a variable of a *native type*. The behavior of an object is defined by the code that implements the class to which the object belongs. For example, a variable of type string is an object whose behavior is controlled by the definition of the string class.

Object code; see *machine code*. This term is unrelated to C++ objects.

An **object code module** is the result of compiling an *implementation file* into *object code*. A number of object code modules are combined to form an *executable program*. This term is unrelated to C++ objects.

Object file; see *object code module*. This term is unrelated to C++ *objects*.

Object-oriented programming is an approach to solving programming problems by creating *objects* to represent the entities being handled by the program, rather than by relying solely on *native data types*. This has the advantage that you can match the language to the needs of the problem you're trying to solve. For example, if you were writing a nurse's station program in C++, you would have objects that represent nurses, doctors, patients, various sorts of equipment, and so on. Each of these objects would display the behavior appropriate to the thing or person it represents.

Off-by-one error; see *fencepost error*.

An **ofstream** (pronounced "o f stream") is a *stream* used for output to a file.

An **op code** is the part of a *machine instruction* that tells the *CPU* what kind of instruction it is and sometimes also specifies a *register* to be operated on.

An **operating system** is a program that deals with the actual *hardware* of your computer. It supplies the lowest level of the software infrastructure needed to run a program. By far the most common operating system for Intel CPUs, at present, is MS-DOS (which is also the basis for Windows 95), followed by OS/2 and Windows NT.

The keyword **operator** is used to indicate that the following symbol is the name of a C++ operator we are redefining, either globally or for a particular class. For example, to redefine =, we have to specify operator = as the name of the function we are writing, rather than just =, so that the compiler does not object to seeing an operator when it expects an identifier.

An **ostream** is a *stream* used for *output*. For example, cout is a predefined ostream that displays characters on the screen.

Output is the process of sending data from the computer to the outside world. The most commonly used source of output for most programs is the screen.

A member function in a derived class is said to **override** the base class *member function* if the derived class function has the same *signature* (name and argument types) as that of the base class member function. The derived class member function will be called instead of the base class member function when the member function is referred to via an object of the derived class. A member function in a derived class with the same name but a different signature from that of a member function in the base class does not override the base class member function. Instead, it "hides" that base class member function, which is no longer accessible as a member function in the derived class.

P

Parent class; see *inheritance*.

A **pointer** is essentially the same as a *memory address*. The main difference is that a memory address is "untyped" (i.e., it can refer to any sort of variable) whereas a pointer always has an associated data type. For example, char* (pronounced "char star") means "pointer to a char". To say "a variable points to a memory location" is almost the same as saying "a variable's value is the address of a memory location". In the specific case of a variable of type char*, to say "the char* x points to a *C string*" is essentially equivalent to saying "x contains the address of the first byte of the C string". Also see *array*.

A **polymorphic object** is a C++ *object* that presents the appearance of a simple object that displays *polymorphism* without exposing the user of the object to the hazards of pointers. The user does not have to know any of the details of the implementation, but merely instantiates an object of the single visible class (the *manager class*). That object does what the user wants with the help of an object of a *worker class*, which is derived from the manager class. Also see *manager/worker idiom*.

Polymorphism is the major organizing principle in C++ that allows us to implement several classes with the same interface and to treat objects of all these classes as though they were of the same class. Polymorphism is a variety of *dynamic typing* that maintains the safety factor of *static type checking*, because the compiler can determine at compile time whether a function call is legal even if it does not know the exact type of the object that will receive that function call at run time. "Polymorphism" is derived from the Greek *poly*, meaning "many", and *morph*, meaning "form". In other words, the same behavior is implemented in different forms.

To **pop** is to remove the top value from a stack.

The **preprocessor** is a part of the C++ compiler that deals with the source code of a program before the rest of the compiler ever sees that source code; thus, the name "preprocessor".

A **preprocessor directive** is a command telling the preprocessor to handle the following source code in a special manner.

A **preprocessor symbol** is a constant value similar to a const, but it is known only to the preprocessor, not to the rest of the compiler. The rules for naming preprocessor symbols are the same as those for other identifiers, but it is customary to use all upper-case letters in preprocessor symbols so that they can be readily distinguished from other identifiers.

The keyword **private** is an *access specifier* that denies *nonmember functions* access to *member functions* and *member variables* of its class.

Creating a class via **private inheritance** means that we are not going to allow outside functions to treat an object of the derived class as an object of the base class. That is, functions that takes a base class object as a parameter will not accept a derived class object in its place. None of the public *member functions* and public data items (if there are any) in the base class will be accessible in a privately derived class object. Contrast with *public inheritance*.

A **program** is a set of instructions specifying the solution to a set of problems, along with the data used by those instructions.

The **program counter** is a *dedicated register* that holds the address of the next instruction to be executed. During a *function call*, a *call instruction* pushes the contents of the program counter on the stack. This enables the *called function* to return to the *calling function* when finished.

Program failure can be defined as a situation in which a program does not behave as intended. The causes of this are legion, ranging from incorrect input data to improper specification of the problem to be solved.

Program maintenance is the process of updating and correcting a program once it has entered service.

Programming is the art and science of solving problems by the following procedure:

1. Find or invent a general solution to a set of problems.

2. Express this solution as an algorithm or set of algorithms.

3. Translate the algorithm(s) into terms so simple that a stupid machine like a computer can follow them to calculate the specific answer for any specific problem in the set.

Warning: This definition may be somewhat misleading, since it implies that the development of a program is straightforward and linear, with no revision. This is known as the "waterfall model" of programming, since water going over a waterfall follows a preordained course in one direction. However, real-life programming doesn't usually work this way; rather, most programs are written in an incremental process as assumptions are changed and errors are found and corrected.

The keyword **protected** is an *access specifier*. When present in a *base class* definition, it allows *derived class* functions access to member variables and functions in the *base class part* of a derived class object, while preventing access by other functions outside the base class.

The keyword **public** is an *access specifier* that allows *nonmember functions* access to *member functions* and *member variables* of its class.

Creating a class via **public inheritance** means that we are going to let outside functions treat an object of the derived class as an object of the base class. That is, any function that takes a base class object as a parameter will accept a derived class object in its place. All of the public *member functions* and public data items (if there are any) in the base class are accessible in a derived class object as well. Contrast with *private inheritance*.

Push means to add another value to a stack.

A **put pointer** holds the address of the next byte in the output area of an *ostream* — that is, where the next byte will be stored if we use << to write data into the stream.

R

RAM is an acronym for Random Access Memory. This is the working storage of a computer, where data and programs are stored while we're using them.

A **reference argument** is another name for a variable from a *calling function* rather than an independent variable in the *called function*. Changing a reference argument therefore affects the corresponding variable in the calling function. Compare with *value argument*.

The **reference-counting idiom** is a mechanism that allows one object (the "reference-counted object") to be shared by several other objects (the "client objects") rather than having to make a copy for each of the client objects.

A **register** is a storage area that is on the same chip as the *CPU* itself. Programs use registers to hold data items that are actively in use; data in registers can be accessed within the time allocated to instruction execution rather than the much longer times needed to access data in *RAM*.

Regression testing means running a modified program and verifying whether previously working functionality is still working.

A **regular member function** is any member function that is not in any of the following categories:

1. constructor,

2. destructor,

3. the assignment operator, operator =.

A *derived class* inherits all regular member functions from its *base class*.

A **retrieval function** is a function that retrieves data that may have been previously stored by a **storage function** or that may be generated when needed by some other method such as calculation according to a formula.

A **return address** is the *memory address* of the next *machine instruction* in a *calling function*. It is used during execution of a *return statement* in a *called function* to transfer execution back to the correct place in the calling function.

A **return statement** is used by a *called function* to transfer execution back to the *calling function*. The return statement can also specify a value of the correct *return type* for the called function. This value is made available to the calling function to be used for further calculation. An example of a return statement is return 0;, which returns the value 0 to the calling function.

A **return type** tells the compiler what sort of data a *called function* returns to the calling function when the *called function* finishes executing. The return value from main is a special case; it can be used to determine what action a batch file should take next.

A **return value** is the value returned from a *called function* to its *calling function*.

RHIDE is the Integrated Development Environment developed by Robert Höhne. It is included on the CD-ROM in the back of this book.

ROM is an abbreviation for *Read-Only Memory.* This is the permanent internal storage of a computer, where the programs needed to start up the computer are stored. As this suggests, ROM does not lose its contents when the power is turned off, as contrasted with RAM.

Run time means "while a (previously compiled) program is being executed".

The **run-time type** of a variable is the type that variable has when the program is being executed. In the presence of *polymorphism*, this type may differ from the type with which the variable was declared at *compile time*.

S

A **scalar variable** has a single value (at any one time); this is contrasted with a vector or an *array*, which contains a number of values, each of which is referred to by its *index*.

The **scope** of a variable is the part of the program in which the variable can be accessed. The scopes with which we are concerned are local, global, and class; see *local scope*, *global scope*, and *class scope* for more details.

A **selection expression** is the part of a switch statement that specifies an expression used to select an alternative section of code.

A **selection sort** is a sorting algorithm that selects the highest (or lowest) element from a set of elements (the "input list") and moves that selected element to another set of elements (the "output list"); the next highest (or lowest) element is then treated in the same manner. This operation is repeated until as many elements as desired have been moved to the output list.

A **short** is a type of *integer variable* that can represent a whole number. With most current C++ compilers, including DJGPP, a short occupies 2 bytes of storage and therefore can represent a number in either the range -32768 to 32767 (if signed) or the range 0 to 65535 (if unsigned).

The **short-circuit evaluation rule** governs the execution of the || and && operators. See *||* and *&&* for details.

A **side effect** is any result of calling a function that persists beyond the execution of that function other than its returning a *return value*. For example, writing data to a file is a side effect.

The **signature** of a function consists of its name and the types of its *arguments*. In the case of a *member function*, the class to which the function belongs is also part of its signature. Every function is uniquely identified by its signature, which is what makes it possible to have more than one function with the same name. This is called *function overloading*.

A **signed char** is a type of *integer variable*. See char for details.

A **signed int** is a type of *integer variable*. See int for details.

A **signed long** is a type of *integer variable*. See long for details.

A **signed short** is a type of *integer variable*. See short for details.

A **signed variable** can represent either negative or positive values. See char, short, int, or long for details.

Slicing is the partial assignment that occurs when a derived class object is assigned to a base class variable. This term is used because in such an assignment only the base class part of the derived class object is assigned while the other fields are "sliced off".

Software refers to the nonphysical components of a computer, the ones you cannot touch. If you can install it on your hard disk, it's software. Examples include a spreadsheet, a word processor, and a database program.

Source code is a program in a form suitable for reading and writing by a human being.

Source code file; see *implementation file*.

Source code module; see *implementation file*.

The **space character** is one of the *nonprinting characters* (or nondisplay characters) that control the format of displayed or printed information.

Special constructor; see *polymorphic object*.

The **square brackets**, **[** and **]**, are used to enclose an *array* or *vector index*, which selects an individual element of the array or vector. Also see [ ].

A **stack** is a data structure with characteristics similar to those of a spring-loaded plate holder such as you might see in a cafeteria. The last plate deposited on the stack of plates will be the first one removed when a customer needs a fresh plate; similarly, the last value deposited (pushed) onto a stack is the first value retrieved (popped).

The **stack pointer** is a *dedicated register*. It is used to keep track of the address of the most recently pushed value on the stack.

A **starting expression** is the part of a for statement that is executed once before the *controlled block* of the for statement is first executed. It is often used to initialize an *index variable* to 0 so that the index variable can be used to refer to the first element of an array or vector. See *for statement* for an example.

A **statement** is a complete operation understood by the C++ compiler. Each statement ends with a semicolon (;).

A **static member function** is a *member function* of a class that can be called without reference to an object of that class. Such a function has no *this pointer* passed to it on entry and therefore cannot refer to member variables of the class.

The **static storage class** is the simplest of the three *storage classes* in C++; variables of this storage class are assigned memory addresses in the *executable program* when the program is *linked*.

Static type checking refers to the practice of checking the correct usage of variables of different types during compilation of a program rather than during execution. C++ uses static type checking. See *type system* for further discussion. Note that this has no particular relation to the keyword static.

Static typing means determining the exact type of a variable when the program is compiled. It is the default typing mechanism in C++. Note that this has no particular relation to the keyword static, nor is it exactly the same as static type checking. See *type system* for further discussion.

Stepwise refinement is the process of developing an algorithm by starting out with a "coarse" solution and "refining" it until the steps are within the capability of the C++ language.

Storage; synonym for *memory*.

A **storage class** is the characteristic of a variable that determines how and when a memory address is assigned to that variable. C++ has three storage classes: static, auto, and dynamic. Please note that the term *storage class* has nothing to do with the C++ term class. See *static storage class*, *auto storage class*, and *dynamic storage class* for more details.

A **storage function** is a function that stores data for later retrieval by a *retrieval function*.

A **stream** is a place to put (in the case of an ostream) or get (in the case of an istream) characters. Some predefined streams are *cin* and *cout*.

A **stream buffer** is the area of memory where the characters put into a stream are stored.

The **string class** defines a type of object that contains a group of chars; the chars in a string can be treated as one unit for purposes of assignment, I/O, and comparison.

A **strstream** is a type of *stream* that exists only in memory rather than being attached to an input or output device. It is often used for formatting of data that is to be further manipulated within the program.

The **switch** statement is functionally equivalent to a number of if/else statements in a row, but is easier to read and modify. The keyword switch is followed by a *selection expression* (in parentheses), which specifies an expression that is used to select an alternative section of code. The various alternatives to be considered are enclosed in a set of curly braces following the selection expression, and are marked off by the keyword case followed by the (constant) value to be matched and a colon.

T

Temporary; see *temporary variable*.

A **temporary variable** is automatically created by the *compiler* for use during a particular operation, such as a *function call* with an *argument* that has to be converted to a different type.

The keyword **this** represents a hidden argument automatically supplied by the compiler in every *member function* call. Its value during the execution of any member function is the address of the class object for which the member function call was made.

To **throw** an *exception* means to cause an interruption in the normal flow control of a program, usually due to an error condition. An exception can be handled via a ***catch*** statement in a function that directly or indirectly called the function that threw the exception.

A **token** is a part of a program that the compiler treats as a separate unit. It's analogous to a word in English, while a *statement* is more like a sentence. For example, string is a token, as are :: and (, whereas x = 5; is a statement.

The keyword **true** is a predefined value representing the result of a conditional expression whose condition is satisfied. For example, in the conditional expression x < y, if x is less than y, the result of the expression will be true.

The keyword **try** is used to control a block from which an *exception* may be generated. If an exception occurs during execution of that block or any functions within that block, the following *catch* statement will be invited to handle the exception, assuming that the specification of the catch statement indicates that it is willing to handle such an exception.

The **type** of an object is the class to which it belongs. The type of a *native variable* is one of the predefined variable types in C++. See *integer variable*, *floating-point variable*, and *bool* for details on the native types.

The **type system** refers to the set of rules the language uses to decide how a variable of a given type may be employed. In C++, these determinations are made by the compiler (*static type checking*). This makes it easier to prevent type errors than it is in languages where type checking is done during execution of the program (*dynamic type checking*). Please note that C++ has both static type checking and *dynamic typing*. This is possible because the set of types that is acceptable in any given situation can be determined at *compile time*, even though the exact type of a given variable may not be known until *run time*.

U

An **uninitialized variable** is one that has never been set to a known value. Attempting to use such a variable is a logical error that can cause a program to act very oddly.

An **unqualified name** is a reference to a *member variable* that doesn't specify which object the member variable belongs to. When we use an unqualified name in a *member function*, the *compiler* assumes that the object we are referring to is the object for which that member function has been called.

An **unsigned char** is a type of *integer variable*. See *char* for details.

An **unsigned int** is a type of *integer variable*. See *int* for details.

An **unsigned long** is a type of *integer variable*. See *long* for details.

An **unsigned short** is a type of *integer variable*. See *short* for details.

An **unsigned** variable is an *integer variable* that represents only positive values (and 0). See *char*, *short*, *int*, and *long* for details.

The term **user** has several meanings in programming. The primary usage in this book is *application programmer*; however, it can also mean *library designer* (in the phrase *user-defined data type*) or even *end user.*

A **user-defined data type** is one that is defined by the user. In this context, user means "someone using language facilities to extend the range of variable types in the language", or *library designer.* The primary mechanism for defining a user-defined type is the *class.*

V

A **value argument** is a variable of *local scope* created when a *function* begins execution. Its initial value is set to the value of the corresponding *argument* in the *calling function.* Changing a value argument does not affect any variable in the calling function. Compare with *reference argument.*

A **variable** is a programming construct that uses a certain part of *RAM* to represent a specific item of data we wish to keep track of in a program. Some examples are the weight of a pumpkin or the number of cartons of milk in the inventory of a store.

A **vector** is a group of variables that can be addressed by their position in the group; each of these variables is called an *element.* A vector has a name, just as a regular variable does, but the elements do not. Instead, each element has an *index* that represents its position in the vector.

Declaring a function to be **virtual** means that it is a member of a set of functions having the same *signatures* and belonging to classes related by *inheritance.* The actual function to be executed as the result of a given function call is selected from this set of functions dynamically (i.e., at run time) based on the actual type of an object referred to via a base class pointer (or base class reference). This is the C++ *dynamic typing* mechanism used to implement polymorphism, in contrast to the *static typing* used for *nonvirtual functions*, which are selected at compile time.

A **void return type specifier** in a *function declaration* indicates that the function in question does not return any value when it finishes executing.

The term **vtable** is an abbreviation for *virtual function address table*. It is where the addresses of all of the *virtual functions* for a given class are stored; every object of that class contains the address of the vtable for that class.

W

A **while statement** is a *loop control statement* that causes its *controlled block* to be executed while a specified logical expression is true.

Worker class: see *polymorphic object*.

Y

A **year number** is an integer value representing the number of years between two dates.

Z

Zero-based indexing refers to the practice of numbering the elements of an *array* or vector starting at 0 rather than 1.

About the Author

Steve Heller had always been fascinated by writing. In his childhood days in the 1950s and 1960s, he often stayed up far past his bedtime reading science fiction. Even in adulthood, if you came across him in his off-hours, he was more likely to be found reading a book than doing anything else.

After college, Steve got into programming more or less by accident; he was working for an actuarial consulting firm and was selected to take charge of programming on their time-sharing terminal because he was making much less than most of the other employees. Finding the programming itself to be more interesting than the actuarial calculations, he decided to become a professional programmer.

Until 1984, Steve remained on the consuming side of the writing craft. Then one day he was reading a magazine article on some programming-related topic and said to himself, "I could do better than that". So he decided to try his hand at technical writing. Steve's first article submission (to the late lamented *Computer Language Magazine*) was published, as were a dozen more over the next ten years.

But although writing magazine articles is an interesting pastime, writing a book is something entirely different. Steve got his chance at this new level of commitment when Harry Helms, then an editor for Academic Press, read one of his articles in *Dr. Dobb's Journal* and wrote him asking whether he would be interested in writing a book for AP. He answered, "Sure, why not?", not having the faintest idea of how much work he was letting himself in for.

The resulting book, *Large Problems, Small Machines*, received favorable reviews for its careful explanation of a number of facets of program optimization, and sold about 20,000 copies within a year after publication of the second edition, entitled *Efficient C/C++ Programming*.

By that time, Steve was hard at work on his next book, *Who's Afraid of C++?*, which was designed to make object-oriented programming intelligible to anyone from the sheerest novice to the programmer with years of experience in languages other than C++. To make sure that his exposition was clear enough for the novice, he posted a message on CompuServe requesting the help of someone new to programming. The responses included one from a woman named Susan, who ended up contributing a great deal to the book. In fact, about 100 pages consisted of email between Steve and Susan. Her contribution was wonderful, but not completely unexpected.

What was unexpected was that Steve and Susan would fall in love during the course of this project, but that's what happened. Since she lived in Texas and he lived in New York, this posed some logistic difficulties. The success of his previous book now became extremely important, as it was the key to Steve's becoming a full-time writer. Writers have been "telecommuting" since before the invention of the telephone, so his conversion from "programmer who writes" to "writer" made it possible for him to relocate to her area, which he promptly did.

Since his move to Texas, Steve has reverted to being a "programmer who writes", as a result of finding a telecommuting position at a wonderful company called Associated Solutions, Inc. In his "spare time", he has continued his writing by updating his advanced algorithms book, the latest version of which was published as *Optimizing C++* in 1998.

Steve and Susan were married in 1997.

Index

Symbols

#define preprocessor directive 860, 863, 994

:: (class membership operator) 316, 329, 331, 341, 343, 353, 356, 379—380, 382—385, 407, 415, 430, 439, 451, 453—454, 466, 470, 643, 678, 740—742, 1002, 1036

-> 466, 645, 711

~ 469

~ 469

A

access specifier 324, 334—336, 345, 503, 541, 557, 590, 597—598, 600, 603, 995, 1002, 1026, 1028

AddItem function 794, 798—799, 810, 814, 853—854, 857, 924, 952, 984

aliasing 753—754, 816, 830, 995

application programmer 310, 338—339, 368, 461, 568, 591, 619, 659, 661, 694—695, 700, 866—867, 995, 1001, 1008, 1038

array 362, 479, 494—496, 498—503, 511—512, 521, 528, 532—533, 540, 546—548, 550—551, 554, 644, 754, 825—828, 854—855, 988, 996, 1007, 1009, 1013—1014, 1020, 1025, 1031, 1033, 1040

array initialization list 754, 827, 996

automatic conversion 483, 486, 557, 829, 869, 997

D

H

I

N

O

P

S

T

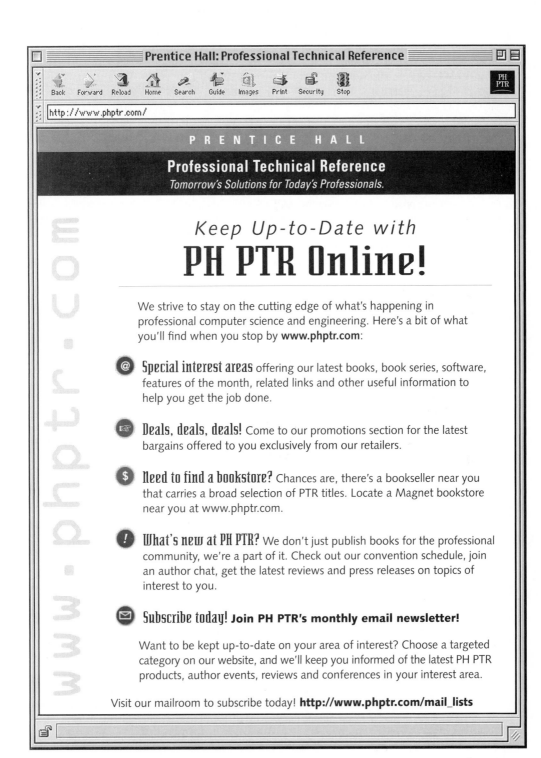

LICENSE AGREEMENT AND LIMITED WARRANTY

READ THE FOLLOWING TERMS AND CONDITIONS CAREFULLY BEFORE OPENING THIS SOFTWARE MEDIA PACKAGE. THIS LEGAL DOCUMENT IS AN AGREEMENT BETWEEN YOU AND PRENTICE-HALL, INC. (THE "COMPANY"). BY OPENING THIS SEALED SOFTWARE MEDIA PACKAGE, YOU ARE AGREEING TO BE BOUND BY THESE TERMS AND CONDITIONS. IF YOU DO NOT AGREE WITH THESE TERMS AND CONDITIONS, DO NOT OPEN THE SOFTWARE MEDIA PACKAGE. PROMPTLY RETURN THE UNOPENED SOFTWARE MEDIA PACKAGE AND ALL ACCOMPANYING ITEMS TO THE PLACE YOU OBTAINED THEM FOR A FULL REFUND OF ANY SUMS YOU HAVE PAID.

1. **GRANT OF LICENSE:** In consideration of your payment of the license fee, which is part of the price you paid for this product, and your agreement to abide by the terms and conditions of this Agreement, the Company grants to you a nonexclusive right to use and display the copy of the enclosed software program (hereinafter the "SOFTWARE") on a single computer (i.e., with a single CPU) at a single location so long as you comply with the terms of this Agreement. The Company reserves all rights not expressly granted to you under this Agreement.

2. **OWNERSHIP OF SOFTWARE:** You own only the magnetic or physical media (the enclosed SOFTWARE) on which the SOFTWARE is recorded or fixed, but the Company retains all the rights, title, and ownership to the SOFTWARE recorded on the original SOFTWARE copy(ies) and all subsequent copies of the SOFTWARE, regardless of the form or media on which the original or other copies may exist. This license is not a sale of the original SOFTWARE or any copy to you.

3. **COPY RESTRICTIONS:** This SOFTWARE and the accompanying printed materials and user manual (the "Documentation") are the subject of copyright. You may not copy the Documentation or the SOFTWARE, except that you may make a single copy of the SOFTWARE for backup or archival purposes only. You may be held legally responsible for any copying or copyright infringement which is caused or encouraged by your failure to abide by the terms of this restriction.

4. **USE RESTRICTIONS:** You may not network the SOFTWARE or otherwise use it on more than one computer or computer terminal at the same time. You may physically transfer the SOFTWARE from one computer to another provided that the SOFTWARE is used on only one computer at a time. You may not distribute copies of the SOFTWARE or Documentation to others. You may not reverse engineer, disassemble, decompile, modify, adapt, translate, or create derivative works based on the SOFTWARE or the Documentation without the prior written consent of the Company.

5. **TRANSFER RESTRICTIONS:** The enclosed SOFTWARE is licensed only to you and may not be transferred to any one else without the prior written consent of the Company. Any unauthorized transfer of the SOFTWARE shall result in the immediate termination of this Agreement.

6. **TERMINATION:** This license is effective until terminated. This license will terminate automatically without notice from the Company and become null and void if you fail to comply with any provisions or limitations of this license. Upon termination, you shall destroy the Documentation and all copies of the SOFTWARE. All provisions of this Agreement as to warranties, limitation of liability, remedies or damages, and our ownership rights shall survive termination.

7. **MISCELLANEOUS:** This Agreement shall be construed in accordance with the laws of the United States of America and the State of New York and shall benefit the Company, its affiliates, and assignees.

8. **LIMITED WARRANTY AND DISCLAIMER OF WARRANTY:** The Company warrants that the SOFTWARE, when properly used in accordance with the Documentation, will operate in substantial conformity with the description of the SOFTWARE set forth in the Documentation. The Company does not warrant that the SOFTWARE will meet your requirements or that the operation of the SOFTWARE will be uninterrupted or error-free. The Company warrants that the

media on which the SOFTWARE is delivered shall be free from defects in materials and workmanship under normal use for a period of thirty (30) days from the date of your purchase. Your only remedy and the Company's only obligation under these limited warranties is, at the Company's option, return of the warranted item for a refund of any amounts paid by you or replacement of the item. Any replacement of SOFTWARE or media under the warranties shall not extend the original warranty period. The limited warranty set forth above shall not apply to any SOFTWARE which the Company determines in good faith has been subject to misuse, neglect, improper installation, repair, alteration, or damage by you. EXCEPT FOR THE EXPRESSED WARRANTIES SET FORTH ABOVE, THE COMPANY DISCLAIMS ALL WARRANTIES, EXPRESS OR IMPLIED, INCLUDING WITHOUT LIMITATION, THE IMPLIED WARRANTIES OF MERCHANTABILITY AND FITNESS FOR A PARTICULAR PURPOSE. EXCEPT FOR THE EXPRESS WARRANTY SET FORTH ABOVE, THE COMPANY DOES NOT WARRANT, GUARANTEE, OR MAKE ANY REPRESENTATION REGARDING THE USE OR THE RESULTS OF THE USE OF THE SOFTWARE IN TERMS OF ITS CORRECTNESS, ACCURACY, RELIABILITY, CURRENTNESS, OR OTHERWISE.

IN NO EVENT, SHALL THE COMPANY OR ITS EMPLOYEES, AGENTS, SUPPLIERS, OR CONTRACTORS BE LIABLE FOR ANY INCIDENTAL, INDIRECT, SPECIAL, OR CONSEQUENTIAL DAMAGES ARISING OUT OF OR IN CONNECTION WITH THE LICENSE GRANTED UNDER THIS AGREEMENT, OR FOR LOSS OF USE, LOSS OF DATA, LOSS OF INCOME OR PROFIT, OR OTHER LOSSES, SUSTAINED AS A RESULT OF INJURY TO ANY PERSON, OR LOSS OF OR DAMAGE TO PROPERTY, OR CLAIMS OF THIRD PARTIES, EVEN IF THE COMPANY OR AN AUTHORIZED REPRESENTATIVE OF THE COMPANY HAS BEEN ADVISED OF THE POSSIBILITY OF SUCH DAMAGES. IN NO EVENT SHALL LIABILITY OF THE COMPANY FOR DAMAGES WITH RESPECT TO THE SOFTWARE EXCEED THE AMOUNTS ACTUALLY PAID BY YOU, IF ANY, FOR THE SOFTWARE.

SOME JURISDICTIONS DO NOT ALLOW THE LIMITATION OF IMPLIED WARRANTIES OR LIABILITY FOR INCIDENTAL, INDIRECT, SPECIAL, OR CONSEQUENTIAL DAMAGES, SO THE ABOVE LIMITATIONS MAY NOT ALWAYS APPLY. THE WARRANTIES IN THIS AGREEMENT GIVE YOU SPECIFIC LEGAL RIGHTS AND YOU MAY ALSO HAVE OTHER RIGHTS WHICH VARY IN ACCORDANCE WITH LOCAL LAW.

ACKNOWLEDGMENT

YOU ACKNOWLEDGE THAT YOU HAVE READ THIS AGREEMENT, UNDERSTAND IT, AND AGREE TO BE BOUND BY ITS TERMS AND CONDITIONS. YOU ALSO AGREE THAT THIS AGREEMENT IS THE COMPLETE AND EXCLUSIVE STATEMENT OF THE AGREEMENT BETWEEN YOU AND THE COMPANY AND SUPERSEDES ALL PROPOSALS OR PRIOR AGREEMENTS, ORAL, OR WRITTEN, AND ANY OTHER COMMUNICATIONS BETWEEN YOU AND THE COMPANY OR ANY REPRESENTATIVE OF THE COMPANY RELATING TO THE SUBJECT MATTER OF THIS AGREEMENT.

Should you have any questions concerning this Agreement or if you wish to contact the Company for any reason, please contact in writing at the address below.

Robin Short
Prentice Hall PTR
One Lake Street
Upper Saddle River, New Jersey 07458

About the CD

The CD-ROM accompanying this book contains:

1. The DJGPP compiler, copyright by DJ Delorie

2. ZIP files containing the source code for this compiler and its associated programs

3. The source code and executable program for RHIDE, the Integrated Development Environment for DJGPP

Please see the Readme.txt file on the CD-ROM for complete requirements and instructions for compiler installation.

Technical Assistance

If you have any problems setting up the compiler or compiling the sample code, or have any other questions, you might want to check my web page, http://www.steveheller.com, for updates to the instructions or sample code.

If you have questions that aren't answered by the information on my home page, you can email me at:

steve@steveheller.com